MCAT®
ORGANIC CHEMISTRY
REVIEW

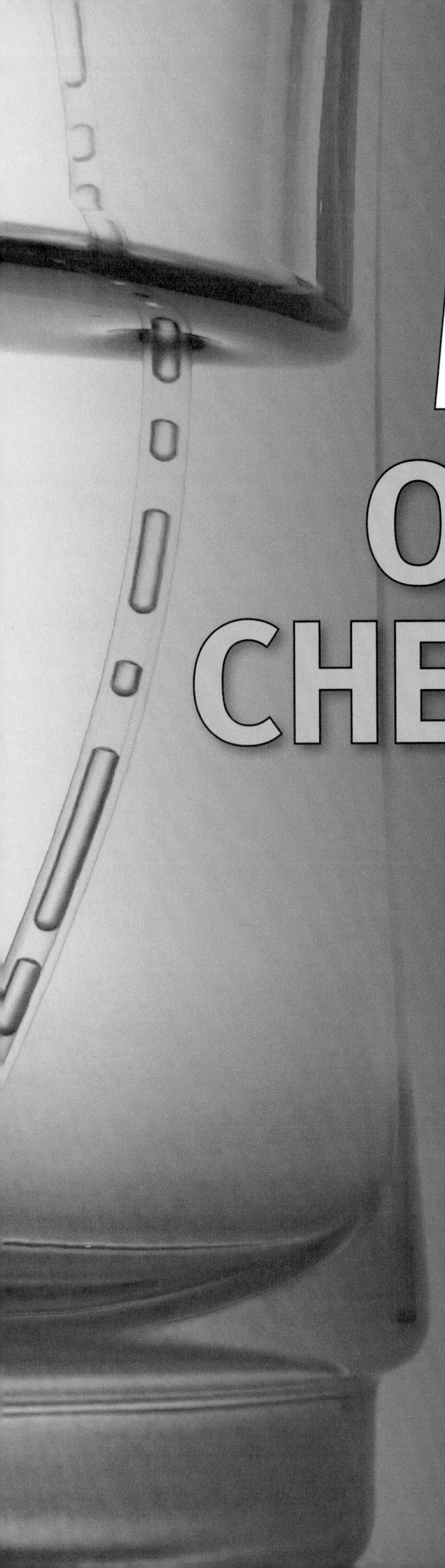

MCAT®

ORGANIC CHEMISTRY REVIEW

REVIEW

The Staff of Kaplan

KAPLAN) PUBLISHING

New York

Published by Kaplan Publishing, a division of Kaplan, Inc.
395 Hudson Street
New York, NY 10014

Printed in the United States of America

10 9 8 7 6 5 4

ISBN: 978-1-60714-641-4

Kaplan Publishing books are available at special quantity discounts to use for sales promotions, employee premiums, or educational purposes. For more information or to purchase books, please call the Simon & Schuster special sales department at 866-506-1949.

Contents

KAPLAN'S EXPERT MCAT TEAM

Kaplan has been preparing premeds for the MCAT for more than 40 years. In the past 15 years alone, we've helped more than 400,000 students prepare for this important exam and improve their chances for medical school admission.

Marilyn Engle
MCAT Master Teacher; Teacher Trainer; Kaplan National Teacher of the Year, 2006; Westwood Teacher of the Year, 2007; Westwood Trainer of the Year, 2007; Encino Trainer of the Year, 2005

John Michael Linick
MCAT Teacher; Boulder Teacher of the Year, 2007; Summer Intensive Program Faculty Member

Dr. Glen Pearlstein
MCAT Master Teacher; Teacher Trainer; Westwood Teacher of the Year, 2006

Matthew B. Wilkinson
MCAT Teacher; Teacher Trainer; Lone Star Trainer of the Year, 2007

Thanks to Jason Baserman, Jessica Brookman, Da Chang, John Cummins, David Elson, Jeff Koetje, Alex Macnow, Andrew Molloy, Josh Rohrig and Amjed Sarfarini

ABOUT SCIENTIFIC AMERICAN

As the world's premier science and technology magazine, and the oldest continuously published magazine in the United States, *Scientific American* is committed to bringing the most important developments in modern science, medicine, and technology to 3.5 million readers worldwide in an understandable, credible, and provocative format.

Founded in 1845 and on the "cutting edge" ever since, *Scientific American* boasts over 140 Nobel laureate authors, including Albert Einstein, Francis Crick, Stanley Prusiner, and Richard Axel. *Scientific American* is a forum where scientific theories and discoveries are explained to a broader audience.

Scientific American published its first foreign edition in 1890 and, in 1979, was the first Western magazine published in the People's Republic of China. Today, *Scientific American* is published in 17 foreign language editions with a total circulation of more than 1 million worldwide. *Scientific American* is also a leading online destination (www.ScientificAmerican.com), providing the latest science news and exclusive features to more than 2 million unique visitors monthly.

The knowledge that fills our pages has the power to inspire—to spark new ideas, paradigms, and visions for the future. As science races forward, *Scientific American* continues to cover the promising strides, inevitable setbacks and challenges, and new medical discoveries as they unfold.

How to Use this Book

Kaplan MCAT Organic Chemistry, along with the other four books in our MCAT Review series, brings the Kaplan classroom experience to you—right in your home, at your convenience. This book offers the same Kaplan content review, strategies, and practice that make Kaplan the #1 choice for MCAT prep. All that's missing is the teacher.

To guide you through this complex content, we've consulted our best MCAT instructors to call out **Key Concept**, to offer **Bridge** to better understanding of the material, and **Mnemonic** devices to assist in learning retention. When you see these sidebars, you will know you're getting the same insight and knowledge that classroom students receive in person. Look for these as well as references to the **Real World** and **MCAT expertise** callouts throughout the book.

HIGH-YIELD MCAT REVIEW

Following the content section, you will find a **High-Yield Questions** section. These questions tackle the most frequently tested topics found on the MCAT. For each type of problem, you will be provided with a stepwise technique for solving the question, as well as important directional points on how to solve it—specifically for the MCAT.

Our experts have again called out the **Key Concepts**, which show you which terms to review. Next, the **Takeaways** box offers a concise summary of the problem-solving approach best used. **Things to Watch Out For** points out any caveats to the approach discussed, which can lead to wrong answer choices. Finally, **Similar Questions** allows you to practice the stepwise technique on analogous open-ended questions.

STAR RATING

The star rating is a Kaplan-exclusive system to help you focus your studies, using a 6-star scale. Two factors are considered when determining the rating for each topic: the "learnability" of the topic—or how easy it is to master—and the frequency with which it appears on the MCAT exam. For example, a topic that presents relatively little difficulty to master and appears with relatively high frequency on the MCAT would receive a higher star rating (e.g., 5 or 6 stars) than a topic which is very difficult to master and appears less frequently on the test. The combination of these two factors represented by the star rating will help you prioritize and direct your MCAT studies.

We're confident that this guide and our award-winning instructors can help you achieve your goals of MCAT success and admission to med school. Good luck!

Introduction to the MCAT

The Medical College Admission Test (MCAT) is different from any other test you've encountered in your academic career. It's not like the knowledge-based exams from high school and college, where emphasis was on memorizing and regurgitating information. Medical schools can assess your academic prowess by looking at your transcript. The MCAT isn't even like other standardized tests you may have taken, where the focus was on proving your general skills.

Medical schools use MCAT scores to assess whether you possess the foundation upon which to build a successful medical career. Though you certainly need to know the content to do well, the stress is on thought process, because the MCAT is above all else a critical thinking test. That's why it emphasizes reasoning, analytical thinking, reading comprehension, data analysis, writing, and problem-solving skills.

Though the MCAT places more weight on your thought process, you must have a strong grasp of the required core knowledge. The MCAT may not be a perfect gauge of your abilities, but it is a relatively objective way to compare you with students from different backgrounds and undergraduate institutions.

The MCAT's power comes from its use as an indicator of your abilities. Good scores can open doors. Your power comes from preparation and mindset because the key to MCAT success is knowing what you're up against. That's where this section of this book comes in. We'll explain the philosophy behind the test, review the sections one by one, show you sample questions, share some of Kaplan's proven methods, and clue you in to what the test makers are really after. You'll get a handle on the process, find a confident new perspective, and achieve your highest possible scores.

ABOUT THE MCAT

Information about the MCAT CBT is included below. For the latest information about the MCAT, visit www.kaptest.com/mcat.

MCAT CBT

Format	U.S.—All administrations on computer
	International—Most on computer with limited paper and pencil in a few isolated areas
Essay Grading	One human and one computer grader
Breaks	Optional break between each section
Length of MCAT Day	Approximately 5.5 hours
Test Dates	Multiple dates in January, April, May, June, July, August, and September
	Total of 24 administrations each year.
Delivery of Results	Within 30 days. If scores are delayed notification will be posted online at www.aamc.org/mcat
	Electronic and paper
Security	Government-issued ID
	Electronic thumbprint
	Electronic signature verification
Testing Centers	Small computer testing sites

Go online and sign up for a local Kaplan Pre-Med Edge event to get the latest information on the test.

PLANNING FOR THE TEST

As you look toward your preparation for the MCAT consider the following advice:

Complete your core course requirements as soon as possible. Take a strategic eye to your schedule and get core requirements out of the way now.

Take the MCAT once. The MCAT is a notoriously grueling standardized exam that requires extensive preparation. It is longer than the graduate admissions exams for business school (GMAT, 3½ hours), law school (LSAT, 3¼ hours) and graduate school (GRE, 2½ hours). You do not want to take it twice. Plan and prepare accordingly.

THE ROLE OF THE MCAT IN ADMISSIONS

More and more people are applying to medical school and more and more people are taking the MCAT. It's important for you to recognize that while a high MCAT score is a critical component in getting admitted to top med schools, it's not the only factor. Medical school admissions officers weigh grades, interviews, MCAT scores, level of involvement in extracurricular activities, as well as personal essays.

In a Kaplan survey of 130 pre-med advisors, 84 percent called the interview a "very important" part of the admissions process, followed closely by college grades (83%) and MCAT scores (76%). Kaplan's college admissions consulting practice works with students on all these issues so they can position themselves as strongly as possible. In addition, the AAMC has made it clear that scores will continue to be valid for three years, and that the scoring of the computer-based MCAT will not differ from that of the paper and pencil version.

REGISTRATION

The only way to register for the MCAT is online. The registration site is: www.aamc.org/mcat.

You will be able to access the site approximately six months before your test date. Payment must be made by MasterCard or Visa.

Go to www.aamc.org/mcat/registration.htm and download *MCAT Essentials* for information about registration, fees, test administration, and preparation. For other questions, contact:

MCAT Care Team
Association of American Medical Colleges
Section for Applicant Assessment Services
2450 N. St., NW
Washington, DC 20037
www.aamc.org/mcat
Email: mcat@aamc.org

Keep in mind that you will need to take the MCAT in the year prior to your planned med school start date. Don't drag your feet gathering information. You'll need time not only to prepare and practice for the test, but also to get all your registration work done.

The MCAT should be viewed just like any other part of your application: as an opportunity to show the medical schools who you are and what you can do. Take control of your MCAT experience.

ANATOMY OF THE MCAT

Before mastering strategies, you need to know exactly what you're dealing with on the MCAT. Let's start with the basics: The MCAT is, among other things, an endurance test.

If you can't approach it with confidence and stamina, you'll quickly lose your composure. That's why it's so important that you take control of the test.

The MCAT consists of four timed sections: Physical Sciences, Verbal Reasoning, Writing Sample, and Biological Sciences. Later in this section we'll take an in-depth look at each MCAT section, including sample question types and specific test-smart hints, but here's a general overview, reflecting the order of the test sections and number of questions in each.

Physical Sciences

Time	70 minutes
Format	• 52 multiple-choice questions: approximately 7–9 passages with 4–8 questions each • approximately 10 stand-alone questions (not passage-based)
What it tests	basic general chemistry concepts, basic physics concepts, analytical reasoning, data interpretation

Verbal Reasoning

Time	60 minutes
Format	• 40 multiple-choice questions: approximately 7 passages with 5–7 questions each
What it tests	critical reading

Writing Sample

Time	60 minutes
Format	• 2 essay questions (30 minutes per essay)
What it tests	critical thinking, intellectual organization, written communication skills

Biological Sciences

Time	70 minutes
Format	• 52 multiple-choice questions: approximately 7–9 passages with 4–8 questions each • approximately 10 stand-alone questions (not passage-based)
What it tests	basic biology concepts, basic organic chemistry concepts, analytical reasoning, data interpretation

The sections of the test always appear in the same order:

Physical Sciences
[optional 10-minute break]
Verbal Reasoning
[optional 10-minute break]
Writing Sample
[optional 10-minute break]
Biological Sciences

SCORING

Each MCAT section receives its own score. Physical Sciences, Verbal Reasoning, and Biological Sciences are each scored on a scale ranging from 1–15, with 15 as the highest. The Writing Sample essays are scored alphabetically on a scale ranging from J to T, with T as the highest. The two essays are each evaluated by two official readers, so four critiques combine to make the alphabetical score.

The number of multiple-choice questions that you answer correctly per section is your "raw score." Your raw score will then be converted to yield the "scaled score"—the one that will fall somewhere in that 1–15 range. These scaled scores are what are reported to medical schools as your MCAT scores. All multiple-choice questions are worth the same amount—one raw point—and *there's no penalty for guessing*. That means that *you should always select an answer for every question, whether you get to that question or not!* This is an important piece of advice, so pay it heed. Never let time run out on any section without selecting an answer for every question.

The raw score of each administration is converted to a scaled score. The conversion varies with administrations. Hence, the same raw score will not always give you the same scaled score.

Your score report will tell you—and your potential medical schools—not only your scaled scores, but also the national mean score for each section, standard deviation, national scoring profile for each section, and your percentile ranking.

WHAT'S A GOOD SCORE?

There's no such thing as a cut-and-dry "good score." Much depends on the strength of the rest of your application (if your transcript is first rate, the pressure to strut your stuff on the MCAT isn't as intense) and on where you want to go to school (different schools have different score expectations). Here are a few interesting statistics:

For each MCAT administration, the average scaled scores are approximately 8s for Physical Sciences, Verbal Reasoning, and Biological Sciences, and N for the Writing Sample. You need scores of at least 10–11s to be considered competitive by most medical schools, and if you're aiming for the top you've got to do even better, and score 12s and above.

You don't have to be perfect to do well. For instance, on the AAMC's Practice Test 5R, you could get as many as 10 questions wrong in Verbal Reasoning, 17 in Physical Sciences, and 16 in Biological Sciences and still score in the 80th percentile. To score in the 90th percentile, you could get as many as 7 wrong in Verbal Reasoning, 12 in Physical Sciences, and 12 in Biological Sciences. Even students who receive perfect scaled scores usually get a handful of questions wrong.

It's important to maximize your performance on every question. Just a few questions one way or the other can make a big difference in your scaled score. Here's a look at recent score profiles so you can get an idea of the shape of a typical score distribution.

Physical Sciences				Verbal Reasoning		
Scaled Score	Percent Achieving Score	Percentile Rank Range		Scaled Score	Percent Achieving Score	Percentile Rank Range
15	0.1	99.9–99.9		15	0.1	99.9–99.9
14	1.2	98.7–99.8		14	0.2	99.7–99.8
13	2.5	96.2–98.6		13	1.8	97.9–99.6
12	5.1	91.1–96.1		12	3.6	94.3–97.8
11	7.2	83.9–91.0		11	10.5	83.8–94.2
10	12.1	71.8–83.8		10	15.6	68.2–83.7
9	12.9	58.9–71.1		9	17.2	51.0–68.1
8	16.5	42.4–58.5		8	15.4	35.6–50.9
7	16.7	25.7–42.3		7	10.3	25.3–35.5
6	13.0	12.7–25.6		6	10.9	14.4–25.2
5	7.9	04.8–12.6		5	6.9	07.5–14.3
4	3.3	01.5–04.7		4	3.9	03.6–07.4
3	1.3	00.2–01.4		3	2.0	01.6–03.5
2	0.1	00.1–00.1		2	0.5	00.1–01.5
1	0.0	00.0–00.0		1	0.0	00.0–00.0
Scaled Score Mean = 8.1 Standard Deviation = 2.32				Scaled Score Mean = 8.0 Standard Deviation = 2.43		

Writing Sample		
Scaled Score	Percent Achieving Score	Percentile Rank Range
T	0.5	99.9–99.9
S	2.8	94.7–99.8
R	7.2	96.0–99.3
Q	14.2	91.0–95.9
P	9.7	81.2–90.9
O	17.9	64.0–81.1
N	14.7	47.1–63.9
M	18.8	30.4–47.0
L	9.5	21.2–30.3
K	3.6	13.5–21.1
J	1.2	06.8–13.4
		02.9–06.7
		00.9–02.8
		00.2–00.8
		00.0–00.1
75th Percentile = Q 50th Percentile = O 25th Percentile = M		

Biological Sciences		
Scaled Score	Percent Achieving Score	Percentile Rank Range
15	0.1	99.9–99.9
14	1.2	98.7–99.8
13	2.5	96.2–98.6
12	5.1	91.1–96.1
11	7.2	83.9–91.0
10	12.1	71.8–83.8
9	12.9	58.9–71.1
8	16.5	42.4–58.5
7	16.7	25.7–42.3
6	13.0	12.7–25.6
5	7.9	04.8–12.6
4	3.3	01.5–04.7
3	1.3	00.2–01.4
2	0.1	00.1–00.1
1	0.0	00.0–00.0
Scaled Score Mean = 8.2 Standard Deviation = 2.39		

WHAT THE MCAT REALLY TESTS

It's important to grasp not only the nuts and bolts of the MCAT, so you'll know *what* to do on Test Day, but also the underlying principles of the test so you'll know *why* you're doing what you're doing on Test Day. We'll cover the straightforward MCAT facts later. Now it's time to examine the heart and soul of the MCAT, to see what it's really about.

THE MYTH

Most people preparing for the MCAT fall prey to the myth that the MCAT is a straightforward science test. They think something like this:

> *"It covers the four years of science I had to take in school: biology, chemistry, physics, and organic chemistry. It even has equations. OK, so it has Verbal Reasoning and Writing, but those sections are just to see if we're literate, right? The important stuff is the science. After all, we're going to be doctors."*

Well, here's the little secret no one seems to want you to know: The MCAT is not just a science test; it's also a thinking test. This means that the test is designed to let you demonstrate your thought process, not only your thought content.

The implications are vast. Once you shift your test-taking paradigm to match the MCAT modus operandi, you'll find a new level of confidence and control over the test. You'll begin to work with the nature of the MCAT rather than against it. You'll be more efficient and insightful as you prepare for the test, and you'll be more relaxed on Test Day. In fact, you'll be able to see the MCAT for what it is rather than for what it's dressed up to be. We want your Test Day to feel like a visit with a familiar friend instead of an awkward blind date.

THE ZEN OF MCAT

Medical schools do not need to rely on the MCAT to see what you already know. Admission committees can measure your subject-area proficiency using your undergraduate coursework and grades. Schools are most interested in the potential of your mind.

In recent years, many medical schools have shifted pedagogic focus away from an information-heavy curriculum to a concept-based curriculum. There is currently more emphasis placed on problem solving, holistic thinking, and cross-disciplinary study. Be careful not to dismiss this important point, figuring you'll wait to worry about academic trends until you're actually in medical school. This trend affects you right now, because it's reflected in the MCAT. Every good tool matches its task. In this case the tool is the test, used to measure you and other candidates, and the task is to quantify how likely it is that you'll succeed in medical school.

Your intellectual potential—how skillfully you annex new territory into your mental boundaries, how quickly you build "thought highways" between ideas, how confidently and creatively you solve problems—is far more important to admission committees than your ability to recite Young's modulus for every material known to man. The schools assume they can expand your knowledge base. They choose applicants carefully because expansive knowledge is not enough to succeed in medical school or in the profession. There's something more. It's this "something more" that the MCAT is trying to measure.

Every section on the MCAT tests essentially the same higher-order thinking skills: analytical reasoning, abstract thinking, and problem solving. Most test takers get trapped into thinking they are being tested strictly about biology, chemistry, and so on. Thus, they approach each section with a new outlook on what's expected. This constant mental gear-shifting can be exhausting, not to mention counterproductive. Instead of perceiving the test as parsed into radically different sections, you need to maintain your focus on the underlying nature of the test: It's designed to test your thinking skills, not your information-recall skills. Each test section presents a variation on the same theme.

WHAT ABOUT THE SCIENCE?

With this perspective, you may be left asking these questions: "What about the science? What about the content? Don't I need to know the basics?" The answer is a resounding "Yes!" You must be fluent in the different languages of the test. You cannot do well on the MCAT if you don't know the basics of physics, general chemistry, biology, and organic chemistry. We recommend that you take one year each of biology, general chemistry, organic chemistry, and physics before taking the MCAT, and that you review the content in this book thoroughly. Knowing these basics is just the beginning of doing well on the MCAT. That's a shock to most test takers. They presume that once they recall or relearn their undergraduate science, they are ready to do battle against the MCAT. Wrong! They merely have directions to the battlefield. They lack what they need to beat the test: a copy of the test maker's battle plan!

You won't be drilled on facts and formulas on the MCAT. You'll need to demonstrate ability to reason based on ideas and concepts. The science questions are painted with a broad brush, testing your general understanding.

KAPLAN

TAKE CONTROL: THE MCAT MINDSET

In addition to being a thinking test, as we've stressed, the MCAT is a standardized test. As such, it has its own consistent patterns and idiosyncrasies that can actually work in your favor. This is the key to why test preparation works. You have the opportunity to familiarize yourself with those consistent peculiarities, to adopt the proper test-taking mindset.

The following are some overriding principles of the MCAT mindset that will be covered in depth in the chapters to come:

- Read actively and critically.
- Translate prose into your own words.
- Save the toughest questions for last.
- Know the test and its components inside and out.
- Do MCAT-style problems in each topic area after you've reviewed it.
- Allow your confidence to build on itself.
- Take full-length practice tests a week or two before the test to break down the mystique of the real experience.
- Learn from your mistakes—get the most out of your practice tests.
- Look at the MCAT as a challenge, the first step in your medical career, rather than as an arbitrary obstacle.

That's what the MCAT mindset boils down to: Taking control. Being proactive. Being on top of the testing experience so that you can get as many points as you can as quickly and as easily as possible. Keep this in mind as you read and work through the material in this book and, of course, as you face the challenge on Test Day.

Now that you have a better idea of what the MCAT is all about, let's take a tour of the individual test sections. Although the underlying skills being tested are similar, each MCAT section requires that you call into play a different domain of knowledge. So, though we encourage you to think of the MCAT as a holistic and unified test, we also recognize that the test is segmented by discipline and that there are characteristics unique to each section. In the overviews, we'll review sample questions and answers and discuss section-specific strategies. For each of the sections—Verbal Reasoning, Physical/Biological Sciences, and the Writing Sample—we'll present you with the following:

- **The Big Picture**
  You'll get a clear view of the section and familiarize yourself with what it's really evaluating.

- **A Closer Look**
  You'll explore the types of questions that will appear and master the strategies you'll need to deal with them successfully.

- **Highlights**
  The key approaches to each section are outlined, for reinforcement and quick review.

TEST EXPERTISE

The first year of medical school is a frenzied experience for most students. In order to meet the requirements of a rigorous work schedule, students either learn to prioritize and budget their time or else fall hopelessly behind. It's no surprise, then, that the MCAT, the test specifically designed to predict success in the first year of medical school, is a high-speed, time-intensive test. It demands excellent time-management skills as well as that sine qua non of the successful physician—grace under pressure.

It's one thing to answer a Verbal Reasoning question correctly; it's quite another to answer several correctly in a limited time frame. The same goes for Physical and Biological Sciences—it's a whole new ballgame once you move from doing an individual passage at your leisure to handling a full section under actual timed conditions. You also need to budget your time for the Writing Sample, but this section isn't as time sensitive. However, when it comes to the multiple-choice sections, time pressure is a factor that affects virtually every test taker.

So when you're comfortable with the content of the test, your next challenge will be to take it to the next level—test expertise—which will enable you to manage the all-important time element of the test.

THE FIVE BASIC PRINCIPLES OF TEST EXPERTISE

On some tests, if a question seems particularly difficult you'll spend significantly more time on it, as you'll probably be given more points for correctly answering a hard question. Not so on the MCAT. Remember, every MCAT question, no matter how hard, is worth a single point. There's no partial credit or "A" for effort, and because there are so many questions to do in so little time, you'd be a fool to spend 10 minutes getting a point for a hard question and then not have time to get a couple of quick points from three easy questions later in the section.

Given this combination—limited time, all questions equal in weight—you've got to develop a way of handling the test sections to make sure you get as many points as you can as quickly and easily as you can. Here are the principles that will help you do that:

1. FEEL FREE TO SKIP AROUND

One of the most valuable strategies to help you finish the sections in time is to learn to recognize and deal first with the questions that are easier and more familiar to you. That means you must temporarily skip those that promise to be difficult and time-consuming, if you feel comfortable doing so. You can always come back to these at the end, and if you run out of time, you're much better off not getting to questions you may have had difficulty with, rather than not getting to potentially feasible material. Of course, because there's no guessing penalty, always put an answer to every question on the test, whether you get to it or not. (It's not practical to skip passages, so do those in order.)

This strategy is difficult for most test takers; we're conditioned to do things in order. Nevertheless, give it a try when you practice. Remember, if you do the test in the exact order given, you're letting the test makers control you. You control how you take this test. On the other hand, if skipping around goes against your moral fiber and makes you a nervous wreck—don't do it. Just be mindful of the clock, and don't get bogged down with the tough questions.

2. LEARN TO RECOGNIZE AND SEEK OUT QUESTIONS YOU CAN DO

Another thing to remember about managing the test sections is that MCAT questions and passages, unlike items on the SAT and other standardized tests, are not presented in order of difficulty. There's no rule that says you have to work through the sections in any particular order; in fact, the test makers scatter the easy and difficult questions throughout the section, in effect rewarding those who actually get to the end. Don't lose sight of what you're being tested for along with your reading and thinking skills: efficiency and cleverness.

Don't waste time on questions you can't do. We know that skipping a possibly tough question is easier said than done; we all have the natural instinct to plow through test sections in their given order, but it just doesn't pay off on the MCAT. The computer won't be impressed if you get the toughest question right. If you dig in your heels on a tough question, refusing to move on until you've cracked it, well, you're letting your ego get in the way of your test score. A test section (not to mention life itself) is too short to waste on lost causes.

3. USE A PROCESS OF ANSWER ELIMINATION

Using a process of elimination is another way to answer questions both quickly and effectively. There are two ways to get all the answers right on the MCAT. You either know all the right answers, or you know all the wrong answers. Because there are three times as many wrong answers, you should be able to eliminate some if not all of them. By doing so you either get to the correct response or increase your chances of guessing the correct response. You start out with a 25 percent chance of picking the right answer, and with each eliminated answer your odds go up. Eliminate one, and you'll have a $33\frac{1}{3}$ percent chance of picking the right one, eliminate two, and you'll have a 50 percent chance, and, of course, eliminate three, and you'll have a 100 percent chance. Increase your efficiency by actually crossing out the wrong choices on the screen using the strike-through feature. Remember to look for wrong-answer traps when you're eliminating. Some answers are designed to seduce you by distorting the correct answer.

4. REMAIN CALM

It's imperative that you remain calm and composed while working through a section. You can't allow yourself to become so rattled by one hard reading passage that it throws off your performance on the rest of the section. Expect to find at least one killer passage in every section, but remember, you won't be the only one to have trouble with it. The test is curved to take the tough material into account. Having trouble with a difficult question isn't going to ruin your score—but getting upset about it and letting it throw you off track will. When you understand that part of the test maker's goal is to reward those who keep their composure, you'll recognize the importance of not panicking when you run into challenging material.

5. KEEP TRACK OF TIME

Of course, the last thing you want to happen is to have time called on a particular section before you've gotten to half the questions. Therefore, it's essential that you pace yourself, keeping in mind the general guidelines for how long to spend on any individual question or passage. Have a sense of how long you have to do each question, so you know when you're exceeding the limit and should start to move faster.

So, when working on a section, always remember to keep track of time. Don't spend a wildly disproportionate amount of time on any one question or group of questions. Also, give yourself 30 seconds or so at the end of each section to fill in answers for any questions you haven't gotten to.

SECTION-SPECIFIC PACING

Let's now look at the section-specific timing requirements and some tips for meeting them. Keep in mind that the times per question or passage are only averages; there are bound to be some that take less time and some that take more. Try to stay balanced. Remember, too, that every question is of equal worth, so don't get hung up on any one. Think about it: If a question is so hard that it takes you a long time to answer it, chances are you may get it wrong anyway. In that case, you'd have nothing to show for your extra time but a lower score.

VERBAL REASONING

Allow yourself approximately eight to ten minutes per passage and respective questions. It may sound like a lot of time, but it goes quickly. Keep in mind that some passages are longer than others. On average, give yourself about three or four minutes to read and then four to six minutes for the questions.

PHYSICAL AND BIOLOGICAL SCIENCES

Averaging over each section, you'll have about one minute and 20 seconds per question. Some questions, of course, will take more time, some less. A science passage plus accompanying questions should take about eight to nine minutes, depending on how many questions there are. Stand-alone questions can take anywhere from a few seconds to a minute or more. Again, the rule is to do your best work first. Also, don't feel that you have to understand everything in a passage before you go on to the questions. You may not need that deep an understanding to answer questions, because a lot of information may be extraneous. You should overcome your perfectionism and use your time wisely.

WRITING SAMPLE

You have exactly 30 minutes for each essay. As mentioned in discussion of the seven-step approach to this section, you should allow approximately five minutes to prewrite the essay, 23 minutes to write the essay, and two minutes to proofread. It's important that you budget your time, so you don't get cut off.

COMPUTER-BASED TESTING STRATEGIES

ARRIVE AT THE TESTING CENTER EARLY

Get to the testing center early to jump-start your brain. However, if they allow you to begin your test early, decline.

USE THE MOUSE TO YOUR ADVANTAGE

If you are right-handed, practice using the mouse with your left hand for Test Day. This way, you'll increase speed by keeping the pencil in your right hand to write on your scratch paper. If you are left-handed, use your right hand for the mouse.

KNOW THE TUTORIAL BEFORE TEST DAY

You will save time on Test Day by knowing exactly how the test will work. Click through any tutorial pages and save time.

PRACTICE WITH SCRATCH PAPER

Going forward, always practice using scratch paper when solving questions because this is how you will do it on Test Day. Never write directly on a written test.

GET NEW SCRATCH PAPER

Between sections, get a new piece of scratch paper even if you only used part of the old one. This will maximize the available space for each section and minimize the likelihood of you running out of paper to write on.

REMEMBER YOU CAN ALWAYS GO BACK

Just because you finish a passage or move on, remember you can come back to questions about which you are uncertain. You have the "marking" option to your advantage. However, as a general rule minimize the amount of questions you mark or skip.

MARK INCOMPLETE WORK

If you need to go back to a question, clearly mark the work you've done on the scratch paper with the question number. This way, you will be able to find your work easily when you come back to tackle the question.

LOOK AWAY AT TIMES

Taking the test on computer leads to faster eye-muscle fatigue. Use the Kaplan strategy of looking at a distant object at regular intervals. This will keep you fresher at the end of the test.

PRACTICE ON THE COMPUTER

This is the most critical aspect of adapting to computer-based testing. Like anything else, in order to perform well on computer-based tests you must practice. Spend time reading passages and answering questions on the computer. You often will have to scroll when reading passages.

Part I
Review

Nomenclature

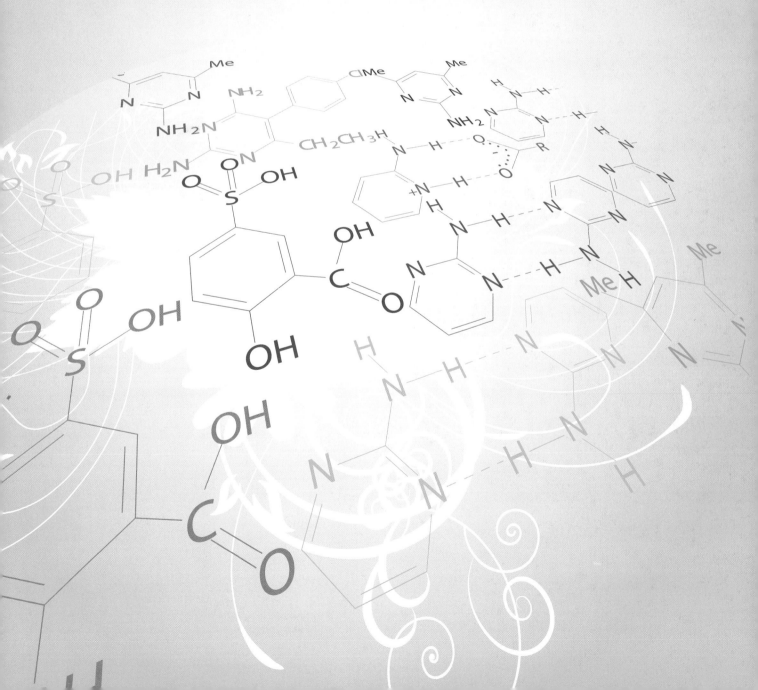

Early in my undergraduate career, I was warned, as I'm sure all of you were, about the dangers of Organic Chemistry. We've heard that the course is designed to weed out unworthy premeds, that it's both a GPA and a spirit breaker for optimistic future doctors. With these horror stories being passed down from generation to generation, it's no surprise that I, too, feared Organic Chemistry long before even setting foot in the classroom. While my expectations of fire, brimstone, and failing grades never actually came to pass, it did turn out to be one of the most challenging classes of my college career.

After surviving both Organic Chemistry I and II, I still didn't really understand the material. I could answer most of the questions with fairly decent accuracy and get good grades (owing to the strong curve), but I never really felt all that confident in the material. It wasn't until I started preparing for the MCAT that I actually began to comprehend what was happening in these reactions. You see, Organic Chemistry on the MCAT is a lot different from what it was in your Organic Chemistry classes. You will no longer be tested on your ability to memorize scattered reactions; instead, you will be tested on your understanding of the fundamental characteristics that drive reactions.

In fact, Organic Chemistry is a lot like chess—just as every piece on the board is capable of different motions, so is each element. It's actually a bit simpler than chess, because there are really only two different actions the atom can take in a reaction: Does it attack a nucleus with its excess electrons (negative charge), or does it get attacked as a result of its electron deficiency (positive charge)? You can decide between these two actions by considering a few important questions: How electronegative is the atom? Can it resonate its electrons? Are other atoms inductively pulling its electron density away? Learning the game of Organic Chemistry is much like learning any other game—if we want to play correctly, we need to know the rules.

Before we jump into examining reactions and solving problems, let's lay out the rules for naming organic compounds. Attempting to solve chemistry problems without knowing nomenclature is like trying to read *A Tale of Two Cities* without knowing English. Whereas the rules of English can sometimes seem unpredictable and inexact, the International Union of Pure and Applied Chemistry (IUPAC) established a precise and comprehensive language for Organic Chemistry. This means that learning IUPAC nomenclature will be infinitely easier than learning English—and, hey, you've already done that!

The MCAT occasionally employs a second dialect, known as a chemical's "common name." These names are based on the traditional names that were used before the IUPAC system (and, like reading Shakespeare, can sometimes seem like a completely different language), but they follow certain trends as well. There are only a handful of common names that you'll need to know on Test Day, and we'll point them out throughout the course of this book.

With a solid understanding of organic nomenclature, you should be able to both draw out the structure of any IUPAC name and give the IUPAC name for any structure you are given. We will provide you with the tools to learn the language of Organic Chemistry, though as with any language, fluency can only come with practice.

Alkanes

STRAIGHT-CHAIN ALKANES

Alkanes are the bare bones of the Organic Chemistry world; they are the simplest of the organic molecules, just a chain of carbons connected by single bonds with hydrogen atoms attached. Alkanes include commonly used fuels such as propane, butane, and octane.

The four simplest straight-chain alkanes are these:

$$CH_4 \qquad CH_3CH_3 \qquad CH_3CH_2CH_3 \qquad CH_3CH_2CH_2CH_3$$

methane   ethane   propane   butane

The general formula for alkanes is C_nH_{2n+2} (where n is an integer).

When the carbon chain contains five or more carbons, the naming gets a little simpler. Just use the Greek root for the number of carbons followed by the ending **–ane**.

$C_5H_{12} =$ **pent**ane $C_9H_{20} =$ **non**ane

$C_6H_{14} =$ **hex**ane $C_{10}H_{22} =$ **dec**ane

$C_7H_{16} =$ **hept**ane $C_{11}H_{24} =$ **undec**ane

$C_8H_{18} =$ **oct**ane $C_{12}H_{26} =$ **dodec**ane

BRANCHED-CHAIN ALKANES

Whenever we have a chain of carbon atoms with smaller carbon chains branching off it, IUPAC gives us an organized system of naming the compound in five easy steps.

Step 1: Find the Longest Chain in the Compound

Finding the longest possible chain might sound easy, but be careful. Sometimes a molecule will be drawn so the backbone is actually composed of what looks like a side branch. Figure 1.1 shows a branched-chain alkane with its backbone.

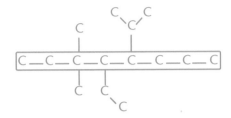

Figure 1.1

If there are two or more chains of equal length, the most substituted chain (the one with the most stuff attached to it) gets priority.

Step 2: Number the Chain

Number the chain such that most substituents get the lowest numbers possible. If you're not sure, just number it both ways and find the sum of each chain (see Figure 1.2). And then, well... it's like golf: The lowest wins.

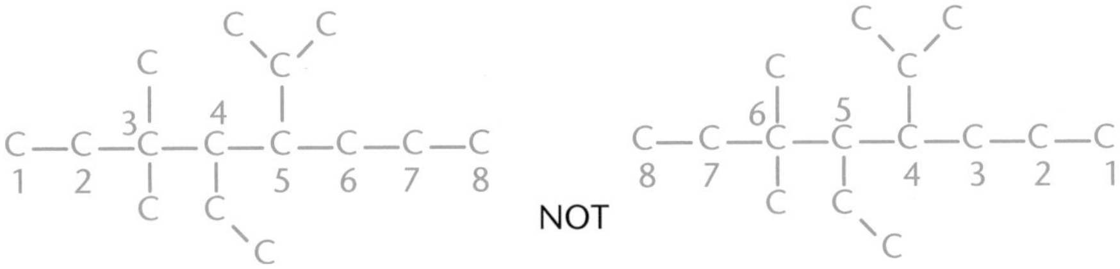

Figure 1.2

Step 3: Name the Substituents

Carbon chain **substituents** are named according to their Greek number root followed by the suffix **–yl**. This term is placed at the beginning of the compound, followed by the name of the longest side chain. Here are examples of some common substituents are.

CH_3–	CH_3CH_2–	$CH_3CH_2CH_2$–
methyl	ethyl	*n*-propyl

The prefix ***n*-**, as we see in *n*-propyl above, simply stands for "normal." The normal designation indicates that the substituent is a straight-chain alkane that attaches to the backbone at one end of its chain. Sometimes the *n*- will be left out, but it's safe for you to assume that a molecule is normal, unless specified otherwise.

So what do abnormal substituents look like? The most common examples of alkane side chains that are not normal are shown in Figure 1.3.

MCAT Expertise

While this is an important rule, the MCAT is not looking to trick you—although they do reserve the right to do so! Most often, you will have smaller chains and not have to work too hard to find the longest carbon chain.

MCAT Expertise

Memorize these structures!

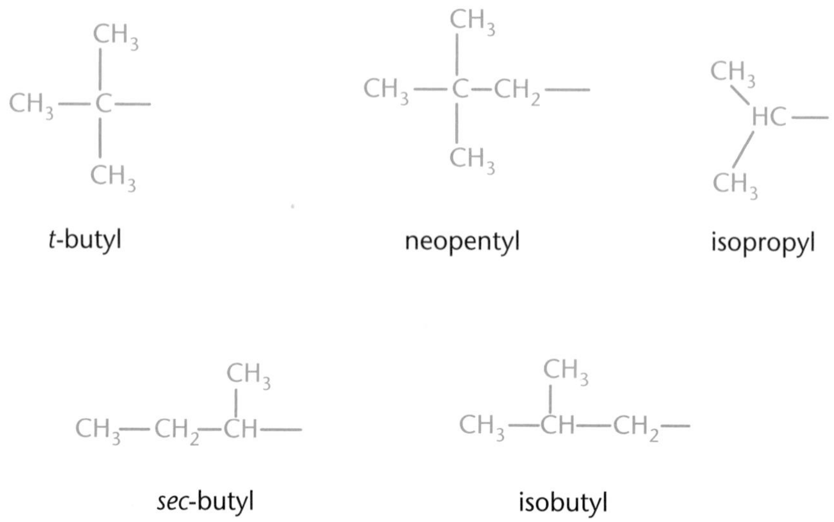

t-butyl neopentyl isopropyl

sec-butyl isobutyl

Figure 1.3

If there are multiple identical substituents, then we use the roots **di–, tri–, tetra–,** and so on.

Step 4: Assign a Number to Each Substituent.

Each substituent is assigned a number to designate its place on the principal chain. If the prefixes di–, tri–, and tetra– are used, we still assign a number for each group, even if those groups are attached to the same carbon. Don't worry if this sounds confusing; we will piece it all together in the next step.

Step 5: Complete the Name.

Names will always begin with the substituents listed in *alphabetical order,* with each substituent name preceded by its assigned number. Here's the tricky part. Numerical prefixes such as **di–, tri–,** and so on, as well as the hyphenated prefixes (***tert–*** [or ***t–***], ***sec–,*** and ***n–***) are ignored in alphabetizing. In contrast to this, nonhyphenated roots that *are* part of the name, such as **iso–, neo–,** or **cyclo–,** *are* alphabetized. We then separate numbers from numbers with commas, and we separate numbers from words with hyphens. Remember that the end of every name will be the name of the backbone chain. Figure 1.4 shows an example.

MCAT Expertise

The MCAT is not a "picky" exam, so you probably won't be asked to choose between two answers that differ only in their alphabetization, but the rule about the prefixes may come in handy.

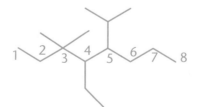

4-ethyl-5-isopropyl-3,3-dimethyl octane

Figure 1.4

CYCLOALKANES

Alkanes can also form rings; these are named by the number of carbon atoms in the ring with the prefix **cyclo–** (see Figure 1.5).

cyclopropane   cyclobutane   cyclooctane

Figure 1.5

The general formula for **cycloalkanes** is C_nH_{2n}. For every ring in the structure, there will be two fewer hydrogens than in the straight-chain counterpart. Let's think about what happens to those two hydrogens. We know that straight-chain hydrocarbons must end with $-CH_3$ groups, and we form a ring by connecting the two ends of the chain. Each carbon must lose a hydrogen to make an additional bond with the other carbon. This loss of hydrogens is also called a "degree of unsaturation." For example, an alkane with two rings present will have the general formula C_nH_{2n-2}, or two degrees of unsaturation.

As long as the ring itself is the longest carbon chain, substituted cycloalkanes will be named as derivatives of the parent ring. *The ring is numbered starting at the point of greatest substitution.* Once again, this means that the carbon with the most stuff attached to it will be assigned the number 1. Afterward, the goal is to give the lowest series of numbers as described in rule 2. If the ring structure is *not* part of the largest carbon chain, it will be listed as a substituent. Figure 1.6 shows two examples.

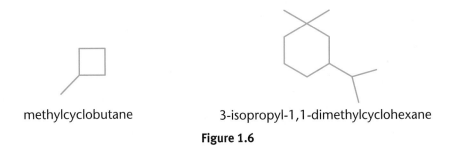

methylcyclobutane   3-isopropyl-1,1-dimethylcyclohexane

Figure 1.6

> **Key Concept**
>
> The general formula for both cycloalkanes and straight-chain alkenes is C_nH_{2n}.

> **Key Concept**
>
> Rings are numbered starting at the point of greatest substitution, and as always, try to get the lowest possible numbers.

> **MCAT Expertise**
>
> The MCAT is a multiple-choice exam. Therefore, it will be more advantageous for you to identify nomenclature errors quickly than to write out the exact name of a giant structure. Remember, speed is going to be one of your greatest assets on the MCAT.

More Complicated Molecules ★★★★★★

All other molecules can be named using this five-step process, although as the molecules get more complicated, we will have more considerations to incorporate. The biggest difference between simple alkanes and these more complicated molecules is this: (You'd better be ready because this is huge!) *When counting out the longest chain of carbons, it MUST include the highest-priority functional group, this group must receive the lowest possible number, and the compound's name must end with the suffix of this group.* What do we mean by priority? Whereas Rolexes and celebrity escorts usually bestow priority upon people trying to get into fancy clubs, molecules just need to be more oxidized than all of their neighbors. We'll return to the concept of oxidation later, but for now, let's begin discussing **alkenes**.

Multiple Bonds

ALKENES

Alkenes (sometimes referred to by their common name, **olefins**) are compounds that contain carbon–carbon double bonds. You'll use the same root as an alkane of equivalent length, but instead of ending with **–ane**, alkenes end with **–ene**.

The general formula for an alkene is C_nH_{2n}. Similar to cyclic alkanes, each double bond leads to two fewer hydrogens on the molecule, or one degree of unsaturation. For example, if we were to have a molecule with one ring and three double bonds, the molecule would have eight fewer hydrogens than its corresponding straight-chain alkane and, thus, four degrees of unsaturation.

As stated before, we need to incorporate the highest priority group when selecting the longest chain and assigning numbers. If there are multiple double bonds, select the chain that contains the greatest number of double bonds, and give the carbons the lowest numbers possible.

NOT

Figure 1.7

Our old rules still apply, so if there are multiple double bonds, they must be named using the numerical prefixes (di–, tri–, etc.) and each bond must receive a number. Also, you may need to name the configurational isomer (*cis/trans*, *Z/E*). This topic will be discussed further in Chapter 2. Substituents are named in the same manner as they are for alkanes, and their positions are specified by their respective numbers.

Frequently, an alkene group must be named as a substituent. In these cases, the systematic names may be used, but the common names are more popular. **Vinyl** derivatives are monosubstituted ethylenes (**ethenyl–**), which is actually just a carbon–carbon double bond as a substituent. You will likely see **allyl** derivatives on the MCAT; these are propylenes attached to a backbone at the C–3 position (**2-propenyl–**), meaning the double bond is at the end of the chain and the single-bonded carbon is attached to the rest of the chain. **Methylene–** refers to the $=CH_2$ group, where the substituent is only one carbon that is double bonded to the rest of the molecule. Examples of all three of these are shown in Figure 1.8.

Bridge

A carbon backbone with alternating single and double bonds is called a conjugated system. Conjugation gives the molecule notable stability because its electrons can be delocalized, a phenomenon that has important consequences for our later discussion of aromatic compounds in Chapter 6.

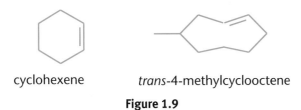

| chloroethene (vinyl chloride) | 3-bromo-1-propene (allyl bromide) | methylene cyclohexane |

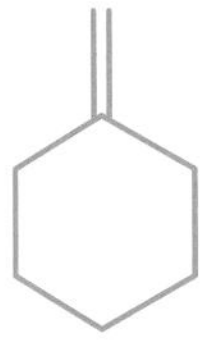

Figure 1.8

CYCLOALKENES

Cycloalkenes (rings containing one or more double bonds) are named like cycloalkanes but with the suffix **–ene** rather than **–ane** (see Figure 1.9). If there is only one double bond and no other substituents, the ring does not have to be numbered.

cyclohexene   *trans*-4-methylcyclooctene

Figure 1.9

ALKYNES

Alkynes are compounds with carbon–carbon triple bonds. The nomenclature rules are the same, but the suffix **–yne** replaces **–ane** from the parent alkane. If necessary, a number indicates the position of the triple bond. No matter how the triple bonds are depicted, they are always linear. Figure 1.10 shows some examples. (*Common name alert:* Two triple-bonded carbons are known by the common name **acetylene**. The IUPAC name **ethyne** is almost never used.)

Key Concept

The general formula for an alkyne is C_nH_{2n-2}. An alkyne has two degrees of unsaturation because it has two pi bonds.

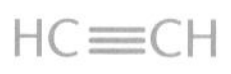

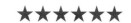

ethyne (acetylene)

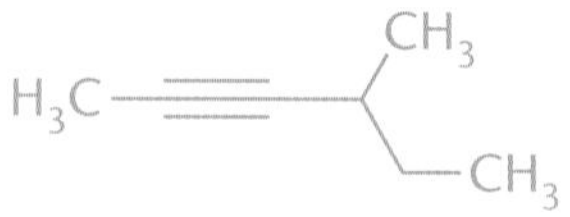

4-methylhex-2-yne

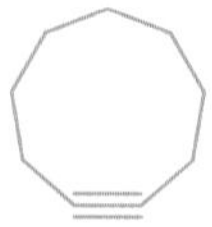

cyclononyne

Figure 1.10

Although this is not likely to come up on the MCAT, when there are both double and triple bonds in a molecule, the molecule's name ends in "*y*-*root*-en-*x*-yne," where the first number *y* describes the position of the double bond, the second number *x* describes the position of the triple bond, and *root* is the prefix representing the length of the principal carbon chain. These numbers must be chosen so that the sum of *x* and *y* is as small as possible, and (as stated before) the double bond is given the lowest number where there is a choice.

Substituted Alkanes ★★★★★★

HALOALKANES

Compounds that contain a **halogen** (F, Cl, Br, or I) substituent are named **haloalkanes**. The substituents are numbered as alkyl groups; thus, the lowest number is determined alphabetically. Notice that the presence of the halide does not dramatically affect the numbering of the chain; we still proceed so that substituents receive the lowest possible numbers. Figure 1.11 shows two examples.

MCAT Expertise

Halogens are great leaving groups and, as such, are likely to be seen on the MCAT (and later in this book) as part of many reactions.

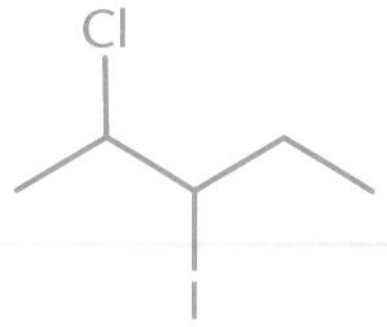

2-chloro-3-iodopentane

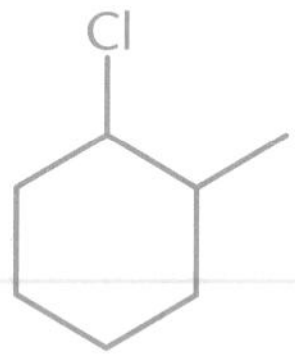

1-chloro-2-methylcyclohexane

Figure 1.11

Alternatively, you may see some haloalkanes on the MCAT named as **alkyl halides**. Remember that the MCAT is a multiple-choice exam, so it is far more important for you to see a name and know what the structure should look like than to decide whether to name the molecule as a haloalkane or an alkyl halide. For example, chloroethane is called **ethyl chloride** using the alkyl halide-naming convention. Two more examples are shown in Figure 1.12.

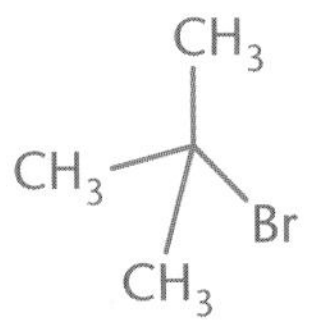

2-bromo-2-methylpropane
(*t*-butyl bromide)

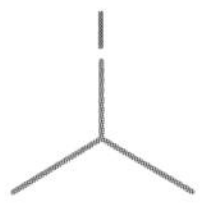

2-iodopropane
(isopropyl iodide)

Figure 1.12

ALCOHOLS

According to the IUPAC system, **alcohols** are named by replacing the –**e** of the corresponding alkane with –**ol**. The chain is numbered so that the carbon attached to the hydroxyl group (–OH) receives the lowest number possible. Even when there is a double bond in the molecule, the –OH group still takes precedence and is given the lowest number. Figure 1.13 shows some exmples.

Key Concept

–OH has priority over double and triple bonds when numbering the chain.

ethanol

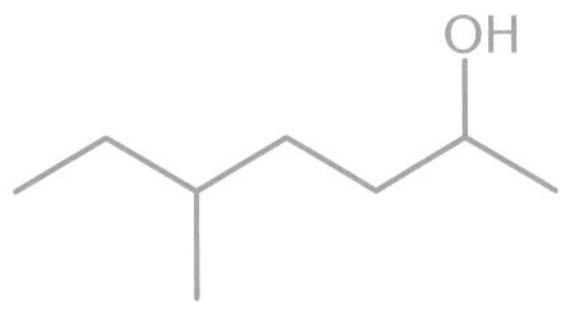

5-methyl-2-heptanol

hept-6-en-1-ol

Figure 1.13

Common name alert: A common system of nomenclature exists for simple alcohols in which the name of the alkyl group is simply followed by the word *alcohol*. For example, ethanol may be named **ethyl alcohol**, or 2-propanol may be named **isopropyl alcohol**.

Molecules with two hydroxyl groups are called **diols** (or **glycols**) and are named with the suffix –**diol**. Two numbers are necessary to distinguish the two functional groups. For example, ethane-1,2-diol is an ethane molecule with an –OH group attached to each carbon, and it is known by its common name **ethylene glycol**. Diols with hydroxyl groups on adjacent carbons are referred to as **vicinal**, and diols with hydroxyl groups on the same carbon are **geminal**. Geminal diols (also called **hydrates**) are not commonly observed because they spontaneously lose water (dehydrate) to produce carbonyl compounds (containing C=O, as we will see in Chapter 8).

Mnemonic

Vicinal diols are in the *vicinity* of each other—that is, from adjacent carbons.

Mnemonic

Geminal diols (like the astrological sign Gemini) are *twins* of each other—that is, from the same carbon.

ETHERS

Following the system from our friends at IUPAC, ethers are named as derivatives of alkanes; once again, the largest alkyl group is chosen as the backbone. The backbone chain is numbered to give the carbon bound to the oxygen the lowest position. The ether functionality is specified by an **alkoxy–** prefix, indicating the presence of an ether (–oxy–) and the corresponding smaller alkyl group (alk–). To make sense of this language, imagine an ether that has its oxygen connected with an ethyl group on one side and a methyl group on the other. The methyl group is named as a substituent and termed a **methoxy**, and the ethane is simply named (because it is the larger group): hence, **methoxyethane**.

Common name alert: Common names for ethers are frequently used. They are derived by naming the two alkyl groups in alphabetical order and adding the word *ether*. The generic term *ether* refers to diethyl ether, a commonly used solvent and one of the original anesthetics. For cyclic ethers, the numbering of the ring begins at the oxygen and proceeds to provide the lowest numbers for the substituents (same way we always do). Three-membered rings are called **oxiranes** by IUPAC, but they are almost always referred to as **epoxides**.

MCAT Expertise

On the MCAT, you will see ethers named in IUPAC as frequently as they are named by common names, so know them both well.

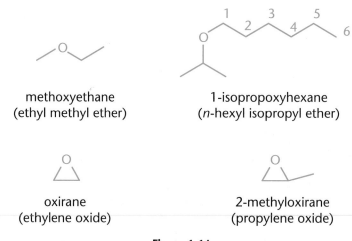

methoxyethane
(ethyl methyl ether)

1-isopropoxyhexane
(*n*-hexyl isopropyl ether)

oxirane
(ethylene oxide)

2-methyloxirane
(propylene oxide)

Figure 1.14

tetrahydrofuran
(THF)

Figure 1.15

ALDEHYDES AND KETONES

Before jumping into the differences between aldehydes and ketones, let's first talk about what makes them *similar*. Both of these compounds have a **carbonyl**, which is a carbon double-bonded to an oxygen. What makes them *different* is simply the placement of the carbonyl within the molecule. In **aldehydes**, the carbonyl is located at the end of the chain. Because the functional group is terminal, it will always receive the number 1, so we do not need to state the number in its name. The only thing we have to do is replace the **–e**, from the parent alkane, and replace it with **–al**, and we've named our aldehyde (see Figure 1.16).

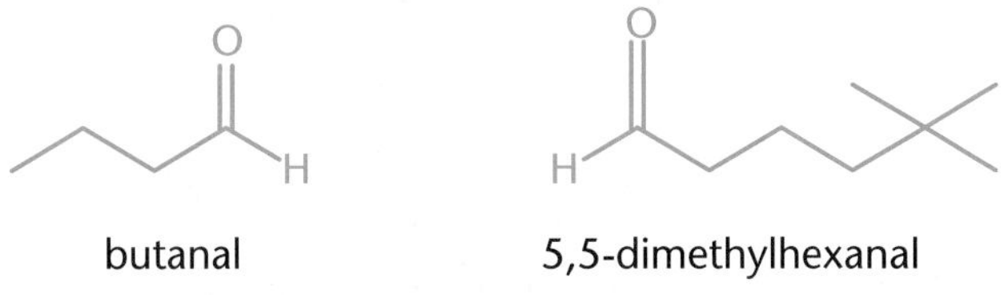

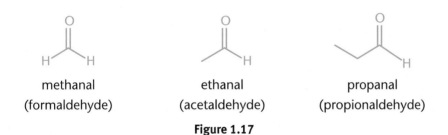

butanal   5,5-dimethylhexanal

Figure 1.16

Common name alert: The common names **formaldehyde**, **acetaldehyde**, and **propionaldehyde** are used almost exclusively instead of their respective IUPAC names **methanal**, **ethanal**, and **propanal** (see Figure 1.17).

methanal   ethanal   propanal
(formaldehyde)   (acetaldehyde)   (propionaldehyde)

Figure 1.17

MCAT Expertise

Common name alert: On the MCAT, the common names *formic acid*, *acetic acid*, and *propanoic acid* are used almost exclusively. *Make sure you know these!*

Ketones are similar to aldehydes, except that the carbonyl is located somewhere in the middle of the carbon chain. As such, a number must be assigned to the carbonyl, and the suffix **–one** is used instead of the **–e** of the parent alkane (see Figure 1.18). As always, our goal in assigning numbers is to give the highest-priority functional group (in this case, the carbonyl) the lowest possible number.

Common name alert: To determine the common name of a ketone, simply list the alkyl groups in alphabetical order followed by the word *ketone*.

In a more complex molecule containing a group with higher priority, the carbonyl group (yes, whether it's a ketone *or* an aldehyde) is named as a substituent with the prefix **oxo–** (because of the oxygen).

MCAT Expertise

On the MCAT, *formaldehyde*, *acetaldehyde*, and *acetone* are used almost exclusively. *Make sure you know these!*

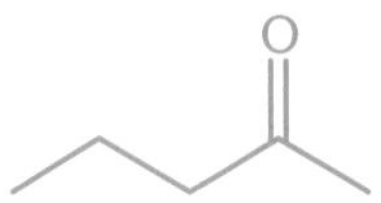

2-pentanone

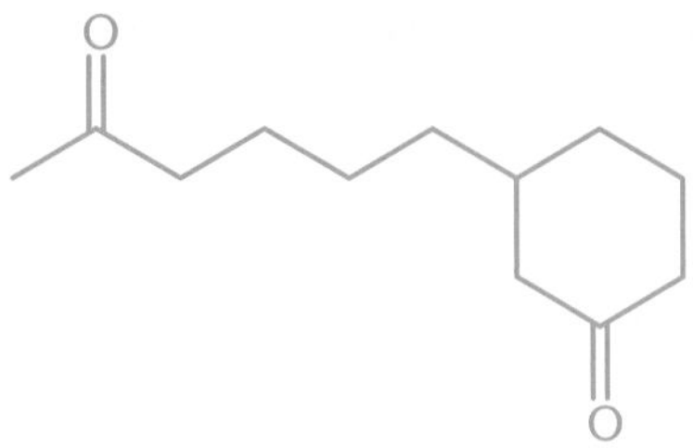

3-(5-oxohexyl)cyclohexanone

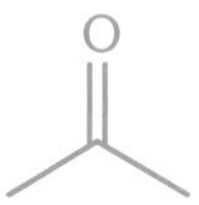

2-propanone
(dimethyl ketone)
(acetone)

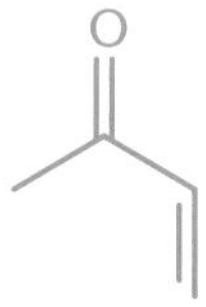

3-butene-2-one
(methyl vinyl ketone)

Figure 1.18

On the MCAT, you will probably come across an alternative to the numeric designations discussed thus far, a convention that names all of the carbons relative to the carbonyl group. In this convention, we call the carbon atom adjacent to the carbonyl alpha (α), and the carbon atoms successively along the chain are named beta (β), gamma (γ), delta (δ), etc. These Greek letter names apply on both sides of the carbonyl, which means the carbons on either side of a ketone are called α carbons. This system is encountered with dicarbonyl compounds with halocarbonyl compounds, or when referring to α-hydrogen acidity, as we will do often when we start reviewing aldehydes and ketones (Chapter 8).

Key Concept

Carbons adjacent to a carbonyl are named α carbons; the carbons next to that are named β carbons. All of the hydrogens attached to those carbons have the same name as the carbon to which they are bound.

CARBOXYLIC ACIDS

Like aldehydes, **carboxylic acids** are terminal functional groups, and the carbonyl will always receive the number 1 when the chain is numbered. Carboxylic acids contain a carbonyl *and* an –OH group, making them quite oxidized. In fact, they are the most oxidized functional group, with three bonds to oxygen. The only carbon that is more oxidized is carbon dioxide, which has four bonds to oxygen. Carboxylic acids are the highest-priority functional group, so every other functional group on a carboxylic acid will be named as a substituent. Figure 1.19 shows some examples.

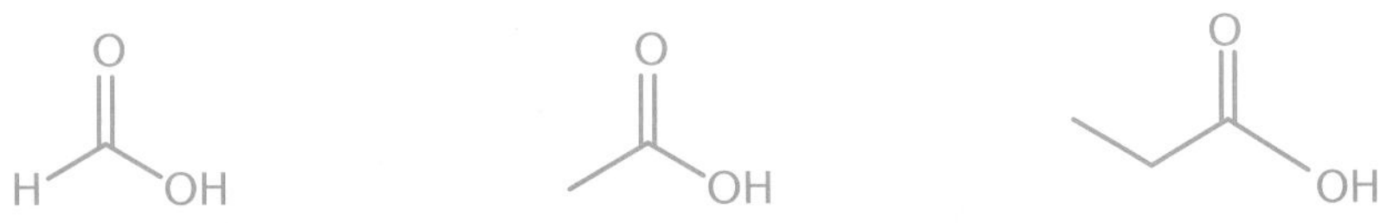

methanoic acid
(formic acid)

ethanoic acid
(acetic acid)

propanoic acid
(propionic acid)

Figure 1.19

AMINES

When naming **amines**, which are nitrogen-containing compounds, the longest chain attached to the nitrogen atom is used as the backbone. When dealing with simple compounds, you simply name the alkane and replace the final –**e** with –**amine**. More complex molecules, with higher-priority functional groups, are named using the prefix **amino–** (see Figure 1.20).

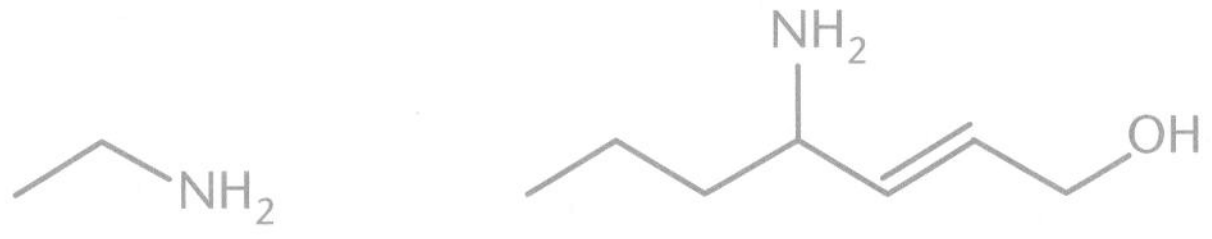

ethanamine

4-aminohept-2-en-1-ol

Figure 1.20

When additional groups are attached to the nitrogen atom, we can designate their position by using the prefix N– (see Figure 1.21).

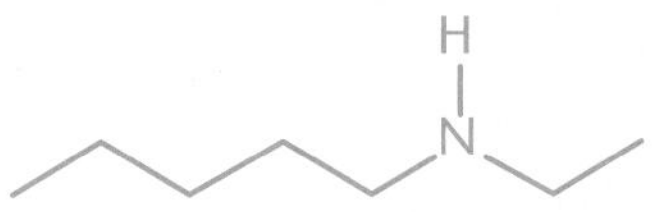

N-ethylpentanamine
(ethylpentylamine)

Figure 1.21

Summary of Functional Groups ★★★★★★

Table 1.1 lists all the major functional groups you need to know for the MCAT. Both prefixes and suffixes are given. If the functional group is the highest-priority group on the molecule, the suffix is used. If the functional group does *not* hold the highest priority, it is named as a substituent, and the prefix is used.

Table 1.1. Major Functional Groups

Functional Group	Structure	IUPAC Prefix	IUPAC Suffix
Carboxylic acid	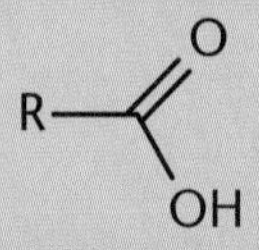 R–C(=O)–OH	carboxy-	-oic acid
Ester	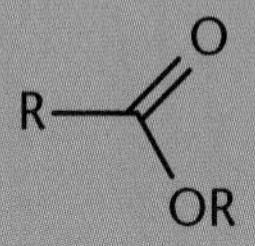 R–C(=O)–OR	alkoxycarbonyl-	-oate
Acyl halide	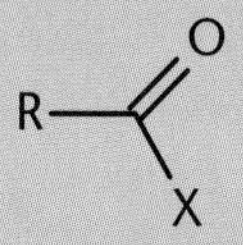 R–C(=O)–X	halocarbonyl-	-oyl halide
Amide	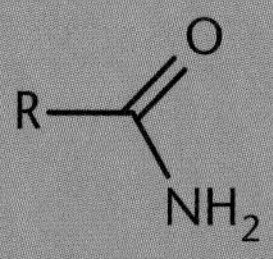 R–C(=O)–NH$_2$	amido-	-amide
Nitrile/Cyanide	$RC \equiv N$	cyano-	-nitrile
Aldehyde	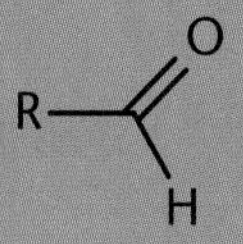 R–C(=O)–H	oxo-	-al
Ketone	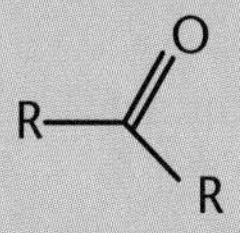 R–C(=O)–R	oxo-	-one
Alcohol	ROH	hydroxy-	-ol
Thiol	RSH	sulfhydryl-	-thiol
Amine	RNH$_2$	amino-	-amine
Imine	R$_2$C=NR'	imino-	-imine
Ether	ROR	alkoxy-	-ether
Sulfide	R$_2$S	alkylthio-	
Halide	-I, -Br, -Cl, -F	halo-	
Nitro	RNO$_2$	nitro-	
Azide	RN$_3$	azido-	
Diazo	RN$_2$	diazo-	

Key Concept

The more oxidized a functional group is, the higher its priority. Table 1.1 lists the functional groups in order of priority, with the highest priority being at the top.

Conclusion

This chapter may not have transformed you into a Grand Chemistry Master, but it does contain all of the nomenclature knowledge that you will need for the MCAT. We also got our first look at the various functional groups that may be present in a molecule. Often, the ability to recognize functional groups (from either the structure or the name) will get you halfway to the correct answer. That's why knowing the rules of nomenclature is such a vital skill and the first topic we introduce you to in this review. A strong foundation in organic nomenclature is requisite for every one of the topics to follow and, ultimately, for success on Test Day. Learning a new language is tough, and although the ability to speak it fluently would be nice, it may not be necessary. Remember that the MCAT is a multiple-choice exam, and any nomenclature that is tested will either be stated in the question stem or in the answer choices. The ability to recognize names will often prove to be nearly as useful as the ability to recall them from memory. If learning other languages had a similar multiple-choice shortcut, far more of us would spend our summers traveling the world.

CONCEPTS TO REMEMBER

☐ Identify the backbone (longest chain of carbons).

☐ Number the chain, keeping numbers for the substituents as low as possible.

☐ Name substituents.

☐ Assign numbers.

☐ Put the whole name together, remembering to alphabetize substituents.

☐ Multiple bonds should be on the main carbon backbone whenever possible.

☐ –OH is a high-priority functional group, placed above multiple bonds in numbering. More oxidized groups have even higher priority.

☐ Haloalkanes, ethers, and ketones are often given common names (e.g., methyl chloride, ethyl methyl ether, diethyl ketone).

☐ Aldehydes and carboxylic acids are terminal functional groups. If present, they define C–1 of the carbon chain.

☐ Remember to specify the isomer, if relevant (such as *cis* or *trans*, *R* or *S*, etc.).

Practice Questions

1. What is the IUPAC name of the following compound?

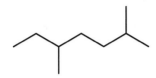

    A. 2,5-Dimethylheptane

    B. 2-Ethyl-5-methylhexane

    C. 3,6-Dimethylheptane

    D. 5-Ethyl-2-methylhexane

2. What is the name of the following compound?

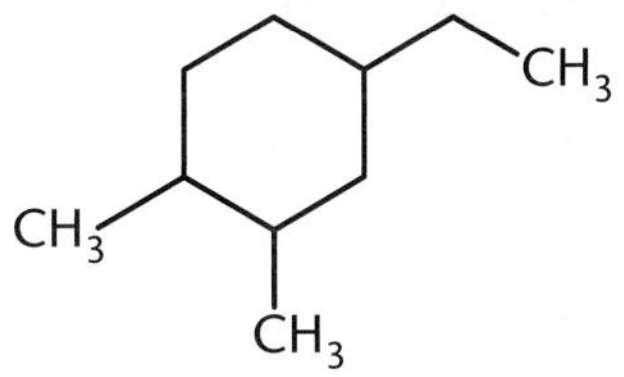

    A. 1-Ethyl-3,4-dimethylcycloheptane

    B. 2-Ethyl-4,5-dimethylcyclohexane

    C. 1-Ethyl-3,4-dimethylcyclohexane

    D. 4-Ethyl-1,2-dimethylcyclohexane

3. What is the name of the following compound?

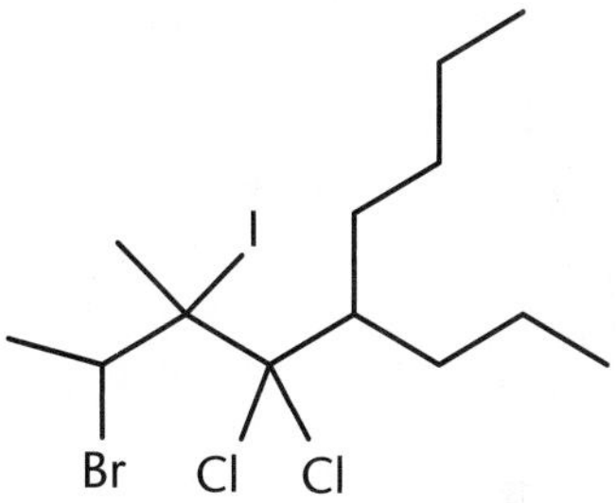

    A. 2-Bromo-5-butyl-4,4-dichloro-3-iodo-
       3-methyloctane

    B. 7-Bromo-4-butyl-5,5-dichloro-6-iodo-
       6-methyloctane

    C. 2-Bromo-4,4-dichloro-3-iodo-3-methyl-
       5-propylnonane

    D. 2-Bromo-5-butyl-4,4-dichloro-3-iodo-
       3-methylnonane

4. What is the name of the following compound?

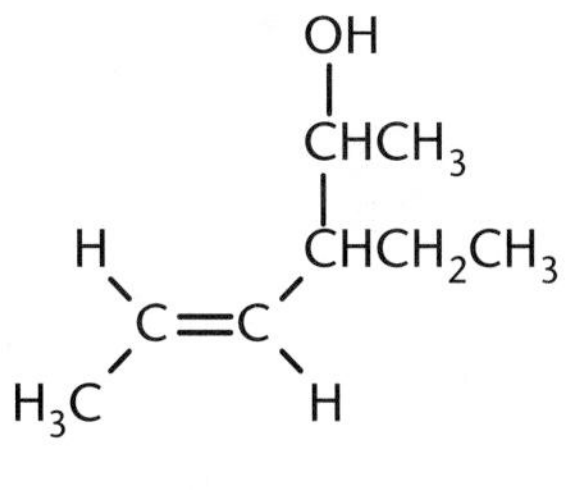

    A. *trans*-3-Ethyl-4-hexen-2-ol

    B. *trans*-4-Ethyl-2-hexen-5-ol

    C. *trans*-3-Ethanol-2-hexene

    D. *trans*-4-Ethanol-2-hexene

5. What is the correct structure for *cis*-1-ethoxy-2-methoxycyclopentane?

A.

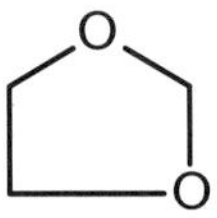

B.

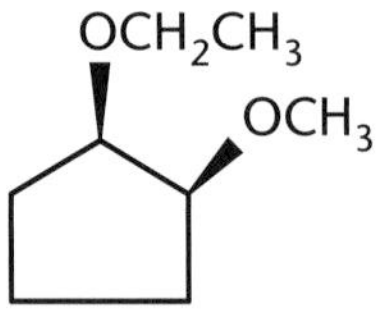

OCH₂CH₃
OCH₃

C.

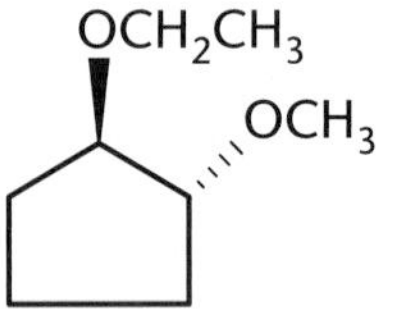

OCH₂CH₃
OCH₃

D.

OCH₃

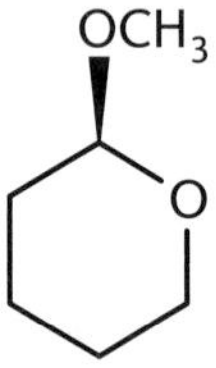

6. Which of the following are considered terminal functional groups?

A. Aldehydes
B. Ketones
C. Carboxylic acids
D. Both (A) and (C)

7. In the figure below, what is the correct name for the molecule shown in the Haworth projection?

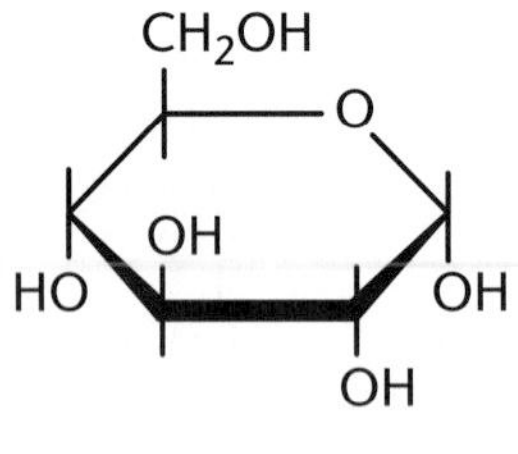

CH₂OH
O
OH
HO
OH
OH

A. α-D-Glucose
B. β-D-Glucose
C. β-L-Glucose
D. σ-L-Glucose

8. The IUPAC name for the structure below ends with what suffix?

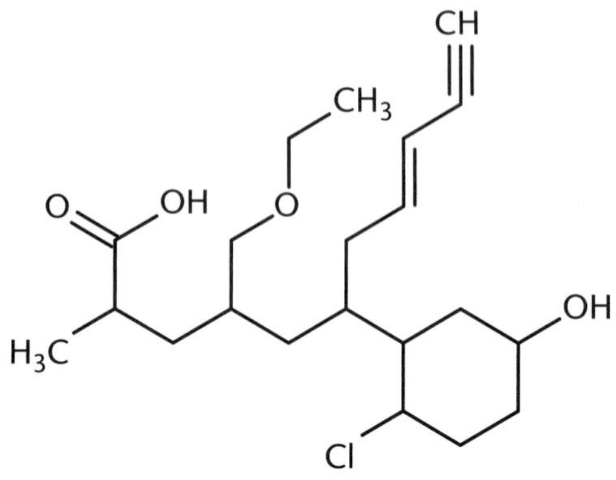

CH
CH₃
O
OH
O
H₃C
OH
Cl

A. –ol
B. –ide
C. –oic acid
D. –yne

Small Group Questions

1. Pyruvic acid is also known as acetylformic acid. Draw the structure of pyruvate, one of the end products of glycolysis.

2. NAD⁺ is a coenzyme that releases high-energy electrons in the electron transport chain. It is known as nicotinamide adenine dinucleotide, as well as diphosphopyridine nucleotide. Using what you know about naming conventions, what functional groups would you expect this molecule to have?

Explanations to Practice Questions

1. A

The first task in naming alkanes is identifying the longest carbon chain. In this case, the longest chain has seven carbons, so the parent alkane ends in –heptane. Choices (B) and (D) can be eliminated. Making sure that the carbons are numbered so that the substituents' position numbers are as small as possible, let's identify those substituents. This compound has two methyl groups at carbons 2 and 5, so the correct IUPAC name is 2,5-dimethylheptane. Choice (C) is wrong because the position numbers of the substituents are not minimized.

2. D

Substituted cycloalkanes are named as derivatives of their parent cycloalkane, which in this case is cyclohexane. Thus, choice (A) can be ruled out immediately. Then the substituents are listed in alphabetical order, and the carbons are numbered so as to give the lowest sum of substituent numbers. This cyclohexane has an ethyl and two methyl substituents; it is therefore an ethyl dimethyl cyclohexane. All of the remaining answer choices recognize this; they differ only in the numbers assigned. To give the lowest sum of substituent numbers, the two methyl substituents must be numbered 1 and 2, and the ethyl substituent must be numbered 4. The correct name for this compound is thus 4-ethyl-1,2-dimethylcyclohexane.

3. C

This question requires the application of the same set of rules used in question 1. The longest backbone has nine carbons, so the compound is a nonane. Thus, choices (A) and (B) can be ruled out immediately. The substituent groups are, in alphabetical order, bromo, chloro, iodo, methyl, and propyl. These substituents must be given the lowest possible position numbers on the hydrocarbon back-bone. The resulting name is 2-bromo-4,4-dichloro-3-iodo-3-methyl-5-propylnonane.

4. A

The first step is to locate the longest carbon chain containing the functional groups (C=C and OH). The backbone has six carbons (–hex–). Because the alcohol group has higher priority than the double bond, it dictates the ending (–ol) and is given the lower position (2). The alkene is named according to the position of the double bond on the backbone followed by *ene* (or *en* if it's not the highest-priority substituent). Thus, the chain is called 4–hexen–2–ol. There is also an ethyl group at C–3, so we can conclude that answer choice (A), *trans*-3-ethyl-4-hexen-2-ol, is correct.

5. B

A cyclopentane is a cyclic alkane with five carbons. A *cis* cyclic compound has both of its top-priority substituents on the same side of the ring. Only choices (B) and (C) have two substituents, so (A) and (D) can be ruled out. In fact, choice (C) is a *trans* compound, so the correct answer must be (B). *Ethoxy* and *methoxy* represent ether substituents, and as shown in choice (B), they must be on adjacent carbons on the same side of the molecule. Thus, the structure of *cis*-1-ethoxy-2-methoxycyclopentane is given by choice (B).

6. D

Aldehyde and carboxylic acid functional groups are characterized by their positions at terminal ends of carbon backbones. As a result, the carbons to which they are attached are named C–1. Ketones (B) are internal by definition, as there must be a carbon on either side of the carbonyl. Choice (D) is correct.

7. A

Starting from the anomeric carbon (hemiacetal), we see that the anomeric –OH group is pointing downward and is positioned *trans*- to the –CH$_2$OH group. Therefore, it is an α-sugar, which rules out answer choices (B), (C), and (D). *Sigma* (D) is not a term used to classify sugars.

8. C

Among the functional groups presented, carboxylic acids have the highest priority, so their parent compounds end with an –oic acid suffix. Answer (A) denotes an alcohol, (B) a halide, and (D) an alkyne, all of which have lower priorities than carboxylic acids.

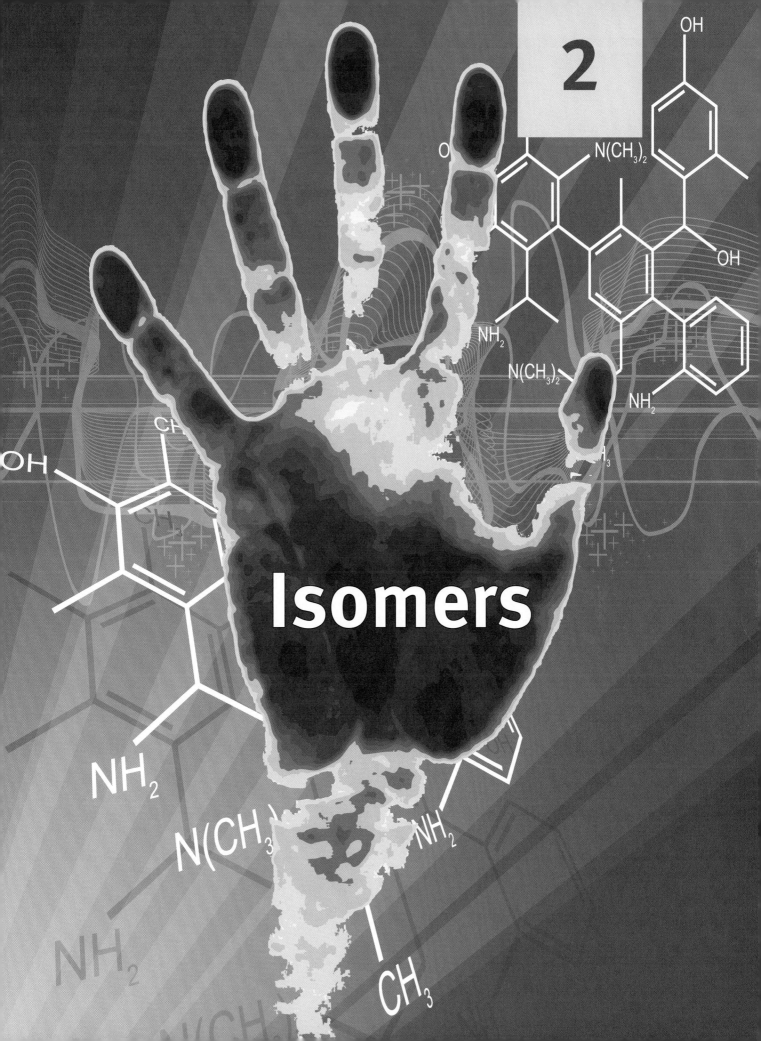

2

Isomers

The more time we spend with chemistry, the more we may start to imagine that molecules have their own personalities and that many of our human characteristics can be projected onto them. For instance, many of the relationships that describe similarities among humans can be ascribed to members of the molecular world. We can imagine that isomers are much like siblings. After all, siblings come from the same formula: mom + dad = child, although as I'm sure you've noticed, each child has his or her own specific characteristics. It's the same way with isomers. Isomers have the same molecular formula, but their differences can be as substantial as those between you and your weird brother who ate bugs on the playground. Keep in mind that isomers describe a relationship; there is no such thing as a single isomer. Just as you need at least two children for them to be siblings, two molecules can be isomers to each other, but no molecule can simply be an isomer by itself. Throughout this chapter, we will learn how to identify these relationships and describe the similarities and differences between isomers.

> **Key Concept**
>
> Isomers = same molecular formula, different structure.

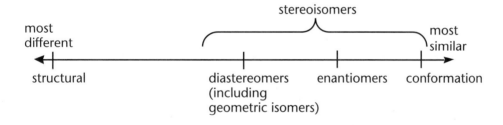

Structural Isomerism ★★☆☆☆

Remember your weird bug-eating brother who seems as if he might even be of a different species? Well, you two are the structural isomers of the social world. Structural isomers are the least similar of all isomers.

In fact, the only thing that **structural isomers** (also called **constitutional isomers**) do share is their molecular formula, meaning that their molecular weights must also be the same. Otherwise, these are completely different molecules, with different chemical and physical properties. This would probably be a good time to make sure we hammer down these concepts, because it is prime MCAT material. **Physical properties** are characteristics such as melting point, boiling point, and solubility. **Chemical properties** determine how the molecule reacts with other molecules. For example, five different structures exist for compounds with the formula C_6H_{14}.

> **Key Concept**
>
> Physical properties: MP, BP, solubility.
> Chemical properties: How it reacts.

> **Bridge**
>
> Physical properties are determined by intermolecular forces; we'll talk more about those in Chapter 3.

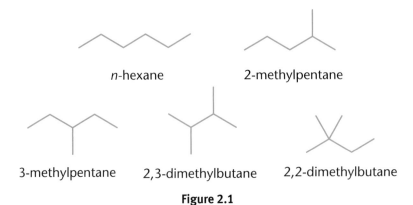

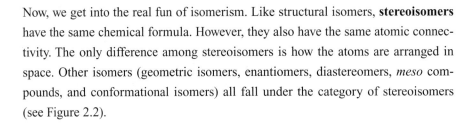

Figure 2.1

Although all of the molecules look totally different, they share the same number of carbon and hydrogen atoms.

Stereoisomerism ★★★★★★

Now, we get into the real fun of isomerism. Like structural isomers, **stereoisomers** have the same chemical formula. However, they also have the same atomic connectivity. The only difference among stereoisomers is how the atoms are arranged in space. Other isomers (geometric isomers, enantiomers, diastereomers, *meso* compounds, and conformational isomers) all fall under the category of stereoisomers (see Figure 2.2).

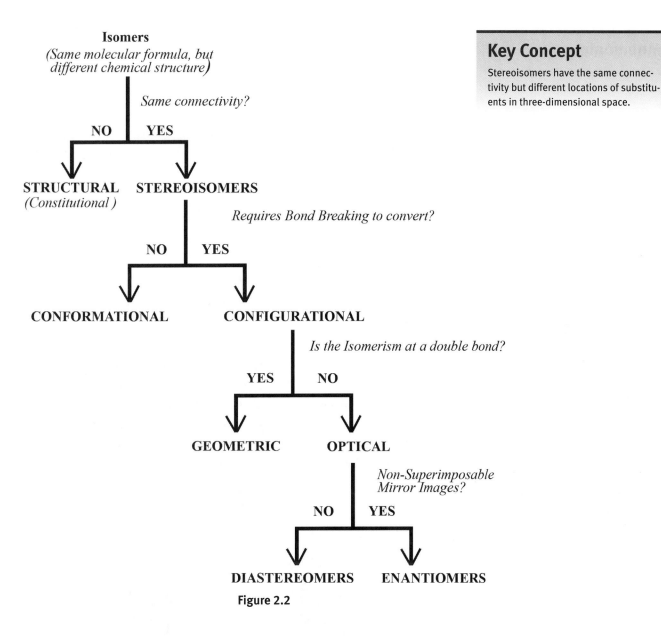

Figure 2.2

GEOMETRIC ISOMERS

Geometric isomers are compounds that differ in the position of substituents attached to a double bond or a cycloalkane. In simple compounds with only one substituent on either side of the double bond (hydrogen doesn't count as a substituent), we use the terms *cis* or *trans*. If two substituents are on the same side, the double bond is called *cis*. If they are on opposite sides, it is a *trans* double bond. For more complicated compounds with polysubstituted double bonds, an alternative method of naming is employed. First, the highest-priority substituent attached to each double-bonded carbon has to be determined. Using the nomenclature convention, the higher the atomic number, the higher the priority, and if the atomic numbers are equal, priority is de-

Mnemonic

Z = "*z*"ame side; *E* = "*e*" opposite side.

termined by the substituents attached to these atoms. The alkene is named **(*Z*)** (from German *zusammen*, meaning "together") if the two highest-priority substituents on each carbon are on the same side of the double bond and **(*E*)** (from German *entgegen*, meaning "opposite") if they are on opposite sides (see Figure 2.3). Don't worry if you aren't fluent in German; this is one of the few times we will use it in Organic Chemistry. If you did have the time to learn a language, Greek or Latin would be far more useful, but who has time to learn a language when they're studying for the MCAT?

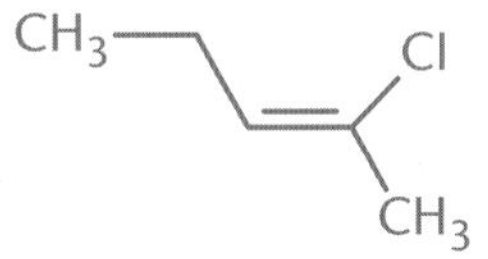

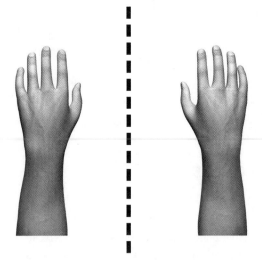

(*Z*)-2-chloro-2-pentene

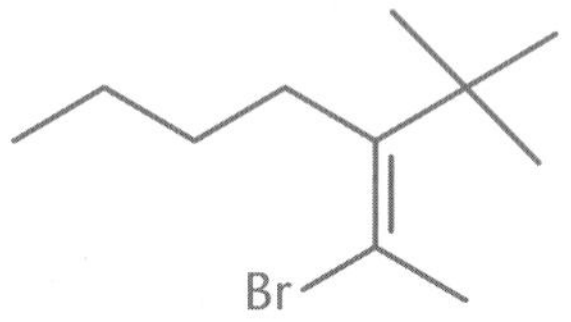

(*E*)-2-bromo-3-*t*-butyl-2-heptene

Figure 2.3

CHIRALITY

An object that is not superimposable upon its mirror image is **chiral**. An example of chirality that you've undoubtedly seen before are your right and left hands (see Figure 2.4). Although essentially identical, they differ in their ability to fit into a right-handed glove. They are mirror images of each other yet cannot be superimposed. Achiral objects have mirror images that *can* be superimposed; for example, a fork is identical to its mirror image and therefore achiral.

Key Concept

Chirality = handedness.

nonsuperimposable mirror images

Figure 2.4

MCAT Expertise

Whenever you see a carbon with four different substituents, *think chirality!*

On the MCAT, we will see this concept tested whenever there is a carbon with *four different* substituents. These carbons, known as **chiral centers**, lack a plane of symmetry. For example, the C–1 carbon atom in 1-bromo-1-chloroethane has four different substituents. The molecule is chiral because it is not superimposable on its mirror image (see Figure 2.5). The nonsuperimposable mirror images of chiral objects are called their **enantiomers**, a specific type of stereoisomer.

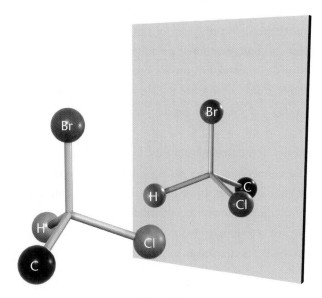

Figure 2.5

Alternatively, a carbon atom with only *three different* substituents, such as 1,1-dibro-moethane, has a plane of symmetry and is therefore **achiral** (not chiral). A simple 180° rotation around a vertical axis allows the compound to be superimposed upon its mirror image. Rotating a molecule in space does not change its chirality (see Figure 2.6).

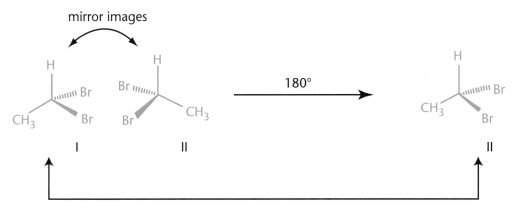

Figure 2.6

Relative and Absolute Configuration

The **configuration** is the spatial arrangement of the atoms or groups of a stereoisomer (enantiomers are configurational isomers). The **relative configuration** of a chiral molecule is its configuration in relation to another chiral molecule (often through chemical interconversion). We will use this to determine whether molecules are enantiomers, diastereomers, or simply the same molecule. On the other hand, the **absolute configuration** of a chiral molecule describes the exact spatial arrangement of these atoms or groups, independent of other molecules. Next, we will go through the set sequence to determine the absolute configuration of a molecule at a single chiral, or stereogenic, center.

Key Concept

When assigning priority, look *only* at the first atom attached to the chiral carbon, not at the group as a whole. The higher the atomic number of this first atom, the higher the priority—this same system is used to determine *Z* and *E* isomers.

Step 1:

Assign priority to the four substituents, looking only at the atoms directly attached to the chiral center. Once again, higher atomic number takes precedence over lower atomic number. If the atomic numbers are equal, priority is determined by the combination of the atoms attached to these atoms. If you come across a tie, just keep looking to the next atoms until you find a winner. If there is a double bond, it is counted as two bonds. Figure 2.7 shows an example.

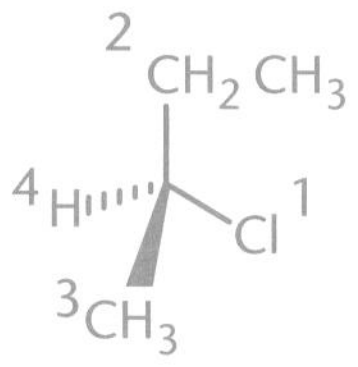

Figure 2.7

Step 2:

Orient the molecule in space so that the atom with the lowest priority (it will usually be hydrogen) is at the back of the molecule. Another way to think of this is to arrange your point of view so that your line of sight proceeds down the bond from the asymmetric carbon atom (the chiral center) to the substituent with lowest priority. The three substituents with higher priority should then radiate out from the central carbon, either coming out of the page or on the plane of the page (see Figure 2.8).

Step 2 (Modified Version):

If you find it difficult to rotate three-dimensional structures in your mind, we have a trick to get around this step. All you need to do is switch the lowest-priority group and the group at the back of the molecule (the substituent projecting *into* the page). This will give us the results of the standard step 2, with one big difference. We now have the *opposite* configuration. So if we use this modified step, we need to remember to switch our final answer (either *R* to *S*, or *S* to *R*. Don't worry, we'll get there next).

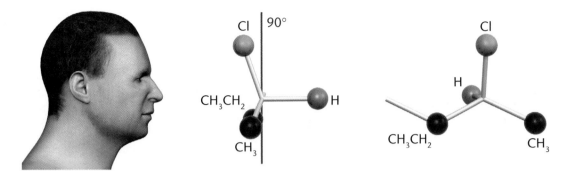

Figure 2.8

Step 3:

Now, imagine drawing a circle connecting the substituents from number 1 to number 2 to number 3. Don't pay attention to the lowest-priority group; it can simply be skipped because it projects into the page. If the circle is drawn clockwise, the asymmetric atom is called **R** (from Latin *rectus,* meaning "right"). If it is counterclockwise, it is called **S** (from Latin *sinister,* meaning "left"), as shown in Figure 2.9.

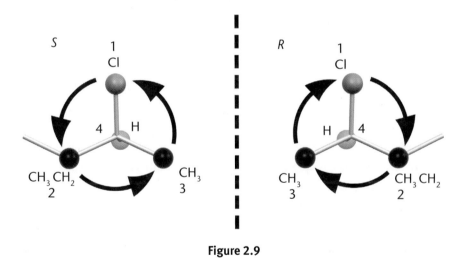

Figure 2.9

Step 4:

Name the compound. The terms *R* and *S* are put in parentheses and separated from the rest of the name by a dash. If we have a compound with more than one chiral center, location is specified by a number preceding the *R* or *S* within the parentheses without a dash.

Fischer Projections

On the MCAT, there is another way to represent three-dimensional molecules, called **Fischer projections**. In this system, horizontal lines indicate bonds that project out from the plane of the page, whereas vertical lines indicate bonds going

Mnemonic

Clockwise is like turning the steering wheel clockwise, which makes the car turn *Right*—so the chirality at that center is *R*. Or think of the way you write an *R* and an *S*. An *R* is drawn with a clockwise movement, whereas an *S* is drawn with a counterclockwise movement.

Key Concept

To determine the absolute configuration at a single chiral center:

1. Assign priority by atomic number.
2. Orient the molecule with the lowest-priority substituent in the back.
3. Move around the molecule from highest to lowest priority ($1 \rightarrow 2 \rightarrow 3$).
4. Clockwise = *R*; counterclockwise = *S*.

into (or behind) the plane of the page. The point of intersection of the lines represents a carbon atom.

To determine configurations using Fischer projections, we follow the same rules, so we have to make sure that the lowest-priority group projects *into* the page. A benefit of Fischer projections is that the lowest-priority group can be on the top *or* on the bottom and still project *into* the page. Along with this, we can manipulate Fischer projections without changing the compound. By interchanging any two pairs of substituents, or by rotating the projection on the plane of the page by 180°, we still have the same compound (see Figure 2.10). However, if only one pair of substituents is interchanged, or if the molecule is rotated by 90°, the mirror image of the original compound is obtained (*R* instead of *S*, or *S* instead of *R*).

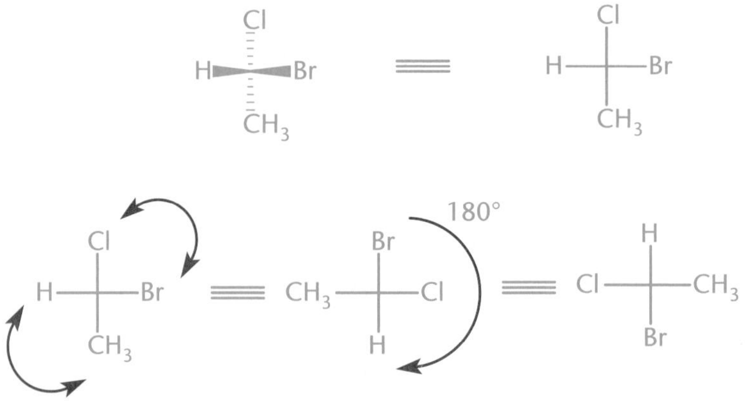

Figure 2.10

But what if our lowest-priority group is pointing to the side and, as such, pointing out of the page? Just as before, we've got a couple of different tricks you can pick from to answer the question.

Option 1
Go ahead and determine the order of substituents as normal, number 1 → number 2 → number 3. Remember, number 4 doesn't count, so just skip right over it when determining the order. Then obtain the designation (*R* or *S*). The *true* designation will be the opposite of what you just obtained.

Option 2
Make a single switch: Just swap the lowest-priority group with one of the groups on the vertical axis. Obtain the designation (*R* or *S*), and once again, the *true* designation will be the opposite of what you just found.

Option 3
The final option is to make *two* switches. Basically, just use option 2, moving the lowest-priority group into the correct position. Then, switch the other two groups as well. Because we made two switches, this molecule will have the same

Mnemonic

Think of a man with a bowtie on. This will remind you that horizontal lines come out of the page.

designation as the initial molecule. This is the same as holding one substituent in place and rotating the other three in order—like the rotation of a methyl group.

Optical Activity

Enantiomers (nonsuperimposable mirror images) are molecules that have the opposite configuration at their one chiral center. Or, if there are multiple chiral centers, they *must* have the opposite configuration at *every one* of their chiral centers to be enantiomers. Much like identical human twins, enantiomers have identical physical properties and most of the same chemical properties. However, enantiomers have two exceptions (as opposed to the possible thousands of exceptions with identical twins): optical activity and how they react in chiral environments. Let's start by discussing optical activity. A compound is optically active if it has the ability to rotate plane-polarized light. Ordinary light is unpolarized, which means it consists of waves vibrating in all possible planes perpendicular to its direction of motion. A polarizer allows light waves oscillating only in a particular direction to pass through, producing plane-polarized light (see Figure 2.11).

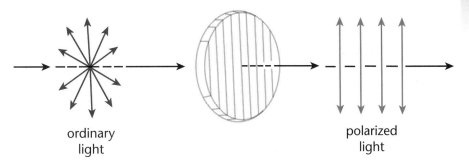

ordinary
light

polarized
light

Figure 2.11

Polarizers have become a popular feature of many sunglasses. By allowing only one plane of light to pass through, they help reduce glare. However, a possible problem with these glasses arises when they are used to view an already polarized light source. If polarized light passes though a polarizer at a perpendicular angle (90° or 270°), no light will be able to pass though. You can try this out with a fancy MP3 player and some polarized glasses.

Returning to a molecular level, if plane-polarized light is passed through an optically active compound, the orientation of the plane is rotated by an angle α. The enantiomer of this compound will rotate light by the same amount but in the *opposite* direction. A compound that rotates the plane of polarized light to the right, or clockwise (from the point of view of an observer watching the light approach), is dextrorotatory and is labeled (+). A compound that rotates light toward the left, or counterclockwise, is levorotatory and is labeled (−). The direction of rotation cannot be determined from the structure of a molecule and must be determined experimentally. That is, it is not related to the absolute configuration of the molecule.

The amount of rotation depends on the number of molecules that a light wave encounters. This depends on *two* factors: the concentration of the optically active compound and the length of the tube through which the light passes. Chemists have set standard conditions of 1 g/mL for concentration and 1 dm for length to compare the optical activities of different compounds. Rotations measured at different concentrations and tube lengths can be converted to a standardized specific rotation ($[\alpha]$) using the following equation:

$$\text{specific rotation } ([\alpha]) = \frac{\text{observed rotation } (\alpha)}{\text{concentration (g/mL)} \times \text{length (dm)}}$$

When both (+) and (−) enantionmers are present in equal concentrations, we call the mixture a **racemic mixture**. In these mixtures, the rotations cancel each other out, and no optical activity is observed. Racemic mixtures are analogous to ambidextrous people, who will use their left hand in one instance and their right hand in another; thus, it would appear to an observer that ambidextrous people possess no handedness at all.

OTHER CHIRAL COMPOUNDS

Diastereomers

Diastereomers are non–mirror image configurational isomers. *cis* and *trans* alkenes are diastereomers. Diastereomers are also possible when a molecule has two or more stereogenic centers and differ at some, but not all, of these centers. This means that diastereomers are required to have *multiple chiral centers*. For any molecule with *n* chiral centers, there are 2^n possible stereoisomers. Thus, if a compound has two chiral carbon atoms, it has a maximum of four possible stereoisomers, as is shown in Figure 2.12.

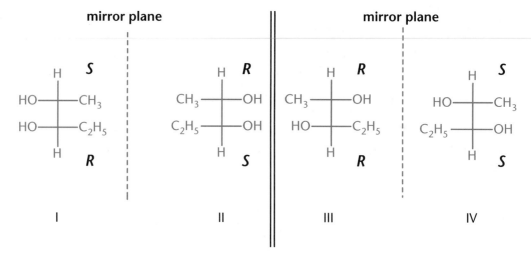

Figure 2.12

I and II are mirror images of each other and are therefore enantiomers. Similarly, III and IV are enantiomers. However, I and III are not. They are stereoisomers that are not mirror images and are thus diastereomers. Notice that other combinations of non–mirror image stereoisomers are also diastereomeric. Hence, I and IV, II and III, I and III, and II and IV are all pairs of diastereomers.

Meso Compounds

The criterion for optical activity of a molecule containing any number of chiral centers is that it has *no* plane of symmetry. If a plane of symmetry exists, the molecule is not optically active, even though it possesses chiral centers. This plane of symmetry can occur either through the chiral center or between chiral centers. As long as there is a plane of symmetry, the compound is *not* chiral. A molecule with an internal plane of symmetry is called a *meso* **compound**. Figure 2.13 shows some examples.

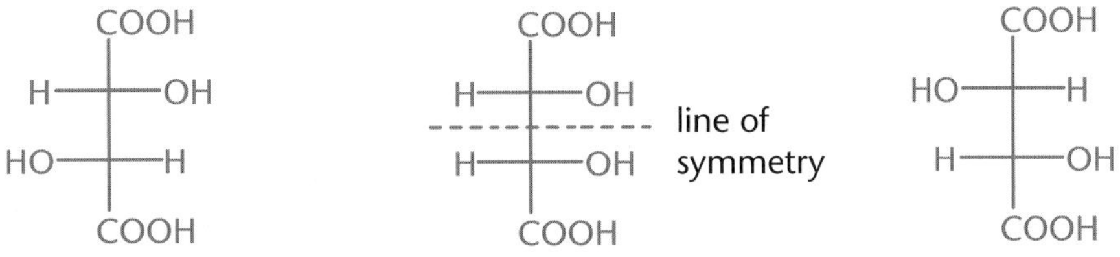

L-tartaric acid   ***meso*-tartaric acid**   **D-tartaric acid**

Figure 2.13

> **Key Concept**
>
> *Meso* compounds are made up of two halves that are mirror images. Thus, they are not optically active.

> **Mnemonic**
>
> *MeSo* compounds have a *Mirror* plane of *Symmetry*.

As you can see above, D- and L-tartaric acid are both optically active, but *meso*-tartaric acid has a plane of symmetry and is not optically active. This means that even though *meso*-tartaric acid has two chiral carbon atoms, the molecule as a whole does not display optical activity.

> **Bridge**
>
> See Chapter 14 for an explanation of D versus L configurations.

CONFORMATIONAL ISOMERISM

Of all the isomers we have discussed so far, **conformational isomers**, or **conformers**, are the most similar. In fact, conformational isomers are the same molecules, only at different points in their natural rotation. Whereas double bonds hold molecules in a specific position (as we saw with geometric isomers), single bonds are free to rotate. So we are no longer looking at the relationships between siblings but are instead talking about the same person who changes slightly throughout the day. As the day goes on, a person can be in different positions, sometimes stressful (perhaps taking an Orgo exam) and sometimes relaxed (celebrating the completion of said Orgo exam). Conformational isomers simply describe the different positions atoms can take around one or more of their single bonds. These different conformations can be seen when the molecule is depicted in a **Newman projection**, in which the line of sight extends along a carbon–carbon bond axis. The conformations are shown as the molecule is rotated about this axis. The classic example for demonstrating

> **Key Concept**
>
> Think of conformational isomers as being different positions (conformations) of a compound—like a person who may be standing up or sitting down. Thus, they are often easily interconverted.

conformational isomerism in a straight chain is butane. In a Newman projection, the line of sight extends through the C2–C3 bond axis.

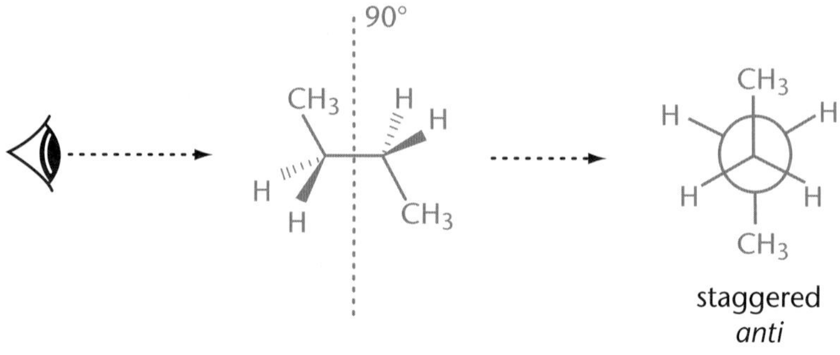

Figure 2.14

Straight-chain Conformations

The most stable conformation is when the two methyl groups (C–1 and C–4) are oriented 180° from each other. In this position, there is minimal steric repulsion between the atoms' electron clouds (they are far apart as they can possibly be), and thus the atoms are "happiest." Because there is no overlap of atoms along the line of sight (besides C–2 and C–3), the molecule is said to be in a **staggered** conformation. Specifically, it is called the *anti* conformation (the most favorable type of staggered conformation) because the two methyl groups are antiperiplanar to each other.

The other type of staggered conformation, called *gauche*, occurs when the two methyl groups are 60° apart. To convert from the *anti* to the *gauche* conformation, the molecule must pass through an eclipsed conformation, in which the two methyl groups are 120° apart and overlap with the H atoms on the adjacent carbon. When the two methyl groups overlap with each other, with 0° separation, the molecule is said to be **totally eclipsed** and is in its highest energy state (see Figure 2.15). This makes the compound quite "unhappy," energetically speaking.

Figure 2.15

Figure 2.16 shows plot of the potential energy versus degree of rotation about the C2–C3 bond in butane. It shows the relative minima and maxima potential energy

Mnemonic

It's *gauche* (or inappropriate) for one methyl group to stand too close to another group!

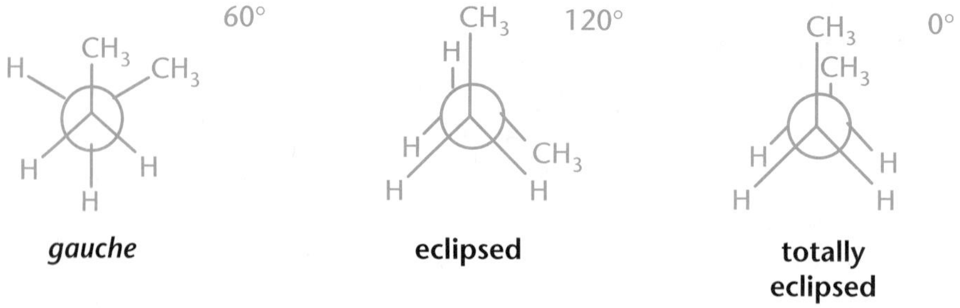

Mnemonic

Groups are *eclipsed* when they are completely in line with one another—think of a solar eclipse!

of the molecule throughout its various conformations. Remember that every molecule wants to be in the lowest energy state possible (something most of us life-forms share, especially when trying to get out of bed on cold days), so the higher the relative energy, the less time the molecule will spend in that energetically unfavorable state.

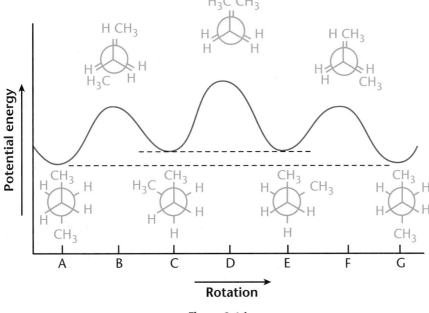

Figure 2.16

These barriers are small (3–4 kcal/mol) and are easily overcome at room temperature. Nevertheless, at very low temperatures, conformational interconversions will dramatically slow. If the molecules do not possess sufficient energy to cross the energy barrier, they may not rotate at all (as happens to all molecules at 0 K).

Cyclic Conformations

Cycloalkanes can be pretty happy (stable) compounds, but if their conditions aren't right, they can get really upset (unstable). This anger comes from **ring strain**, which arises from three factors: angle strain, torsional strain, and nonbonded strain (sometimes referred to as steric strain). **Angle strain** results when bond angles deviate from their ideal values. **Torsional strain** results when cyclic molecules must assume conformations that have eclipsed interactions. **Nonbonded strain** (van der Waals repulsion) results when *nonadjacent* atoms or groups compete for the same space. Nonbonded, or steric, strain is the dominant source of energy in the **flagpole interactions** of the boat conformation. To alleviate this strain, cycloalkanes attempt to adopt various nonplanar conformations. Cyclobutane puckers into a slight *V* shape, cyclopentane adopts what is called the envelope conformation, and cyclohexane (the one you will undoubtedly see the most) exists mainly in three conformations called the **chair**, the **boat**, and the **twist** or **skew-boat** (see Figure 2.17).

| puckered cyclobutane | envelope cyclopentane | chair cyclohexane | boat cyclohexane | twist-boat cyclohexane |

Figure 2.17. Conformations of Cyclic Hydrocarbons

Cyclohexane

Unsubstituted

The most stable conformation of cyclohexane is the chair conformation. In this conformation, all three types of strain are eliminated. The hydrogen atoms that are perpendicular to the plane of the ring (sticking up or down) are called *axial*, and those parallel (sticking out) are called *equatorial*. The axial–equatorial orientations alternate around the ring.

The boat conformation is adopted as an intermediate state when the chair flips and converts to another chair (known as a **ring flip**). In such a process, hydrogen atoms in the equatorial position become axial, and vice versa, in the new chair. In the boat conformation, all of the atoms are eclipsed, creating a high-energy state. To avoid this strain, the boat can twist into a slightly more stable form called the *twist* or *skew-boat* conformation.

Monosubstituted

The interconversion between the two chair conformations can be slowed if a sterically bulky group is attached to the ring (*t*-butyl is the standard bulky group on the MCAT). For a bulky group, the equatorial position is favored over the axial position, because in the axial position, there is steric repulsion with the other axial substituents. Remember: Large groups such as *t*-butyl are most stable in the equatorial position.

> **Mnemonic**
>
> Axial substituents are on a vertical axis, like your axial skeleton (skull and spine). Equatorial substituents go around the middle, like the earth's equator.

> **Mnemonic**
>
> When you have low energy, you sit down in a *chair* to rest. *Boats* can be tippy, so they are less stable.

> **Key Concept**
>
> A bulky substituent will favor one of the two chair conformations. Remember that the bulky groups will prefer to be equatorial, so they will minimize the steric repulsion.

Figure 2.18

Disubstituted

Even when we have disubstituted cycloalkanes, we can still only have two different conformations, which can be interconverted with a ring flip. When doing this, the molecule will put the biggest or bulkiest group into the equatorial position. If both substituents are located on the same side of the ring, the molecule is called *cis*; if the two groups are on opposite sides of the ring, it is called *trans* (see Figure 2.19). This doesn't change with a ring flip; it simply moves them from equatorial to axial, and vice versa.

cis-1,2-dimethylcyclohexane *trans*-1,2-dimethylcyclohexane

Figure 2.19

In *trans*-1,4-dimethylcyclohexane, both of the methyl groups are equatorial in one chair conformation and axial in the other, but in either case, they point in opposite directions relative to the plane of the ring (see Figure 2.20).

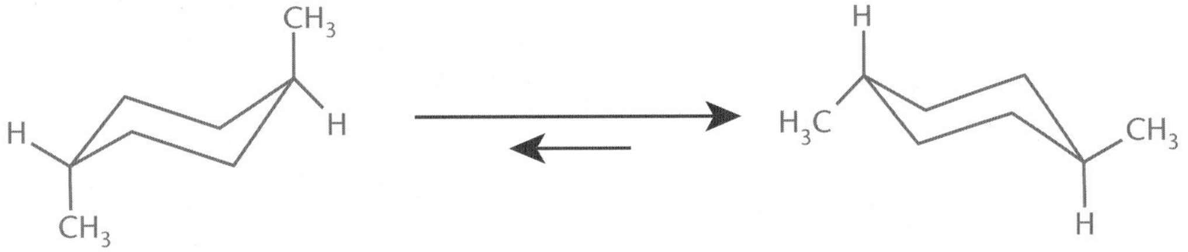

trans-1,4-dimethylcyclohexane

Figure 2.20

Conclusion

Throughout this chapter, we've seen just how many different characteristics and personalities can be derived from the same molecular formula. Although their personalities aren't quite as unique as those seen on the playground, they'll be a lot more useful on Test Day. In fact, this information is going to be essential on the MCAT—not only questions on isomerism itself but on every single Organic Chemistry problem you encounter. Most of the compounds we come across will have different possible isomers, and you need to be prepared to differentiate among them to find the one and only correct answer.

MCAT Expertise

Cis and *trans* are not only used for simple alkenes but also for multisubstituted cycloalkanes. On the MCAT, be sure to keep stereochemistry in mind, because many a wrong answer will include an incorrect stereochemical designation or lack one that is needed.

CONCEPTS TO REMEMBER

☐ Structural isomers share only a molecular formula; they have different physical and chemical properties.

☐ Stereoisomers share the same molecular formula and the same atomic connectivity, but differ in their three-dimensional shape.

☐ Geometric isomers differ in positioning around a double bond, and they differ in many chemical and physical properties.

☐ A chiral (stereogenic) center has four different groups attached to the central carbon and is given the absolute configuration of either *R* or *S*. A lone pair may also be considered as one of the four different groups.

☐ Enantiomers have the same chemical and physical properties in an achiral environment; they differ only in the way they rotate plane-polarized light and how they react in chiral environments.

☐ Diasteromers (non–mirror image stereoisomers), which differ at some but not all chiral centers, have different chemical and physical properties. *cis-trans* isomers are also diastereomers.

☐ *Meso* compounds have an internal plane of symmetry and are not optically active.

☐ Conformational isomers are the same compound at different points in rotation around a single bond.

☐ The chair conformation is the most favored position for cyclohexane.

☐ In ring structures, big bulky groups prefer to be in the equatorial position.

Practice Questions

1. Which of the following do not show optical activity?

   A. (*R*)-2-Butanol
   B. (*S*)-2-Butanol
   C. A solution containing 1 M (*R*)-2-butanol and 2 M (*S*)-2-butanol
   D. A solution containing 2 M (*R*)-2-butanol and 2 M (*S*)-2-butanol

2. How many stereoisomers exist for the following aldehyde?

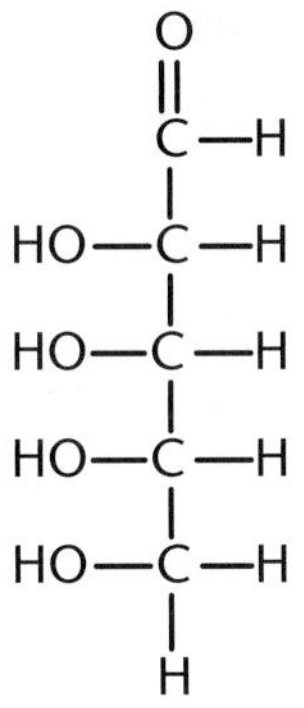

   A. 2
   B. 4
   C. 8
   D. 16

3. Which of the following compounds is optically inactive?

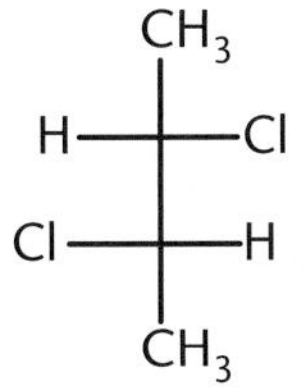

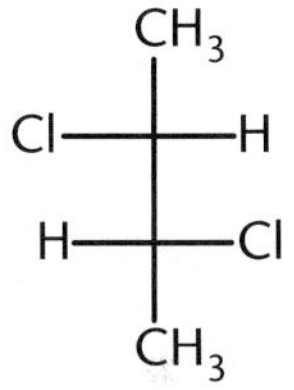

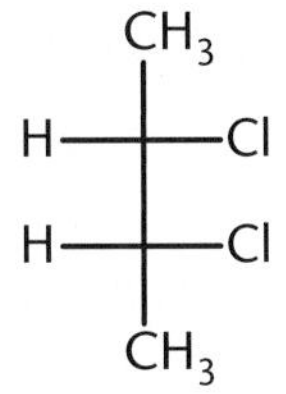

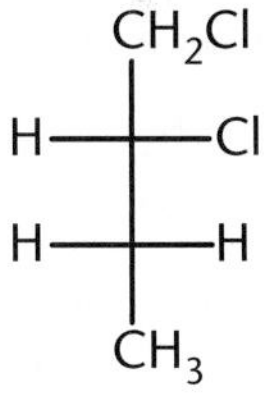

4. Cholesterol, shown below, contains how many chiral centers?

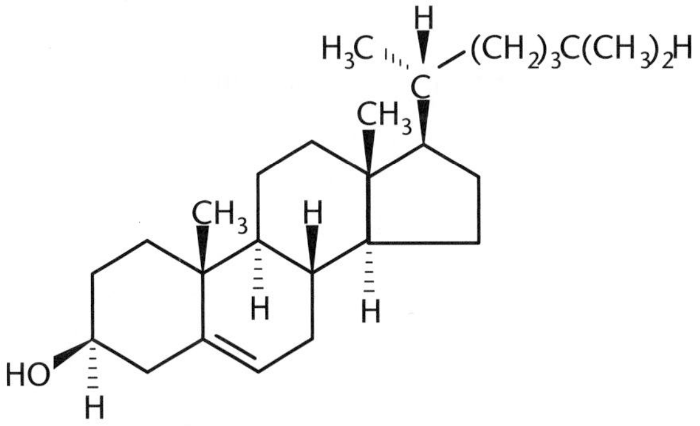

   cholesterol

   A. 5
   B. 7
   C. 8
   D. 9

5. Which isomer of the following compound is the most stable?

A.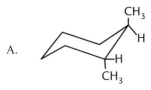

B.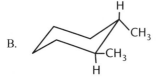

C.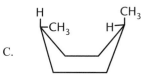

D.   They are all equally stable.

6. The following reaction results in

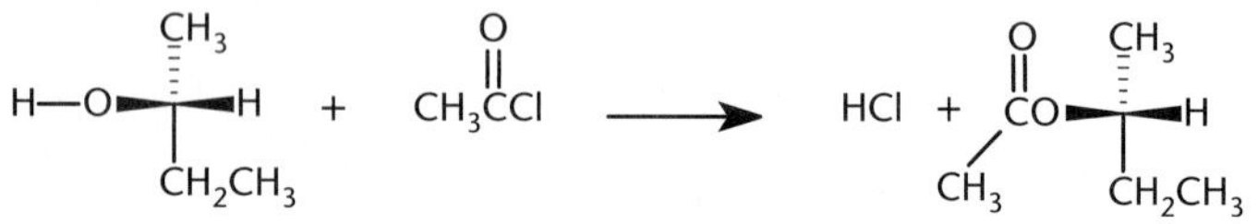

$$H-O\!\!-\!\!\overset{CH_3}{\underset{CH_2CH_3}{\rule{0pt}{1.5em}\overset{\text{\large$\vdots$}}{\underset{\text{\large$\vdots$}}{C}}}}\!\!-\!\!H \;+\; CH_3\overset{O}{\overset{\|}{C}}Cl \;\longrightarrow\; HCl \;+\; \overset{O}{\overset{\|}{C}}O\!\!-\!\!\overset{CH_3}{\underset{CH_2CH_3}{\rule{0pt}{1.5em}\overset{\text{\large$\vdots$}}{\underset{\text{\large$\vdots$}}{C}}}}\!\!-\!\!H$$

A. retention of relative configuration and a change in the absolute configuration.

B. a change in the relative and absolute configurations.

C. retention of the relative and absolute configurations.

D. retention of the absolute configuration and a change in the relative configuration.

7. The following is a pair of what structures?

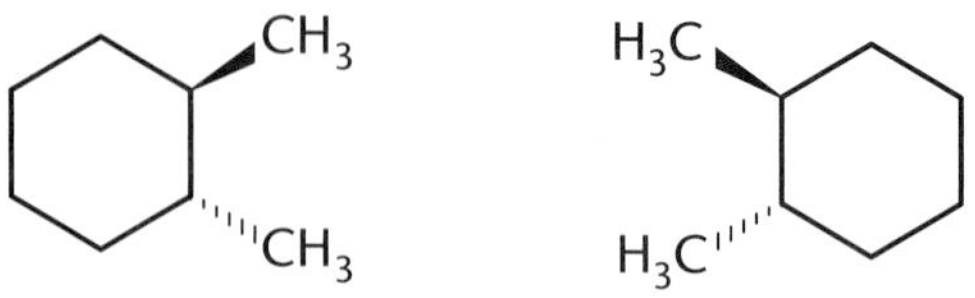

I

II

A. Enantiomers

B. Diastereomers

C. *meso* compounds

D. Structural isomers

Small Group Questions

1. Compare the energies (with respect to torsional strain) of the different conformational isomers of 2-dimethyl propane (neopentane) using Newman projections.

2. How are diastereomers used to separate racemic mixtures into their enantiomers?

Explanations to Practice Questions

1. D

Choice (D) is a racemic mixture of 2-butanol because it consists of equimolar amounts of (R)-2-butanol and (S)-2-butanol. The (R)-2-butanol molecule rotates the plane of polarized light in one direction, and the (S)-2-butanol molecule rotates it by the same angle but in the opposite direction. For every (R)-2-butanol molecule, there is an (S)-2-butanol molecule; as a result, each rotation is canceled out. No net rotation of polarized light is observed. Choice (A) is wrong because all the molecules of the (R)-2-butanol solution rotate the plane of light in the same direction, so rotations do not cancel and optical activity is observed. For the same reason, the (S)-2-butanol solution (B) also shows optical activity. Thus, choices (A) and (B) are incorrect. Choice (C) has more (S)-2-butanol molecules than (R)-2-butanol molecules. The entire rotation produced by the (R)-2-butanol molecules is canceled by half of the (S)-2-butanol molecules; the rotation produced by the other half of (S)-2-butanol molecules contributes to the optical activity observed in this solution. Thus, choice (C) is incorrect.

2. C

The maximum number of stereoisomers of a compound equals 2^n, where n is the number of chiral carbons in the compound. Here, there are three chiral carbon atoms ($n = 3$), marked by asterisks in the following figure:

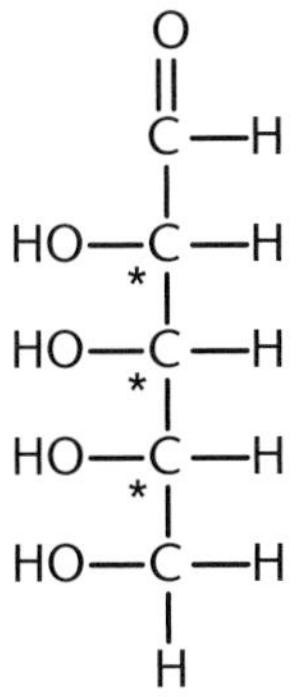

Thus, the number of stereoisomers it can form is $2^n = 2^3 = 8$. Hence, the correct choice is (C).

3. C

The answer choice is an example of a *meso* compound: a compound that contains chiral centers but is superimposable on its mirror image. A *meso* compound can also be recognized by the fact that one half of the compound is the mirror image of the other half:

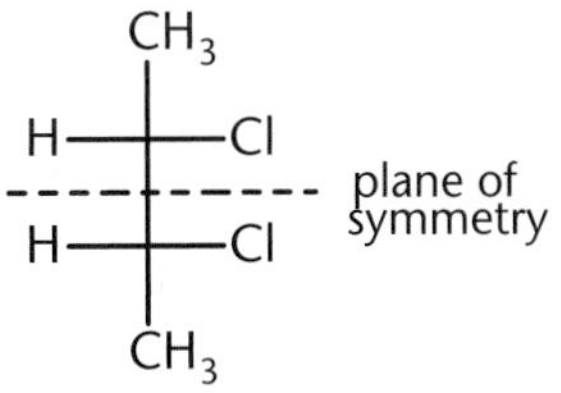

Owing to this internal plane of symmetry, the molecule is achiral and, hence, optically inactive. Choices (A) and (B) are enantiomers of each other and will certainly show optical activity on their own. Choice (D), because it contains a chiral carbon and no internal plane of symmetry, is optically active as well.

4. C

To be considered a chiral center, a carbon must have four different substituents. There are eight stereocenters in this molecule, which are marked below with asterisks.

cholestrol

The other carbons are not chiral for various reasons. Many are bonded to two hydrogens; others participate in double bonds, which count as two bonds to the same thing.

5. B

Choice (B) is a chair conformation in which the two equatorial methyl groups are *trans* to each other. Because the axial methyl hydrogens do not compete for the same space as the hydrogens attached to the ring, this conformation ensures the least amount of steric strain. Choice (A) would be less stable than choice (B) because the diaxial methyl group hydrogens are closer to the hydrogens on the ring, causing greater steric strain. Choice (C) is wrong because it is in the more unstable boat conformation. Choice (D) is incorrect because we can definitively order these structures from most to least stable.

6. C

The relative configuration is retained because the bonds of the stereocenter are not broken. The cleaved bond is between a substituent of the stereocenter (the O atom) and

another atom attached to the substituent (the H attached to the O). The absolute configuration is also retained, because the (R)/(S) designation is the same for the reactant and the product.

7. A

The correct answer is choice (A), enantiomers. If you look at the two structures, you can see that they are mirror images of each other. To make our analysis a bit easier, we can rotate structure II by 180° to give structure III. Structures I and III are nonsuperimposable mirror images, which means they are enantiomers.

Choice (B) is incorrect because diastereomers are stereoisomers, which are not mirror images of each other. Choice (C) is incorrect because for a compound to be designated as a *meso* compound, it must have a plane of symmetry, and neither of these do. Choice (D) is wrong because structural isomers are compounds with the same molecular formula but different atomic connections. These compounds do have the same atomic connections. The only difference is that they differ in their spatial arrangement of atoms. As a result, they are in the class of stereoisomers, not structural isomers.

3

Bonding

Now that we have an understanding of language and structures, we are ready to start examining the real backbone of chemistry: bonding. Bonding determines which atoms come together to form molecules, and it governs the way those molecules interact with the other molecules in their environment.

Any Organic Chemistry student knows that Orgo is really the study of carbon and carbon compounds. What makes carbon so special? Why does one element get an entire branch of chemistry to itself? The simple answer is bonding or, more specifically, that carbon has special bonding properties. Carbon is tetravalent, which means that it can form bonds with up to four other atoms, allowing for the massive versatility required to form the foundation of life. This versatility is compounded by the fact that carbon, located near the center of the periodic table, can form bonds with many different elements. In addition, because carbon atoms are fairly small, the bonds that they form are strong and stable.

Needless to say, to really understand Organic Chemistry, we first have to understand what's going on behind the scenes during bonding. If you haven't yet read up on your General Chemistry, do so now. Periodic trends such as differences in electronegativity are what determine the kind of bonding that will occur between two atoms. Remember that there are two types of chemical bonds. The first is **ionic**, in which electrons are transferred from one atom to another; the second is **covalent**, in which electrons are shared between atoms. Organic Chemistry is deeply rooted in covalent bonding. Understand covalent bonding, and you'll understand the organic world.

> **MCAT Expertise**
>
> In Organic Chemistry, we will be primarily concerned with polar and nonpolar covalent bonds. These will have effects on the physical properties, which will be discussed in Chapter 12: Purification and Separation.

Atomic Orbitals ★★★★★☆

Bonding occurs in the outermost electron shell of atoms, so if we want to understand bonding, we first need to understand orbitals, which tell us where the electrons in an atom are located. The first three quantum numbers, **n**, **l**, and **m**, describe the size, shape, and number of atomic orbitals an element possesses. The principal quantum number n, which can equal 1, 2, 3, etc., corresponds to the energy levels in an atom and is essentially a measure of size. The smaller the number, the closer the orbital is to the nucleus, and the lower its energy.

Within each electron shell, there can be several types of orbitals (s, p, d, f, etc., corresponding to the azimuthal quantum numbers $l = 0, 1, 2, 3$, and so forth). Each type of atomic orbital has a specific shape. An **s-orbital** is spherical and symmetrical, centered on the nucleus. A **p-orbital** is composed of two lobes located symmetrically about the nucleus and contains a **node** (an area where the probability of finding an electron is zero) in the nucleus. You can picture the p-orbital as a dumbbell that can be positioned in three different orientations, along the x-, y-, or z-axis (see Figure 3.7).

A **_d_-orbital** is composed of four symmetrical lobes and contains two nodes. Four of the _d_-orbitals are clover-shaped, and the fifth looks like a donut wrapped around the center of a _p_-orbital. Thankfully, the multiple, complex shapes of _d_- and _f_-orbitals are rarely encountered in Organic Chemistry.

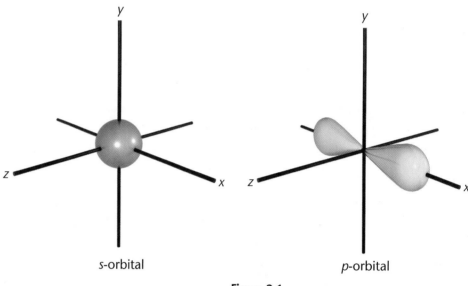

s-orbital   p-orbital

Figure 3.1

Molecular Orbitals

 ★★★★☆☆

SINGLE BONDS

Now that we are equipped with an understanding of atomic orbitals, we are ready to get to the good stuff. When two atomic orbitals combine, they form a **molecular orbital**. Molecular orbitals are obtained mathematically by adding or subtracting the wave functions of the atomic orbitals. Don't worry: You won't have to do this math on the MCAT, but it can be tested visually, as shown in Figure 3.2. If the signs of the wave functions are the same, a lower-energy (more stable) **bonding orbital** is produced. If the signs are different, a higher-energy (less stable) **antibonding orbital** is produced. In other words, molecular orbitals don't comply with the old adage that opposites attract. Just as with a bond between friends, you need to have things in common (in the case of orbitals, a sign) to form a bond. A low-stress (low-energy) friendship will ensue. Conversely, people with conflicting personalities, or orbitals with opposite signs, are likely to be repelled by each other and are forced to endure tense (high-energy) interactions.

MCAT Expertise

Orbitals are more likely to be tested in the Physical Sciences section, but a good understanding of this topic will help in the Biological Sciences section as well.

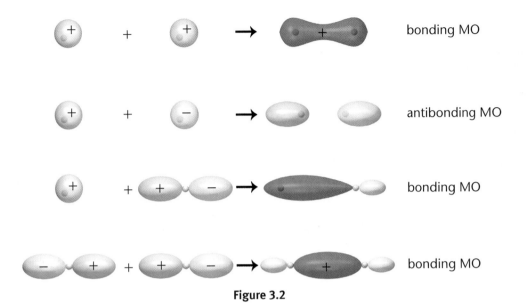

Figure 3.2

When a molecular orbital is formed by head-to-head or tail-to-tail overlap, as in Figure 3.2, the resulting bond is called a **sigma (σ) bond**. *All single bonds are sigma bonds,* accommodating two electrons. Shorter bonds hold atoms more closely together and are stronger than longer bonds. This is true with all kinds of bonds, including single bonds.

DOUBLE AND TRIPLE BONDS

When two *p*-orbitals line up in a parallel (side-by-side) fashion, their electron clouds overlap, and a bonding molecular orbital, called a **pi (π) bond**, is formed (Fig. 3.3). One pi bond on top of an existing single bond is called a **double bond**. A sigma bond and two pi bonds is a **triple bond**. Unlike single bonds, which allow free rotation of atoms around the bond axis, double and triple bonds hinder rotation, and, in effect, lock the atoms into position.

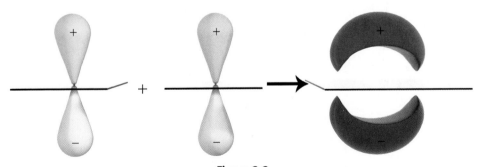

Figure 3.3

One important fact to remember is that a pi bond cannot exist independently of a sigma bond. Only after the formation of a sigma bond will the *p*-orbitals of adjacent carbons be parallel and in position to form the pi bond. This makes sense; after all, you can't expect someone to be your best friend (or best friend forever) if you aren't even friends to begin with. The more bonds that are formed between atoms, the shorter the overall bond length. Therefore, a double bond is shorter than a single bond, and a triple bond is shorter than a double bond. The shorter the bond length, the greater the strength of the bond.

However, individual pi bonds are weaker than sigma bonds, and it is possible to break only one of the bonds in a double bond, leaving a single bond intact. This happens often in Organic Chemistry, as geometric isomers are converted between *cis* and *trans* conformations. Breaking a single bond requires far more energy, so it happens much less often.

Hybridization

Every MCAT student should know that the carbon atom has the electron configuration $1s^2 2s^2 2p^2$ and, therefore, needs four electrons to complete its octet. A typical molecule formed by carbon (perhaps by the bacteria in your large intestine after that bean burrito) is methane, CH_4. Experimentation shows that the four sigma bonds in methane are equivalent. Wait a second—four equal bonds is inconsistent with what we know about the asymmetrical distribution of carbon's valence electrons: two electrons in the $2s$-orbital, one in the p_x-orbital, one in the p_y-orbital, and none in the p_z-orbital. Rest assured, one of your predecessors in Organic Chemistry (Linus Pauling) developed the theory of orbital hybridization to account for this apparent discrepancy.

sp^3

Hybrid orbitals are formed by mixing different types of orbitals. Just as with molecular orbitals, we can use math to combine three p-orbitals and one s-orbital. The result? Four identical sp^3 orbitals with a brand-new, hybrid shape (see Figure 3.4).

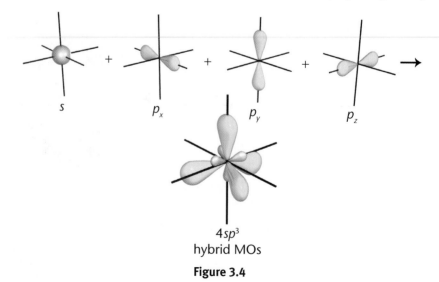

Figure 3.4

All four of these orbitals point toward the vertices of a tetrahedron to minimize repulsion, which explains why carbon prefers a tetrahedral geometry. The hybridization is accomplished by promoting one of the 2s electrons into the $2p_z$ orbital (see Figure 3.5). This produces four valence orbitals, each with one electron, which can be mathematically mixed to provide the hybrids.

Key Concept

Hybridization is a way of making all of the bonds to a central atom equivalent to each other. The sp^3 orbitals are the reason for the tetrahedral shape that is a hallmark of carbon-containing compounds.

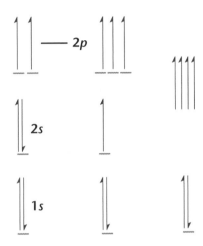

unhybridized   unhybridized   hybridized
ground state   excited state   ground state

Figure 3.5

On the MCAT, you will sometimes be tested about how much "s character" a certain hybrid bond has. To solve these problems, we simply need to determine what type of hybridization it is and use the name to solve the problem. For example, in sp^3, we have one s and three p, so the bond therefore has 25 percent s character and 75 percent p character.

sp^2

Although carbon is most often bound with sp^3 hybridization, there are two other possibilities. For example, when one s-orbital is mixed with two p-orbitals (33% s, 66% p), three sp^2 hybrid orbitals are formed (see Figure 3.6).

This is the hybridization seen in alkenes. The third p-orbital of each carbon is left unhybridized—this is the orbital that participates in the pi bond. The three sp^2 orbitals are oriented 120° apart, which allows for maximum separation because, just like Americans, orbitals need their elbow room. So we know that the unhybridized p-orbital is tied up in the pi bond of the double bond, but what about the hybrid orbitals? In ethylene (ethene), for example, two of the sp^2 hybrids will participate in C–H single bonds, and the other hybrid orbital will line up with the pi bond and form the C=C double bond.

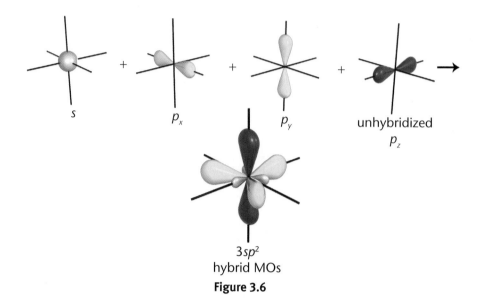

3*sp²*
hybrid MOs

Figure 3.6

sp

To form a triple bond, we need two of the *p*-orbitals to form pi bonds, and the third *p*-orbital will combine with the *s*-orbital to form two *sp*-hybrid orbitals (50% *s* character, 50% *p* character; see Figure 3.7). These orbitals are oriented 180° apart, which explains the linear structure of molecules such as acetylene.

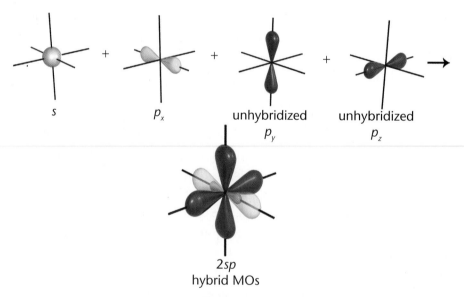

2*sp*
hybrid MOs

Figure 3.7

Conclusion

You may have thought this chapter was a bit brief; that's because the specifics of bonding fall mostly under the domain of General Chemistry. However, without a solid grasp of electronegativity, orbitals, and bonding, it will be difficult to succeed on the Organic Chemistry (or General Chemistry, for that matter) portion of the MCAT. In the Biological Sciences section, the focus will likewise be on the topics detailed in this chapter: atomic orbitals, molecular orbitals, and hybridization. The ability of carbon to form single, double, and triple bonds (or to form sigma and multiple pi bonds) and to form hybrid orbitals gives rise to an entire branch of chemistry; less than half of a section on your MCAT; and, of course, to you and every living thing on this planet. Avoid compartmentalizing the information you learn throughout the course of your studies; all the subjects within science blend together into a seemingly complicated, yet beautifully simple, picture of the universe. The sooner you begin to appreciate this fact, the more manageable and more rewarding your studying will become.

Bonding Summary

Table 3.1 summarizes all the major features of bonding in organic molecules that will likely appear on Test Day. Remember, the geometry specifies the hybridization.

Table 3.1. Bonds of Organic Molecules

Bond Order	Component Bonds	Hybridization	Angles	Examples
single	sigma	sp^3	109.5°	C–C; C–H
double	sigma pi	sp^2	120°	C=C; C=O
triple	sigma pi pi	sp	180°	C≡C; C≡N

MCAT Expertise

Remember that charts and tables are important not only in the passages on the MCAT but also as you go through this book. Always come back to these pages to see the central points of information being presented.

CONCEPTS TO REMEMBER

☐ The principal quantum number, n, determines distance from nucleus and energy level; Possible values = 1, 2, 3, etc.

☐ The azimuthal quantum number, l, determines the shape of the orbital; possible values are $0 \rightarrow n - 1$ (corresponding to s-, p-, d-, and f-orbitals).

☐ Bonding orbitals share the same sign and are energetically favorable.

☐ Antibonding orbitals have opposite signs and are energetically unfavorable.

☐ Single bond = one sigma bond, sp^3 hybridized, 109.5° bond angles; examples: C–C, C–H.

☐ Double bond = one sigma bond + one pi bond, sp^2 hybridized, 120° bond angles; examples: C=C, C=O.

☐ Triple bond = one sigma bond + two pi bonds, sp hybridized, 180° bond angles; examples: C≡C, C≡N.

Practice Questions

1. Within one principal quantum level, which orbital has the least energy?

   A. *s*
   B. *p*
   C. *d*
   D. *f*

2. Which of the following compounds possesses at least one σ bond?

   A. CH_4
   B. C_2H_2
   C. C_2H_4
   D. All of the above

3. In a double-bonded carbon atom (C=C)

   A. hybridization occurs between the *s*-orbital and one *p*-orbital.
   B. hybridization occurs between the *s*-orbital and two *p*-orbitals.
   C. hybridization occurs between the *s*-orbital and three *p*-orbitals.
   D. no hybridization occurs between the *s*-and *p*-orbitals.

4. The hybridization of the carbon atom and the nitrogen atom in the ion CN⁻ are

   A. sp^3 and sp^3, respectively.
   B. sp^3 and sp, respectively.
   C. sp and sp^3, respectively.
   D. sp and sp, respectively.

5. Which of the following hybridizations does the Be atom in BeH_2 assume?

   A. *sp*
   B. sp^2
   C. sp^3
   D. None of the above

6. Two atomic orbitals combine to form

   I. a bonding molecular orbital.

   II. an antibonding molecular orbital.

   III. new atomic orbitals.

   A. I only
   B. I, II, and III
   C. III only
   D. I and II only

7. Molecular orbitals can contain a maximum of

   A. one electron.
   B. two electrons.
   C. four electrons.
   D. $2n^2$ electrons, where *n* is the principal quantum number of the combining atomic orbitals.

8. π bonds are formed by which of the following orbitals?

   A. Two *s*-orbitals
   B. Two *p*-orbitals
   C. One *s*- and one *p*-orbital
   D. All of the above

9. How many σ bonds and π bonds are present in the following compound?

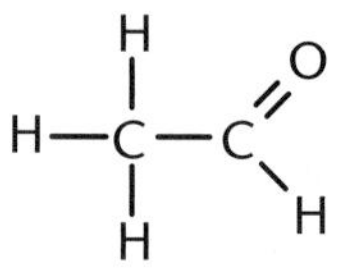

A. Six σ bonds and one π bond
B. Six σ bonds and two π bonds
C. Seven σ bonds and one π bond
D. Seven σ bonds and two π bonds

10. The four C–H bonds of CH_4 point toward the vertices of a tetrahedron. This indicates that the hybridization of a carbon atom is

A. *sp*.
B. *sp²*.
C. *sp³*.
D. None of the above.

Small Group Questions

1. Why is a single bond stronger than a pi bond?

2. Draw an orbital diagram for allene ($H_2C=C=CH_2$). What is the hybridization of all three carbons? What is the shape of the molecule? What other (more common) molecule is reminiscent of allene?

Explanations to Practice Questions

1. A

The energies of the subshells within a principal quantum number are as follows: $s < p < d < f$.

2. D

σ bonds are formed when orbitals overlap end to end. All single bonds are σ bonds; double and triple bonds each contain one σ bond in addition to their π bonds. The compounds CH_4, C_2H_2, and C_2H_4 (choices (A), (B), and (C), respectively) all contain at least one single bond, so the correct answer is (D).

3. B

In a double-bonded carbon, sp^2 hybridization occurs—that is, one s-orbital hybridizes with two p-orbitals to form three sp^2 hybrid orbitals. Therefore, the correct choice is (B). The third p-orbital of the carbon atom remains unhybridized and takes part in the formation of the π bond of the double bond.

4. D

The carbon atom and the nitrogen atoms are connected by a triple bond in CN^-.

$$:N\equiv C:^-$$

A triple-bonded atom is sp hybridized; one s-orbital hybridizes with one p-orbital to form two sp-hybridized orbitals. The two remaining unhybridized p-orbitals take part in the formation of two π bonds. The correct choice, therefore, is (D).

5. A

BeH_2 is a linear molecule, which means that the angle between the two Be–H bonds is 180°. Because sp-orbitals are oriented at an angle of 180°, the Be atom is sp-hybridized. Therefore, the correct choice is (A).

6. D

When atomic orbitals combine to form molecular orbitals, the number of molecular orbitals obtained equals the number of atomic orbitals that take part in the process. Half of the molecular orbitals formed are bonding molecular orbitals, and the other half are antibonding molecular orbitals. In this case, two atomic orbitals combine to form one low-energy bonding molecular orbital and one high-energy antibonding molecular orbital. New atomic orbitals do not form, so answer choices (B) and (C) can be eliminated. The correct choice is (D).

7. B

Like atomic orbitals, molecular orbitals each can contain a maximum of two electrons with opposite spins.

8. B

π bonds are formed by the parallel overlap of unhybridized p-orbitals. The electron density is concentrated above and below the bonding axis. A σ bond, on the other hand, can be formed by the head-to-head overlap of two s-orbitals, two p-orbitals, or one s- and one p-orbital. Here, the density of the electrons is concentrated between the two nuclei of the bonding atoms.

9. A

Each single bond has one σ bond, and each double bond has one σ bond and one π bond. In this question, there are five single bonds (five σ bonds) and one double bond (one σ bond and one π bond), which gives a total of six σ bonds and one π bond. Thus, the correct choice is (A).

10. C

The four bonds point to the vertices of a tetrahedron, which means that the angle between two bonds is 109.5°, which is characteristic of sp^3 orbitals. Hence, the carbon atom of CH_4 is sp^3 hybridized. The correct choice, therefore, is (C).

Alkanes, Alkyl Halides, and Substitution Reactions

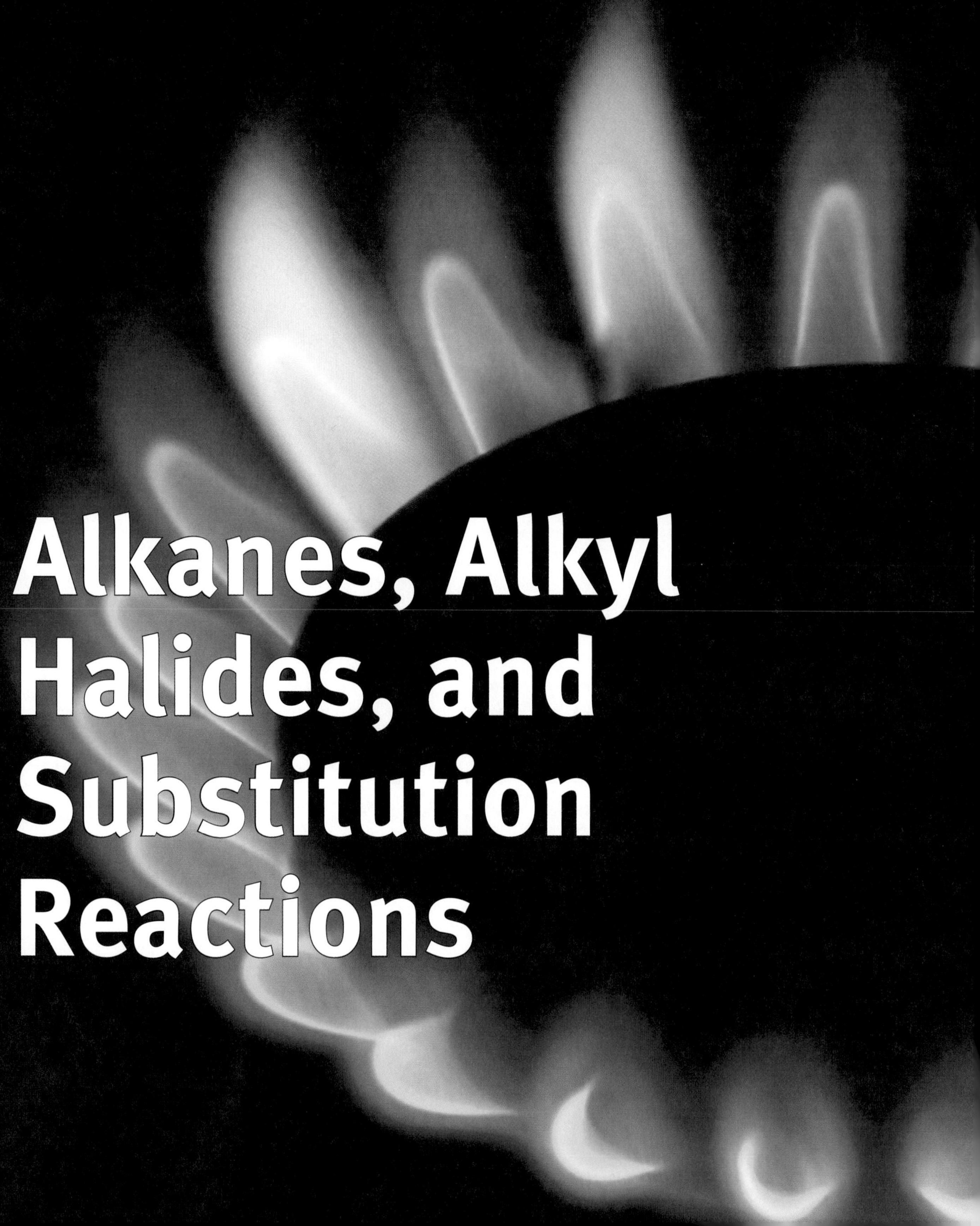

In Chapter 3, we talked about the backbone of Organic Chemistry: bonding. In this chapter, we will begin discussing the simplest type of molecules with a carbon backbone: alkanes. They are our basic organic molecules, containing only carbon and hydrogen. As fully **saturated hydrocarbons**, they have no double bonds, and thus each carbon is *saturated* with the maximum number of hydrogens it can hold. This is reflected in the general formula for alkanes, which you probably recall from Chapter 1 to be C_nH_{2n+2}.

In our modern world, it is incredibly difficult, if not downright impossible, to go a single day without using alkanes. If you've ever cooked with a gas grill (propane), driven a car (octane), or sparked up a lighter (butane), you've used alkanes. As you can see from these examples, most alkanes are combustible liquids and gases. The first four alkanes (methane, ethane, propane, and butane) are probably the most familiar to you, as they are used primarily for heating and cooking. Longer alkanes tend to exist as liquids and are used as fuels in internal combustion engines (such as the one in your car), diesel engines, and jet engines. As alkanes increase even further in length, they are used as oils, waxes, and tars. We are almost guaranteed to come into contact with alkanes in the real world, but how will we see alkanes on Test Day? This chapter will cover all the information you'll need to know about alkanes and their much more reactive derivatives, alkyl halides (alkanes with a halogen in place of hydrogen).

Nomenclature ★★★☆☆☆

As we mentioned in Chapter 1, there are a couple of common names for alkanes that you will frequently encounter on the MCAT, including those shown in Figure 4.1.

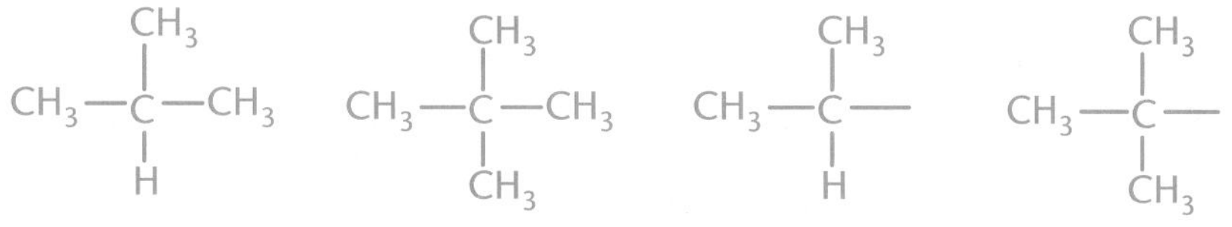

| isobutane | neopentane | isopropyl | *t*-butyl |

Figure 4.1

We classify carbons by the number of other carbon atoms to which they are directly bonded. A **primary** carbon atom (written as **1°**) is bonded to only one other carbon atom. A **secondary (2°)** carbon is bonded to two, a **tertiary (3°)** to three, and a **quaternary (4°)** to four other carbon atoms (see Figure 4.2). In addition, we also classify the hydrogen atoms attached to 1°, 2°, or 3° carbon atoms as 1°, 2°, and 3°, respectively. In fact, the hydrogens attached to carbons will always carry the same name as their parent carbon atom.

> **Bridge**
>
> Refer to Chapter 1 for the general rules of nomenclature for alkanes.

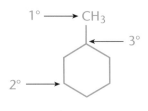

Figure 4.2

Physical Properties ★★★★★★

The physical properties of alkanes (melting point, boiling point, density, etc.) are all prime information to be tested on the MCAT. The nice thing about physical properties is that they vary in a predictable manner. As the molecular weight increases, so do the melting point, boiling point, and density. This is logical; the heavier the molecule is, the harder it should be for the molecule to break away from others and enter the higher-energy gas phase. That's why, at room temperature, straight-chain compounds of up to 4 carbons are found in the gaseous state, chains of 5 to 16 carbons exist as liquids, and the longer-chain compounds are waxes and harder solids. Branched molecules follow a similar trend, but they have slightly lower boiling points than their straight-chain isomers. This is because greater branching reduces the surface area of the molecule available for interactions with neighboring molecules. The weakened intermolecular attractive forces (van der Waals forces) result in a decreased boiling point. Whereas the boiling point follows a perfectly predictable trend, the trend for melting points tends to be a little funky. Generally, the melting point does follow the same trend—after all, with greater branching, the molecules cannot stack up as close to each other as they would prefer. Imagine trying to stack up whole trees instead of just logs. Tough, right? But for a given number of carbons, what really matters is how symmetrical the molecule is. Think about the trees again: It would be much easier to stack symmetrical trees than irregular ones. Therefore, the more symmetrical a molecule, the higher the melting point.

Reactions ★★★★★☆

Alkanes are very stable molecules; they don't react easily with other compounds—that is, unless we agitate them into reacting. As we've seen with fuels, they can sit on shelves for years without concern, but as soon as they are exposed to a spark and some oxygen . . . fire in the hole!

COMBUSTION

Combustion is the reaction of alkanes with molecular oxygen to form carbon dioxide, water, and heat. The combustion reaction has been a favorite among humans for a long time, although its mechanism isn't as simple as striking a match. The reaction is believed to proceed through a radical process, and because it is complex, the mechanism is not within the scope of the MCAT. What *is* within the scope of the MCAT is the equation for combustion:

$$C_3H_8 + 5\ O_2 \rightarrow 3\ CO_2 + 4\ H_2O + heat$$

One problem that arises is that combustion is often incomplete. This dangerous incompletion results in significant quantities of carbon monoxide instead of carbon dioxide. This carbon monoxide production is a major cause of air pollution.

FREE RADICAL HALOGENATION

One of the frequently encountered alkane reactions on the MCAT is **halogenation**, in which one or more hydrogen atoms are replaced with a halogen atom (Cl, Br, or I) via a **free-radical substitution** mechanism. These reactions involve three steps, but the second step can occur multiple times before the final step occurs.

Initiation

Diatomic halogens are homolytically cleaved (the two electrons of the sigma bond are split equally) by either heat or ultraviolet light, resulting in the formation of two free radicals. Free radicals are neutral species with unpaired electrons (such as Cl• or R_3C•). They are extremely reactive and readily attack alkanes, or pretty much anything that gets near them. Free radicals act in the same manner as political radicals (easily roused citizens who will readily take part in a rally or demonstration).

$$\text{Initiation:}\quad X_2 \xrightarrow[\text{or } \Delta]{h\nu} 2X\bullet$$

Propagation

A propagation step is one in which a radical produces another radical that can continue the reaction. A free radical reacts with an alkane, removing a hydrogen atom to form HX and creating an alkyl radical. The alkyl radical can then react with X_2 to form an alkyl halide, generating X•. We can always identify a propagation step because it is the only step that both begins and ends with a radical. Note that the product of the first propagation step is the starting material of the second, and the product of the second is the starting material for the first step (a chain reaction). Just as with the propagation of a species, the end goal is to make more of the same thing.

$$\text{Propagation:}\quad X\bullet + RH \rightarrow HX + R\bullet$$
$$R\bullet + X_2 \rightarrow RX + X\bullet$$

Real World

Nitrogen in the air is often oxidized accidentally in the internal combustion engine, whereas nitrous oxide injection systems can be purposely (and illegally) installed to increase the engine power of a car. Unfortunately, various nitrogen oxides are major contributors to air pollution.

Bridge

Foods high in antioxidants reportedly help remove the free radicals naturally produced within the body from oxidative phosphorylation.

Termination

Propagation will continue until two free radicals combine with one another to form a stable molecule, ending the reaction.

$$\text{Termination:} \quad 2X\bullet \rightarrow X_2$$
$$X\bullet + R\bullet \rightarrow RX$$
$$2R\bullet \rightarrow R_2$$

Larger alkanes have many hydrogens available for the free radical to attack. Bromine radicals react fairly slowly and primarily attack the hydrogens on the carbon atom that can form the most stable free radical (i.e., the most substituted carbon atom). This is a good general rule to get down now: *The more stable the intermediate is, the more likely the reaction is to occur.*

$$\bullet CR_3 > \bullet CR_2H > \bullet CRH_2 > \bullet CH_3$$
$$3° > 2° > 1° > \text{methyl}$$

MCAT Expertise

Always think of carbocations and free radicals as electron-deficient because both species have fewer than the eight electrons needed to be complete. In this way, we can remember the trends of stability of both of these species: 3° > 2° > 1° > methyl.

Thus, a tertiary radical is the most likely to be formed in a free radical bromination reaction (see Figure 4.3).

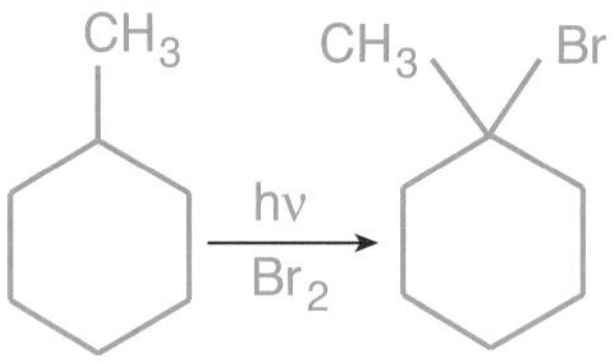

Figure 4.3

Free-radical chlorination is a more rapid process and thus depends not only on the stability of the intermediate but also on the number of hydrogens present. Free-radical chlorination reactions are more likely to replace primary hydrogens if they are the most abundant type of hydrogen present, despite the relative instability of primary radicals. Because of this decreased selectivity, free-radical chlorination reactions yield mixtures of products and are useful only when just one type of hydrogen is present.

PYROLYSIS

MCAT Expertise

When a reaction involves UV light, you will almost always see a free radical. When a reaction involves heat, you should consider the possibility of free radicals and elimination reactions (which do not involve radicals and will be discussed in Chapter 5).

Pyrolysis occurs when a molecule is broken down by heat. You can remember the name of this reaction by breaking it down into components: *Pyro* indicates that the reaction needs heat (just as a pyromaniac needs to light things on fire), and *lysis* is a term we use to talk about breaking molecules (or cell membranes, in the case of cell death). Pyrolysis, also known as **cracking**, is most commonly used to reduce the average molecular weight of heavy oils and increase the production of the more desirable volatile compounds. In the pyrolysis of alkanes, the C–C bonds are cleaved, producing smaller-chain alkyl radicals. These radicals can recombine to form a variety of alkanes, as shown in Figure 4.4.

$$CH_3CH_2CH_3 \xrightarrow[\Delta]{} CH_3\bullet + \bullet CH_2CH_3$$

$$2\ CH_3\bullet \longrightarrow CH_3CH_3$$

$$2\ \bullet CH_2CH_3 \longrightarrow CH_3CH_2CH_2CH_3$$

Figure 4.4

Alternatively, in a process called **disproportionation**, a radical transfers a hydrogen atom to another radical, producing an alkane and an alkene, as shown in Figure 4.5.

$$CH_3\bullet + \bullet CH_2CH_3 \rightarrow CH_4 + CH_2 = CH_2$$

Figure 4.5

Substitution Reactions of Alkyl Halides ★★★★★★

Alkyl halides and other substituted carbon atoms can take part in nucleophilic substitution reactions. **Nucleophiles** ("nucleus lovers") are electron-rich species that are attracted to positively charged or positively polarized atoms (known as **electrophiles**, or "electron lovers"). Alkyl halides are some of the most common substrates you will see undergoing nucleophilic substitution reactions on the MCAT. In these reactions, and with every reaction you see on the MCAT, the first thing we need to do is identify the nucleophile and the electrophile.

Key Concept

A rule of thumb is that basicity and nucleophilicity are directly related because both imply that the compound wants to donate electrons, but the solvent may stabilize these species and alter that trend. In aprotic solvents, the trend stays intact.

NUCLEOPHILES

Basicity

When comparing two nucleophiles, if both have the same attacking atom (for example, oxygen), nucleophilicity is roughly correlated to basicity. This seems logical: After all, the stronger the base is, the more likely it is to attract a positively charged proton. (Aha! Our Brønsted-Lowry definition of a base!) Because nucleophilic strength also measures how much the atom wants to find a positive charge, these two traits strongly correlate. For example, nucleophilic strength decreases in this order:

$$RO^- > HO^- > RCO_2^- > ROH > H_2O$$

Size and Polarizability

If the attacking atoms differ, or if the conditions differ, nucleophilic ability doesn't necessarily correlate with basicity. For example, in a **protic** solvent (solvents with protons in solution, such as water or alcohols), large atoms tend to be better nucleophiles because they can shed the solvating protons surrounding them and are more polarizable. Let's think about this: If we had a small, incredibly electronegative atom such as fluoride in a protic solvent, what would happen? Would it even make it to the electrophile? Probably not. It would probably pick up a proton out of solution the second it could. But what if we had a big old iodide atom? Well, it's not nearly as electronegative, so it would be less likely to pick up a proton the second it hit the solution. Furthermore, it's so big that it can be polarized, meaning the electrons can shift around, making some areas more negative than others, giving it a much better chance to make it to the electrophile while it is still negative enough to attack. Hence, nucleophilic strength decreases in this order:

$$CN^- > I^- > RO^- > HO^- > Br^- > Cl^- > F^- > H_2O$$

In **aprotic** (without protons) solvents, however, the nucleophiles don't have fancy proton coats surrounding them; they are not solvated. In this situation, nucleophilic strength *is* related to basicity. For example, in the aprotic solvent dimethylsulfoxide, the order of nucleophillic strength is the same as base strength:

$$F^- > Cl^- > Br^- > I^-$$

Note that this is the opposite of the trend in protic solvents.

LEAVING GROUPS

The ease with which nucleophilic substitution takes place also depends on how good a leaving group is present. Good leaving groups are easy to detect: The best leaving groups are those that are weak bases or, if you like, stable anions or neutral species. That is, they can easily accommodate an electron pair. Good leaving groups (weak bases) are the conjugate bases of strong acids. In the case of the halogens, this is the opposite of base strength (the pK_a of HI is −10.4, whereas the pK_a of HF is 3.1):

$$I^- > Br^- > Cl^- > F^-$$

S$_N$1 REACTIONS

S$_N$1 is the designation for a **unimolecular nucleophilic substitution** reaction. The term *unimolecular* tells us that the rate of the reaction depends on only one species, the **substrate** (the original molecule) itself. The rate-determining step is the dissociation of this species to form a stable, *positively charged* ion called a **carbocation.**

Mechanism of S$_N$1 Reactions

S$_N$1 reactions involve two steps: the dissociation of a molecule into a carbocation and a good leaving group, followed by the combination of the carbocation with a nucleophile (see Figure 4.6).

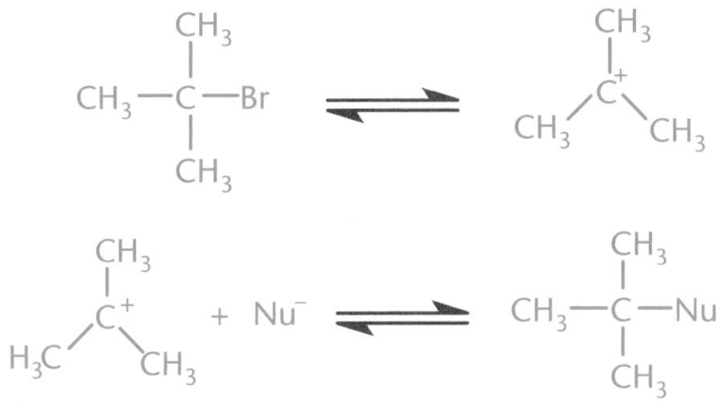

Figure 4.6

The first step of this mechanism is interesting. Notice that carbon is happily located with the other nonmetals on the right side of the periodic table, a place where atoms don't like to have positive charges. As such, it takes a little bit of coaxing to get carbon to become a carbocation. This can be accomplished using polar protic solvents with lone electron pairs, because the electron-rich groups can solvate the carbocation and help stabilize it. Carbocations are also stabilized by charge delocalization. The more highly substituted the cation is, the more stable it will be. This means the order of stability is as follows:

tertiary > secondary > primary > methyl

If we want to get a particular product from an S$_N$1 reaction, we need to make sure that the original substituent is a better leaving group than the nucleophile; otherwise, the reverse reaction will outcompete the forward reaction. This is an important factor, because it means that S$_N$1 reactions *do not* require strong nucleophiles, however, the more reactive the nucleophile the more likely an S$_N$2 reaction will result. Since the carbocation is *such* a strong electrophile, it will basically pick up anything that comes near it with lone electrons.

Rate of S$_N$1 Reactions

Like a relay race team, the rate at which a reaction occurs depends on its slowest step. Such a step is termed the **rate-limiting** or **rate-determining step** of the reaction, because it limits the speed of the reaction. In an S$_N$1 reaction, the slowest step is the dissociation of the molecule to form the carbocation, which we said was energetically unfavorable. In other words, the formation of a carbocation is the rate-limiting step. The only reactant in this step is the original molecule (substrate), so the rate of the entire reaction, under a given set of conditions, depends only on the

> **MCAT Expertise**
>
> The carbocation intermediate is the hallmark of the S$_N$1 reaction, and our understanding of the intermediate will be essential in determining all of the facts surrounding the reaction, including the rate and the products.

> **Key Concept**
>
> The kinetics of unimolecular reactions are first order.

concentration of this original molecule, rate = k[RX] (a so-called first-order reaction). The rate does not depend on the concentration or the nature of the nucleophile because it is not involved in the rate-determining step.

The rate of an S_N1 reaction can be increased by anything that accelerates the formation of the carbocation. The most important factors that we have already discussed are summarized below.

Structural Factors

Highly substituted alkyl halides allow for distribution of the positive charge over a greater number of carbon atoms and, thus, form the most stable carbocations.

Solvent Effects

Highly polar solvents are better at surrounding and isolating ions than less polar solvents. Polar protic solvents, such as water, work best because solvation stabilizes the intermediate state.

Nature of the Leaving Group

Weak bases dissociate more easily from the alkyl chain and thus make better leaving groups, increasing the rate of carbocation formation.

> **Key Concept**
>
> The pentacoordinate (five-coordinate) transition state, where one bond is forming and the other is breaking, is the hallmark of the S_N2 reaction. The increased crowding around that central atom will guide the rate and products of the reaction.

S_N2 REACTIONS

Under certain conditions, the formation of a carbocation is unlikely, if not downright impossible. Even under such conditions, substitution reactions can still proceed, but they must occur by a different mechanism that avoids the carbocation altogether. Enter S_N2: An **S_N2 (bimolecular nucleophilic substitution)** reaction involves a strong nucleophile pushing its way into a compound, while simultaneously displacing the leaving group in one concerted step (see Figure 4.7). Because this reaction has only one step, it must be the rate-determining step. The reaction is called bimolecular because the rate-determining step involves two molecules, as we will soon discuss.

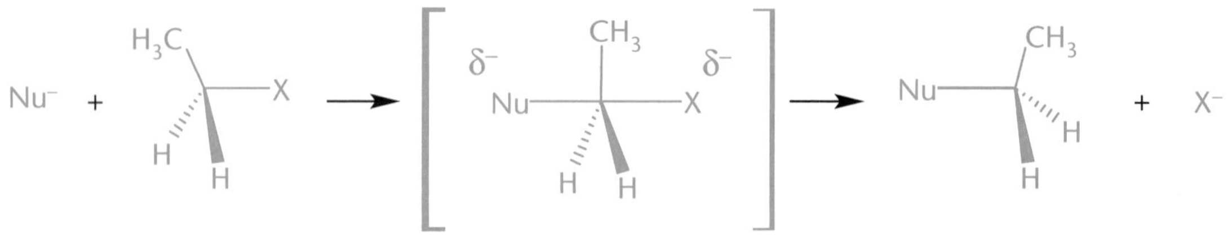

Figure 4.7

Mechanism of S_N2 Reactions

In S_N2 reactions, the nucleophile actively displaces the leaving group in an in-line attack. This is sometimes called a *backside attack*. For this to occur, the nucleophile must be strong, and the substrate cannot be sterically hindered. This tells us something important about the reactivity of substrates: Primary substrates are the most likely to undergo S_N2 reactions, followed by secondary, whereas tertiary substrates are just too crowded to participate in this mechanism. Notice that this is the opposite of the trend for S_N1 reactions. The nucleophile attacks the reactant from the backside of the leaving group, forming a **trigonal bipyramidal** transition state (sp^2). As the reaction progresses, the bond to the nucleophile strengthens, while the bond to the leaving group weakens. The leaving group is displaced as the bond to the nucleophile becomes complete.

Rate of S_N2 Reactions

The single step of an S_N2 reaction involves *two* reacting species: the substrate (the molecule with a leaving group, often an alkyl halide or a tosylate) and the nucleophile. Therefore, the concentrations of both have a role in determining the rate of an S_N2 reaction; the two species must meet in solution, and raising the concentration of either will make such a meeting more likely. Because the rate of the S_N2 reaction depends on the concentration of two reactants, it follows **second-order kinetics** (rate = k[Nu] [RX]).

S_N1 Versus S_N2 ★★★★★☆

Now, we come to the real stuff the MCAT loves to test: What conditions favor one mechanism over the other? As you try to decide which mechanism or mechanisms are occurring, be sure to consider such factors as sterics, nucleophilic strength, leaving group ability, reaction conditions, and solvent effects.

Stereochemsitry of Substitution Reactions ★★★★★☆

S_N1 STEREOCHEMISTRY

The S_N1 mechanism involves a carbocation intermediate in which the carbon only has three groups bound to it. With only three substituents, the molecule takes on a planar shape, with 120° between each of the bonds. That means that the carbons are sp^2 hybridized. Because the molecule is planar (and therefore achiral), the nucleophile can attack either the top *or* the bottom of the compound. This means that as long as the end product has four different groups, we can have two different products, depending on whether the nucleophile attacks from the top or the bottom (see Figure 4.8).

Key Concept

An intermediate is distinct from a transition state. An intermediate is a well-defined species with a finite life-time and must be at a relative minimum energy for this to occur. On the other hand, a transition state is a theoretical structure used to define a mechanism. The transition state represents a maximum (in energy) between two minima on a reaction coordinate.

Key Concept

The kinetics of S_N2 reactions are second order.

MCAT Expertise

The comparison of molecules and which mechanism will be favored by particular reactants under particular conditions is a common topic on the MCAT.

Key Concept

S_N1 leads to loss of stereochemistry; S_N2 leads to a *relative* inversion of stereochemistry owing to backside attack. Be careful, though, because the *absolute* configuration may remain the same if the leaving group and the nucleophile do not maintain the same priority.

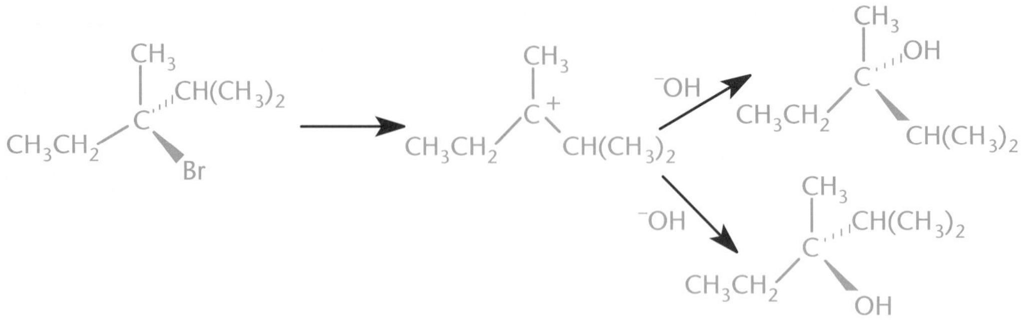

Figure 4.8

Bridge

Refer to Chapter 2 for further discussion of optical activity.

So, if the original compound was optically active, the product will be a racemic mixture and, thus, no longer optically active.

S$_N$2 STEREOCHEMISTRY

In the S$_N$2 mechanism, the nucleophile must attack the backside of the molecule, because the leaving group leaves from the other side. If a chiral molecule undergoes an S$_N$2 reaction, the molecule will flip, and an inversion of configuration will take place (see Figure 4.9). We've all had the unpleasant experience of trying to use an umbrella on a blustery day. When the wind blows your umbrella inside out, the original configuration of the umbrella is inverted. Your umbrella has been S$_N$2-ed!

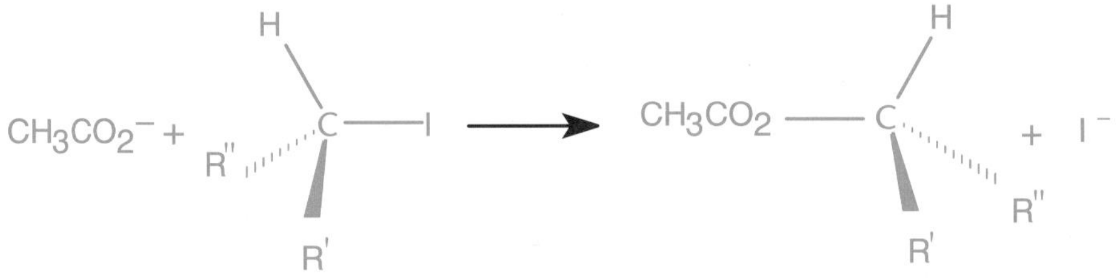

Figure 4.9

One important thing to be aware of is that this inversion of stereochemistry will lead to an inversion of the *absolute* configuration only if the leaving group and the nucleophile have the same priority (*R* will be changed to *S*, and vice versa). If the nucleophile and the leaving group have *different* priorities, even though the molecule will still flip, the designation will *not* be changed.

Table 4.1 summarizes S$_N$1 and S$_N$2 reactions.

Table 4.1. S_N1 and S_N2 Reactions

S_N1	S_N2
• 2 steps	• 1 step
• Favored in polar protic solvents.	• Favored in polar aprotic solvents.
• $3° > 2° \gg 1° >$ methyl.	• $1° > 2° \gg 3°$.
• Rate = k[RX].	• Rate = k[Nu] [RX].
• Racemic products.	• Optically active/inverted products.
• Favored with the use of bulky nucleophiles.	

MCAT Expertise

Here's another important table to refer to many times before Test Day.

Conclusion

Although alkanes are a relatively simple part of Organic Chemistry, they are an essential part of the MCAT and will definitely show up on Test Day. Because alkanes are stable (or not very reactive) molecules, there aren't many reactions to commit to memory—but remember that alkanes will undergo combustion, free-radical halogenation, and pyrolysis (cracking) when agitated into reacting. As soon as we swap out a hydrogen atom for a halogen (creating an alkyl halide), the game changes entirely. Because alkyl halides are equipped with good leaving groups, they can undergo nucleophilic substitution reactions. We saw that there are two possible mechanisms of nucleophilic substitutions, unimolecular (S_N1) and bimolecular (S_N2), which occur through mechanisms with two steps and one step, respectively. Make sure you are completely confident on S_N1 and S_N2 reactions and the conditions under which each will occur. This is one of the most important concepts in MCAT Organic Chemistry.

CONCEPTS TO REMEMBER

☐ Physical properties of alkanes: ↑ chain length, ↑ boiling point, ↑ melting point, ↑ density

☐ Physical properties of alkanes: ↑ branching, ↓ boiling point, ↓ density

☐ Free radical halogenation steps: initiation, propagation, termination

☐ Nucleophiles = electron rich; electrophiles = electron deficient.

☐ Solvents affect nucleophilicity.

☐ Weak bases make good leaving groups.

☐ S_N1: two steps; S_N2: one step

☐ S_N1: favored in protic solvents; S_N2: favored in aprotic solvents.

☐ S_N1: 3° > 2° >> 1°; S_N2: 1° > 2° >> 3°.

☐ S_N1: rate = $k[RX]$; S_N2: rate = $k[Nu][RX]$.

☐ S_N1: racemic products; S_N2: inverted product

Practice Questions

1. Under the following conditions,

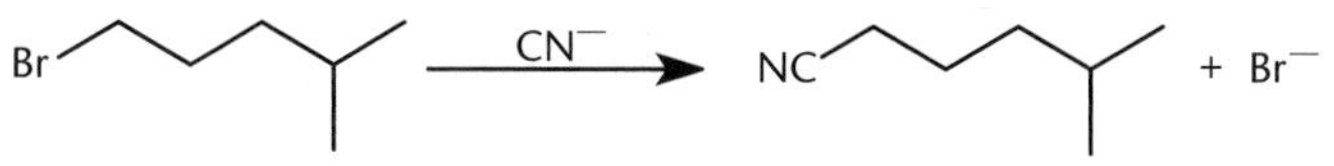

1-bromo-4-methylpentane will most probably react via

A. S_N1.
B. S_N2.
C. both S_N1 and S_N2.
D. neither S_N1 nor S_N2.

2. The following molecule can be classified as having

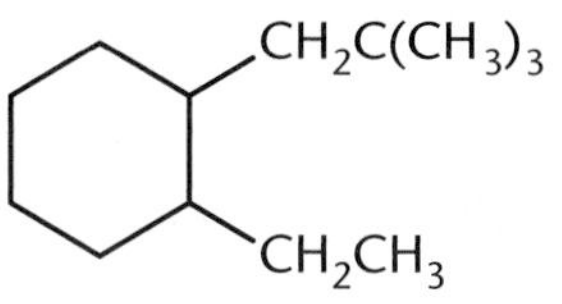

A. four primary, two secondary, four tertiary, and three quaternary carbon atoms.
B. three methyl groups, two ethyl groups, and four secondary carbon atoms.
C. four primary, six secondary, two tertiary, and one quaternary carbon atoms.
D. three primary, three secondary, four tertiary, and three quaternary carbon atoms.

3. S_N1 reactions show first-order kinetics because

A. the rate-limiting step is the first step to occur in the reaction.
B. the rate-limiting step involves only one molecule.
C. there is only one rate-limiting step.
D. the reaction involves only one molecule.

4. The following reaction sequence is typical of S_N1 reactions. Identify the rate-limiting step(s).

Step 1
$$(CH_3)_3C\text{—}Cl \longrightarrow (CH_3)_3C^+ + Cl^-$$

Step 2
$$(CH_3)_3C^+ \xrightarrow{CH_3CH_2OH} (CH_3)_3C\overset{+}{\underset{H}{\text{—}O\text{—}}}CH_2CH_3$$

Step 3
$$(CH_3)_3C\overset{+}{\underset{H}{\text{—}O\text{—}}}CH_2CH_3 \longrightarrow (CH_3)_3C\text{—}O\text{—}CH_2CH_3 + H^+$$

A. Step 1
B. Step 2
C. Step 3
D. Steps 1 and 2

5. Which of the following would be the best solvent for an S_N2 reaction?

A. H_2O
B. CH_3CH_2OH
C. CH_3SOCH_3
D. $CH_3CH_2CH_2CH_2CH_2CH_3$

6. Which of the following conditions, listed as leaving group and nucleophile, respectively, would most favor an S_N2 reaction?

A. I^-, Cl^-
B. EtO^-, tosylate
C. tosylate, CN^-
D. OH^-, H_2O

7. What would be the major product of the following reaction?

$$CH_3CH_2CH_3 + Br_2 \xrightarrow{h\upsilon}$$

A. $CH_3CH_2CH_2Br$
B. $CH_3CH_2CH_2CH_2CH_2CH_3$
C. $(CH_3)_2CHBr$
D. CH_3CH_2Br

8. Treatment of (S)-2-bromobutane with sodium hydroxide results in the production of a compound with an (R) configuration. The reaction has most likely taken place through

A. an S_N1 mechanism.
B. an S_N2 mechanism.
C. both an S_N1 and S_N2 reaction.
D. cannot be determined.

9. What is the correct order of the boiling points of the following compounds?

  I. *n*-hexane

  II. 2-methylpentane

  III. 2,2-dimethylbutane

  IV. *n*-heptane

A. I > IV > II > III
B. IV > III > II > I
C. IV > I > II > III
D. I > II > III > IV

10. The reaction of isobutane with an unknown halogen is catalyzed by light. The two major products obtained are

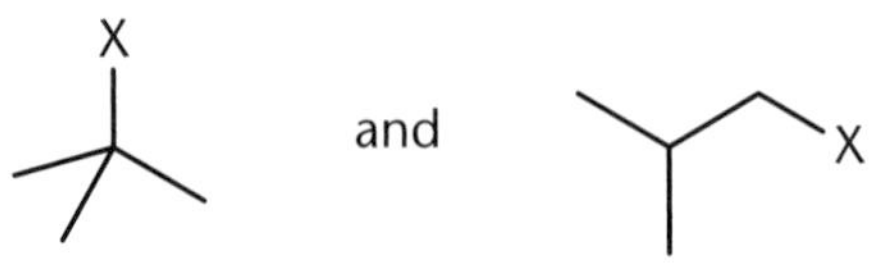

What is the unknown halogen?

A. Cl_2
B. Br_2
C. I_2
D. F_2

Small Group Questions

1. In free-radical halogenation, why is bromine more selective than chlorine?

2. What is the difference between an intermediate and a transition state?

Explanations to Practice Questions

1. B

In this question, a primary alkyl halide is treated with cyanide, which is a good nucleophile. Primary alkyl halides are not sterically hindered and are therefore readily displaced in S_N2 reactions. Cyanide will displace the bromide to produce 5-methylheptanenitrile in good yield. An S_N1 reaction will probably not occur because formation of a primary carbocation is very unstable.

2. C

The molecule shown in question 2 is 2-ethyl-1-neopentyl-cyclohexane. A primary carbon atom is one that is bonded to only one other carbon atom, a secondary carbon atom is bonded to two, a tertiary to three, and a quaternary to four. Thus, this molecule has four primary, six secondary, two tertiary, and one quaternary carbon atoms, so choice (C) is correct.

3. B

An S_N1 reaction is a first-order nucleophilic substitution reaction. It is called first-order because the rate-limiting step involves only one molecule; thus, the correct answer is choice (B). Choice (A) is incorrect because the rate-limiting step is not necessarily the first step to occur in a reaction. It is simply the slowest step. Choice (C) is a true statement but is incorrect because it is irrelevant to the term *first-order*. Finally, choice (D) is incorrect because it is the rate-limiting step, not the reaction, that involves only one molecule.

4. A

The formation of a carbocation is always the rate-limiting step for S_N1 reactions. This step is the slowest to occur, and its rate determines the rate of the reaction. Step 2 is a nucleophilic attack on the carbocation by ethanol. In step 3, a proton is lost from the protonated ether. Steps 2 and 3 both occur very rapidly in solution and are not rate-limiting steps. Answer choice (D) is incorrect because there can be only one rate-limiting step.

5. C

S_N2 reactions are most successful in polar aprotic solvents, such as dimethylsulfoxide. S_N2 reactions occur via a one-step mechanism in which a nucleophile attacks a substrate. Polar aprotic solvents accelerate this reaction by allowing the nucleophile to be "naked" (i.e., not surrounded by hydrogen-bonded solvation spheres). This allows the nucleophile easy access to the substrate. In addition, the solvent should be polar to dissolve the reactants. Choice (A), water, and choice (B), ethanol, are both incorrect because although they are polar, they are also protic and would diminish the power of the nucleophile. Choice (D) is hexane and is incorrect because it is a nonpolar solvent.

6. C

This reaction is S_N2, and for it to occur there must be a good leaving group and a strong incoming nucleophile. In choice (C), X is tosylate, an excellent leaving group, and Y is cyanide, an excellent nucleophile. Therefore, choice (C) is the correct answer. Choice (A) is incorrect because, although iodide is a good leaving group (favoring the forward reaction), it is also a great nucleophile (favoring the reverse reaction). Choice (B) is incorrect because ethoxide is a poor leaving group and tosylate is a weak nucleophile. Finally, choice (D) is incorrect because again, hydroxide is a poor leaving group and water is a poor nucleophile.

7. C

This question concerns the free-radical bromination of an alkane. The bromination reaction occurs in such a way as to produce the most stable alkyl radical. This is because bromine radicals are selective, as opposed to chlorine radicals, which react indiscriminately. In this question, the most stable radical is a secondary radical, which further reacts to form 2-bromopropane, which is the correct answer. Choice (A) is incorrect because 1-bromopropane results from reaction of a primary radical, and although this may occur to an extent, the major product will be 2-bromopropane. Choice (B) would result from the combination of two primary radicals and is expected to be a minor product. Finally, choice (D) is incorrect because a carbon atom is lost in the reaction, which does not occur in free-radical bromination.

8. B

When (S)-2-bromobutane is treated with hydroxide, a compound with an (R) configuration is obtained. The most likely occurrence is a substitution reaction, and the fact that the absolute configuration has changed suggests an S_N2 reaction. Inversion of configuration is a hallmark of the S_N2 mechanism, whereas racemization is typical of S_N1 reactions.

9. C

The correct answer is choice (C), IV > I > II > III, corresponding to n-heptane > n-hexane > 2-methylpentane > 2,2-dimethylbutane. As the chain length of a straight-chain alkane is increased, the boiling point also increases, approximately 25° to 30°C for each additional carbon atom. Therefore, n-heptane is expected to boil at a higher temperature than n-hexane. Isomeric alkanes also follow a trend: As branching increases, boiling point decreases. Compounds I, II, and III are isomeric hexanes, listed in increasing order of branching. Therefore, n-hexane boils at a higher temperature than 2-methylpentane, which boils at a higher temperature than 2,2-dimethylbutane.

10. A

Free-radical halogenation reactions are practical only for bromine and chlorine; iodine (C) and fluorine (D) do not react efficiently and can therefore be eliminated. Bromine radicals (B) react slowly compared with chlorine radicals and are, therefore, more likely to react in a manner that forms the most stable alkyl radical (i.e., the most substituted radical). This leads to the production of one major bromination product. Chlorine radicals, on the other hand, react so quickly that they become indiscriminate and generally produce several different products. In this particular reaction, two different products are isolated in comparable yields, so the halogen used must have been chlorine.

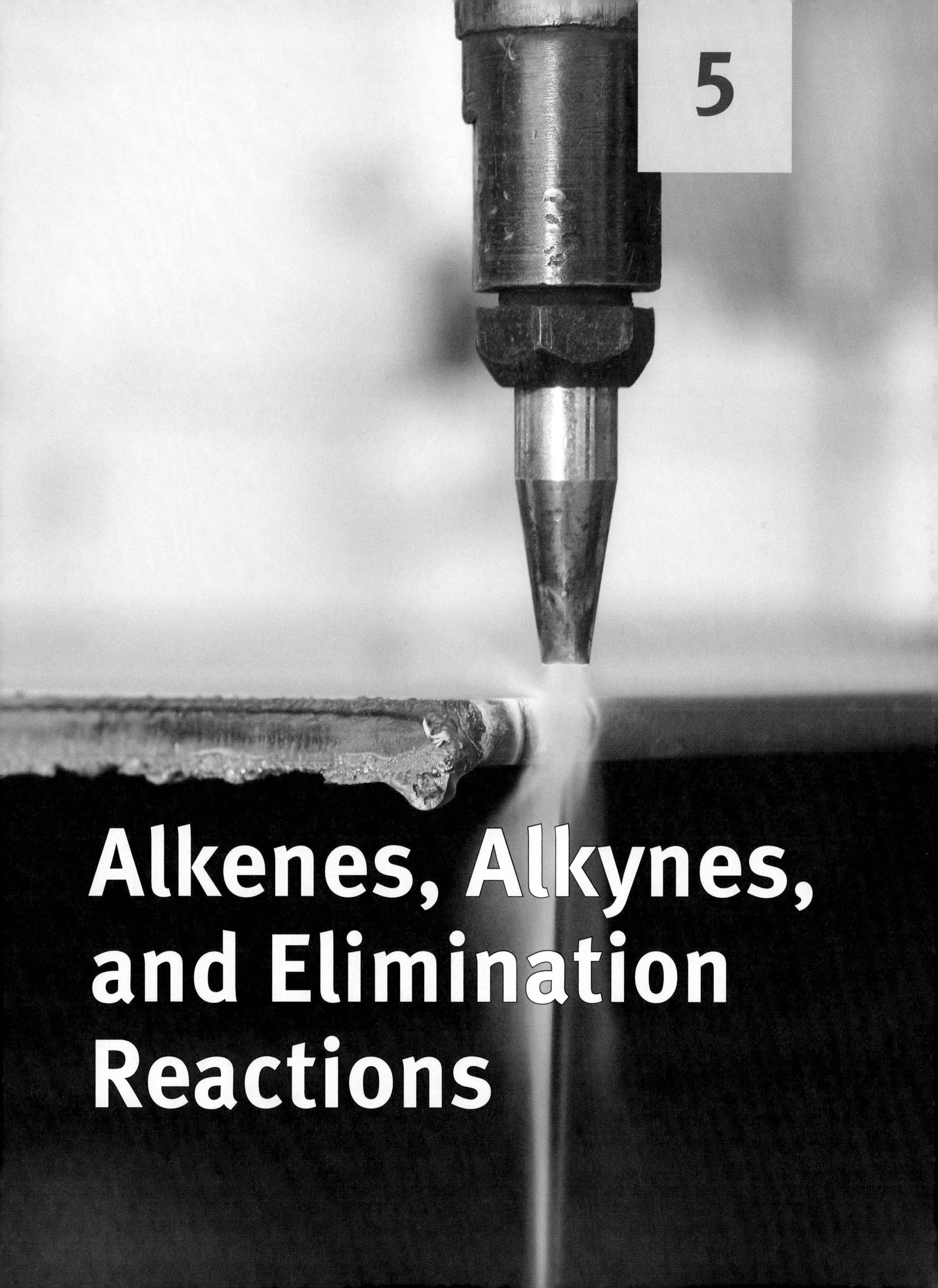

Alkenes, Alkynes, and Elimination Reactions

We've mentioned several times so far that carbon is the basis of life. In fact, carbon does more than just constitute living things; it is also extremely useful and versatile in its pure form. As children, we write with graphite pencils, leaving beautiful silver streaks of math on wide-ruled paper (until the teacher covers them in red ink). As adults, we exchange diamond rings made of pure carbon as a symbol of engagement. Although pure carbon is pretty neat, it gets much more interesting when we mix it with hydrogen (as we saw in the last chapter). In this chapter, we'll learn some different recipes, combining carbon and hydrogens to create unsaturated molecules. Remember from Chapter 1 that each double bond or ring in a molecule will result in a degree of unsaturation, and each triple bond will give the molecule two degrees of unsaturation. This may sound like new terminology, but it isn't. We've all heard of unsaturated fats—these are just fatty carbon chains with one or more double bonds. Remember that double bonds are considered functional groups, and as it turns out, alkenes are more reactive than their corresponding alkanes.

Alkenes are useful and abundant in both industry and nature. The simplest alkene, ethene (known almost exclusively as ethylene), is the starting material in the production of polyethylene (a polymer used to make the plastic bags that are rapidly disappearing from grocery stores). In nature, ethylene is a hormone that induces fruit ripening. Alkynes, which contain at least one triple bond, are unstable and very reactive—pretty much the opposite of their corresponding alkanes. Industrial processes such as welding take advantage of the extremely hot (over 3,330°C!) flame that results from the combustion of acetylyne, or ethyne.

Alkenes and alkynes both contain π bonds, which endow them with many similar properties. π bonds are commonly formed through elimination reactions, a required and heavily tested concept on the MCAT. Luckily, they can be studied in relation to the substitution reactions discussed in Chapter 4.

Alkenes ★★★★★★

NOMENCLATURE

Here's a quick review. Alkenes are sometimes called **olefins**, and their stereochemistry is described by *cis*, *trans*, *E*, and *Z*. The common names *ethylene*, *propylene*, and *isobutylene* are used more often than their corresponding IUPAC names (see Figure 5.1).

MCAT Expertise

Alkenes and alkynes are not going to be tested directly on the MCAT, and if they appear, most of the relevant information will be included in the passage and/or question stem. Elimination reactions, however, *will* be tested because they are related to the substitution reactions discussed in Chapter 3.

Bridge

See Chapter 1 for a review of nomenclature and Chapter 2 for a review of stereochemistry.

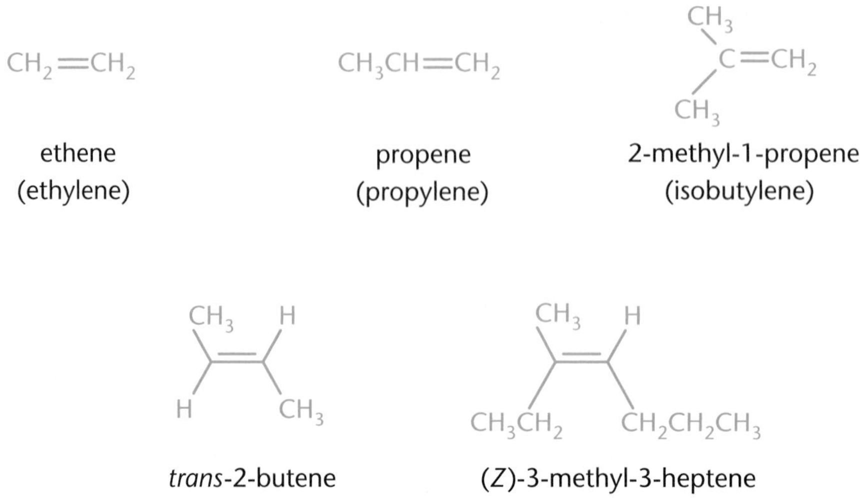

ethene
(ethylene)

propene
(propylene)

2-methyl-1-propene
(isobutylene)

trans-2-butene

(Z)-3-methyl-3-heptene

Figure 5.1

PHYSICAL PROPERTIES

The physical properties of alkenes are similar to those of alkanes. For example, the melting and boiling points increase with increasing molecular weight and are even similar in value to those of corresponding alkanes. However, when dealing with alkenes, we must take stereochemistry into account. *Trans*-alkenes generally have higher melting points than *cis*-alkenes because they are more symmetric, which allows for better packing in the solid state. *Trans*-alkenes also tend to have lower boiling points than *cis*-alkenes because they are less polar.

Polarity is the result of an asymmetrical distribution of electrons in a molecule. This causes the molecule to have one partially negative region, and another that is partially positive. In alkenes, unequal electron distribution creates dipole moments that point from the electropositive alkyl groups toward the electronegative alkene. That is, the sp^3 carbons donate electrons to the sp^2 carbons. Why? Because sp^3 carbons have less s-character (25%) than sp^2 carbons (33%), and s-electrons can be found at the positive nucleus, making them more stable. When you draw these dipole moments, make sure that the arrows always point toward electron density, as in Figure 5.2. In *trans*-2-butene, the two dipole moments are oriented in opposite directions and cancel each other out. This means that the compound possesses no net dipole moment and is *nonpolar*. On the other hand, *cis*-2-butene, with its same-side orientation, *does* have a net dipole moment, resulting from the addition of the two smaller dipoles. The additional intermolecular forces that arise from this polarity tend to raise the boiling point.

Key Concept

trans-alkenes have higher melting points than *cis*-alkenes owing to higher symmetry, which allows for more efficient packing in the solid state. *cis*-alkenes have higher boiling points than *trans*-alkenes because they are polar (as we see in Figure 5.2).

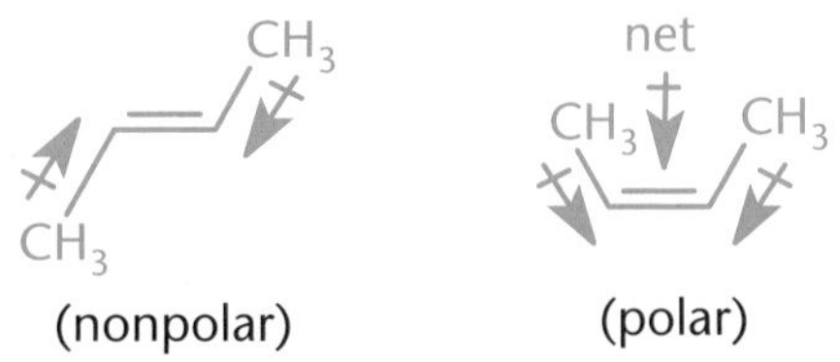

Figure 5.2

SYNTHESIS

Although there are many ways to synthesize alkenes, the most common method involves **elimination reactions** of either alcohols or alkyl halides. In elimination reactions, the carbon backbone kicks off (or eliminates) a hydrogen and a halide (dehydrohalogenation), or a molecule of water (dehydration), and forms a double bond (see Figure 5.3).

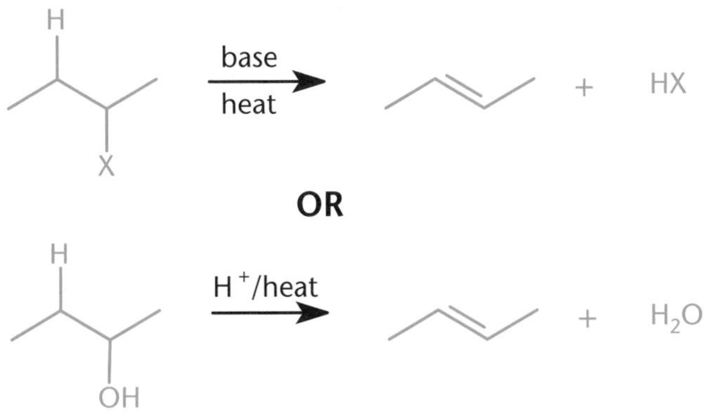

Figure 5.3

There are two mechanisms of elimination, unimolecular and bimolecular, referred to as **E1** and **E2** respectively. Getting down the rules of elimination reactions won't require too much extra brain space, because the concepts behind these reactions are the same as those behind the S_N1 and S_N2 reactions discussed in Chapter 4. We will need to keep track of certain conditions that will favor elimination over substitution, and vice versa.

Unimolecular Elimination

Unimolecular elimination, abbreviated E1, is a two-step process, and the rate of reaction depends on the concentration of only one species, the substrate. The first step of E1 is the same as the first step of S_N1: departure of a leaving group and formation of a carbocation intermediate. In the second step, a proton on an adjacent carbon (the β-carbon) is removed by a weak base, and the double bond is formed with the electrons from the now broken carbon–hydrogen bond. We'll see shortly that if a strong base is present, the E2 mechanism will be more likely.

MCAT Expertise

When a reaction involves heat, you should consider the possibility of elimination reactions and free radicals (which were discussed in Chapter 4).

Key Concept

The carbocation intermediate is the hallmark of the E1 reaction, just as in the S_N1 reaction. Our understanding of the intermediate will be essential in determining all the facts surrounding the reaction, including the rate and the products. E1 and S_N1 reactions compete because the formation of the intermediate, which is the slow step in both, is the same.

Key Concept

E1 reactions typically favor the more stable alkene as the major product (i.e., more highly substituted carbon product).

Key Concept

E2 and S_N2 are in direct competition like the unimolecular reactions.

MCAT Expertise

If you ever see a big bulky strong base, *think E2!*

E1 is favored by the same factors that favor S_N1: polar protic solvents, the ability to form a stable carbocation, highly branched carbon chains, good leaving groups, and the absence of a good nucleophile. Because both mechanisms occur under similar conditions, the two are competitive, and directing a reaction toward either E1 or S_N1 alone is difficult. Remember that both reactions require a stable carbocation and that higher temperatures tend to favor the E1 pathway.

Bimolecular Elimination

Similar to S_N2, bimolecular elimination (E2) occurs in one step. As the name suggests, the rate of an E2 reaction depends on two species, the substrate and the base (nucleophile). As a strong base (such as the ethoxide ion, $C_2H_5O^-$) removes a proton, a halide ion ***anti*** (see Chapter 2 for a discussion of *anti*) to the proton leaves, resulting in the formation of a double bond (see Figure 5.4).

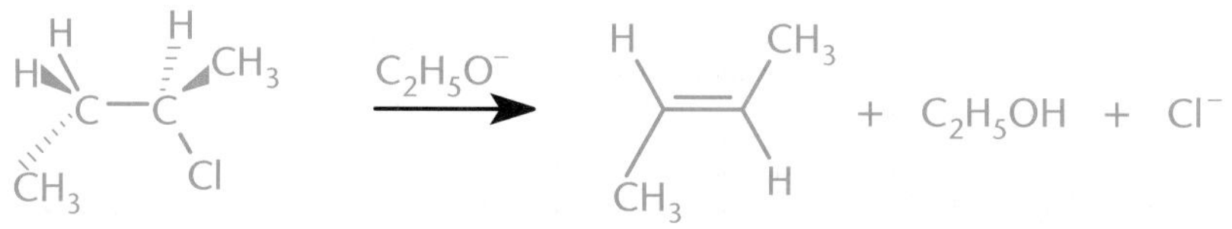

Figure 5.4

E2 reactions will often have two possible products. The double bond can form on either side of the departing halide, but the more substituted double bond will constitute a larger percentage of the products. If the molecule can form either of the two geometric isomers, the *trans*-isomer will be the predominate product, because it is more stable than the sterically strained *cis*-isomer.

It is easier to control E2 versus S_N2 than it is to control E1 versus S_N1. Two ways to control between E2 and S_N2 are listed below:

1. Steric hindrance is important in E2 reactions. Highly substituted carbon chains, which form the most stable alkenes, undergo E2 easily and S_N2 rarely. The bulk of the base (nucleophile) also has a large impact on the dominant mechanism. A bulky base nucleophile will have a hard time getting to the backside of the α-carbon (the carbon with the leaving group) for an inline attack. It is much easier to pluck off a hydrogen from the neighboring carbon, and besides, there are many more hydrogens from which to choose.
2. A stronger base favors E2 over S_N2. S_N2 is favored over E2 by weak Lewis bases (strong nucleophiles). Excellent nucleophiles such as cyanide, ^-CN, and iodide, I^-, are commonly used for S_N2 because they are poor bases. A strong base will pull off a β-hydrogen before it can reach the α-carbon atom of the substrate, resulting in an E2 reaction.

Controlling S_N1 versus E1 is done by controlling the conditions, specifically factors such as the polarity of the solvent, or, most important, the temperature. S_N2 versus E2 depends more on the properties of the substrate and the base. E1 is the least likely mechanism of the four. Remember that we will usually form the most substituted double bond possible in elimination reactions.

REACTIONS

Throughout the following reactions, and the remainder of this text, we will frequently use the terms *oxidation* and *reduction*. You may remember from your studies in General Chemistry that if a species is *oxidized,* it *loses electrons* and if it is *reduced, electrons are gained*. For our purposes in Organic Chemistry, we don't need to worry about counting electrons. In fact, all we need to do is look at hydrogen. If a species is reduced, it will be getting more hydrogen; if it is oxidized, it will be losing hydrogen and, thus, gaining double bonds and, often, oxygen.

Reduction

Catalytic hydrogenation is a fancy name for reducing an alkene by adding molecular hydrogen to the double bond with the aid of a metal catalyst (see Figure 5.5). Typical catalysts you will see on the MCAT are platinum **(Pt)**, palladium **(Pd)**, and nickel **(Ni)** (usually Raney nickel, a special powdered form, but that's not the kind of thing the MCAT will test you on). Occasionally rhodium, iridium, or ruthenium are used, but you are unlikely to see them on Test Day.

Catalytic hydrogenation is unique because it actually takes place on the surface of the metal. One face of the π bond becomes coordinated to the metal surface where molecular hydrogen is bound. That's why the two hydrogen atoms are added to the same face of the double bond. Think of it as a moon lander (the double bond) landing on the surface of the moon (the metal catalyst): The reaction takes place where the two touch. This type of addition is called *syn* **addition**.

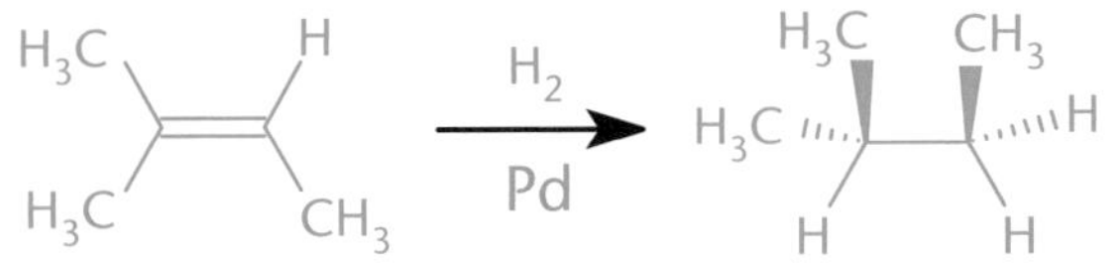

Figure 5.5

> **Key Concept**
>
> Reactions where only one stereoisomer is formed are called stereospecific reactions.

Electrophilic Additions

In Chapter 3, we discovered that the π bond is relatively weak and higher in energy and, thus, more reactive compared with the σ bond. Therefore, it can be broken without breaking the σ bond. As a result, we can add compounds to double bonds while leaving the carbon skeleton intact. Although many different **addition reactions** are possible, most operate via the same essential mechanism.

Mnemonic

Lewis *Acids Accept* electron pairs; Lewis bases donate electron pairs.

Key Concept

Markovnikov's rule refers to the addition of a group to the more substituted carbon of the double bond. It does so because the more stable carbocation intermediate (the more highly substituted) will form in the slow first step and the nucleophile will then attack that positive charge in the fast second step.

Because the electrons of the π bond are particularly reactive, they are easily attacked by molecules seeking to accept an electron pair (Lewis acids). Recall that these seekers (or "lovers") of electrons are called **electrophiles**.

Addition of HX

The electrons in the double bond act as a Lewis base and react with the partially positive hydrogen of HX molecules. The first step yields a carbocation intermediate. In cases where the alkene is asymmetrical, the initial protonation occurs to produce the most stable carbocation. Be careful here; this means that the proton will actually add to the *least* substituted carbon atom (the carbon atom with the most protons). This addition will form the carbocation on the adjacent carbon (that is *more* substituted), because alkyl substituents stabilize carbocations. This phenomenon is called **Markovnikov's rule**, and the goal is to produce the most stable carbocation. In the second step, the halide ion combines with the carbocation to yield an alkyl halide. Figure 5.6 shows an example.

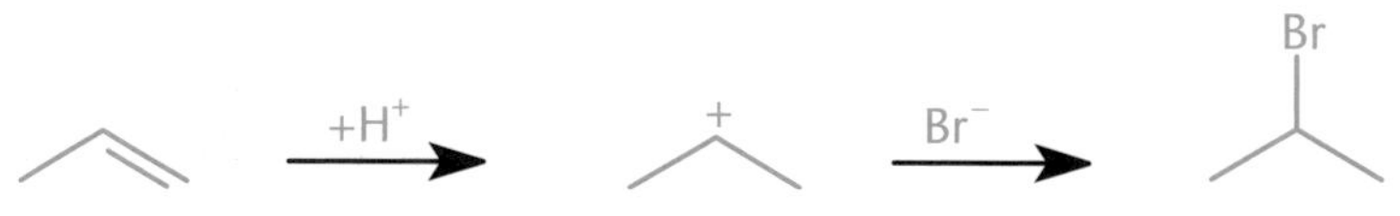

Figure 5.6

Addition of X$_2$

The addition of diatomic halogens to a double bond is a rapid process. In fact, it is frequently used as a diagnostic tool to test for the presence of double bonds. The double bond acts as a nucleophile again in this reaction, attacking one half of an X$_2$ molecule and displacing X$^-$ from the other side. The second halogen is just acting, as usual, as the leaving group. The first step results in a **cyclic halonium ion** (bromonium and chloronium ions are known to exist), which can dissipate the positive charge with a trinuclear intermediate. X$^-$ then attacks the ion on the opposite face because the bromine is blocking the other side (*anti*-addition!), resulting in the **dihalo** compound (see Figure 5.7).

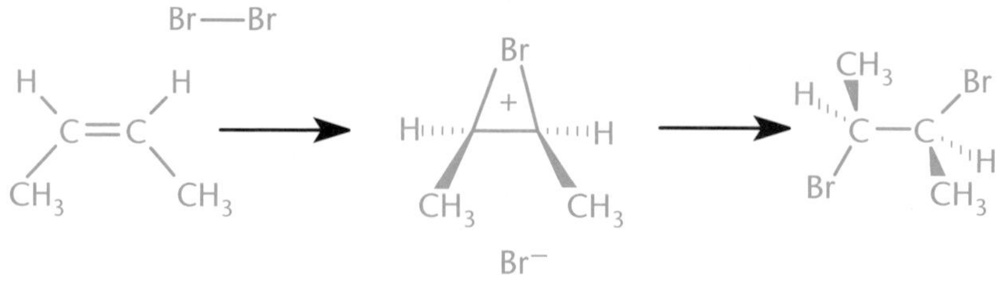

anti-addition

Figure 5.7

If this reaction is carried out in a nucleophilic solvent, the cyclic halonium ion can be attacked by solvent molecules before the halogen ion gets a chance to do so. For example, if the reaction is run with water as a solvent, this can produce a halo alcohol.

Addition of H₂O

Water can be added to alkenes under acidic conditions (most commonly H_2SO_4). The first step? Once again, the double bond is protonated according to Markovnikov's rule, forming the most stable carbocation. This carbocation then reacts with water, yielding a protonated alcohol, which then loses a proton to become an alcohol (see Figure 5.8). We have to perform this reaction at low temperatures because at high temperatures, the reverse reaction, acid-catalyzed dehydration, is heavily favored. Remember, if heat is part of the reaction, look for the formation of a double bond. Adding water will break the double bond, so we'll need low temperatures. Hydration of the double bond can also be achieved under mild conditions with oxymercuration-reduction. As with acid-catalyzed hydration, which is consider harsh, Markovnikov regiochemistry is observed.

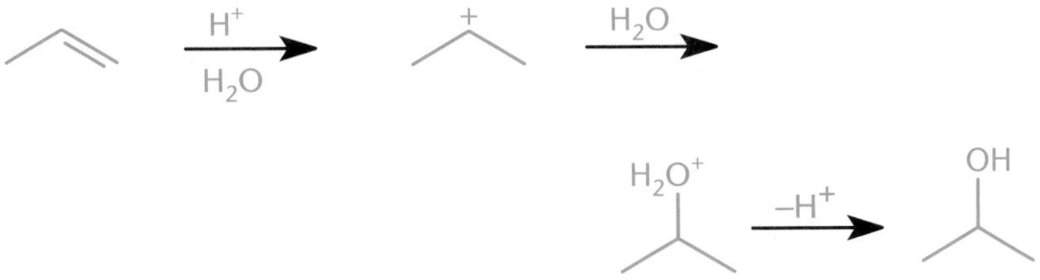

Figure 5.8

Free Radical Additions

There's another way to add HX to alkenes: through a mechanism that uses free-radical intermediates. This reaction occurs in the presence of peroxides, oxygen, or ultraviolet light. Free-radical additions disobey the Markovnikov rule because X• adds first to the double bond, producing the most stable free radical. As you can see in Figure 5.9, this means that the halogen will end up on the least substituted carbon. This is in contrast to standard electrophilic additions, where H^+ adds first to produce the most stable carbocation. The important thing to realize here is that both of these mechanisms are in place to create the most stable intermediate. This reaction is useful for HBr, but it is not practical for HCl or HI, because they are energetically unfavorable.

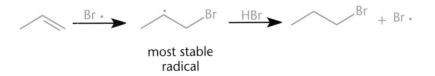

most stable
radical

Figure 5.9

MCAT Expertise

When peroxides or UV light are present, expect free radical reactions that do not follow Markovnikov's rule.

Key Concept

In anti-Markovnikov reactions, we can see that the most stable radical forms on the most substituted carbon (just as the most stable carbocation formed before), but because the halogen adds first, it ends up on the least substituted carbon. Remember, the most stable intermediate and least energetic transition state will *always* determine the favored products.

Hydroboration

Diborane (B_2H_6; often written as *borane*: BH_3) adds readily to double bonds. The boron atom (owing to its incomplete octet) is a Lewis acid and attaches to the less sterically hindered carbon atom. At the same time, a hydride is transferred to the adjacent carbon (a concerted mechanism). The second step is an oxidation-hydrolysis with peroxide and aqueous base that directly transfers water to the bond with boron, producing an alcohol with overall anti-Markovnikov, *syn* orientation (see Figure 5.10).

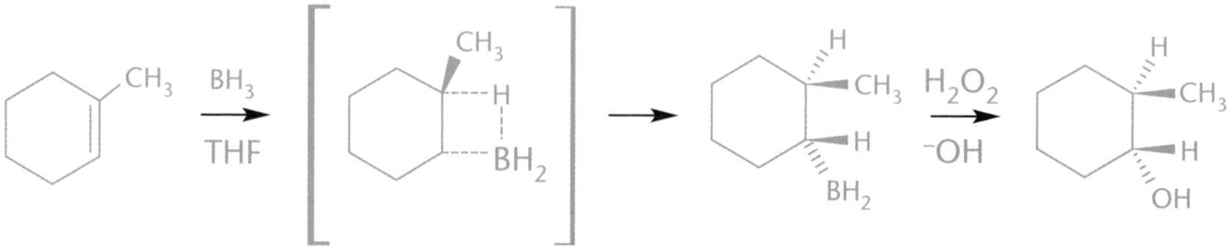

Figure 5.10

Oxidation

Oxidation is *prime* MCAT material, and luckily there's a useful trick to figure out if we're looking at an oxidation reaction. As a general rule, if a reagent has a whole bunch of oxygen in it, chances are that it's an oxidizing agent. In this chapter, we will discuss only a few of these reagents, but we will introduce you to the rest of the oxidizing reagents that you'll need to know on Test Day as we discuss aldehydes, ketones, and carboxylic acids later in this text.

Potassium Permanganate

Alkenes can be oxidized with $KMnO_4$ (potassium permanganate), although depending on the reaction conditions, we can end up with drastically different products (see Figure 5.11). If we make our conditions as mild as possible, using cold, dilute, basic $KMnO_4$, the product simply has –OH groups added to each side of the double bond. Such products are called 1,2 diols (vicinal diols), or glycols, and they have *syn* orientation.

> ### Key Concept
>
> Cold, basic, and dilute conditions should always make you think of a mild or weak reaction (adding alcohols to a double bond). Hot, acidic conditions should make you think of rigorous or strong reactions (breaking the double bond altogether and forming carboxylic acids).

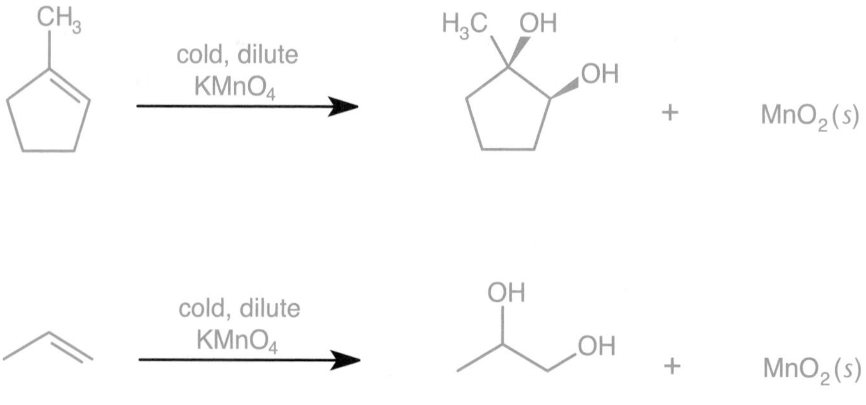

Figure 5.11

Alternatively, we can kick it up a notch and use a hot, basic solution of potassium permanganate, followed by an acid wash (see Figure 5.12). When we do this, nonterminal alkenes are cleaved to form two molar equivalents of carboxylic acid, and terminal alkenes are cleaved to form a carboxylic acid and carbon dioxide. If the nonterminal double-bonded carbon is disubstituted, a ketone will be formed. Under these intense conditions, we simply chop the double bond in half and make those cleaved carbons as oxidized as possible.

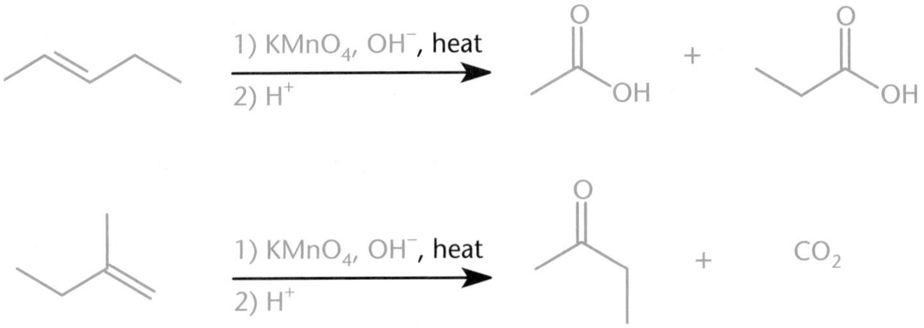

Figure 5.12

Ozonolysis

Ozonolysis is another strong oxidative process, but it can be made more selective than hot, acidic $KMnO_4$. Although it still cleaves the double bond in half, it only oxidizes the carbon to an aldehyde (or a ketone if the starting molecule is disubstituted) under reducing conditions (Zn/H^+ or $(CH_3)_2S$; see Figure 5.13). Ozonolysis under oxidizing conditions (H_2O_2) yields the same products as hot, acidic $KMnO_4$.

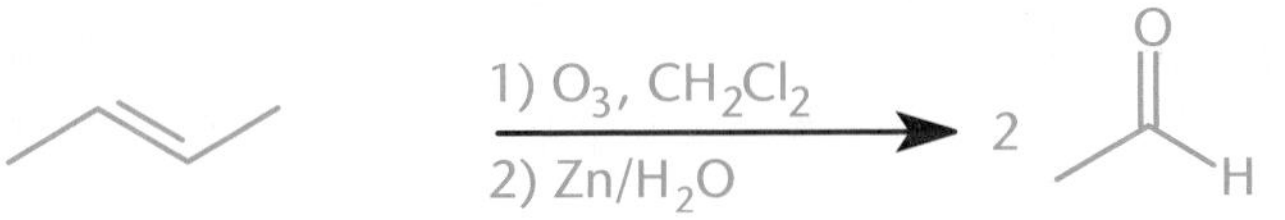

Figure 5.13

We can also obtain alcohols from this reaction; all we need to do is reduce the aldehyde or ketone products with a mild reducing agent, such as sodium borohydride ($NaBH_4$), or the more potent $LiAlH_4$ (see Figure 5.14).

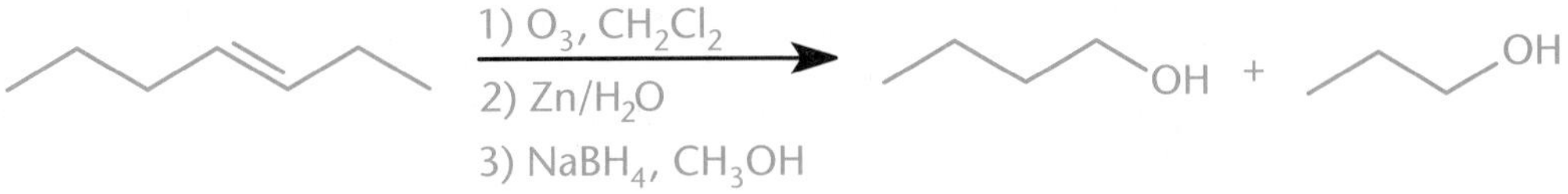

Figure 5.14

Peroxycarboxylic Acids

Alkenes can also be oxidized with peroxycarboxylic acids, which are strong oxidizing agents. Peroxyacetic acid (CH_3CO_3H) and *m*-chloroperoxybenzoic acid (MCPBA) are commonly used. The unique thing about this reaction is that the products are **epoxides** (also called **oxiranes**). This reaction is an example of syn addition:

MCPBA
O

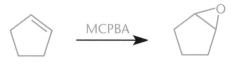

Figure 5.15

Polymerization

Polymerization is the creation of long, high-molecular-weight chains **(polymers)** composed of repeating subunits (called **monomers**). Polymerization usually occurs through a radical mechanism, although anionic and even cationic polymerizations are commonly observed. A typical example is the formation of polyethylene from ethylene (ethene) that requires high temperatures and pressures (this is the reaction used to make those grocery store plastic bags), shown in Figure 5.16.

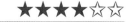

Key Concept

When heat is present, consider the possibility of a radical mechanism.

$$CH_2{=}CH_2 \xrightarrow[\text{high pressure}]{R\cdot,\ \text{heat}} RCH_2CH_2(CH_2CH_2)_nCH_2CH_2R$$

Figure 5.16

MCAT Expertise

Alkynes will not be directly tested and will probably show up even less than alkenes on the MCAT. However, notice that alkynes undergo many reactions that are similar to those of alkenes, because they both have pi bonds.

Alkynes ★★★★☆☆

Alkynes are hydrocarbons that possess one or more carbon–carbon triple bonds. All triple bonds form straight lines with 180° between carbons as a result of the *sp* hybridization.

NOMENCLATURE

To name alkynes, use the suffix **–yne** and specify the position of the triple bond when it is necessary (see Figure 5.17). A common exception to the IUPAC rules is ethyne, which is almost exclusively called **acetylene**. Frequently, compounds are named as derivatives of acetylene.

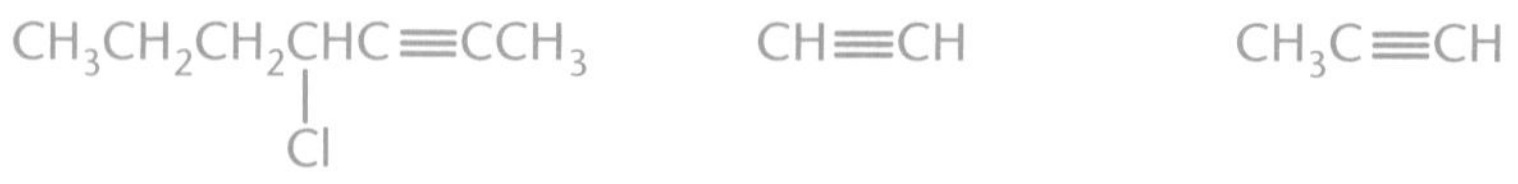
CH3CH2CH2CHC≡CCH3
Cl
CH≡CH
CH3C≡CH

4-chloro-2-heptyne | ethyne (acetylene) | propyne (methylacetylene)

Figure 5.17

PHYSICAL PROPERTIES

As we'd expect, the physical properties of the alkynes are similar to those of analogous alkenes and alkanes. In general, similar to alkanes and alkenes, the shorter-chain compounds are gases, but alkynes boil at somewhat higher temperatures than their corresponding alkenes. Internal alkynes, like alkenes, boil at higher temperatures than terminal alkynes.

Asymmetrical distribution of electron density causes alkynes to have dipole moments larger than those of alkenes but still small in magnitude. Thus, we can assume that solutions of alkynes will be slightly polar, or at least more polar than a solution of alkenes.

One unique property to remember is that terminal alkynes are fairly acidic (at least for a carbon atom); they have pK_a's of approximately 25. This means that terminal alkynes can stabilize a negative charge fairly well, something that is uncommon for carbon atoms. As stated earlier, this stabilization stems from the 50 percent *s*-character. Recall that *s*-electrons have some probability of being found at the nucleus (negative electrons are happier in the positive nucleus). This property is exploited in some of the reactions of alkynes, which we will discuss soon.

> ### MCAT Expertise
>
> The acidity of the hydrogen on a terminal alkyne is the one major difference from all other hydrocarbon molecules. If anything about alkynes shows up on the MCAT, it will likely be in a question about acidity or a synthesis passage involving the reactions below.

SYNTHESIS

One way to make triple bonds is through two rounds of elimination of a geminal (remember twins, from the same carbon) or vicinal (neighbors in the vicinity) dihalide.

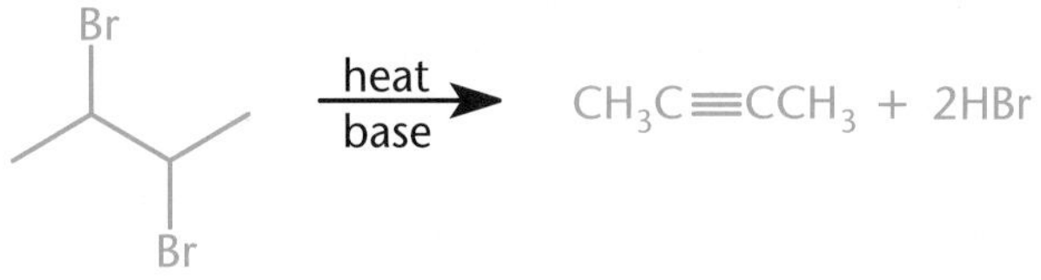

$$CH_3C \equiv CCH_3 + 2HBr$$

Figure 5.18

As you can see in Figure 5.19, this reaction requires high temperatures and a strong base, and so it's not always practical. A more useful method adds an already existing triple bond into a new carbon skeleton. To do this, a terminal triple bond is converted into a nucleophile by removing its acidic proton with a strong base ($NaNH_2$ or *n*-BuLi), producing an *acetylide ion*. Remember that terminal alkynes are fairly acidic, so this is a reasonable process. Once formed, the ion will perform nucleophilic displacements on primary alkyl halides at room temperature, as shown in Figure 5.19.

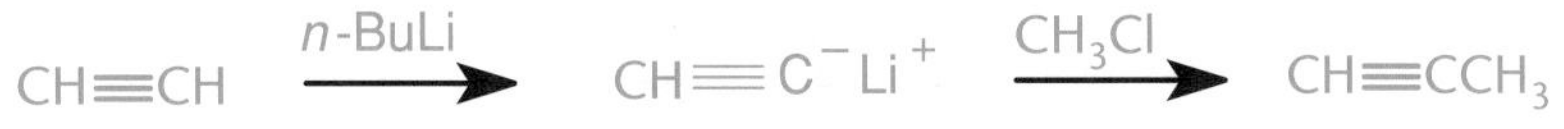

$$CH \equiv CH \xrightarrow{\textit{n}\text{-BuLi}} CH \equiv C^- Li^+ \xrightarrow{CH_3Cl} CH \equiv CCH_3$$

Figure 5.19

REACTIONS

Reductions

Alkynes, just like alkenes, can be hydrogenated (reduced) with a catalyst to produce alkanes. If we want alkenes as our final product, we need to stop the reduction after addition of just one equivalent of H_2. This partial hydrogenation can take place in two ways (see Figure 5.20). The first uses **Lindlar's catalyst**, which is palladium on barium sulfate ($BaSO_4$) with quinoline, a heterocyclic aromatic poison that stops the reaction at the alkene stage. Because the reaction occurs on a metal surface, the alkene product is the *cis*-isomer (just like the other reduction reactions we discussed using metal catalysts). The second method uses sodium in liquid ammonia at temperatures below –33°C (the boiling point of ammonia) and produces the *trans*-isomer of the alkene via a free-radical mechanism.

MCAT Expertise

In Organic Chemistry, think about reduction as adding bonds to hydrogen and oxidation as adding bonds to oxygen.

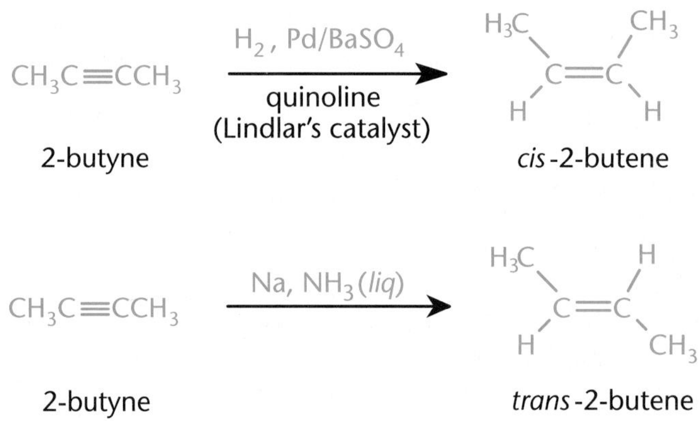

Figure 5.20

Addition

Electrophilic

Electrophilic addition to alkynes occurs in the same manner as it does to alkenes. The products form according to Markovnikov's rule. Addition can be stopped at the intermediate alkene stage or carried further. Of course, if we want to go all the way to the alkane stage, we will need two equivalents of reactants (see Figure 5.21).

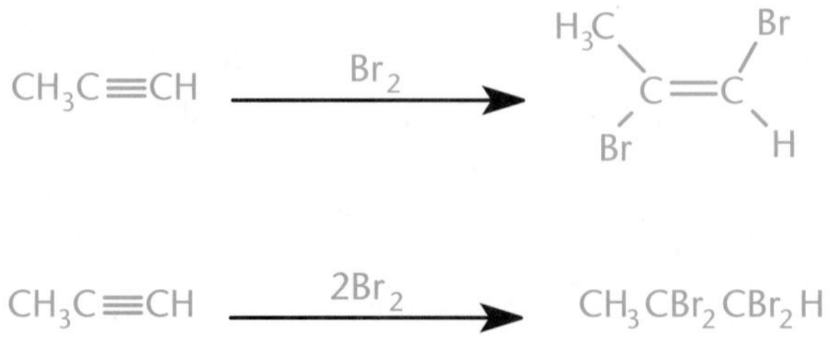

Figure 5.21

Free Radical

Radicals add to triple bonds just as they do to double bonds, with anti-Markovnikov orientation (see Figure 5.22). Be aware that the reaction product is usually the *trans*-isomer. This is because the intermediate vinyl radical can isomerize to its more stable form.

Key Concept

As always, the most stable electron-deficient species forms. In this reaction, we get an anti-Markovnikov product.

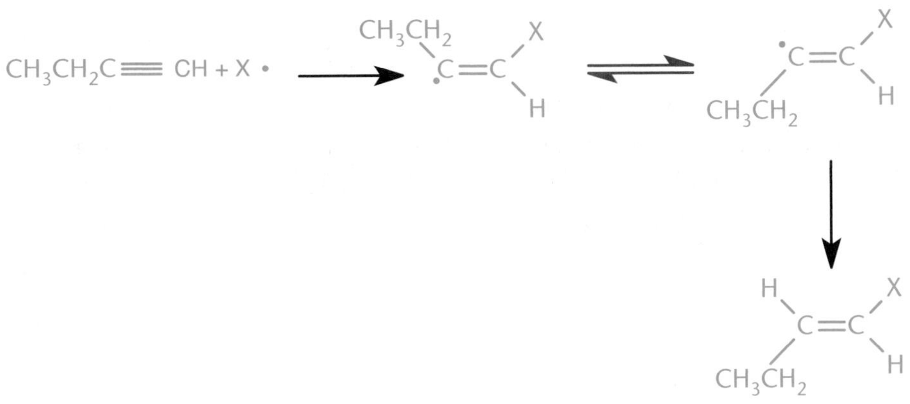

Figure 5.22

Hydroboration

As we'd expect, the addition of boron to triple bonds occurs by the same method as addition of boron to double bonds. Addition is *syn,* and the boron atom adds first. Notice that in the intermediate below, the boron is bound to three different substituents. If we follow the reaction with an acetic acid wash, the boron atom can be removed, and each substituent will have a proton from acetic acid in its place. This produces a *cis*-alkene, as shown in Figure 5.23.

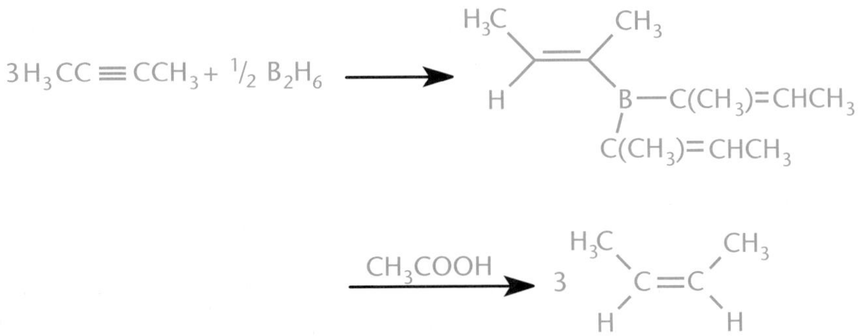

Figure 5.23

If we're dealing with terminal alkynes, a disubstituted borane is used to prevent further boration of the vinylic intermediate to an alkane. The vinylic borane intermediate can be oxidatively cleaved with hydrogen peroxide (H_2O_2), creating an intermediate vinyl alcohol (an enol), which tautomerizes to the more stable carbonyl compound (via keto-enol tautomerism; see Figure 5.24).

Bridge

Keto-enol tautomerism will be discussed in Chapter 8.

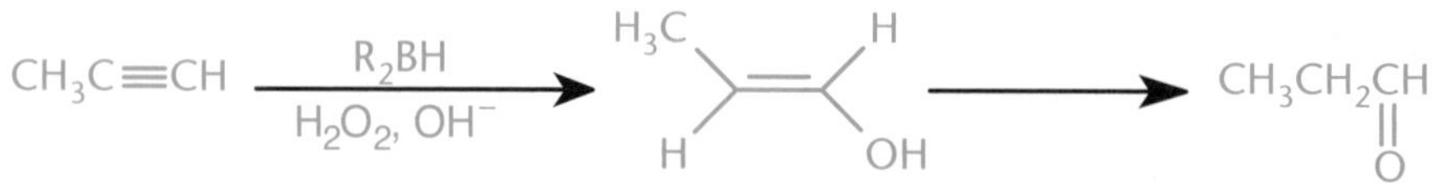

Figure 5.24

Oxidation

Just like their alkene counterparts, alkynes can be oxidatively cleaved with either hot, basic potassium permangenate, $KMnO_4$ (followed by acidification) or with ozone (see Figure 5.25). Notice that both alkenes and alkynes will give the same product when reacted with hot, acidic $KMnO_4$. The difference here is with ozone. Remember that when alkenes react with ozone under reducing conditions (Zn/CH_3COOH), they yield aldehydes or ketones. However, under oxidizing conditions (H_2O_2) carboxylic acids are obtained instead of aldehydes. When alkynes are reacted with ozone, they yield carboxylic acids or CO_2. Note that triple bonds (with two π bonds) will add two oxygens to each carbon. Terminal alkynes produce CO_2.

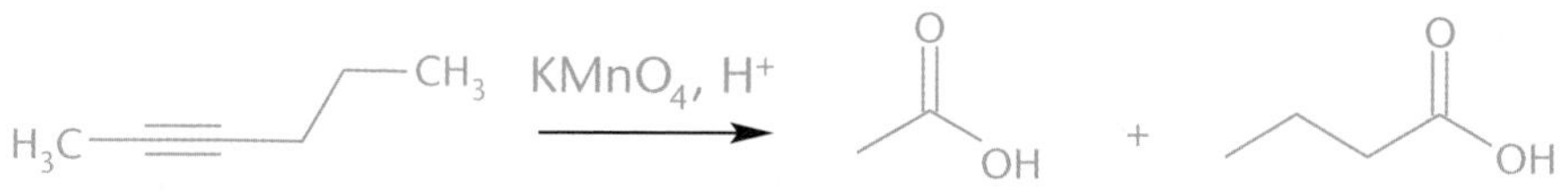

Figure 5.25

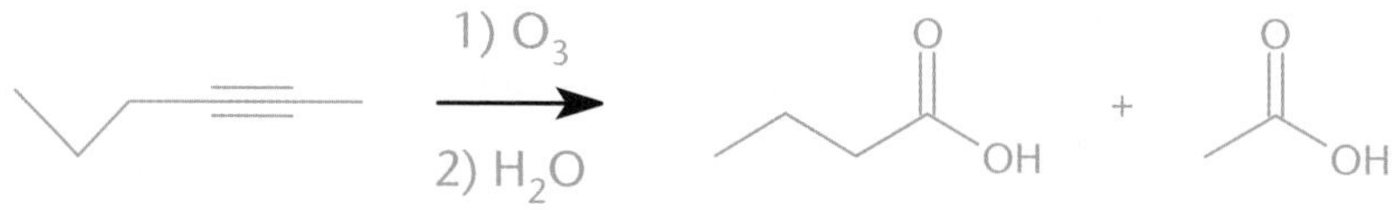

Figure 5.26

Conclusion

It's true that the carbon atom is capable of an astonishingly wide variety of forms and uses. Nevertheless, the alkene and alkyne varieties have similar names, similar structures, and, as you have learned from this chapter, many of the same properties. We saw that alkenes and alkynes can be synthesized by elimination reactions and that, just as in the substitution reactions discussed in Chapter 4, there are two mechanisms of elimination that take place selectively under certain conditions. Unlike the stable alkanes of Chapter 4, alkenes and alkynes can undergo additions, oxidations, and reductions.

We arrive now at one of the greatest lessons in your preparation for the MCAT. Simply put, you should focus on key differences and similarities. This will hold true for all topics and all subjects on the MCAT. The test makers know that memorizing Organic Chemistry in its entirety is an impossible, and ultimately useless, task. By focusing on key concepts, the MCAT gives you the chance to prove that you *understand* Organic Chemistry. It is far more important for you to know the rules of chemistry and understand what the possible products could be than it is to memorize the exact products of every reaction. This is going to be a lot different from your Organic Chemistry class in college and, in all likelihood, much easier.

CONCEPTS TO REMEMBER

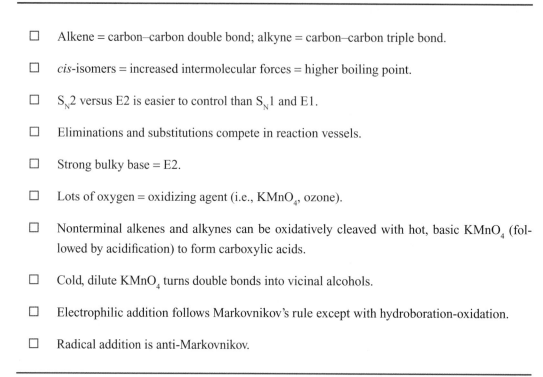

☐ Alkene = carbon–carbon double bond; alkyne = carbon–carbon triple bond.

☐ *cis*-isomers = increased intermolecular forces = higher boiling point.

☐ S_N2 versus E2 is easier to control than S_N1 and E1.

☐ Eliminations and substitutions compete in reaction vessels.

☐ Strong bulky base = E2.

☐ Lots of oxygen = oxidizing agent (i.e., $KMnO_4$, ozone).

☐ Nonterminal alkenes and alkynes can be oxidatively cleaved with hot, basic $KMnO_4$ (followed by acidification) to form carboxylic acids.

☐ Cold, dilute $KMnO_4$ turns double bonds into vicinal alcohols.

☐ Electrophilic addition follows Markovnikov's rule except with hydroboration-oxidation.

☐ Radical addition is anti-Markovnikov.

Practice Questions

1. What is the major product of the reaction below?

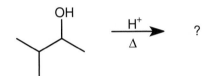

OH
H+
Δ
?

A. 3-methyl-1-butene
B. 2-methyl-3-butene
C. 3-methyl-2-butene
D. 2-methyl-2-butene

2.

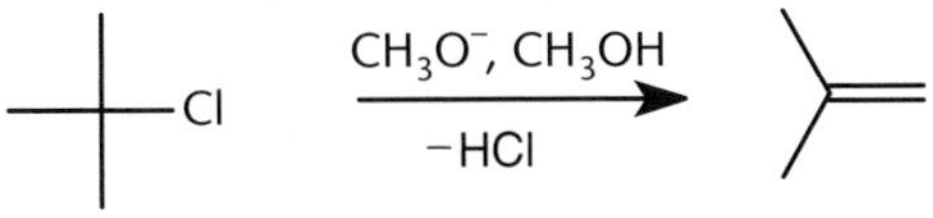

Cl
CH3O−, CH3OH
−HCl

The above reaction takes place mostly by which of the following mechanisms?

A. S_N1
B. S_N2
C. E1
D. E2

3. Which of the following products would be formed if 2-methyl-2-butene were reacted with hot, basic $KMnO_4$?

A. 1 mole of acetic acid and 1 mole of propanoic acid
B. 2 moles of pentanoic acid
C. 1 mole of acetic acid and 1 mole of acetone
D. 2 moles of acetic acid and 1 mole of CO_2

4. What are the products of the following reaction?

1) O3/CH2Cl2
2) Zn, H2O
?

A.
OH
+
O
H
H

B.
O
+
CH3OH

C.
O
+
CO2

D.
O
H
H
+
O

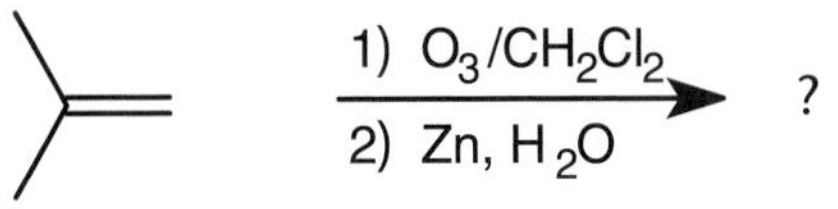

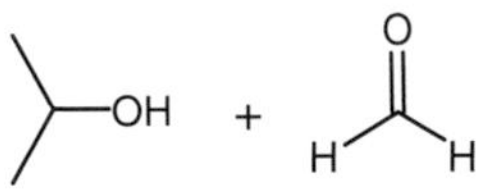

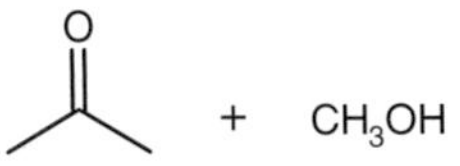

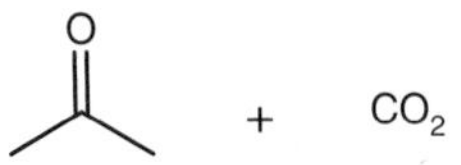

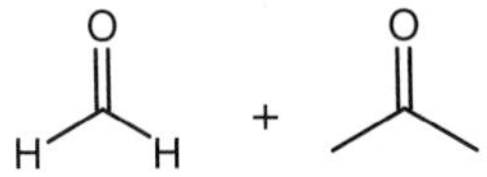

5. What are the products of the following reaction?

CH3
CH3—C≡C—CH
CH3
1) hot KMnO4, OH−
2) H+
?

A.
O
H
+
H
O

B.
O
H
+
HO
O

C.
O
OH
+
HO
O

D.
OH
OH

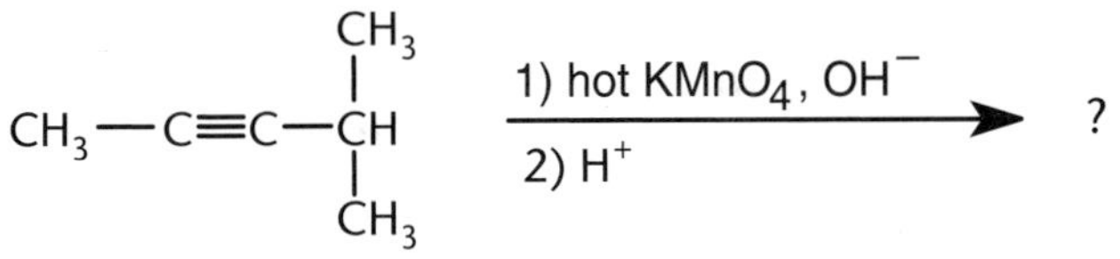

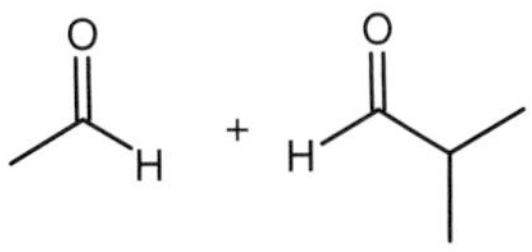

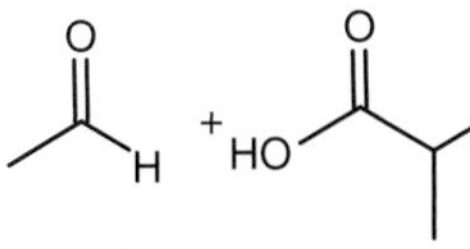

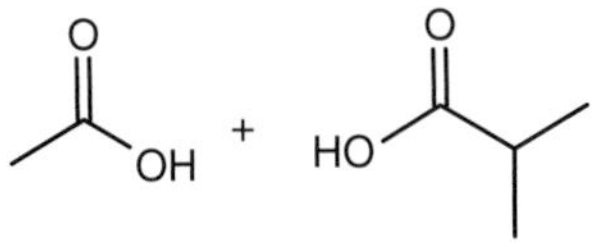

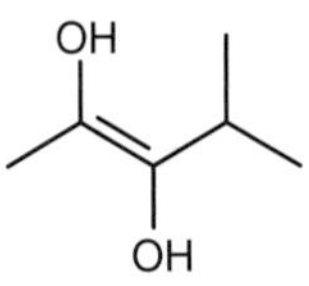

6.

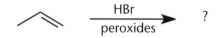

HBr / peroxides → ?

Which of the following represents the product obtained in the above reaction?

A.  Br

B.

C. 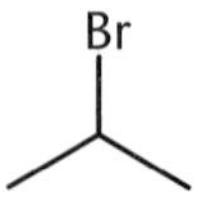 Br

D. 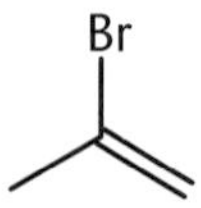 Br

7. What is the major product of the reaction shown below?

H₂ / Lindlar's catalyst → ?

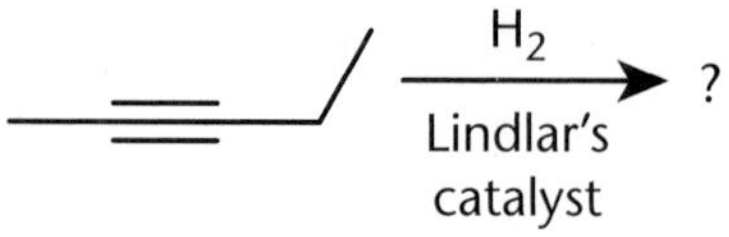

A. (Z)-2-pentene
B. Pentane
C. (E)-2-pentene
D. No reaction

8. Given the reaction shown below, what is the major product, not counting stereoisomers?

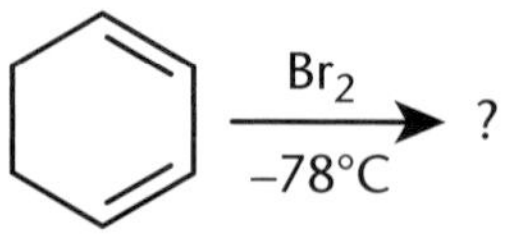

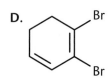 Br_2 / $-78°C$ → ?

A. 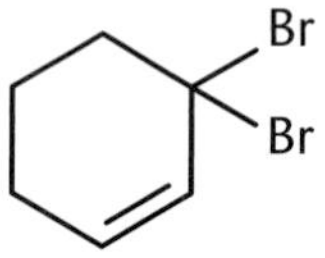 Br Br

B. 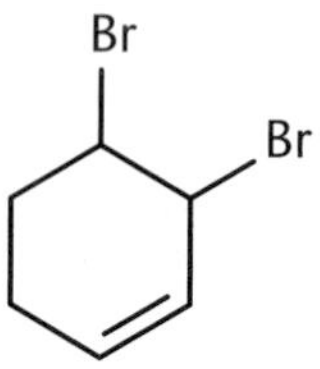 Br Br Br

C. Br Br

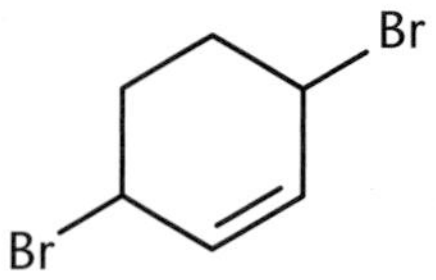

D. Br Br

9. Which of the reagents shown below will furnish 2-butanone starting with either 2-butyne or 1-butyne?

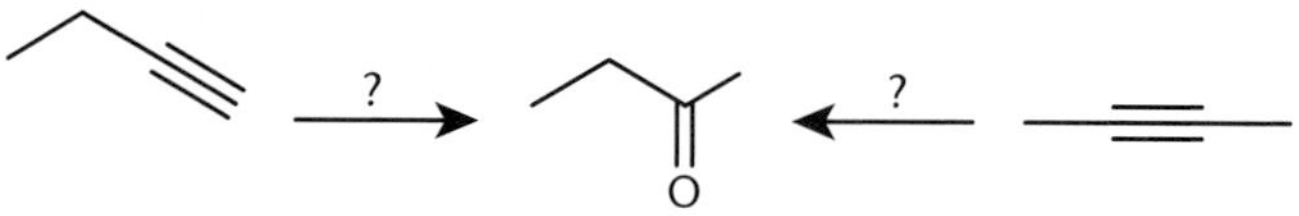

A. H_3O^+/H_2O
B. BH_3/THF, followed by H_2O_2/NaOH
C. Acidic $KMnO_4$, heat
D. H_2SO_4, $HgSO_4$, and H_2O

Small Group Questions

1. What makes I^- such a good leaving group? Why is tosylate a good leaving group as well?

2. Why is E1 least likely to occur of all four substitution and elimination reactions?

Explanations to Practice Questions

1. D

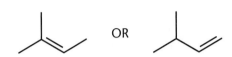

Heating an alcohol generally leads to loss of a water molecule. Multiple products (in this case, two) can be obtained depending on which H atom joins the –OH group to form water. The most stable product will be the most substituted alkene, which in this case is 2-methyl-2-butene.

2. D

Because this reaction converts a tertiary haloalkane into an alkene, it's an elimination. Strong bases favor E2, and weak bases favor E1. Because methoxide is a strong base, elimination occurs by the E2 mechanism in this situation. Choice (D) is the correct response.

3. C

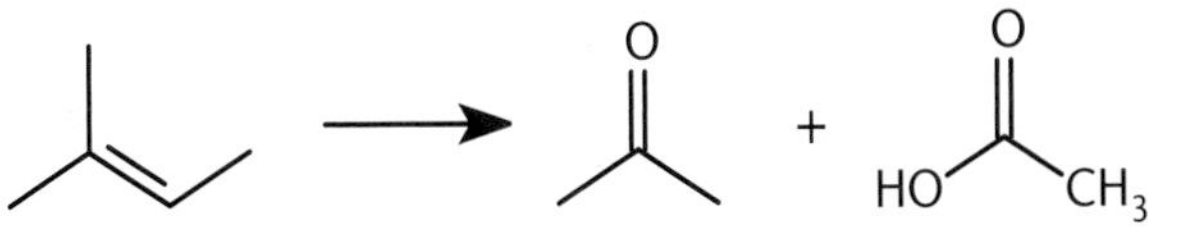

The double bond of 2-methyl-2-butene is cleaved by hot, basic potassium permanganate to form acetone and acetic acid. Cleavage of a primary double-bonded carbon yields a carboxylic acid (in this case, acetic acid), but cleavage of a secondary double-bonded carbon results in a ketone (here, acetone).

4. D

Ozonolysis of an alkene and subsequent treatment with zinc and water produces carbonyl compounds. After cleavage, any or all sides with secondary carbons become ketones, and the remaining side(s) with primary carbons become aldehydes.

5. C

Treating alkynes with hot, basic $KMnO_4$ leads to triple-bond cleavage and the formation of carboxylic acids.

6. A

In the presence of peroxides, the addition of HBr to the double bond takes place in an anti-Markovnikov manner in a series of free-radical reactions initiated by peroxides.

1. $ROOR \xrightarrow{h\nu} 2RO\bullet$
2. $HBr + RO\bullet \longrightarrow ROH + Br\bullet$
3. $CH_3CH = CH_2 + Br\bullet \longrightarrow CH_3-C\bullet H-CH_2Br$
4. $CH_3-C\bullet H-CH_2Br + HBr \longrightarrow CH_3-CH_2-CH_2 Br + Br\bullet$

In step 3, $CH_3-H_2-CH_2Br$ is formed instead of $CH_3-CHBr-H_2$ because the more substituted free radical is more stable than the less substituted one. Thus, the correct choice is (A). Note that in the absence of peroxides, HBr adds to the double bond in a Markovnikov manner and would result in the figure shown in answer (C).

7. A

Hydrogenation with Lindlar's catalyst will partially reduce triple bonds to yield alkenes; thus, answers (B) and (D) are incorrect. The addition of hydrogen occurs in a *syn* fashion (i.e., both hydrogen atoms are added on the same side). This means that the alkene's highest-priority substituents will both be pushed to the same side of the double bond, which is referred to as *Z* geometry.

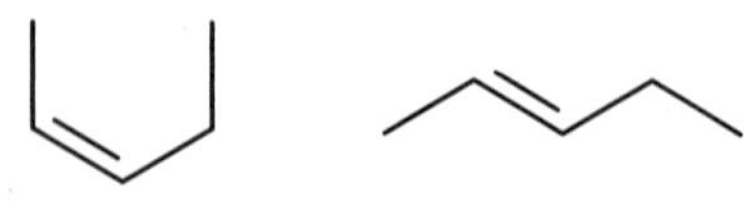

(*Z*)-2-pentene   (*E*)-2-pentene

8. B

The products depend on the reaction conditions. At low temperatures (−78°C), the major product resulting from the addition of bromine across a diene is the kinetically favored product (1,2-addition). Thus answer choice (B) is correct. Answer (C), the thermodynamically favored product (more highly substituted alkene) results from a 1,4-addition and is the major product at higher temperatures. Answer (A) is incorrect because bromine wouldn't add twice to the same carbon. Answer (D) is also incorrect because the addition of bromine would break the double bond.

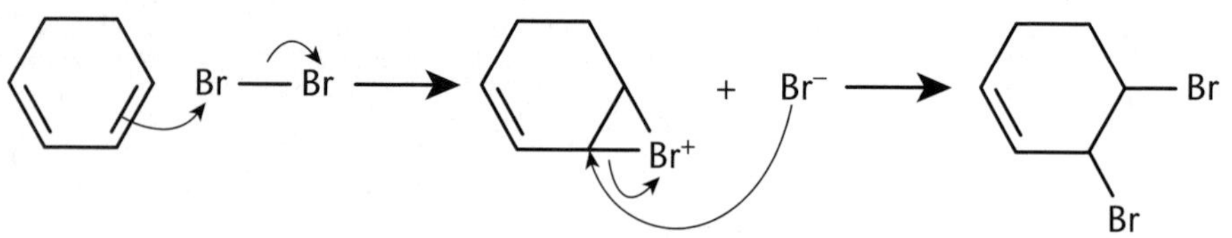

9. D

Answers (A) and (B) add across the triple bond to yield aldehydes when reacted with terminal alkynes and ketones when reacted with internal alkynes, so they are incorrect. Answer (C) is also incorrect because acidic $KMnO_4$ will cleave triple bonds with concurrent oxidation, giving carboxylic acids (and carbon dioxide with terminal alkynes).

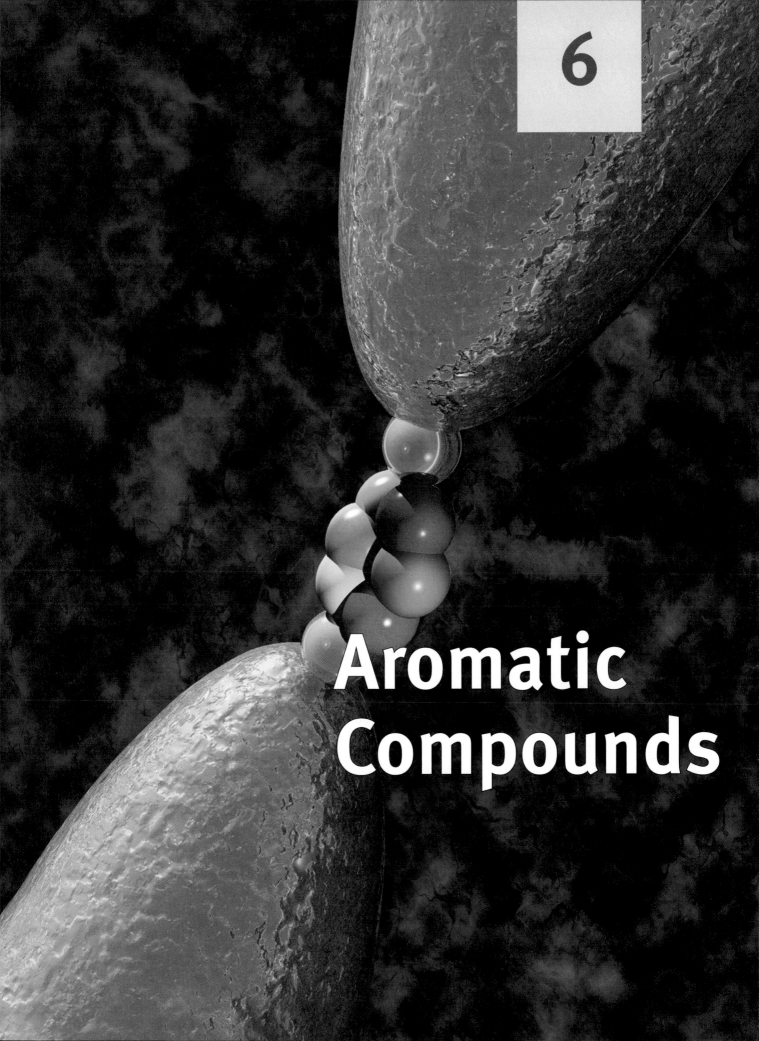

6

Aromatic Compounds

If you've ever stepped inside a Chinese restaurant or a florist, you undoubtedly have a certain association with the word *aromatic*, or *fragrant*. Until now, the word *aromatic* might bring to mind the scent of ginger or roses, but after we're done here, you'll be more likely to experience visions of benzene. (That's a good thing, we promise!) In the Organic Chemistry sense, the term **aromatic** describes any unusually stable ring system. Aromatic compounds are cyclic, conjugated polyenes that possess $4n + 2$ π electrons and adopt planar conformations to allow maximum overlap of their conjugated π orbitals. As we mentioned in our earlier discussion of nomenclature, a system is conjugated if it contains atoms (usually carbon, but sometimes nitrogen or oxygen) connected by alternating single and multiple (double or triple) bonds. The really neat thing is that the same compounds that we traditionally associate with pleasant-smelling aromas tend to exhibit the chemical characteristics of aromaticity.

The criterion of $4n + 2$ π electrons is known as Hückel's rule, and it is an important indicator of aromaticity. In general, if a cyclic conjugated polyene follows Hückel's rule, it is an aromatic compound, with extra stability resulting from filled bonding orbitals. Antiaromatic molecules (to be avoided) have electrons in higher-energy nonbonding or antibonding orbitals. Neutral compounds, anions, and cations all may be aromatic. Any compound that is not aromatic is described as **aliphatic**, or "fatty." Some typical aromatic compounds and ions are shown in Figure 6.1.

MCAT Expertise

Because the MCAT is not going to give you the formula for a 60-carbon fullerene molecule (Buckyball) and make you figure out if it is aromatic, just remember the smaller numbers (2, 6, 10, 14, and 18) and you won't even need to use the formula. The Hückel number is another way of saying that there are odd *pairs* of π electrons (benzene has three, naphthalene has five, and so forth).

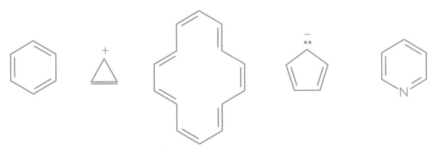

Figure 6.1

If a compound fits all the characteristics of an aromatic compound *except* for Hückel's rule (if it has only has $4n$ π electrons), it is said to **antiaromatic**. These are cyclic, conjugated polyenes that are destabilized. The two antiaromatic compounds you will most likely see on Test Day are shown in Figure 6.2.

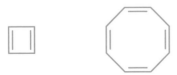

Figure 6.2

Nomenclature ★★★★☆☆

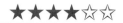

Aromatic compounds are referred to as **aryl** compounds, or **arenes**, and can be represented by the symbol **Ar**. When named as a substituent, benzene is represented by Ph. Do not confuse Benzyl for phenyl: benzyl refers to the $PhCH_2$– group. Aliphatic compounds are called **alkyl** (as we've already seen) and are represented by the symbol **R**. Common names exist for many mono- and disubstituted aromatic compounds. A few that will undoubtedly be used on the MCAT are shown in Figures 6.3 and 6.4.

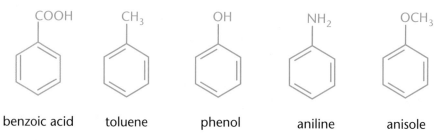

MCAT Expertise

Knowledge of substituted aromatic compounds common names is essential on the MCAT.

COOH
CH3
OH
NH2
OCH3
benzoic acid
toluene
phenol
aniline
anisole

Figure 6.3

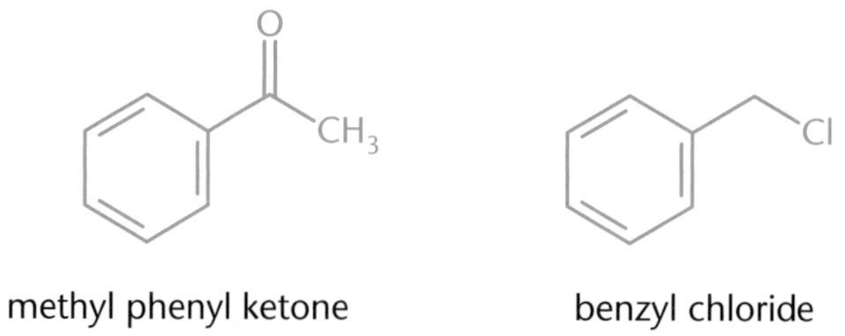

O
CH3
Cl
methyl phenyl ketone
benzyl chloride

Figure 6.4

MCAT Expertise

Because many incorrect answer choices will be missing a carbon or have an extra carbon, we need to pay close attention to the names used in the questions and answers and how they relate to the structures.

Another way we will often see benzene is with the ring itself substituted. These rings are named as alkyl benzenes, although the common names seen in Figures 6.3 and 6.4 are used instead of benzene when appropriate. The substituents are then numbered to produce the lowest sequence, just as we've always done. A 1,2-disubstituted compound is called ***ortho-***, or simply ***o-***; a 1,3-disubstituted compound is called ***meta-***, or ***m-***; and a 1,4-disubstituted compound is called ***para-***, or ***p-***. This all may sound like gibberish, but it's shown much more clearly in Figure 6.5.

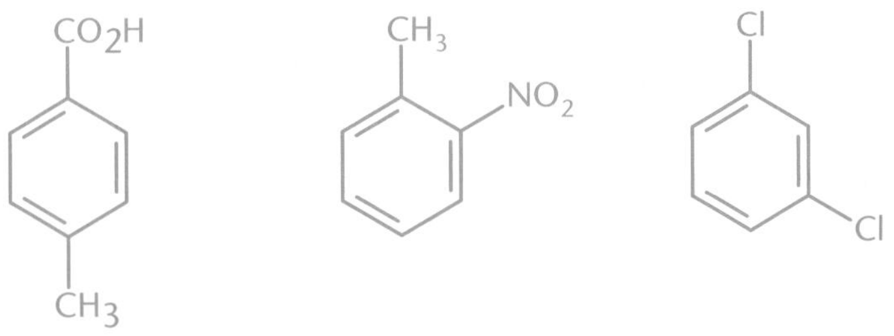

p-methylbenzoic acid *o*-nitrotoluene *m*-dichlorobenzene

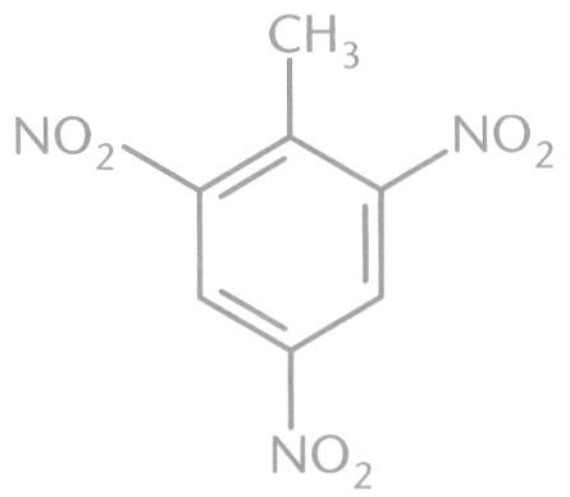

2,4,6-trinitrotoluene
(TNT)

Figure 6.5

MCAT Expertise

Ortho (*o*-), *meta* (*m*-), and *para* (*p*-) are designations with which you should become intimate, because they will have an essential role in our understanding of electrophilic aromatic substitution, discussed later in this chapter.

To mix it up even further, the MCAT can give you polycyclic (multiple connected) or heterocyclic rings (rings made up with atoms other than just carbon) Figure 6.6 shows some of these.

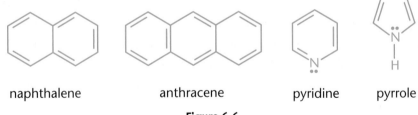

naphthalene anthracene pyridine pyrrole

Figure 6.6

Molecules like these will truly test your knowledge of the *concept* behind aromaticity, not just your ability to memorize names and equations. Let's examine **pyridine** and **pyrrole** using our MCAT-style critical thinking skills.

Looking at these two molecules, we can see that both have lone pairs on their nitrogen atoms, which we know tend to function as bases in a reaction. The interesting thing is that pyridine's lone pair *can* function as a base and pull a proton out of solution, whereas pyrrole's lone pair *cannot*. So, why not? Pyrrole's lone pairs are already occupied; they are the fifth and sixth electrons that give pyrrole the $4n + 2$ π electrons required by Hückel's rule. Because the electrons participate in the aromaticity of the molecule, it would be energetically unfavorable to have them leave their aromatic job to pull a hydrogen out of solution. Thus, pyrrole's lone pair won't react. Pyridine, on the other hand, already has the six necessary π electrons in its ring, and because its lone pair doesn't participate in the aromaticity, it is free to make friends with the protons in solution.

Properties

The physical properties of aromatic compounds are generally similar to those of other hydrocarbons. However, their chemical properties are significantly affected by aromaticity. The characteristic planar shape of benzene permits the ring's six π orbitals to overlap, delocalizing the electron density. All six carbon atoms are sp^2 hybridized, and each of the six orbitals overlaps equally with its two neighbors. As a result, the delocalized electrons form two π electron clouds, one above and one below the plane of the ring. This delocalization stabilizes the molecule, making it fairly unreactive: In particular, aromatic compounds (such as benzene) do not undergo addition reactions like alkenes but prefer to maintain their aromaticity, as it is a great stabilizing influence.

Reactions

ELECTROPHILIC AROMATIC SUBSTITUTION (EAS)

Wait a second. Didn't we just say that benzene didn't undergo addition reactions the way alkenes did? It's true that benzene doesn't undergo *addition* reactions, but it will undergo *substitution* reactions. The key here is that an addition reaction will disrupt the aromaticity of the ring, whereas the end product of a substitution will restore aromaticity. With benzene, a substitution reaction would mean that a hydrogen atom on the ring is replaced by another group. The most common examples of this are halogenation, sulfonation, nitration, alkylation, and acylation.

Halogenation

Aromatic rings react with bromine or chlorine in the presence of a Lewis acid, such as $FeCl_3$, $FeBr_3$, $AlBr_3$, or $AlCl_3$, to produce a good yield of monosubstituted products (see Figure 6.7). Reactions of fluorine or iodine with aromatic rings are less useful, although for opposite reasons. Fluorine, which is highly reactive, tends to produce multisubstituted products, and iodine's lack of reactivity requires special conditions for the reaction to proceed. Halogenation of aromatic rings is a lot like Baby Bear's porridge; it won't work if the halogen is too reactive or too unreactive—it's got to be ju-u-u-ust right.

Key Concept

Because our reactant, benzene, is so stable, we need some kind of catalyst or extreme conditions to drive these reactions. Think potent electrophiles.

Key Concept

Because the aromaticity of benzene provides a significant amount of stability, almost all of the reactions with benzene will involve keeping the aromaticity. In other words, here we see an overall substitution, not an addition to the molecule.

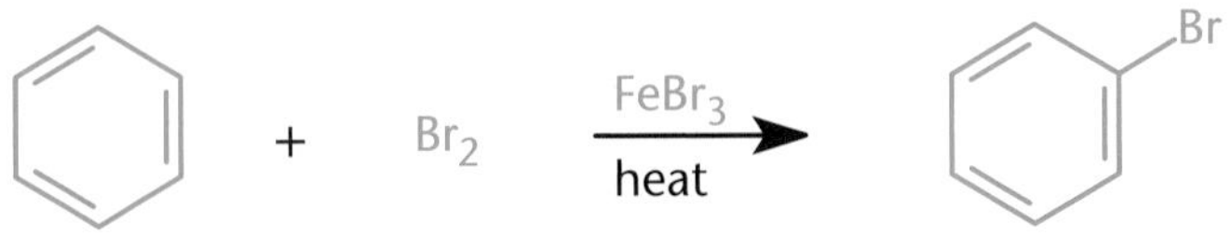

Figure 6.7

Sulfonation

Another substitution reaction aromatic rings can undergo is sulfonation. In this reaction, the aromatic ring reacts with fuming sulfuric acid (not angry acid, but just a really hot mixture of sulfuric acid and sulfur trioxide) to form sulfonic acids (see Figure 6.8). As we've said, benzene isn't very reactive, so it takes intense reaction conditions like these to drive substitution reactions forward. Sulfonation is reversible.

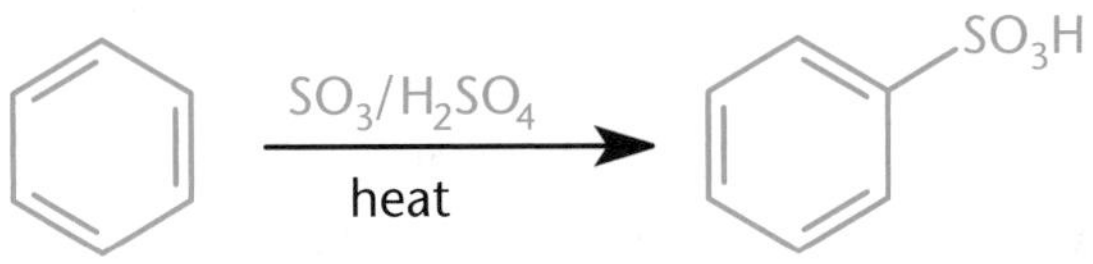

Figure 6.8

Nitration

The nitration of aromatic rings is another synthetically useful reaction. A mixture of nitric and sulfuric acids is used to create the nitronium ion, NO_2^+, a strong electrophile. Nitronium reacts with aromatic rings to produce **nitro** compounds (see Figure 6.9). As we will see later when we discuss substituent effects, the product of this reaction is the *least* reactive substituted aromatic compound, and because it's the least reactive, it tends to show up on the MCAT.

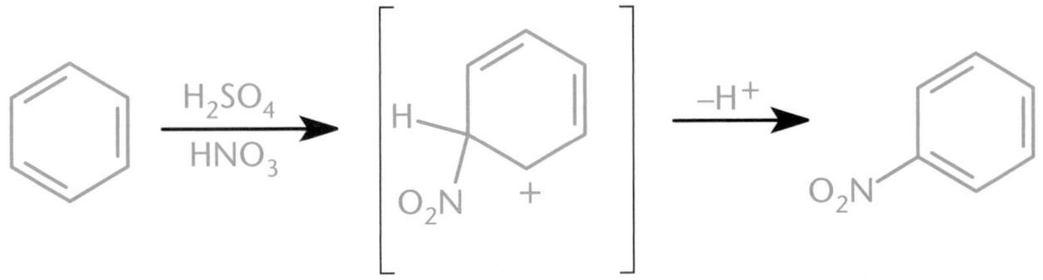

Figure 6.9

Acylation (Friedel-Crafts Reactions)

In the Friedel-Crafts acylation reaction, an acyl group is turned into a carbocation (which, with its full positive charge, is a great electrophile) by a Lewis acid catalyst such as $AlCl_3$. The carbocation acyl group is then incorporated into the aromatic ring (see Figure 6.10).

Key Concept

Friedel-Crafts alkylation reactions can also occur, but these are less useful because the product is attacked faster than the starting material, leading to overalkylation. (See substituent effects below.)

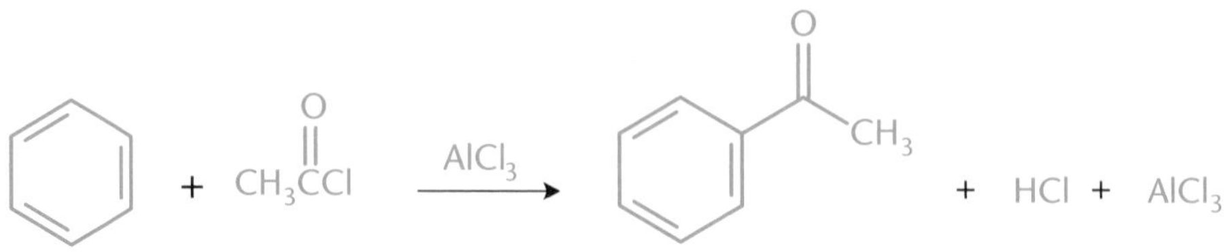

Figure 6.10

Substituent Effects

Substituents on an aromatic ring *strongly* influence the susceptibility of the ring to EAS. Even further, the current substituents also determine the position on the ring where an incoming electrophile will most likely add. Sound crazy? It's not; in fact, everything discussed here is determined by the resonance structures of substituted aromatic rings. If you want some good practice after reading this section, draw out the resonance structures of phenol and nitrobenzene and compare the differences.

Substituents can be grouped into two major categories according to whether they enhance substitution (activating) or inhibit substitution (deactivating). The basis of these categories is rooted in whether the group tends to donate or withdraw electron density. The groups that donate electron density are called *activators,* and groups that withdraw electron density are called *deactivators*. As mentioned above, if a second substitution takes place, the groups that are already attached to the ring will determine where the new group is placed. If an activator is attached to the ring, it will direct new substituents to the *ortho* or *para* position. If a deactivator is attached, a second substitution, although less likely, will occur only at the *meta* position. Halogens are our one exception to the rule, as they are the only deactivators (mildly, at that) that direct to the *ortho* and *para* positions.

For example, when toluene undergoes EAS, the methyl group directs substitution to the *ortho* and *para* positions (see Figure 6.11).

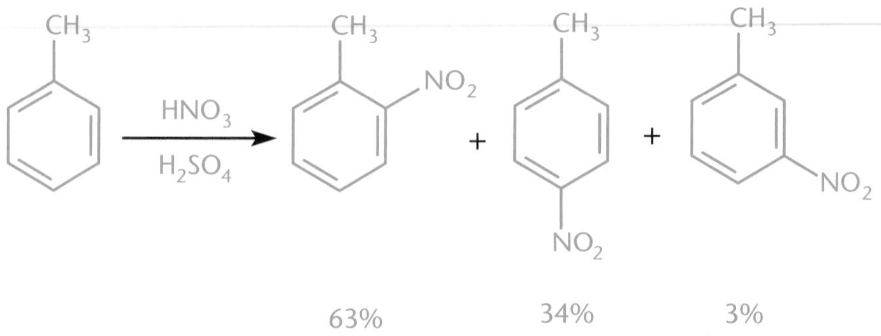

Figure 6.11

Note: Although there are two *ortho* positions, the largest percentage of products with *ortho*/*para* directors is often at the *para* position because of steric hindrance of the substituent.

REDUCTION

Catalytic Reduction

Benzene rings can be reduced to cyclohexane by catalytic hydrogenation, although because of benzene's stability, it only occurs under vigorous conditions (elevated temperature and pressure). Ruthenium or rhodium on carbon are the most common catalysts (see Figure 6.12); platinum or palladium may also be used but require higher pressure.

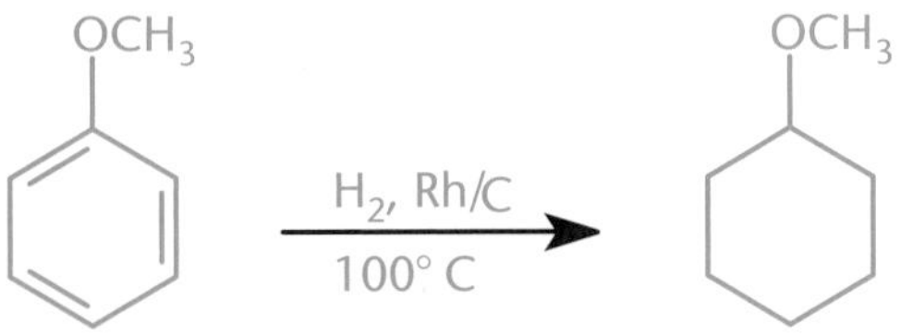

Figure 6.12

Conclusion

The mouthwatering recollections of Chinese food may never completely leave your mind, but your associations with the word *aromaticity* are probably changed forever by Organic Chemistry. The most important thing for you to remember is that aromatic compounds are particularly stable and any reaction that would destroy this stability is not likely to occur. However, reactions that restore the aromatic stability, such as EAS, or reactions that produce aromatic intermediates have a good chance of occurring—and a very good chance of appearing on the MCAT.

CONCEPTS TO REMEMBER

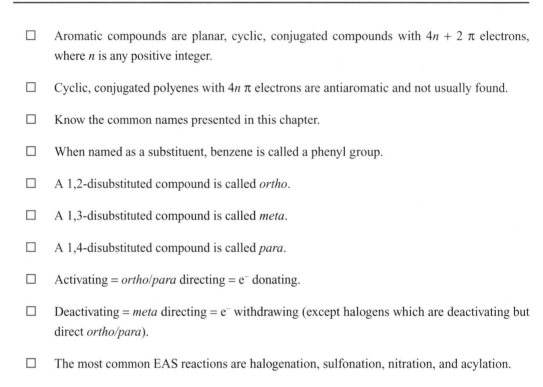

☐ Aromatic compounds are planar, cyclic, conjugated compounds with $4n + 2$ π electrons, where n is any positive integer.

☐ Cyclic, conjugated polyenes with $4n$ π electrons are antiaromatic and not usually found.

☐ Know the common names presented in this chapter.

☐ When named as a substituent, benzene is called a phenyl group.

☐ A 1,2-disubstituted compound is called *ortho*.

☐ A 1,3-disubstituted compound is called *meta*.

☐ A 1,4-disubstituted compound is called *para*.

☐ Activating = *ortho*/*para* directing = e⁻ donating.

☐ Deactivating = *meta* directing = e⁻ withdrawing (except halogens which are deactivating but direct *ortho*/*para*).

☐ The most common EAS reactions are halogenation, sulfonation, nitration, and acylation.

Practice Questions

1. Which of the following represents the correct structure for *para*-nitrotoluene?

   A.

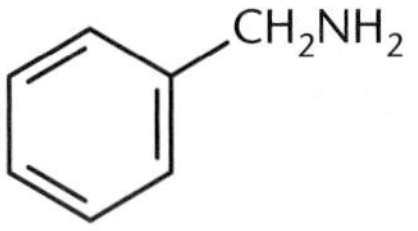

   B.

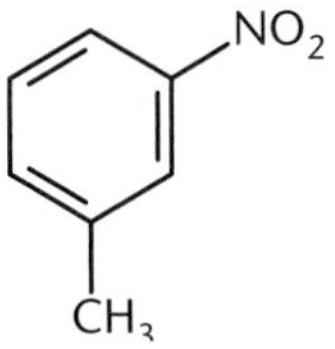

   C.

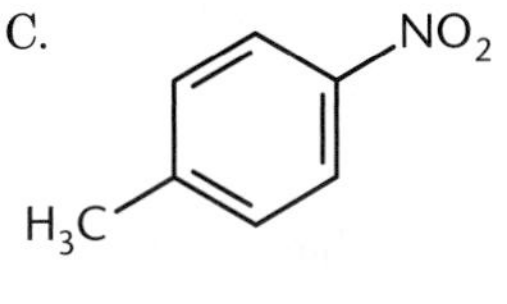

   D.

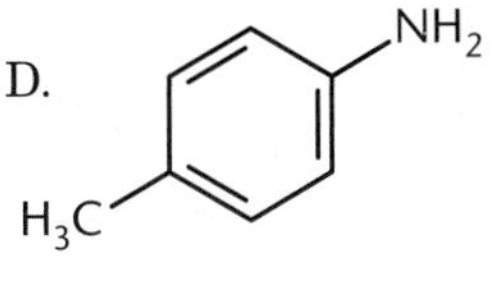

2. What would be the major product of the following reaction?

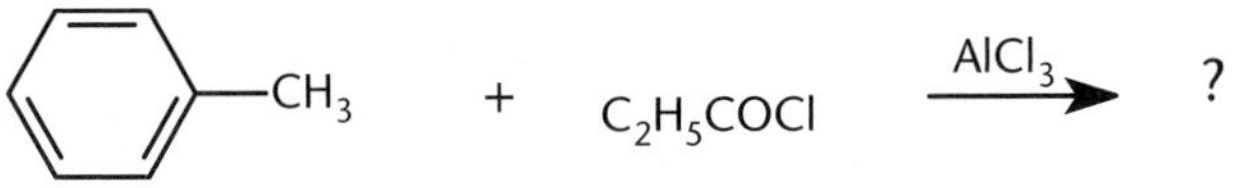

   A.

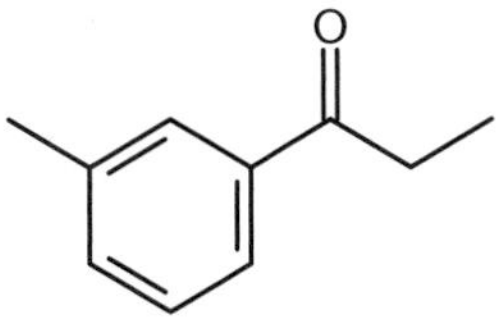

   B.

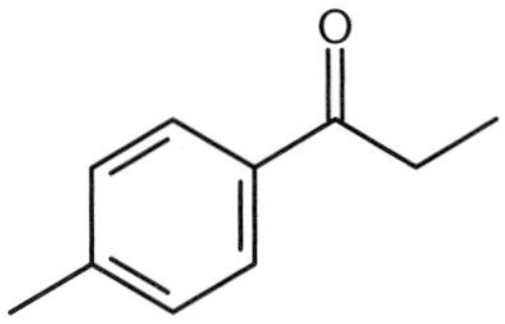

   C.

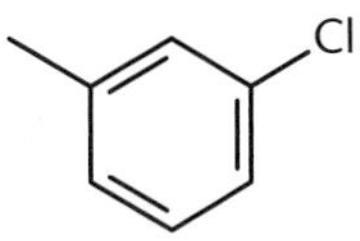

   D.

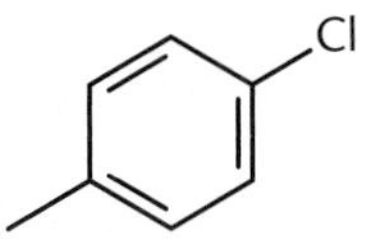

3. Nitration of benzene at 30°C leads to a 95 percent yield of nitrobenzene. When the temperature is increased to 100°C, dinitrobenzene is produced. Which of the following is the predominant product?

   A.

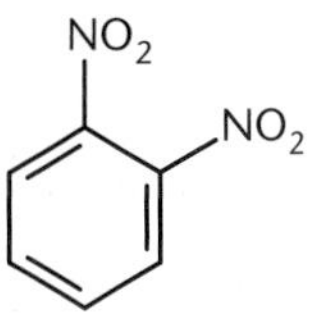

   B.

   C.

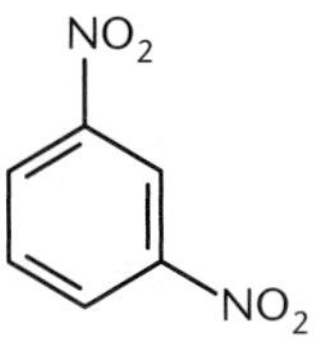

   D.

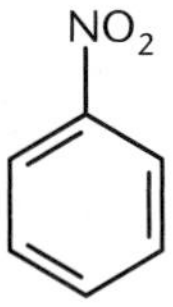

4. What is the major product of the nitration reaction below?

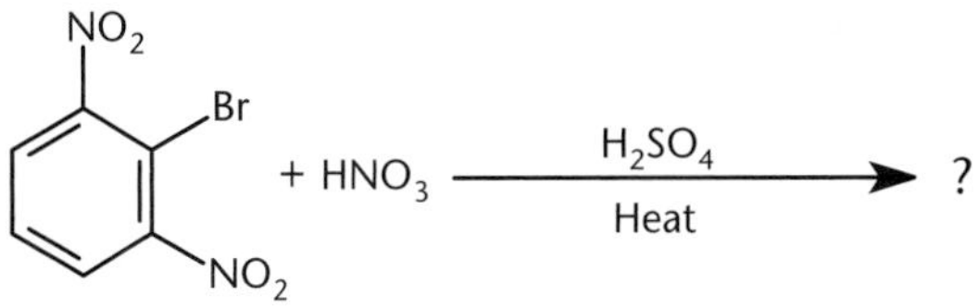

   A.

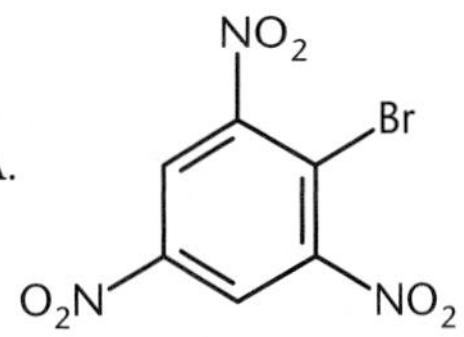

   B.

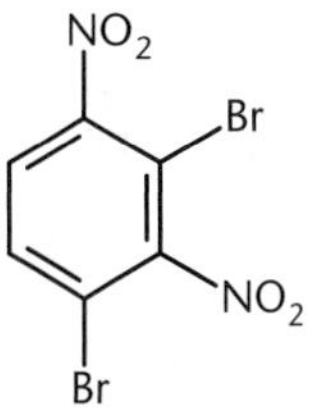

   C.

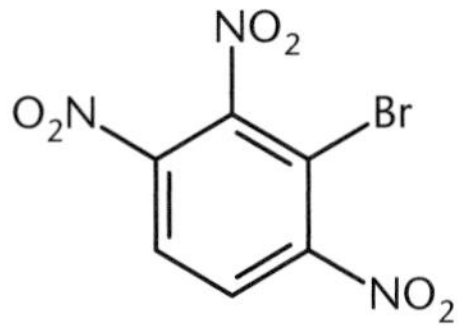

   D.

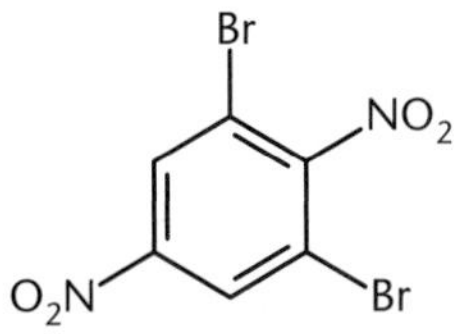

5. Give the predominant product(s) of the reaction below.

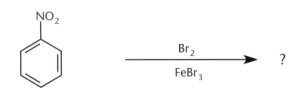

A.

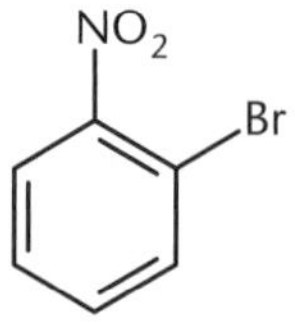

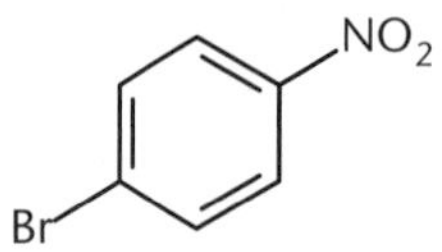

B.

C.

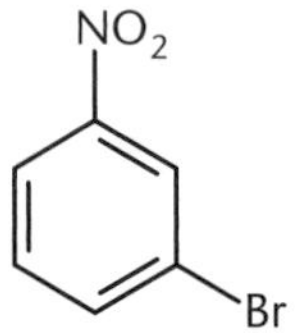

D.

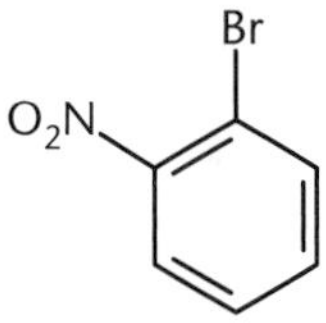

6. Which sequence of reaction conditions should be used to produce the compound below from benzene?

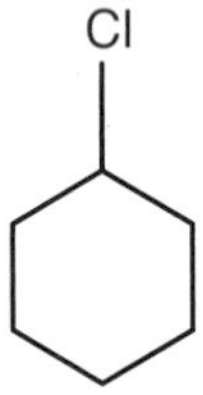

A. $AlCl_3/Cl_2$; $H_2/Rh/C$
B. Cl_2/UV light; $H_2/Rh/C$
C. $H_2/Rh/C$; $AlCl_3/Cl_2$
D. HCl; $H_2/Rh/C$

7. Starting with phenol, what is the major product of the reaction sequence shown below?

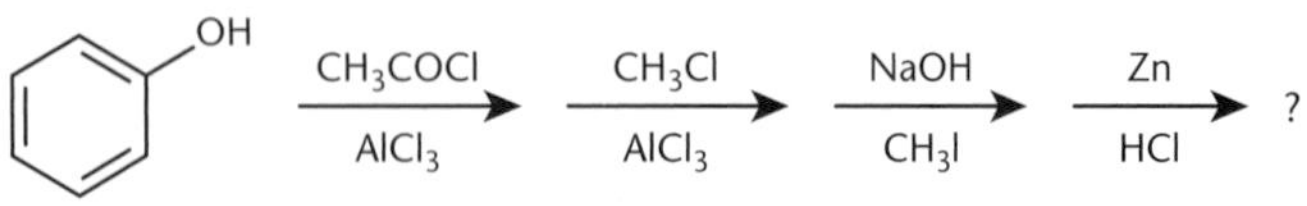

A. Aceto(4-methoxy-3-methyl)phenone
B. 4-Ethyl-2,6-dimethylphenol
C. 4-Ethyl-2-methylanisole
D. 3-Chloro-4-ethyl-2-methylanisole

8. How would an ammonium group affect a benzene ring for subsequent reactions?

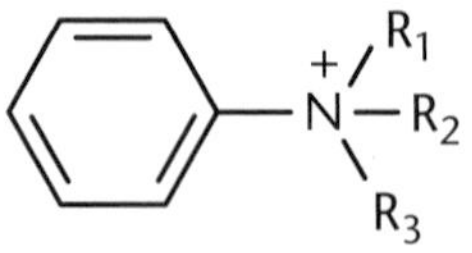

A. Deactivate the ring; *m*-directing
B. Activate the ring, *o/p*-directing
C. Deactivate the ring; *o/p*-directing
D. Activate the ring; *m*-directing

9. Which of the molecules shown below are aromatic?

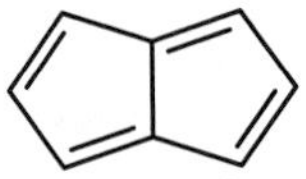

Compound I 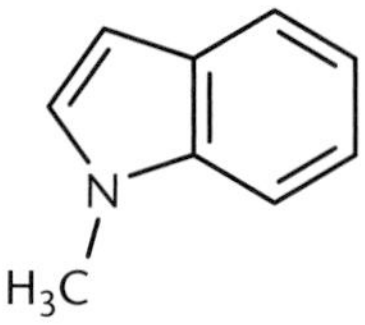   Compound II

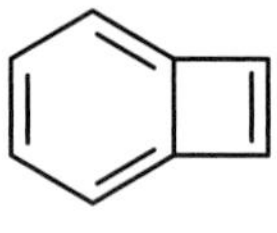

Compound III

A. I only
B. II only
C. I and III only
D. I, II, and III

Small Group Questions

1. Draw the resonance structures of phenol and nitrobenzene and explain how the structures influence the addition of substituents to the ring.

2. Explain why halogens are the exception to the substituent effect rules.

Explanations to Practice Questions

1. C

Toluene is the common name for methylbenzene: a methyl group attached to a benzene ring. In *para*-nitrotoluene, the nitro group ($-NO_2$) is attached to the ring directly across from the methyl group. Choice (C) is the correct response. Choice (B) is wrong because it shows the nitro group as *meta*-, not *para*-substituted relative, to the methyl group. Choices (A) and (D) can be eliminated because neither contains a nitro group.

2. B

The reaction shown, a Friedel-Crafts acylation of toluene, will yield a product containing the original methyl substituent and a new carbonyl substituent. Chlorination of the ring will not occur; although that process also uses $AlCl_3$ as a catalyst, Cl_2 would need to be present. Therefore, choices (C) and (D) (both chlorotoluenes) can be eliminated. Because CH_3 is an activating, *ortho/para*-directing group, the *meta*-isomer, choice (A), would be a minor product at best. The *para*- and *ortho*-isomers would be major products, of which only the *para*-isomer is present in the answer choices (choice (B)).

3. C

meta-dinitrobenzene is the predominant product, because $-NO_2$ is a *meta*-directing group.

4. A

All three substituents of 2-bromo-1,3-dinitrobenzene direct reaction to C–5, which is *meta* to both nitro groups and *para* to the bromine atom. Choice (A) will be the major product. Because all three groups are deactivating, the reaction will be slow and require elevated temperatures.

5. B

This reaction shows the bromination of nitrobenzene. Choices (A) and (D) are different views of the same compound, so both can be eliminated. Choice (B) shows *meta*-bromonitrobenzene, which is the favored product of this reaction because the *nitro*-substituent is *meta*-directing. Choices (A), (C), and (D) show the *ortho*- and *para*-isomers, which are less favored in this reaction.

6. A

To produce chlorocyclohexane, two different procedures must be carried out: The benzene ring must be chlorinated and hydrogenated (reduced). A suitable way to chlorinate the ring is to use Cl_2 and the Lewis acid catalyst $AlCl_3$, which is seen in choices (A) and (C). Now for the second step: hydrogenation. Hydrogenation of the benzene ring can be accomplished by using hydrogen in the presence of a catalyst, also shown in choices (A) and (C). Chlorination must occur first, because reduction removes the ring's characteristic aromatic properties, making EAS no longer possible. Therefore, (A) is the correct answer. Chlorine and ultraviolet light generally pair together for radical reactions, so choice (B) is wrong. Choice (D) is wrong because HCl will not chlorinate the ring.

7. C

The order of reactions is Friedel-Crafts acylation, Friedel-Crafts alkylation, Williamson ether synthesis, and Clemmenson reduction (see below).

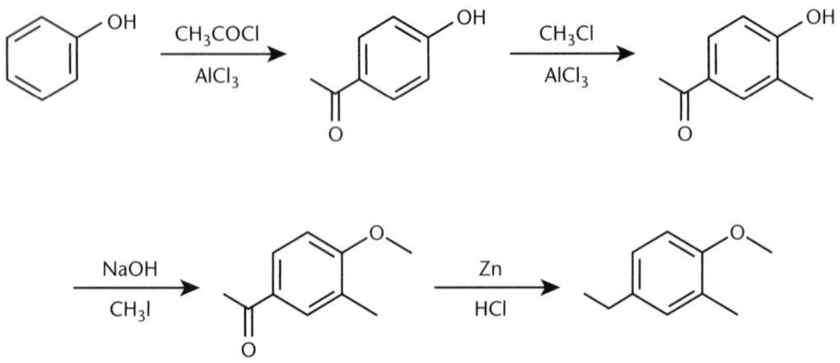

Answer (A) refers to the penultimate product above, whereas answer (B) implies that the Williamson ether synthesis furnishes the benzene with an additional methyl group. Similarly, answer (D) is incorrect because it implies that a chloride from HCl is added to benzene.

8. A

The ammonium group, with a positive charge on nitrogen, deactivates the benzene by pulling electron density away from the ring, directing subsequent groups to the *meta*-positions. Answer (B) is incorrect because it refers to groups that donate electron density into the benzene ring (e.g., alcohols, amines), whereas answer (C) refers to halogens. Finally, answer (D) is incorrect because *meta*-directing groups cannot activate the ring.

9. B

The formula for aromaticity follows Hückel's rule, which states that the number of π electrons in an aromatic compound must be equal to $4n + 2$, where n is any integer. Counting two electrons per double bond or sp^2 atom, compound I has 8 electrons, compound II has 10 (including the lone pair on nitrogen), and compound III has 8. Setting those numbers equal to $4n + 2$ shows us that only in compound II do we find n to be an integer.

Alcohols and Ethers

Alcohols and ethers are probably the two most popular chemicals that you'll encounter in Organic Chemistry, among scientists and laypeople alike. Ethanol, for one, has been popular with humans for more than ten thousand years. It's not just humans, either: Many animals are known to seek out rotten fruits that have fermented enough to contain moderate levels of alcohol. Note that when we talk about consuming alcohol, we are referring exclusively to ethanol. In fact, consuming other alcohols can have drastically negative effects. Methanol, for example, can cause blindness when ingested, an effect that many home distillers during Prohibition learned the hard way.

Ether, on the other hand, is young by comparison (only around 500 years old), but it should be a favorite of the aspiring surgeon. Ether became well known in the 1800s, when it was introduced as one of the first anesthetics for early surgeries. Once again, not just any ether was used as an anesthetic but specifically diethyl ether.

Alcohols ★★★★★★

Alcohols have the general formula ROH. The functional group is –**OH**, and it is referred to as a **hydroxyl** group. One way to think of alcohol is as a water molecule substituent that loses a proton when it attaches to an alkyl group, restoring its neutrality.

NOMENCLATURE

Alcohols are named in the IUPAC system by replacing the –**e** ending of the root alkane with the ending –**ol**. The carbon atom attached to the hydroxyl group must be included in the longest chain and receives the lowest possible number. Some examples are shown in Figure 7.1.

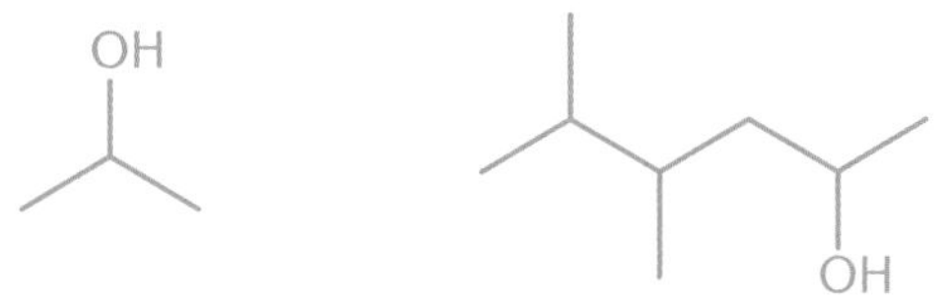

2-propanol   4,5-dimethyl-2-hexanol

Figure 7.1

Alternatively, the alkyl group can be named as a derivative, followed by the word *alcohol*, as in Figure 7.2.

ethyl alcohol   isobutyl alcohol

Figure 7.2

> ### MCAT Expertise
> Alcohols are an important group of compounds. They will be seen on the MCAT as protic solvents, reactants, products, and a prime example of hydrogen bonding.

> ### Key Concept
> The –OH group has high priority, so its C must be in the carbon backbone with the lowest number possible.

We will also see (as we did in Chapter 6) that alcohols can be attached to aromatic rings (see Figure 7.3). These compounds are called phenols and have the general formula ArOH.

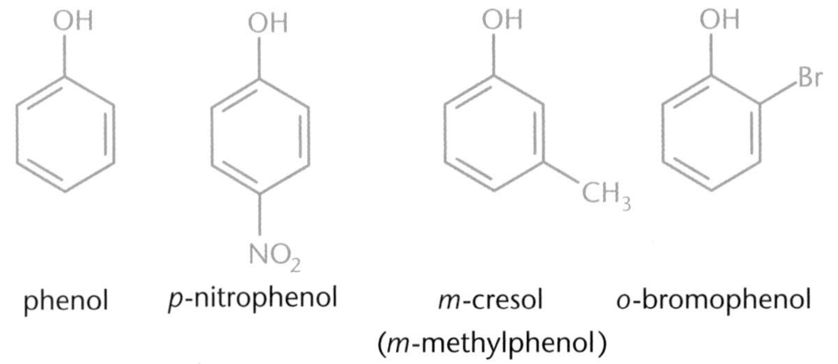

| phenol | *p*-nitrophenol | *m*-cresol (*m*-methylphenol) | *o*-bromophenol |

Figure 7.3

PHYSICAL PROPERTIES

The boiling points of alcohols are significantly higher than those of analogous hydrocarbons, owing to intermolecular **hydrogen bonding** (see Figure 7.4).

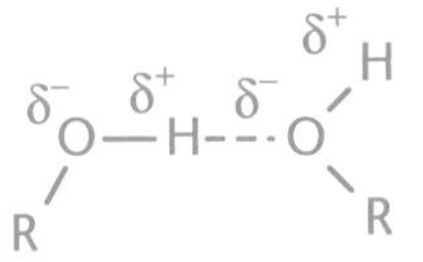

Figure 7.4

Molecules with more than one hydroxyl group show greater degrees of hydrogen bonding, as is evident from the boiling points in Figure 7.5.

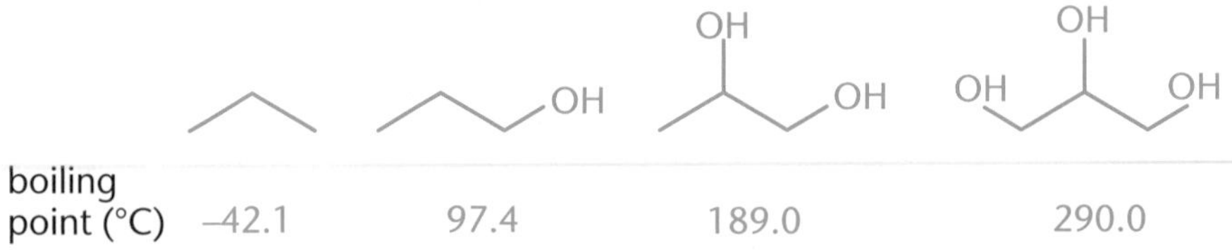

| boiling point (°C) | −42.1 | 97.4 | 189.0 | 290.0 |

Figure 7.5

Hydrogen bonding occurs when hydrogen atoms are attached to highly electronegative atoms: namely nitrogen, oxygen, and fluorine. Hydrogen bonding exists as a result of the extreme polarity of these bonds. Thus, we can expect that HF will have particularly strong hydrogen bonds because the high electronegativity of fluorine causes the HF bond to be highly polarized.

The hydroxyl hydrogen atom is weakly acidic, and alcohols can dissociate into protons and alkoxy ions in the same way that water dissociates into protons and hydroxide ions. Table 7.1 gives pK_a values of several compounds.

Table 7.1

	Dissociation		pK$_a$
H$_2$O	⇌	HO$^-$ + H$^+$	15.7
CH$_3$OH	⇌	CH$_3$O$^-$ + H$^+$	15.5
C$_2$H$_5$OH	⇌	C$_2$H$_5$O$^-$ + H$^+$	15.9
i-PrOH	⇌	*i*-PrO$^-$ + H$^+$	17.1
t-BuOH	⇌	*t*-BuO$^-$ + H$^+$	18.0
CF$_3$CH$_2$OH	⇌	CF$_3$CH$_2$O$^-$ + H$^+$	12.4
PhOH	⇌	PhO$^-$ + H$^+$	≈10.0

Bridge

pK$_a$ = −logK$_a$. Strong acids have high K$_a$'s and small pK$_a$'s. Thus, phenol, which has the smallest pK$_a$, is the most acidic of the alcohols listed.

Looking at Table 7.1, we can see that the hydroxyl hydrogens of phenols are more acidic than those of alcohols. This is because the aromatic nature of the ring allows for the distribution of negative charge throughout the ring, thus stabilizing the anion. As a result, phenols form intermolecular hydrogen bonds and have relatively high melting and boiling points. Phenol is slightly soluble in water (presumably owing to hydrogen bonding), as are some of its derivatives. Because phenols are much more acidic than aliphatic (nonaromatic) alcohols, they can form salts with inorganic bases such as NaOH.

The presence of other substituents on the ring has significant effects on the acidity, boiling points, and melting points of phenols. As with other aromatic compounds, electron-withdrawing substituents increase acidity, and electron-donating groups decrease acidity.

Another interesting trend that you probably noticed from Table 7.1 is that for aliphatic alcohols, the more alkyl groups that are present, the less acidic the molecule is. This is the opposite of the trend for carbocations. Logically enough, it's all based on the same concept. Because alkyl groups donate electron density (as we discussed in Chapter 6), they help *stabilize* a *positive* charge but will *destabilize* a *negative* charge.

Key Concept

Charges like to be spread out as much as possible. Acidity decreases as more alkyl groups (electron donating) are attached because they destabilize the alkoxide anion. Resonance or electron-withdrawing groups stabilize the alkoxy anion, making the alcohol more acidic.

REVIEW

Key Reaction Mechanisms for Alcohols and Ethers

As you read about the synthesis and reactions of alcohols and ethers, you'll see the same basic reaction mechanisms occurring over and over. Rather than memorizing each reaction individually, try to think of them in broad categories. Focus on how the basic mechanism works and how a particular reaction exemplifies it. The Big Three mechanisms for alcohols and ethers are these:

MCAT Expertise

Notice that the first two reactions here are the ones discussed earlier in our chapters on alkanes and alkenes. The third mechanism will get much more attention in the upcoming chapters.

1. *Nucleophilic substitution: S_N1, S_N2*

   Example: $CH_3Br + OH^- \longrightarrow CH_3OH + Br^-$

   See Chapter 4 for an in-depth review of nucleophilic substitution.

2. *Electrophilic addition to a double bond*

   Example: H_2O +

   This and other reactions that add H_2O to double bonds were covered in Chapter 5.

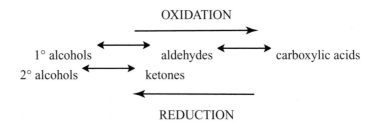

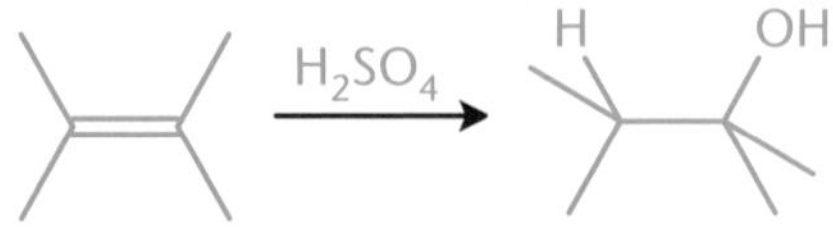

3. *Nucleophilic addition to a carbonyl*

   This mechanism is discussed in great detail in Chapters 8 to 10.

   Example: CH_3MgBr +

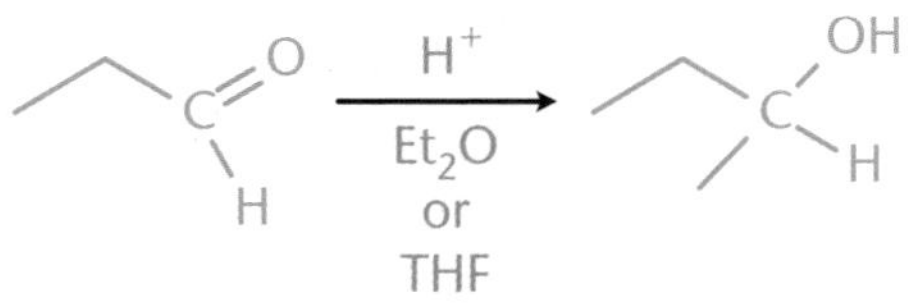

Also, when thinking about alcohols, you should keep in mind their place on the oxidation-reduction continuum:

OXIDATION →

1° alcohols ⟷ aldehydes ⟷ carboxylic acids

2° alcohols ⟷ ketones

← REDUCTION

Mnemonic

More bonds to oxygen = more oxidized. Remember that a double bond counts as two.

As you read about the individual reactions in which alcohols participate, try to fit them into this three-reaction framework. It will work for most of the reactions you will see on Test Day.

SYNTHESIS

Alcohols can be prepared from a variety of compounds. Ethanol can be produced from the fermentation of sugars, as we mentioned in the introduction with the example of rotting fruits. Methanol, on the other hand, is obtained from the destructive distillation of wood and is, therefore, called wood alcohol. As we said, methanol is toxic and can cause blindness if ingested. Ethanol can be metabolized by the body, but is also toxic if consumed in large quantities.

Addition Reactions

In Chapter 5, we discussed the addition of water to double bonds, an addition reaction that prepared alcohols. Alcohols can also be prepared from the addition of organometallic compounds to carbonyl groups; we'll get to this in Chapter 10.

Substitution Reactions

Both S_N1 and S_N2 reactions can be used to produce alcohols under the proper conditions, as discussed in Chapter 4.

Reduction Reactions

Alcohols can be prepared from the reduction of aldehydes, ketones, carboxylic acids, or esters. Lithium aluminum hydride ($LiAlH_4$, or LAH) and sodium borohydride ($NaBH_4$) are the two most common reducing reagents, and they each work a little bit differently (see Figure 7.6). LAH is the powerful one, and it will reduce just about anything (even esters, amides, and carboxylic acids) all the way to an alcohol. $NaBH_4$ is weaker, so although it, too, will reduce aldehydes, ketones, or acyl chlorides, it cannot reduce esters, carboxylic acids, or amides.

> **MCAT Expertise**
>
> Oxidation and reduction reactions are an important tool to the organic chemist and will be important for you to know on the MCAT. Remember: Reducing agents have a lot of Hs ($NaBH_4$ and $LiAlH_4$), and oxidizing agents have a lot of Os ($KMnO_4$ and CrO_3).

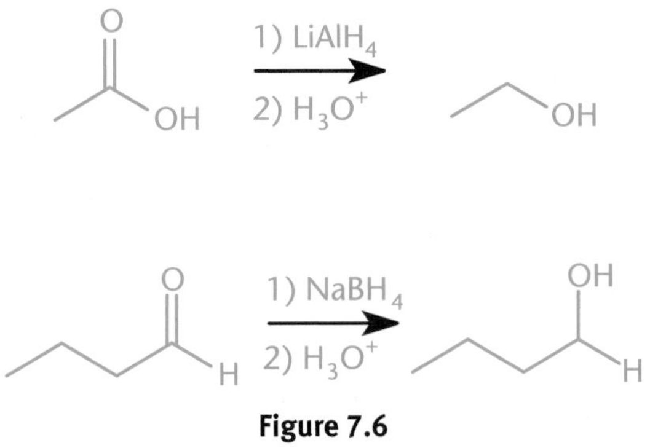

Figure 7.6

Phenol Synthesis

Phenols may be synthesized from arylsulfonic acids with hot NaOH. However, this reaction is useful only for phenol or its alkylated derivatives, as most other functional groups are destroyed by the harsh reaction conditions. A more versatile method of synthesizing phenols is by the hydrolysis of diazonium salts, shown in Figure 7.7.

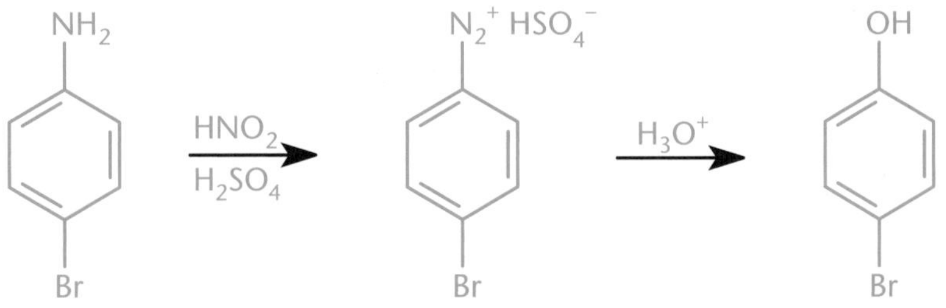

Figure 7.7

REACTIONS

Elimination Reactions

Alcohols can be dehydrated in a strongly acidic solution (usually H_2SO_4) to produce alkenes. The mechanism of this dehydration reaction is E1 for secondary and tertiary alcohols but E2 for primary alcohols. We need an acidic solution so that the –OH group can be protonated and converted to a good leaving group

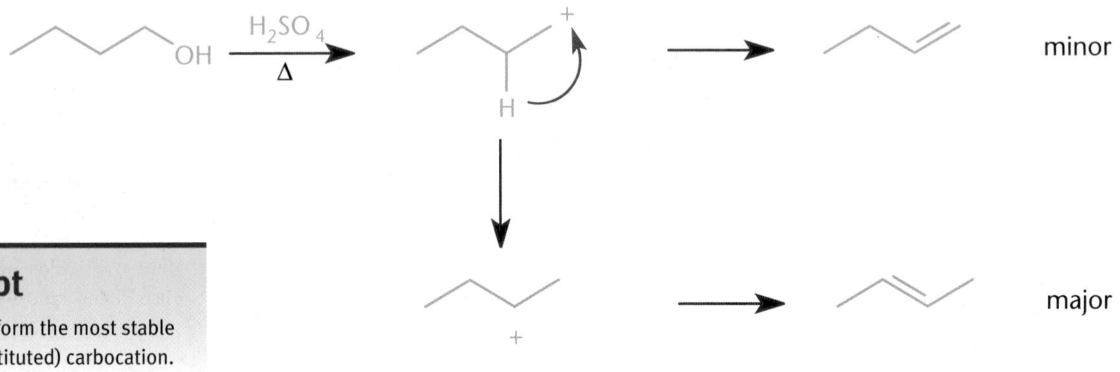

Figure 7.8

Notice in Figure 7.8 that two products are obtained, with the more stable alkene as the major product. This occurs via movement of a proton to produce the more stable 2° carbocation. This type of rearrangement, hydride shift, is commonly encountered with carbocations.

A milder method employs $POCl_3$ (phosphorus oxychloride), which follows an E2 mechanism for primary and secondary alcohols. Again, it converts the –OH group into a good leaving group.

Substitution Reactions

The displacement of hydroxyl groups in substitution reactions is rare because the hydroxide ion is a poor leaving group. If such a transformation is desired, the hydroxyl group must be made into a good leaving group. As we said before, protonating the alcohol makes water a good leaving group for S_N1 reactions. Even better, the alcohol can be converted into a tosylate (*p*-toluenesulfonate) group, which is an excellent leaving group for S_N2 reactions (see Figures 7.9a and 7.9b).

Key Concept

It's like the electrophilic addition of H_2O to a double bond, only this time it's in reverse—elimination.

Key Concept

In E1, you want to form the most stable (that is, most substituted) carbocation.

Key Concept

Alcohols can participate in S_N1/S_N2 reactions but only if you turn the –OH into a better leaving group by one of the following methods:

—Protonate it

—Convert to a tosylate.

—Form an inorganic ester.

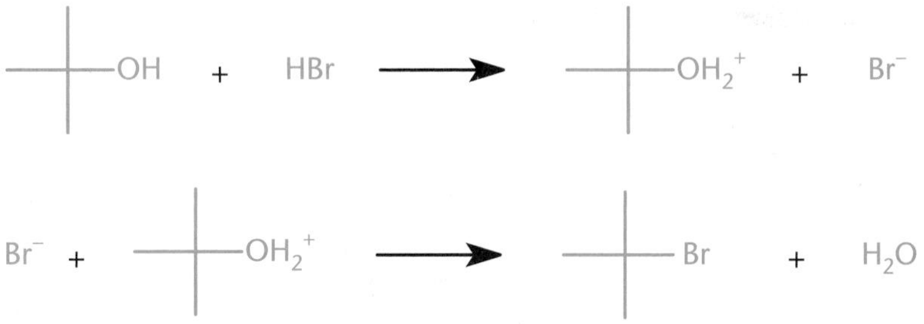

Figure 7.9a

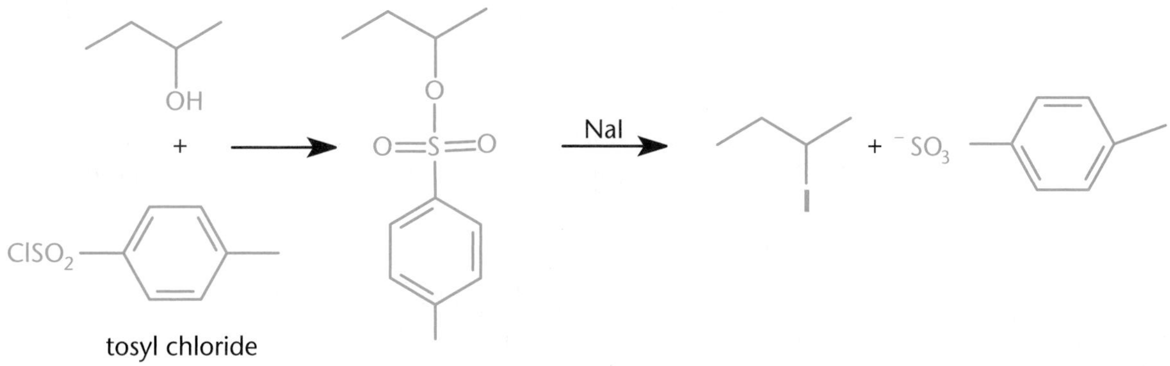

tosyl chloride

Figure 7.9b

Another useful reaction is the conversion of alcohols to alkyl halides. A common method involves the formation of inorganic esters, which readily undergo S_N2 reactions. Alcohols react with thionyl chloride to produce an intermediate inorganic ester (a chlorosulfite) and pyridine. The chloride ion, through an S_N2 mechanism, attacks the backside of the carbon bearing the oxygen (from the alcohol) and the chlorosulfite group. The reaction generates SO_2 and Cl⁻, forming the desired alkyl chloride with inversion of configuration. Take a look at the mechanism outlined in Figure 7.10.

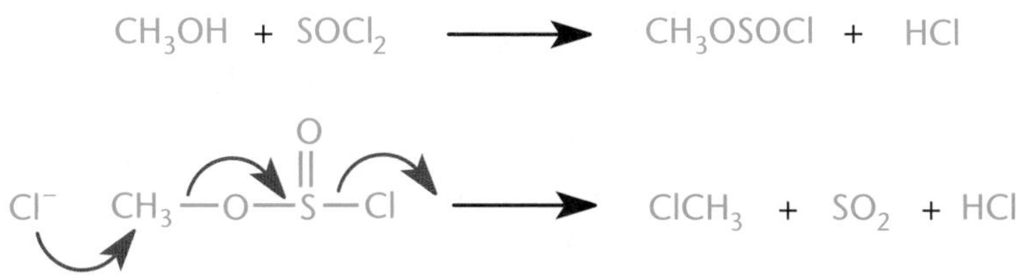

Figure 7.10

An analogous reaction to this, where the alcohol is treated with PBr_3 (in pyridine) instead of thionyl chloride, produces alkyl bromides. In both cases, as with tosylates, the poor alcohol leaving group is converted to a good leaving group.

MCAT Expertise

Phenols are good substrates for the EAS reactions from Chapter 6. Remember that the lone pair from the oxygen makes it an electron-donating substituent. Therefore, the –OH will be activating and *ortho*/*para* directing.

Mnemonic

When you see a transition metal (such as Cr or Mn) with lots of oxygen ($Na_2Cr_2O_7$, CrO_3, or $KMnO_4$), think *oxidation*.

Phenols readily undergo electrophilic aromatic substitution reactions because the lone pairs on the oxygen donate electron density to the ring. This means the –OH group is strongly activating and, thus, an *ortho*/*para*-directing ring substituent (see Chapter 6).

Oxidation Reactions

The oxidation of alcohols generally involves some form of chromium (VI) as the oxidizing agent, which is reduced to chromium (III) during the reaction. Every oxidizing agent we discuss here is a strong oxidizing agent (will convert a primary alcohol into a carboxylic acid) except for one, **PCC**. PCC (**pyridinium chlorochromate**, $C_5H_6NCrO_3Cl$) is the only "mild" (anhydrous) oxidant you need to know on the MCAT. This means it only *partially* oxidizes primary alcohols; thus, it stops after it has been converted to an aldehyde. It does this because it lacks water to hydrate the aldehyde (aldehydes are easily hydrated). When aldehydes are hydrated (gem diols or 1,1-diols), they can be oxidized to carboxylic acids. PCC will also form ketones from 2° alcohols, so the only difference between PCC and all of the other oxidizing agents is how they react with 1° alcohols. Tertiary alcohols are already as oxidized as they can be and so do not react with *any* of the oxidizing agents.

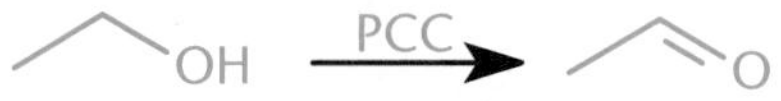

Figure 7.11

Another reagent used to *fully* oxidize primary and secondary alcohols is alkali (either sodium or potassium) dichromate salt. This means it will oxidize 1° alcohols to carboxylic acids and secondary alcohols to ketones.

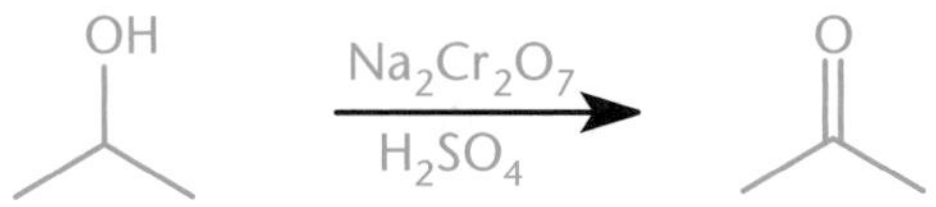

Figure 7.12

An even stronger oxidant is chromium trioxide, CrO_3. This is often dissolved with dilute sulfuric acid in acetone, a reaction called **Jones's oxidation**. This, too, oxidizes primary alcohols to carboxylic acids and secondary alcohols to ketones.

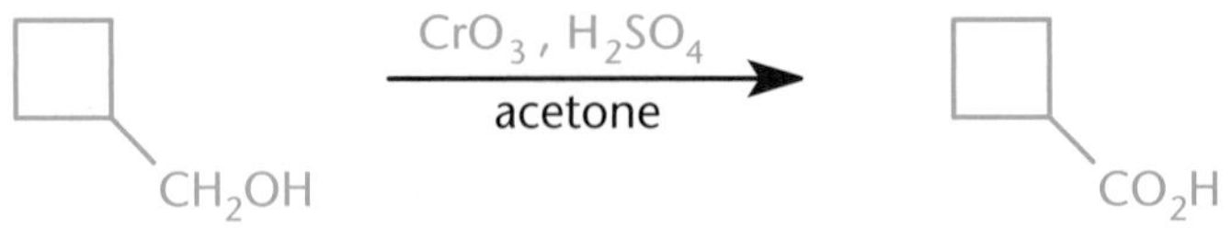

Figure 7.13

Treatment of phenols with oxidizing reagents produces compounds called **quinones** (2,5-cyclohexadiene-1,4-diones).

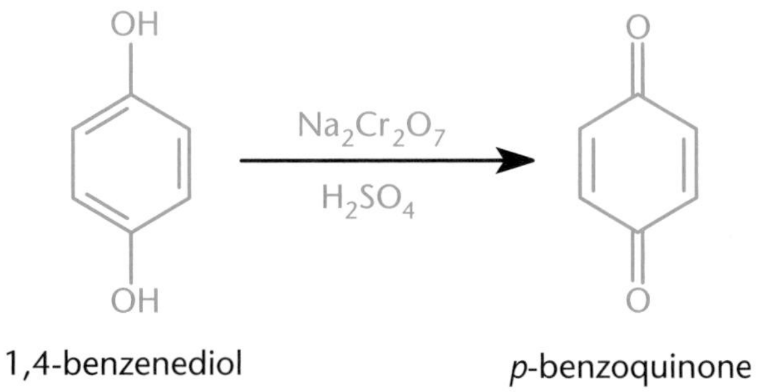

OH
OH
$Na_2Cr_2O_7$
H_2SO_4
O
O
1,4-benzenediol
p-benzoquinone

Figure 7.14

Ethers ★★★☆☆☆

An ether is a compound with two alkyl (or aryl) groups bonded to an oxygen atom. The general formula for ethers is ROR. Ethers can be thought of as disubstituted water molecules. As we mentioned at the beginning of this chapter, the most familiar ether is diethyl ether. Although it is no longer used as a medical anesthetic, it is still often used in the laboratory.

> **Key Concept**
> Ethers, like alcohols, are important solvents, *but* ethers are aprotic and unreactive.

NOMENCLATURE

As explained in Chapter 1, ethers are named according to IUPAC rules as alkoxyalkanes, with the smaller chain as the prefix and the larger chain as the suffix. There is also a common system of nomenclature in which ethers are named as alkyl alkyl ethers, with the substituents alphabetized. For example, *methoxyethane* would be named *ethyl methyl ether* (see Figure 7.15).

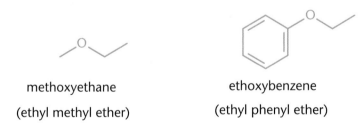

O
O
methoxyethane
(ethyl methyl ether)
ethoxybenzene
(ethyl phenyl ether)

Figure 7.15

Exceptions to these rules occur for cyclic ethers, as there aren't two different alkyl groups attached to them. Many common names exist for these cyclic compounds (see Figure 7.16).

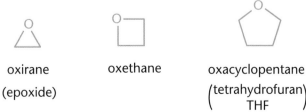

> **Key Concept**
> Remember that smaller rings have more angle strain, making them less stable and more reactive.

O
O
O
oxirane
(epoxide)
oxethane
oxacyclopentane
(tetrahydrofuran THF)

Figure 7.16

Key Concept

Note that the *lack* of hydrogen bonding is significant when determining the physical properties of ethers.

Key Concept

Look, it's S_N2 again! Therefore, you need a strong nucleophile (alkoxides are good) and an unhindered substrate (not bulky or highly substituted).

PHYSICAL PROPERTIES

An important distinction to note about ethers is that they do not undergo hydrogen bonding. Think about it; ethers have no hydrogen atoms bonded to the oxygen atoms, so they can't possibly participate in hydrogen bonding. Ethers therefore boil at relatively low temperatures compared with alcohols; in fact, they boil at approximately the same temperatures as alkanes of comparable molecular weight.

Ethers are only slightly polar and, therefore, only slightly soluble in water. They are inert to most organic reagents and as such, they are frequently used as solvents.

SYNTHESIS

The Williamson ether synthesis, an important reaction for the MCAT, produces ethers from the reaction of metal alkoxides with primary alkyl halides or tosylates. The alkoxides behave as nucleophiles and displace the halide or tosylate via an S_N2 reaction, producing an ether. There's nothing new here; this is a reaction you should already know. Note that it is in competition with E2.

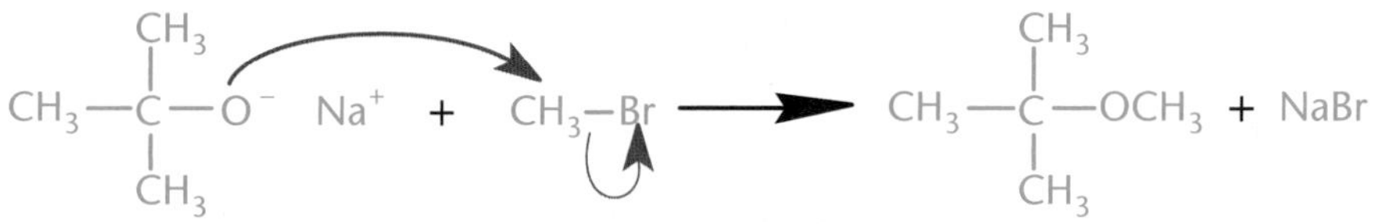

Figure 7.17

Remember that alkoxides will only attack nonhindered halides. Thus, to synthesize the methyl ether shown in Figure 7.17, an alkoxide must attack a methyl halide; the reaction *cannot* be accomplished with the methoxide ion attacking a bulky alkyl halide substrate.

The Williamson ether synthesis can also be applied to phenols (see Figure 7.18). Relatively mild reaction conditions are sufficient, owing to the acidity of phenols.

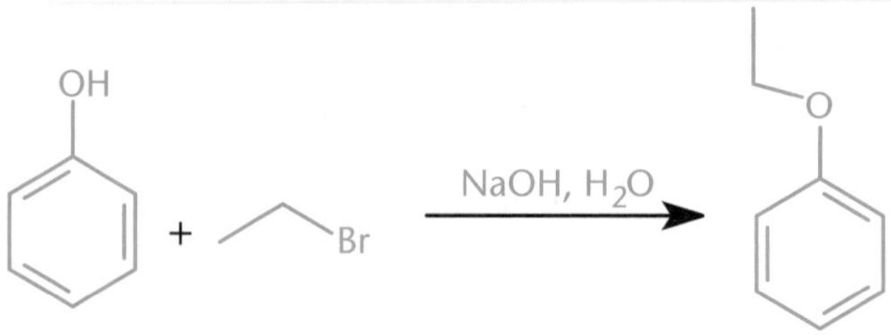

Figure 7.18

Cyclic ethers can be prepared in a number of ways, but you are likely to see it via internal S_N2 displacement. Intramolecular reactions are favored because, as we know, the rate and equilibrium of the reaction are affected by the reagent concentrations. With intramolecular reactions, the reagents see fairly high concentrations of each other; they are basically tied together (see Figure 7.19).

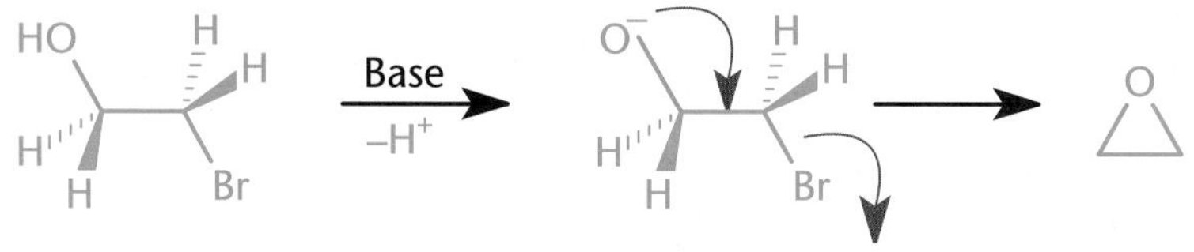

Figure 7.19

Another way to make cyclic ethers is by the oxidation of an alkene with a **peroxy acid** (general formula RCOOOH) such as mcpba (*m*-chloroperoxybenzoic acid). This reaction will also produce an epoxide or oxirane, as in Figure 7.20.

Figure 7.20

REACTIONS

Peroxide Formation

Ethers react with the oxygen in air to form highly explosive compounds called **peroxides** (general formula ROOR). You don't need to worry about the mechanism of this formation, but you should know that the reaction is possible.

Cleavage

Cleavage of straight-chain ethers will take place only under vigorous conditions, usually at high temperatures in the presence of HBr or HI. Cleavage is initiated by protonation of the ether oxygen. The reaction then proceeds by an S_N1 or S_N2 mechanism, depending on the conditions and the structure of the ether (Figure 7.21). Although not shown here, the alcohol products usually react with a second molecule of hydrogen halide to produce an alkyl halide.

Key Concept

More S_N2! This time, however, it's intramolecular—the nucleophile and leaving group are part of the same molecule.

MCAT Expertise

Intramolecular reactions are often seen on the MCAT because they can be confusing to test takers. With every reaction on the MCAT, identify an electrophile (positive) and a nucleophile (negative) first, and you know that they will then come together—even if they are part of the same molecule.

Key Concept

Remember, strong bases are poor leaving groups. Without protonation, the leaving group would be an alkoxide (strongly basic), and the reaction would be unlikely to proceed.

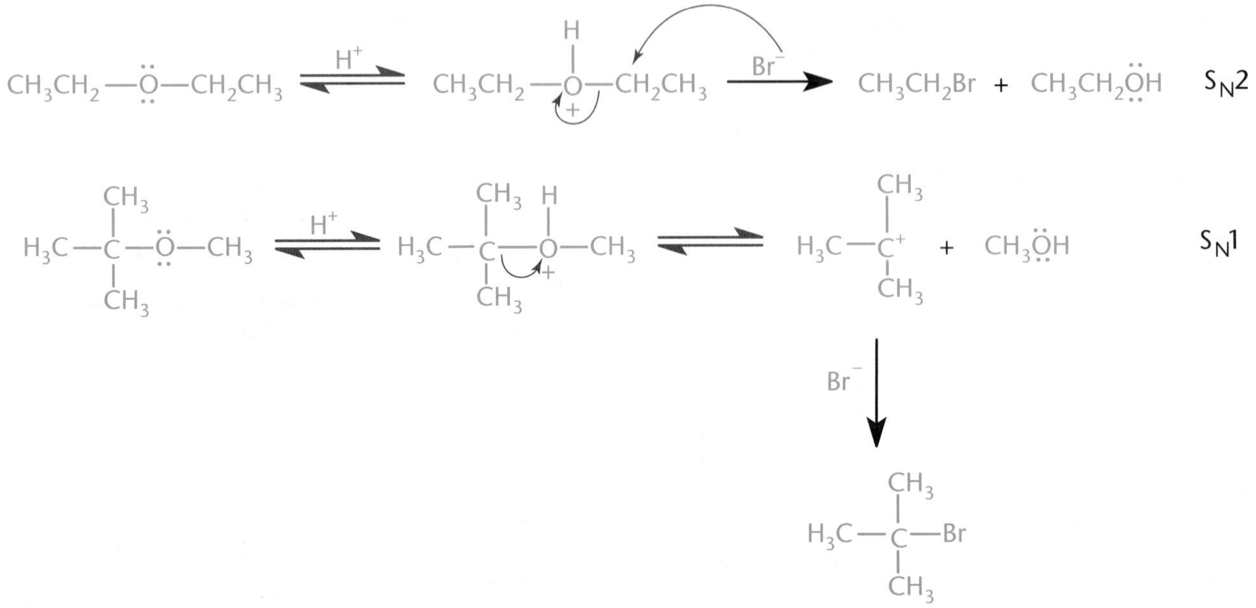

Figure 7.21

Key Concept

Cleavage of straight chain ethers is acid-catalyzed. Cleavage of epoxides can be acid-catalyzed (the nucleophile (e.g., H_2O, ROH) attacks the more substituted carbon of the epoxide) or base-induced (the nucleophile (e.g., RMgX, $LiAlH_4$, OH⁻) attacks the least substituted carbon of the epoxide).

Because epoxides are highly strained cyclic ethers, they are ready to react and, thus, susceptible to S_N2 reactions. Unlike straight-chain ethers, these reactions can be catalyzed by acid or reacted with base (nucleophiles), as shown in Figure 7.22. In symmetrical epoxides, either carbon can be nucleophilically attacked. However, in asymmetrical epoxides, the *most* substituted carbon is nucleophilically attacked when catalyzed with acid, and the *least* substituted carbon is attacked with a nucleophile (basic conditions).

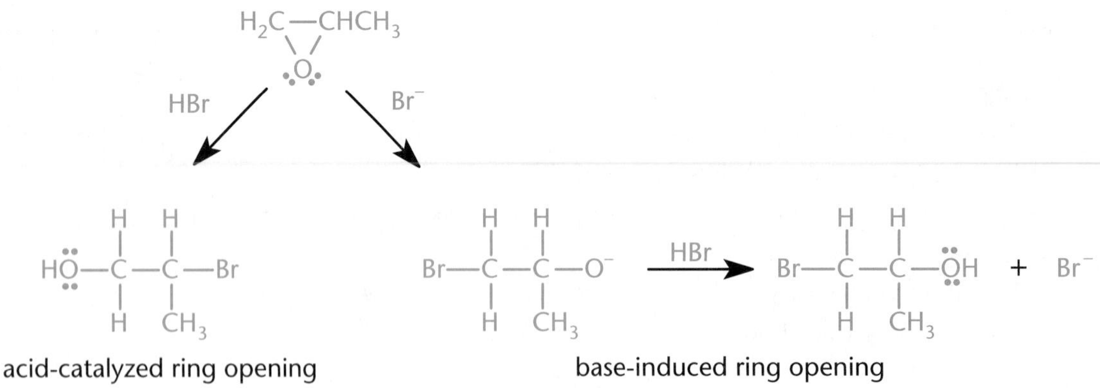

acid-catalyzed ring opening   base-induced ring opening

Figure 7.22

Base (nucleophile) induced cleavage has mostly S_N2 character, so it occurs at the least hindered (least substituted) carbon. Because the environment is basic, it provides a better nucleophile than an acidic environment.

In contrast, acid-catalyzed cleavage is thought to have some S_N1 character and some S_N2 character. The epoxide's oxygen is protonated, converting it to a better leaving group. As a result, the carbons share a bit of the positive charge. Because substitution stabilizes this charge (remember, 3° carbons make the best carbocations), the more substituted carbon becomes a good target for nucleophilic attack.

Key Concept

Base-induced cleavage has mostly S_N2 character, whereas acid-catalyzed cleavage seems to have some S_N1 character.

Conclusion

Alcohols and ethers may be popular among humans and animals, but they are a particular favorite of MCAT test makers. We get our first look at the unique properties that stem from hydrogen bonding: Remember that alcohols can form hydrogen bonds but ethers cannot. Know how alcohols and ethers are synthesized and understand the major reactions in which each participates. From this point forward, oxidation and reduction will be important reactions. Know that an oxidizing agent will have lots of oxygen, and a reducing agent will have lots of hydrogens. Don't let epoxides, ethers, or alcohols intimidate you; the same basic principles and reaction mechanisms that we've seen with more simple compounds apply here as well. Whenever you get a really complicated reaction, just take a step back, figure out what will act as the nucleophile and electrophile, and then go from there.

CONCEPTS TO REMEMBER

- ☐ Alcohol = ROH.

- ☐ Alcohols (and any other compound that has a hydrogen bonded to an O, N, or F) will undergo hydrogen bonding, leading to a relatively high boiling point.

- ☐ Whereas alkyl groups stabilize positive charges, they destabilize negative charges.

- ☐ Alcohols can be made by nucleophilic substitution, electrophilic addition to a double bond, or nucleophilic addition to a carbonyl.

- ☐ If a reactant has a lot of oxygen, it's an oxidizing agent; if it has a lot of hydrogen, it's a reducing agent.

- ☐ Terminal alcohols are oxidized to carboxylic acids, secondary alcohols are oxidized to ketones, and tertiary alcohols cannot be oxidized.

- ☐ PCC only oxidizes terminal (primary) alcohols to aldehydes.

- ☐ The oxygen of alcohols or ethers can be protonated to make them into better leaving groups.

- ☐ Cleavage of straight-chain ethers is acid catalyzed; cleavage of cyclic ethers (epoxides) can be carried out in acid or base.

- ☐ Base-induced epoxide cleavage has S_N2 character; acid-catalyzed cleavage has S_N1 and S_N2 character.

Practice Questions

1. Alcohols have higher boiling points than their analogous ethers and hydrocarbons because

   A. the oxygen atoms in alcohols have shorter bond lengths.
   B. hydrogen bonding is present in alcohols.
   C. alcohols are more acidic than their analogous ethers and hydrocarbons.
   D. All of the above

2. Tertiary alcohols are oxidized with difficulty because

   A. there is no hydrogen attached to the carbon with the hydroxyl group.
   B. there is no hydrogen attached to the α-carbon.
   C. tertiary alcohols contain hydroxyl groups with no polarization.
   D. they are relatively inert.

3. Which of the following reagents should be used to convert $CH_3(CH_2)_3CH_2OH$ into $CH_3(CH_2)_3CHO$?

   A. KMnO4
   B. Jones's reagent
   C. PCC ($C_5H_6NCrO_3Cl$)
   D. LiAlH4

4. The reaction of 1 mole of diethyl ether with excess hydrobromic acid results in the production of

   A. 2 moles of ethyl bromide.
   B. 2 moles of ethanol.
   C. 1 mole of ethylbromide and 1 mole of ethanol.
   D. 1 mole of methylbromide and 1 mole of propanol.

5. Given the reaction shown below with *m*-chloroperoxybenzoic acid, what is the stereochemistry of the product?

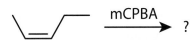

   I. 2(*R*), 3(*R*)

   II. 2(*R*), 3(*S*)

   III. 2(*S*), 3(*R*)

   IV. 2(*S*), 3(*S*)

   A. I and II
   B. II and IV
   C. II and III
   D. I and IV

6. What are the major products of the reaction shown below?

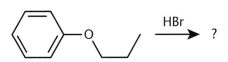

   A. Phenol and bromopropane
   B. Bromobenzene and propanol
   C. Bromobenzene and propane
   D. Benzene and propane

7. Which of the compounds below can undergo oxidation?

A.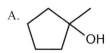

B.

C.

D.

Small Group Questions

1. Why are ethers relatively inert?

2. For epoxide opening, explain the differences in the mechanism between the acid-catalyzed and base-catalyzed reactions.

8. What reagents most effectively produce the following transformation shown below?

? → OH, OCH₃

A. CH_3OH, H^+
B. CH_3Br
C. H_3O^+, CH_3Cl
D. CH_3OH, $CH_3O^-Na^+$

Explanations to Practice Questions

1. B

Alcohols have higher boiling points than their analogous ethers and hydrocarbons as a result of their polarized O–H bonds, in which oxygen is partially negative and hydrogen is partially positive. This enables the oxygen atoms of other alcohol molecules to be attracted to the hydrogen, forming a weak hydrogen bond. Heat is required to break these hydrogen bonds, thereby increasing the boiling point. The analogous hydrocarbons and ethers do not form hydrogen bonds and, therefore, vaporize at lower temperatures. Choice (A) is irrelevant; oxygen's bond length is not a factor in determining a substance's boiling point. Choice (C) is a true statement, but it is also irrelevant to boiling point determination.

2. A

Tertiary alcohols can be oxidized but only under extreme conditions, because their carbon atoms do not have spare hydrogens to give up. Alcohol oxidation involves the removal of such a hydrogen so that carbon can instead make another bond to oxygen. If no hydrogen is present, a carbon–carbon bond must be cleaved, which requires a great deal of energy and will, therefore, occur only under extreme conditions. Choice (B) is incorrect because the number of hydrogens attached to the α-carbon is irrelevant to the mechanism of alcohol oxidation. Choice (C) is incorrect because the hydroxyl group of a tertiary carbon is polarized. Choice (D) is a false statement.

3. C

The best way to prepare aldehydes from primary alcohols is to use PCC (pyridinium chlorochromate, $C_5H_6NCrO_3Cl$), which is choice (C). $KMnO_4$, choice (A), is a strong oxidizing agent and converts a primary alcohol to a carboxylic acid. Jones's reagent, choice (B), also converts a primary

alcohol into a carboxylic acid. $LiAlH_4$, choice (D), is a reducing agent; it cannot reduce an alcohol further and will certainly not oxidize an alcohol to an aldehyde.

4. A

When 1 mole of an ether reacts with HBr, the initial products are 1 mole of alcohol and 1 mole of alkyl bromide, choice (C). However, under these acidic conditions, Br displaces H_2O, resulting ultimately in 1 mole each of two alkyl bromides. In this case, because the ether is symmetric, the product is 2 moles of ethyl bromide, choice (A). Choice (B) is incorrect because under these conditions, the alcohol is protonated, and H_2O (a good leaving group) is replaced by Br to form ethyl bromide. Choice D is wrong because the ether molecule is split at the oxygen atom; it does not rearrange, as would be required to produce a three-carbon and a one-carbon fragment.

5. C

mCPBA is used to form epoxides, which occurs in a *syn* fashion. Starting with (Z)-2-pentene, two products, a pair of enantiomers, are possible:

Answer I is incorrect, as formation of a 2(R), 3(R) product implies that epoxidation occurs in an *anti* fashion.

Answer IV is also incorrect, as a 2(*S*), 3(*S*) product is the enantiomers of 2(*R*), 3(*R*), which does not form. Because answers I and IV are incorrect, answers (A), (B), and (D) are also incorrect.

6. A

In the presence of strong acids, ethers are cleaved via protonation of the oxygen atom, followed by an S_N2 reaction by the bromide ion, forming an alkyl halide and an alcohol. However, because benzene cannot undergo S_N2 reactions, the bromide ion can attack only on the propyl side of the ether, forming phenol and bromopropane:

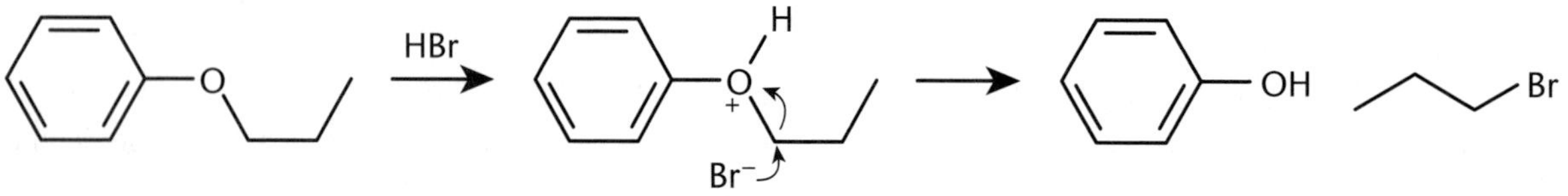

Answers (B) and (C) are incorrect because they require bromide to attack the benzene carbon in an S_N2 fashion. Hydrocarbons do not form during ether cleavage, so answer (D) is incorrect.

7. D

Primary and secondary alcohols can undergo oxidation, whereas tertiary alcohols (A), ketones (B), and carboxylic acids (C) cannot. None of these compounds' central atoms can make another bond to oxygen.

8. D

The product comes from a base-catalyzed opening of the epoxide. Answers (A) and (C) are incorrect, because those are acidic conditions, whereas bromomethane alone (B) is unlikely to elicit any ring opening. Most likely, it will require a catalyst. Base catalysis (D), with sodium methoxide as the base, can effectively open the epoxide ring and furnish the methyl ether in the correct position.

Aldehydes and Ketones

In Chapter 7, we briefly mentioned that alcohols can be oxidized to aldehydes. At the time, this probably looked as unfamiliar as any other reaction on the page, but it may actually be one with which you are intimately, and unfortunately, acquainted. In the human body, the liver enzyme alcohol dehydrogenase facilitates the conversion of ethanol (an alcohol) to acetaldehyde (an aldehyde), a much more toxic substance. The nausea, headache, and slightly fruity stench that linger after a night of heavy drinking are the result of elevated acetaldehyde levels (and, of course, severe dehydration). Ketones are also responsible for some familiar scents and flavors, most of which are much more pleasurable. The two enantiomers of carvone, for instance, give rise to the distinct odors of dill (S–(+)) and spearmint (R–(−)). The most familiar ketone is probably acetone, which lends products such as nail polish and paint thinner their slightly less pleasant scents.

This chapter focuses on what is probably the *most important* class of functional groups on the MCAT: the carbonyls. The two functional groups highlighted here have a lot in common, because they both contain a carbonyl—a double bond between a carbon atom and an oxygen atom. The only difference between the two is what is *attached* to the carbonyl. A **ketone** has two alkyl (or aryl) groups bonded to the carbonyl, whereas an **aldehyde** has one alkyl (or aryl) group and one hydrogen. This hydrogen tells us that the aldehyde must be at an end of the chain, or as we chemistry folk like to call it, at the terminal position.

The carbonyl group is one of the most important functional groups in Organic Chemistry for two reasons. First, the carbonyl is a component of many different functional groups. In addition to aldehydes and ketones, the carbonyl is found in carboxylic acids, esters, amides, and several other compounds we'll tackle later (mostly in Chapter 11). More important, the carbonyl has the unique ability to behave as either a nucleophile (as in condensation reactions) *or* an electrophile (as in nucleophilic addition reactions), essentially taking on opposite characteristics. Whereas this duplicity can have negative consequences in humans (as we learned from the tale of Dr. Jekyll and Mr. Hyde), it simply gives the carbonyl more opportunities to react with other molecules.

Nomenclature ★★★★★☆

According to the Orgo gurus at IUPAC, aldehydes are named with the suffix **–al**. We won't ever need to specify the position of the aldehyde group because, by definition, it must occupy the terminal (C–1) position. Common names exist for the first five aldehydes: **formaldehyde**, **acetaldehyde**, **propionaldehyde**, **butyraldehyde**, and **valeraldehyde** (see Figure 8.1). Of these names, you are most likely to encounter the first two on the MCAT.

> ### Key Concept
> An aldehyde is a terminal functional group; it defines the C–1 position. A ketone, on the other hand, will always be midchain and can *never* be a terminal functional group.

MCAT Expertise

Uh-oh, more common names! Notice that these common names have a pattern that can help us: *form–* will be seen also in formic acid (a one-carbon carboxylic acid), and *acet–* is seen in many two-carbon compounds (acetylene, acetic acid, and acetyl CoA).

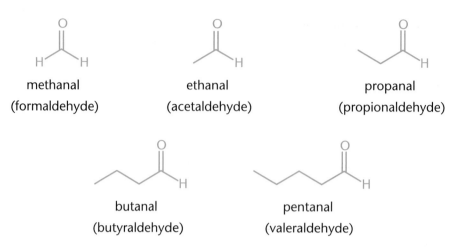

methanal
(formaldehyde)
ethanal
(acetaldehyde)
propanal
(propionaldehyde)
butanal
(butyraldehyde)
pentanal
(valeraldehyde)

Figure 8.1

We must remember two other aspects of aldehyde nomenclature, shown in Figure 8.2. First, if the aldehyde is attached to a ring, we use the suffix **–carbaldehyde**. Second, if the aldehyde does not hold priority in the molecule, we name it as a substituent with the prefix **formyl–**.

cyclopentanecarbaldehyde   *m*-formylbenzoic acid

Figure 8.2

Ketones are quite logically named with the suffix **–one**. As opposed to aldehydes, the location of the carbonyl group on a ketone *must* be specified with a number, with the exception of propanone (acetone), butanone, and cyclic ketones (where it is assumed that the carbonyl occupies the number one position). Naming ketones with the common system of nomenclature is similar to naming ethers. We simply list the two alkyl groups alphabetically, followed by the word *ketone*. When it is necessary to name the ketone as a substituent, we use the prefix **oxo–**. Figure 8.3 shows some examples.

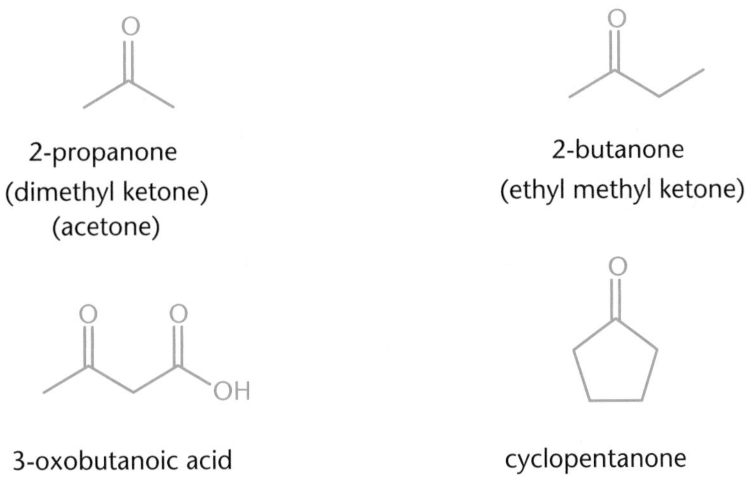

2-propanone
(dimethyl ketone)
(acetone)

2-butanone
(ethyl methyl ketone)

3-oxobutanoic acid

cyclopentanone

Figure 8.3

Physical Properties ★★★★★★

The physical properties of aldehydes and ketones are governed by the presence of the carbonyl group. The dipole of a carbonyl is greater than the dipole of an alcohol, because the carbonyl lacks a hydrogen, which would cancel some of the C–O dipole (see Figure 8.4). In solution, the dipole moments associated with these polar carbonyl groups line up, causing an elevation in boiling point relative to their associated alkanes. However, even though the dipoles are more polar than alcohols, the elevation in boiling point is less than that in alcohols, because no hydrogen bonding is involved. In general, aldehydes are more reactive towards nucleophiles than ketones.

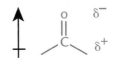

Figure 8.4

Synthesis ★★★★☆☆

There are numerous methods of preparing aldehydes and ketones, but the three methods you will most likely encounter on the MCAT are the following.

OXIDATION OF ALCOHOLS

An aldehyde can be obtained from the partial oxidation of a primary alcohol, and a ketone can be obtained from the oxidation of a secondary alcohol. As we mentioned in Chapter 7, the only reagent you will see that can oxidize a primary alcohol to an aldehyde (and *not* all the way to a carboxylic acid) is PCC (a dry, nonhydrating

Key Concept

The carbonyl group (in aldehydes and ketones) has a dipole moment. Oxygen is more electronegative—it is an "electron hog," pulling the electrons away from the carbon, making the carbon electrophilic.

MCAT Expertise

While the dipole moments in the carbonyl increase their intermolecular forces and boiling points relative to alkanes, it is not as significant as the effect of hydrogen bonding seen in alcohols.

Key Concept

Primary alcohols can be carefully oxidized to aldehydes. Secondary alcohols can be oxidized to ketones.

oxidizing reagent). We have many more options to oxidize a secondary alcohol into a ketone, because there is no risk of oxidizing too far. Sodium or potassium dichromate, chromium trioxide (Jones's reagent), or even PCC will perform this oxidation quite well.

OZONOLYSIS OF ALKENES

Alternatively, double bonds can be oxidatively cleaved to form aldehydes and/or ketones. Whether you get an aldehyde or ketone depends on whether you started with a mono- or disubstituted double bond. This is another one of those reactions where the name tells us almost everything we need to know: Ozonolysis breaks double bonds using ozone. Refer to Chapter 5 for an in-depth discussion.

FRIEDEL-CRAFTS ACYLATION

This reaction was also already discussed (in Chapter 6). In short, it produces aromatic ketones (aldehydes if R = H) in the form of R-CO-Ar.

Reactions ★★★★★★

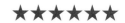

ENOLIZATION AND REACTIONS OF ENOLS

Key Concept

Aldehydes and ketones exist in the traditional keto form (C = O) and as the less common enol tautomer (*enol* = *ene* + *ol*). The enol form can act as a nucleophile.

Alpha protons (protons attached to the carbons adjacent to carbonyls) are relatively acidic ($pK_a \approx 20$) owing to resonance stabilization of the conjugate base. If this doesn't make sense, draw it out; push the leftover electrons up toward the oxygen and see how the extra negative charge can be spread among several atoms. Now, the hydrogen atom that detaches from the α-carbon has a good probability of reattaching to the partially negative oxygen instead of the carbon. Therefore, aldehydes and ketones exist in solution as a mixture of two isomers, the familiar **keto** form, and the **enol** form, representing the unsaturated alcohol (**ene** = the double bond, **ol** = the alcohol, so **ene** + **ol** = **enol**). The two isomers, which differ only in the placement of a proton (and the double bond), are called **tautomers**. The equilibrium between the tautomers lies far to the keto side, so there will be many more keto-isomers in solution. The process of interconverting from the keto to the enol tautomer, shown in Figure 8.5, is called **enolization** or, less specifically, **tautomerization**.

Key Concept

Note that tautomers are *not* resonance structures, because they have different connectivity of atoms.

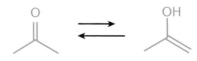

Figure 8.5

Enols are important intermediates in many reactions of aldehydes and ketones. The enolate carbanion, which acts as a nucleophile, can be created with a strong base, such as lithium diisopropyl amide (LDA) or potassium hydride (KH). A 1,3-dicarbonyl is extra acidic because there are two carbonyls to delocalize negative charge and, as such, is often used to make the carbanion. Once formed, the nucleophilic carbanion reacts via an S_N2 mechanism with alkyl halides (a favorite of most nucleophiles) or α, β-unsaturated carbonyl compounds in reactions called **Michael additions**. In this reaction, the carbanion attaches to the unsaturated carbonyl at the β-position owing to its resonance forms. The more you understand the resonance forms of molecules, the more you will be able to predict the specific location on the molecule where a reaction will take place.

> **Key Concept**
>
> Remember our discussion of hydrogen acidity? The hybrid structures in Figure 8.6 demonstrate why the hydrogen on the α-carbon is acidic and can act as a nucleophile.

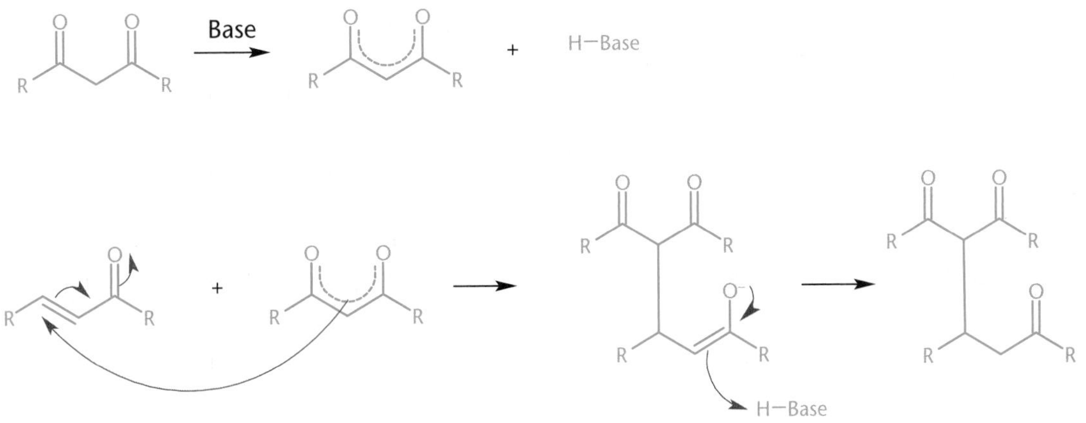

Figure 8.6

ADDITION REACTIONS

Heads-up! This is important. In all of the following reactions, the general reaction mechanism is the same: *nucleophilic addition to a carbonyl*. This is probably one of the most important reactions on the MCAT, and many of the reactions of aldehydes, ketones, and even more complicated molecules share this general reaction mechanism. Rather than memorizing all the possible reactions individually, focus on understanding the basic pattern. Then, you can learn how a particular reaction exemplifies it.

As we saw in Figure 8.4, the C=O bond is polarized, with a partial positive charge on C and a partial negative charge on O. This makes the carbon an electrophile, ripe for nucleophilic attack—kind of like wearing a steak hat while swimming off the southern coast of Africa, if you think of sharks as the nucleophiles.

When a nucleophile attacks, it forms a covalent bond to the carbon, breaking the π bond in the C=O. The electrons from the π bond are pushed up onto the oxygen atom, which, being more electronegative, is relatively happy to hold the negative charge for a while, generating a tetrahedral intermediate. If no good leaving group is present, the carbonyl will not re-form, and the final product will be nearly identical to the intermediate, except that the –O⁻ will usually accept a proton to become

> **MCAT Expertise**
>
> Memorizing one reaction may help you get one question correct on the MCAT, but understanding trends and overarching concepts will allow you to answer many questions correctly. You will see that the carbonyl carbon is a great target for nucleophilic attack in many of the reactions in this chapter.

a hydroxyl (–OH) Group. However, if a good leaving group is present, the carbonyl double bond can re-form and push off the leaving group—but we'll get to that later on with carboxylic acid derivatives.

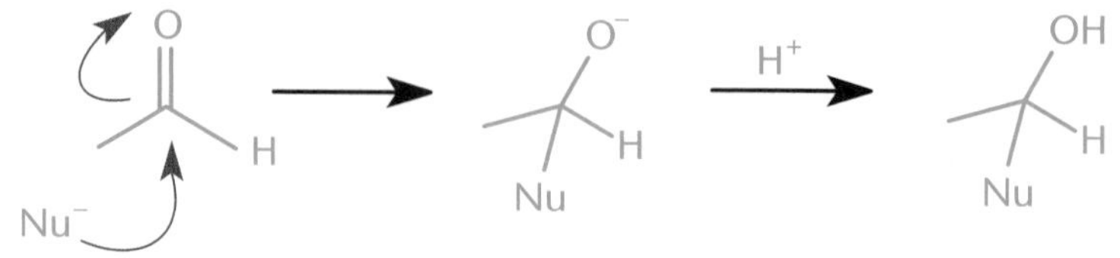

Figure 8.7

Although Figure 8.7 only shows nucleophilic addition to an aldehyde, this mechanism is the same for ketones.

Hydration

In the presence of water, aldehydes and ketones react to form gem-diols (1,1-diols), as shown in Figure 8.8. In this case, the nucleophilic oxygen in water attacks the electrophilic carbonyl carbon. This hydration reaction normally proceeds slowly, but we can increase the rate by adding a small amount of acid or base.

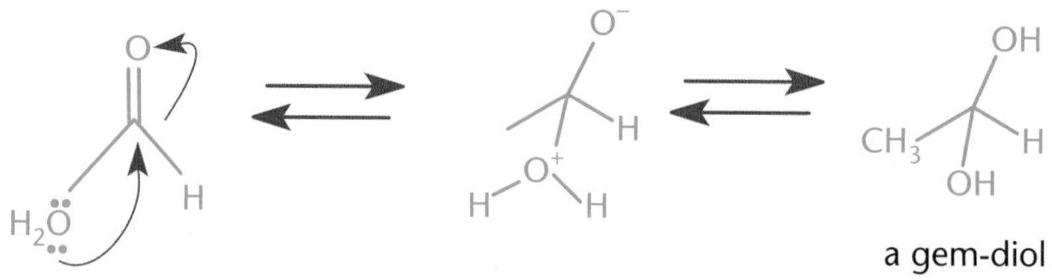

a gem-diol

Figure 8.8

Acetal and Ketal Formation

A similar reaction occurs when aldehydes and ketones are treated with alcohols. When one equivalent of alcohol (the nucleophile in this reaction) is added to an aldehyde or ketone, the product is a hemiacetal or a hemiketal, respectively (see Figure 8.9). We can always recognize a hemiacetal or hemiketal because it will still contain one hydroxyl group. Because the reactions here have only proceeded halfway, the products are termed *hemi*. In base, the reaction would stop here.

When two equivalents of alcohol are added, the reaction proceeds all the way and the product is an acetal or a ketal (see Figure 8.10). Because aldehydes contain a hydrogen on the carbonyl, both hemiacetals and acetals will still contain a hydrogen as a distinguishing characteristic.

The reaction proceeds via the same mechanism as hydration, and it is catalyzed by anhydrous acid. Acetals and ketals, which are comparatively inert, are frequently used as protecting groups for carbonyl functionalities. Ethylene glycol is a popular protecting group, as it is a diol and both alcohol groups come from the same molecule. Molecules with protecting groups can easily be converted back to carbonyls with aqueous acid, and heat.

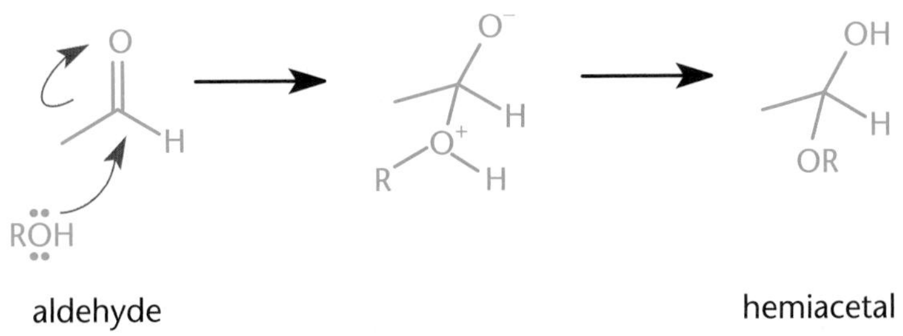

aldehyde   hemiacetal

Figure 8.9

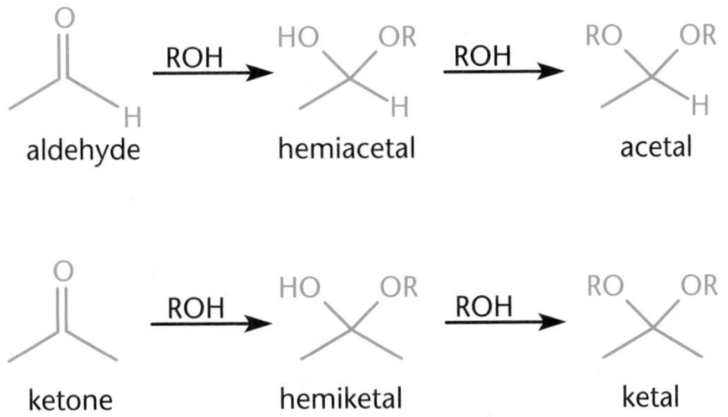

aldehyde   hemiacetal   acetal

ketone   hemiketal   ketal

Figure 8.10

Reactions with Hydrogen Cyanide (HCN)

Hydrogen cyanide is a classic nucleophile on the MCAT. We learned in Chapter 5 that alkynes are fairly acidic because of their triple bonds. Well, HCN has both a triple bond and an electronegative nitrogen atom, so it is even more acidic ($pK_a \approx 9.2$). After the hydrogen dissociates, the nucleophilic cyanide anion can attack the carbonyl carbon atom (see Figure 8.11). Reactions with aldehydes and ketones produce stable compounds called **cyanohydrins** (once the oxygen has been reprotonated). The cyanohydrin gains its stability from the newly formed C–C bond. (In contrast, when a carbonyl reacts with HCl, a weak C–Cl bond is formed, and the resulting chlorohydrin isn't very stable.)

Key Concept

In the formation of acetals and ketals, alcohol is the nucleophile and the carbonyl carbon is the electrophile.

Key Concept

In a reaction with HCN, ⁻CN is the nucleophile, and the carbonyl carbon is the electrophile.

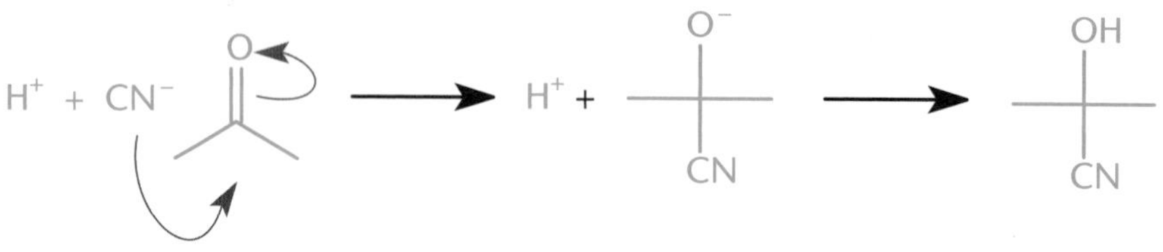

Figure 8.11

Key Concept

Can you see the pattern developing? On the MCAT, when you see a carbonyl carbon, think *electrophile* first!

Condensation with Ammonia Derivatives

Ammonia contains nitrogen, which we expect to act as a nucleophile as long as the lone pair on the nitrogen isn't too busy participating in an aromatic ring. This is the case for ammonia and for many of its derivatives. Because they make good nucleophiles, ammonia derivatives react readily with carbonyls. In the simplest case, ammonia adds to the carbon atom and water is lost, producing an **imine**, a compound with a nitrogen atom double-bonded to a carbon atom. Remember that a reaction in which water is lost between two molecules is called a **condensation reaction**.

In this case, the first part of the reaction follows the nucleophilic addition mechanism that we saw in the last three addition reactions. However, after the formation of a tetrahedral intermediate, this reaction proceeds further: A double bond forms between carbon and nitrogen and a leaving group (water) is kicked off (see Figure 8.12). We said before that a leaving group is usually kicked off by the re-formation of the C=O bond, so condensation with ammonia is unique. This mechanism is called **nucleophilic substitution** on a carbonyl, and we'll examine it in greater detail in Chapter 9.

Some common ammonia derivatives that react with aldehydes and ketones are hydroxylamine (H_2NOH), hydrazine (H_2NNH_2), and semicarbazide ($H_2NNHCONH_2$); these form oximes, hydrazones, and semicarbazones, respectively.

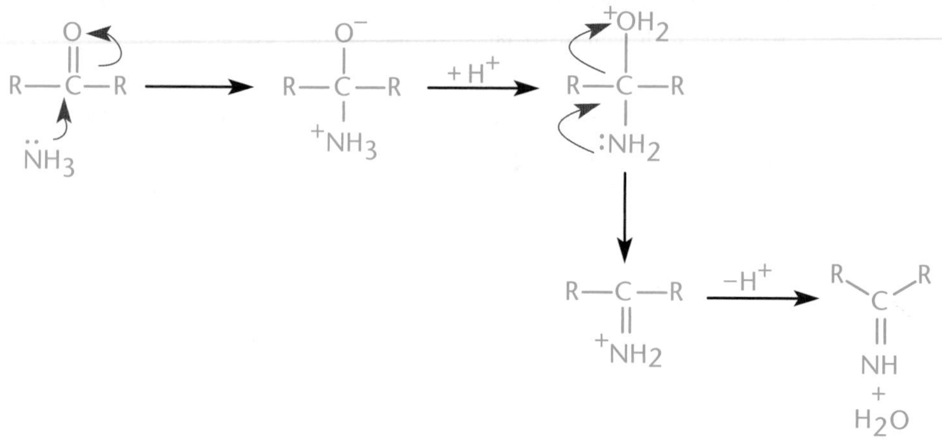

Figure 8.12

Don't worry too much about protons coming and going in reactions on the MCAT; there should be plenty in the solution, so you can use them wherever they are needed to facilitate this reaction. Examples of the other potential nucleophiles that we just mentioned and their respective products are shown in Figure 8.13.

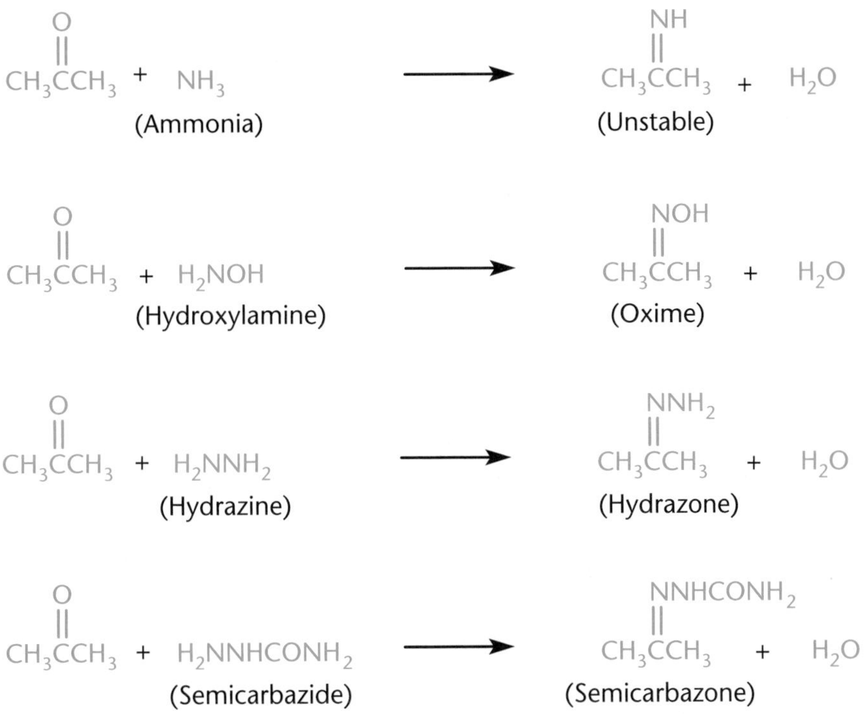

$$CH_3\overset{\overset{\displaystyle O}{\|}}{C}CH_3 \;+\; NH_3 \longrightarrow CH_3\overset{\overset{\displaystyle NH}{\|}}{C}CH_3 \;+\; H_2O$$
(Ammonia)   (Unstable)

$$CH_3\overset{\overset{\displaystyle O}{\|}}{C}CH_3 \;+\; H_2NOH \longrightarrow CH_3\overset{\overset{\displaystyle NOH}{\|}}{C}CH_3 \;+\; H_2O$$
(Hydroxylamine)   (Oxime)

$$CH_3\overset{\overset{\displaystyle O}{\|}}{C}CH_3 \;+\; H_2NNH_2 \longrightarrow CH_3\overset{\overset{\displaystyle NNH_2}{\|}}{C}CH_3 \;+\; H_2O$$
(Hydrazine)   (Hydrazone)

$$CH_3\overset{\overset{\displaystyle O}{\|}}{C}CH_3 \;+\; H_2NNHCONH_2 \longrightarrow CH_3\overset{\overset{\displaystyle NNHCONH_2}{\|}}{C}CH_3 \;+\; H_2O$$
(Semicarbazide)   (Semicarbazone)

Figure 8.13

MCAT Expertise

Nothing new here: just more carbonyl carbons acting as electrophiles with different nucleophiles.

THE ALDOL CONDENSATION

The **aldol condensation** is another vital reaction for MCAT, and it basically follows the same nucleophilic addition mechanism to a carbonyl that was described in the reactions above (see Figure 8.14a). However, in this case, an aldehyde acts both as an electrophile (in its keto form) and a nucleophile (in its enol or enolate form). For example, when acetaldehyde (ethanal) is treated with a catalytic amount of base, an enolate ion is produced. The enolate is more nuclophilic than the enol because it is negatively charged. This nucleophilic enolate ion can react with the carbonyl group (an electrophile) of another acetaldehyde molecule. The key is that you have both species in the same flask; this is why you do not convert all of your aldehyde into an enolate. The product is 3-hydroxybutanal, which contains both alcohol and aldehyde functional groups. This type of compound is called an **aldol**, from **ald**ehyde and alco**hol**.

Key Concept

Finally, something new ... well, sort of. In the aldol condensation, it should be no surprise that the carbonyl carbon acts as an electrophile, but we also have the aldehyde acting as a nucleophile (in the form of an enolate ion)

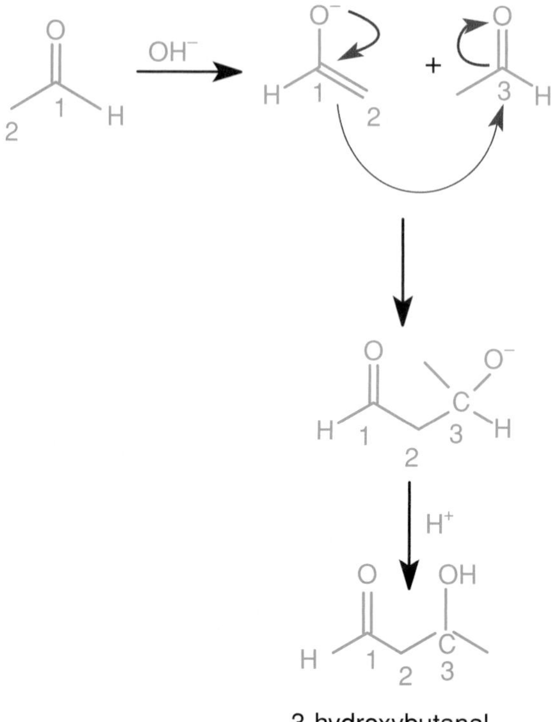

3-hydroxybutanal
(an aldol)

Figure 8.14a

With a strong base and higher temperatures, condensation occurs: We kick off a water molecule and form a double bond, producing an α, β-unsaturated aldehyde (see Figure 8.14b). This type of condensation reaction has become known as the **aldol condensation**.

Figure 8.14b

Aldol condensations are most useful if we only use one type of aldehyde or ketone. If there are multiple aldehydes or ketones, we can't easily control which will act as the nucleophile and which will act as the electrophile, and a mixture of products will result unless one of the molecules is missing an α-hydrogen (like benzaldehyde).

THE WITTIG REACTION

Here's one of the more elaborate reactions that you'll have to know for the MCAT, although it, too, follows the same principles we've already discussed. If you struggle with this one, simply remember that the **Wittig reaction** swaps out a C=O for a C=C.

More specifically, the Wittig reaction forms carbon–carbon double bonds by converting aldehydes and ketones into alkenes (see Figure 8.15). The first step involves the formation of a phosphonium salt from the S_N2 reaction of an alkyl halide with the nucleophile triphenylphosphine, $(C_6H_5)_3P$. This compound is simply a phosphorus atom that has three aromatic phenyl groups attached to it. With its lone pairs and the added electron density from the phenyl groups, the phosphorus makes a great nucleophile and readily attacks the partially positive carbon on the alkyl halide. This phosphonium salt is then deprotonated (losing the proton α to the phosphorus) with a strong base, yielding a neutral compound called an **ylide** (pronounced "ill-id") or **phosphorane**. The ylide form is a **zwitterion** (a molecule with both positive and negative charges), and the phosphorane form has a double bond between carbon and phosphorus. (The phosphorus atom may be drawn as pentavalent, because it can use the low-lying $3d$ atomic orbitals.)

> **Key Concept**
>
> The term *salt* refers to any ionic compound that contains enough cations and anions to be electrically neutral. In Organic Chemistry, this will usually be a one-to-one relationship.

> **Key Concept**
>
> The ylide can act as a nucleophile and attack the carbonyl.

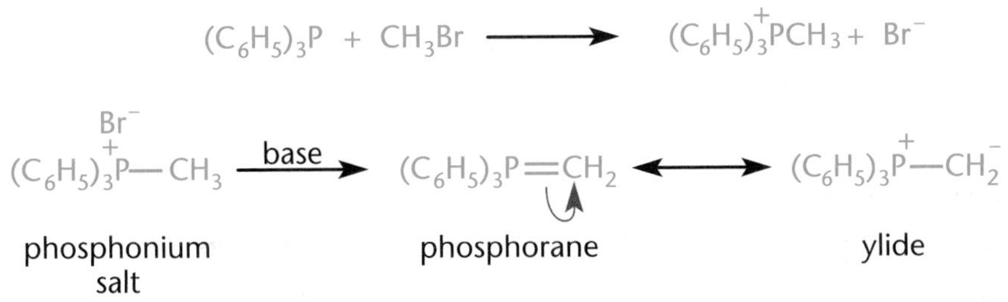

Figure 8.15

Notice that an ylide is a type of carbanion and, thus, has nucleophilic properties. When combined with an aldehyde or ketone, an ylide attacks the carbonyl carbon, giving an intermediate called a *betaine* (a specific kind of zwitterion), which forms a four-membered ring with an ionic bond between the oxygen and the phosphorus. This ringed intermediate is called an *oxaphosphetane,* and it decomposes to yield an alkene and triphenylphosphine oxide, as shown in Figure 8.16.

> **Key Concept**
>
> The Wittig reaction ultimately converts C=O to C=C (aldehydes/ketones to alkenes).

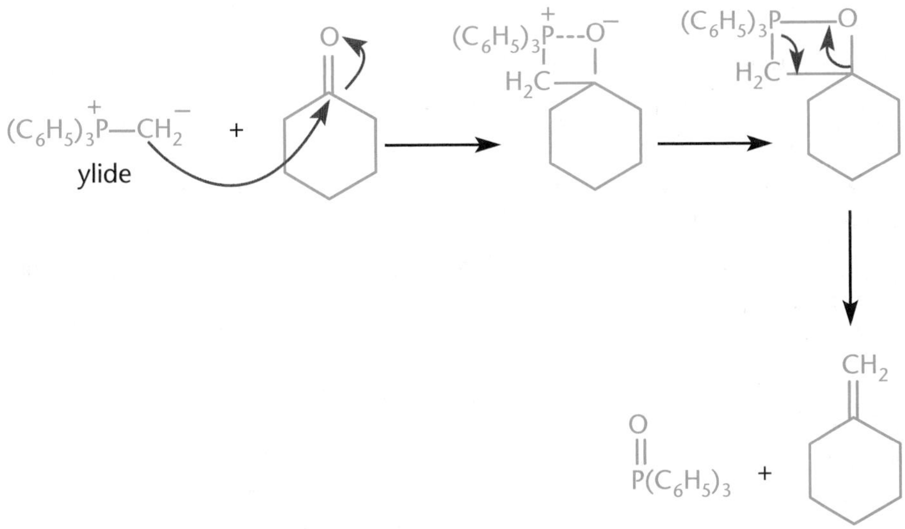

Figure 8.16

This decomposition reaction is driven by the strength of the phosphorus–oxygen bond that is formed.

OXIDATION AND REDUCTION

MCAT Expertise

As mentioned earlier, oxidation and reduction are important reactions of aldehydes and ketones, because aldehydes are midway between alcohols and carboxylic acids on the oxidation spectrum and ketones are maximally oxidized. Also, although knowledge of these mechanisms is not required for the MCAT, it should not be surprising that the carbonyl carbon acts as an electrophile.

Aldehydes occupy the middle of the oxidation–reduction spectrum; they are more oxidized than alcohols but less oxidized than carboxylic acids. Ketones, on the other hand, are as oxidized as secondary carbons can get.

Pretty much any oxidizing agent (except PCC) can oxidize aldehydes into carboxylic acids; some examples are $KMnO_4$, CrO_3, Ag_2O, and H_2O_2.

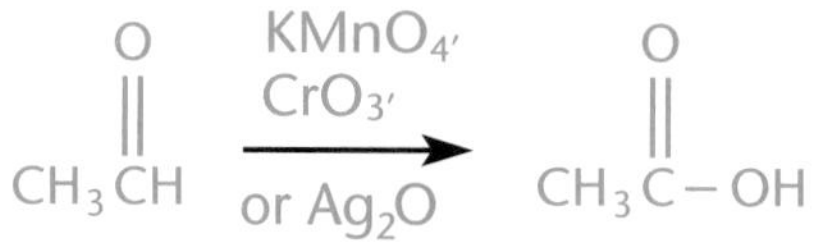

Figure 8.17

A number of different reagents will reduce aldehydes and ketones to alcohols. The most common ones seen on the MCAT, shown in Figure 8.18, are lithium aluminum hydride (LAH) and sodium borohydride ($NaBH_4$), which is often used when milder conditions are needed.

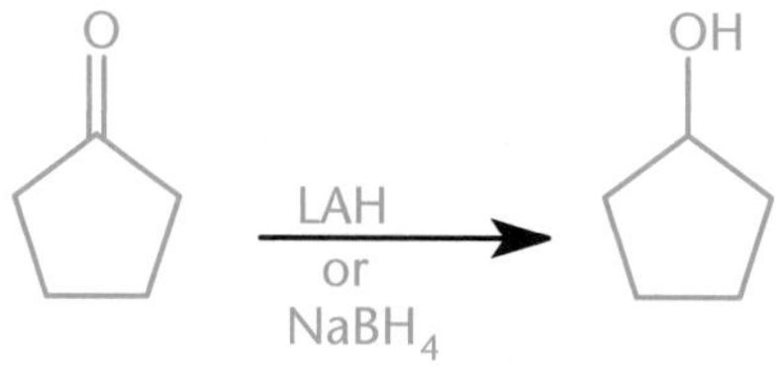

Figure 8.18

If we want to get more extreme, there are two ways to reduce aldehydes and ketones all the way to alkanes. In the **Wolff-Kishner reduction** (Figure 8.19), the carbonyl is first converted to hydrazone (we discussed this reaction earlier in this chapter, under the section on condensation reactions with ammonia derivatives). The hydrazone then releases molecular nitrogen (N_2) when it is heated with a base, forming an alkane. Note that the Wolff-Kishner reaction is useful only when the product is stable under basic conditions.

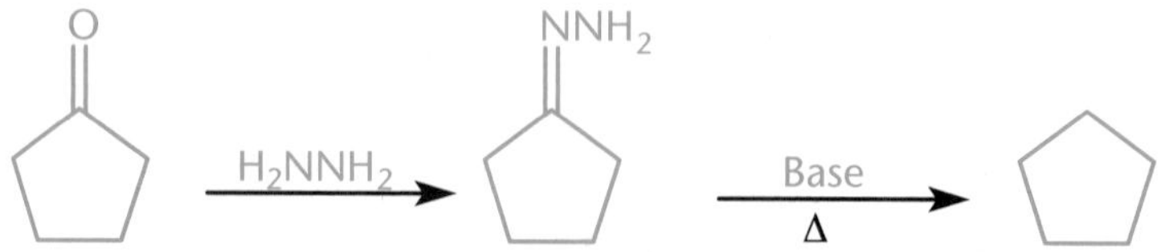

Figure 8.19

An alternative reduction that is not subject to this restriction is the **Clemmensen reduction** (Figure 8.20). In this reaction, an aldehyde or ketone is heated with amalgamated zinc in hydrochloric acid.

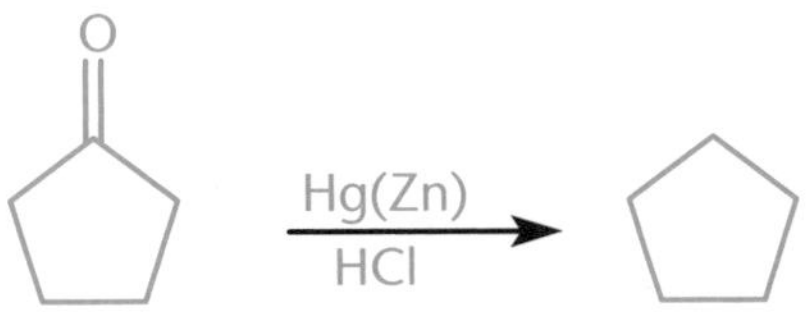

Figure 8.20

Key Concept

Both aldehydes and ketones can be fully reduced to alkanes by:

— Wolff-Kishner (H_2NNH_2, Base (KOH), Ethylene glycol (a high boiling solvent))

—Clemmensen [Hg(Zn), HCl]

Conclusion

We hope we have demonstrated in our review of aldehyde and ketone chemistry that the Organic Chemistry on the MCAT is going to be a lot different from that in your college courses. As the compounds we discuss become more and more reactive, it might feel as if the amount of information you need to learn is growing exponentially. It's true that we now have to be aware of several different synthesis routes and a lot more possible reactions. But remember that we don't need to memorize all the different reactions that take place; what we really need to do is understand the trends that govern every reaction. For instance, we learned that most of the reactions of aldehydes and ketones proceed through a mechanism in which a nucleophile attacks the carbonyl carbon. This electrophilicity and vulnerability to attack are hallmarks of the carbonyl group, as we'll see when we examine its role in other compounds, continuing in Chapter 10 with carboxylic acids.

CONCEPTS TO REMEMBER

☐ In a carbonyl, the carbon is partially positive, and the oxygen is partially negative.

☐ Aldehydes are terminal functional groups; ketones are midchain functional groups.

☐ Aldehydes can be synthesized from primary alcohols with PCC.

☐ Aldehydes can be oxidized to carboxylic acids or reduced to primary alcohols.

☐ Ketones cannot be further oxidized, but they can be reduced to secondary alcohols.

☐ The enol form is significant because it can act as a nucleophile, but it is not prevalent in solution.

☐ Many nucleophiles will add to the electropositive carbonyl carbon.

☐ Ammonia deriviatives often add in condensation reactions, removing water and forming a $C=N$.

☐ The Wittig reaction swaps out a $C=O$ for a $C=C$.

☐ The Wolf-Kishner reduction and the Clemmensen reduction reduce ketones or aldehydes to alkanes.

Practice Questions

1. 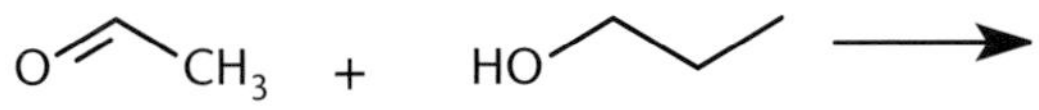 + ⟶

What is the product of the above reaction?

A.

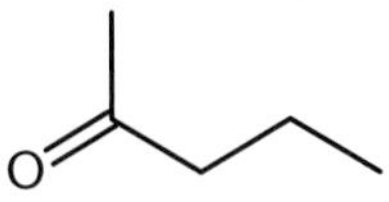

B.

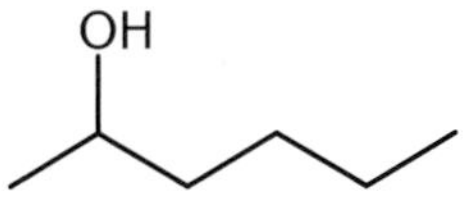

C.

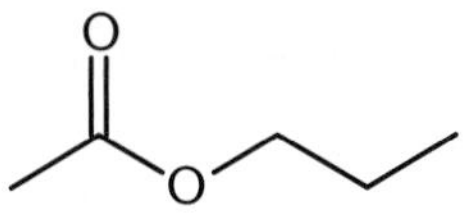

D.

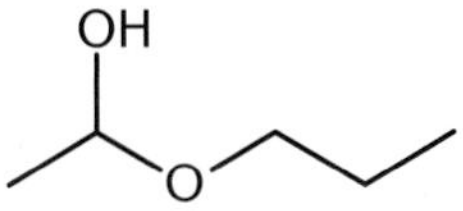

2. 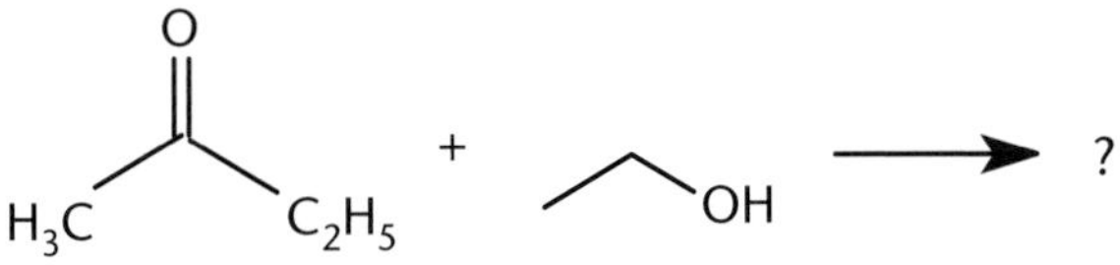 + ⟶ ?

What is the major product of the above reaction?

A. 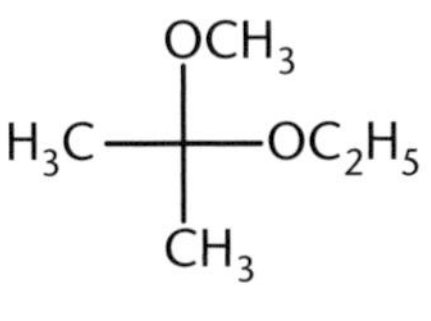 $H_3C-\overset{OCH_3}{\underset{CH_3}{\overset{|}{\underset{|}{C}}}}-OC_2H_5$

B.

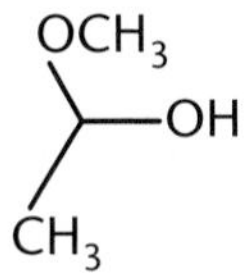

C. $H_3C-\overset{OH}{\underset{C_2H_5}{\overset{|}{\underset{|}{C}}}}-OC_2H_5$

D.

3. 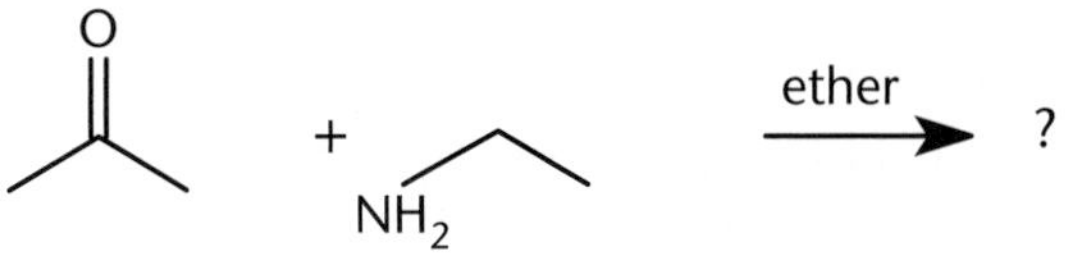 + $\xrightarrow{\text{ether}}$?

What is the product of the above reaction?

A. 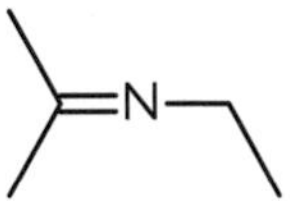   C.

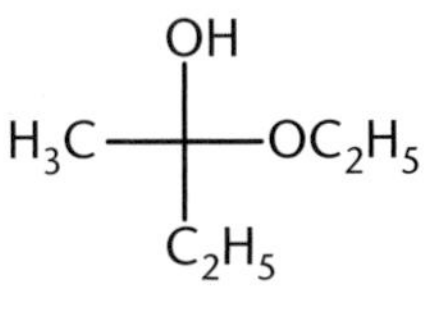

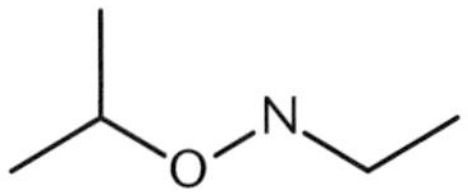

B. 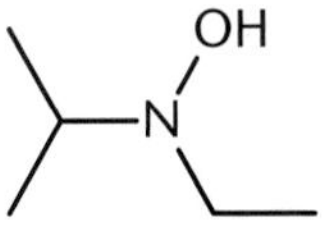   D.

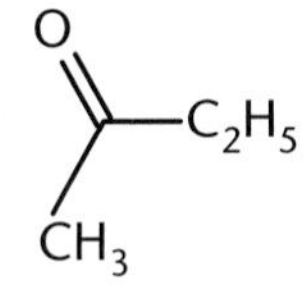

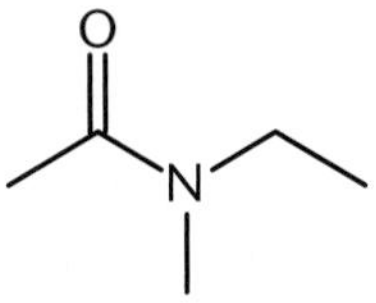

4. All of the following properties are responsible for the reactivity of the carbonyl bond in propanone EXCEPT the fact that

A. the carbonyl carbon is electrophilic.

B. the carbonyl oxygen is electron withdrawing.

C. a resonance structure of the compound places a positive charge on the carbonyl carbon.

D. the π electrons are mobile and are pulled toward the carbonyl carbon.

5. 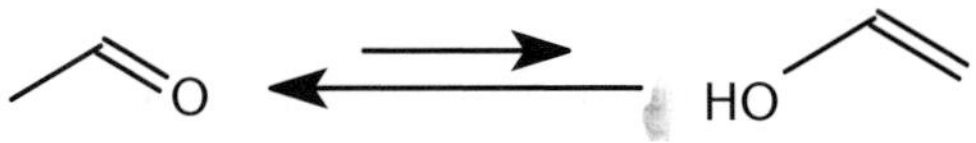 ⇌

The above reaction is an example of

A. esterification.

B. tautomerization.

C. elimination.

D. dehydration.

6.

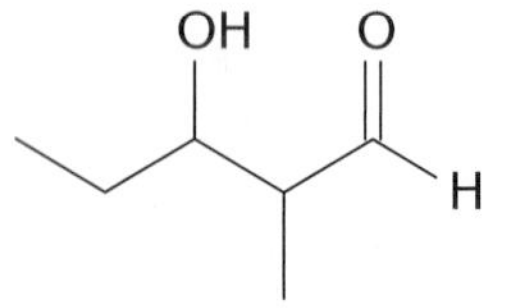

Which of the following reactions produces the above compound?

A. $CH_3CHO + CH_3CH_2CH_2CHO \rightarrow$
B. $CH_3COCH_3 + CH_3CH_2CH_2CHO \rightarrow$
C. $CH_3CH_2COCH_3 + CH_3CHO \rightarrow$
D. $CH_3CH_2CHO + CH_3CH_2CHO \rightarrow$

7.

What is the product of the above reaction?

A. C_3H_7OH
B. C_2H_5COOH
C. C_3H_7CHO
D. CH_3COOH

8. Heating an aldehyde with Zn in HCl produces

A. a ketone.
B. an alkane.
C. an alcohol.
D. a carboxylic acid.

9.

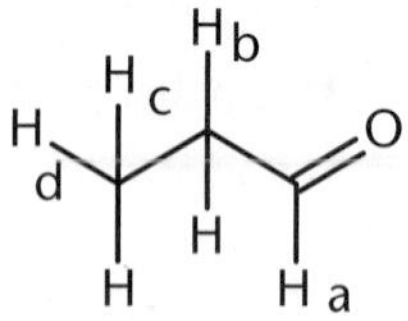

Which hydrogen atom in the above compound is the most acidic?

A. a
B. b
C. c
D. d

10.

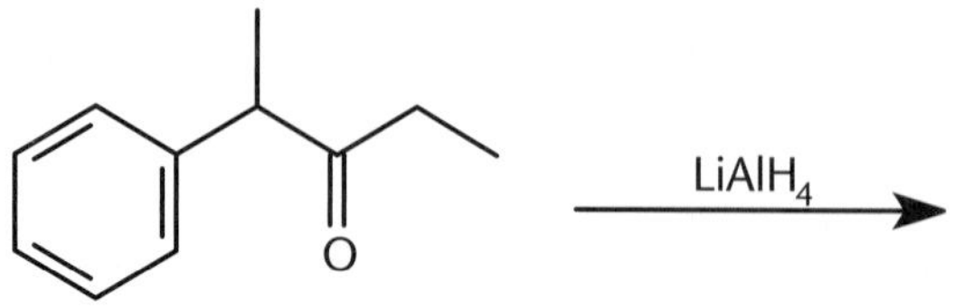

What product is obtained in the above reaction?

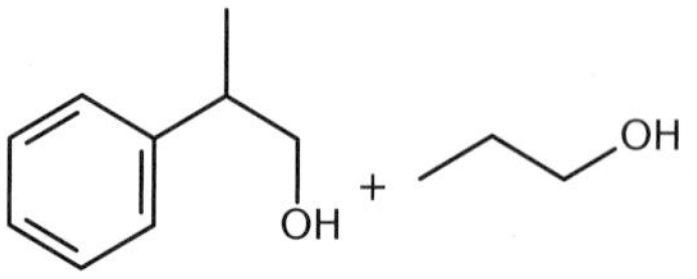

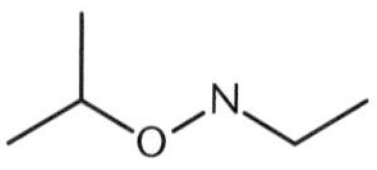

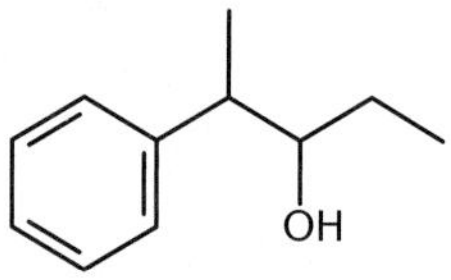

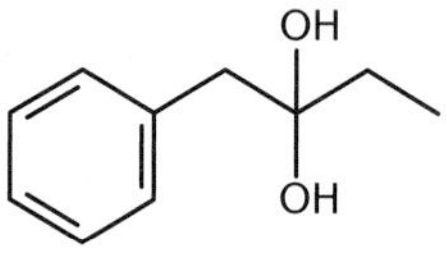

11. What is the product of the reaction between benzaldehyde and an excess of ethanol (C_2H_5OH) in the presence of anhydrous HCl?

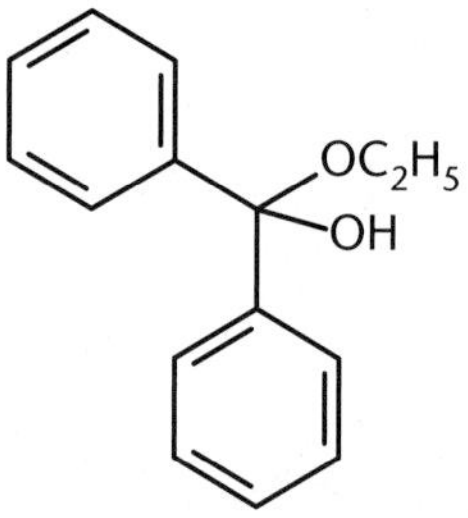

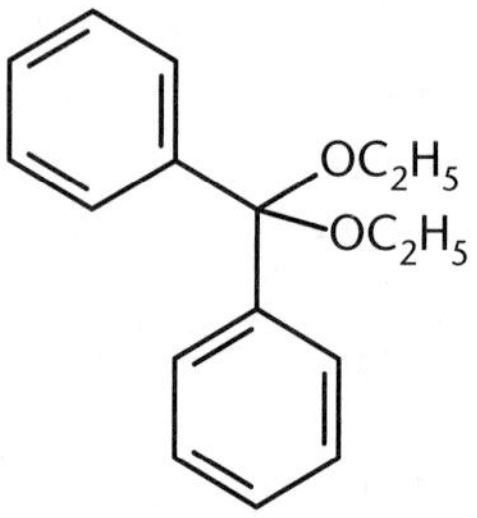

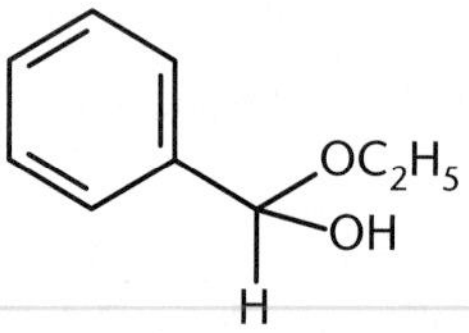

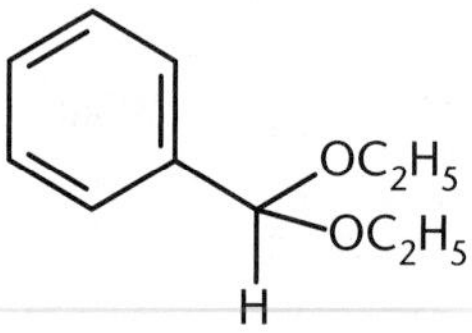

12. A student investigates the reactivity of carboxylic acid derivatives and aldehydes by reacting hydrazine (H_2N-NH_2) with benzaldehyde and benzoyl chloride (C_7H_5ClO). Which of the following statements is true about this reaction?

A. Both compounds undergo substitution reactions but arrive at different products.

B. Both compounds undergo elimination reactions but arrive at the same product.

C. Unlike benzaldehyde, benzoyl chloride undergoes an elimination reaction because chlorine is a good leaving group.

D. Unlike benzaldehyde, benzoyl chloride undergoes a substitution reaction because chlorine is a good leaving group.

13. Assuming a meticulously anhydrous environment, which of the following could be used to form 3-ethylhept-6-en-3-ol?

A.

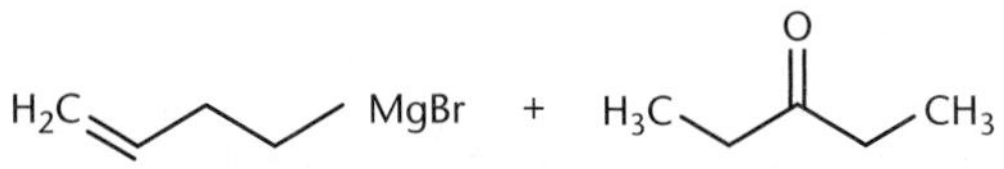

B.

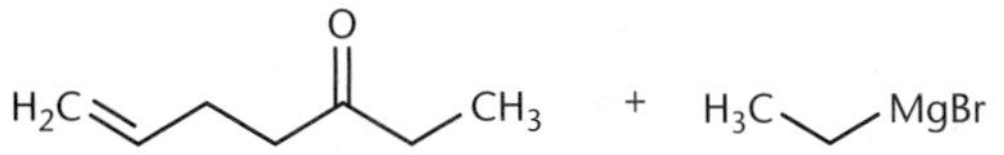

C.

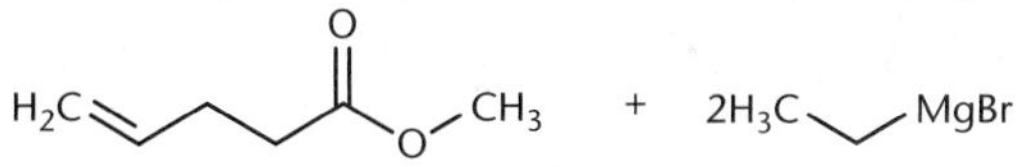

D. All of the above

Small Group Questions

1. Hemiacetals and hemiketals usually keep reacting to form acetals and ketals. Why is it difficult to isolate hemiacetals and hemiketals?

2. Why does the equilibrium between keto and enol tautomers lie far to the keto side?

Explanations to Practice Questions

1. D

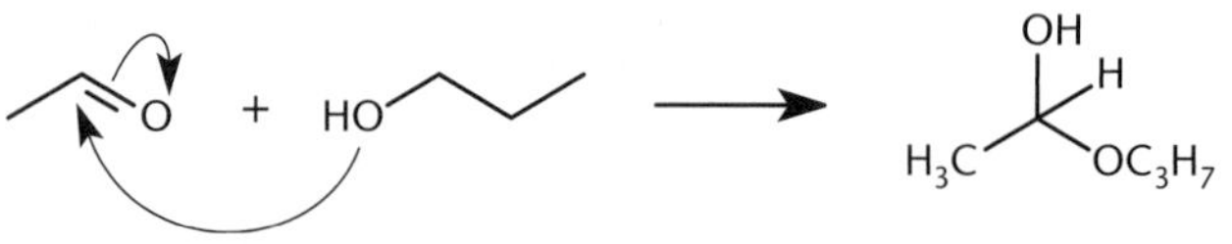

One mole of aldehyde reacts with one mole of alcohol via a nucleophilic addition reaction to form a product called a hemiacetal. In a hemiacetal, an –OH group, an –OR group, an H atom, and an –R group are attached to the same carbon atom.

2. C

The reaction between one mole of a ketone and one mole of an alcohol produces a compound analogous to a hemiacetal, called a hemiketal. This has an –OH group, an –OR group, and two –R groups attached to the same carbon atom. Of the given choices, only choice (C) represents a hemiketal. Choice (A) has two –OR groups and two –R groups attached to the same carbon atom; this compound is called a ketal. Choice (B) is a hemiacetal, with an –OH group, an –OR group, an H atom, and an –R group attached to the same carbon atom. Choice (D) is a ketone. The correct choice, therefore, is (C). Note that a hemiketal is a very unstable compound; it reacts rapidly with a second mole of alcohol to form a ketal.

3. A

Aldehydes and ketones react with ammonia and primary amines to form imines (also called Schiff bases), compounds with a double bond between carbon and nitrogen.

$$(CH_3)_2C=O + H_2N–C_2H_5 \rightarrow (CH_3)_2C=NCH_2CH_3 + H_2O$$

The correct choice is (A).

4. D

The reactivity of the carbonyl bond in propanone, and in aldehydes and ketones in general, can be attributed to the difference in electronegativity between the carbon and oxygen atoms. The more electronegative oxygen atom attracts the bonding electrons toward itself and is, therefore, electron withdrawing. Thus, the carbonyl carbon is electrophilic, and the carbonyl oxygen is nucleophilic. Choices (A) and (B) are true statements and are therefore incorrect answer choices (remember, this is an EXCEPT question). The resonance structure of propanone does have a positive charge on the carbon atom, although this structure is not stable and would not contribute much to the resonance hybrid. Nevertheless, it is a possible resonance structure and cannot be discounted, so choice (C) is incorrect. The π electrons of the carbonyl bond are pulled toward the more electronegative element, which is oxygen, not carbon. D is an incorrect statement, which makes it the correct answer for this EXCEPT question.

5. B

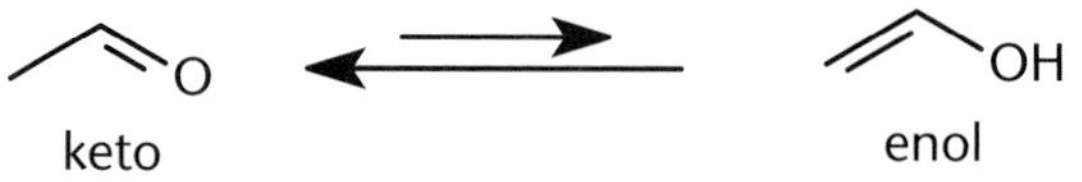

Tautomerization, choice (B), is the interconversion of keto and enol forms of a compound. The above reaction involves an interconversion of the keto and enol forms of ethanal. Note that equilibrium lies to the left in the above reaction, because the keto form is more stable. Esterification, choice (A), is the formation of esters from carboxylic acids and alcohols. Elimination, choice (C), is a reaction in which a part of a reactant is lost and a multiple bond is introduced. Dehydration, choice (D), is one in which a molecule of water is eliminated.

6. D

The reaction is an example of aldol condensation. In the presence of a base, the α-H is abstracted from an aldehyde, forming an enolate ion, $CH_3CH–CHO$. This enolate ion then attacks the carbonyl groups of the other aldehyde molecule, CH_3CH_2CHO, forming the above aldol. The correct choice is (D).

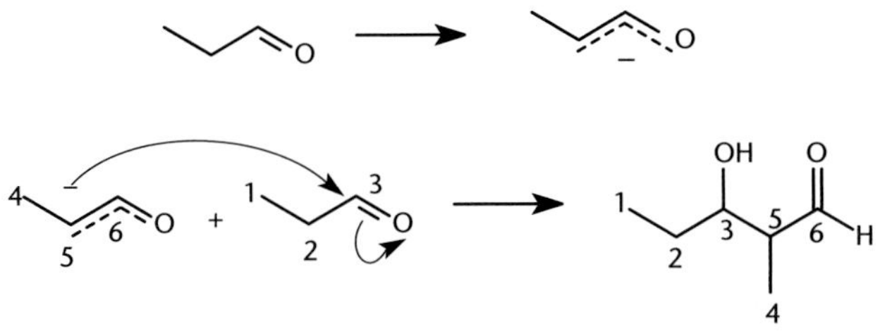

7. B

Aldehydes are easily oxidized to the corresponding carboxylic acids by $KMnO_4$. The –CHO group is converted to –COOH. In this reaction, therefore, C_2H_5CHO is oxidized to C_2H_5COOH, which is choice (B). In choice (A), the aldehyde has been reduced to an alcohol. In choice (C), a –CH_2 group has been added. Thus, choices (A) and (C) are incorrect. In choice (D), the –CHO group has been oxidized to –COOH, but a –CH_2 group has been removed, so choice (D) is incorrect.

8. B

Heating an aldehyde or a ketone with amalgamated Zn/HCl converts it to the corresponding alkane; this reaction is called the Clemmensen reduction. Note that aldehydes and ketones can also be converted to alkanes under basic conditions by reaction with hydrazine (the Wolff-Kishner reduction).

9. B

The hydrogen alpha to the carbonyl group is the most acidic, because the resultant carbanion is resonance-stabilized:

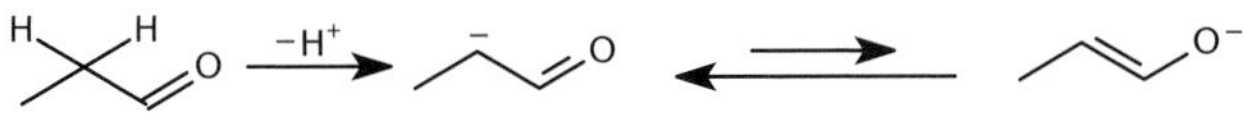

10. B

$LiAlH_4$ reduces carboxylic acids, esters, and aldehydes to primary alcohols and ketones to secondary alcohols. In this reaction, therefore, the ketone is converted to a secondary alcohol. Thus, the correct answer is choice (B), $C_6H_5CH(CH_3)CHOHCH_2CH_3$.

11. D

This molecule corresponds to an acetal: two alkoxyl functionalities bonded to the same carbon. This question states that an excess of ethanol is present, so benzaldehyde will first be converted to a hemiacetal, having an alkoxyl and a hydroxyl functionality bonded to the same carbon, then an acetal. Choices (A) and (B) are wrong because they show the presence of two benzene rings in the final product. Choice (C) shows a hemiacetal, which is not the final product. Because the question indicates an excess of ethanol, we should expect a second reaction between the hemiacetal and ethanol.

12. D

Hydrazine is nucleophilic and attacks the carbonyl carbon of both molecules, forming a negatively charged oxide intermediate. However, for benzoyl chloride, the C=O double bond is re-formed, and chloride is displaced because it is a good leaving group. Therefore, answer (D) is correct since this is an example of a substitution reaction. Benzaldehyde, on the other hand, forms a hydrazone with hydrazine via nucleophilic addition and condensation (the carbonyl oxygen atom leaves as water). Answer (A) is incorrect because benzaldehyde and benzoyl chloride undergo different reactions, answer (B) is incorrect because the final products are clearly different, and answer (C) is incorrect because the reaction types have been transposed.

13. D

The structure of 3-ethylhept-6-en-3-ol is shown below:

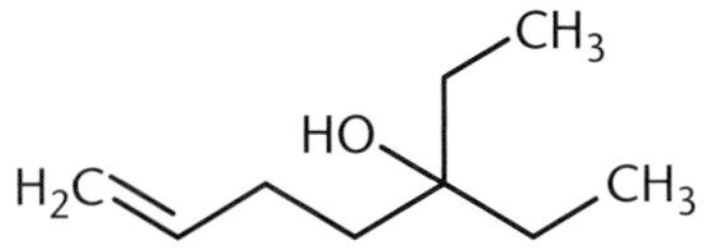

An anhydrous environment implies that Grignard reagents are being used. Because various Grignard reagents are present among the choices, all of them are feasible. Answers (A) and (B) both produce the product required; the only difference is the initial Grignard reagent. Answer (C) also produces the same product, because Grignard reagents will alkylate esters to completion, forming tertiary alcohols. Since answers (A), (B), and (C) all give 3-ethylhept-6-en-3-ol, answer (D) is correct.

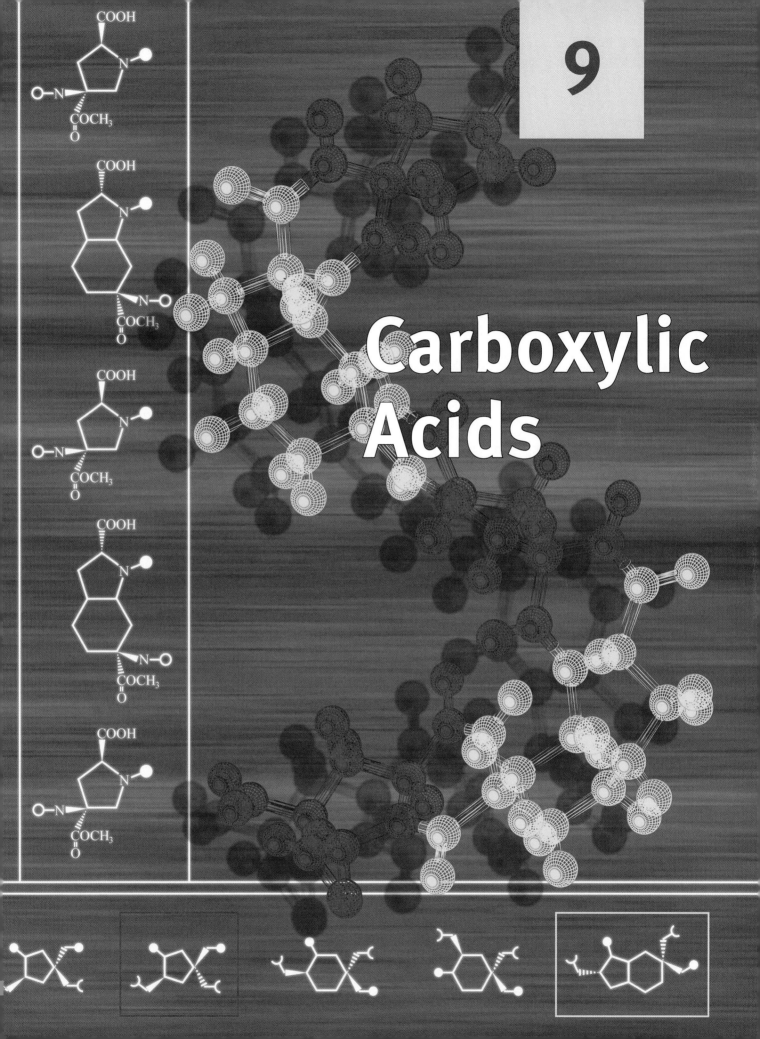

9

Carboxylic Acids

Our exploration of carbonyl compounds brings us to one of the most exciting forms of the carbonyl, the **carboxyl group** (a carbonyl attached to a hydroxyl group). Your first association with carboxylic acids is probably acetic acid, the key ingredient of vinegar. Like acetaldehyde (the hangover-causing nuisance discussed in Chapter 8), acetic acid is derived from ethanol via fermentation. Any alcoholic substance can be transformed into vinegar; all you need is some bacteria and a whole lot of time. The functions and uses of carboxylic acids extend far beyond the cleaning and culinary roles of vinegar. Carboxylic acids are found in soaps, oils, preservatives, skin care products, clothing, and, most important, amino acids (more to come in Chapter 15).

So what makes carboxylic acids so interesting and versatile? First, they're acids, so they like to give away protons. Second, when a carboxylic acid does give away a proton, the leftover electrons are resonated between two oxygen atoms, making the molecule more likely to give off the proton in the first place (pK_a = 3–6). Compare this with alcohols (with only one oxygen), which have pK_a of about 16. Third, a carboxylic acid has a hydrogen bond donor and acceptor in the same functional group, leading to large intermolecular forces and high boiling points. Fourth, the carbonyl carbon is electropositive, so it makes a great electrophile. Fifth, carboxylic acids, a terminal functional group, have the highest priority in nomenclature, so we're talking about the top dog here. Sixth and most important, carboxylic acids occur widely in nature and are synthesized by all living organisms, including you.

MCAT Expertise

Carboxylic acids have an important role in biology and can also be used to flavor your food (vinegar is acetic acid). Carboxylic acids and their derivatives (covered in the next chapter) are doubly important to the premed, because they are sure to show up on the MCAT!

Nomenclature ★★★★★☆

In the IUPAC system of nomenclature, carboxylic acids have the highest priority, so they are always named by adding the suffix **–oic acid** to the alkyl root. This also means that the chain is always numbered so that the carboxyl group receives the lowest possible number. Additional substituents are named in the usual fashion. Figure 9.1 shows two examples.

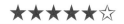

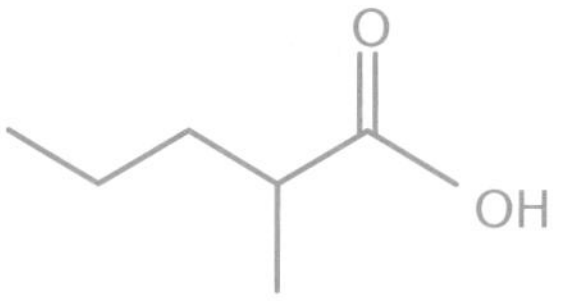

2-methylpentanoic acid

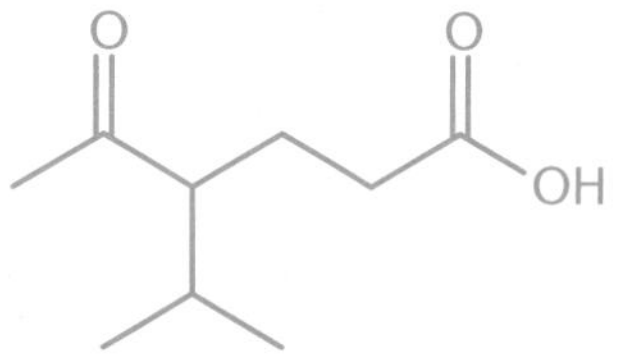

4-isopropyl-5-oxohexanoic acid

Figure 9.1

Key Concept

Besides acidity, the other special property of carboxylic acids that you should expect (especially after the last chapter) is an electrophilic carbonyl carbon.

Carboxylic acids were among the first organic compounds discovered; thus, their original names continue to be used today in the common system of nomenclature. For example, formic acid (from Latin *formica*, meaning "ant") was found in the

MCAT Expertise

We are using the same common name prefixes as before: *form*– for one carbon and *acet*– for two.

venom of biting ants and also in stinging nettles. Butyric acid (from Latin *butyrum*, meaning "butter") was found in rancid butter. Figure 9.2 lists the common and IUPAC names of the first three carboxylic acids.

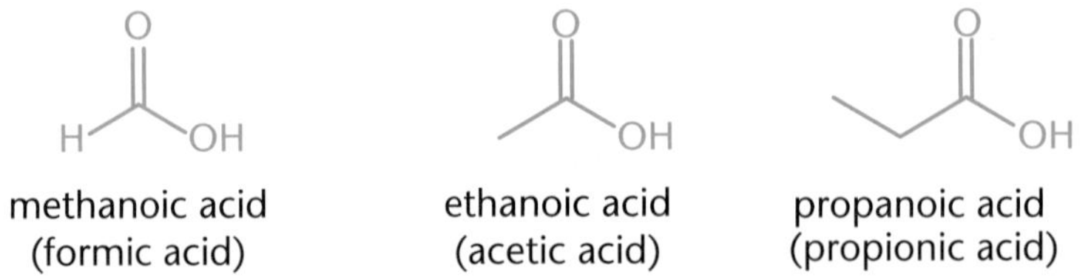

methanoic acid
(formic acid)

ethanoic acid
(acetic acid)

propanoic acid
(propionic acid)

Figure 9.2

Cyclic carboxylic acids are usually named as cycloalkane carboxylic acids. The carbon atom to which the carboxyl group is attached is numbered 1, and all other groups are given the lowest possible numbers. Salts of carboxylic acids are named beginning with the cation, followed by the name of the acid with the ending **–ate** replacing **–ic acid**. Typical examples are shown in Figure 9.3.

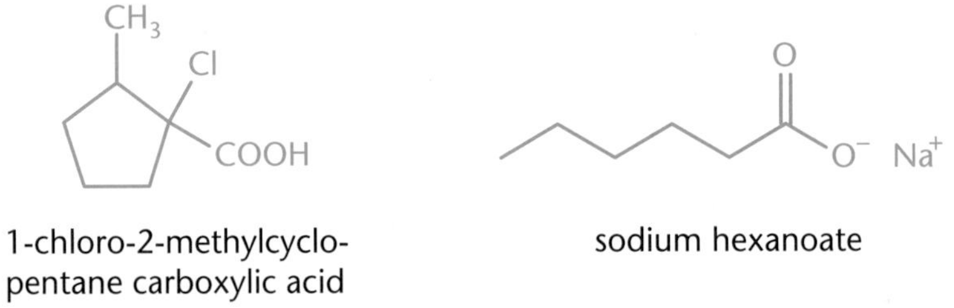

1-chloro-2-methylcyclo-
pentane carboxylic acid

sodium hexanoate

Figure 9.3

Another complication we can encounter on the MCAT is molecules with two carboxyl groups on the same molecule. Dicarboxylic acids are common in biological systems, and you are likely to see a few on Test Day. The first six straight-chain terminal dicarboxylic acids are oxalic (2C), malonic (3C), succinic (4C), glutaric (5C), adipic (6C), and pimelic (7C) acids. Their IUPAC names are ethanedioic acid, propanedioic acid, butanedioic acid, pentanedioic acid, hexanedioic acid, and heptanedioic acid.

Physical Properties ★★★★★★

Key Concept

Carboxylic acids are polar and can form hydrogen bonds. Their acidity is due to resonance stabilization and can be enhanced by adding electronegative groups or other potential resonance structures.

HYDROGEN BONDING

Carboxylic acids are polar and form hydrogen bonds with each other. Not only can carboxylic acids hydrogen bond, they can hydrogen bond *really* well, because there are two different points that can participate in hydrogen bonding. As a result, carboxylic acids form dimers: pairs of molecules connected by two hydrogen bonds.

Multiple hydrogen bonds elevate the boiling and melting points of carboxylic acids even higher than those of the corresponding alcohols. As usual, the boiling points also increase with increasing molecular weight.

ACIDITY

As we mentioned before, the acidity of carboxylic acids is due to the resonance stabilization of the carboxylate anion (the conjugate base). When the hydroxyl proton dissociates from the acid, the negative charge left on the carboxylate group is delocalized between the two oxygen atoms (see Figure 9.4). The more stable the conjugate base is, the more likely the proton is to leave, and thus, the stronger the acid.

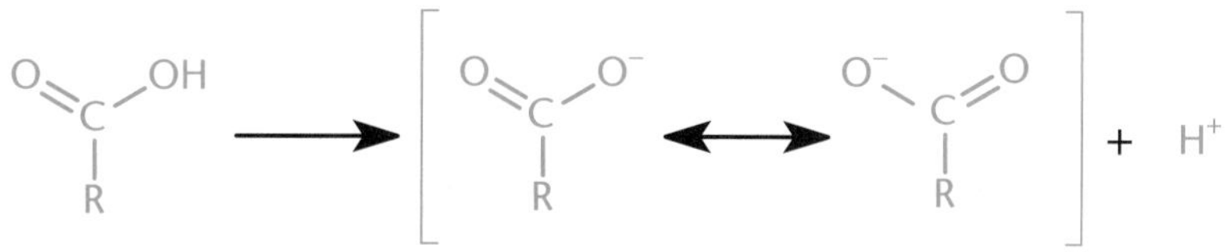

Figure 9.4

Substituents on carbon atoms near a carboxyl group will influence its acidity. Electron-withdrawing groups, such as –Cl or –NO$_2$, further absorb the negative charge and increase acidity. Electron-donating groups, such as –NH$_2$ or –OCH$_3$, donate additional electron density and destabilize the negative charge, making the compound less acidic. The closer the substituent groups are to the carboxyl group, the greater the effect will be.

In dicarboxylic acids, one –COOH group (which is electron withdrawing owing to the partial positive charge on carbon) influences the other, making the compound *more* acidic than the analogous monocarboxylic acid. The catch here is that once the proton leaves, and the carboxylate anion has formed, it will make the second carboxyl group *less* acidic. Think about it: If the second group were deprotonated, it would create a doubly charged species in which the two negative charges repel each other. Because this is unfavorable, the second proton is even less acidic than the alpha proton of a monocarboxylic acid.

Beta-dicarboxylic acids are notable for the high acidity of the α-hydrogens located on the carbon between the two carboxyl groups (pK$_a$ ~ 10). Loss of this acidic hydrogen atom produces a carbanion, which is stabilized by the electron-withdrawing effect of *two* carboxyl groups (see Figure 9.5).

Key Concept

Other ways to stabilize the negative charge (and thus increase acidity) are

- electron-withdrawing groups (e.g., halides) and
- groups that allow more resonance stabilization (e.g., benzyl or allyl substituents).

The more of these groups that exist, and the closer they are to the acid, the stronger the acid is.

Bridge

This is just another example of what we discussed in Chapter 8 with 1,3-dicarbonyls.

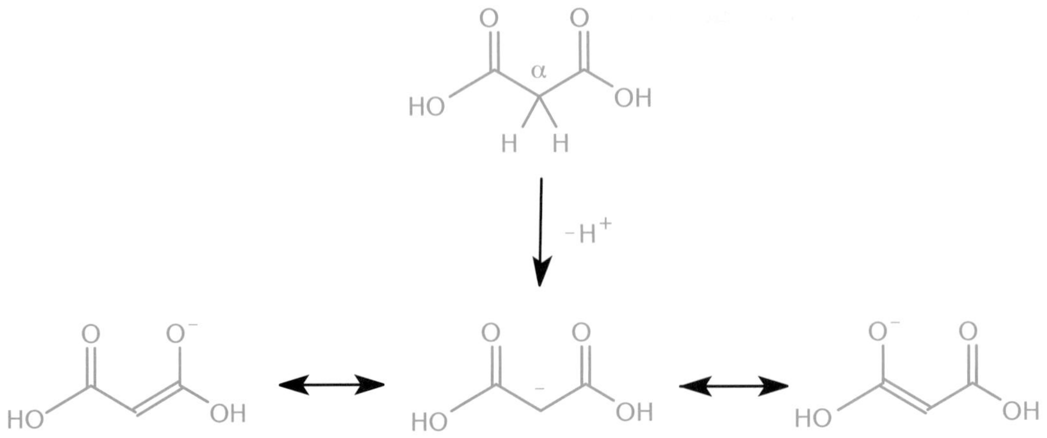

Figure 9.5

This acidity also applies to the α-hydrogens of β-ketoacids and other molecules that share this 1,3-dicarbonyl structure (see Figure 9.6).

Real World

These β-ketoacids will come up again in medical school when you are studying diabetic ketoacidosis, but let's leave that to the future, because only the significant acidity of their α-hydrogen will be tested on the MCAT.

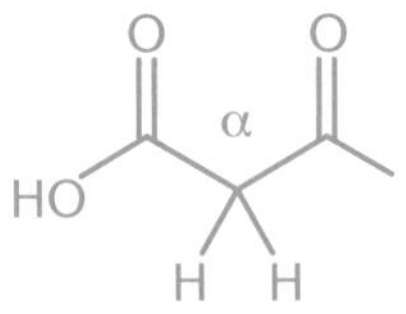

Figure 9.6

Synthesis ★★★★★☆

Mnemonic

Carb*oxy*lic acids are the most *oxi*dized.

OXIDATION REACTIONS

Carboxylic acids can be prepared via oxidation of aldehydes, primary alcohols, and certain alkylbenzenes. The oxidant is usually potassium permanganate, $KMnO_4$, as shown in Figure 9.7, but several other oxidizing agents we've mentioned will work as well. Remember that secondary and tertiary alcohols cannot be oxidized to carboxylic acids because of valence limitations.

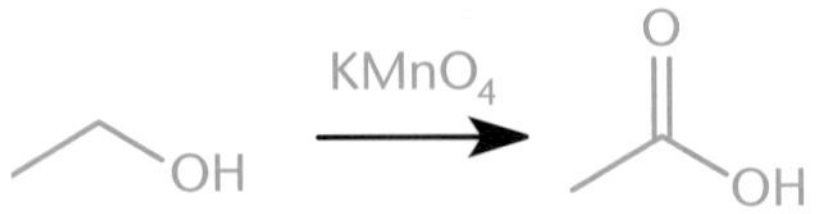

Figure 9.7

CARBOXYLATION OF ORGANOMETALLIC REAGENTS

Organometallic reagents, such as Grignard reagents, react with carbon dioxide (CO_2) to form carboxylic acids (see Figure 9.8). This reaction is useful for the conversion of tertiary alkyl halides into carboxylic acids, which, as we just mentioned, cannot be accomplished through other methods. Note that this reaction adds one carbon atom to the chain (because we are adding the CO_2 and not just oxidizing a carbon already on the molecule).

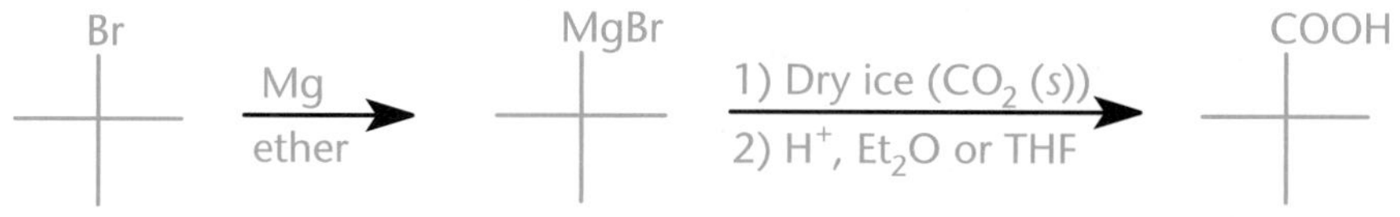

> **Key Concept**
>
> In the second reaction, the nucleophile is essentially a carbanion that is coordinated with a positively charged magnesium, and the electrophile is the carbon of the CO_2 (which is similar to any other carbonyl or carboxylic carbon).

Br — $\xrightarrow[\text{ether}]{\text{Mg}}$ — MgBr — $\xrightarrow[\text{2) H}^+\text{, Et}_2\text{O or THF}]{\text{1) Dry ice (CO}_2\text{ (s))}}$ — COOH

Figure 9.8

HYDROLYSIS OF NITRILES

Nitriles, also called cyanides, are compounds containing the functional group $-C\equiv N$. The cyanide anion ($-C\equiv N$) carries the negative charge on the carbon atom, making it a great nucleophile but not a great base. It will displace primary and secondary halides in typical S_N2 fashion. Nitriles can then be hydrolyzed under either acidic or basic conditions, producing carboxylic acids and ammonia (or ammonium salts), as shown in Figure 9.9. Note that all carboxylic acid derivatives may be hydrolyzed to their parent carboxylic acid.

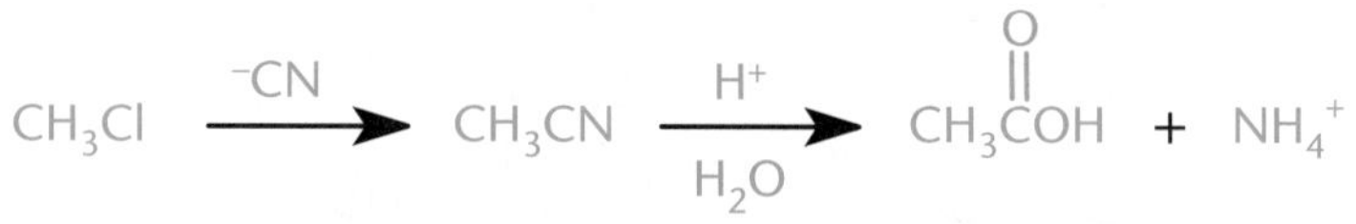

$$CH_3Cl \xrightarrow{^-CN} CH_3CN \xrightarrow[H_2O]{H^+} CH_3\overset{\displaystyle O}{\overset{\displaystyle \|}{C}}OH + NH_4^+$$

Figure 9.9

This reaction allows for the conversion of alkyl halides into carboxylic acids. As in the carboxylation reaction, an additional carbon is introduced into the chain. For instance, if you wanted to synthesize acetic acid, a possible starting material would be methyl chloride (as is shown in Figure 9.9).

Reactions ★★★★★★

SOAP FORMATION

When long-chain carboxylic acids react with sodium or potassium hydroxide, they form salts. This can be done in practice by mixing fat (triglycerides: three carboxylic acids

MCAT Expertise

RCOOH + NaOH

RCOO⁻Na⁺
(a soap)
+
H₂O

connected by a glycerol) with lye (sodium hydroxide). These salts (which we call soaps) are useful, because they can solvate nonpolar organic compounds in aqueous solutions since they possess both a nonpolar tail and a polar carboxylate head (see Figure 9.10).

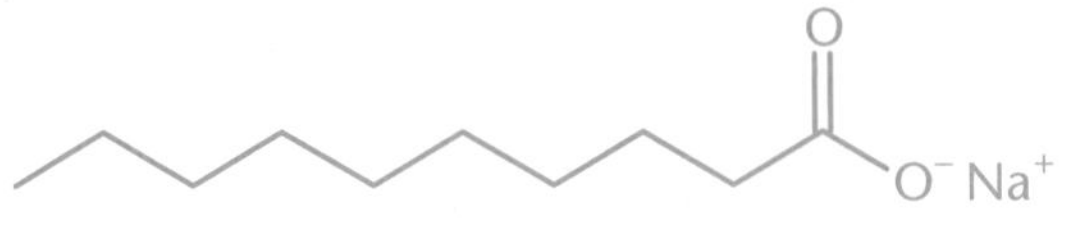

nonpolar tail   polar head

Figure 9.10

When placed in aqueous solution, soap molecules arrange themselves into spherical structures called **micelles**. The polar heads face outward, where they can be solubilized by water, and the nonpolar hydrocarbon chains are oriented toward the inside of the sphere, protected from the solvent. Nonpolar molecules, such as grease, can dissolve in the hydrocarbon interior of the spherical micelle, whereas the micelle as a whole is hydrophilic owing to its polar shell. Thus, when you wash your hands, the soap molecules arrange themselves in a micelle around nonpolar dirt and grease, and the whole micelle dissolves in water and rinses off.

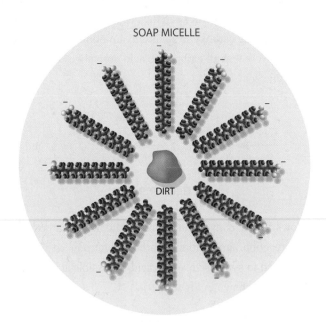

Figure 9.11

NUCLEOPHILIC ACYL SUBSTITUTION

Many of the reactions in which carboxylic acids (and their derivatives) participate proceed via a single mechanism: nucleophilic acyl *substitution*. This mechanism is similar to nucleophilic *addition* to a carbonyl, which we went over in the preceding

Real World

In the small intestine, consumed fat is solubilized in micelles, not with detergent but with bile salts, which have a structure similar to soaps—hydrophobic tail and hydrophilic head.

chapter. The key difference: Nucleophilic substitution concludes with re-formation of the C=O double bond and elimination of a leaving group (see Figure 9.12).

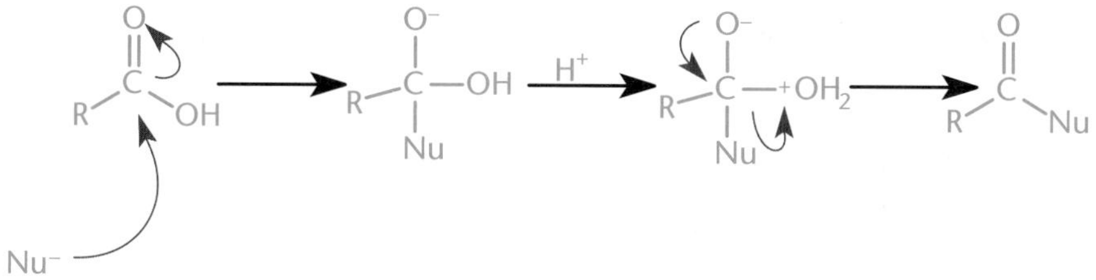

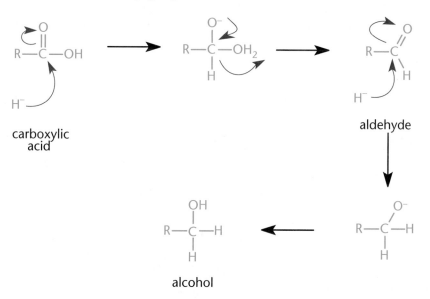

Figure 9.12

Key Concept

Carboxylic acids and esters can only be reduced by $LiAlH_4$ and not the less reactive $NaBH_4$.

Reduction

We know by now that carboxylic acids occupy the most oxidized end of the oxidation–reduction continuum. That means that they can't be further oxidized. However, carboxylic acids can definitely be reduced. Lithium aluminum hydride (LAH) reduces carboxylic acids to their corresponding alcohols (see Figure 9.13). Aldehyde intermediates may be formed in the course of the reaction, but they, too, will be reduced to the alcohol. The reaction occurs by nucleophilic addition of hydride to the carbonyl group.

Figure 9.13

Ester Formation

Esters, named after your great aunt, twice removed (just kidding, that's Great Aunt Esther), are a kind of hybrid between a carboxylic acid and an ether. To make esters, we react carboxylic acids with alcohols under acidic conditions. This is a condensation reaction, so water is a side product.

Key Concept

Protonating the C=O makes the C even more ripe for nucleophilic attack.

In an acidic solution, the O on the C=O can be protonated. This enhances the polarity of the bond, putting more positive charge on the C and making it *even more* susceptible to nucleophilic attack. This condensation reaction occurs most rapidly with primary alcohols.

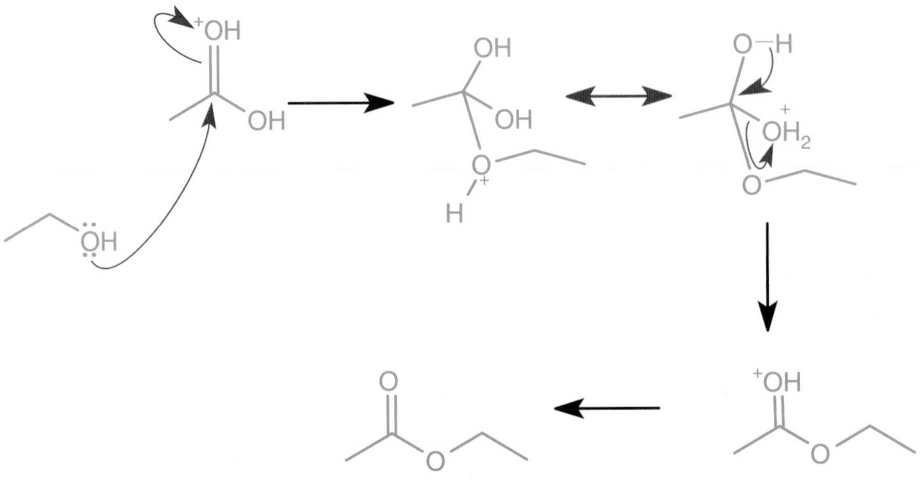

Figure 9.14

Esters are named in the same manner as salts of carboxylic acids. For example, the ester shown in the reaction in Figure 9.14 has the common name *ethyl acetate,* or the IUPAC name *ethyl ethanoate*.

Key Concept

Acid chlorides are among the highest-energy (least stable and most reactive) members of the carbonyl family.

Acyl Halide Formation

Acyl halides, also called acid halides, are compounds with carbonyl groups bonded to halides. Several reagents can convert carboxylic acids into acyl halides, but **thionyl chloride**, $SOCl_2$, is the one you are most likely to see on Test Day (see Figure 9.15).

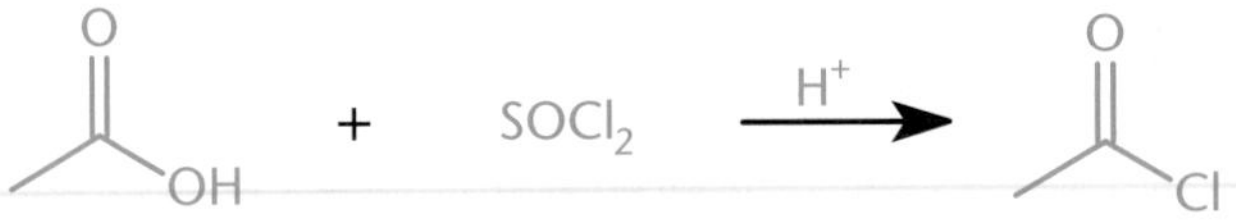

Figure 9.15

Real World

Decarboxylation is common in biochemical pathways in the body, such as the Krebs cycle.

These compounds are important because acid chlorides are reactive. The greater electron-withdrawing power of the $-Cl^-$ makes the carbonyl carbon even more susceptible to nucleophilic attack than the carbonyl carbon of a carboxylic acid. As such, acid chlorides are frequently used as intermediates in the conversion of carboxylic acids to esters and amides. We'll introduce these reactions in Chapter 10.

DECARBOXYLATION

Carboxylic acids can undergo **decarboxylation** reactions, which mean exactly what it sounds like—losing a carbon. Whenever we want to get rid of a carbon on the MCAT, it will be lost in the form of carbon dioxide.

1,3-Dicarboxylic acids and other β-keto acids may spontaneously decarboxylate when heated. Under these conditions, the carboxyl group is lost and replaced with hydrogen. Because both electrophile and nucleophile are in the same molecule, the reaction proceeds through a six-membered ring transition state (as seen in Figure 9.16). The enol that is initially formed from the destruction of the ring tautomerizes to the more stable keto form.

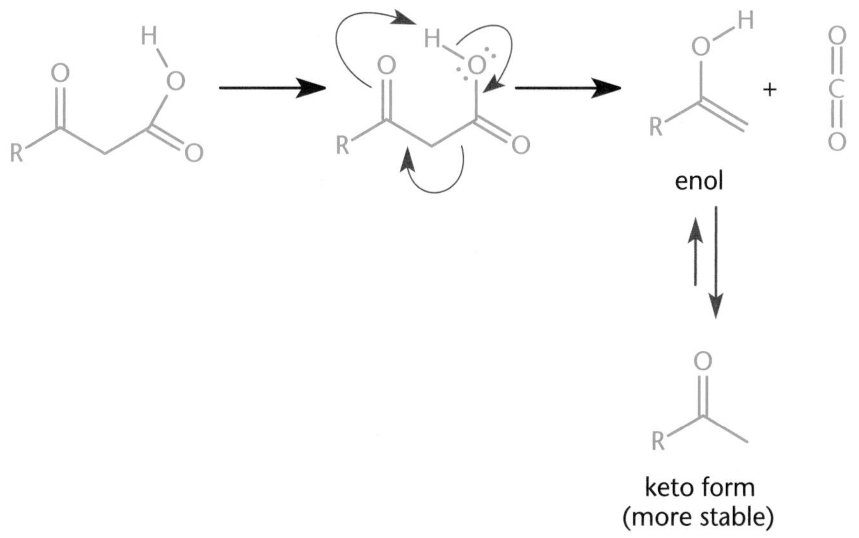

enol

keto form
(more stable)

Figure 9.16

Conclusion

We hope that you have been impressed with the various exciting aspects of carboxylic acids, because we sure were. In fact, we find them *so* exciting that the next chapter will be devoted to the different derivatives that can be formed from carboxylic acids. Acids are an important concept on the MCAT; they can be tested in either General Chemistry or Organic Chemistry. The underlying concept in both subjects is the same: The more stable the conjugate base is, the more likely it is that the proton will leave. This stability is determined by three factors: periodic trends (electronegativity and, thus, induction), size of the anion (HF is a weaker acid than HI), and resonance. Understanding inductive and resonance effects is a major key to success on Test Day.

CONCEPTS TO REMEMBER

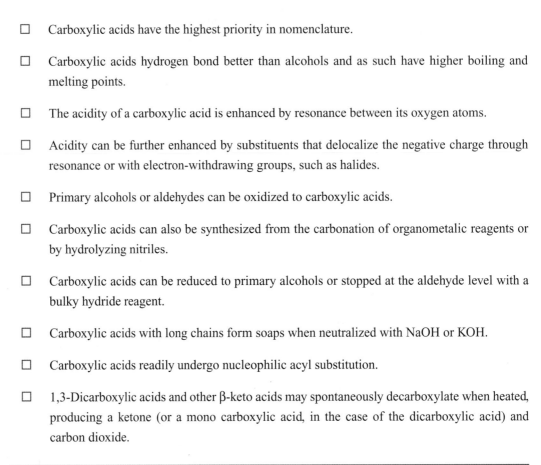

☐ Carboxylic acids have the highest priority in nomenclature.

☐ Carboxylic acids hydrogen bond better than alcohols and as such have higher boiling and melting points.

☐ The acidity of a carboxylic acid is enhanced by resonance between its oxygen atoms.

☐ Acidity can be further enhanced by substituents that delocalize the negative charge through resonance or with electron-withdrawing groups, such as halides.

☐ Primary alcohols or aldehydes can be oxidized to carboxylic acids.

☐ Carboxylic acids can also be synthesized from the carbonation of organometalic reagents or by hydrolyzing nitriles.

☐ Carboxylic acids can be reduced to primary alcohols or stopped at the aldehyde level with a bulky hydride reagent.

☐ Carboxylic acids with long chains form soaps when neutralized with NaOH or KOH.

☐ Carboxylic acids readily undergo nucleophilic acyl substitution.

☐ 1,3-Dicarboxylic acids and other β-keto acids may spontaneously decarboxylate when heated, producing a ketone (or a mono carboxylic acid, in the case of the dicarboxylic acid) and carbon dioxide.

Practice Questions

1. Which of these molecules could be classified as a soap?

   A. $CH_3(CH_2)_{17}CH_2COOH$
   B. CH_3COOH
   C. $CH_3(CH_2)_{19}CH_2COO^-Na^+$
   D. $CH_3COO^-Na^+$

2. Which of these compounds would be expected to decarboxylate when heated?

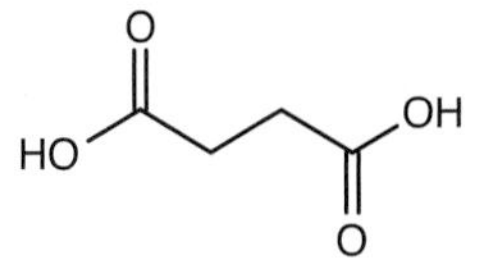

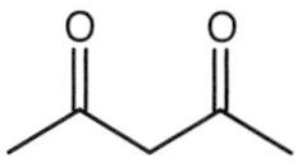

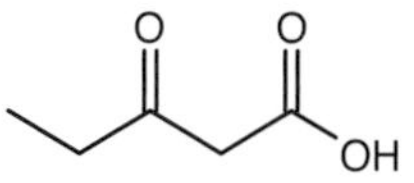

3. Oxidation of which of the following compounds is most likely to yield a carboxylic acid?

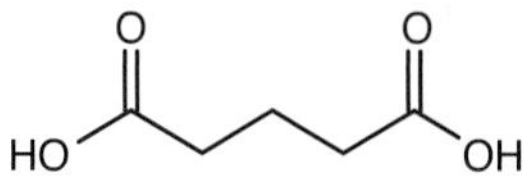

   A. Acetone
   B. Cyclohexanone
   C. 2-Propanol
   D. Methanol

4. Carboxylic acids have higher boiling points than the corresponding alcohols because

   A. molecular weight is increased by the additional carboxyl group.
   B. the pH of the compound in solution is lower.
   C. acid salts are soluble in water.
   D. hydrogen bonding is much stronger than in alcohols.

5. Which of the following carboxylic acids will be the most acidic?

   A. $CH_3CHClCH_2COOH$
   B. $CH_3CH_2CCl_2COOH$
   C. $CH_3CH_2CHClCOOH$
   D. $CH_3CH_2CH_2COOH$

6. Which of the following substituted benzoic acid compounds will be the least acidic?

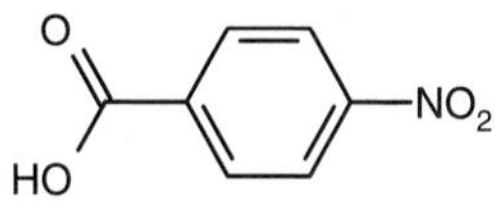

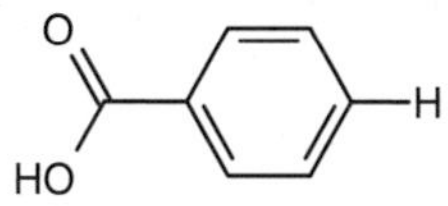

7. Predict the final product of the following reaction.

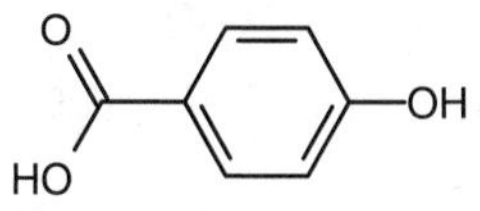

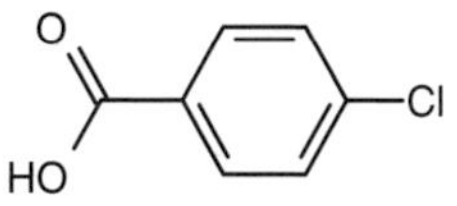

$$CH_3(CH_2)_4CH_2OH \xrightarrow[\text{acetone}]{CrO_3,\ H_2SO_4} ?$$

1-hexanol

   A. $CH_3(CH_2)_4CHO$
   B. $CH_3(CH_2)_4COOH$
   C. $CH_3(CH_2)_4CH_3$
   D. $HOOC(CH_2)_4COOH$

8. Carboxylic acids can be reacted in one step to form all of the following compounds EXCEPT

   A. acyl halides.
   B. amides.
   C. alkenes.
   D. alcohols.

9. The reduction of a carboxylic acid by lithium aluminum hydride will yield what final product?

A. An aldehyde
B. An ester
C. A ketone
D. An alcohol

10. Which of the following CANNOT be used to convert butanoic acid to butanoyl chloride?

A. PCl_3
B. PCl_5
C. CCl_4
D. $SOCl_2$

11. Which of the following reagents will reduce butanoic acid to butanol?

A. $LiAlH_4$
B. $LiAlH_4$, H_2O
C. $NaBH_4$
D. All of the above

12. In the presence of an acid catalyst, the major product of ethanoic acid and ethanol is

A. acetic anhydride.
B. butene.
C. diethyl ether.
D. ethyl acetate.

Small Group Questions

1. What is the difference between a carboxylate anion and an alkoxide anion?

2. Recall that the α-hydrogen on a carboxylic acid is especially acidic. Is it more or less acidic than the hydroxyl hydrogen?

Explanations to Practice Questions

1. C

A soap is a long-chain hydrocarbon with a highly polar end. Generally, this polar end, or head, is a salt of a carboxylic acid. Choice (C) fits these criteria and is the correct answer. The remaining choices all fail one or both of the criteria and are therefore wrong. Choice (A) is not a salt. Choice (B) is acetic acid, which is not a salt and does not possess a long chain. Choice (D) is sodium acetate, which is a salt but does not have a long hydrocarbon chain.

2. D

This compound is a β-keto acid: a keto functionality β to a carboxyl functionality. Decarboxylation occurs with β-keto acids and 1,3-diacids, because they can form a cyclic transition state that permits simultaneous hydrogen transfer and loss of carbon dioxide. Choice (B) is a diketone and does not have a single carboxyl group. Choices (A) and (C) are 1,4- and 1,5-diacids, respectively, and will decarboxylate but with more difficulty. The correct answer is choice (D).

3. D

Oxidation of methanol, choice (D), will yield first formaldehyde and then formic acid; this is the correct answer. Acetone, choice (A), cannot be oxidized further unless extremely harsh conditions are used. This is because the carbonyl carbon is bonded to two alkyl groups and further oxidation would necessitate cleavage of a carbon–carbon bond. Choice (B), cyclohexanone, is likewise limited in its options for further oxidation. Choice (C), 2-propanol, can be oxidized to acetone but no further without harsh conditions.

4. D

The boiling points of compounds depend on the strength of the attractive forces between molecules. In both alcohols and carboxylic acids, the major form of intermolecular attraction is hydrogen bonding; however, the hydrogen bonds of carboxylic acids are much stronger than those of alcohols, because the acids are much more polar. This makes the boiling points of carboxylic acids higher than those of the corresponding alcohols, so choice (D) is correct. Boiling points also depend on molecular weight, choice (A), but in this case, the difference in molecular weight has a smaller influence than the effect of hydrogen bonding. Therefore, choice (A) is wrong. Choice (B) is a correct statement but does not sufficiently explain the difference in boiling points. Choice (C) discusses the behavior of an acid's salt in solution, which is wrong for the same reason.

5. B

The acidity of carboxylic acids is significantly increased by the presence of highly electronegative functional groups. Their electron-withdrawing effect upon the carboxyl group increases the stability of the carboxylate anion, favoring proton dissociation. This effect increases as the number of electronegative groups on the chain increases, and it also increases as the distance between the acid, functionality and electronegative group decreases. Among the carboxylic acids listed, choice (D) is the only unsubstituted acid, and therefore, must have the lowest acidity. Choice (A) is β-halogenated, whereas choices (B) and (C) are α-halogenated, so we can reject (A). Finally, choice (B) contains two α-halogens and choice (C) includes only one, so the electron-withdrawing effect in choice (B) is stronger, and (B) is the correct answer.

6. C

The effects of different substituents upon the acidity of benzoic acid compounds are correlated with their effects on the reactivity of the benzene ring (see Chapter 6). Activating substituents donate electron density into the benzene ring, and the ring in turn donates electron density to the carboxyl group, destabilizing the benzoate ion formed and therefore decreasing a compound's acidity. Deactivating substituents have the opposite effect: They withdraw electrons from the ring, which in turn withdraws negative charge from the carboxyl group, thus stabilizing the carboxylate anion and increasing the compound's acidity. Choice (A) contains a nitro group attached to the ring, and choice (B) has a chloride; both of these substituents have deactivating effects, so these choices can be eliminated. Choice (D) is unsubstituted benzoic acid, whereas choice (C) has a strongly activating hydroxyl substituent. Thus, choice (C) will be the least acidic and is the correct answer.

7. B

Jones's reagent (chromium trioxide in aqueous sulfuric acid) oxidizes primary alcohols directly to monocarboxylic acids, so choice (B) is correct. This reagent is too strong an oxidizing agent to give an aldehyde as the final product (an aldehyde will be formed but will immediately be oxidized further), so choice (A) is wrong. Choice (D), a dicarboxylic acid, cannot form because there is no functional group handle on the other end of the molecule for the reagent to attack and it cannot attack the inert alkane. Nor will it reduce an alkane such as choice (C), so this is also wrong.

8. C

Carboxylic acids cannot be converted into alkenes in one step. Acyl halides (A) are formed with thionyl chloride. Amides (B) are formed by reaction with ammonia. Alcohols (D) may be formed using a variety of reducing agents. To form alkenes (C), carboxylic acids may be reduced to alcohols, which can then be transformed into alkenes by elimination.

9. D

Lithium aluminum hydride (LAH) is a strong reducing agent. LAH can completely reduce carboxylic acids to primary alcohols, choice (D). Aldehydes are intermediate products of this reaction; therefore, choice (A) is wrong. Esters are formed from carboxylic acids by reaction with alcohols, so choice (B) is wrong. Ketones are formed by the Friedel-Crafts acylation of the acyl chloride derivatives of acids, so choice (C) is wrong.

10. C

PCl_3 (A), PCl_5 (B), and $SOCl_2$ (D) are all reactive enough to donate a chloride to a carboxylic acid to form the acyl chloride. Carbon tetrachloride is more often used as a solvent than as a reagent, because its C–Cl bond is stable and is not a good source of Cl$^-$ nucleophiles.

11. A

Lithium aluminum hydride ($LiAlH_4$) is an effective reducing agent for carboxylic acids. It is also reactive with water, so performing the reaction as it is listed in choice (B) does not work. Although sodium tetrahydroborate (C) is a reducing agent, it is not strong enough to dissolve two carbon-oxygen bonds.

12. D

The reaction described is a Fischer esterification, in which the –OH group of ethanoic acid is first protonated to form water, which is a good leaving group. The nucleophilic oxygen atom of ethanol then attacks the electrophilic carbonyl carbon of ethanoic acid, ultimately displacing water to form ethyl acetate. The acid catalyst is regenerated from ethanol's released proton. Although acetic anhydride can form via the coupling of two acetic acid molecules, it would not be a major product given the conditions listed in the question, so answer (A) is incorrect. Ethers and alkenes do not form under these conditions, either, so answers (B) and (C) are incorrect.

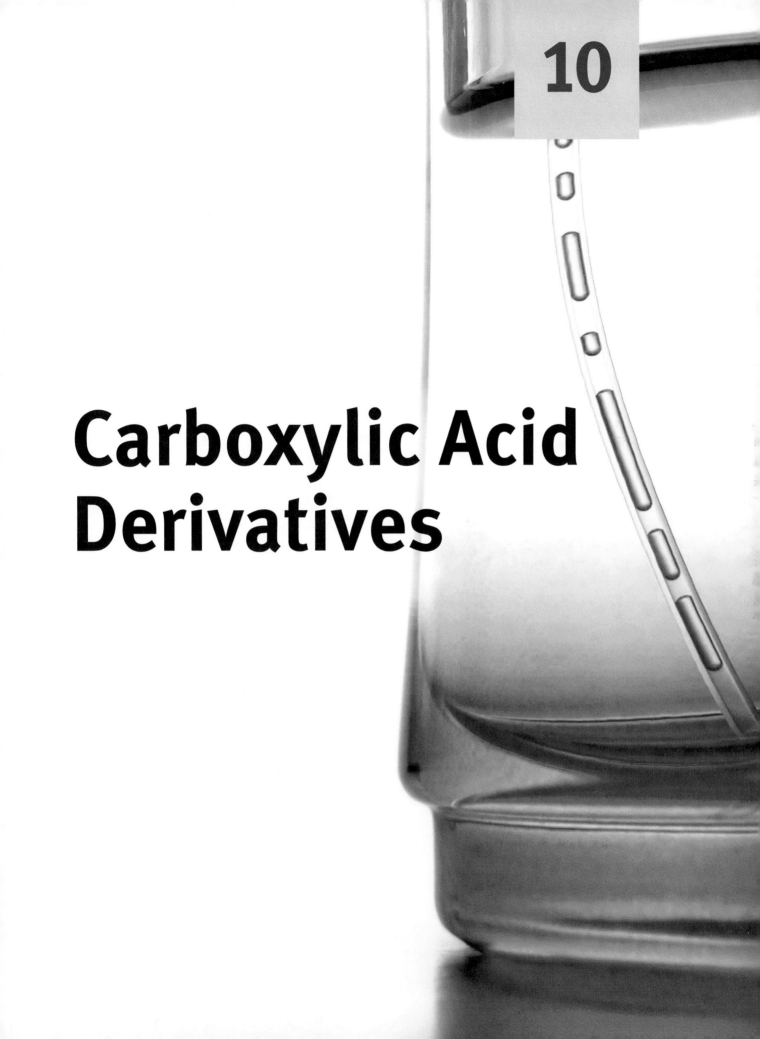

Carboxylic Acid Derivatives

10

If you're one of those poor souls who still doesn't believe carboxylic acids are all that thrilling, we can't blame you. They don't always seem too exciting, at least to the human eye. But if you were a molecule with free electrons, you'd probably think that carboxylic acids were a party. It's true: carboxylic acids have many of the same characteristics as parties. First, they provide a place where all nucleophiles are welcome. We saw this in the last chapter, where the carbonyl is susceptible to attack by everything from water to amines to other carbonyls (in the enol form). In addition, it's just like a party where the guests keep coming and going; some guests stay for a while (amines), and others just pop in and out to make an appearance (halides). Throughout this chapter, we will discuss this party and the different names the carboxylic acid derivative carries, depending on the guests that are present. The big ones on which we will focus are **acyl halides**, **anhydrides**, **amides**, and **esters**. Each of these molecules replaces the –OH on the carboxyl group with **–X**, **–OCOR**, **–NH$_2$**, or **–OR**, respectively. The nice thing about this party is that, similar to parties with humans, everyone comes in the same way. Some people drive and some take cabs, but everyone must walk through the same front door. We will notice a common mechanism with all of the following reactions.

Acyl Halides   ★★★★☆

NOMENCLATURE

Acyl halides are also called **acid** or **alkanoyl halides**. (Remember that the acyl group is RCO–.) Acyl halides are the most reactive of the carboxylic acid derivatives. They are named in the IUPAC system by changing the –oic acid ending of the carboxylic acid to **–oyl halide**. Some typical examples, shown in Figure 10.1, are ethanoyl chloride (also called acetyl chloride), benzoyl chloride, and *n*-butanoyl bromide.

> **MCAT Expertise**
>
> Order of carboxylic acid derivative reactivity: acyl halides > anhydrides > esters = carboxylic acids > amides.

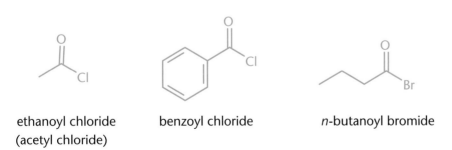

| ethanoyl chloride (acetyl chloride) | benzoyl chloride | *n*-butanoyl bromide |

Figure 10.1

SYNTHESIS

The most common acyl halides are acid chlorides, although you may occasionally encounter acid bromides and iodides. Acid chlorides are prepared by reacting a carboxylic acid with thionyl chloride, SOCl$_2$. SO$_2$ and HCl are the other products, and the evolution of SO_2 drives this reaction (see Figure 10.2). Alternatively, PCl_3 or PCl_5 (or PBr_3, to make an acid bromide) will accomplish the same transformation.

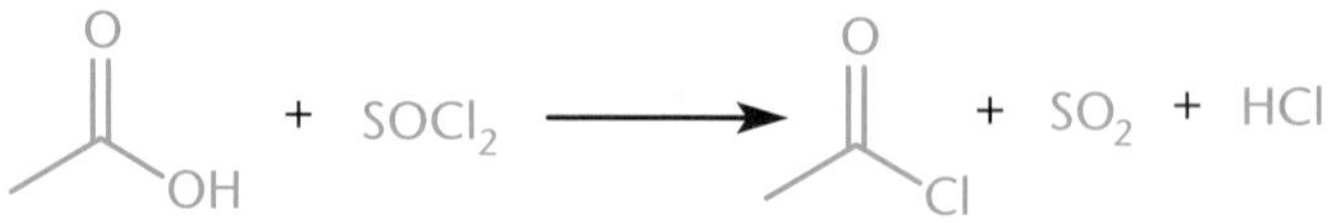

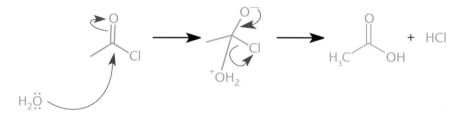

Figure 10.2

REACTIONS: NUCLEOPHILIC ACYL SUBSTITUTION

As we'd expect, all of the reactions of acyl halides occur via nucleophilic acyl substitution, as discussed in Chapter 9.

Hydrolysis

The simplest reaction we'll see is the conversion of an acid halide back into its corresponding carboxylic acid. Acid halides react rapidly with water to form their carboxylic acid and HCl (see Figure 10.3). This makes acid halides dangerous: If they are exposed to either your eyes or airways, they will react with the water in those spaces, forming HCl and carboxylic acid *on you*, a sensation you'd probably not wish to experience.

Figure 10.3

Conversion into Esters

Another similar reaction is the conversion of acyl halides into esters. The basic mechanism is the same as hydrolysis, once again proceeding through a tetrahedral intermediate. This time, though, we use *alcohol* as the nucleophile. The leaving group is still chlorine, which can pick up a hydrogen in solution, making HCl as a side product (see Figure 10.4).

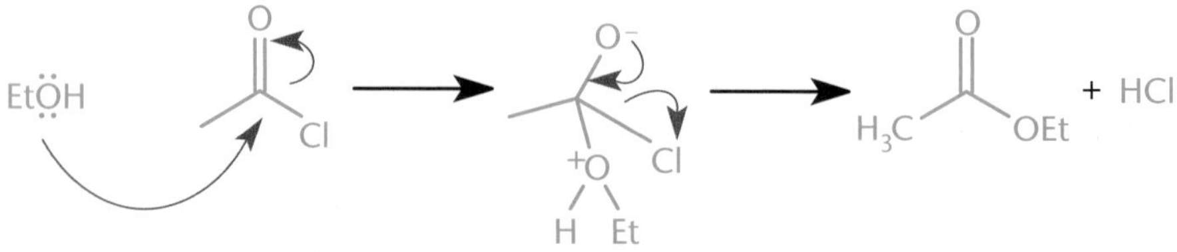

Figure 10.4

Key Concept

The steps are the same for all of these reactions. The carbonyl carbon acts as an electrophile and is attacked by a nucleophile. In the second step, the leaving group takes the extra electrons. Note: Aldehydes and ketones do not have a leaving group. That is why they undergo nucleophilic *additions*.

Mnemonic

Hydrolysis = *hydro* + *lysis*, or cleavage by water.

Conversion into Amides

Acyl halides can be converted into amides (compounds of the general formula $RCONR_2$) by an analogous reaction with amines. The lone pairs on nucleophilic amines, such as ammonia, attack the carbonyl group, displacing chloride. The side product is ammonium chloride (a salt—remember this means an ionic compound), formed from excess ammonia and HCl (see Figure 10.5).

Whereas *acyl halides* react with amines to form amides, if we were to react *ketones* with amines, the product would be an *imine* (discussed in Chapter 8).

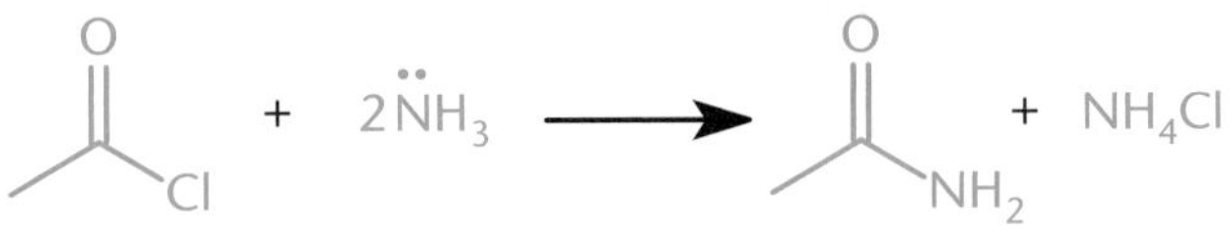

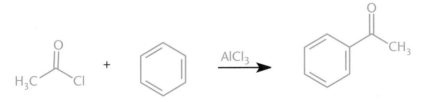

Figure 10.5

OTHER REACTIONS

Friedel-Crafts Acylation

Aromatic rings can be acylated in a Friedel-Crafts reaction (as discussed in Chapter 6), a type of electrophilic aromatic substitution. The nucleophile is the aromatic ring, and the electrophile, as we'd expect, is the carbonyl. However, when the acyl chloride attacks, its bond to chlorine is almost completely broken by the reaction with $AlCl_3$. The pi electrons of the aromatic system act as a nucleophile, attacking the electrophilic acyl cation or acylium ion (RCO^+). The product, as we can see in Figure 10.6, is an alkyl aryl ketone.

> **MCAT Expertise**
>
> This mechanism is a two-in-one for us! The electrophile, of course, is the carbonyl carbon and the nucleophile is the benzene ring. So, we have either a nucleophilic acyl substitution or an electrophilic aromatic substitution, depending on your perspective.

Figure 10.6

Reduction

Acid halides can be reduced to alcohols or selectively reduced to the intermediate aldehydes using a bulky hydride reagent that has only one hydride to transfer: $LiAlH(OC(CH_3)_3)_3$.

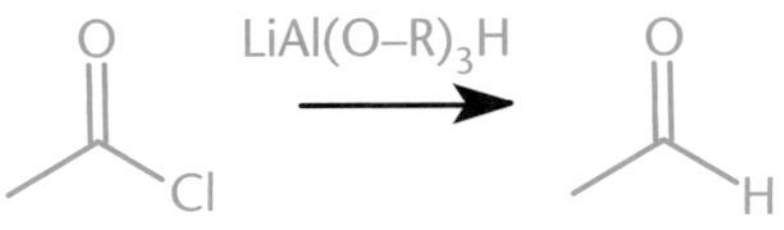

Figure 10.7

Anhydrides

NOMENCLATURE

Anhydrides, also called **acid anhydrides**, are the condensation dimers of carboxylic acids with the general formula RCOOCOR. They are named by substituting the word *anhydride* for the word *acid* in an alkanoic acid. The most common and important anhydride is **acetic anhydride**, the dimer of acetic acid. You should be able to recognize that succinic, maleic, and phthalic anhydrides, shown in Figure 10.8, are cyclic anhydrides arising from intramolecular condensation or dehydration of diacids, but you won't need to memorize their names.

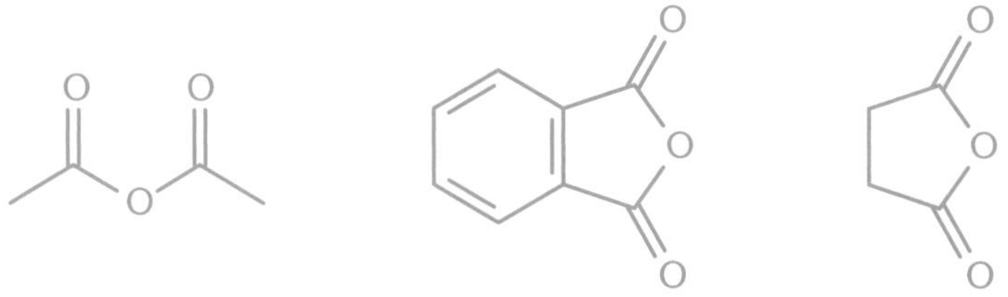

acetic anhydride
(ethanoic anhydride)

phthalic anhydride

succinic anhydride

Figure 10.8

SYNTHESIS

As we just mentioned, anhydrides are the product of a condensation reaction between two carboxylic acids (see Figure 10.9). The mechanism is a combination of a few reactions we've already discussed. The hydroxide group of one acid acts as the nucleophile, and (of course) the carbonyl is the electrophile. One molecule is of water is lost in the condensation.

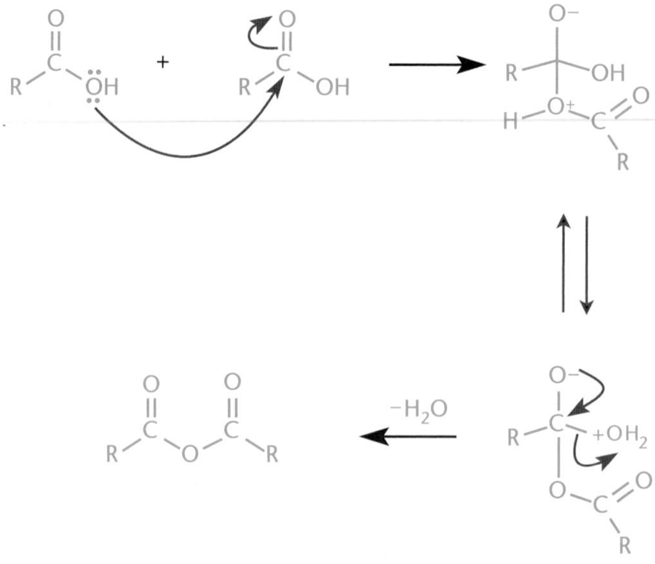

Figure 10.9

Anhydrides can also be synthesized by the reaction of an acid chloride and a carboxylate anion, as shown in Figure 10.10.

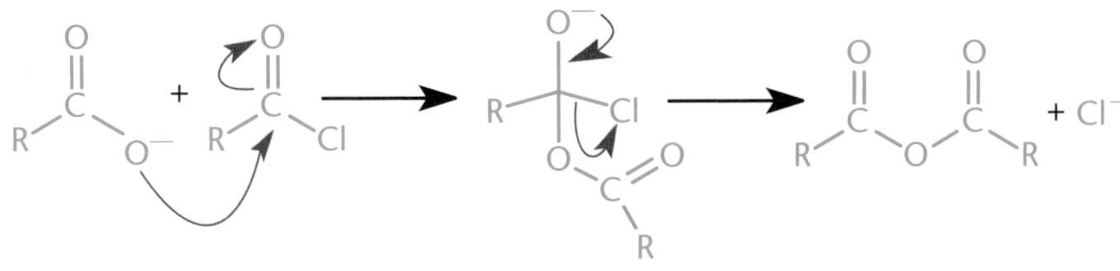

Figure 10.10

Certain cyclic anhydrides can be formed simply by heating carboxylic acids (see Figure 10.11). The reaction is driven forward by the increased stability of the newly formed ring; as such, only five- and six-membered ring anhydrides are easily made. In this reaction, the hydroxyl group of one –COOH acts as the nucleophile, attacking the carbonyl on the other –COOH.

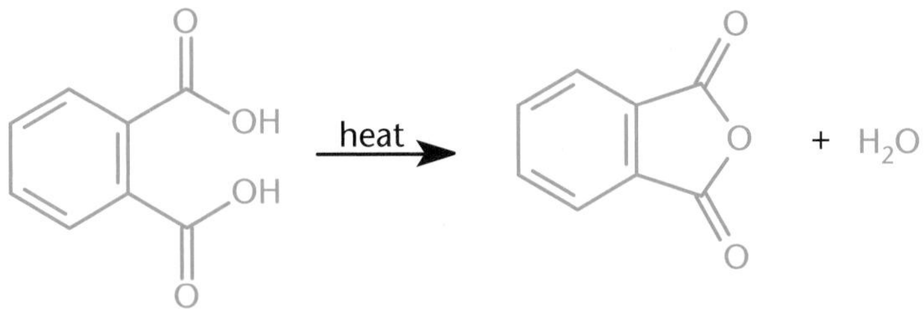

o-phtalic acid   phthalic anhydride

Figure 10.11

> **MCAT Expertise**
>
> Always remember that intramolecular reactions are more likely to occur than a reaction involving two separate molecules. Think about two people handcuffed together; they are much more likely to get into a fight than two random people passing each other on the street.

REACTIONS

Anhydrides react under the same conditions as acid chlorides, but because they are more stable, they are less reactive. The reactions are slower, and no matter what the nucleophile, they will produce a carboxylic acid side product (wasting all that carbon!) instead of the HCl produced by acid halides. Cyclic anhydrides are also subject to the following reactions, which cause ring opening at the anhydride group along with formation of the new functional groups.

Hydrolysis

We can break up anhydrides into two equivalents of carboxylic acids by exposing them to water. For these reactions to be useful, the anhydride must be symmetric.

Key Concept

The carbonyl compound is the electrophile, the nucleophile is water, and the leaving group is a carboxylic acid (which is not as good a leaving group as the halogens in the acyl halide reactions).

Figure 10.12

Key Concept

Reactions that convert compounds to amides only differ in the attacking nucleophile.

Note that in the reaction shown in Figure 10.12, the leaving group is actually a carboxylic acid.

Conversion into Amides

Anhydrides can also be cleaved by ammonia, producing amides and carboxylic acids (see Figure 10.13a).

There's a problem here, though. One of our products is a carboxylic acid, and we're carrying out the reaction in an environment filled with ammonia. That means we've now got an acid in a basic environment. The two will react, forming a salt, specifically **ammonium carboxylate** (see Figure 10.13b).

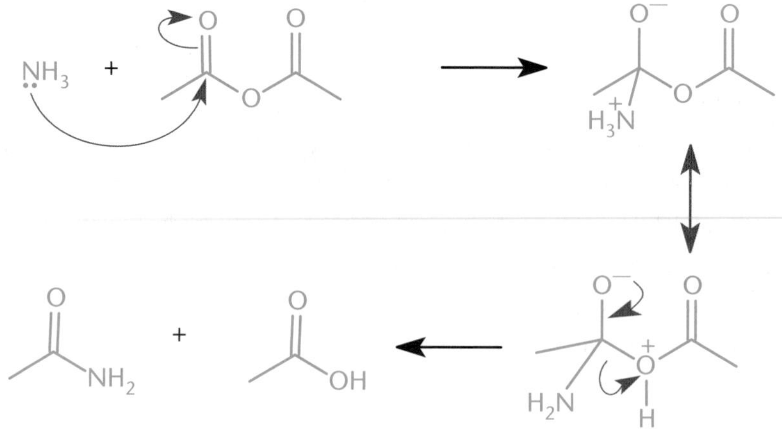

Figure 10.13a

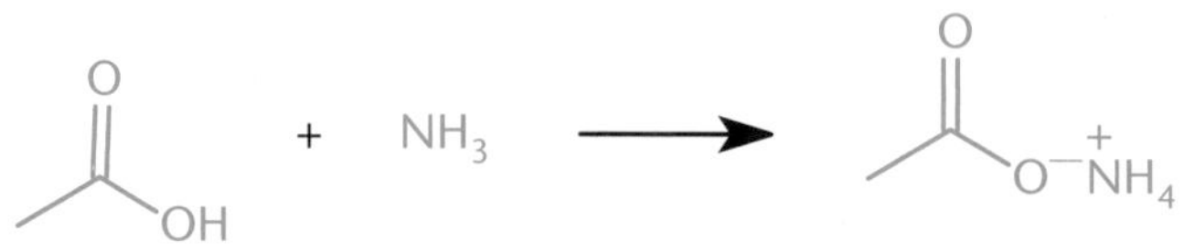

Key Concept

Acid chlorides can be converted into any of the other derivatives, anhydrides can make any of the less reactive derivatives (esters and amides), and esters can be converted into amides.

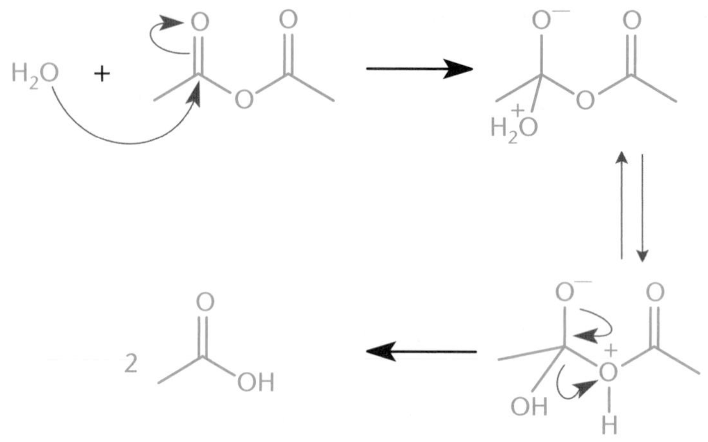

Figure 10.13b

So, even though the leaving group is actually a carboxylic acid, the final products will be an amide and the ammonium salt of a carboxylate anion.

Conversion into Esters and Carboxylic Acids

Another nucleophile we can plug into this formula is an alcohol; this reaction will form esters and carboxylic acids (see Figure 10.14).

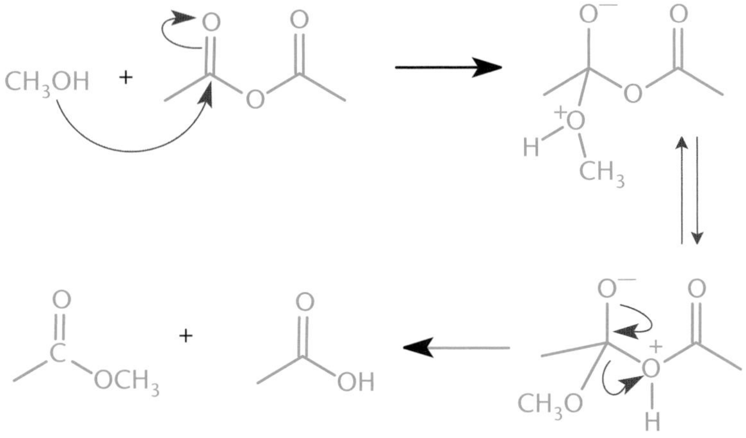

Figure 10.14

Acylation

Once again, we return to Friedel-Crafts acylation. When we add $AlCl_3$ or another Lewis acid catalyst (see Figure 10.15), the reaction will occur readily.

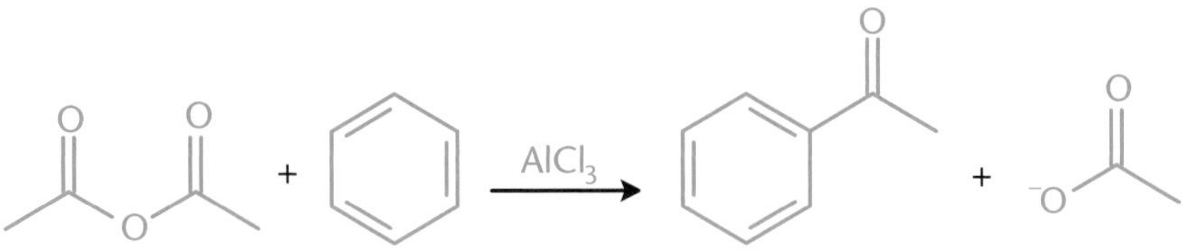

Figure 10.15

Amides ★★★★☆

NOMENCLATURE

Amides are compounds with the general formula $RCONR_2$. They are named by replacing the –oic acid ending with **–amide**. Alkyl substituents on the nitrogen atom are listed as prefixes, and their location is specified with the letter *N*. Figure 10.16 shows one example.

MCAT Expertise

This reaction is the same as the earlier two-in-one involving both EAS and nucleophilic acyl substitution.

Bridge

The peptide bond is an amide linkage that possesses double-bond character from resonance and is the most stable carboxylic acid derivative.

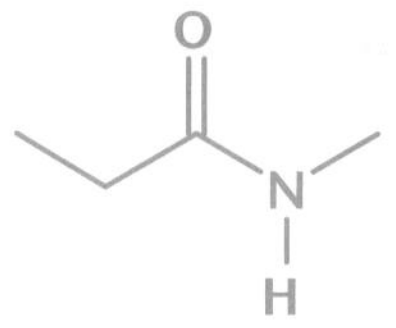

N-methylpropanamide

Figure 10.16

Key Concept

Only primary and secondary amines can be used to form amides.

SYNTHESIS

Amides are generally synthesized by the reaction of acid chlorides with amines or by the reaction of acid anhydrides with ammonia, as we just discussed. Note that loss of hydrogen is required for these reactions to take place. Thus, only primary and secondary amines will undergo this reaction.

REACTIONS

Amides are the most stable of the carboxylic acid derivatives, so once they're bound to the carbonyl, they're staying around for a while. They're like the guests at a party who're still around at 3 A.M. and just can't take the hint that we want them to leave. It takes extreme conditions to get them to leave; while faking a big argument with your significant other works well for unwanted human guests, acidic or basic conditions will do the trick at the molecular level.

Real World

Extreme conditions (e.g., strong acid) are necessary to hydrolyze an amide, which is why we have stomach acid: to help provide the catalysis necessary for proteases to break down proteins.

Hydrolysis

Amides can be hydrolyzed under acidic conditions via nucleophilic substitution. The acidic conditions allow the carbonyl oxygen to become protonated, making it more susceptible to nucleophilic attack by a water molecule. The product of this reaction is a carboxylic acid and ammonia, as shown in Figure 10.17.

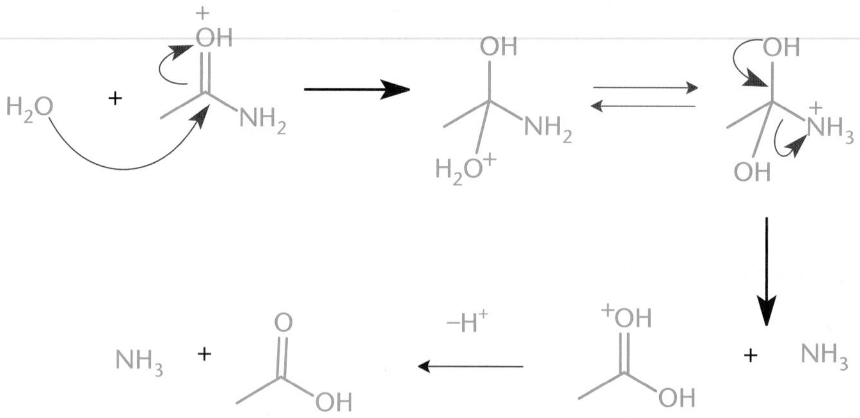

Figure 10.17

Hydrolysis can also occur if conditions are basic enough. The reaction is similar, except that the carbonyl oxygen is not protonated and the nucleophile is a hydroxide ion. The product of this reaction will be the carboxylate ion.

Hofmann Rearrangement

The Hofmann rearrangement converts amides to primary amines with the loss of the carbonyl carbon as CO_2. The initial reactants are bromine and sodium hydroxide, which react to form *sodium hypobromite* (as seen in Figure 10.18). The mechanism is fairly intense. As such, it is most important for you to focus on the reactants and products.

The mechanism involves the formation of a **nitrene**, the nitrogen analog of a *carbene*. This nitrene is attached to the carbonyl, and like a carbene, it only has six electrons; thus, it is an electrophile looking for more electrons. The electron deficiency is resolved by rearranging to form an **isocyanate**, which has a double bond on either side of the carbon, one to oxygen and one to nitrogen (hence, *iso–*, meaning *equal*). The isocyanate molecule is then hydrolyzed to form the amine, with CO_2 as a leaving group.

> ### Key Concept
> Hofmann rearrangement = amide $\longrightarrow$ primary amine (with loss of a carbon, as CO_2).

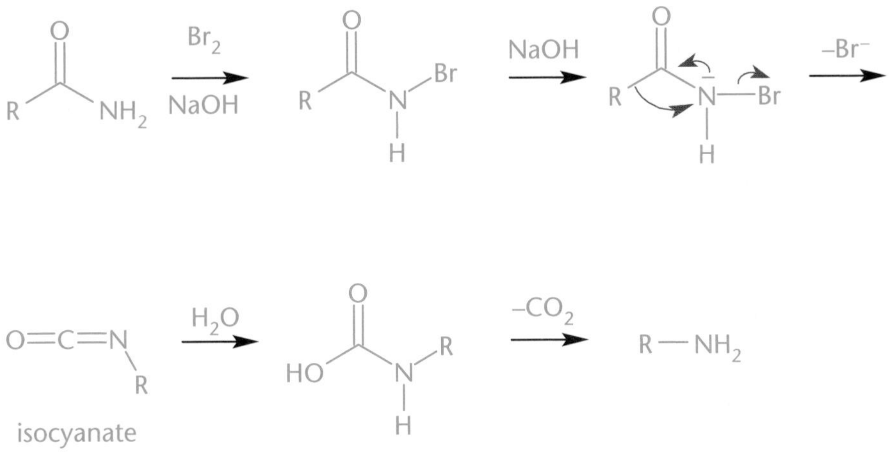

Figure 10.18

Reduction

Amides can be reduced with lithium aluminum hydride (LAH) to their corresponding amine (see Figure 10.19). Although this reaction also gives an amine product, it is different from the Hofmann rearrangement because there is no loss of carbon. LAH just does the good old-fashioned reduction we've seen before.

> ### Key Concept
> Reduction also produces amines, but no carbon is lost.

Figure 10.19

Esters ★★★★☆☆

NOMENCLATURE

Esters, the dehydration products of carboxylic acids and alcohols, are found in many fruits and perfumes (items also commonly found at your Great Aunt Esther's house . . . coincidence?). They are named in the IUPAC system as **alkyl** or **aryl alkanoates**. As we mentioned in the last chapter, *ethyl acetate*, derived from the condensation of acetic acid and ethanol, is called *ethyl ethanoate* according to IUPAC nomenclature.

SYNTHESIS

Key Concept

Acid + alcohol = ester.

Under acidic conditions, mixtures of carboxylic acids and alcohols will condense (losing water) into esters. This is called Fischer esterification. Esters can also be obtained from reaction of acid chlorides or anhydrides with alcohols, as we saw in previous sections. Phenolic (aromatic) esters are produced in the same way, although the aromatic acid chlorides are less reactive than aliphatic (nonaromatic) acid chlorides, so we need to kick up the reaction conditions by adding a base as a catalyst (see Figure 10.20).

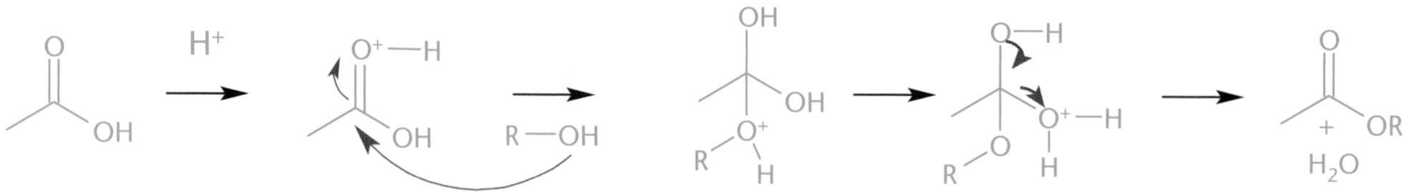

Figure 10.20

REACTIONS

MCAT Expertise

Hydrolysis, especially of esters, is a popular topic on the MCAT.

Hydrolysis

Esters, just like every other derivative of carboxylic acids, can be hydrolyzed. Hydrolysis of esters produces carboxylic acids and alcohols. Because esters and carboxylic acids (the products) are equally reactive, we can drive the reaction forward by using either acidic or basic conditions.

Under acidic conditions, the mechanism is as shown in Figure 10.21.

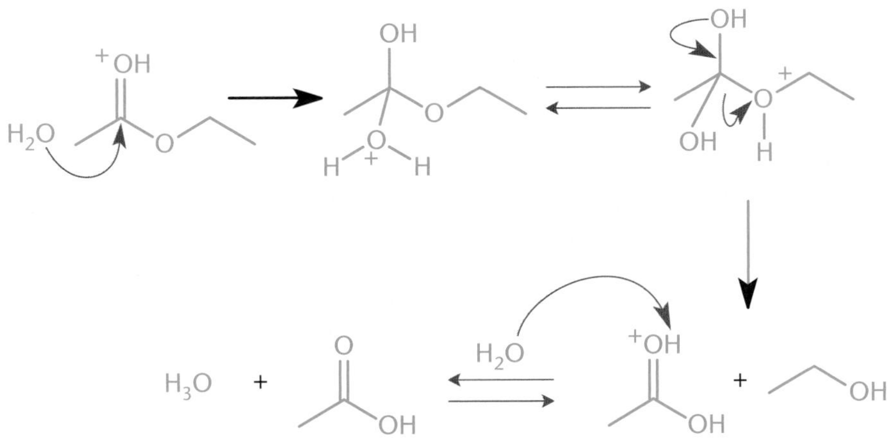

Figure 10.21

The reaction proceeds similarly under basic conditions, except that the oxygen on the C=O is not protonated and the nucleophile is OH⁻ instead of water.

Triacylglycerols, also called fats, are esters of long-chain carboxylic acids (fatty acids) and glycerol (1,2,3-propanetriol). **Saponification** is the process by which fats are hydrolyzed under basic conditions to produce soaps (see Figure 10.22). Alternatively, acidification of the soap regenerates triacylglycerol. This process is sometimes used on solutions of free fatty acids to increase the caloric content of animal feed, but we don't recommend trying it with your hand soap—it tastes pretty bad, as anyone who has had his mouth washed out with soap can attest.

> **Bridge**
>
> Triacylglycerols are actually esters, with glycerol as the alcohol (ROH) and free fatty acids as RCOOH.

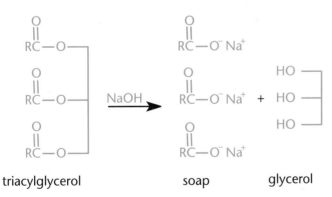

triacylglycerol   soap   glycerol

Figure 10.22

Conversion into Amides

As we saw before, nitrogen bases, such as ammonia, will attack the electron-deficient carbonyl carbon atom, displacing an alkoxide to yield an amide and an alcohol side product (see Figure 10.23). This reaction is not very common because it's much more effective to start with acid chloride.

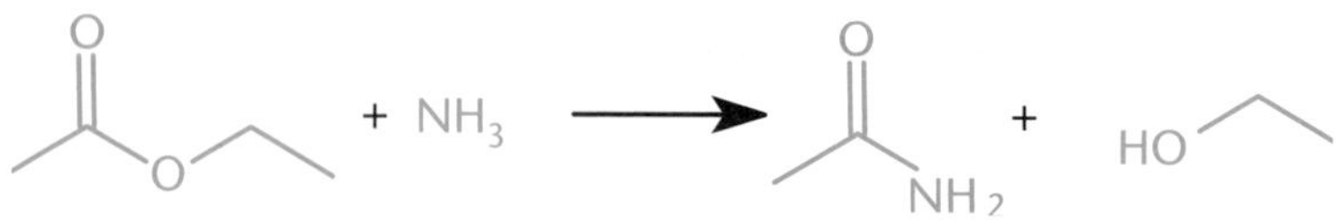

Figure 10.23

Transesterification

Other alcohols can act as nucleophiles and displace the alkoxy groups on esters. This process, which simply transforms one ester into another, is aptly named **transesterification** (see Figure 10.24).

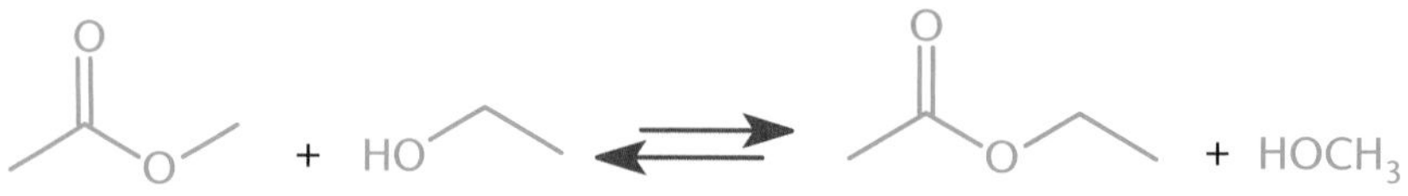

Figure 10.24

Grignard Addition

The negatively charged carbon of a Grignard reagent adds to the carbonyl group of esters. This reaction results in a ketone, as the carbonyl is re-formed and the alkoxy group is kicked off. There's a catch, though: The ketone product will be more reactive than the initial ester and, thus, readily attacked by more Grignard reagent. To get around this problem, two equivalents of Grignard reagent can be used to produce tertiary alcohols with good yield. (The intermediate ketone can be isolated only if the alkyl groups are sufficiently bulky to prevent further attack.) The first round of this reaction proceeds just like all the others in this chapter, as nucleophilic substitution, but the second round is nucleophilic addition, because the carbonyl is turned into an alcohol instead of being re-formed (see Figure 10.25).

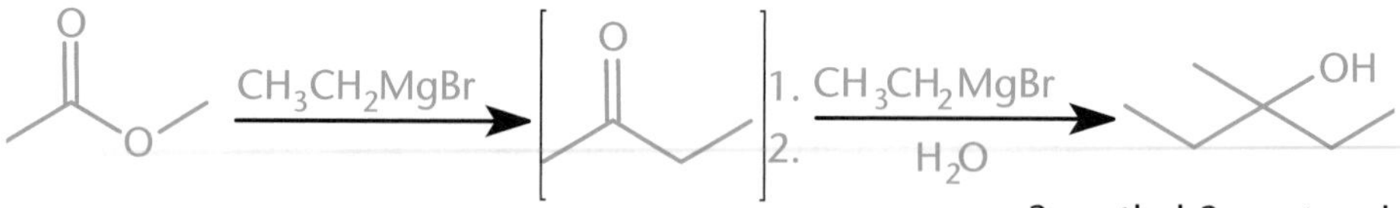

3-methyl-3-pentanol

Figure 10.25

Condensation Reactions

Another ester reaction you're likely to see on Test Day is the **Claisen condensation**. In the simplest case, two moles of ethyl acetate react under basic conditions to produce a β-keto-ester, specifically, *ethyl 3-oxobutanoate*, or *acetoacetic ester* by its common name. (The Claisen condensation is also called the *acetoacetic ester condensation*.) The reaction proceeds by addition of an enolate anion (created by the basic conditions) to the carbonyl group of another ester, followed by displacement of an ethoxide ion (see Figure 10.26). Don't worry if that all sounds confusing; this is the same mechanism we learned in Chapter 8 for aldol condensation, but now we're using esters, which have built-in leaving groups, as our reactants.

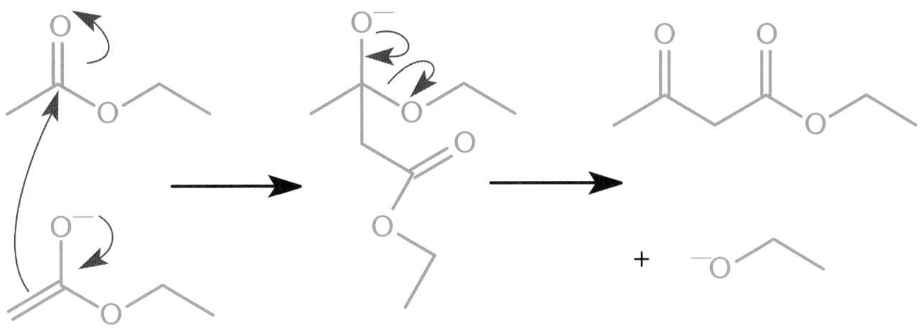

Figure 10.26

Reduction

Esters can be reduced to primary alcohols with LAH but *not* with the weaker $NaBH_4$. This is a helpful trait for chemists, because it allows for selective reduction in molecules with multiple functional groups. Note in Figure 10.27 that the products are two alcohols.

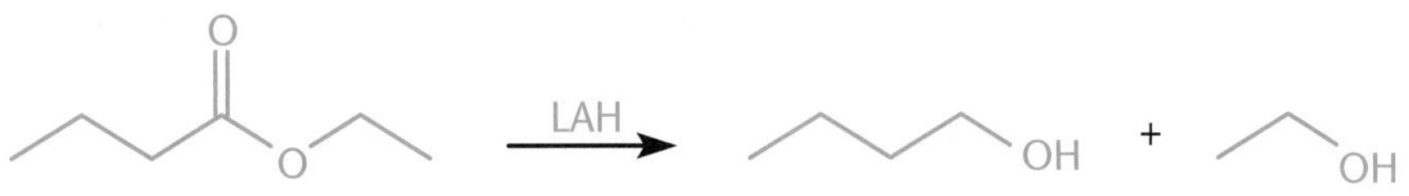

Figure 10.27

PHOSPHATE ESTERS

Let's switch gears for a minute and talk about phosphate esters. Although phosphoric acid derivatives are not carboxylic acid derivatives, they do form esters similar to those that we've discussed so far.

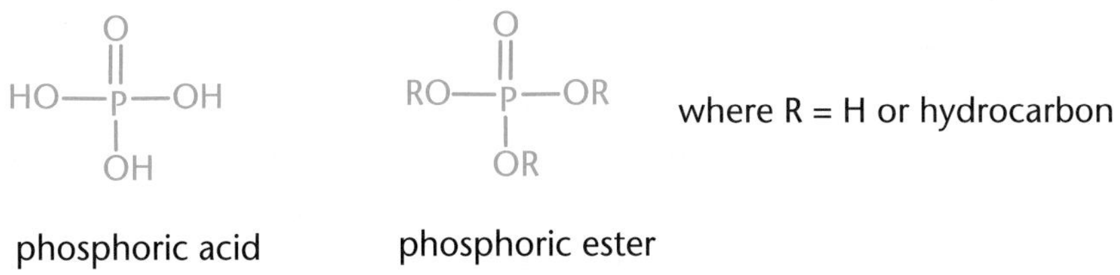

where R = H or hydrocarbon

phosphoric acid   phosphoric ester

Figure 10.28

Phosphoric acid and the mono- and diesters are acidic (more so than carboxylic acids), so they usually exist as anions. Like all esters, they can be cleaved under acidic conditions into the parent acid (in Figure 10.28, H_3PO_4) and alcohols.

Many living systems are literally covered in phosphate esters in the form of phospholipids (phosphoglycerides), shown in Figure 10.29, in which glycerol is attached to two carboxylic acids and one phosphoric acid.

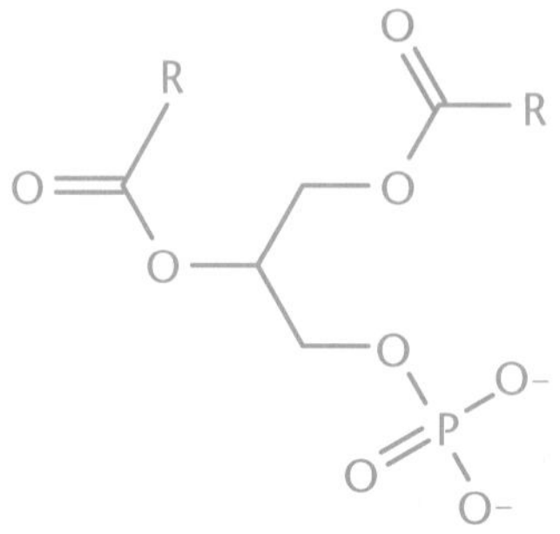

Bridge

Phosphodiester bonds should look familiar to you from your studies of molecular biology. They are responsible for holding the DNA backbone together, connecting nucleotides with covalent linkages.

phosphatidic acid
diacylglycerol phosphate
(a phosphoglyceride)

Figure 10.29

Phospholipids are the main component of cell membranes, and phospholipid/carbohydrate polymers form the backbone of nucleic acids, the hereditary material of life. The nucleic acid derivative adenosine triphosphate (ATP), the fuel that drives our cellular engines, can give up or regain one or more phosphate groups. ATP facilitates many biological reactions by releasing phosphate groups (via hydrolysis) to other compounds, thereby increasing their reactivity. This reaction is downhill in free energy, so it is thermodynamically favorable and drives many biological reactions.

Conclusion

That was a whole lot of information in only a handful of pages, but as we're sure you noticed, it's actually only a few reactions happening in a wide variety of contexts. The MCAT test makers don't want you to memorize all the possible reactions; they simply want you truly to understand the trends and the underlying reasons for these reactions. Make sure you know the order of reactivity of the derivative (from acyl halides, the restless party guest, to amides, the guest who just won't go home). Also, learn the general mechanism for nucleophilic substitutions and the special reactions of esters and amides. Your study of amides will pay off right away. The next chapter introduces nitrogen-containing compounds, and we will return to the *very* special case of amino acids in the final chapter.

CONCEPTS TO REMEMBER

The most important derivatives of carboxylic acids are acyl halides, anhydrides, esters, and amides. We decided to organize these derivatives from most reactive (least stable) to least reactive (most stable).

ACYL HALIDES

- ☐ Can be formed by adding $RCOOH + SOCl_2$, PCl_3 or PCl_5, or PBr_3.

- ☐ Undergo many different nucleophilic substitutions; H_2O yields carboxylic acid, ROH yields an ester, and NH_3 yields an amide.

- ☐ Can participate in Friedel-Crafts acylation to form an alkyl aryl ketone.

- ☐ Can be reduced to alcohols or, selectively, to aldehydes.

ANHYDRIDES

- ☐ Can be formed by RCOOH + RCOOH (condensation) or $RCOO^-$ + RCOCl (substitution).

- ☐ Undergo many nucleophilic substitution reactions, forming products that include carboxylic acids, amides, and esters.

- ☐ Can participate in Friedel-Crafts acylation.

ESTERS

- ☐ Formed by RCOOH + ROH or, even more easily, by acid chlorides or anhydrides + ROH.

- ☐ Hydrolyze to yield acids + alcohols; adding ammonia yields an amide.

- ☐ Reaction with Grignard reagent (2 moles) produces a tertiary alcohol.

- ☐ In the Claisen condensation, analogous to the aldol condensation, the ester acts both as nucleophile and electrophile—but note the product difference.

- ☐ Are very important in biological processes, particularly phosphate esters, which can be found in membranes, nucleic acids, and metabolic reactions.

AMIDES

- ☐ Can be formed by acid chlorides + amines or acid anhydrides + ammonia.

- ☐ Hydrolysis yields carboxylic acids or carboxylate anions.

- ☐ Can be transformed to primary amines via Hofmann rearrangement or reduction.

Practice Questions

1.

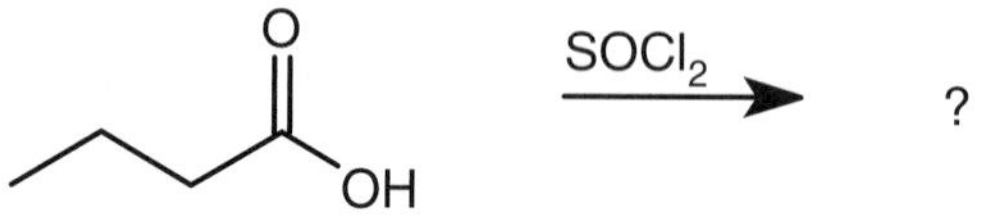

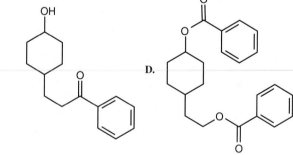

What would be the product of the above reaction?

A.

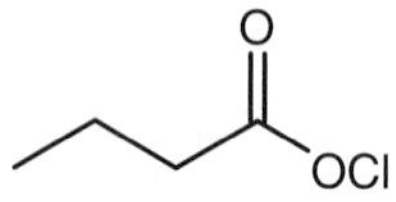

B.

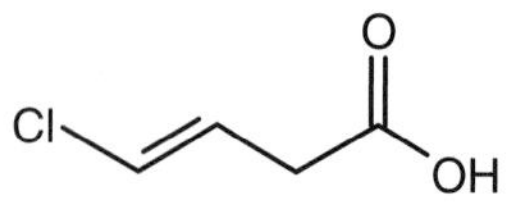

C.

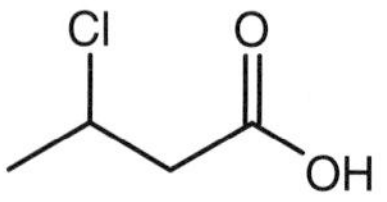

D.

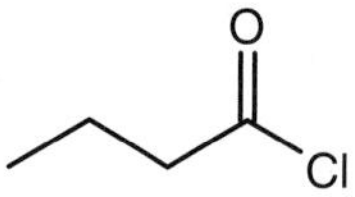

2. During the hydrolysis of an acid chloride, pyridine (a base) is usually added to the reaction vessel. This is done because

A. the reaction leads to the production of hydroxide ions.

B. the acyl chloride is unreactive.

C. the hydrolysis reaction leads to the formation of HCl.

D. the pyridine reacts in a side reaction with the carboxylic acid product.

3.

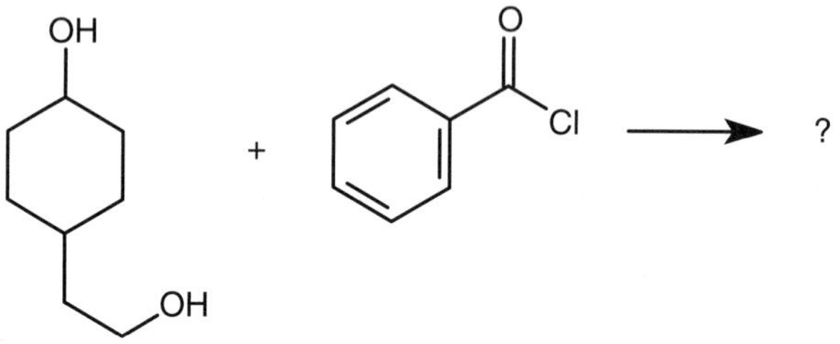

What would be the primary product of the above reaction?

A.

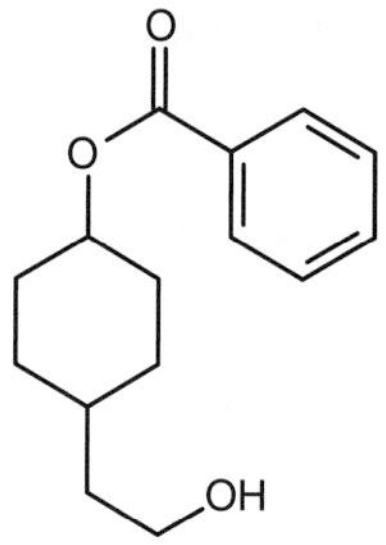

B.

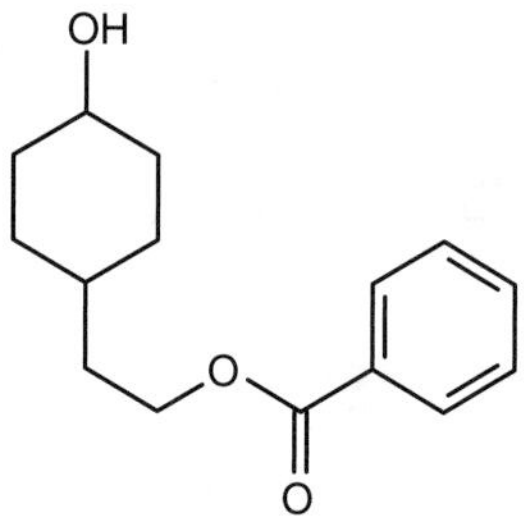

C.

D.

4. To produce a primary amide, an acid chloride should be treated with

A. ammonia.

B. an alcohol.

C. a primary amine.

D. a tertiary amine.

5. Which of the following would be the best method of producing methyl propanoate?

A. Reacting propanoic acid and methanol in the presence of a mineral acid
B. Reacting ethanol with propanoyl chloride in the presence of a base
C. Reacting propanoyl chloride with an aqueous base
D. Reacting propanoic acid with ethanol in the presence of a mineral acid

6.

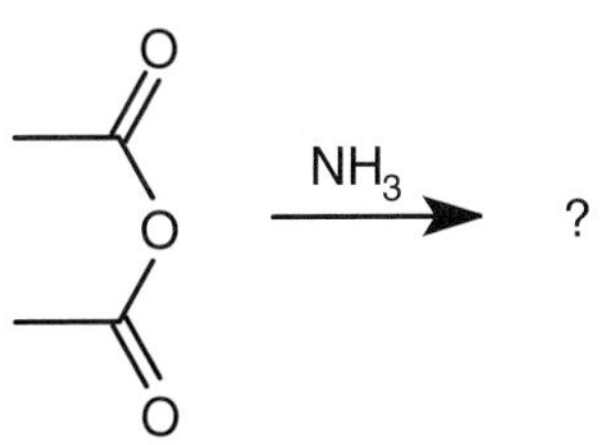

What would be the product(s) of the above reaction?

A. 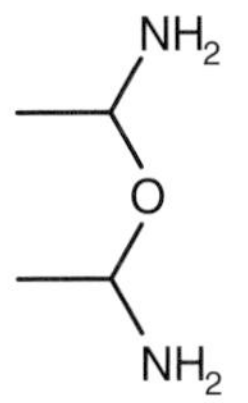

B. 2 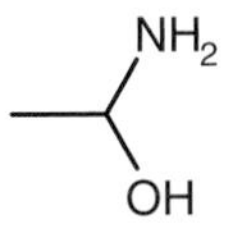

C. 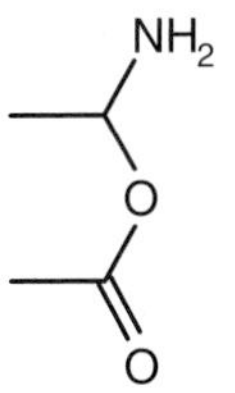

D. 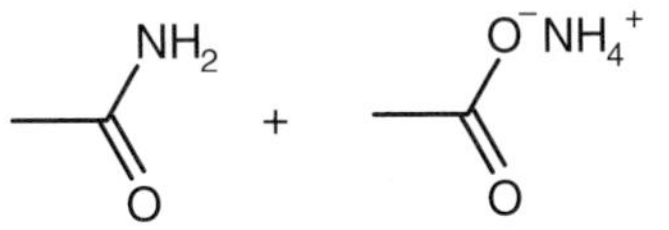

7.

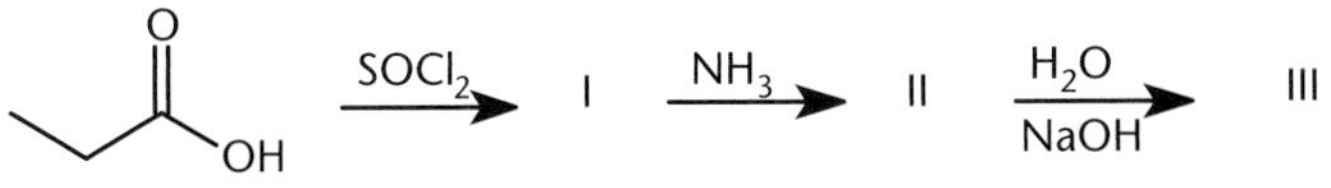

Which of the following correctly shows the intermediates and products of the reaction above?

A. 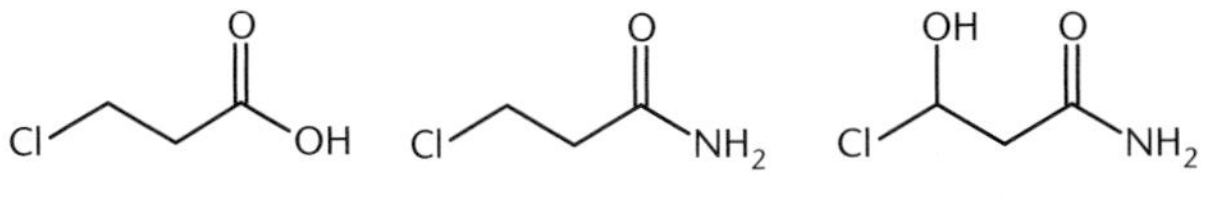

I II III

B. 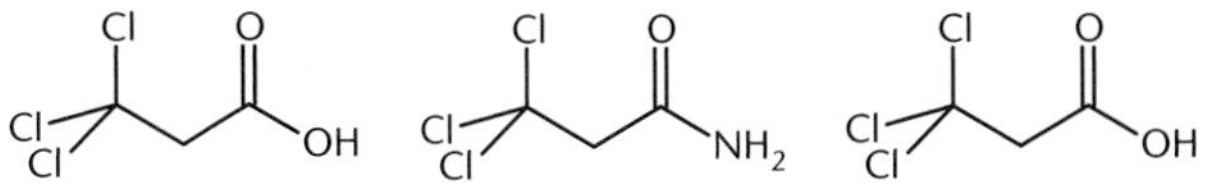

I II III

C. 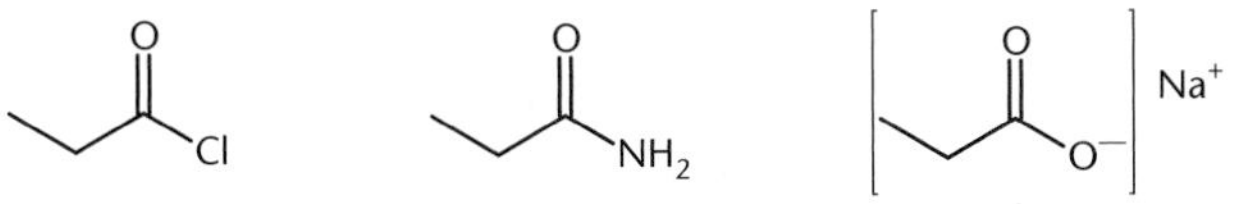

I II III

D. 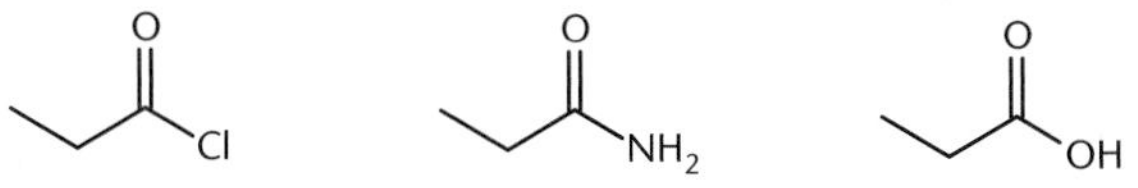

I II III

8. Which conversion between carboxylic acid derivatives is NOT possible by nucleophilic reaction?

A. Acid chloride → ester
B. Acid chloride → anhydride
C. Anhydride → amide
D. Ester → anhydride

9. Acyl halides make excellent reactants in carboxylic acid derivative synthesis because

A. halides are amenable to nucleophilic attack.
B. halides are amenable to electrophilic attack.
C. halide ions are good leaving groups.
D. there is a lack of rotation around the C=O bond.

10. Which of the following undergoes a Fischer esterification most rapidly?

A.

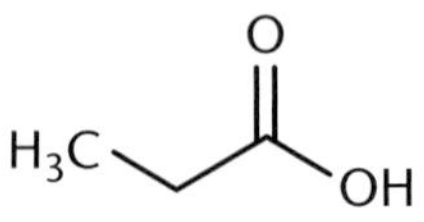

B.

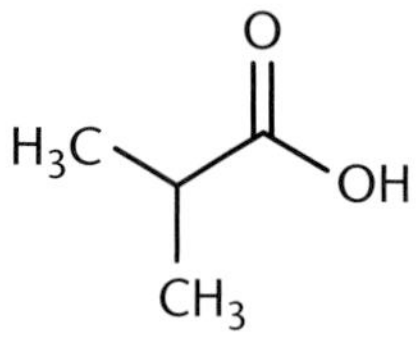

C.

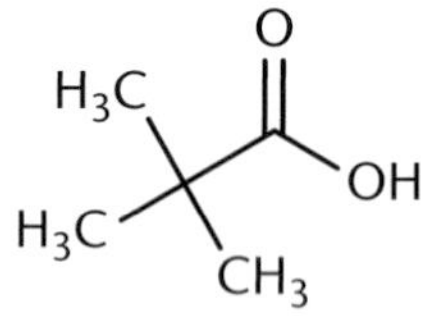

D.

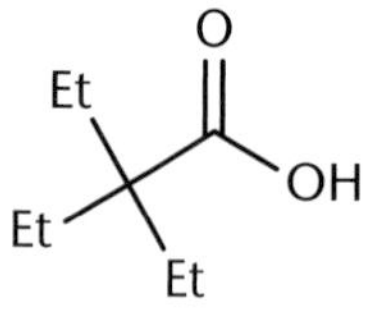

Small Group Questions

1. We provided the mechanism for acid-catalyzed hydrolysis of esters. Draw out the mechanism for base-catalyzed hydrolysis and examine the similarities and differences between the mechanisms.

2. Why is the hydrolysis of esters (saponification) irreversible?

Explanations to Practice Questions

1. D

Treating a carboxylic acid with thionyl chloride results in the production of an acyl chloride. In this reaction, butanoic acid is converted to butanoyl chloride, which is choice (D).

2. C

Hydrolysis of an acid chloride results in the formation of a carboxylic acid and HCl. Therefore, basic pyridine serves to neutralize acidic HCl. The reaction does not result in the formation of hydroxide ions, so choice (A) is wrong. We can assume that pyridine does not neutralize carboxylic acid (D) because if it did, the reaction would be unsuccessful. No scientist would add a reagent that would consume the desired product! Thus, HCl must be the acid that pyridine neutralizes. Finally, choice (B) is incorrect because reactivity is characteristic of acyl chlorides. Again, the correct answer is choice (C).

3. B

In this question, an acid chloride is treated with an alcohol, and the product will be an ester. However, the esterification process is affected by the presence of bulky side chains on either reactant, as it is easier to esterify an unhindered alcohol than a hindered one. In this reaction, the primary hydroxyl group is less hindered and will react with benzoyl chloride more rapidly, so choice (B) is correct. Choice (A) is incorrect because the hydroxyl group is secondary and therefore more hindered and the reaction rate will be slower. Choice (C) is incorrect because it is not an ester. Choice (D) is prevented by the same steric issues that hold back choice (A).

4. A

Acid chlorides react with ammonia or other amines to form amides. These amines must have a hydrogen to give up so that they can form a bond with carbon; therefore, only ammonia and primary or secondary amines can undergo this reaction. A primary amide is one in which only one carbon substituent is bound to nitrogen, so it must be the carbonyl carbon. Therefore, nitrogen cannot come with any pre-existing bonds to other carbons. Ammonia, choice (A), must be used. The reaction of an alcohol with an acid chloride produces an ester, so choice (B) is incorrect. A primary amine reacting with an acid chloride would result in a secondary amide; thus, choice (C) is incorrect. Choice (D) is wrong because tertiary amines will not react with acid chlorides, as nitrogen has no leaving groups that it can release in exchange for new bonds.

5. A

Methyl propanoate is an ester; it can be synthesized by reacting a carboxylic acid with an alcohol in the presence of acid (A). Reacting ethanol with propanoyl chloride (B) will also result in the formation of an ester, but because ethanol is used, ethyl propanoate will be formed, not methyl propanoate. This is also the case for choice (D), because ethanol is used here as well. Choice (C) is incorrect because propanoyl chloride will not form an ester in the presence of base alone. Therefore, choice (A) is the correct response.

6. D

This question asks for the products when ammonia reacts with acetic anhydride. Recall from the notes that an amide and an ammonium carboxylate will be formed. The only choice showing such a pair is (D), acetamide and ammonium acetate.

7. C

This question gives a reaction scheme for the conversion of propanoic acid to various derivatives, and it asks what intermediate products are formed. The first reaction involves the formation of an acid chloride using thionyl chloride. Thus, choices (A) and (B), which depict intact carboxylic acid functionalities, can be eliminated. The second reaction is an ammonolysis of propanoyl chloride. The product should be propanamide, because ammonia will replace the chloride on the carbonyl carbon. This does not help us choose between (C) and (D), but it is an important concept to know for Test Day. The final reaction involves amide hydrolysis. Hydrolysis leads to carboxylic acid formation. Distinguishing between choices (C) and (D), which both have a carboxylic acid as the third product, involves understanding how carboxylic acids exist in acidic and basic conditions. In acidic solution, the carboxyl group will be protonated, whereas in basic solution, the carboxyl group will be deprotonated. This reaction involves hydrolysis in the presence of base; therefore, the resulting carboxylic acid will exist in solution as a carboxylate salt. Thus, choice (C) is the correct answer, because it has sodium propanoate as the product of the third reaction.

8. D

There is a hierarchy to the reactivity of carboxylic acid derivatives that dictates how reactive they are toward nucleophilic attack. This order, from highest to lowest, is acid chlorides > anhydrides > esters > amides. In practical terms, this means that derivatives of higher reactivity can form derivatives of lower activity but not vice versa. Acid chlorides are more reactive than anhydrides and esters; thus, answers (A) and (B) are incorrect. Anhydrides are more reactive than amides, making answer (C) incorrect. Nucleophilic attack of an ester cannot result in the corresponding anhydride. Esters can only be converted into amides. (D) is the correct answer.

9. C

Halide ions are excellent leaving groups, which make acyl halides reactive compounds (i.e., ready to kick off their halides in favor of substitution). The halides themselves are open to neither electrophilic nor nucleophilic attack, making (A) and (B) incorrect. Rotation about the carbonyl bond (D) is irrelevant because halides do not participate in that bond.

10. A

A Fischer esterification involves refluxing a carboxylic acid and a primary or secondary alcohol with an acid catalyst. Under these conditions, the carbonyl carbon is open to attack by the oxygen atom in the alcohol acting as a nucleophile. The rate of this reaction depends on the amount of steric hindrance around the carbonyl carbon, because there must be room for the alcohol to approach the carboxylic acid substrate. The molecule in choice (A) is the least sterically hindered; thus, the reaction will take place most rapidly and is the correct answer. Answers (B) through (D) have increasing amounts of steric crowding, which correlate with decreasing rates of esterification. As a result of having fewer alkyl groups, choice (A) also shows the least electron density being donated to the partially positive carbonyl carbon (in other words, choice (A) has the strongest carbonyl electrophile). Although this effect is minimal compared with the steric issues we discussed above, it does help us confirm that we chose the right answer.

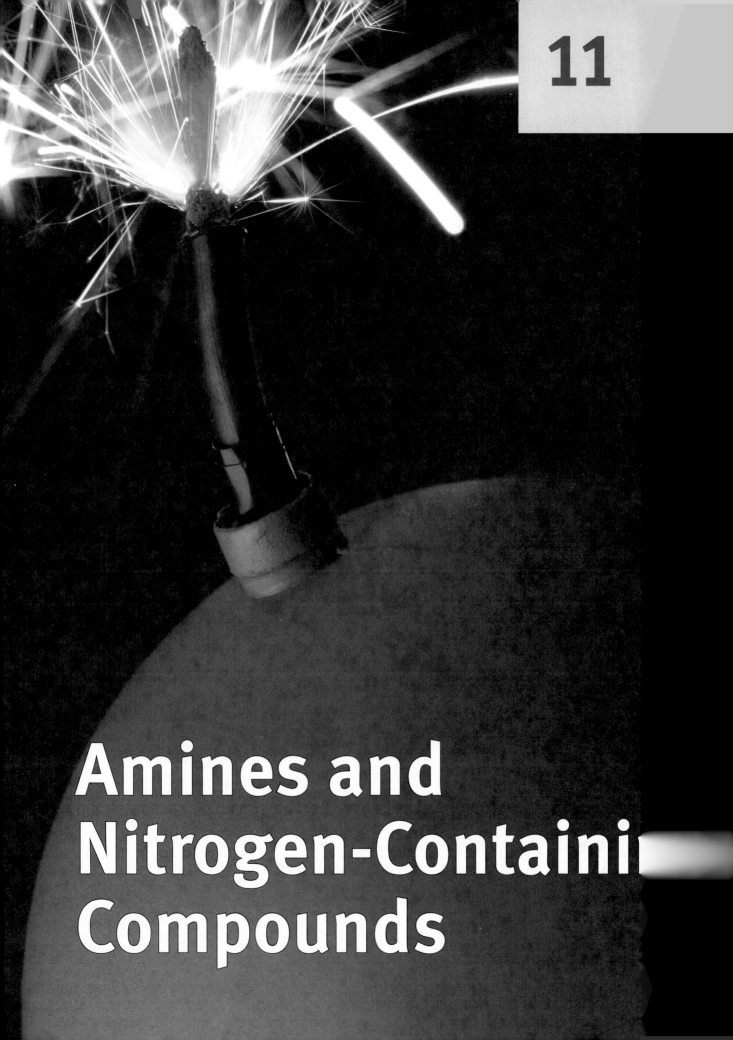

Amines and Nitrogen-Containing Compounds

We're willing to bet that the most intimidating reactions on your college Orgo exams were full of nitrogen-containing compounds. And we understand that nitrogen-containing compounds can look really scary—especially when the test makers choose to relate the story of melamine, the nitrogen-rich aromatic compound that caused the pet food recalls in 2007. However, we'll let you in on a little secret here: It doesn't matter if you get a compound you've never seen before. In fact, we're pretty sure that you *will* get a compound you've never seen before. The truth is, every nitrogen-containing compound has similar characteristics, and as long we have the fundamentals down, we won't care if it is melamine (1,3,5-triazine-2,4,6-triamine) or trinitrotoluene (TNT). This is the last chapter that will focus on specific functional groups, so make sure you're comfortable with all of the fundamentals before moving on.

MCAT Expertise

Amino groups are common in biological molecules and can hydrogen bond, so they are very likely to show up on the MCAT.

Nomenclature ★★★★☆☆

Amines have the general formula NR_3, so they normally have a lone pair of electrons. They are classified according to the number of alkyl (or aryl) groups to which they are bound. A **primary (1°)** amine is attached to one alkyl group, a **secondary (2°)** amine to two, and a **tertiary (3°)** amine to three. A nitrogen atom attached to four alkyl groups will carry a positive charge, as it has lost its lone pair forming the fourth bond. This ion is called a **quaternary ammonium compound**, and it exists as a salt owing to its positive charge.

In the common system, amines are generally named as alkylamines. The groups are designated individually, or if there are identical groups, we use the prefixes *di*– or *tri*– (just as we always do). In the IUPAC system, amines are named by substituting the suffix **–amine** for the final *e* of the name of the longest alkane to which the nitrogen is attached. *N* is used to label substituents attached to the nitrogen in secondary or tertiary amines, and we have to list a separate *N* for each different substituent attached to the nitrogen (see Table 11.1). If there is another functional group on the molecule with higher priority (more oxidized), the prefix **amino–** is used. Aromatic amines are named as derivatives of aniline ($C_6H_5NH_2$) using the common system or as derivatives of benzenamine with the IUPAC system.

Table 11.1. Amine Nomenclature

Formula:	$CH_3CH_2NH_2$	$CH_3CH_2N(CH_3)_2$	$(CH_3)_2NCH_2CH_2CH_2CH_2CH_3$
IUPAC:	ethanamine	*N,N*-dimethylethanamine	*N,N*-dimethylhexanamine
Common:	ethylamine	dimethylethylamine	dimethylhexylamine

MCAT Expertise

The naming of amines is complicated because the common names are often more, well, *common* than IUPAC. Again, don't spend a lot of time trying to figure out how to name every amine; just get a general idea. Always remember that when *N* precedes the name of a group, this means the substituent is on the nitrogen itself.

There are many other nitrogen-containing organic compounds, but we've talked about a lot of them already. **Amides** are the condensation products of carboxylic acids and amines, as we discussed in Chapter 10. **Carbamates** are compounds with the general formula RNHC(O)OR′. Because they have nitrogen attached to a carbonyl, carbamates also fall into the category of amides. But they're a special type of amide because they have an oxygen on the other side of the carbonyl with an alkyl or aryl group attached to it. Carbamates are derived from compounds called **isocyanates** (general formula RNCO, as discussed in Chapter 10 with the Hofmann rearrangement). Because isocyanates have a carbon double-bonded to both an oxygen and a nitrogen, the carbon is polar and ripe for nucleophilic attack. When the isocyante is attacked by alcohol, a carbamate is formed. Carbamates are also called **urethanes**, and they can form **polyurethanes**, an extremely useful and versatile polymer found in foams, hard plastics, and even Spandex!

Enamines are the nitrogen analogs of enols: Instead of a hydroxide group, an amine group is attached to the carbon–carbon double bond. (Thus, enamines are to nitrogen what enols are to oxygen.) **Imines** contain nitrogen–carbon double bonds. **Nitriles**, or **cyanides**, are compounds with a triple bond between a carbon atom and a nitrogen atom. They are named with either the prefix **cyano**– or the suffix –**nitrile**. **Nitro** compounds contain the nitro group, NO_2 (as discussed in Chapter 6).

Here's another hint that may help on Test Day: If you ever see a compound with **az** in its name, it contains a nitrogen. For example, the **diazo** compounds, as the name suggests, contain an N_2 functionality, with two nitrogens at the end of a chain resonating between a double and a triple bond. They tend to lose the N_2 as nitrogen gas and form **carbenes**, highly reactive carbons with only six valence electrons. This is usually seen as a carbon with two R groups and a lone pair of electrons. **Azides** are compounds with a linear N_3 functionality (double bonds between three nitrogens). When azides lose nitrogen gas (N_2), they form **nitrenes**, the nitrogen analogs of carbenes. Nitrenes tend to have their six valence electrons distributed in one bond to an R group and two lone pairs of electrons. Examples of the various nitrogen-containing compounds are shown in Figure 11.1.

Bridge

As you might guess, all amino acids are amines. Peptide bonds between amino acids in proteins are amide bonds. Urea, a molecule used to store ammonia for removal from the body, is also an amide.

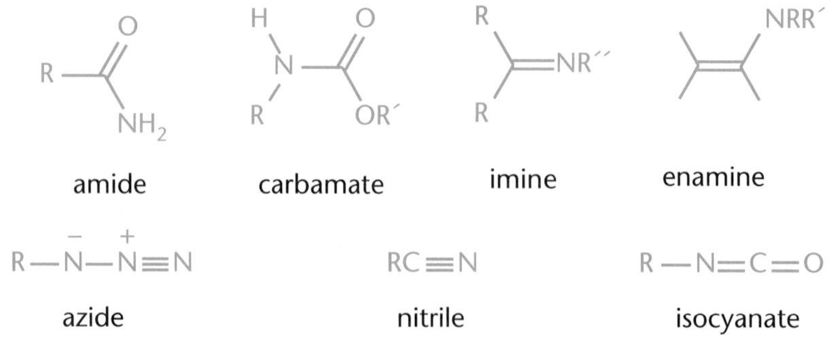

Figure 11.1

Properties

★★★★★★

The boiling points of amines lie between those of alkanes and alcohols. For example, ammonia boils at −33°C, whereas methane boils at −161°C and methanol boils at 64.5°C. Following the general trend, as molecular weight increases, so do boiling points. Primary and secondary amines can form hydrogen bonds, but because nitrogen is not as electronegative as oxygen, the hydrogen bonds of amines are not as strong as those of alcohols. Tertiary amines, on the other hand, cannot even hydrogen bond at all (they have no hydrogen!) and, thus, have lower boiling points than their other amine counterparts.

The nitrogen atom in an amine is approximately sp^3 hybridized. Nitrogen must bond to only three substituents to complete its octet; a lone pair occupies the last sp^3-orbital. The lone pair of electrons on nitrogen is the determining characteristic of nitrogen chemistry. It endows nitrogen-containing compounds with their basic and nucleophilic properties. In addition, nitrogen is more electronegative than carbon but less than oxygen, which will indicate the distribution of electron density on a molecule. Just keep these two facts in mind whenever you approach reactants with nitrogen.

Nitrogen atoms bonded to three different substituents are technically chiral because of the geometry of the orbitals. However, these enantiomers cannot be isolated because they interconvert rapidly in a process called **nitrogen inversion**: an inversion of the sp^3-orbital occupied by the lone pair (see Figure 11.2). The activation energy for this process is only 6 kcal/mol, so the nitrogen will not be optically active. However at very low temperatures, or if the structure prevents the inversion of the molecule, it will be optically active. An example would be the quaternary ammonium salts, which, lacking a lone pair, do not interconvert.

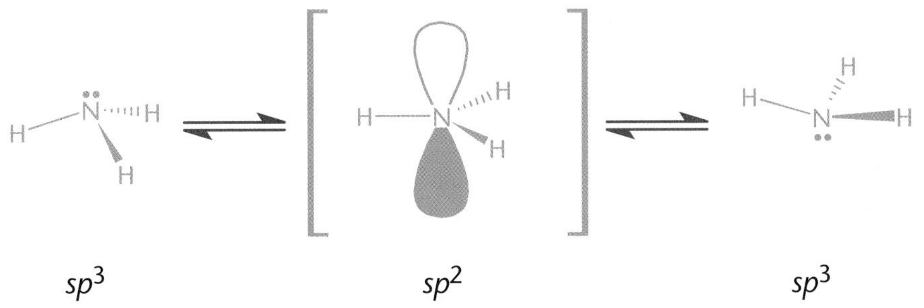

sp^3 sp^2 sp^3

Figure 11.2

Amines are bases, so they readily accept protons to form ammonium ions. The pK_b value of alkyl amines is around 4, making them slightly more basic than ammonia ($pK_b = 4.76$) but less basic than hydroxide ($pK_b = −1.7$). Aromatic amines such as aniline (pK_b = 9.42) are far less basic than aliphatic amines, because the electron-withdrawing effect of the ring reduces the basicity of the amino group. The presence of other substituents on the ring also alters the basicity of anilines: Electron-donating groups (such as $-OH$, $-CH_3$, and $-NH_2$) increase basicity, whereas electron-withdrawing groups (such as NO_2) reduce basicity (discussed in Chapter 6).

Amines also function as weak acids. The pK_a's of amines are around 35; thus, a strong base is required for deprotonation. For example, the proton of diisopropylamine may be removed with the superbase butyllithium, forming the sterically hindered base lithium diisopropylamide (LDA) and butane shown in Figure 11.3.

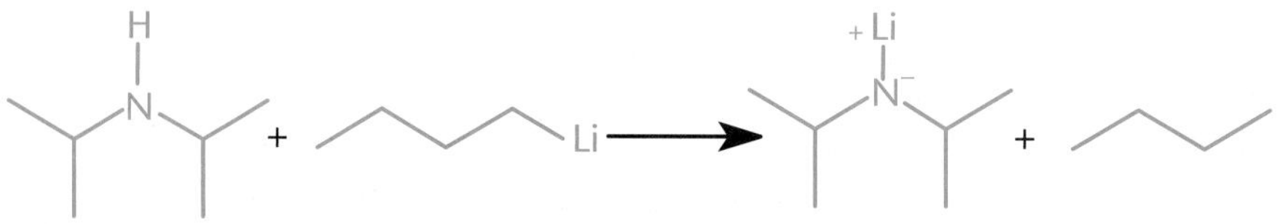

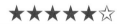

Figure 11.3

Real World

An interesting property of several nitrogen-containing compounds, such as nitroglycerin and nitrous oxide, is their ability to act as relaxants. Nitroglycerine is given sublingually (under the tongue) to relieve coronary artery spasms in people with chest pain, and nitrous oxide (laughing gas) is a common dental anesthetic. Nitroglycerine has the additional property of rapidly decomposing to form gas and, thus, is fairly explosive.

Synthesis ★★★★★☆

ALKYLATION OF AMMONIA

Direct

Alkyl halides react with ammonia to produce alkylammonium halide salts, shown below, as in Figure 11.4. Ammonia functions as a nucleophile and displaces the halide atom. When the salt is treated with base, the alkylamine product is formed.

$$CH_3Br + NH_3 \longrightarrow CH_3\overset{+}{N}H_3Br^- \xrightarrow{NaOH} CH_3NH_2 + NaBr + H_2O$$

Figure 11.4

Key Concept

This is an S_N2 reaction mechanism. The product will actually be a better nucleophile than the original nucleophile, because the electron-donating properties of the alkyl group cause further substitution.

This reaction can often lead to side products. The alkylamine formed is itself nucleophilic because of the lone pair on the nitrogen, and it can react with the alkyl halide to form more complex products.

Gabriel Synthesis

The Gabriel synthesis converts a primary alkyl halide to a primary amine. To do this, we must first create a disguised form of ammonia (deprotonated phthalimide) to prevent side product formation (see Figure 11.5).

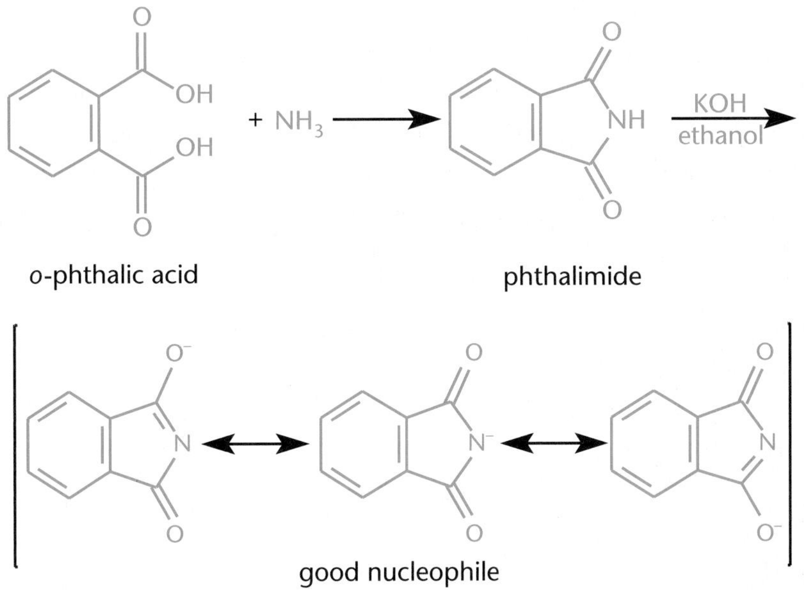

o-phthalic acid   phthalimide

good nucleophile

Figure 11.5

Phthalimide, the condensation product of phthalic acid and ammonia, acts as a good nucleophile when deprotonated. It displaces halide ions, forming *N*-alkylphthalimides, which do not react with other alkyl halides. When the reaction is complete, the *N*-alkylphthalimide can be hydrolyzed with aqueous base to produce our product, the alkylamine (see Figure 11.6).

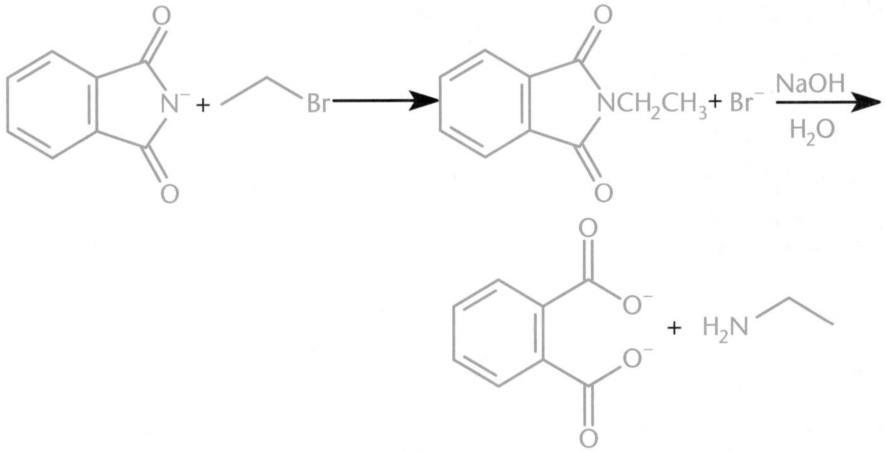

Figure 11.6

> ## Key Concept
>
> Addition of ammonia to an alkyl halide and the Gabriel synthesis are both S_N2 reactions. With its unshared electron pair, ammonia is a good nucleophile, whereas the halides (except fluorine) are all good leaving groups (see Chapter 4).

REDUCTION

Amines can be obtained from other nitrogen-containing compounds via reduction reactions.

Nitro Compounds

We can easily reduce nitro compounds to primary amines. The most common reducing agent is iron or zinc used with dilute hydrochloric acid (see Figure 11.7), although many other reagents can be used. This reaction is especially useful for aromatic compounds, because nitration of aromatic rings is easy and the reduction converts a deactivating group into an activating group.

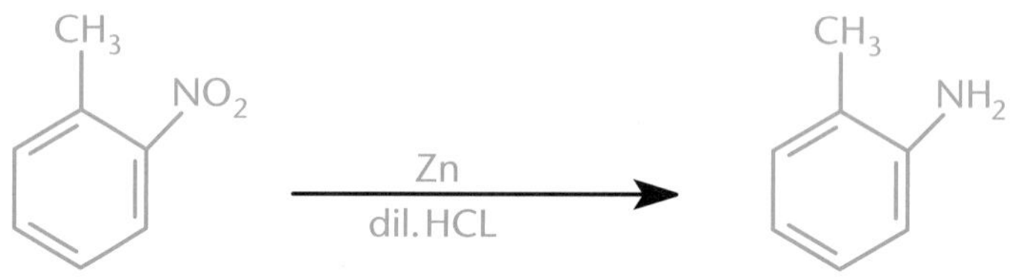

Figure 11.7

Nitriles

Nitriles can be reduced with hydrogen and a metal catalyst, or with lithium aluminum hydride (LAH) as shown in Figure 11.8, yielding primary amines.

$$CH_3CH_2C{\equiv}N \xrightarrow{\text{LAH}} CH_3CH_2CH_2NH_2$$

Figure 11.8

Imines

Another method for synthesizing amines is **reductive amination**. We start with an aldehyde or ketone and react it with ammonia, a primary amine, or a secondary amine. This reaction yields a primary, secondary, or tertiary amine, respectively, and the carbonyl becomes an –OH group (a carbinolamine). The carbinolamine loses water to form an imine, but when the imine is exposed to hydrogen and a metal catalyst, it will undergo reduction in much the same way that a carbonyl does, producing the amine.

Key Concept

An imine is a nitrogen double bonded to a carbon atom. It looks like a carbonyl and acts like one, too, with similar polarity and similar reactivity.

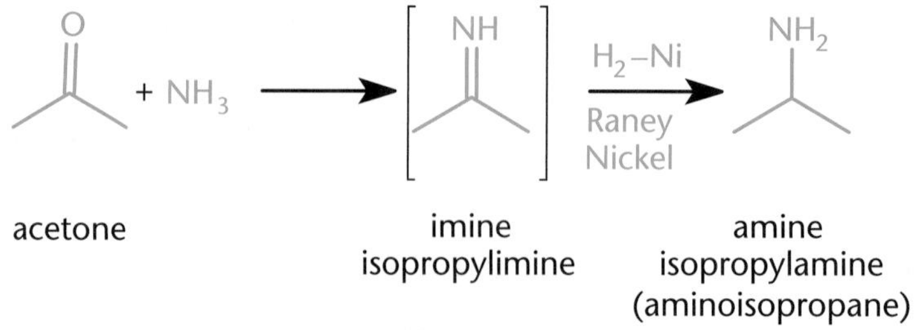

Figure 11.9

Amides

Amides can be reduced with LAH to form amines, as discussed in Chapter 10, (see Figure 11.10).

Figure 11.10

Reactions ★★★☆☆

EXHAUSTIVE METHYLATION

Exhaustive methylation is also known as **Hofmann elimination**. In this process, an amine is converted to quaternary ammonium iodide by treatment with excess methyl iodide. In other words, the nitrogen now has methyl groups in all the positions where it used to have hydrogens or lone pairs. Treatment with silver oxide and water displaces the iodide ion and converts the molecule to ammonium hydroxide, which, when heated, undergoes elimination to form an alkene and an amine (see Figure 11.11). The predominant alkene formed is the least substituted, in contrast with normal elimination reactions, where the predominant alkene product is the most substituted. The least substituted alkene is formed because of the bulk of the quarternary ammonium salt leaving group.

> **Key Concept**
>
> Amines can be formed by the following:
>
> 1) S_N2 reactions:
>   - Ammonia reacting with alkyl halides
>   - Gabriel synthesis
>
> 2) Reduction of:
>   - Amides
>   - Aniline and its derivatives
>   - Nitriles
>   - Imines
>
> Amines can be converted to alkenes by exhaustive methylation followed by an E2 reaction forming the less-substituted alkene.

Figure 11.11

Conclusion

There are a lot of functional groups to remember in this chapter, and we urge you to learn them all. Once you've taken the time to learn the basics, make sure you take the time to *practice using them*. Look under the sink, flip through this book, or grab your old textbook from college—just pick some reactants and figure out what could happen. If you're not sure, ask a classmate; figure it out together. The best way to learn is to teach each other.

This isn't the last time you will see nitrogen-containing compounds in this book. Nitrogen returns in the final chapter in the form of amino acids (along with carbon, of course!), which combine to create the peptides and proteins that establish the structure and functions of every living thing. But once again, even as we deal with bigger and more complex molecules, the chemistry comes down to functional groups and general trends.

We hope this chapter has helped you realize that no matter what molecule the MCAT throws at you, as long as you know the characteristics of nitrogen-containing functional groups, you will be able to find the *best* answer. Even if that molecule is … melamine.

CONCEPTS TO REMEMBER

☐ The suffix *–amine* is used when the amine has the highest priority.

☐ The prefix *amino–* is used when the amine does not have the highest priority.

☐ Remember the nitrogen-containing functional groups: amides; carbamates = urethanes; isocyanates; enamines; imines; nitriles = cyanides; nitro; diazo; azide; carbene; nitrene.

☐ The boiling point of amines is between that of alcohols and alkanes.

☐ Certain amines can be optically active if inversion is inhibited by sterics.

☐ Amines have lone pairs, so they are bases/nucleophiles.

☐ A nitrogen double-bonded to carbon (imine) acts like an oxygen double-bonded to carbon (carbonyl).

☐ Addition of ammonia to an alkyl halide and the Gabriel synthesis are both S_N2 reactions.

☐ Many nitrogen-containing function groups are easily reduced to amines.

☐ Exhaustive methylation = Hofmann elimination. In this reaction, the nitrogen of an amine is released as trimethylamine, and the substituent is converted into the least substituted alkene.

Practice Questions

1. A compound with the general formula $R_4N^+X^-$ is classified as a

   A. secondary amine.
   B. quaternary ammonium salt.
   C. tertiary amine.
   D. primary amine.

2. Amines have lower boiling points than the corresponding alcohols because

   A. they have higher molecular weights.
   B. they form stronger hydrogen bonds.
   C. they form weaker hydrogen bonds.
   D. There is no systematic difference between the boiling points of amines and alcohols.

3. Which of the following would be formed if methyl bromide were reacted with phthalimide and followed by hydrolysis with aqueous base?

   A. $C_2H_5NH_2$
   B. CH_3NH_2
   C. $(C_2H_5)_3N$
   D. $(CH_3)_4N^+Br^-$

4. The reaction of benzamide with $LiAlH_4$ yields which of the following compounds?

   A. Benzoic acid
   B. Benzonitrile
   C. Benzylamine
   D. Ammonium benzoate

5. Which of the following amines has the highest boiling point?

   A. CH_3NH_2
   B. $CH_3(CH_2)_6NH_2$
   C. $CH_3(CH_2)_3NH_2$
   D. $(CH_3)_3CNH_2$

6. If 2-amino-3-methylbutane were treated with excess methyl iodide, silver oxide, and water, what would be the major reaction products?

   A. Ammonia and 2-methyl-2-butene
   B. Trimethylamine and 3-methyl-1-butene
   C. Trimethylamine and 2-methyl-2-butene
   D. Ammonia and 3-methyl-1-butene

7. Nylon, a polyamide, is produced from hexanediamine and a substance X. This substance X is most probably

   A. an amine.
   B. a carboxylic acid.
   C. a nitrile.
   D. an alcohol.

8. What is the IUPAC name for the compound shown below?

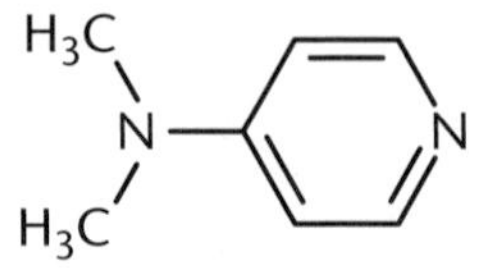

   A. 4-(*N*-dimethylamino)pyridine
   B. Dimethylaminopyridine
   C. 4-(*N,N*-dimethylamino)pyridine
   D. *N,N*-dimethylaminopyridine

9. Pyrrolidine is an excellent base with a pK_a of 11.27. In contrast, pyrrole, which has a similar structure, is a poor base with a pK_a of 0.4. Why is pyrrole such a poor base compared with pyrrolidine?

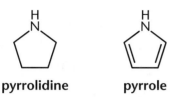

pyrrolidine   **pyrrole**

A. Pyrrole is aromatic.

B. Pyrrolidine is antiaromatic.

C. The nitrogen atom in pyrrole does not have any lone pairs.

D. The nitrogen in pyrrolidine contains an extra lone pair.

10. What product is formed from the following reaction?

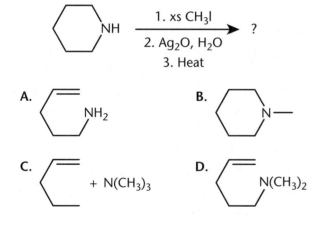

Small Group Questions

1. Why is the C–N bond of an amide planar?

2. Does a protonated amide have resonance stabilization?

Explanations to Practice Questions

1. B

A quaternary ammonium salt has four substituents attached to the central nitrogen, resulting in a positive charge. As a result, this compound forms a salt, where X^- is usually a halide. Primary amines have the general formula RNH_2, secondary amines have the general formula R_2NH, and tertiary amines have the general formula R_3N. Therefore, choices (A), (C), and (D) are incorrect.

2. C

Amines form weaker hydrogen bonds than alcohols, because nitrogen has a lower electronegativity than oxygen. The molecules are not held together as tightly and are therefore more volatile.

3. B

The reaction between methyl bromide and phthalimide results in the formation of methyl phthalimide. Subsequent hydrolysis then yields methylamine, so choice (B) is the correct response. Therefore, the overall reaction is the conversion of a primary alkyl halide into a primary amine (known as the Gabriel synthesis). Choice (A) is wrong because it contains an ethyl group, not a methyl group. To form this compound, the initial reactant should be ethyl bromide. Choices (C) and (D) are incorrect because these are tertiary and quaternary nitrogen compounds, respectively, and the reaction only converts primary alkyl halides into primary amines.

4. C

Lithium aluminum hydride is a good reducing agent and is used to reduce amides to amines. Reduction of benzamide will result in the formation of benzylamine (C). Hydrolysis of benzamide would result in the formation of benzoic acid, so choice (A) is incorrect. Benzonitrile would be formed by amide dehydration, so choice (B) is also wrong. To form ammonium benzoate (D), benzamide would first have to be hydrolyzed and then reacted with ammonia, so this answer choice is also incorrect.

5. B

As the molecular weights of amines increase, so do their boiling points. Of the choices given, choice (B), heptylamine, has the highest molecular weight and therefore the highest boiling point, 142°C–144°C. For comparison's sake, choice (A), methylamine, has a boiling point of −6.3°C, butylamine, choice (C), has a boiling point of 77.5°C, and *t*-butylamine, choice (D), has a boiling point of 44.4°C.

6. B

Treatment of an amine with excess methyl iodide, silver oxide, and water is called exhaustive methylation or Hofmann elimination. A trisubstituted amine and an alkene are the products formed. 2-Amino-3-methylbutane is a primary amine; therefore, it will be able to pick up three methyl groups after separating from the alkyl chain. The trisubstituted amine produced will be trimethylamine. The predominant alkene product will be the least substituted alkene, because removal of a secondary hydrogen is sterically hindered. Therefore, this reaction will produce 3-methyl-1-butene, plus trimethylamine (B). Choices (A) and (D) are incorrect; ammonia cannot be a product of this reaction because the mechanism involves the addition of methyl groups. Choice (C) is incorrect because 2-methyl-2-butene, the more substituted alkene, would not be the predominant product.

7. B

An amide is formed from an amine and a carboxyl group or its acyl derivatives. In this question, an amine is already given; the compound to be identified must be an acyl compound. The only acyl compound among the choices given is a carboxylic acid, choice (B).

8. C

All groups (except hydrogen atoms) bonded to nitrogen need to be specified by the *N–* prefix, followed by the group. This prefix is repeated for each group. Answer (A) is incorrect because it fails to provide an *N–* prefix per methyl substituent, whereas answer (B) is incorrect because it lacks both a numerical position and *N–* prefixes. Answer (D) is incorrect because the position of the amino substituent is not specified.

9. A

The nitrogen atoms in pyrrolidine and pyrrole each have one lone pair (with three bond pairs) when neutral, so answers (C) and (D) are incorrect. An antiaromatic system has $4n$ electrons, where n is an integer. Because pyrrolidine lacks such a system, answer (B) is incorrect. Pyrrole is indeed aromatic, because it has six π electrons. Aromatic compounds have stable electron systems and prefer to remain undisturbed.

10. D

This is an exhaustive methylation reaction. The amine is not an individual product; rather, it is tethered to the alkene. Answer (B) shows an incomplete reaction, as there is no alkene present. Answer (A) is incorrect because the amine must be trisubstituted. Answer (C) is incorrect because the nitrogen can only pick up two methyl groups, based on the number of carbons to which it is already bound.

Purification and Separation

We've spent a lot of time discussing how to get various products from a plethora of discussed reagents, but as we're sure you learned in your Organic Chemistry labs, chemistry isn't as straightforward in the real world as it is on paper. Although the reaction itself may be completed in a matter of minutes, separating out the desired product can be difficult and tends to take up the majority of our time in lab. In fact, much of the actual work we end up doing in Organic Chemistry is concerned with the isolation and purification of the desired product. Throughout this chapter, we will discuss several techniques to isolate products. In addition, we have some good news for you: There is no lab practical on the MCAT, so if you were that clumsy student who managed to break three separatory funnels, the test makers will never know. Just understand *when* to use these techniques and understand *why* they work; and you'll do great.

Basic Techniques ★★★★☆

EXTRACTION

One of the simplest ways to separate out a desired product is through **extraction**, the transfer of a dissolved compound (the desired product) from a starting solvent into a solvent in which the product is more soluble. Extraction is based on the fundamental concept that *like dissolves like*. This principle tells us that a polar substance will dissolve best in polar solvents and a nonpolar substance will stick with the nonpolar solvents. If we selectively take advantage of this characteristic, we can extract our desired product, leaving most of the impurities behind in the first solvent.

When we perform extractions, it is important to make sure that the two solvents are immiscible (form two layers that do not mix, such as vinegar and oil). The two layers are temporarily mixed (when shaken like a Polaroid picture) so that solute can pass from one solvent to the other. For example, in a solution of isobutyric acid and diethyl ether, we can extract the isobutyric acid with water. Isobutyric acid, with its polar carboxy group, is more soluble in water than in ether, so when the two solvents are mixed together, isobutyric acid will transfer to the water in the aqueous phase.

After we mix the two layers together, how do we get our desired product out? The water (aqueous) and ether (organic) phases will separate on their own if we give them enough time to settle in a specialized piece of glassware called a **separatory funnel** (see Figure 12.1). Gravitational forces cause the heavier layer to sink to the bottom of the funnel, and the bottom layer can be removed. The separatory funnel is a lot like a normal funnel, just with a stopper on the bottom and a much bigger price tag. In general, the organic layer will be on the top and the aqueous layer will be on the bottom, although the opposite can also occur, because the order of the layers is determined by their relative densities. Once we drain out the aqueous layer from the bottom of the funnel, we will have removed most of the isobutyric acid from the mixture, but a small amount will remain dissolved in the ether phase. To retrieve the rest of the acid, we repeat the extraction several times with fresh solvent (water). We will get more of the product out of the mixture if we perform multiple extractions, meaning that we will get higher yield if we perform three consecutive extractions of 10 mL than if we perform one extraction of 30 mL. This is analogous to the fact that it is more effective to wash dirty clothes three times than it is to wash them once with three times the detergent (unless you're trying to have a suds party). Once our compound has been isolated in the solvent, we can obtain the compound alone by evaporating the solvent, usually using a rotary evaporator (Rotovap).

Figure 12.1

Another way to take advantage of solubility properties is to perform the reverse of the extraction we just described and remove unwanted impurities. This process is called a **wash**, because it is washing the product of unwanted impurities.

FILTRATION

Another simple purification technique is **filtration**, which isolates a solid from a liquid. This technique is governed by the same concept you use to separate your cooked spaghetti from boiling water. It's much easier to pour the entire contents of the pot into a colander than it is to try to suck out the boiling water. In the chemistry lab, we pour our liquid-solid mixture onto a paper filter that allows only the solvent to pass through (much like a coffee filter in an automatic coffee pot). At the end of a filtration, we have a solid (often called the residue) on the filter paper and a flask full of the liquid that passed through the filter, known as the **filtrate**.

We will encounter two basic types of filtration on the MCAT: gravity filtration and vacuum filtration. In **gravity filtration**, the solvent's own weight pulls it through the filter, just like what happens in our coffee pot. Frequently, however, the pores of the filter become clogged with solid, slowing the rate of filtration and possibly resulting in a big mess. For this reason, when we use gravity filtration we want the substance of interest to be in solution (dissolved in the solvent), and for any impurities to remain undissolved. This is exactly what happens when we make coffee. Furthermore, because we want to ensure that the product remains dissolved, gravity filtration is usually carried out with hot solvent (hot coffee anyone?).

Alternatively, we can use **vacuum filtration** to separate our liquid-solid mixture. In this method, the solvent is forced through the filter by a vacuum on the other side. To do this, you need a specific flask that has a valve on the side to attach the vacuum, called a Büchner flask, although it is often referred to simply as a vacuum flask (see Figure 12.2). This method works much faster, so vacuum filtration is used when you need to isolate relatively large quantities of solid, particularly when the solid is the desired product. Remember that we don't hook up a vacuum system to make coffee, and you'll remember that the solid is our desired product for vacuum filtration.

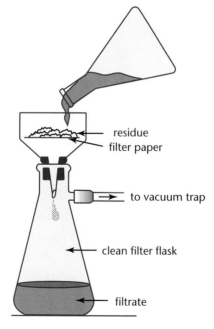

residue
filter paper

to vacuum trap

clean filter flask

filtrate

Figure 12.2

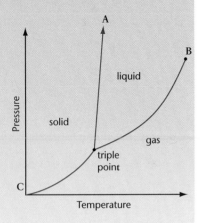
RECRYSTALLIZATION

When we use vacuum filtration to isolate a solid product, significant impurities may still be present. At this point, we can use recrystallization to purify our solid product even further. In this process, we dissolve our product in a minimum of hot solvent, and let it recrystallize as it cools—but we need to be really picky about our choice of solvent. We want to make sure that our solid product is soluble in the solvent at *high temperatures only*. In other words, we want our product to be insoluble at cold (or even room) temperature. This way, when we heat up the solvent, the entire solid product will dissolve (our desired product and all the impurities). When it cools, however, only our desired product will recrystallize out of solution, because the solute's defined crystal lattice tends to exclude the impurities.

We must also consider the polarity of the solvent, because polar solvents dissolve polar compounds and nonpolar solvents dissolve nonpolar compounds. On Test Day, you are likely to be given a chart that describes the solubilities of all the possible solvents (there's no time for trial-and-error experiments). If the solubility information is not available, a solvent with intermediate polarity is generally desirable for recrystallization. In addition, our solvent should have a low enough freezing point so that the solution may be sufficiently cooled without a chance of freezing.

In some instances, a mixed solvent system may be used for recrystallization. First, we dissolve the crude compound in a solvent in which it is highly soluble. Then we slowly add another solvent in which the compound is less soluble. This second solvent is added in drops, just until the solid begins to precipitate. We then heat the solution again, enough to redissolve the precipitate. After it dissolves, we slowly cool the mixture to induce crystal formation, which can then be isolated with vacuum filtration.

SUBLIMATION

Sublimation is one of the great stage acts of chemistry. Recall from General Chemistry that sublimation occurs when a heated solid turns directly into a gas without passing through an intermediate liquid stage. Sublimation can be used as a method of purification because the impurities found in most reaction mixtures will not sublime easily.

To perform sublimation, we produce vapors that condense on a chilled glass tube called a **cold finger** (see Figure 12.3). What exactly is a cold finger, you ask? It's just a piece of glassware chilled by packing with dry ice or running cold water through it. Most sublimations are performed under vacuum, because at lower pressures, compounds will be less likely to pass through a liquid phase and will sublime instead. Another benefit of using a vacuum is that the low pressure reduces the temperature required for sublimation (just as low-pressure conditions reduce the temperature for evaporation) and, thus, the danger that the compound will decompose. The optimal conditions depend on the compound we are purifying (because each compound has a different phase diagram), although most compounds (other than water) have a phase diagram similar to the one seen in the key concept margin note on page 214.

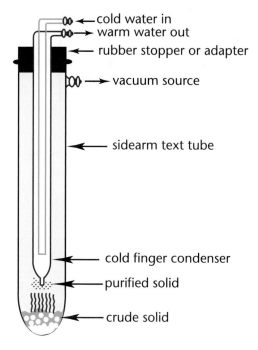

cold water in
warm water out
rubber stopper or adapter
vacuum source

sidearm text tube

cold finger condenser
purified solid
crude solid

Figure 12.3

CENTRIFUGATION

Have you ever been on the Gravitron ride at a carnival? That giant spinning contraption is simply a huge, slowed-down version of a centrifuge. Centrifugation relies on the fact that particles in a solution settle (sediment) at different rates depending on their mass, density, and shape. This means that the heavy, dense particles will settle at the bottom of the solution and the lighter particles end up on top. This natural process can be completed at hyperspeed by spinning the solution around really, *really* fast via a centrifuge (see Figure 12.4). Inside a centrifuge, the solution (in test tubes) is subjected to centrifugal forces, causing the compounds of greater mass and density to settle toward the bottom of the test tubes, while lighter compounds remain near the top (the same as what would happen if you just let the test tube sit, only much faster). We use this method of separation frequently in biochemistry, when we separate large particles such as cells, organelles, and biological macromolecules.

Real World

Centrifugation is generally used to separate large things from each other. For example, you can

- centrifuge blood to separate cells (red blood cells, white blood cells, and platelets) from plasma;

- centrifuge cell debris to separate out organelles of interest, such as mitochondria;

- centrifuge (at extremely high speeds—called ultracentrifugation) to separate big DNA molecules, such as bacterial chromosomes, from smaller ones, such as plasmids. Large quantities of pure DNA are obtained using this method.

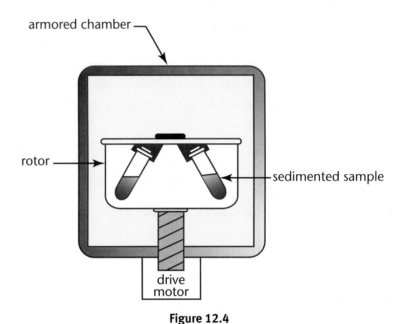

armored chamber

rotor

sedimented sample

drive motor

Figure 12.4

Mnemonic

*Se*Dimentation depends on *Si*ze (mass) and *D*ensity.

Distillation

★★★☆☆

All of the techniques we've discussed so far have been methods to separate compounds that don't mix together perfectly. But what happens when we have two separate liquids that have similar polarities and are, therefore, soluble in each other? This is where distillation comes in handy. Distillation takes advantage of differences in boiling point to separate two liquids by vaporization and condensation. The liquid with the lower boiling point will vaporize first, and the vapors rise up and condense in a water-cooled distillation column, dripping down the column into a vessel that catches the distillate. The temperature is kept low enough so the liquid with the higher boiling point will never boil and, thus, remain liquid in the initial container. This is the process that is used to make liquor (at a *distill*ery). Because ethanol boils at a lower temperature than water, we can use distillation to make beverages with high ethanol contents.

SIMPLE DISTILLATION

Simple distillation is just what it sounds like, the most basic kind of distillation. It is exactly like the distillation described above. Because there are no special factors involved in this distillation, it should only be used to separate liquids that boil below 150°C and that have at least a 25°C difference in boiling point. This way, the temperature is low enough that the compounds won't degrade, and there is a large enough difference in boiling points that we won't accidentally cause the second compound to boil off into the distillate. The apparatus itself consists of a distilling flask containing the two liquids, a distillation column consisting of a thermometer and a condenser, and a receiving flask to collect the distillate.

VACUUM DISTILLATION

We use **vacuum distillation** whenever we want to distill a liquid that has a boiling point over 150°C. By using a vacuum, we are lowering the pressure over the surface of the liquid. This decreases the temperature that the liquid must reach to boil (the same reason water boils at a lower temperature in the mountains of Colorado than it does in New York City: less air pressure). This way, we don't have to worry about degrading the compound with excessively high heat, and we get the liquid to boil faster, a win-win situation. The apparatus shown in Figure 12.5 is for vacuum distillation, but notice that if we were to remove the vacuum, it would be a simple distillation.

Bridge

Remember from General Chemistry that liquids boil when their vapor pressure equals atmospheric pressure. In vacuum distillation, we lower the atmospheric pressure so that the liquid can boil at lower temperatures.

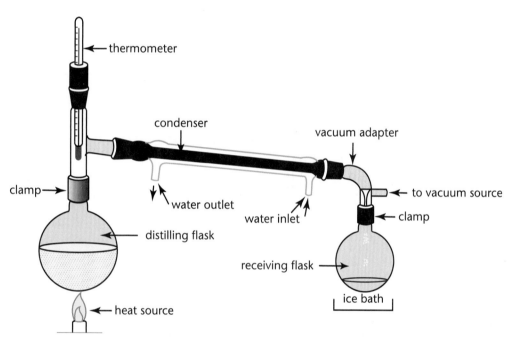

Figure 12.5

FRACTIONAL DISTILLATION

When we want to separate two liquids with similar boiling points (less than 25°C apart), we use **fractional distillation**. In this distillation, we use a fractioning column to connect the distilling flask to the distillation column (see Figure 12.6). A fractioning column is basically any column filled with inert objects, such as glass beads or steel wool, which act to increase the surface area of the column. As the vapors rise up the column they will condense on the available surfaces, and then as more heat rises, the condensation will re-evaporate and rise up further, thus recondensing even higher on the column. Each time the condensations evaporate, the vapors will contain a greater proportion of the lower–boiling point component. By the time the vapors make it to the top of the fractioning column, the vapor is composed of only our desired substance, which then condenses in the distillation column and drips down to the receiving flask.

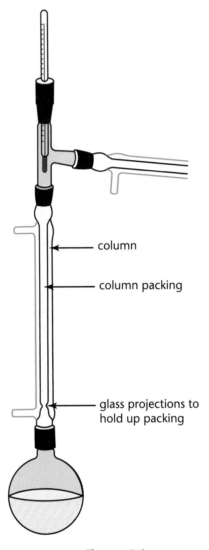

column

column packing

glass projections to hold up packing

Figure 12.6

Chromatography ★★★★☆☆

Chromatography is another tool that uses physical and chemical properties to separate and identify compounds from a complex mixture. In all forms of chromatography discussed here, the concept is identical: The more similar the compound is to its surroundings (whether by polarity, charge, etc.), the more it will stick and move slowly through its surroundings.

The process begins by placing our sample onto a solid medium called the **stationary phase** or **adsorbent**. We then run the **mobile phase**, usually a liquid (or gas in gas chromatography) through the stationary phase. This will displace (elute) the sample and carry it through the stationary phase. Depending on the substance and the polarity of the mobile phase, it will adhere to the stationary phase with different strengths, causing the different substances to migrate at different speeds. This is called partitioning, and it represents an equilibrium between the two phases. Different compounds will have different equilibrium constants and elute at different rates. This results in each compound separating within the stationary phase, allowing us to isolate them individually.

We can use a plethora of different media as our stationary phase, each one exploiting different properties that allow us to separate out our compound. Within this crowd, the property you will most likely see on the MCAT is polarity. For instance, **thin-layer chromatography (TLC)**, which we will soon discuss, uses silica gel, a highly polar substance, as its stationary phase. This means that any polar compound will adhere to the gel quite well and thus move (elute) slowly. In addition, when using **column chromatography**, size and charge both have a role in how quickly a compound moves through the stationary phase. Even strong interactions, such as antibody-ligand binding, are used in chromatography. The possibilities are virtually endless.

We've said that this whole analysis is based on the speed at which substances move through media, but we don't get out a radar gun to clock their speeds. In practice, we either measure how far each substance travels in a given amount of time (as in TLC), or we time how long it takes the substance to elute off the column (as in column or gas chromatography).

The four types of chromatography that we'll see on the MCAT are **TLC**, **column chromatography**, **gas chromatography (GC)**, and **high-pressure** (or **performance**) **liquid chromatography (HPLC)**.

THIN-LAYER CHROMATOGRAPHY

The adsorbent we use in TLC is either a piece of paper or a thin layer of silica gel or alumina adhered to an inert carrier sheet (glass or plastic). We then place the mixture that we want to separate onto the adsorbent itself; this is called **spotting** because we apply a small, well-defined spot of our mixture onto the plate. The TLC plate is then **developed**, which involves placing the adsorbent upright in a developing chamber (usually a beaker with a lid or a wide-mouthed jar) containing a shallow pool of **eluant** (solvent) at the bottom. We have to make sure that the initial spots on the plate are above the level of the solvent. If not, they'll simply elute off the plate and into the solvent, rather than moving up the plate. If everything's set up correctly, the solvent will creep up the plate via capillary action, carrying the different compounds with it at varying rates.

> **Key Concept**
>
> Chromatography separates compounds based on how strongly they adhere to the solid, or stationary, phase (or, in other words, how easily they come off into the mobile phase).

When the solvent front nears the top of the plate, the plate is removed from the chamber and allowed to dry.

As we mentioned before, TLC is often done with silica gel, which is polar and hydrophilic. The mobile phase on the other hand, is usually an organic solvent (often a mixture) of weak to moderate polarity, so it doesn't bind well to the gel. Because of this, nonpolar compounds hang out with the organic solvent and move quickly as the solvent moves up the plate, whereas the more polar molecules are stuck to the gel. **Reverse-phase chromatography** is the exact opposite. Here, the stationary phase is very nonpolar, so polar molecules move up the plate very quickly, whereas nonpolar molecules stick more tightly to the stationary phase.

The spots of individual compounds are usually white, which makes them difficult or impossible to see on the white TLC plate. To get around this problem, we can place the developed TLC plate under ultraviolet light, which will show any compounds that are ultraviolet sensitive (like forensic detectives searching a crime scene for DNA). Alternatively, we can use iodine, phosphomolybdic acid, or vanillin (yep, the kind that tastes good) to stain the spots. The problem with this is that the stain will destroy the compound (usually by oxidation), so we can't recover it.

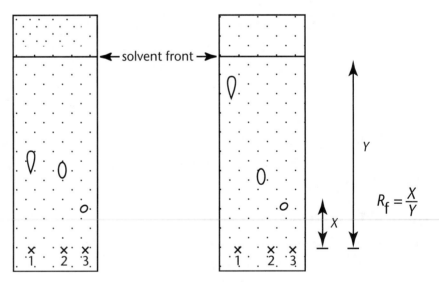

Figure 12.7

Key Concept

If the sample travels farther, it is similar to the solvent.

Now let's get into the math behind TLC. We take the distance that the compound travels and divide it by the distance that the solvent travels (which will always be a larger number). This ratio is called the R_f **value** (see Figure 12.7). This is a relatively constant value for a particular compound in a given solvent, so we can use the R_f value to find the identity of an unknown compound.

Because we generally perform this technique on a small scale, TLC is frequently used only for qualitative identification (determining the identity of a compound). If we really wanted to, we could use TLC on a larger scale as a means of purification. **Preparative** or **prep TLC** uses a large TLC plate that has a big streak of a mixture on it. As the plate develops, the streak splits into bands of individual compounds, just as it did in the small-scale version. Because the streak is so large, we can scrape the bands off and rinse them with a polar solvent, recovering the pure compounds from the silica.

COLUMN CHROMATOGRAPHY

The principle behind column chromatography is the same as for TLC. The difference with column chromatography is that it uses a column filled with silica or alumina beads as an adsorbent, allowing for much greater separation (see Figure 12.8). In addition, TLC uses capillary action to move the solvent and compounds up the plate, whereas in column chromatography, solvent and compounds move down the column by gravity. To speed up the process, we can force the solvent through the column with nitrogen gas, a technique called **flash column chromatography**. In column chromatography, the solvent polarity can easily be changed to help elute our compound.

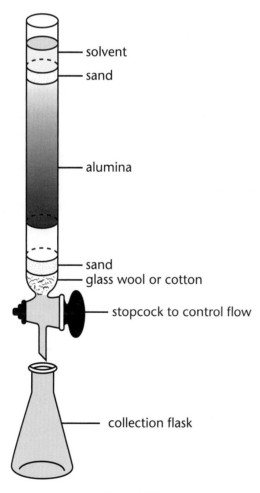

Figure 12.8

Eventually, the solvent drips out of the end of the column, and we can collect the different fractions that leave the column at varying times. Each fraction contains bands that correspond to different compounds. After collection, we can evaporate the solvent and isolate the compounds we want to keep. Column chromatography is particularly useful in biochemistry because it can be used to separate macromolecules such as proteins or nucleic acids. Several techniques can be used to isolate specific materials.

Ion Exchange Chromatography

In this method, the beads in the column are coated with charged substances, so they attract or bind compounds that have an opposite charge. For instance, a positively charged column will attract and hold the negatively charged backbone of DNA as it passes though the column, either increasing its retention time or retaining it completely. A salt gradient is used to elute the charged molecules that have stuck to the column.

Size-Exclusion Chromatography

In this method, the beads used in the column contain tiny pores of varying sizes. These tiny pores allow small compounds to enter the beads, thus slowing them down. Large compounds can't fit into the pores, so they will move around them and travel through the column faster. It is important to remember that in this type of chromatography, the small compounds are slowed down and retained longer. The size of the pores may be varied so that different molecular weight molecules may be fractionated. A common approach in protein purification is to use an ion exchange column followed by a size-exclusion column.

Affinity Chromatography

We can also customize columns to bind any substance of interest. For example, if we wanted to purify substance A, we could use a column of beads coated with something that binds A very tightly (hence the name *affinity* chromatography), such as a receptor for A, A's biological target, or even a specific antibody. This means that A will bind to the column very tightly and it will likely stay inside the column. Later, we can elute A by washing the column with a free receptor (or target or antibody), which will compete with the bead-bound receptor and ultimately free substance A from the column. The only drawback of the elution is that we now have our inhibitor or receptor bound to our biological target. This inhibitor can be difficult to remove if it binds tightly.

GAS CHROMATOGRAPHY

Gas chromatography (GC) is another method we have for qualitative separation. GC, also called **vapor-phase chromatography (VPC)**, is similar to all other types of chromatography that we've discussed (see Figure 12.9). The main difference, conceptually, is that the eluant is a gas (usually helium or nitrogen) instead of a liquid.

Key Concept

All chromatography is about how "like" the substance is to the mobile and stationary phases *except* for size-exclusion chromatography.

The adsorbent is inside a 30-foot column that is coiled and kept inside an oven to control its temperature. The mixture is then injected into the column and vaporized. The gaseous compounds travel through the column at different rates, because they adhere to the adsorbent to different degrees and will separate by the time they reach the end of the column. The requirement for the compounds that we inject is that they be volatile: low-melting-point, sublimable solids or liquids. The major difference in practice between GC and the other methods we have discussed is that in GC, we leave the analysis in the hands of computers. The compounds are registered by a detector, which records the presence of a compound as a peak on a chart. It is common to separate molecules using GC and then to inject the pure molecules into a mass spectrometer for molecular weight determination (GC-mass spec).

> **Key Concept**
>
> To identify a compound or distinguish two different compounds, look at their retention times—that is, how long it took for each to travel through the column.

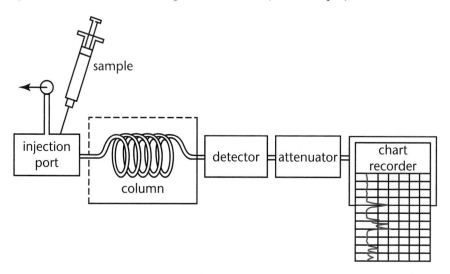

Figure 12.9

HPLC

HPLC stands for either **high-pressure** or **high-performance liquid chromatography**. As the name suggests, the eluant is a liquid, and it travels through a column of a defined composition. There are a variety of columns whose stationary phase is chosen depending on our target molecule and whose size is chosen depending on the quantity of material that needs to be purified. This is similar to a GC column, only a liquid is the eluent. In the past, very high pressures were used, but recent advances allow for much lower pressures, which is why the name changed from *high-pressure* to *high-performance*. In HPLC, a small sample is injected into the column, and separation occurs as it flows through. The compounds pass through a detector and are collected as the solvent flows out the end of the apparatus. It looks similar to GC, because computers do all the work for us, but we use liquid under pressure instead of gas. As the whole process is under computer control, sophisticated solvent gradients can be applied to the column to help resolve the various components in our mixture.

Electrophoresis

Another way we can separate a mixture of compounds that carry a charge is with **electrophoresis**. In molecular biology, this is one of the most important analytical techniques. This works by subjecting our compounds, usually macromolecules such as proteins or DNA, to an electric field, which moves them according to their charge and size. Negatively charged compounds (such as DNA) will migrate toward the positively charged anode, and positively charged compounds will migrate toward the negatively charged cathode. The velocity of this migration, known as the **migration velocity**, v, of a molecule, is directly proportional to the electric field strength, E, and to the net charge on the molecule, z, and is inversely proportional to a frictional coefficient, f, which depends on the mass and shape of the migrating molecules.

$$v = \frac{Ez}{f}$$

Generally speaking, the more charged the molecule or the stronger the electric field is, the faster it will migrate through the medium. Conversely, the bigger and more convoluted the molecule is, the slower it will migrate.

AGAROSE GEL ELECTROPHORESIS

There's a good possibility that once upon a time, in a college biology lab far, far away, you used **agarose gel electrophoresis** (see Figure 12.10) to separate pieces of nucleic acid (usually deoxyribonucleic acid [DNA] but sometimes ribonucleic acid [RNA]). The medium used in this type of electrophoresis is **agarose**, a plant gel derived from seaweed. Agarose is a great tool because it is nontoxic and easy to manipulate (unlike sodium dodecyl sulfate-polyacrylamide [SDS-PAGE]). Because every piece of nucleic acid is negatively charged (from its phosphate-sugar backbone), nucleic acids can be separated on the basis of size and shape alone (even without the charge-masking qualities of SDS, which we will soon discuss). It is also useful to stain agarose gels with a compound called *ethidium bromide*, which binds to nucleic acids and allows us to visualize our results by fluorescence under ultraviolet light. The staining process is toxic, however. Agarose gel electrophoresis can also be used to obtain our compound (preparatively) by cutting the desired band out of the gel and eluting out the nucleic acid.

SDS-PAGE

Sodium dodecyl sulfate-polyacrylamide gel electrophoresis is a useful tool because it separates proteins on the basis of mass alone; the procedure typically denatures the proteins. Polyacrylamide gel is the standard medium for electrophoresis and functions much in the same way as agarose gel. What makes it interesting is that SDS disrupts all noncovalent interactions. It binds to proteins and creates large chains with net negative charges, thereby neutralizing the protein's original charge. As the proteins move through the gel, the only variable affecting their velocity is f, the frictional coefficient, which depends on mass. After separation, we can stain the gel so the protein bands can be visualized and our results recorded. If you do not want to have your protein denatured, so-called "native" gels may be run.

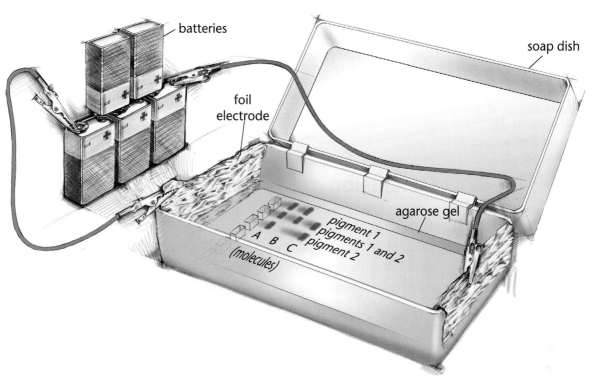

Figure 12.10

ISOELECTRIC FOCUSING

We also have a technique that exploits the acidic and basic properties of amino acids: **isoelectric focusing**. Each protein may be characterized by its **isoelectric point**, **pI**, which is the pH at which its net charge (the sum of all the charges on all of its amino acids) is zero (we will discuss this further in Chapter 15). If we take a mixture of proteins and place them in a electric field that exists across a gel with a pH gradient (acidic on one end, basic on the other, and neutral in the middle), the proteins will move until they reach the point that has a pH equal to their pI. At this pH, the protein's net charge is zero, so it will stop moving.

Let's go through an example to show how this works, as the concept behind this is essential for both Organic and General Chemistry. Let's say that we have protein with a pI of 9. As we know, this means that when the protein is in an environment

Key Concept

Because amino acids and proteins are organic molecules, the fundamental principle of acid-base chemistry apply to them as well.

- At a low pH, $[H^+]$ is relatively high. Thus, at a pH < pI, proteins will tend to be protonated and positively charged. As a result, they will migrate towards the cathode.

- At a relatively high (basic) pH, $[H^+]$ is lower and proteins will tend to be deprotonated and negatively charged. As a result, they will migrate towards the anode.

with a pH of 9, it will carry no charge; if it is at a pH that is higher or lower than 9, it will carry a charge. If we place this protein onto the gel at a pH of 7, there will be more protons around the protein (is more acidic than 9: thus, more protons in solution). These protons will attach to the available basic sites on the protein, creating a net positive charge on the molecule. This charge will then carry the protein toward the negatively charged cathode, which rests on the basic side of the gradient. As the protein moves closer to the cathode, there are fewer protons in the gel (the pH increases). Eventually, as the concentration of free protons drops and we near a pH of 9, the protons creating the positive charge will dissociate, and the protein will become neutral. A quick way to remember the charge of each end of the gel is to recall that we associate acids with protons, which carry a positive charge, and thus the anode is positively charged. We associate bases with the negatively charged hydroxide ion, which gives us the negatively charged cathode.

Conclusion

We hope that reading this chapter brought back loving memories of your Organic Chemistry lab, but if it didn't, don't worry—the MCAT doesn't care about your laboratory skills. As long as you understand the principles governing these techniques and when you should apply them, you'll be in great shape for the MCAT. Remember that purification and separation techniques exploit physical properties to obtain a purified product. The key factors are polarity, solubility, size and shape, boiling point, and charge. These factors can be traced back to the intermolecular forces or properties of the molecules themselves. Having a variety of tools and methods to separate and collect a purified product is essential in practical Organic Chemistry, but choosing the proper techniques often requires a great deal of knowledge and consideration of the product. In the next chapter, we'll take a look at some methods that will help identify, and sometimes separate out, an unknown product.

CONCEPTS TO REMEMBER

☐ Extraction separates dissolved substances based on differential solubility in aqueous versus organic solvents.

☐ Filtration separates solids from liquids.

☐ Recrystallization separates solids based on differential solubility; temperature is really important here.

☐ Sublimation separates solids based on their ability to sublime.

☐ Centrifugation separates large things (such as cells, organelles, and macromolecules) based on mass and density.

☐ Distillation separates liquids based on boiling point, which in turn depends on intermolecular forces.

☐ Chromatography uses a stationary phase and a mobile phase to separate compounds based on how tightly they adhere (generally due to polarity, size, or charge).

☐ Electrophoresis separates biological macromolecules (such as proteins or nucleic acids) based on size and sometimes charge.

Practice Questions

1. A mixture of sand, benzoic acid, and naphthalene in ether is best separated by

   B. filtration, followed by acidic extraction, followed by recrystallization.
   C. filtration, followed by basic extraction, followed by evaporation.
   D. extraction, followed by sublimation, followed by GC.
   E. filtration, followed by electrophoresis, followed by extraction.

2. Fractional distillation would most likely be used to separate which of the following compounds?

   A. Methylene chloride (boiling point of 41°C) and water (boiling point of 100°C)
   B. Ethyl acetate (boiling point of 77°C) and ethanol (boiling point of 80°C)
   C. Aniline (boiling point of 184°C) and benzyl alcohol (boiling point of 22°C).
   D. Aniline (boiling point of 184°C) and water (boiling point of 100°C).

3. Which of the following compounds would be the most effective in extracting benzoic acid from a diethyl ether solution?

   A. Tetrahydrofuran
   B. Aqueous hydrochloric acid
   C. Aqueous sodium hydroxide
   D. Water

4. Which of the following techniques would best separate red blood cells from blood plasma?

   A. Gel electrophoresis
   B. Centrifugation
   C. Isoelectric focusing
   D. HPLC

5. What would be the effect on the R_f values if the TLC described below were run with hexane rather than ether as the eluant?

Compound	Distance Travelled
benzyl alcohol	1.0 cm
benzyl acetate	2.6 cm
p-nitrophenol	2.3 cm
naphthalene	4.0 cm

   A. No effect
   B. Increase tenfold
   C. Double
   D. Decrease

6. If benzyl alcohol, benzyl acetate, *p*-nitrophenol, and naphthalene were separated by column chromatography with ether on silica gel, which compound would elute first?

   A. Benzyl alcohol
   B. Benzyl acetate
   C. *p*-nitrophenol
   D. Naphthalene

7. Which of the following would be the best procedure for extracting acetaldehyde from an aqueous solution?

A. A single extraction with 100 mL of ether
B. Two successive extractions with 50 mL portions of ether
C. Three successive extractions with 33.3 mL portions of ether
D. Four successive extractions with 25 mL portions of ether

8.

	pI	*MW*
Protein A	4.5	25,000
Protein B	6.0	10,000
Protein C	9.5	12,000

At what pH can the above proteins be separated by isoelectric focusing?

A. 4.5
B. 6
C. 9.5
D. 7

9. Four compounds, I, II, III, and IV, are separated by thin-layer chromatography (TLC). Compound III is the most polar, II the least polar, and I and IV have intermediate polarity. The solvent system is 85:15 ethanol:methylene chloride. Which spot belongs to compound III?

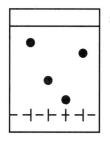 solvent front

A. Spot with the smallest R_f
B. Spot with the second largest R_f
C. Spot with the largest R_f
D. More information is needed.

10. What is the function of sodium dodecyl sulfate (SDS) in SDS-PAGE?

A. SDS stabilizes the gel matrix, improving resolution during electrophoresis.
B. SDS solubilizes proteins to give them uniformly negative charges, so separation is based purely on size.
C. SDS raises the pH of the gel, separating multiunit proteins into individual subunits.
D. SDS solubilizes proteins to give them uniformly positive charges, so separation is based purely on pH.

11. Suppose an extraction with methylene chloride ($d = 1.4$ g/ml) is performed, with the desired compound initially in brine ($d \approx 1$ g/ml). In a separatory funnel, which layer will be the organic layer?

A. Bottom layer
B. No layers are observed; methylene chloride and brine are 100 percent miscible.
C. Top layer
D. More information is needed.

Small Group Questions

1. Silica gel is often used in thin-layer chromatography. What properties does silica gel probably possess?

2. Discuss the advantages and disadvantages of the purification and separation techniques. Which is the most time-intensive? The most labor-intensive? The most destructive? The most exact?

Explanations to Practice Questions

1. B

In this question, three substances must be separated using a combination of techniques. The first step should be the most obvious: removal of the sand by filtration. Sand is an insoluble impurity and cannot be extracted. Thus, choice (C) is wrong. After filtration, the remaining compounds are still dissolved in ether. If the solution is extracted with aqueous base, the benzoate anion is formed and becomes dissolved in the aqueous layer, while naphthalene, a non-polar compound, remains in the ether. The compounds are now separated, and evaporation of the ether will yield purified naphthalene. (The benzoic acid can be isolated by acidifying the aqueous layer and filtering the precipitate.) This combination of techniques is given in choice (B), the correct answer. Choice (A) is wrong because the benzoic acid will not dissociate in an acidic solution and so will not become water soluble (on the other hand, if the solvent were basic, it would separate benzoic acid). Choice (D) is incorrect, electrophoresis will not separate the two organic compounds, because they have the same charge.

2. B

Fractional distillation is the most effective procedure for separating two liquids that boil within a few degrees of each other. Ethyl acetate and ethanol, choice (B), boil within three degrees of each other and thus would be good candidates for fractional distillation. In choice (A), the compounds have widely separated, and relatively low, boiling points, so a simple distillation would suffice. Vacuum distillation is needed for answer choices (C) and (D), because the boiling point of aniline is over 150 degrees.

3. C

By extracting with sodium hydroxide (C), benzoic acid will be converted to its sodium salt, sodium benzoate. Sodium benzoate, unlike its acid counterpart, will dissolve in an aqueous solution. The aqueous layer simply has to be acidified to retrieve benzoic acid. Choice (A) is wrong because diethyl ether and tetrahydrofuran are miscible; this answer choice can be discarded. Hydrochloric acid will not transform benzoic acid into a soluble salt, so choice (B) is incorrect. Finally, choice (D) is wrong because benzoic acid is insoluble in water.

4. B

Red blood cells suspended in blood plasma are best separated by centrifugation. In this technique, the blood cells would be forced to the bottom of the tube, which could then be separated from the plasma. Because this is essentially a phase difference, a solid and a liquid, electrophoresis does not have to be employed, so choices (A) and (C) can be eliminated. Choice (D) is wrong because HPLC is used to separate smaller organic compounds.

5. D

Hexane is less polar than ether and, therefore, is less likely to displace compounds adsorbed to the silica gel. This would decrease the distance the compounds would travel, decreasing the R_f values.

6. D

In column chromatography, as in TLC, the least polar compound travels most rapidly. This means that naphthalene, with an R_f value of 0.4, would travel most rapidly and would be the first to elute from the column.

7. D

It is more effective to perform four successive extractions with small amounts of ether than to perform one extraction with a large amount of ether.

8. B

The three proteins may be separated when the isoelectric point of one of these proteins is equal to the pH of the solution. In this problem, protein B has the intermediate pI (6), so the proteins can best be separated when the pH of the solution equals the pI of B, or 6. Because protein A is neutral at pH = 4.5, it becomes basic (negatively charged) at pH = 6, thus, at this pH, protein A migrates to the anode. On the other hand, protein C is neutral at pH = 9.5. Therefore, at pH = 6 it becomes acidic (positively charged) and migrates to the cathode. Finally, protein B remains in the solution because at pH equal to its isoelectric point, its molecules are uncharged and, therefore, are not affected by the potential difference. Thus, the three proteins are separated.

9. C

R_f, or retention value, is a quotient between the distance moved by the spot (sample) over the distance traveled by the solvent front. In other words, the closer the spot is to the solvent front, the larger the R_f will be. The solvent system is polar, which means that the most polar compound will stay with the polar mobile phase the longest, resulting in the largest R_f. This gives compound III the largest R_f.

Answer (B) is incorrect, as the second-largest R_f can belong to either compound I or IV, which have intermediate polarity. The spot with the smallest R_f (A) belongs to compound II, the most nonpolar compound of the four.

10. B

Sodium dodecyl sulfate is a detergent and will digest proteins, forming micelles with uniformly negative charges. Because the protein is sequestered within the micelle, other factors, such as charge of the protein and shape, have minimal roles during separation; in essence, the protein micelles can be modeled as being spheres of different sizes. SDS has no effect on the gel matrix (polyacrylamide), so answers (A) and (C) are incorrect (reducing agents such as mercaptoethanol are used to break up multiunit proteins). Answer (D) incorrectly describes the micelles as being positively charged.

11. A

Because methylene chloride is denser than brine (salt water), the organic layer will settle at the bottom of the funnel (A), making answer (C) incorrect. Answer (B) is also incorrect, because methylene chloride is nonpolar, so it cannot mix with brine.

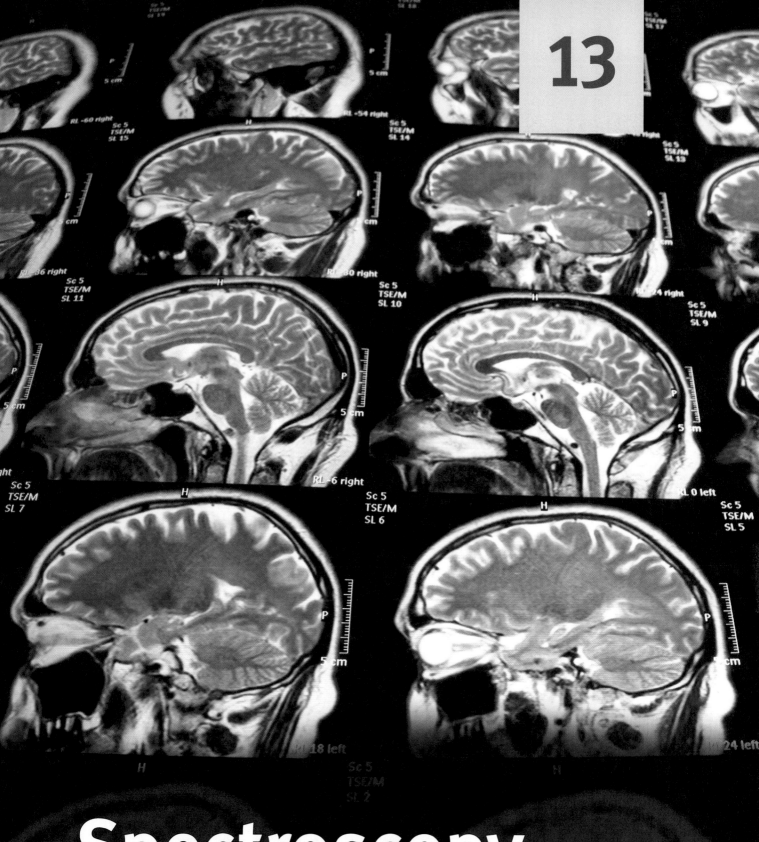

Spectroscopy

In the last chapter, we discussed various techniques for isolating, purifying, and identifying compounds. To use these methods, we usually have to have an idea about the identity of the compound we're trying to isolate. If the compound we are testing is completely unknown, we could use the previous chapter's techniques to determine many of its properties, and we could spend hours comparing its boiling point and melting point with literature values, hoping to find a match. However, there is a much more efficient way to identify a new unknown compound specifically and definitively. **Spectroscopy** measures the energy differences between the possible states of a molecular system by determining the frequencies of electromagnetic radiation (light) absorbed by the molecules. These possible states are quantized energy levels associated with different types of molecular motion, such as molecular rotation, vibration of bonds, nuclear spin transitions, and electron absorption. Different types of spectroscopy measure these different types of molecular properties, allowing us to identify the presence of specific functional groups and even to determine how they are connected.

One of the big advantages of spectroscopy is that only a small quantity of sample is needed. Also, the sample may be reused after a test is performed (except after mass spectroscopy). The downside of spectroscopy is that it's difficult to do in your kitchen (unlike finding boiling points). But, as long you have a chemistry lab available, these are some of the best techniques to identify compounds.

Infrared ★★★☆☆

BASIC THEORY

Infrared (IR) spectroscopy measures molecular vibrations, which can be seen as **bond stretching**, **bending**, or combinations of different vibrational modes. The useful absorptions of IR light occur at wavelengths of 3,000 to 30,000 nm, although when we represent IR on a graph, we use an analog of frequency called **wavenumber** (3,000 to 30,000 nm corresponds to 3,500 to 300 cm^{-1} in wavenumbers). When light of these frequencies/wavenumbers is absorbed, the molecules enter excited vibrational states. Bond stretching (which can be either symmetric or asymmetric) involves the largest change in energy and, thus, is observed in the higher frequency region of 4,000 to 1,500 cm^{-1}. Bending vibrations are observed in the lower frequency region of 1,500 to 400 cm^{-1}. The four types of vibration that can occur are shown in Figure 13.1.

MCAT Expertise

You will likely see a question or passage dealing with IR and/or ^{1}H-NMR on your exam. Pay attention to the tips on the following pages to be sure to get the high-yield information.

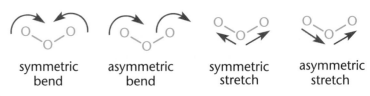

symmetric | asymmetric | symmetric | asymmetric
bend | bend | stretch | stretch

Figure 13.1

In addition to these bending and stretching vibrations, there can be vibrations that incorporate a combination of bending, stretching, and rotating. Furthermore, even more complex vibration patterns, caused by the motion of the molecule as a whole, can be seen in the 1,500 to 400 cm⁻¹ region. This is called the **fingerprint region**, as it is characteristic of each individual molecule. Spectroscopy experts can use this region to identify a substance, but you won't ever need to use it on the MCAT.

For an absorption to be recorded, the vibration must result in a change in the bond dipole moment. This means that molecules that do not experience a changing dipole moment, such as those composed of atoms with the same electronegativity or molecules that are symmetrical, do not exhibit absorption. For example, we cannot get an absorption from O_2 or Br_2, but we can from HCl or CO. Symmetric bonds will also be silent (the triple bond in acetylene, for example).

To get a spectrum, simply pass IR light (4,000 to 400 cm⁻¹) through a sample and record the absorption pattern. Percent transmittance is plotted versus frequency, where percent transmittance equals absorption minus one ($\%T = A - 1$); this means that maximum absorptions appear as the bottom of valleys on the spectrum.

CHARACTERISTIC ABSORPTIONS

For the MCAT, you only need to memorize a few absorptions. In fact, there are two that are more important than all the others. The first is alcohol (or anything else with an –OH group), which absorbs around 3,300 cm⁻¹ with a broad peak, and the second is the carbonyl, which absorbs around 1,700 cm⁻¹ with a sharp peak (compared with the –OH stretch). Fairly simply, huh? Don't get us wrong; it would be to your advantage to memorize all of Table 13.1, but unless you love memorizing numbers, we'd suggest spending your time on higher-yield concepts. One way to do this is to study the trends and differences in the table. Notice how the bond between any atom and hydrogen always has a relatively high frequency and how, as we add more bonds between carbon atoms, the frequency at which they will absorb increases. Or notice how N–H bonds are in the same region as O–H bonds, except they have a sharp peak instead of a broad one. This sort of information will be given to you in tables on the MCAT, so practice finding the trends now; it is an *essential* skill for Test Day.

Key Concept

Symmetric stretches do not show up in IR spectra because they involve no net change in dipole moment.

Key Concept

Wavenumbers (cm⁻¹) are an analog of frequency.

$f = \dfrac{c}{\lambda}$, whereas wavenumber $= \dfrac{1}{\lambda}$.

Table 13.1   Absorption Frequencies

Functional Group	Frequency (cm^{-1})	Vibration
Alkanes	2,800–3,000	C–H
	1,200	C–C
Alkenes	3,080–3,140	=C–H
	1,645	C=C
Alkynes	2,200	C≡C
	3,300	≡C–H
Aromatic	2,900–3,100	C–H
	1,475–1,625	C–C
Alcohols	3,100–3,500	O–H (broad)
Ethers	1,050–1,150	C–O
Aldehydes	2,700–2,900	(O)C–H
	1,725–1,750	C=O
Ketones	1,700–1,750	C=O
Acids	1,700–1,750	C–O
	2,900–3,300	O–H (broad)
Amines	3,100–3,500	N–H (sharp)

APPLICATION

We can learn a great deal of information from an IR spectrum, and most of that information comes from the frequencies between 1,400 and 4,000 cm^{-1}; everything lower is out of scope for the MCAT.

> **MCAT Expertise**
>
> Infrared spectroscopy is best used for identification of functional groups. The most important peaks to know are those for the –OH (*broad* peak above 2,900 cm^{-1}) and the carbonyl peak (*sharp* peak near 1,700 cm^{-1}). If you know nothing else here, *know these!*

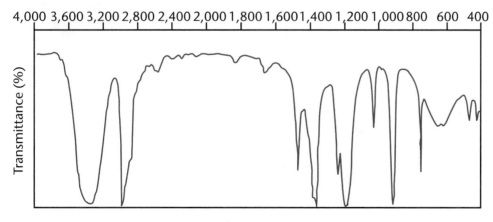

Figure 13.2

Figure 13.2 shows the IR spectrum for an aliphatic alcohol: The large broad peak at 3,300 cm^{-1} is due to the presence of a hydroxyl group, whereas the sharper peak at 3,000 cm^{-1} is due to the carbon–hydrogen bonds in the alkane portion of the molecule.

Nuclear Magnetic Resonance ★★★★☆

BASIC THEORY

Nuclear magnetic resonance (NMR) spectroscopy is one of the most widely used spectroscopic tools in Organic Chemistry, and it's the most important technique to understand for the MCAT. NMR spectroscopy is based on the fact that certain nuclei have magnetic moments that are oriented at random. When such nuclei are placed in a magnetic field, their magnetic moments tend to align either with or against the direction of this applied field. Nuclei whose magnetic moments are aligned with the field are said to be in the **α-state** (lower energy), whereas those whose moments are aligned against the field are said to be in the **β-state** (higher energy). The nuclei can then be irradiated with radio frequency pulses that match the energy gap between the two states, which will excite some lower-energy nuclei into the β-state. The absorption of this radiation leads to excitation at different frequencies, depending on an atom's magnetic environment. In addition, the nuclear magnetic moments of each atom are affected by nearby atoms that also possess magnetic moments. Hence, a compound may contain many nuclei that resonate at different frequencies, producing a complex spectrum.

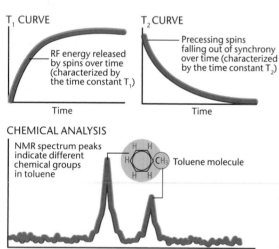

Results ▶

The computer registers the time it takes for each type of spin to release the absorbed radio energy (T_1 graph). The system can also monitor the precessing spins as they fall randomly out of sync (T_2 graph). At the same time, it records the precession frequency of the spins of different chemical groups, which are summarized by a value called the chemical shift. The shift forms the basis of NMR spectra plots that identify constituent chemical groups in a sample, such as those in the hydrocarbon molecule toluene (chemical analysis graph). MRI machines combine all these NMR data to produce views of internal body tissues, including images of the human brain (above right).

Figure 13.3

A typical NMR spectrum is a plot of frequency versus absorption of energy during resonance. Note that frequency decreases from left to right, just as it does for IR spectra. Alternatively, we can plot varying magnetic fields on the *x*-axis, increasing toward the right. Because different NMR spectrometers operate at different magnetic field strengths, a standardized method of plotting the NMR spectrum has been adopted. This standardized method, which is the only one seen on the MCAT, uses an arbitrary variable, called **chemical shift** (represented by the symbol δ), with units of **parts per million (ppm)** of spectrometer frequency. The chemical shift is plotted on the *x*-axis, and it increases toward the left (referred to as **downfield**). To make sure that we know just how far downfield compounds are, we use a reference peak to mark the location of 0 δ. TMS (tetramethylsilane) is the calibration standard and appears on every spectrum to mark 0 ppm.

Nuclear magnetic resonance is most commonly used to study ^{1}H nuclei (protons) and ^{13}C nuclei, although any atom possessing a nuclear spin (any nucleus with an odd atomic number or odd mass number) can be studied, such as ^{19}F, ^{17}O, ^{5}N, and ^{31}P.

^{1}H-NMR

Most ^{1}H nuclei come into resonance 0 to 10 ppm downfield from TMS. Each distinct set of nuclei gives rise to a separate peak. This means that if multiple nuclei are in relatively identical locations, they will give the same peak. For example, Figure 13.4 depicts the ^{1}H-NMR of dichloromethyl methyl ether which has two distinct sets of ^{1}H nuclei. The single proton attached to the dichloromethyl group is in a different magnetic environment from the three protons on the methyl group (which are all magnetically identical), so the two classes will resonate at different frequencies. The three protons on the methyl group are magnetically equivalent because this group rotates freely and, on average, each proton sees an identical environment. As a result, the three protons all resonate at the same frequency. Thus, as we can see in Figure 13.4, the spectrum for dichloromethyl methyl ether will have two separate peaks (the peak on the far right is TMS, not from our compound).

> **Bridge**
>
> Nuclei with odd mass or odd atomic numbers, or both, will have a magnetic moment when placed in a magnetic field. Not all nuclei have magnetic moments (^{12}C, for example).

> **Key Concept**
>
> TMS provides a reference peak. The signal for its H atoms is assigned $\delta = 0$.

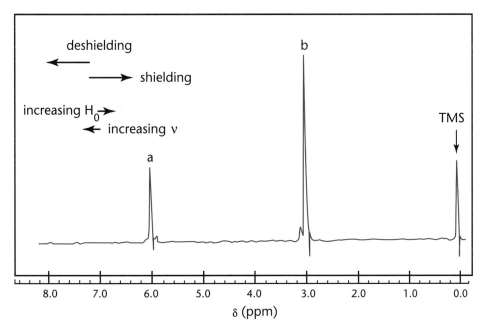

Figure 13.4

The peak on the left (a) is from the single dichloromethyl proton, and the taller middle peak is from three methyl protons (b). The height difference isn't a coincidence; the taller peak represents the greater number of protons that caused it. Specifically, if we were to analyze the area under the peaks, we would find that the ratio of (b) to (a) is 3:1, corresponding exactly to the number of protons that produced each peak.

Now that we know which peak is which, let's talk about their respective positions on the graph. We can see that the peak for the single proton (a) is fairly far downfield compared with the other protons. This is because it is attached to a carbon with two electronegative groups (chlorine). These atoms pull electron density away from the surrounding atoms, thus **deshielding** the proton from its electron cloud. The more the proton's electron density is pulled away, the less it can shield itself from the applied magnetic field, resulting in a reading further downfield. With this same reasoning, we know that if we had an electron-donating group, such as the silica atom in TMS, it would help **shield** the ^{1}H nucleus and give it a position further upfield. That's why we use TMS as the reference peak, assigned to a value of zero; everything else will be more deshielded than TMS.

Now, let's make it a little more interesting. Consider a compound containing protons that are within three bonds of each other: in other words, a compound in which there are two adjacent atoms (generally C, N, or O) that each have protons attached. When we have two protons in such close proximity to each other, that are *not* magnetically identical, **coupling (splitting)** occurs. Let's use an example to illustrate the concept; see Figure 13.5.

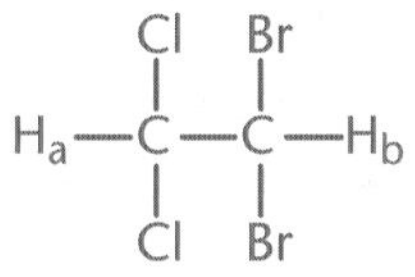

$$H_a - \overset{\overset{\displaystyle Cl}{|}}{\underset{\underset{\displaystyle Cl}{|}}{C}} - \overset{\overset{\displaystyle Br}{|}}{\underset{\underset{\displaystyle Br}{|}}{C}} - H_b$$

Figure 13.5

Notice the two protons, H_a and H_b, on 1,1-dibromo-2,2-dichloroethane. Because of their proximity, the magnetic environment of H_a can be affected by H_b, and vice versa. Thus, at any given time, H_a can experience two different magnetic environments, because H_b can be in either the α- or the β-state. The different states of H_b influence the nucleus of H_a (because the two H atoms are within three bonds of each other), causing slight upfield and downfield shifts. There is approximately a 50 percent chance that H_b will be in one of the two states, so the resulting absorption is a **doublet**, two peaks of identical intensity, equally spaced around the true chemical shift of H_a. H_a and H_b will both appear as doublets, because each one is coupled with one other hydrogen. To determine the number of peaks present (doublet, triplet, etc.), we use the $n + 1$ rule, where n is the number of protons that are three bonds away from our proton of interest. The magnitude of this splitting, measured in Hertz, is called the **coupling constant, J**.

Let's try a molecule that has even more coupled protons. In 1,1-dibromo-2-chloroethane (Figure 13.6), the H_a nucleus is affected by two nearby H_b nuclei and, thus, can experience four different states: αα, αβ, βα, or ββ.

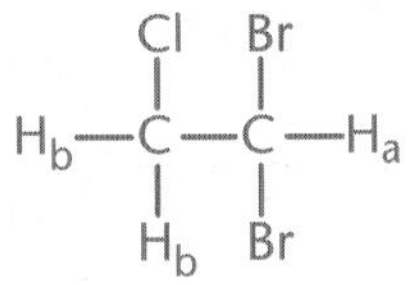

Figure 13.6

Although there are technically four different states, αβ has the same effect as βα (just as 3 × 4 is equal to 4 × 3), so both of these resonances occur at the same frequency. This means we will have three unique frequencies, αα, ββ, and αβ/βα. H_a will appear as three peaks (a **triplet**) centered on the true chemical shift, with an area ratio of 1:2:1.

Table 13.2 shows the area ratios for up to seven adjacent hydrogens, but it isn't necessary to know this table for the MCAT. Just remember that you simply add up the number of coupled hydrogens and add one (for our proton of interest itself) to determine the number of peaks. In addition, peaks that have more than four shifts will sometimes be referred to as a **multiplet**.

Now let's move on to H_b. Because both hydrogens are attached to the same carbon, they will be magnetically identical (this doesn't apply to alkenes, since they can't freely rotate around the double bond). These hydrogens are within three bonds of one other hydrogen, H_a. This means that they will appear as a doublet, but because there are two of them, the peak for H_b will be taller than the peak for H_a.

Table 13.2. Area Ratios for Adjacent Hydrogens

Number of Adjacent Hydrogens	Total Number of Peaks	Area Ratios
0	1	1
1	2	1:1
2	3	1:2:1
3	4	1:3:3:1
4	5	1:4:6:4:1
5	6	1:5:10:10:5:1
6	7	1:6:15:20:15:6:1
7	8	1:7:21:35:35:21:7:1

Table 13.3 indicates the chemical shift ranges of several different types of protons.

Key Concept

The splitting of the peak represents the number of adjacent hydrogens. A peak will be split into $n + 1$ peaks, where n is the number of adjacent hydrogens.

Key Concept

Proton NMR is good for

1. determining the relative number of protons and their relative chemical environments.
2. showing how many adjacent protons there are by splitting patterns.
3. showing certain functional groups.

MCAT Expertise

If you know nothing else about ^{1}H-NMR for the MCAT, know that the peaks for alkyl groups are upfield (1 to 3 ppm), peaks for alkenes are further downfield (4 to 7 ppm), peaks for aldehydes are even further downfield (9 to 10 ppm), and carboxylic acids are the furthest downfield (10 to 12 ppm). Also, just counting the number of the peaks and unique hydrogens may get you the correct answer.

Table 13.3. Proton Chemical Shift Ranges

Type of Proton	Approximate Chemical Shift δ (ppm) Downfield from TMS
RCH$_3$	0.9
RCH$_2$	1.25
R$_3$CH	1.5
2CH5CH	4.6–6.0
2C;CH	2.0–3.0
Ar2H	6.0–8.5
2CHX	2.0–4.5
2CHOH/2CHOR	3.4–4.0
RCHO	9.0–10.0
RCHCO2	2.0–2.5
2CHCOOH/2CHCOOR	2.0–2.6
2CHOH2CH$_2$OH	1.0–5.5
ArOH	4.0–12.0
2COOH	10.5–12.0
2NH$_2$	1.0–5.0

It would be to your advantage to memorize all of these values, but it's fairly low-yield information. The values that are useful to memorize are the outliers, the incredibly deshielded ones, like the aldehyde at 9 to 10 ppm, and the even more deshielded carboxylic acid between 10.5 and 12 ppm. Another popular peak on the MCAT is the hydrogen of an aromatic ring, which lies between 6.5 and 8.5 ppm. Once again, it's more helpful for you to learn to recognize trends than to memorize numbers. You already understand how electronegativity works, so just apply that concept here. The more electron density that is pulled away from the proton, the more deshielded it will be.

^{13}C-NMR

^{13}C-Nuclear magnetic resonance imaging is similar to ^{1}H-NMR, although there are a few key differences. First and foremost, it appears far less on the MCAT than ^{1}H-NMR, which means our main job is to know how it differs from ^{1}H-NMR. The most obvious difference is that ^{13}C-NMR signals occur 0 to 210 δ downfield from the carbon peak of TMS, quite a bit further than the 0 to 12 δ downfield that we saw with ^{1}H-NMR. We should also note that ^{13}C atoms are rare (although not as rare as the ^{14}C atoms used for carbon dating). In fact, ^{13}C atoms account for only 1.1 percent of all carbon atoms. This has two effects: First, a much larger sample is needed to run a ^{13}C spectrum (about 50 mg compared with 1 mg for ^{1}H-NMR), and second, coupling

MCAT Expertise

Don't spend too much time on ^{13}C-NMR. Just know that the same principle applies with regard to electrons as in ^{1}H-NMR: the more deshielded, the further downfield.

between carbon atoms is generally not observed (the probability of two ^{13}C atoms being adjacent is 0.011×0.011, or roughly 1 in 1,000).

However, coupling is observed between carbon atoms and the protons that are directly attached to them. This one-bond coupling works analogously to the three-bond coupling we saw in ^1H-NMR. For example, if a carbon atom is attached to two protons, it can experience three different states of those protons ($\alpha\alpha$, $\alpha\beta/\beta\alpha$, and $\beta\beta$), and the carbon signal is split into a triplet with the area ratio 1:2:1.

An additional feature of ^{13}C-NMR is the ability to record a spectrum without the coupling of adjacent protons. This is called **spin decoupling**, and it produces a spectrum of singlets, each corresponding to a separate, magnetically equivalent carbon atom. For example, compare the two following spectra of 1,1,2-trichloropropane. One (Figure 13.7) is a typical spin-decoupled spectrum, and the other (Figure 13.8) is spin-coupled. The number of ^{13}C resonances (except for symmetrically disposed atoms) will give us a carbon count in our molecule.

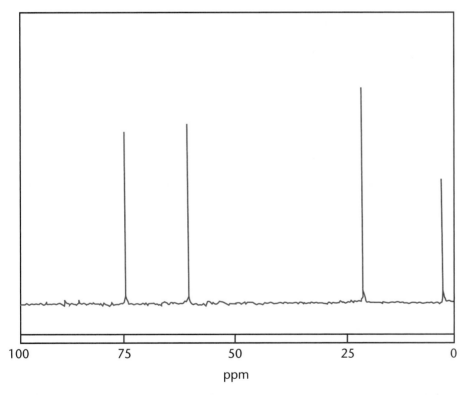

Figure 13.7

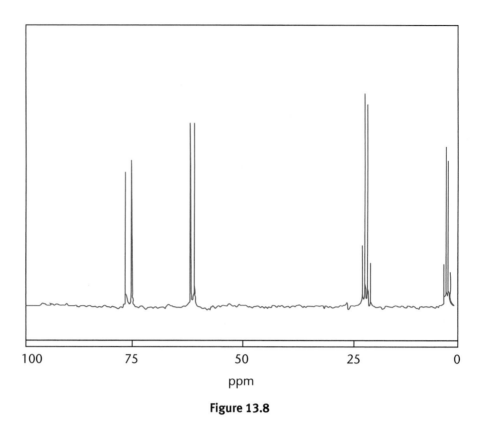

Figure 13.8

In general, we can use NMR spectroscopy to learn about the carbon skeleton of a compound, and we can get hints as to what the functional groups are. Specifically, NMR provides us with the following four types of information:

1. The number of nonequivalent nuclei, determined from the number of peaks

2. The magnetic environment of a nucleus, determined by the chemical shift

3. The relative numbers of nuclei, determined by integrating the peak areas in ^{1}H-NMR

4. The number of neighboring nuclei, determined by the splitting pattern observed (except for ^{13}C in the spin-decoupled mode)

Ultraviolet Spectroscopy

BASIC THEORY

Although you will never have to interpret **ultraviolet (UV) spectroscopy** data on the MCAT, it is fair game to be discussed, so a basic understanding of how it works and when it is used will suffice. Ultraviolet spectra are obtained by passing ultraviolet light through a sample (usually dissolved in an inert, nonabsorbing solvent), and the absorbance is plotted against wavelength. The absorbance is caused by electronic transitions between orbitals. The biggest piece of information we get from this technique is the wavelength of maximum absorbance, which tells us the extent of conjugation within conjugated systems, as well as other structural and compositional information. The take-home point here is that if you see UV spectroscopy on the MCAT, the compound being tested has conjugated bonds. The more conjugated, the lower the energy of the transition.

Mass Spectroscopy

BASIC THEORY

Mass spectrometry differs from most of the other methods we've discussed in this chapter, because it is actually not true spectroscopy (no absorption of electromagnetic radiation is involved) and because it is a destructive technique. Mass spectrometry destroys the compound, so we cannot reuse the sample once the analysis is complete. Most mass spectrometers use a high-speed beam of electrons to ionize the sample (eject an electron), a particle accelerator to put the charged particles in flight, a magnetic field to deflect the accelerated cationic fragments, and a detector that records the number of particles of each mass that exit the deflector area.

The initially formed ion is the molecular radical-cation (M^+), which results from a single electron being removed from a molecule of the sample. This unstable species usually decomposes rapidly into a cationic fragment and a radical fragment. Because there are many molecules in the sample and usually more than one way for the initially formed radical-cation to decompose into fragments, a typical mass spectrum is composed of many lines, each corresponding to a specific mass/charge ratio (m/z). The spectrum itself plots mass/charge on the horizontal axis and relative abundance of the various cationic fragments on the vertical axis (see Figure 13.9).

CHARACTERISTICS

The tallest peak (highest intensity) belongs to the most common ion, called the **base peak**, and is assigned the relative abundance value of 100 percent. The peak with the highest m/z ratio (the peak furthest to the right in Figure 13.9) is generally the **molecular ion peak (parent ion peak)** or simply **M^+**. Because this is the original compound with one electron missing, we can use it to find the molecular weight. Even further, because it has only lost one electron, the charge value is usually 1; hence, the m/z ratio can usually be read as the mass of the fragment itself.

APPLICATION

Fragmentation patterns can provide information that helps us identify or distinguish certain compounds. In particular, the fragmentation pattern provides clues to the compound's structure by way of molecular mass. For example, whereas IR spectroscopy would be of little use in distinguishing between propionaldehyde and butyraldehyde, a mass spectrum would give us unambiguous data distinguishing the two.

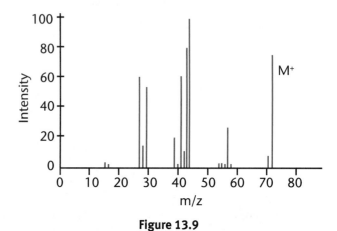

Figure 13.9

Figure 13.9 shows the mass spectrum of butyraldehyde. The peak at m/e = 72 corresponds to the molecular cation-radical M⁺; this alone tells us that the compound has a molecular weight of 72 g/mol, meaning it must be butyraldehyde.

Looking further, we can see the base peak at m/e = 44, which corresponds to the cationic fragment resulting from the loss of a fragment weighing 28 g/mol (since $72 - 44 = 28$). Some quick math will show us that this is a C_2H_4 fragment, resulting from one of the most common rearrangements, the McLafferty rearrangement (an example of which is shown in Figure 13.10). Another peak to note is the one at 57 (which corresponds to the loss of a 15 g/mol fragment, a CH_3 radical).

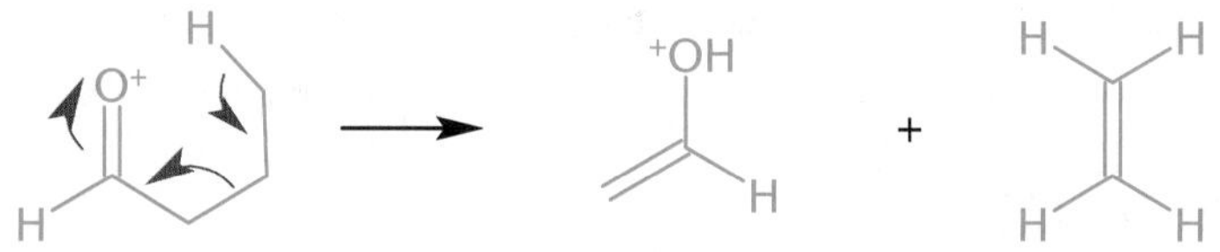

Figure 13.10

Mass spectroscopy is basically a math game, with each peak showing the weight of the molecule with a different fragment missing. Just remember that carbon is 12, hydrogen is +1, and oxygen is 16; then plug in the numbers and see what kinds of groups could have been fragmented off.

Conclusion

This chapter was full of numbers and values, but the most important thing to know about spectroscopy on the MCAT is that you don't need to know a lot of numbers. The numbers that you *do* need to know have already been stressed heavily in this chapter, but as always, your focus should be on the general mechanisms and principles. You should know the properties of molecules that each spectroscopy method exploits, and you should be able to make a rudimentary evaluation of each method's spectroscopic data. Know that IR is best for identifying the presence (or, more important, the absence) of functional groups and that NMR can help you figure out the configuration of these functional groups. Proton NMR will be much more common on the MCAT, but be aware that ^{13}C-NMR exists and that it measures chemical shift on a much higher scale. Know how to interpret the graphs—the chemical shift of deshielded protons will be downfield, or toward the left of the graph. Make sure that you can interpret split peaks (interference from neighboring hydrogens) and peak magnitude (number of magnetically identical hydrogens). A cursory understanding of UV spectroscopy (test for conjugation!) and mass spectroscopy (fragments based on mass) will suffice. In many MCAT passages, you will be given spectroscopic data, even though you will likely be able to solve the problems without even using it. If you *are* knowledgeable about spectroscopy, you'll be able simply to look at the data and circle the answer, saving yourself lots of time, a precious resource on the MCAT. Make sure that you have all the fundamental concepts in Organic Chemistry down first and then start perfecting your analysis of spectroscopic data.

CONCEPTS TO REMEMBER

- ☐ Infrared spectroscopy is used to find functional groups.

- ☐ Carbonyls = sharp peak at 1,700 cm^{-1}.

- ☐ Hydroxides = broad peak at 3,300 cm^{-1}.

- ☐ Amines = sharper peaks at 3,300 and 3,400 cm^{-1} for primary amines; secondary amines have one peak.

- ☐ ^{1}H-NMR is useful to find the structure of a compound and can also reveal the functional groups.

- ☐ ^{1}H-NMR measures how deshielded (how much electron density has been pulled away) protons are on a molecule. $\delta = 0$–12 ppm. The more deshielded the proton is, the further downfield it will be.

- ☐ In ^{1}H-NMR, protons three bonds apart experience coupling. If there is one proton three bonds away, it is a doublet; if there are two, it is a triplet; three, it is a quartet.

- ☐ ^{13}C-NMR is similar to ^{1}H-NMR, but $\delta = 0$–210 ppm.

- ☐ UV spectroscopy is useful for conjugated compounds.

- ☐ Mass spectroscopy can be used to find the mass of the compound and the masses of fragments of the compound.

Practice Questions

1. IR spectroscopy is most useful for distinguishing

    A. double and triple bonds.

    B. C–H bonds.

    C. chirality of molecules.

    D. composition of racemic mixtures.

2. Oxygen (O_2) does not exhibit an IR spectrum because

    A. it has no molecular motions.

    B: it is not possible to record IR spectra of a gaseous molecule.

    C: molecular vibrations do not result in a change in the dipole moment of the O_2 molecule.

    D. None of the above

3. If IR spectroscopy were employed to monitor the oxidation of benzyl alcohol to benzaldehyde, which of the following would provide the best evidence that the reaction was proceeding as planned?

    A. Comparing the fingerprint region of the spectra of starting material and product

    B. Noting the change in intensity of the peaks corresponding to the phenyl ring

    C. Noting the appearance of a broad absorption peak in the region of $3,100$–$3,500$ cm^{-1}

    D. Noting the appearance of a strong absorption in the region of $1,700$ cm^{-1}

4. Which of the following chemical shifts would correspond to an aldehyde proton signal in a ^{1}H-NMR spectrum?

    A. 9.5 ppm

    B. 7.0 ppm

    C. 11.0 ppm

    D. 1.0 ppm

5. The isotope ^{12}C is not useful for NMR because

    A. it is not abundant in nature.

    B. its resonances are not sensitive to the presence of neighboring atoms.

    C. it has no magnetic moment.

    D. the signal-to-noise ratio in the spectrum is too low.

6. In ^{13}C-NMR, splitting of spectral lines is due to

    A. coupling between a carbon atom and protons attached to that carbon atom.

    B. coupling between a carbon atom and protons attached to adjacent carbon atoms.

    C. coupling between adjacent carbon atoms.

    D. coupling between two adjacent protons.

7. Ultraviolet spectroscopy is most useful for detecting

    A. aldehydes and ketones.

    B. unconjugated alkenes.

    C. conjugated alkenes.

    D. aliphatic acids and amines.

8. Mass spectroscopy results in the separation of fragments according to

A. atomic mass.

B. mass-to-charge ratio.

C. viscosity.

D. absorption wavelength.

9. Alkyl benzenes often provide mass spectra with a large peak at m/z 91. What aromatic fragment is responsible for the observed peak?

A.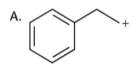

B.

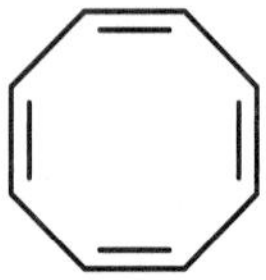

C.

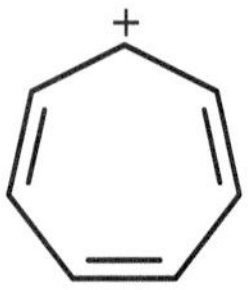

D.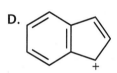

10. Using ¹H-NMR, and focusing on the 0–4.5 ppm region only, how is the spectrum for ethanol distinguished from the spectrum for isopropanol?

A. They cannot be distinguished from ¹H-NMR alone.

B. A triplet and quartet are observed for ethanol, whereas a doublet and septet are observed for isopropanol.

C. A triplet and quartet are observed for isopropanol, whereas a doublet and septet are observed for ethanol.

D. The alcohol hydrogen in ethanol will appear within that region, whereas the alcohol hydrogen in isopropanol will not appear in that region.

11. For the compound below, how many distinct signals are observed in the ¹³C-NMR spectrum?

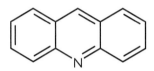

A. 13

B. 6

C. 7

D. 9

12. In an IR spectrum, how does extended conjugation of double bonds affect the absorbance band of carbonyl (C=O) stretches compared with normal absorption at 1,720 cm^{-1}?

A. The absorbance band will occur at a lower wavenumber.

B. The absorbance band will occur at a higher wavenumber.

C. The absorbance band will occur at the same wavenumber.

D. The absorbance band will disappear.

Small Group Questions

1. Why is ¹H-NMR more useful than ¹³C-NMR?

2. Will two enantiomers have identical IR spectra?

Explanations to Practice Questions

1. A

Infrared spectroscopy is most useful for distinguishing between different functional groups. Almost all organic compounds have C–H bonds (B), so except for fingerprinting a compound, these absorptions are not useful. Little information about the optical properties of a compound, such as choices (C) and (D), can be obtained by IR spectroscopy.

2. C

Because molecular oxygen is homonuclear and diatomic, there is no net change in its dipole moment during vibration or rotation; in other words, the compound does not absorb in the infrared. Diatomic nitrogen and chlorine exhibit similar behavior. IR spectroscopy is based on the principle that when the molecule vibrates or rotates, there is a change in dipole moment; therefore, choice (C) is the correct answer. Choice (A) is wrong because oxygen does have molecular motions. Choice (B) is wrong because it is possible to record the IR of a gaseous molecule, as long as it shows a change in its dipole moment when it vibrates.

3. D

In this reaction, the functional group is changing from a hydroxyl to an aldehyde. This means that a sharp stretching peak will appear at around 1,700 cm^{-1}, which corresponds to the carbonyl functionality. Therefore, choice (D) is the correct response. Choice (C) is the opposite; the reaction will be characterized by the disappearance of a peak at 3,100 to 3,500 cm^{-1}, not the appearance of one (this peak corresponds to the hydroxyl functionality). Choice (A) is certainly useful, but it is not as good a method as choice (D). Choice (B) is the least useful, as it is the C=O and –OH stretches that need to be considered.

4. A

The peak at 9.5 ppm (A) corresponds to an aldehyde proton. This signal lies downfield because the carbonyl oxygen is electron withdrawing and deshields the proton. Choice (C) corresponds to a carboxyl proton, and is even further downfield, because the acidic proton is deshielded to a greater degree than the aldehyde proton. Choice (B) is wrong because this chemical shift corresponds to aromatic protons. Choice (D) is wrong because this upfield signal is characteristic of an alkyl proton.

5. C

This isotope has no magnetic moment and will therefore not exhibit resonance. Nuclei that possess a magnetic moment are typically nuclei with odd-numbered masses (^{1}H, ^{11}B, ^{13}C, ^{15}N, ^{19}F, etc.) or those with an even mass but an odd atomic number (^{2}H, ^{10}B). Note that ^{12}C is abundant in nature.

6. A

Coupling between adjacent carbon atoms (C) is rarely seen owing to the low abundance of ^{13}C. Coupling between carbon and protons on the adjacent carbon (B) is never observed. Because proton coupling is relevant only to ^{1}H-NMR, choice (D) is incorrect.

7. C

Most conjugated alkenes (C) give an intense ultraviolet absorption. Aldehydes, ketones, acids, and amines all absorb in the ultraviolet range. However, other forms of spectroscopy (mainly IR and NMR) are more useful for precise identification. Isolated alkenes, choice (B), can rarely be identified by UV.

8. B

In mass spectrometry, a molecule is broken down into smaller, charged fragments. These fragments are passed through a magnetic field and are identified according to their mass-to-charge ratios; therefore, choice (B) is the correct answer. Choice (D) is the basis for IR and NMR, not mass spectrometry, so this is incorrect. Viscosity, (C), doesn't form the basis for any of the spectroscopic techniques discussed, so it is also wrong. Finally, choice (A) is incorrect because the separation of fragments does not depend solely on mass but on charge as well, and the fragments are mostly polyatomic.

9. C

Alkyl benzenes commonly break apart to form a benzyl fragment (m/z 91), which rearranges to a tropylium fragment, which is aromatic (the empty *p*-orbital is part of the continuous π-system.) The answer can also be found by calculating the weights of the fragments for each choice: 105 for (A), 104 for (B) (note: the structure is cyclooctatetraene, which is nonaromatic as it is nonplanar and fails to satisfy Hückel's rule), and 103 for (D).

10. B

The region in question often gives information about the types of alkyl groups present. Specifically, an ethyl group will give a characteristic triplet (for the methyl group, which is coupled to –CH$_2$) and a quartet (for –CH$_2$, which is coupled to the methyl group), whereas a septet (for the –CH group, which is coupled to two methyl groups) and a doublet (for the two methyl groups coupled to –CH) are characteristic of an isopropyl group. Answer (C) is incorrect, because the alkyl group to peak relationship is reversed, whereas the alcohol hydrogen (D) is an unreliable check, since that peak can occur anywhere between 0 and 10 ppm, depending on the alcohol.

ethanol   isopropanol

11. C

The molecule is symmetric, with a mirror plane present that bisects the nitrogen and carbon atoms in the center ring, so many carbon atoms will have identical chemical shifts in the ^{13}C-NMR spectrum.

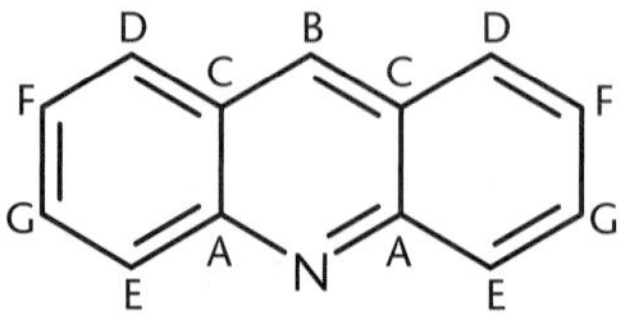

In the figure above, the 7 pairs of equivalent carbons are labeled A–G.

(A), (B), and (D) are incorrect because they fail to account fully for the mirror plane giving rise to identical signals.

12. A

Carbonyl groups (C=O) in conjugation with double bonds tend to absorb at lower wavenumbers, because the delocalization of π electrons causes the C=O bond to lose double-bond character, shifting the stretching frequency closer to C–O stretches, which occur between 1,000 and 1,250 cm^{-1}. For this reason, (B) and (C) are incorrect. (D) is incorrect because, for the C=O stretch to disappear, the bond needs to be fully broken, which does not happen during conjugation.

Carbohydrates

Carbohydrates (or, as they are known colloquially, carbs) have experienced a tumultuous few decades in American culinary culture. Remember the food pyramid, which advised that we consume 6 to 11 servings of carbohydrates (in the form of bread, cereal, rice, and pasta) per day? Nowadays, we're inundated with no-carb or low-carb diets, but the truth is, carbohydrates still make up most of the food and drinks that fill our refrigerators and cupboards. It's a good thing, too, because carbohydrates are the most direct source of chemical energy for organisms ranging from protozoa to plants to people.

Carbohydrates are compounds that contain carbon, hydrogen, and oxygen in the form of polyhydroxylated aldehydes or ketones with the general formula $C_n(H_2O)_n$ (hence *carbo-hydrate)*.

A single carbohydrate unit is called a **monosaccharide** (simple sugar) and, logically, a molecule with two sugars is called a **disaccharide**. **Oligosaccharides** are short carbohydrate chains (*oligos* is Greek for "a few"), whereas **polysaccharides** are long carbohydrate chains.

MCAT Expertise

The MCAT likes to take complicated molecules and test you on the most basic information about them. Therefore, when dealing with carbohydrates on the exam, look for the functional groups we have seen in all of the previous chapters and realize that they will always act the same.

Monosaccharides ★★★★☆

We classify monosaccharides the same way we classify most organic compounds: according to the number of carbons they possess. However, to name monosaccharides, we use the numerical prefix followed by the suffix *–ose* (think gluc*ose*). For example, **trioses**, **tetroses**, **pentoses**, and **hexoses** have three, four, five, and six carbons, respectively. The basic structure of monosaccharides is exemplified by the simplest of them all, glyceraldehyde, shown in Figure 14.1.

Key Concept

Monosaccharides are the simplest units and are classified by the number of carbons.

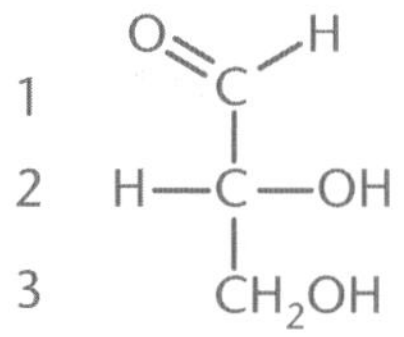

glyceraldehyde

Figure 14.1

Glyceraldehyde is a polyhydroxylated aldehyde, also known as an **aldose** (aldehyde sugar). The numbering of the carbon atoms in monosaccharides begins with the carbon closest to the carbonyl group. Thus, with aldoses, the aldehyde will always have the number C–1. Earlier we said that carbohydrates could be polyhydroxylated aldehydes or ketones, so let's go through the simplest ketone sugar, shown in Figure 14.2.

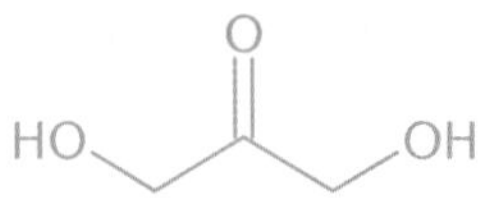

Figure 14.2

The simplest ketone sugar **(ketose)** is dihydroxyacetone. As we just mentioned, the ketone will receive the lowest possible number; in fact, every ketose that we will encounter on the MCAT will have the ketone group on C–2.

Notice that on every monosaccharide, every carbon *other* than the carbonyl will carry a hydroxyl group.

STEREOCHEMISTRY

Let's review the stereochemistry of monosaccharides by using Fischer projections to study the enantiomeric configurations of glyceraldehyde (see Figure 14.3).

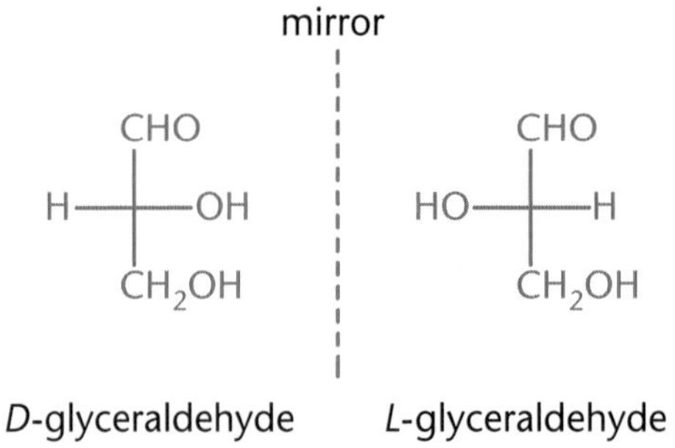

Figure 14.3

Key Concept

D and L are based on the stereochemistry of glyceraldehyde. These are not related to the + and – designations denoting optical rotation.

Early in the 20th century, scientists used glyceraldehyde to learn about the optical rotation of sugars. The results of this early study (which occurred before the *R* and *S* designations were used), led to the designation of **D** and **L** configurations. D-Glyceraldehyde was later determined to exhibit a positive rotation (designated as D-(+)-glyceraldehyde), and L-glyceraldehyde a negative rotation (designated as L-(−)-glyceraldehyde). On the MCAT, all other monosaccharides are assigned the D or L configuration based upon their relationship to glyceraldehyde. Therefore, if a molecule whose highest numbered chiral center (the chiral center farthest from the carbonyl) has the same configuration as D-(+)-glyceraldehyde, it is classified as a D sugar. A molecule that has its highest numbered chiral center in the same configuration as L-(−)-glyceraldehyde is classified as an L sugar. This is illustrated with glucose in Figure 14.4.

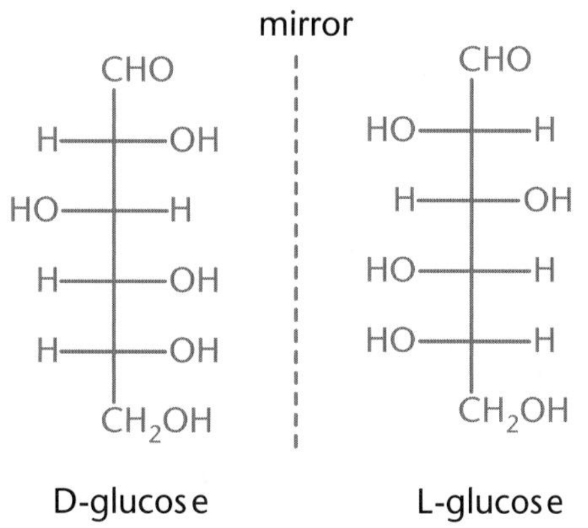

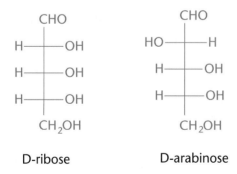

D-glucose   L-glucose

Figure 14.4

This serves as the basis of division for two optical families of sugars, the D family and the L family. All D sugars will have the hydroxide of their highest numbered chiral center on the right, and all L sugars will have that hydroxide on the left. Make sure that you are familiar with these three types of stereoisomers.

1. The same sugars, in different optical families, are enantiomers (such as D-glucose and L-glucose).

2. All nonidentical (nonmirror image) sugars within the same family (as long as both are ketoses/aldoses, and have the same number of carbons) are diastereomers.

3. Diastereomers that only differ at only one chiral center are known as **epimers** (such as D-ribose and D-arabinose, which only differ at C–2; see Figure 14.5).

> **Mnemonic**
>
> In a Fischer projection, if the *Lowest* –OH is on the *Left*, the molecule is *L*. If the –OH is on the *Right*, it's *D* (from the Latin root *dextro*, meaning "right").

> **Key Concept**
>
> Epimers differ in configuration at only one carbon.

D-ribose   D-arabinose

Figure 14.5

Some of the most important monosaccharides that you should memorize for the MCAT are shown in Figure 14.6.

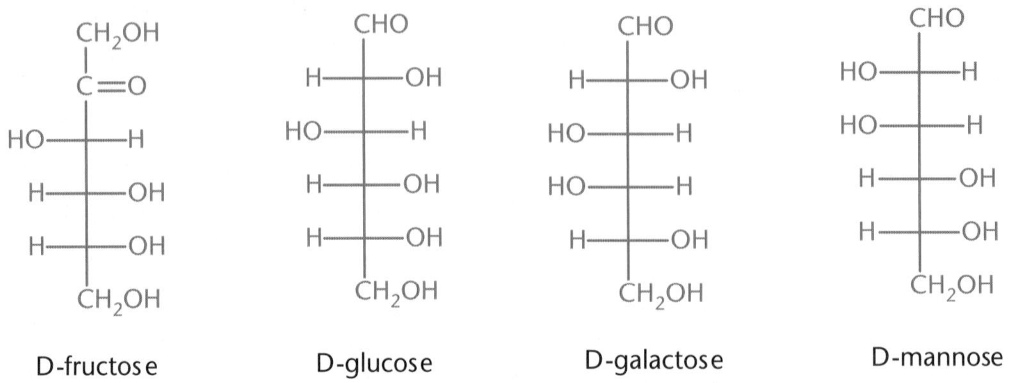

Figure 14.6

Note that in Figure 14.6, fructose is a ketose, whereas glucose, galactose, and mannose are all aldoses.

RING PROPERTIES

Because monosaccharides contain both a hydroxyl group (a nucleophile) and a carbonyl group (an electrophile), they can undergo intramolecular reactions to form cyclic hemiacetals (from aldoses) and hemiketals (from ketoses). Because of ring strain, the only cyclic molecules that are stable in solution are six-membered **pyranose** rings or five-membered **furanose** rings. Note that the hydroxide group is the nucleophile in the ring formation, so oxygen becomes a member of the ring structure.

Like cyclohexane, the pyranose rings adopt a chairlike configuration, and the substituents assume axial or equatorial positions to minimize steric hindrance. When we convert the monosaccharide from its straight-chain Fischer projection to the Haworth projection (shown in Figure 14.7), any group on the right of the Fischer projection will point down, and any group on the left side of the Fischer projection will point up. The reaction scheme in Figure 14.7 depicts the formation of a cyclic hemiacetal from D-glucose.

Key Concept

Note that the carbonyl carbon is (as always) a good electrophile and the many –OH groups can act as nucleophiles. What do you think will happen when these two groups are handcuffed together in the same molecule? Well, of course, an intramolecular nucleophilic acyl substitution!

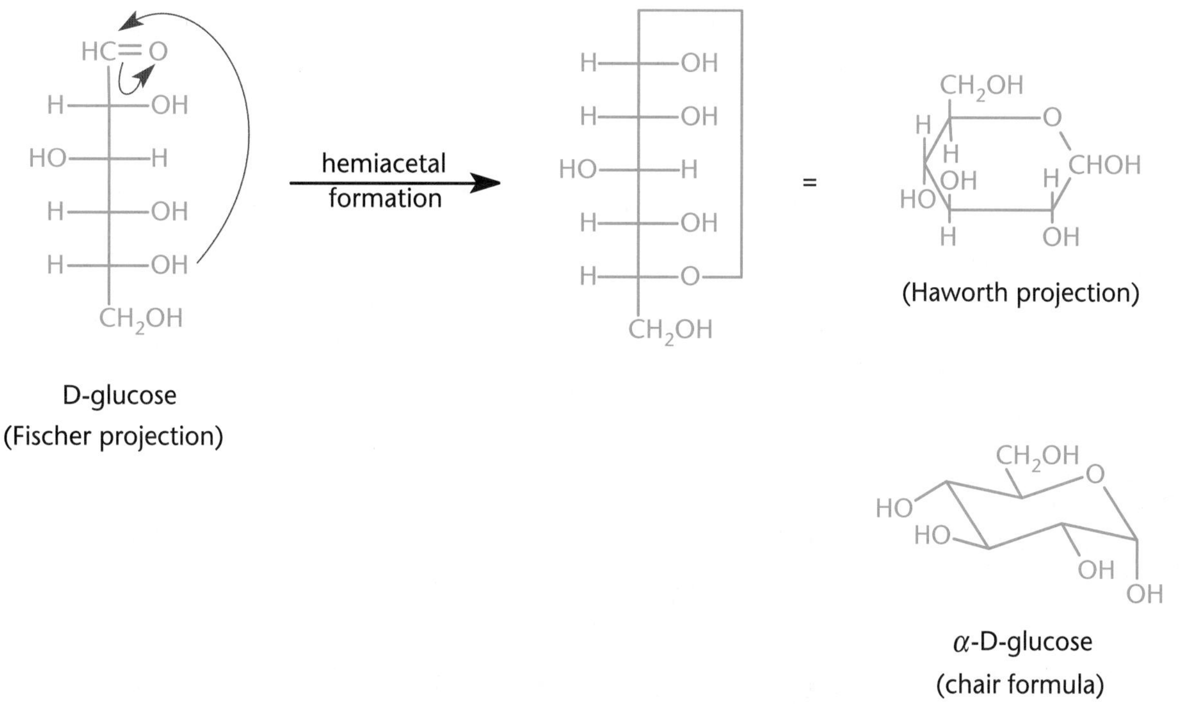

D-glucose
(Fischer projection)

hemiacetal formation

(Haworth projection)

α-D-glucose
(chair formula)

Figure 14.7

Because the oxygen of the hydroxide on the highest-numbered chiral group (the same one that determines whether it is D or L) functions as the nucleophile in ring formation, six-membered rings are formed from six carbon aldoses or seven carbon ketoses. Alternatively, five-membered rings are formed from five carbon aldoses or six carbon ketoses.

When we convert a straight-chain monosaccharide into its cyclic form, the carbonyl carbon (C–1 for glucose) becomes chiral. Cyclic stereoisomers that differ about the new chiral carbon are known as **anomers**. In fact, the carbon that becomes chiral is named for this characteristic, labeled the **anomeric carbon**. When a sugar is drawn in ring form, it is easy to identify the anomeric carbon: Simply find the carbon that is attached to both the oxygen in the ring and a hydroxide group. In glucose, the **alpha** (α) anomer has the –OH group of C–1 *trans* to the CH$_2$OH substituent (pointing down), whereas the **beta** (β) anomer has the –OH group of C–1 *cis* to the CH$_2$OH substituent (pointing up).

When we expose hemiacetal rings to water (see Figure 14.8), they will spontaneously open and re-form. Because the substituents on the single bond between C–1 and C–2 can rotate freely, either the α or β anomer can be formed. This spontaneous change of configuration about C–1 is known as **mutarotation**, and it occurs more rapidly when we catalyze it with an acid or base. Mutarotation results in a mixture that contains both anomers at their equilibrium concentrations (for glucose: 36% α, 64% β).

Key Concept

Anomers differ in configuration only at the newly formed chiral center, which is created by the attack of the alcohol on two different sides of the planar carbonyl carbon. α = *trans* to the –CH$_2$OH (down in glucose). β = *cis* to the –CH$_2$OH (up in glucose).

MCAT Expertise

Here is a clarification of often confusing terms:

Anomerization—the forming of one anomer or another from the straight-chain sugar

Mutarotation—the process of one anomer changing into the other anomer by opening and reclosing

The α configuration is less favored because the hydroxyl group of the anomeric carbon is axial, adding to the steric strain of the molecule.

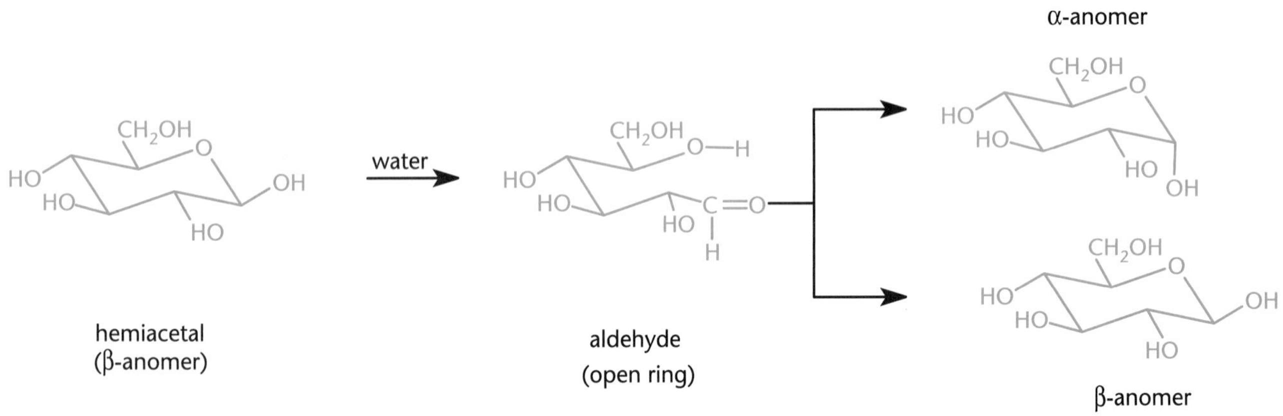

Figure 14.8

MONOSACCHARIDE REACTIONS

Ester Formation

Key Concept

Reaction types are determined by the functional groups present. Think of alcohols and carbonyls.

The MCAT test makers love to test on compounds such as monosaccharides, because even though they look confusing at first, their component parts still react the same as they would in a smaller molecule. Because monosaccharides contain hydroxyl groups, they undergo many of the same reactions as simple alcohols. Specifically, we can convert monosaccharides to esters, using acid anhydride and a base. In this reaction, all of the hydroxyl groups will be esterified. The reaction in Figure 14.9 is an example of glucose esterification.

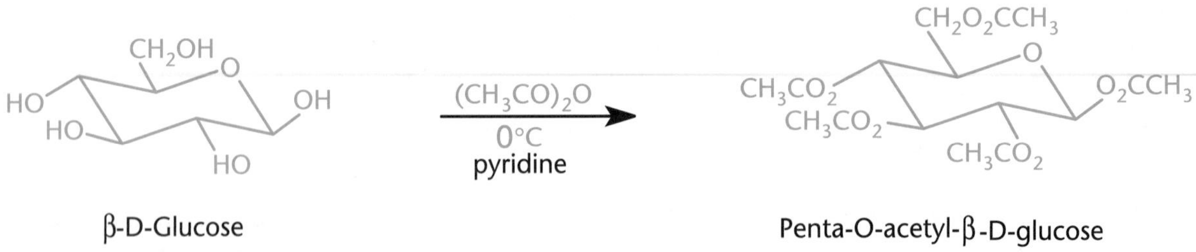

Figure 14.9

Oxidation of Monosaccharides

As monosaccharides switch between anomeric configurations, the hemiacetal rings spend a short period of time in the open-chain aldehyde form. Just like other aldehydes, they can be oxidized to carboxylic acids; these oxidized aldoses are called **aldonic acids**. Because aldoses can be oxidized, they are considered reducing agents. Therefore, any monosaccharide with a hemiacetal ring (–OH on C–1) is considered a **reducing sugar**. Both Tollens's reagent and Benedict's reagent can be used to detect the presence of reducing sugars. A positive Tollens's test involves the reduction of Ag^+ to form metallic silver. When Benedict's reagent is used, a red precipitate of Cu_2O indicates the presence of a reducing sugar (see Figure 14.10).

An interesting phenomenon to be aware of is that ketose sugars are also reducing sugars and give positive Tollens's and Benedict's tests. Although ketones cannot be oxidized to carboxylic acids, they can isomerize to aldoses via keto-enol shifts. While in the aldose form, they can react with Tollens's or Benedict's reagents to form the carboxylic acid. A more powerful oxidizing agent, such as dilute nitric acid will oxidize both the aldehyde and the primary alcohol (C–6) to carboxylic acids.

Real World

Benedict's test can be used to detect glucose in the urine of diabetics.

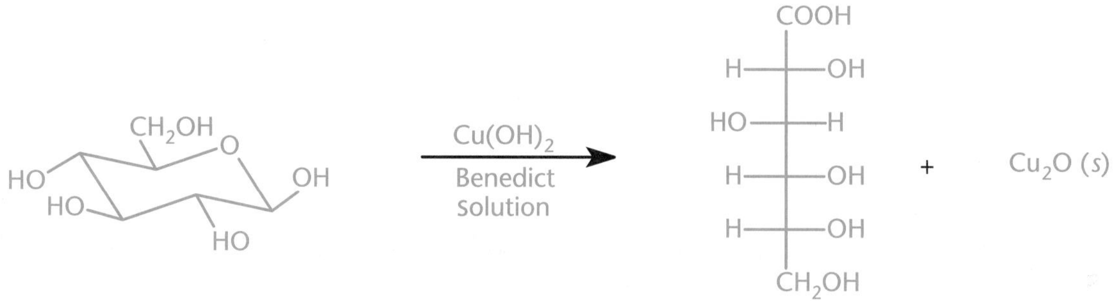

β-D-Glucose   D-Gluconic Acid (an aldonic acid)   (red solid)

Figure 14.10

Glycosidic Reactions

As we remember from Chapter 8, hemiacetals will react with alcohol to form acetals. True to form, hemiacetal monosaccharides will react with alcohol under acidic conditions. The anomeric hydroxyl group is transformed into an alkoxy group, yielding a mixture of the α- and β-acetals (with water as a leaving group). The resulting C–O bond is called a **glycosidic linkage**, and the acetal is known as a **glycoside**. An example is the reaction of glucose with ethanol shown in Figure 14.11.

Key Concept

This reaction is not new to us, either; it is really just a dressed-up S_N2 reaction with the sugar acting as the nucleophile.

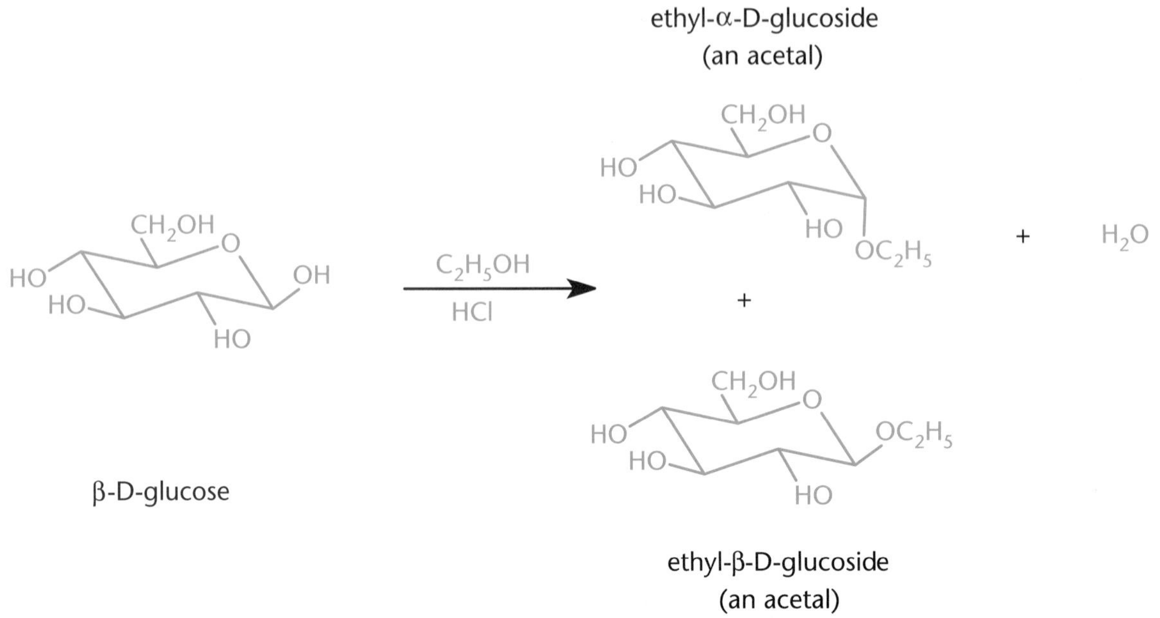

ethyl-α-D-glucoside
(an acetal)

+ H₂O

+

ethyl-β-D-glucoside
(an acetal)

Figure 14.11

Disaccharides ★★★★☆☆

As discussed previously, a monosaccharide may react with alcohols to give acetals. Notice that monosaccharides also have hydroxide groups, so they, too, can function as the alcohol in reactions with other monosaccharides. When two monosaccharides react in this way, the product is called a **disaccharide**. The formation of a disaccharide is shown in Figure 14.12.

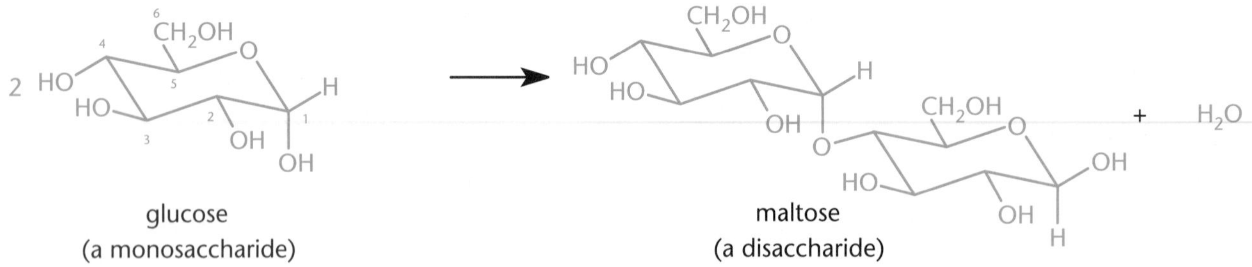

glucose
(a monosaccharide)

maltose
(a disaccharide)

+ H₂O

Figure 14.12

The most common glycosidic linkage occurs between C–1 of the first sugar and C–4 of the second, designated as a 1,4′ linkage; it is the one you will most likely see on the MCAT. 1,6′ and 1,2′ bonds are also observed. The glycosidic bonds may be either α or β, depending on the orientation of the hydroxyl group on the anomeric carbon. In Figure 14.13, the product has a 1,4′-α linkage (maltose). Two glucose monosaccharides joined by a 1,4′-β linkage yield cellobiose.

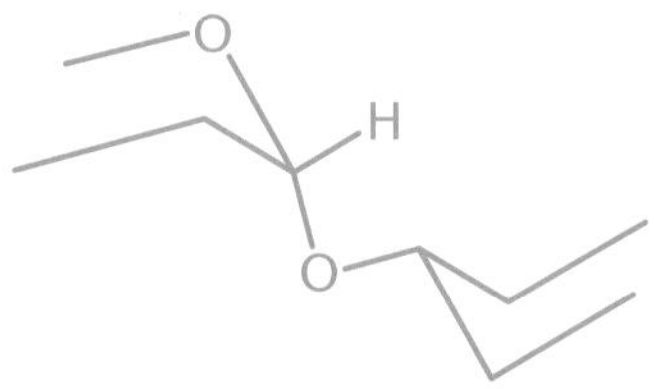

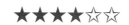

α-glycosidic linkage

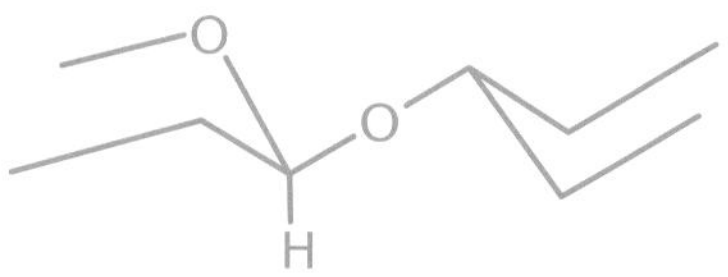

β-glycosidic linkage

Figure 14.13

Glycosidic linkages are often cleaved in the presence of aqueous acid. For example, we can cleave the glycosidic linkage of the disaccharide maltose into two molecules of glucose.

Polysaccharides ★★★★☆☆

Polysaccharides are large chains of monosaccharides linked together by glycosidic bonds. The three most important biological polysaccharides are cellulose, starch, and glycogen. Although these three polysaccharides have different functions, they are all composed of the same monosaccharide, D-glucose. In cellulose, the chain of glucose molecules is linked by 1,4'-β-glycosidic bonds. Cellulose is the structural component of plants and is not digestible (think fiber), at least by humans. Cows on the other hand, can't get enough of the stuff. Starch is a polysaccharide that is more digestible by humans. Plants store energy as starch molecules by linking glucose molecules primarily in 1,4′-α-glycosidic bonds, although occasional 1,6′-α-glycosidic bonds form branches off the chain. Animals, on the other hand, store their excess glucose as glycogen. Glycogen is similar to starch, except that it has more 1,6′-α-glycosidic bonds (approximately 1 for every 12 glucose molecules), which makes it a highly branched compound (dendrimer). All three polysaccharides are composed of glucose subunits, but they differ in their configuration about the anomeric carbon and the position of glycosidic bonds, resulting in notable biological differences (see Figure 14.14).

Real World

In lactose intolerance, a person is missing the enzyme lactase, which breaks the disaccharide lactose into glucose and galactose molecules.

Bridge

Key biological polysaccharides are cellulose (1,4′-β), starch, and glycogen (mostly 1,4′-α, although some are 1,6′-α).

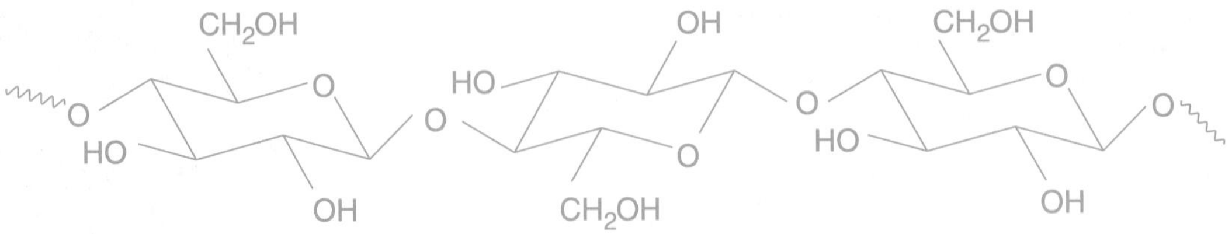

cellulose, a 1,4′-β-D-glucose polymer

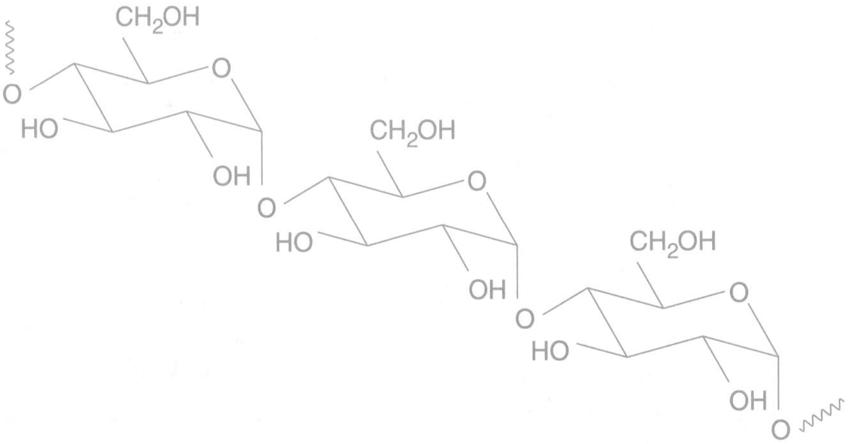

starch, a 1,4′-α-D-glucose polymer

Figure 14.14

Conclusion

This chapter was an introduction to the world of macromolecules, and as such, we began with the smallest of them all, simple carbohydrates. Although macromolecules are likely to appear on the MCAT, it's important to realize that no matter how big the molecule is, it will still follow the same rules that govern the smallest of molecules. In all of Organic Chemistry, our focus should be on nucleophiles and electrophiles. The only difference with macromolecules is that the nucleophile and electrophile may be on the same molecule. Keep this in mind, because things are going to get much bigger as we enter the last chapter of this text and begin our discussion of the nitrogen-containing macromolecules: proteins.

CONCEPTS TO REMEMBER

☐ Carbohydrates have the general formula $C_n(H_2O)_n$.

☐ Aldoses are sugars with aldehydes at the C–1 position; ketoses are sugars with ketones at the C–2 position.

☐ L-sugars have the highest-numbered chiral hydroxyl group on the left side of the sugar; D-sugars have the highest-numbered chiral hydroxyl group on the right (in a Fischer projection).

☐ D-glucose and L-glucose are enantiomers (nonsuperimposable mirror images).

☐ Any sugars that differ at only one chiral center are known as epimers.

☐ Sugars can undergo intramolecular reactions that form rings. Pyranose rings are six-membered sugar rings; furanose rings are five-membered rings.

☐ C–1 becomes chiral when a ring is formed; this newly chiral atom is known as the anomeric carbon. For glucose, the anomeric carbon can either be α (down) or β (up).

☐ Changing back and forth between the α and β position is known as mutarotation.

☐ The key reactions of monosaccharides are ester formation, oxidation, and glycosidic reactions.

☐ Polysaccharides: Cellulose is a chain of glucose with 1,4′-β-glycosidic bonds; starch and glycogen are mostly 1,4′-α-glycosidic bonds (with some 1,6′-β-glycosidic bonds that form branches off the chain).

Practice Questions

1. When glucose is in a straight-chain formation, it

   A. is an aldoketose.
   B. is a pentose.
   C. has five chiral carbons.
   D. is 1 of 16 stereoisomers.

2. All of the following are true of epimers EXCEPT

   A. they differ in configuration about only one carbon.
   B. they usually have slightly different chemical and physical properties.
   C. they are diastereomers (with the exception of glyceraldehyde).
   D. they always have equal but opposite optical activities.

3.

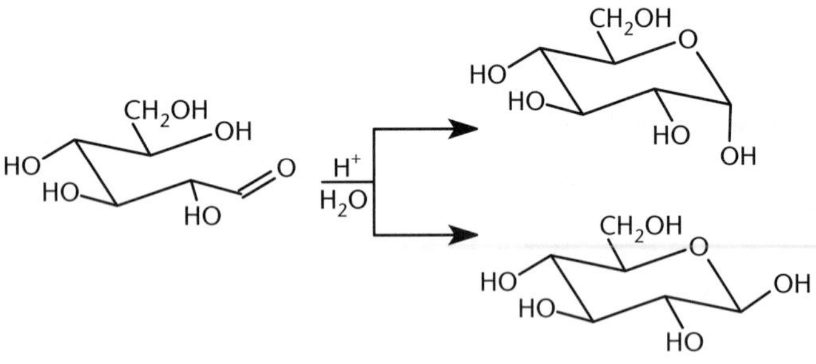

   The above reaction is an example of one step in

   A. aldehyde formation.
   B. hemiketal formation.
   C. mutarotation.
   D. glycosidic bond cleavage.

4. What is the product of the following reaction?

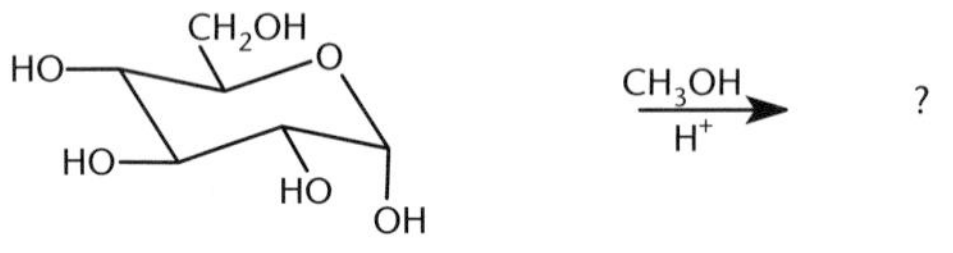

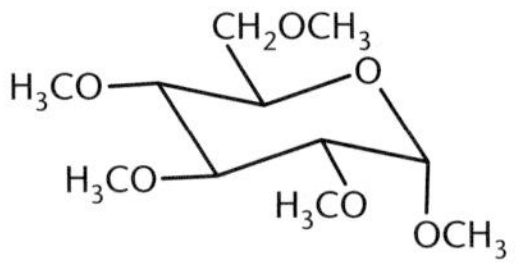

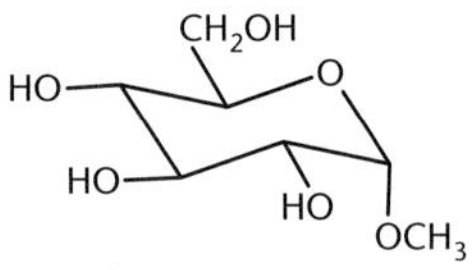

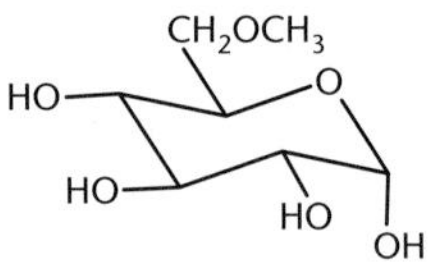

5. Which of the following compounds is not a monosaccharide?

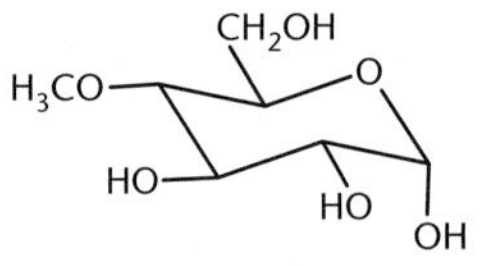

   A. Deoxyribose
   B. Fructose
   C. Glucose
   D. Maltose

6. The cyclic forms of monosaccharides are

   I. Hemiacetals
   II. Hemiketals
   III. Acetals

   A. I only
   B. III only
   C. I and II only
   D. I, II, and III

7. When the following straight-chain Fischer projection is converted to a chair or ring conformation, what will be its structure?

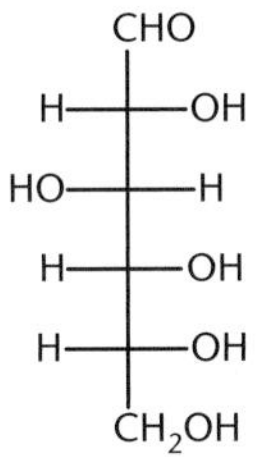

CHO
H——OH
HO——H
H——OH
H——OH
CH₂OH

A.

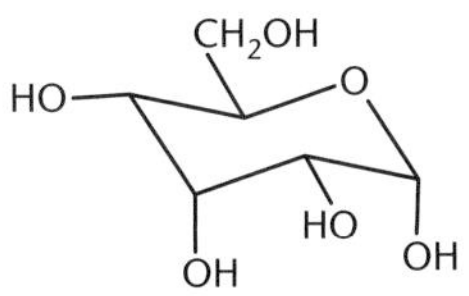

CH₂OH
HO
HO OH
OH OH

B.

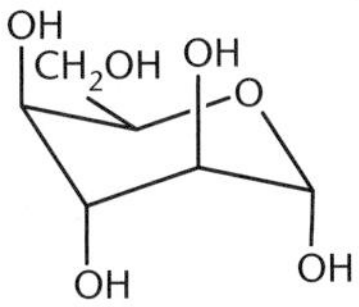

OH
CH₂OH OH
O
OH OH

C.

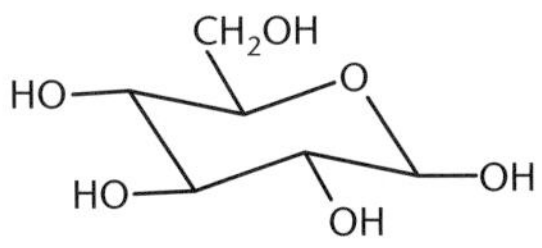

CH₂OH
HO
HO OH
OH

D.

OH
CH₂OH OH
O
HO OH

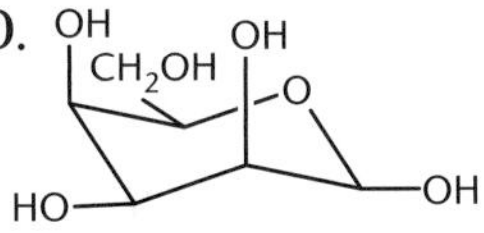

8. What would be the product of the following reaction?

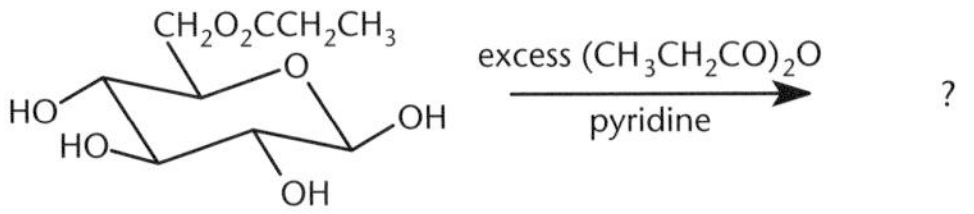

CH₂O₂CCH₂CH₃
O
HO
HO OH
OH

excess (CH₃CH₂CO)₂O
——————————→ ?
pyridine

A.

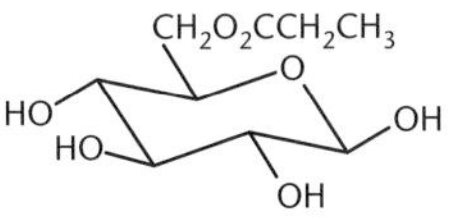

CH₂O₂CCH₂CH₃
O
HO
HO OH
OH

B.

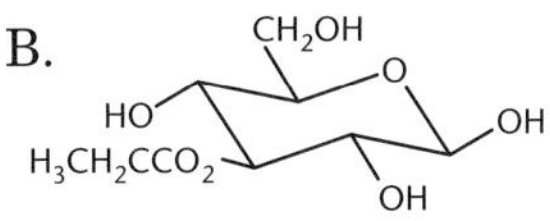

CH₂OH
O
HO
H₃CH₂CCO₂ OH
OH

C.

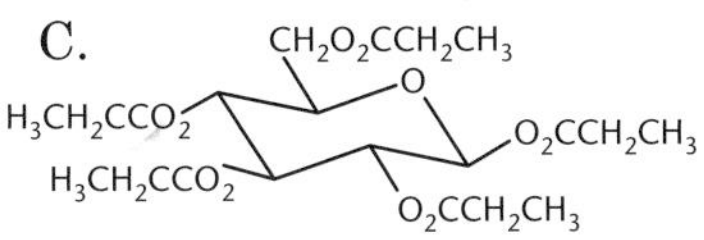

CH₂O₂CCH₂CH₃
O
H₃CH₂CCO₂
H₃CH₂CCO₂ O₂CCH₂CH₃
O₂CCH₂CH₃

D.

CH₂OH
O
HO
HO O₂CCH₂CH₃
OH

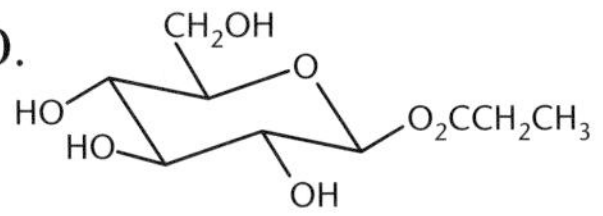

9. Which of the following are reducing sugars?

A. Fructose
B. Galactose
C. Glucose
D. All of the above

10. What description best fits the pair of sugars shown below?

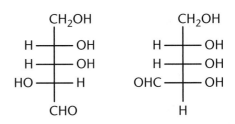

A. They are enantiomers.
B. They are diastereomers.
C. They are meso compounds.
D. They are identical.

11. Galactose is the C–4 epimer of glucose. Which structure below is galactose?

A.

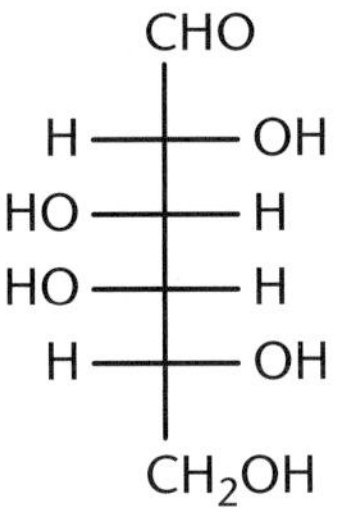

CHO
H——OH
HO——H
HO——H
H——OH
CH₂OH

B.

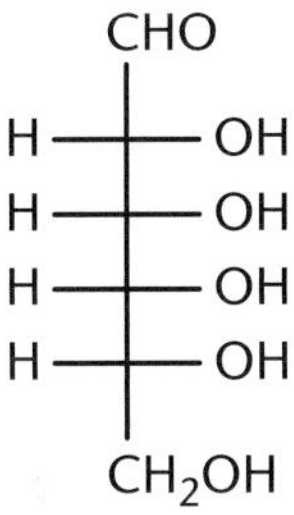

CHO
H——OH
H——OH
H——OH
H——OH
CH₂OH

C.

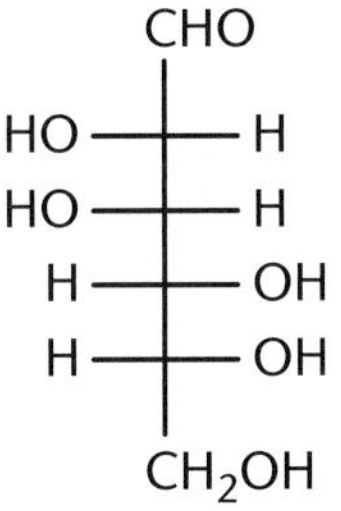

CHO
HO——H
HO——H
H——OH
H——OH
CH₂OH

D.

CHO
H——OH
HO——H
H——OH
HO——H
CH₂OH

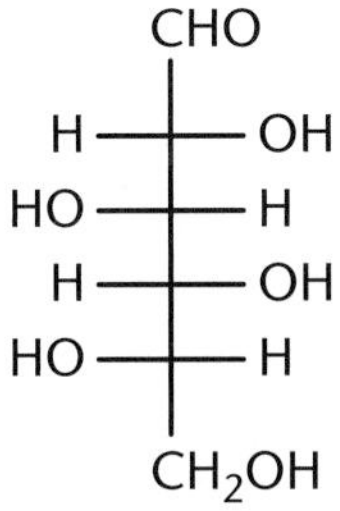

12. Under strongly acidic conditions, aldoses become oxidized to dicarboxylic acids called *aldaric acids*. An unknown pentose X, which is optically active, produces an optically inactive aldaric acid upon treatment with HNO_3. What is the structure of pentose X?

A.
```
       CHO
   H ——— OH
  HO ——— H
  HO ——— H
      CH₂OH
```

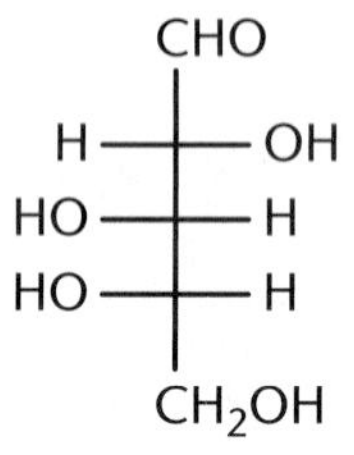

B.
```
       CHO
  HO ——— H
  HO ——— H
   H ——— OH
      CH₂OH
```

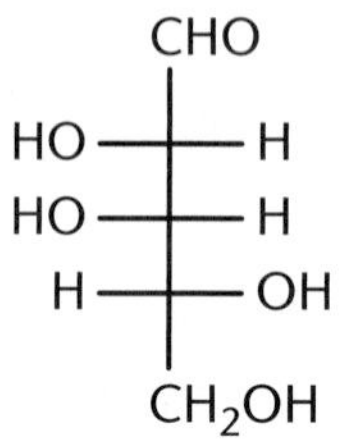

C.
```
      CH₂OH
  HO ——— H
  HO ——— H
   H ——— OH
       CHO
```

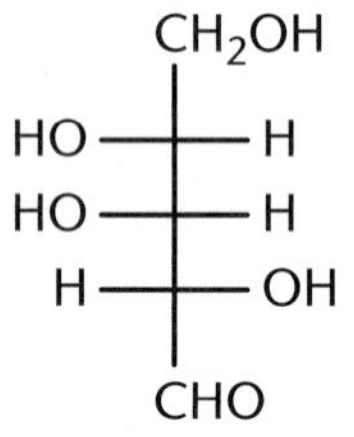

D.
```
       CHO
   H ——— OH
   H ——— OH
   H ——— OH
      CH₂OH
```

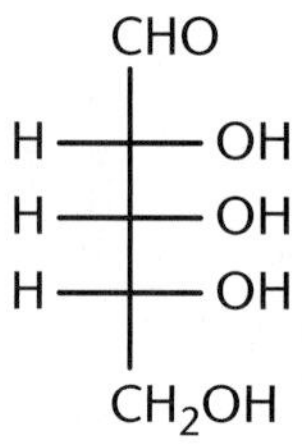

Small Group Questions

1. How many possible aldotetroses are there?

2. How do you convert from a Fischer projection to a chair conformation?

Explanations to Practice Questions

1. D

Glucose is an aldohexose, meaning that it has one aldehyde group and six carbons. Given this information, choices (A) and (B) can be eliminated. In aldose sugars, each nonterminal carbon is chiral. Therefore, glucose has four chiral centers, not five (C). The number of stereoisomers possible for a chiral molecule is 2^n, where n is the number of chiral carbons. Because glucose has four chiral centers, there are $2^4 = 16$ stereoisomers possible. Thus, choice (D) is correct.

2. D

Epimers are monosaccharide diastereomers that differ in their configuration about only one carbon (A). As with all diastereomers (C), epimers have different chemical and physical properties (B), and their optical activities have no relation to each other. Enantiomers have equal but opposite optical activities. Therefore, choice (D) is the only statement that does not apply to epimers.

3. C

In solution, the hemiacetal ring of glucose will break open spontaneously and then re-form. When the ring is broken, bond rotation occurs between C–1 and C–2 to produce either the α- or the β-anomer. The reaction given in this question depicts the mutarotation of glucose, corresponding to (C). Choice (A) is incorrect because the reactant is an aldehyde, not the product. Choice (B) is incorrect because a hemiketal has an –OH group and an –OR group. In addition, hemiketals are formed from ketones, and our starting product is an aldehyde. Finally, choice (D) is incorrect because there is no glycosidic bond in the starting product.

4. B

When glucose is reacted with ethanol under acid catalysis, the hemiacetal is converted to an acetal via replacement of the anomeric hydroxyl group with an alkoxy group. The result is a type of acetal known as a glycoside. This corresponds with choice (B). (A) is incorrect because the –OH on the C–6 carbon would not be converted to –OCH_3.

5. D

Maltose is a disaccharide made of two glucoses, making choice (D) the correct answer. All the other choices are monosaccharides.

6. C

Monosaccharides can exist as hemiacetals (I) or hemiketals (II), depending on whether they are aldoses (monosaccharides that contain an aldehyde functionality in their open-chain forms) or ketoses (monosaccharides that contain a ketone functionality in their open-chain forms). When a monosaccharide is in its cyclic form, the anomeric carbon is attached to the oxygen in the ring (which constitutes the acetal or ketal group) and is also attached to a hydroxyl functionality (hence, it is only a hemiacetal or hemiketal, since a full acetal or ketal would involve the conversion of this functionality to an alkoxy group). Therefore, choices I and II are true, making choice (C) the correct response.

7. C

Start by drawing out the Haworth projection. Recall that all the groups on the right in the Fischer projection will go on the bottom of the Haworth projection, and all the groups on the left will go on the top. Next, draw the chair structure, with the oxygen in the back right vertex. Label the carbons in the ring, 1 through 5, moving clockwise around the ring from the oxygen. Now, draw in the lines for all the axial substituents, alternating above and below the ring. Remember to start on the anomeric C–1 carbon, where the axial substituent points down. Now start filling in the substituents. The substituent can be in either position on the anomeric carbon, so skip that one for now. Look back to C–2 on the Haworth; the –OH is below the ring. That means that we'll put it in the equatorial position on the ring, because the axial position is pointing up. The –OH on C–3 is above the ring in the Haworth, so it should also go in the equatorial position on the ring, because the axial position points down. The –OH on C–4 is below the ring in the Haworth and will also end up in the equatorial position on the ring, because the axial position points up. Finally, the –CH$_2$OH group is above the ring in the Haworth, so it will go in the equatorial position in the ring (as the axial position points down). The only possible answer choice, therefore, is (C), which represents the β-anomer.

8. C

Glucose, because it has hydroxyl groups, can react like any alcohol and be converted to an ester. Therefore, the reaction of glucose with an anhydride in the presence of base, shown in this question, creates an ester group at each hydroxyl position. Choice (C) is the only answer that shows every hydroxyl group esterified.

9. D

All aldose sugars are considered reducing sugars, since they are easily oxidized to carboxylic acids by such reagents as Tollens's and Benedict's solutions. Galactose (B) and glucose (C) are aldoses; thus, they are reducing sugars. Although fructose (A) is not an aldose, it can be oxidized because it can isomerize to an aldose via a few keto-enol shifts in a basic solution. Therefore, all three monosaccharides are reducing sugars, and choice (D) is correct.

10. D

The easiest way to answer this question is to determine the stereochemistry of C–2 (counting from the aldehyde), which for both sugars is *R*. Since the other chiral carbons for both sugars are the same, they are identical; (A) and (B) are incorrect. (C) is incorrect because there is no internal plane of symmetry.

11. A

Galactose is a diastereomer of glucose, with the stereochemistry at C–4 (counting from the aldehyde) reversed. Being able to identify C–4 is enough to answer this question, even if you do not remember what glucose looks like. Since (B), (C), and (D) have identical stereochemistry at C–4, they are incorrect.

12. D

To answer this question, replace the ends of each sugar with carboxylic acids and then find the *meso* sugar. (B) is incorrect, since the aldaric acid remains optically active (no internal mirror plane), while (A) and (C) are identical (one is the 180° flip of the other.)

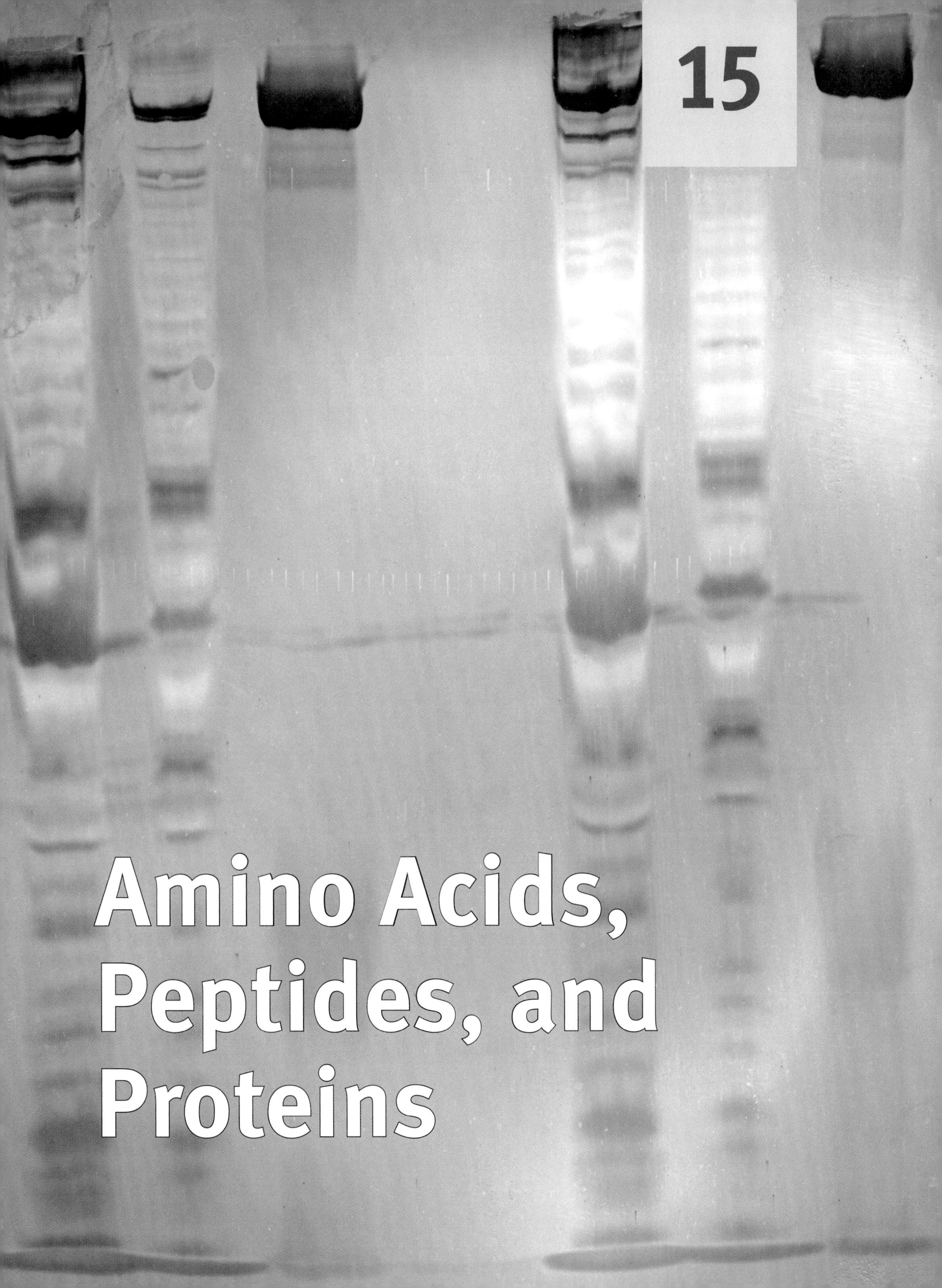

Amino Acids, Peptides, and Proteins

Congratulations! Welcome to the last chapter of this book, in which everything we've learned so far is put together. This chapter continues our discussion of macromolecules, although we will make things a bit more complicated than the carbohydrates in the previous chapter. Not only will, we be discussing C, O, and H, we will throw N into the mix as well via the building blocks of proteins, amino acids. To really understand amino acids, we need to know all about nucleophilicity, electrophilicity, acidity, basicity, resonance, intermolecular forces—basically the trends that we've discussed throughout this book. This extra complexity isn't surprising, because proteins have many more functions in our bodies than petroleum has uses in our commercial world. Proteins do everything from providing structure (keratin) to communicating signals (peptide hormones) to catalyzing reactions (enzymes). Proteins are the largest compounds that you will need to know for Organic Chemistry on Test Day, but they will still behave in the same way as other compounds containing the same functional groups. Go in with confidence; you already know how all these molecules work.

Amino Acids

★★★★☆☆

Amino acids contain an amine group and a carboxyl group attached to a single carbon atom (the α-carbon). The other two substituents of the α-carbon are a hydrogen atom and a variable side chain referred to as the **R-group**. It is helpful to think of the α-carbon as the central atom of the amino acid, because it is the atom that has all of the different functional groups attached to it (see Figure 15.1).

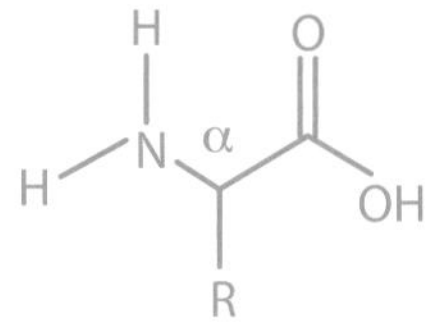

Figure 15.1

The α-carbon, with its four different groups, is a chiral (stereogenic) center (except in **glycine**, the simplest amino acid, where R = H and it only has three different groups attached to it), so all amino acids (except for glycine) are optically active. Naturally occurring amino acids (of which there are 20) are all L-enantiomers (as discussed in Chapters 2 and 14). Therefore, by convention, the Fischer projection for an amino acid is drawn with the amino group on the left (L = left). L-Amino acids have *S* configurations, except for cysteine, which is *R* because of the change in priority caused by the sulfur.

MCAT Expertise

Many of the Organic Chemistry topics we have already encountered can be tested with amino acids and proteins: carboxylic acid derivatives (peptide bond = amide linkage), hydrogen bonding, electrophoresis, stereochemistry, and acid-base properties. Expect to be tested on the basics, even when dealing with more complicated molecules.

Key Concept

With the exception of glycine, all amino acids are chiral.

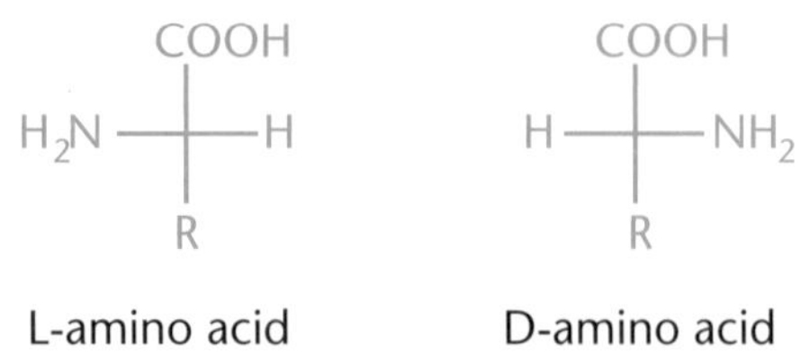

L-amino acid   D-amino acid

Figure 15.2

ACID-BASE CHARACTERISTICS

Acid-base chemistry just doesn't get any more interesting than amino acids, because they have both a basic amino group *and* an acidic carboxyl group. Species that can act as both acids and bases are described as **amphoteric** (water is also an amphoteric species). You can think of amino acids as double agents: They can play either role, depending on the terms and conditions. Whereas double agents will switch sides for money or protection, amino acids function as either acids or bases depending on the pH of their environment. This means that if there are lots of protons in solution (acidic, low pH), the amino acid will pick up a proton, thus functioning as a base. On the other hand, if there are few protons in solution (basic, high pH), the amino acid will donate a proton, thus functioning as an acid. Remember that science is all about equilibrium; if conditions go too extreme in one direction, something will occur to try to bring the system back to normal. Amino acids are a great example of this, and whether they are put into a highly acidic or highly basic environment, they will function to bring the system back toward neutral.

Now that we've discussed the theory behind amino acids, let's get into how we are likely to see them on Test Day. Recall from previous chapters that amino groups take on positive charges when protonated and carboxyl groups take on negative charges when deprotonated. This means that when an amino acid is put into solution, as shown in Figure 15.3, it will take on both of these charges, forming a dipolar ion, or **zwitterion** (from German *zwitter*, or "hybrid"). The two oppositely charged halves of the molecule neutralize each other, so at a neutral pH, amino acids exist in the form of internal salts.

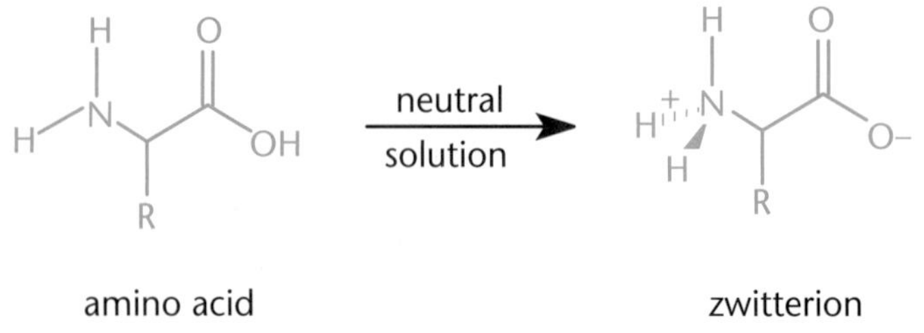

amino acid   zwitterion

Figure 15.3

Because there are two different locations that can either be protonated or deprotonated, amino acids have at least two different dissociation constants, K_{a1} and K_{a2} relative to the pH, or K_{b1} and K_{b2} relative to the pOH.

If we put a neutral amino acid into an acidic solution, as shown in Figure 15.4, it will become fully protonated. The amino group is protonated fairly easily (because it is protonated even at neutral pH), but it takes a fairly acidic environment to protonate the carboxyl group.

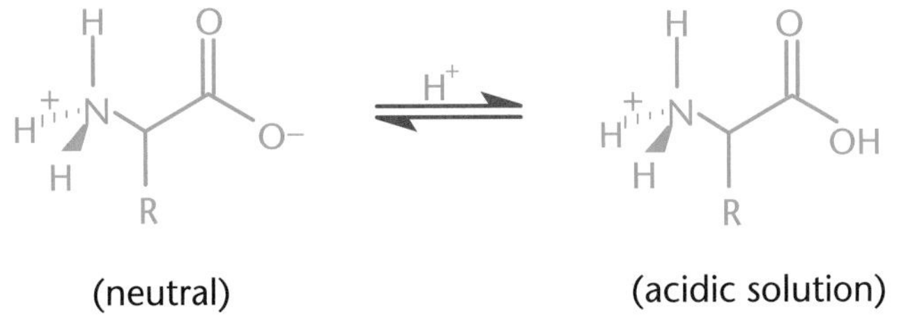

(neutral)   (acidic solution)

Figure 15.4

If we were to take a neutral amino acid and drop it into a basic solution, as shown in Figure 15.5, the opposite would occur, and the amino acid would become fully deprotonated. Here, the carboxyl group is easy to deprotonate (because it is deprotonated even at neutral pH), but it takes a more alkaline environment to deprotonate the amino group.

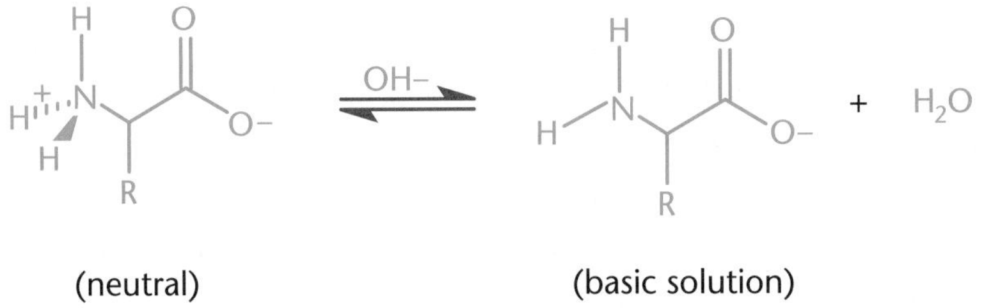

(neutral)   (basic solution)

Figure 15.5

This means that at a low pH, the amino acid will carry an excess positive charge and at a high pH, it will carry an excess negative charge. The intermediate pH, at which the amino acid exists as a zwitterion, is known as the **isoelectric point (pI)**, or **isoelectric pH**, of the amino acid.

This isoelectric pH must lie between pK_{a1} and pK_{a2}. Remember that pK_a is simply the pH at which dissociation occurs. As we should remember, p(anything) implies an inverse relationship. This means that a high K_a will have a low pK_a, just as a high proton concentration $[H^+]$ will have a low pH.

TITRATION OF AMINO ACIDS

Because amino acids have acidic and basic properties, they are great candidates for titration. The titration of each proton occurs as a distinct step, resembling that of a simple monoprotic acid. Thus, the titration curve ends up looking like a combination of two or three monoprotic acids (three if the amino acid has an acidic or basic R-group) all tied together. Figure 15.6 shows the titration curve for glycine.

Key Concept

At its isoelectric point, an amino acid is uncharged.

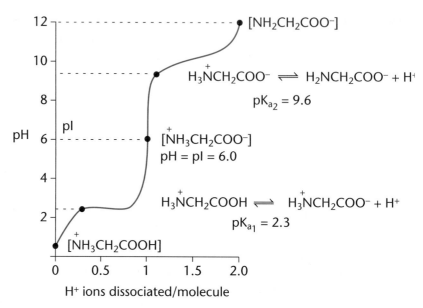

Figure 15.7

A 1 M glycine solution is acidic, which means glycine exists predominantly as $^+NH_3CH_2COOH$: fully protonated and with a positive charge. As the solution is titrated with NaOH, the carboxyl group, as it is the most acidic, will be the first to lose a proton. During this stage, the amino acid acts as a buffer, and the pH changes very slowly. When 0.5 moles of base have been added to the amino acid solution, the concentrations of the initial glycine $^+NH_3CH_2COOH$ and $^+NH_3CH_2COO^-$ (its zwitterion) are equimolar. At this point, the pH is equal to pK_{a1}, and the solution is buffered against pH changes. This is an important point to remember: When pH = pK_a, the solution is in a buffer zone, represented by a flat horizontal line on the graph (because there is no change in pH).

As we add more base, more and more of the carboxyl groups will become de-protonated. The amino acid starts to lose its buffering capacity, and the pH will start to rise quickly during this phase. By the time 1 mole of base has been added (remember that we started with 1 mole of glycine), glycine exists exclusively as $^+NH_3CH_2COO^-$. Because we have added equal amounts of glycine and base, each molecule of glycine has been deprotonated at the carboxyl group. This means that every amino acid is now electrically neutral; thus, the pH at this point is equal to the isolelectric point (pI) of glycine. This is our second point to remember: When we've added equal amounts of amino acid and base, pH = pI, and we have a vertical line on our graph.

As we continue adding base, glycine passes through a second buffering stage, during which the pH change is held steady again. But now, because we've already deproto-nated all of the carboxyl groups, the less acidic amino groups start to deprotonate.

Key Concept

Titration with base: First the carboxyl group is deprotonated, then the amino group.

When 1.5 moles of base have been added, the concentrations of $^+NH_3CH_2COO^-$ and $NH_2CH_2COO^-$ are equimolar, and the pH is equal to pK_{a2}. This is our second buffering zone, which we need to remember occurs when $pH = pK_{a2}$, and once again appears as a roughly horizontal line on the graph.

Continuing with our theme, as we add another 0.5 moles of base (2 moles total), the remaining amino groups are deprotonated, leaving only $NH_2CH_2COO^-$ in solution.

Here are some of the key concepts you'll need to remember for the MCAT, although we highly recommend studying titrations (see General Chemistry Chapter 10: Acids and Bases), as they are often tested in the Physical Sciences section of the MCAT:

1. When adding base, the carboxyl groups lose their protons first; after all of the carboxyl groups are fully deprotonated, the amino groups start to lose their acidic protons.
2. Two moles of base must be added to deprotonate one mole of most amino acids. The first mole deprotonates the carboxyl group, whereas the second deprotonates the amino group.
3. The buffering capacity of the amino acid is greatest at or near the pH of the two dissociation constants, pK_{a1} and pK_{a2}. At the isoelectric point (which can be found by determining the average of pK_{a1} and pK_{a2}), its buffering capacity is minimal, and the graph appears as a vertical line.
4. Some amino acids contain acidic or basic side chains. To find the pI of these amino acids, simply average the two acidic pK_a's if the side chain is acidic. If the side chain is basic, take the average of the two basic pK_a's.
5. It is possible to perform the titration in reverse, from alkaline pH to acidic pH, with the addition of acid; in that case, the sequence of events is reversed.

HENDERSON-HASSELBALCH EQUATION

This is another topic that often appears in the General Chemistry portion of the MCAT, so we will discuss it briefly here. As we've just discussed, the ratio of protonated to deprotonated amino acids that exist in solution depends on the pH of the solution. The Henderson-Hasselbalch equation defines this relationship by relating the pH to the ratio of conjugate acid to conjugate base. It also provides a mathematical expression for the dissociation constants of amino acids.

$$pH = pK_a + \log \frac{[\text{conjugate base}]}{[\text{conjugate acid}]}$$

When the pK_{a1} of glycine is known, the ratio of acid to its conjugate base for a particular pH can be determined. For example, at pH 3.3, glycine, which has a pK_a of 2.3, will have these ratios:

Key Concept

Amino acids pass through at least two buffering stages, one at each pK_a.

Bridge

Make sure you take the time to study and practice the chemistry of acids and bases and the Henderson-Hasselbalch equation. A solid understanding of these topics is even more essential for the Physical Sciences section of the MCAT.

$$3.3 = 2.3 + \log \frac{[^+H_3NCH_2COO^-]}{[H_3N^+CH_2COH]}$$

$$\text{By subtraction: } \log \frac{[H_3N^+CH_2COO^-]}{[H_3N^+CH_2COOH]} = 1$$

$$\text{The antilog of } 1 = 10; \text{ thus, } \frac{[H_3N^+CH_2COO^-]}{[H_3N^+CH_2COOH]} = \frac{10}{1}$$

Therefore, in this example, there are ten times as many zwitterions as there are fully protonated amino acids. We can also do this with the pK_{a2} of glycine (if it is given); we would simply change the conjugate base to $NH_2CH_2COO^-$ and the conjugate acid to $^+NH_3CH_2COO^-$. We can use the Henderson-Hasselbalch equation experimentally to prepare effective buffer solutions of amino acids. The best buffering regions of amino acids occur within one pH unit of the pK_a or pK_b.

AMINO ACID SIDE CHAINS

This is where we begin to see the real functionality of amino acids; after all, the side chains (R-groups) give each amino acid its unique character. Furthermore, it is the combination of these different side chains that give different proteins their distinguishing features. The 20 naturally occurring amino acids are grouped into four categories: **nonpolar**, **polar** (but *uncharged*), **acidic**, and **basic**. Although you definitely don't need to memorize the structure of each amino acid for the MCAT, it is important to know the function of each amino acid. If you remember which category each amino acid fits into, you'll be in great shape for Test Day.

Nonpolar Amino Acids

Most nonpolar amino acids (see Figures 15.7a and b) have R-groups that are saturated hydrocarbons. This means that these R-groups are hydrophobic and, thus, decrease the solubility of the amino acid in water. For this reason, these amino acids prefer to be buried inside proteins, away from the aqueous cellular environment. An interesting example of how this preference can lead to disastrous effects is sickle cell anemia. This disorder affects hemoglobin by replacing the hydrophilic amino acid glutamic acid with hydrophobic valine. Because the glutamic acid is normally on the aqueous exterior of the molecule, replacing it with hydrophobic valine causes the molecule to contort into a sickle shape in an attempt to bury the valine in the molecule's interior.

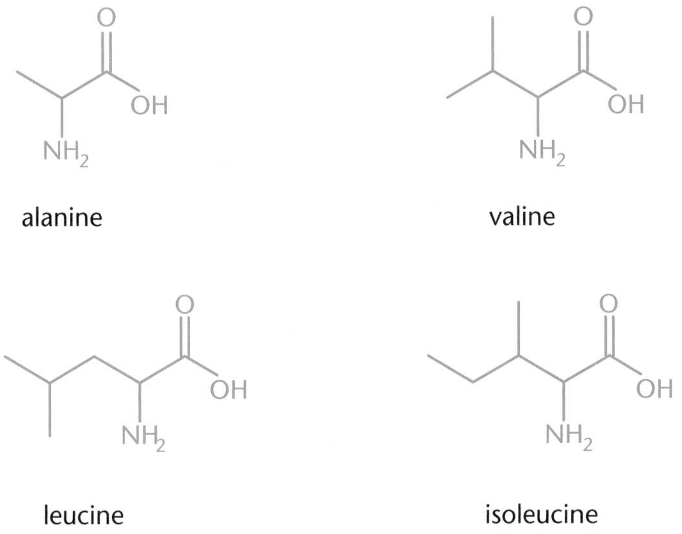

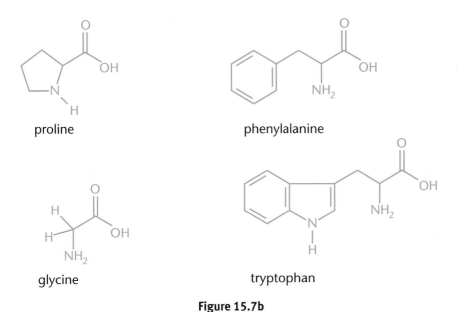

Figure 15.7a

In addition to fully saturated hydrocarbons, there are a few other nonpolar amino acid side chains (see Figure 15.7b). Also, note that although tryptophan has a nitrogen atom with a lone pair, the electrons are resonated through the aromatic ring, so it does not exhibit basic properties. The tryptophan ring, which is large and hydrophobic, is often a nucleating residue when proteins fold.

Key Concept

Nonpolar amino acids are often found at the core of globular proteins or in transmembrane regions of proteins that are in contact with the hydrophobic portion of the phospholipid membrane.

Figure 15.7b

Polar Amino Acids

Polar amino acids (Figures 15.8a and b) have uncharged polar R-groups that are hydrophilic. This polarity increases their solubility in water, so they are often found on the surface of proteins.

Key Concept

The other types of amino acids (polar, acidic, and basic) are found in regions of proteins that are exposed to the aqueous, polar environment (that is, the surface of the protein).

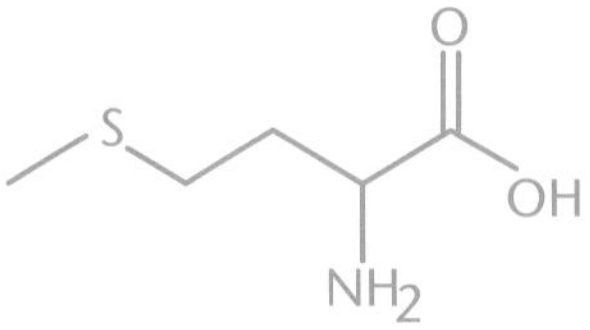

methionine

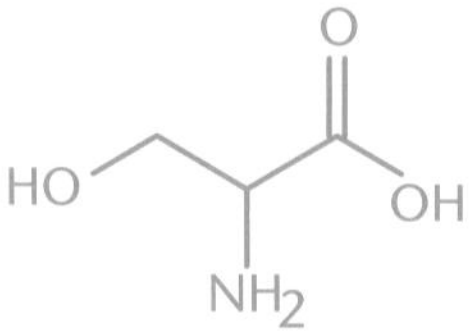

serine

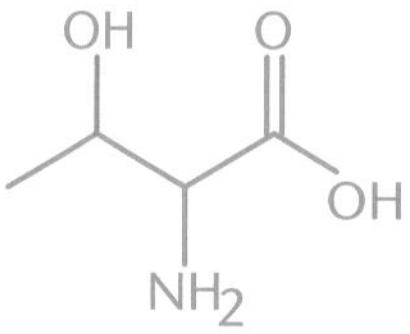

threonine

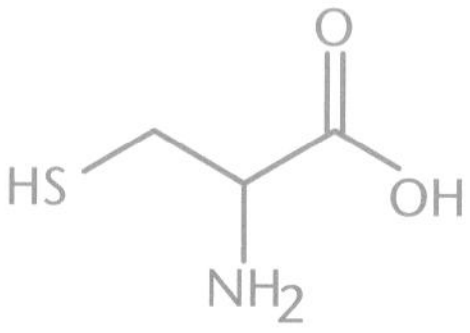

cysteine

Figure 15.8a

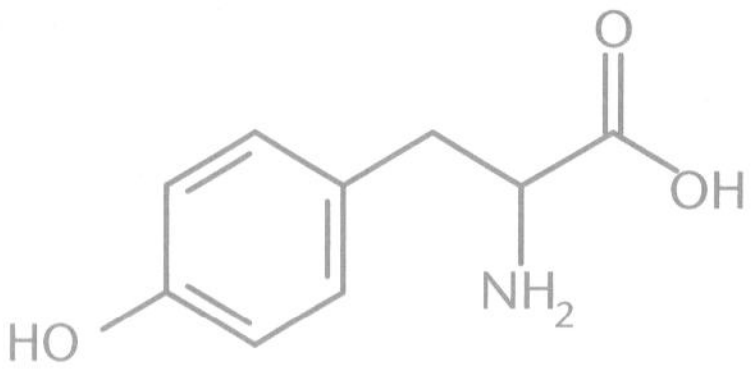

tyrosine

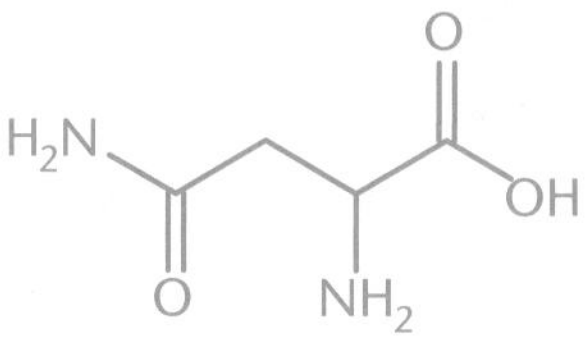

asparagine

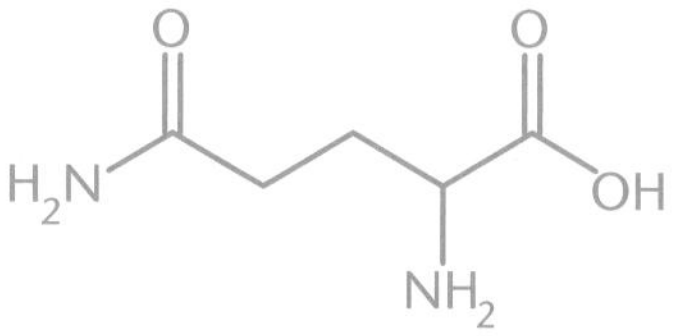

glutamine

Figure 15.8b

Key Concept

Acidic amino acids have a negative charge at physiological pH (7.4). They have three distinct pK_a's.

Acidic Amino Acids

Acidic amino acids (Figure 15.9) have an R-group that contains a carboxyl group. They have a net negative charge at physiological pH (7.4), so they exist in salt form in the body. Acidic amino acids have important roles in the substrate-binding sites of enzymes and reactions that require a proton transfer. Proteases provide examples of enzymes that use the acid-base properties of acidic side chains. The nice thing about the acidic amino acids is that their names both end in *acid*, making it easier to remember which group they belong to.

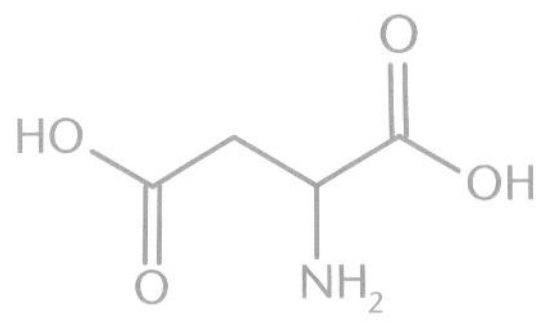

aspartic acid

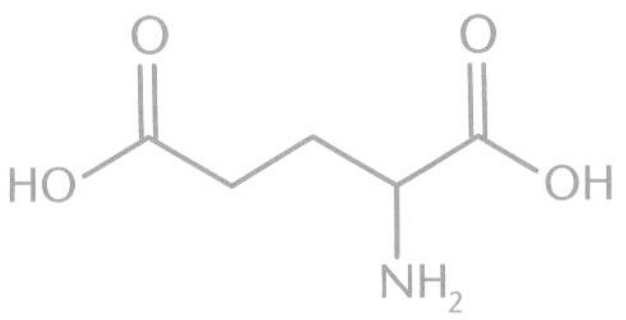

glutamic acid

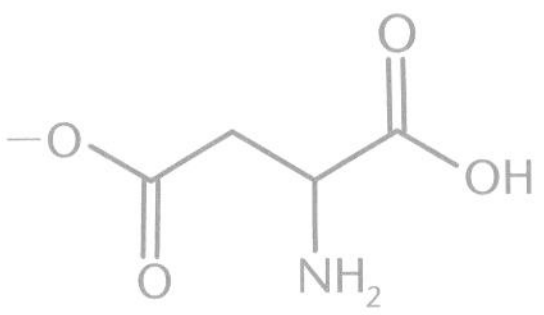

(salt is aspartate.)

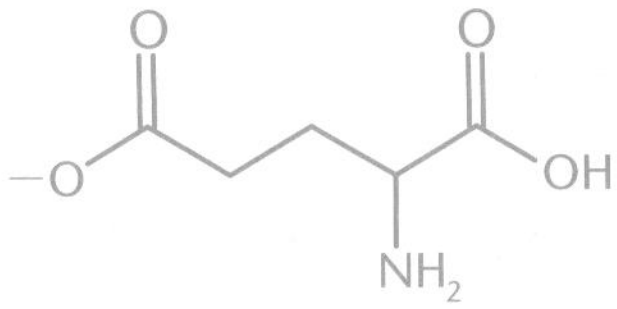

(salt is glutamate.)

Figure 15.9

Aspartic acid and glutamic acid each have three groups that must be neutralized during titration (two –COOH and one –NH$_3^+$). Therefore, their titration curve is different from the standard curve that we saw for glycine. This also means that these molecules have three distinct dissociation constants—pK$_{a1}$, pK$_{a2}$, and pK$_{a3}$—although the neutralization curves of the two carboxyl groups overlap to a certain extent. Because of the additional carboxyl group, the isoelectric point is shifted toward an acidic pH and can be found by averaging both of the acidic pK$_a$'s together. In addition, three groups require three moles of base to deprotonate each mole of the acidic amino acid.

Basic Amino Acids

Amino acids whose side chains contain an amino group are called basic amino acids (see Figure 15.10). These will carry a net positive charge at physiological pH (7.4).

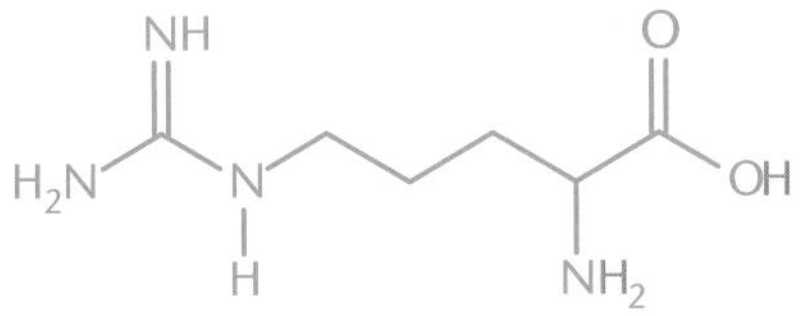

arginine

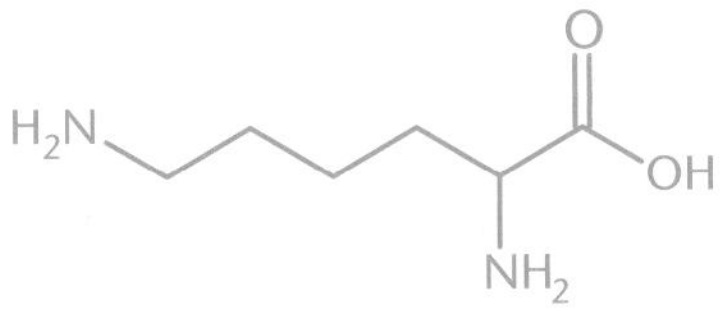

lysine

histidine

Figure 15.10

> **Key Concept**
>
> At physiological pH, basic amino acids have a net positive charge. They also have three dissociation constants.

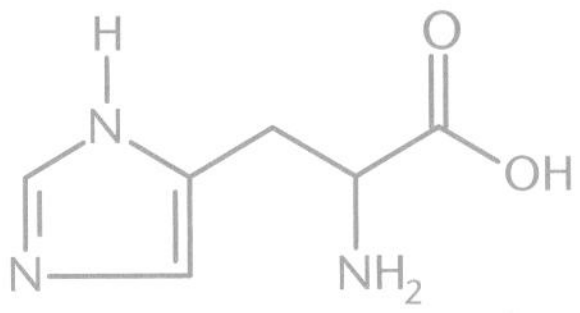

Similar to acidic amino acids, the titration curve of basic amino acids is modified by the additional amino group that must be neutralized. These amino acids also have three dissociation constants, and the neutralization curves for the two amino groups overlap somewhat. The isoelectric point is shifted toward an alkaline pH and can be found by averaging the two basic pK_as together. Once again, three moles of acid are needed to neutralize one mole of a basic amino acid.

Understanding titration curves and isoelectric points helps us to predict the charge of any particular amino acid at a given pH. For example, in a mixture of glycine, glutamic acid, and lysine at pH 6, glycine will be neutral, glutamic acid will be negatively charged, and lysine will be positively charged.

Peptides ★★☆☆☆

Peptides are composed of amino acid subunits, sometimes called **residues** (see Figure 15.11). We know that amino acids have a carboxyl group on one end and an amino group on the other, so when two amino acids with these groups combine, a **peptide bond**, which is simply an amide bond, forms between them. Peptides are basically small proteins (the distinction between a peptide and protein is vague, but it is generally accepted that peptides contain fewer than about 50 residues). Two amino acids joined together form a **dipeptide**, three form a **tripeptide**, and many amino acids linked together form a **polypeptide**.

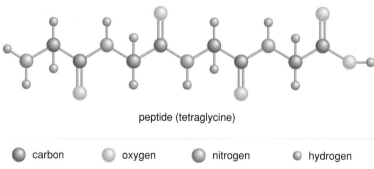

peptide (tetraglycine)

● carbon   ● oxygen   ● nitrogen   ● hydrogen

Figure 15.11

REACTIONS

As we mentioned, amino acids are joined by peptide bonds (amide bonds) between the carboxyl group of one amino acid and the amino group of another. To form this bond, a condensation reaction occurs (water is lost). The reverse reaction, hydrolysis (cleavage by adding water) of the peptide bond, is catalyzed by an acid or base, as we saw earlier (see Figure 15.12).

In addition, certain enzymes digest the chain at specific peptide linkages. For example, trypsin cleaves at the carboxyl end of arginine and lysine, and chymotrypsin cleaves at the carboxyl end of phenylalanine, tyrosine, and tryptophan. Although you don't need to memorize where these enzymes cleave amino acids, they will often be described in a passage on the MCAT, so you should be comfortable identifying the location of peptide bonds within a peptide.

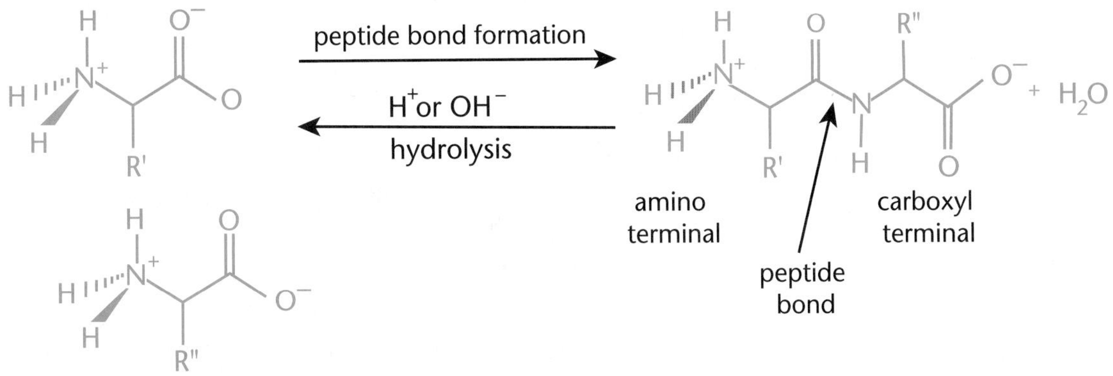

Figure 15.12

PROPERTIES

The terminal amino acid with a free α-amino group is known as the **amino-terminal** or **N-terminal** residue, whereas the terminal residue with a free carboxyl group is called the **carboxy-terminal** or **C-terminal** residue. By convention, peptides are drawn with the N-terminal end on the left and the C-terminal end on the right.

As we remember from previous chapters, amides have two resonance structures, so the true structure is a hybrid with partial double-bond character between the nitrogen and the carbonyl carbon (see Figure 15.13). This double-bond character leads to an important property: Rotation about the C–N bond is restricted. This restriction adds to the rigidity and stability of the backbone of proteins. The bonds on either side of the peptide unit, on the other hand, can rotate however they like, because they are only single bonds.

> **Key Concept**
>
> Rotation is limited around the peptide bond because resonance gives the C–N bond partial double-bond character.

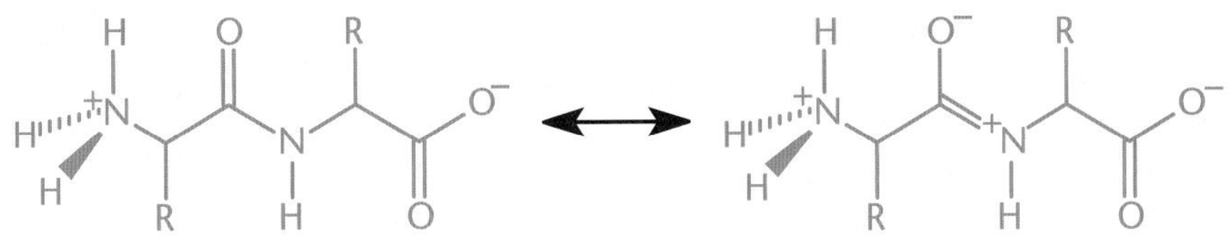

Figure 15.13

MCAT Expertise

The levels of protein structure are often tested on the MCAT, so be familiar with the primary, secondary, tertiary, and quaternary structure elements and the factors that affect them.

Proteins

Proteins are polypeptides that range from only a few to more than a thousand amino acids in length. They serve a vast array of functions in biological systems, acting as enzymes, hormones, membrane pores, receptors, and elements of cell structure. Proteins are the main actors of biological systems; after all, our genetic code is simply a grocery list of different protein codes. There are four levels of protein structure—**primary**, **secondary**, **tertiary**, and **quaternary**.

PRIMARY STRUCTURE

The primary structure of proteins is the structure that is coded into the DNA of the organism. It is the sequence of amino acids, listed from the N-terminus to the C-terminus, each linked by peptide bonds.

This is the most fundamental structure of the protein; it is the sequence that determines all higher levels of protein structure. In other words, a protein will assume whatever secondary, tertiary, and quaternary structures are the most energetically favorable for the given primary structure and the environment. This primary structure can be determined in a laboratory using a procedure called **sequencing**. This is most easily done on the DNA (the gene) that produced the protein.

SECONDARY STRUCTURE

The secondary structure is the local structure of neighboring amino acids. The most important thing to remember about secondary structure is that it is primarily the result of hydrogen bonding between nearby amino acids. Also, know that the two most common types of secondary structure are the **α-helix** and the **β-pleated sheet** (sometimes simply called **β-sheet**). β-sheets may be parallel or antiparallel. Some turns are also considered elements of secondary structure.

MCAT Expertise

Hydrogen bonds show up in all kinds of interesting places in this book and on the MCAT. Always be on the lookout for these strong interactions and what role they might have.

α-Helix

The α-helix is a rodlike structure in which the peptide chain coils clockwise about a central axis. This helix is stabilized by the intramolecular hydrogen bonds between carbonyl oxygen atoms and amide hydrogen atoms four residues away from each other ($n + 4$ hydrogen bond). The side chains of these amino acids point away from the helix's core, interacting with the cellular environment. A typical protein with this structure is **keratin**, a fibrous structural protein that is found in our hair and fingernails.

β-Pleated Sheet

In β-pleated sheets, the peptide chains lie alongside each other, forming rows. As we said before, these chains are held together by intramolecular hydrogen bonds between the carbonyl oxygen atoms on one peptide chain and the amine hydrogen atoms on another. To accommodate the greatest possible number of hydrogen bonds, the β-pleated sheet assumes a rippled, or pleated, shape (see Figure 15.14). The R-groups of amino residues point above and below the plane of the β-pleated sheet. Silk fibers are composed of β-pleated sheets.

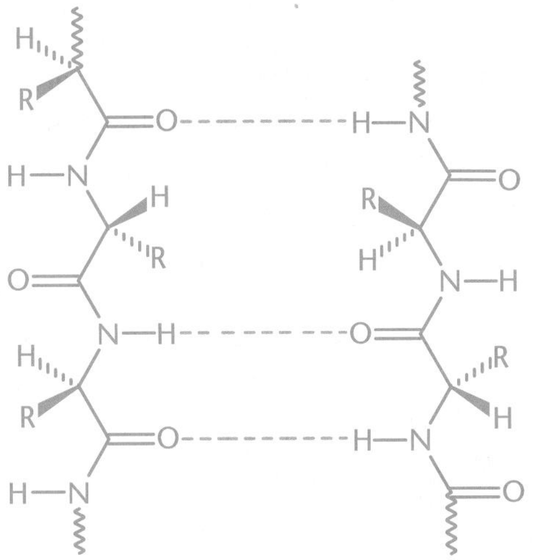

Figure 15.14

TERTIARY STRUCTURE

Tertiary structure refers to the three-dimensional shape of the protein. It is mostly determined by hydrophilic and hydrophobic interactions between the R-groups of amino acids. This three-dimensional structure is also determined by the distribution of disulfide bonds. A disulfide bond results when two **cysteine** molecules become oxidized to form **cystine** as shown in Figure 15.15. Disulfide bonds create loops in the protein chain. Disulfide bonds determine how wavy or curly our hair is; in fact, as many people learned in the 1980s, you can add more disulfide bonds to your hair—it's called a perm.

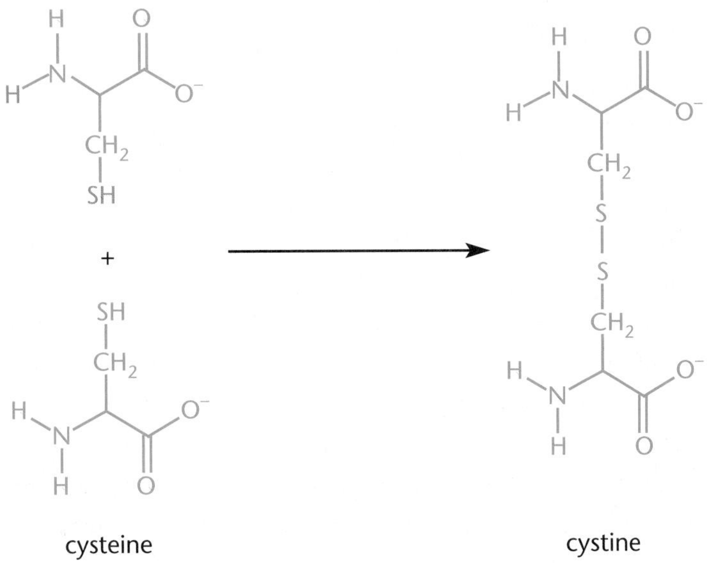

cysteine   cystine

Figure 15.15

Amino acids other than cysteine can have significant effects on tertiary structures as well. For instance, proline, because of its ring shape, cannot fit into every location in an α-helix, so it causes a kink in the chain.

Amino acids with hydrophilic (polar or charged) R-groups tend to arrange themselves toward the outside of the protein, where they interact with the aqueous cellular environment. Amino acids with hydrophobic R-groups tend to be found close together, and they protect themselves from the aqueous environment by burying themselves in the middle of the protein.

Proteins are divided into two major classifications on the basis of their tertiary structure. **Fibrous proteins**, such as **collagen**, are found as sheets or long strands, whereas **globular proteins** (think *globe*), such as myoglobin, are spherical.

QUARTERNARY STRUCTURE

A protein can have quaternary structure only if it contains more than one polypeptide subunit. The quaternary structure refers to the way these subunits arrange themselves to yield a functional protein. The classic example of quaternary structure is **hemoglobin**, the oxygen-transporting machines that fill our red blood cells. Hemoglobin is composed of four different globular protein subunits.

CONJUGATED PROTEINS

Conjugated proteins derive part of their function from covalently attached molecules called **prosthetic groups**. These prosthetic groups can be organic molecules, such as vitamins, or even metal ions, such as iron. Proteins with lipid, carbohydrate, and nucleic acid prosthetic groups are referred to as **lipoproteins**, **glycoproteins**, and **nucleoproteins**, respectively. These prosthetic groups have major roles in determining the function of their respective proteins. For example, each of hemoglobin's subunits (as well as myoglobin) contains a prosthetic group known as the **heme group**. This heme group is composed of an organic porphyrin ring with an iron atom bound in the center. The heme group itself binds to and carries oxygen; as such, hemoglobin would be inactive without the heme group.

DENATURATION OF PROTEINS

Denaturation, or **melting**, is the process by which proteins lose their three-dimensional structure and revert to a **random-coil** state. Because this process destroys the protein's tertiary structure, it renders it completely functionless. There are several methods we can use to denature a protein—with a detergent, change in pH, temperature, or even solute concentration. The weak intermolecular forces that keep the protein stable and functional can be disrupted by any of these factors. When a protein denatures, the damage is usually permanent. However, certain gentle denaturing agents (such as urea) do not permanently disrupt the protein. Removing the reagent might allow the protein to **renature** (regain its structure and function). That is, the denaturation is reversible.

Conclusion

It's pretty amazing to examine the vastly different functions that are derived from various combinations of the same 20 amino acids. Even more interesting is that the same 20 amino acids comprising all of the proteins in our bodies are the same 20 amino acids that make the proteins of almost every single form of life on this planet, from *Escherichia coli* to aspen trees.

Many Organic Chemistry textbooks open with the sweeping claim that Orgo is the "chemistry of life"; we'd like to end with it. It's undeniably true that the molecules and reactions we study in Orgo are essential to the functions we use as qualifications for life: the ability to self-replicate and use energy from the environment. However, in the years since the term was coined, *organic chemistry* has come to include a great deal more than life processes. In fact, you've been using Orgo from just about the moment you woke up this morning: the gas in your car (Alkanes—Chapter 4), the plastic shopping bag lining your trash can (Alkenes and Alkynes—Chapter 5), the flowery scent of your perfume (Aromatic Compounds—Chapter 6), the aerosol propellant that allowed you to spritz on your perfume (Alcohols and Ethers—Chapter 7), the spearmint flavor of your toothpaste (Aldehydes and Ketones—Chapter 8), the preservative that keeps your toothpaste fresh (Carboxylic Acids—Chapter 9), the nail polish remover you used to clean off your chipped toenails (Carboxylic Acid Derivatives—Chapter 10) . . . all the way down to the carpet fibers that cushioned your toes as you stepped out of bed (Amines and Nitrogen-Containing Compounds—Chapter 11). Undoubtedly, extraction, filtration, or distillation was used to prepare the food and drink that you will consume today (Purification and Separation—Chapter 12), and odds are that someday (we hope not today!) you will need an MRI scan to assess or diagnose an injury or illness (Spectroscopy—Chapter 13). Of course, Organic Chemistry still includes the "chemistry of life": The bagel that you ate for breakfast (Carbohydrates—Chapter 14) is broken down into energy, which your body uses to build proteins, giving rise to every structure and function in your body (Amino Acids, Peptides, and Proteins—Chapter 15).

Despite the subject's compelling relevance to everyday life, college Organic Chemistry still manages to terrify and alienate its students, as we noted in the beginning of this book. The MCAT, on the other hand, doesn't ask you to memorize tables of reactants or regurgitate hundreds of named reactions from scratch. Instead, the

Real World

Denaturation is the loss of three-dimensional structure. Permanent denaturation occurs when cooking egg whites. They denature and form a solid, rubbery mass that cannot be transformed back to its clear liquid form.

MCAT asks you to look at the bigger picture, to know trends, to participate. We hope that studying for the MCAT has given you a chance to start over with Orgo—to focus on the *how* and the *why* instead of the *what*. Organic Chemistry, like the MCAT as a whole, should be seen not as an obstacle but as an opportunity. So work hard, have some fun along the way, and keep thinking about where you're heading . . . you can almost feel that white (polyester!) coat.

CONCEPTS TO REMEMBER

☐ Amino acids contain a carboxyl group, an amino group, a hydrogen, and an R-group attached to a central α-carbon.

☐ There are 20 naturally occurring amino acids, all of which are L-enantiomers, except for glycine which is achiral.

☐ Amino acids are amphoteric species (they can function as acids or bases).

☐ In a neutral solution, nonpolar and polar amino acids exist as zwitterions, acidic amino acids exist as negatively charged ions, and basic amino acids exist as positive ions.

☐ All amino acids have at least two pK_a's, and the isoelectric point (pI) is between the two pK_a's. For acidic amino acids with three pK_a's, the pI is between the two largest pK_a's; for basic amino acids with three pK_a's, the pI is between the two lowest pK_a's.

☐ During titration, when $pH = pK_a$, concentration of the protonated species is equal to that of the deprotonated species. This region is known as the buffer zone, and pH changes very little during this region (appears as a horizontal line).

☐ During titration, when $pH = pI$, all of the species have been deprotonated, and pH changes drastically (appears as a somewhat vertical line).

☐ Nonpolar amino acids are hydrophobic, so they are often found buried within protein molecules.

☐ Polar, acid, and basic amino acids are hydrophilic and are often found on the surface of proteins.

☐ Primary structure is determined by the amino acid sequence (N → C); secondary structure is determined by local hydrogen bonding; tertiary structure (the three-dimensional shape) is determined largely by hydrophobic and hydrophilic interactions but also by disulfide bonds; quaternary structure is from the aggregation of more than one polypeptide subunits.

☐ Conjugated proteins derive part of their function from prosthetic groups (which can be either organic molecules or metal ions).

Practice Questions

1. If a mixture of alanine (pI = 6) and aspartic acid (pI = 3) is subjected to electrophoresis at pH 3, which of the following would you expect to occur?

   A. Alanine will migrate to the cathode, while aspartic acid migrates to the anode.
   B. Alanine will not move, while aspartic acid migrates to the cathode.
   C. Aspartic acid will not move, while alanine migrates to the cathode.
   D. Alanine will migrate to the anode, while aspartic acid migrates to the cathode.

2. In a neutral solution, most amino acids exist as

   A. positively charged compounds.
   B. zwitterions.
   C. negatively charged compounds.
   D. hydrophobic molecules.

3. What would be the charge of glutamic acid at pH 7?

   A. Neutral
   B. Negative
   C. Positive
   D. None of the above

4. If an amino acid (pI = 9.74) in acidic solution is completely titrated with sodium hydroxide, what will be its charge at pH 3, 7, and 11, respectively?

   A. Positive, neutral, negative
   B. Negative, neutral, positive
   C. Neutral, positive, positive
   D. Positive, positive, negative

5. Amino acids with nonpolar R-groups have which of the following characteristics in aqueous solution?

   A. They are hydrophilic and found buried within proteins.
   B. They are hydrophobic and found buried within proteins.
   C. They are hydrophobic and found on protein surfaces.
   D. They are hydrophilic and found on protein surfaces.

6. All of the following statements concerning peptide bonds are true EXCEPT

   A. their formation involves a reaction between an amine group and a carboxyl group.
   B. they are the primary bonds found in proteins.
   C. they have partial double-bond character.
   D. their formation involves hydration reactions.

7. How many different tripeptides can be formed that contain one valine, one alanine, and one leucine?

   A. 5
   B. 6
   C. 7
   D. 8

8. Beside peptide bonds, what other covalent bonds are commonly found in peptides?

   A. Hydrogen
   B. Ether
   C. Disulfide
   D. Hydrophobic

9. α-helices are secondary structures characterized by

A. intramolecular hydrogen bonds.

B. disulfide bonds.

C. a rippled effect.

D. intermolecular hydrogen bonds.

10. Denaturation involves the loss of what type(s) of structure?

A. Primary

B. Secondary

C. Tertiary

D. Both (B) and (C)

Small Group Questions

1. Amino acids naturally exist as L-enantiomers. What specific effect might a mutation that causes production of D-enantiomers have on a eukaryotic cell?

2. Can amino acids with multiple charges be used in buffer systems?

Explanations to Practice Questions

1. C

At pH 6, alanine will exist as a neutral, dipolar ion: The amino group will be protonated, whereas the carboxyl group will be deprotonated. At a pH of 3, there will be excess hydrogen ions in solution, which will protonate the carboxyl group, and the molecule will assume an overall positive charge. Alanine will therefore migrate to the cathode. On the other hand, aspartic acid will exist as a neutral dipolar ion at a pH of 3 because this is equivalent to its isoelectric point. Therefore, when it is subjected to electrophoresis, it will not move. In summary, alanine will migrate to the cathode, while aspartic acid will not move, making choice (C) the correct response.

2. B

Most amino acids (with the exception of the acidic and basic amino acids) have two sites for protonation, the carboxylic acid and the amine group. At a neutral pH, the carboxylic acid will be deprotonated (negatively charged), and the amine group will remain protonated (positively charged). This dipolar ion is called a zwitterion; therefore, (B) is the correct answer.

3. B

The amino acid in question is glutamic acid, which is an acidic amino acid because it contains an extra carboxyl group. At neutral pH, both of the carboxyl groups are ionized, so there are two negative charges on the molecule. Only one of the charges is neutralized by the positive charge on the amino group, so the molecule has an overall negative charge. Thus, the answer is choice (B).

4. D

With a pI = 9.74, the amino acid must have two basic groups. At pH 3, the two amine groups and the carboxyl group will be protonated to give a net positive charge. As the pH rises to 7, the proton will first dissociate from the carboxyl, but both amine groups will still be fully protonated, so the charge will still be positive. At pH 11, the molecule is above its isoelectric point and will be fully deprotonated, resulting in two neutral amine groups and a negatively charged carboxylate group, so the charge at pH 11 will be negative. Therefore, the correct sequence of charges is positive, positive, negative, corresponding to choice (D).

5. B

Nonpolar molecules or groups are those whose negative and positive centers of charge coincide. They are not soluble in water and are thus hydrophobic. Amino acids with hydrophobic R-groups tend to be found buried within protein molecules, where they do not have to interact with the aqueous cellular environment. This makes choice (B) the correct answer. Choices (A) and (D) are incorrect because nonpolar R-groups cannot be hydrophilic. Choice (C) is incorrect because nonpolar molecules are seldom located on the surface of proteins, where they would interact unfavorably with the aqueous cellular environment.

6. D

Formation of a peptide bond, which is the primary covalent bond found in proteins (B), involves a condensation reaction between the amine group of one amino acid and the carboxyl group of an adjacent amino acid (A). As a result of the carbonyl group present at the bond, the double bond resonates between C=O and C=N. This resonance gives the peptide bond a partial double-bond character (C) and limits rotation about the bond.

From this information, it can be seen that choices (A), (B), and (C) are all characteristics of the peptide bond.

Choice (D) is false because the formation of the peptide bond is a condensation reaction, involving the loss of water, rather than a hydration reaction, which involves the addition of water.

7. B

The six tripeptides that can be formed are these:

Val-Ala-Leu, Val-Leu-Ala,

Ala-Val-Leu, Ala-Leu-Val,

Leu-Val-Ala, Leu-Ala-Val

8. C

The key word in this question is *covalent*. Although hydrogen bonds (A) and hydrophobic bonds (D) are involved in peptide structure, they are not considered covalent bonds, because they do not involve sharing electrons. Therefore, choices (A) and (D) are incorrect. Ether bonds (B) are covalent bonds, but they are not found in peptides. The correct answer is disulfide bonds, choice (C). Disulfide bonds are covalent bonds forming between the sulfur-bearing R-groups of cysteines. The resulting cystine molecule constitutes a disulfide bridge and often causes a loop in the peptide chain.

9. A

When discussing secondary structure, the most important bond is the hydrogen bond. The rigid α-helices are held together by hydrogen bonds between the carbonyl oxygen of one peptide bond and the amine hydrogen of a peptide bond four residues removed. This hydrogen bond is intramolecular, so choice (A) is correct. Disulfide bonds are covalent bonds usually associated with primary and tertiary structure; therefore, choice (B) is incorrect. Choices (C) and (D) are incorrect because the rippled effect and intermolecular hydrogen bonds are both characteristic of β-pleated sheets.

10. D

Protein denaturation involves the loss of three-dimensional structure and function. Because the three-dimensional shape of a protein is conferred by secondary and tertiary structures, denaturation disrupts these structures. Therefore, both choices (B) and (C) are correct. Denaturation does not cause a loss of primary structure because it does not cause peptide bonds to break; thus, choice (A) is incorrect.

High-Yield Problem Solving Guide for Organic Chemistry

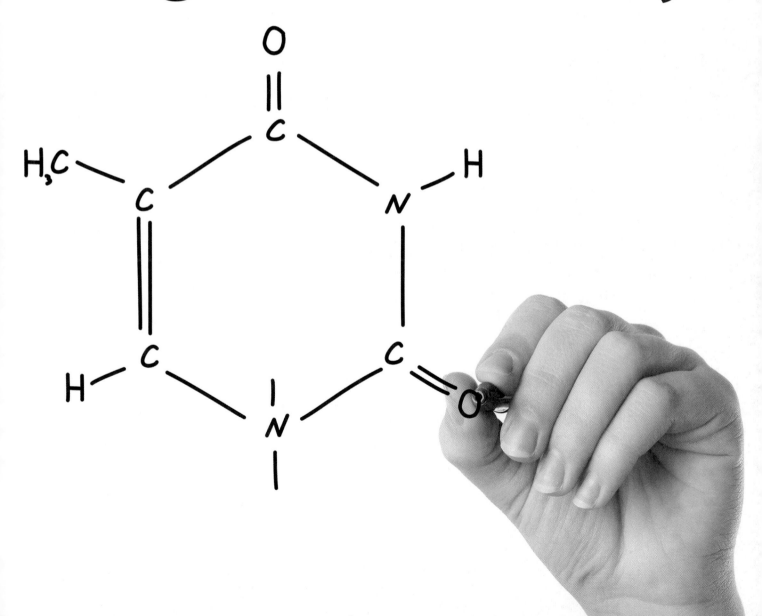

High-Yield MCAT Review

This is a **High-Yield Questions section**. These questions tackle the most frequently tested topics found on the MCAT. For each type of problem, you will be provided with a stepwise technique for solving the question and key directional points on how to solve for the MCAT specifically.

For each topic, you will find a "Takeaways" box, which gives a concise summary of the problem-solving approach, and a "Things to Watch Out For" box, which points out any caveats to the approach discussed above that usually lead to wrong answer choices. Finally, there is a "Similar Questions" box at the end so you can test your ability to apply the stepwise technique to analogous questions.

We're confident that this guide can help you achieve your goals of MCAT success and admission into medical school!

Good luck!

Nomenclature

What is the IUPAC name for the following compound?

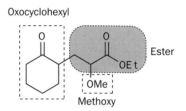

1) Identify the highest-priority functional group.

In this case, the highest-priority functional group is the ester. Therefore, we will name everything attached to the ester as a substituent, including the cyclohexyl ring on the left.

2) Determine the longest continuous carbon chain attached to the highest-priority functional group and number them accordingly.

In this case, the longest continuous chain is three carbons, with carbon 1 being the carbonyl carbon (because the ester is the highest-priority functional group). Because the ester has three carbons, it will be a propanoate ester.

3) Locate the substituents on the carbon chain identified in step 2 and name and number them.

The first substituent is the ethyl group on the ester, which we will name by placing the word *ethyl* in front of the ester name.

Next, there is a methyl group attached to an oxygen at carbon 2, which will be named as a methoxy group.

Finally, how do we handle the ring attached to carbon 3? If there were nothing attached to the ring, we would name the ring as a cyclohexyl substituent. However, there is a ketone on the ring. When aldehydes or ketones are named as substituents recall that they are named as "oxo" groups. The numbering works by assigning the carbon attached to the ester carbon chain as carbon 1 as shown.

Therefore, the ketone on the ring will be at carbon 2. We'll name the whole ring as a (2-oxocyclohexyl) substituent and put it in parentheses so that we don't confuse the two numbering systems.

---

4) Put it all together.
The name of our compound will therefore be this:

ethyl 2–methoxy–3–(2–oxocyclohexyl)propanoate

Similar Questions

1) How would the name be altered if the alkyl group attached to the ester oxygen contained substituents?

2) Upon reduction with sodium borohydride, followed by dilute acid workup, the molecule below gave two products in unequal yield. Draw them and provide the correct IUPAC name for each.

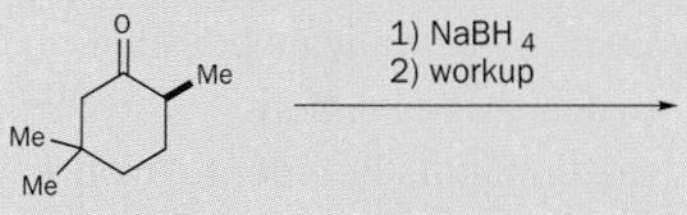

3) What are the two possible products of the reaction shown below? Draw and provide IUPAC names for both.

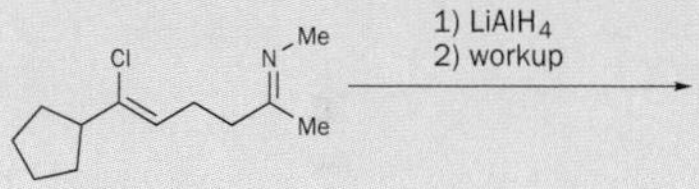

Key Concepts

Chapter 2

Isomers

Enantiomers

Diastereomers

Isomers

The reagent *meta*-chloroperoxybenzoic acid (mCPBA) is often used to convert alkenes to epoxides. If the alkene shown below is treated with mCPBA, two products result. Draw these products and determine their isomeric relationship.

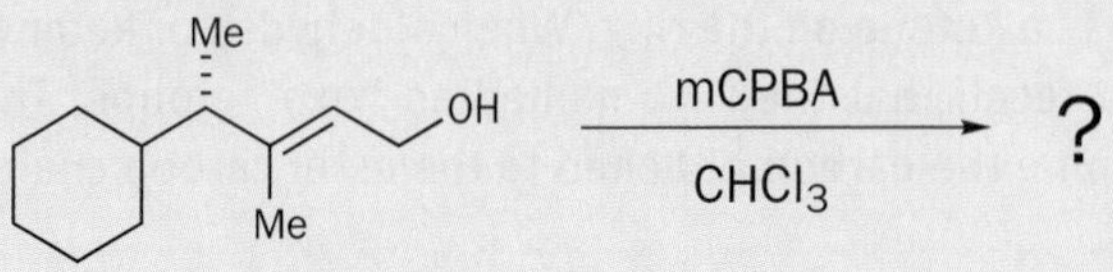

Takeaways

Be as systematic as possible in assigning isomeric relationships in order to avoid making mistakes and missing easy points on Test Day!

1) Draw the product(s) and note the major differences between them.

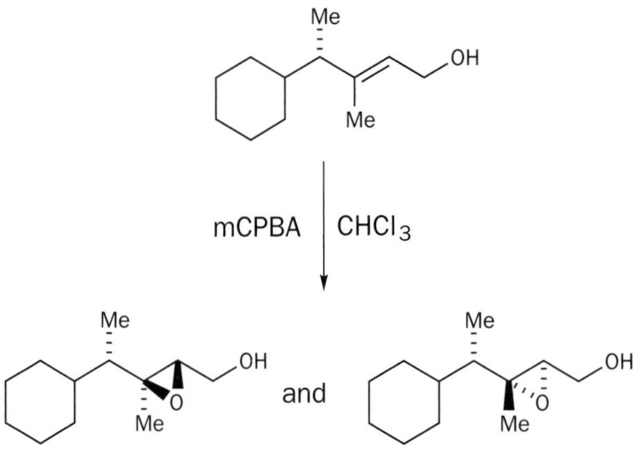

Recall that alkenes are flat due to both carbons being sp^2 hybridized. Therefore, the epoxide can form on either face of the alkene, giving rise to two possible products.

Notice that each isomer differs only in the stereochemical sense.

Things to Watch Out For

Avoid confusing *enantiomers* and *diastereomers*. This is where a great many mistakes are made on MCAT questions. Remember that if two molecules are nonsuperimposable mirror images, they are enantiomers. Provided that you have determined that the molecules are configurational isomers without a plane of symmetry, *any other molecules are diastereomers.*

2) Determine the isomeric relationship.
The first question you should ask yourself is whether or not the molecules have the same connectivity. Here they do, because they differ only in the orientation of two stereocenters, so they are not structural isomers.

Next, you need to figure out whether bond breaking would be required to interconvert them. Here, that is definitely true because to convert the top isomer to the bottom one, you would have to break both epoxide carbon–oxygen bonds and reassemble them on the opposite face of the molecule. Therefore, our molecules are configurational isomers.

Then, you will want to see if the molecules are nonsuperimposable mirror images of one another.

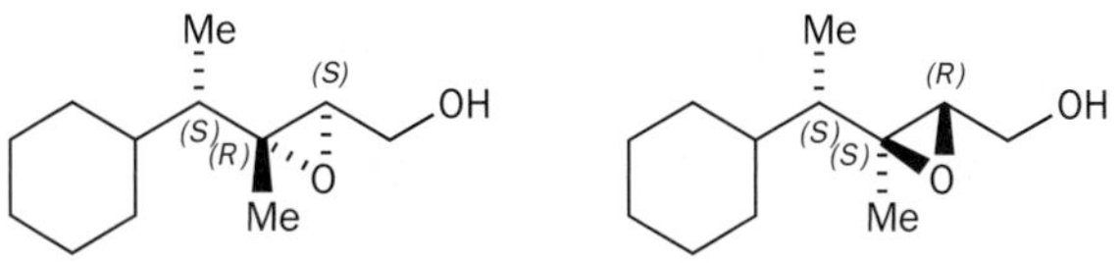

The molecules are not nonsuperimposable mirror images of one another because the stereocenter adjacent to the cyclohexyl ring has the same orientation in both products. (Note that the carbon where the ring is joined to the acyclic portion of the molecule is *not* a stereocenter. Why?) Therefore, our two molecules are *diastereomers*.

You can confirm this by assigning *R/S* designations to each stereocenter and then seeing that some of the stereocenters have the same orientation and some are different. For our two molecules to be *enantiomers,* each stereocenter would have to have the opposite orientation in each product.

Similar Questions

1) Alkynes can be reduced to alkenes selectively by manipulating the reaction conditions. Examine the reaction scheme below and determine the relationship between the two products.

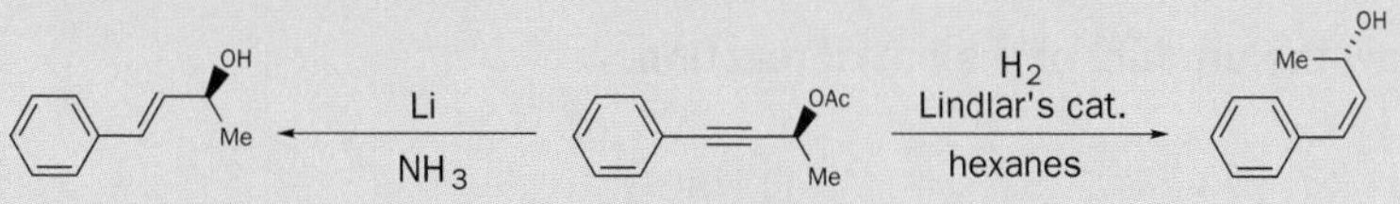

2) If the alkenes in question 1 were reduced with Pd/H$_2$, would the isomeric relationship change?

3) Would the physical properties of the alkenes in question 1 be the same or different? What about when the alkenes were reduced?

Key Concepts

Chapter 2

Stereochemistry

Fischer projections

Oxidation/reduction

meso compounds

meso Compounds

A student wanted to prepare chiral polyols by taking sugars and reacting them with sodium borohydride. She took D-xylose, shown below, and treated it with sodium borohydride, followed by a dilute aqueous acid workup. On purifying and isolating the product, she found that it did not rotate plane-polarized light. What was the structure of the product, and why did it not rotate light?

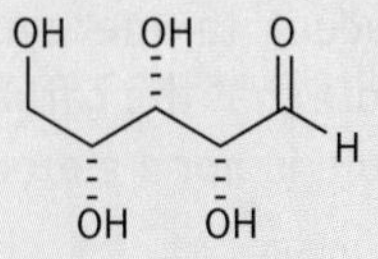

D-xylose

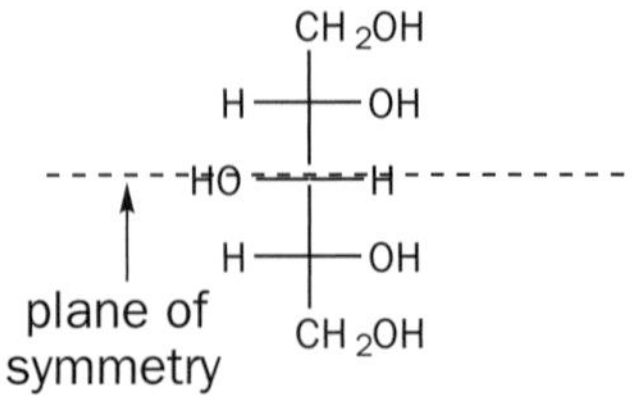

Takeaways

Anytime a molecule with stereocenters behaves as an achiral molecule, there must be a plane of symmetry somewhere in the molecule.

1) Convert the molecule from standard projection to Fischer projection.

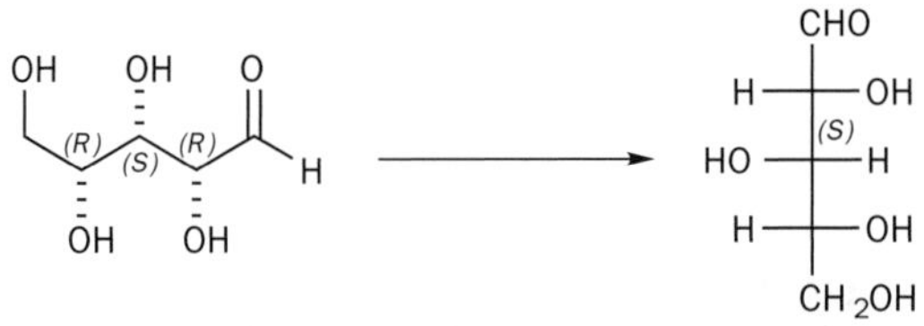

This will enable you to see stereochemical relationships much more clearly.

2) Draw the product of the initial reaction.

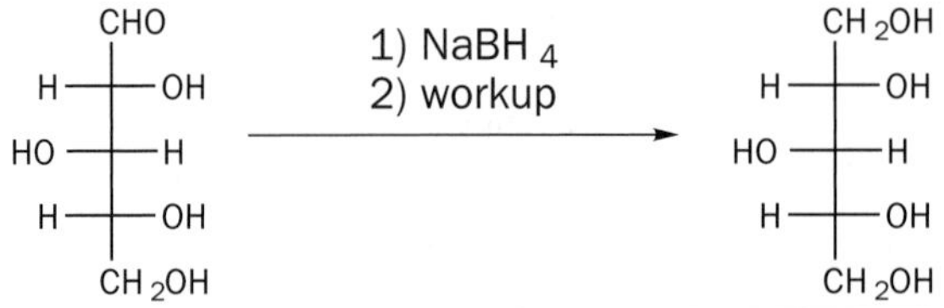

In this case, sodium borohydride reduces the aldehyde to an alcohol.

Things to Watch Out For

With molecules with multiple stereocenters, be sure to draw them as Fischer projections to be able to spot the symmetry planes easily.

3) Look for planes of symmetry in the product.

plane of
symmetry

The fact that a molecule possesses stereocenters but is achiral is a dead giveaway that the molecule must be a *meso* compound. This would be caused by a plane of symmetry in the molecule. The plane of symmetry runs right through C3 in this case.

Similar Questions

1) Which of the remaining three D-aldopentoses (shown below) would result in achiral polyols when subjected to borohydride reduction?

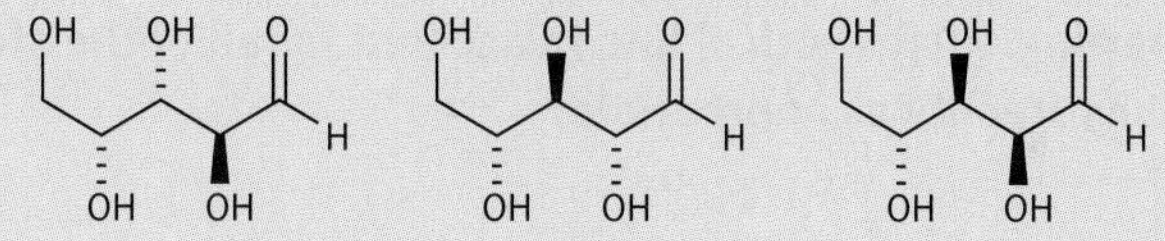

Key Concepts

Chapter 2

Stereochemistry

Fischer projections

Stereocenter

Fischer Projections

Redraw the following molecule in a Fischer projection:

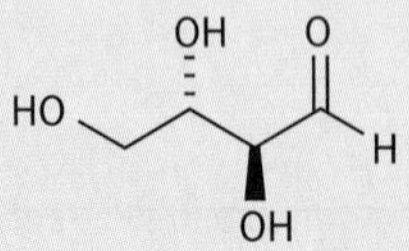

1) Begin by drawing a flat, vertical line to account for all of the stereocenters. Draw in end substituents as appropriate.

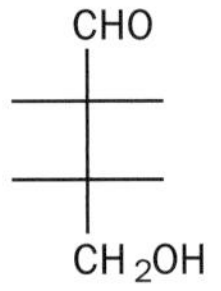

2) Determine the stereochemical orientation of the stereocenters in the original molecule by assigning R/S to each.

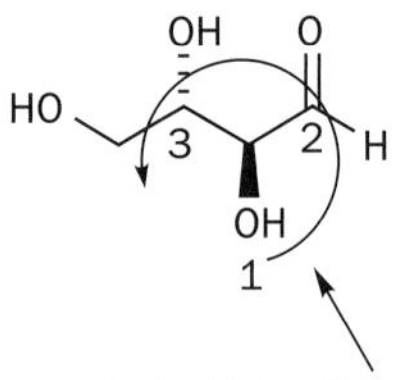

Going from 1 to 2 to 3 means turning to the left.

Takeaways

Assigning priorities is based on atomic number and is done one atom at a time. When you "turn" from the highest-priority to the lowest-priority substituent, think about the three highest-priority substituents as being on a steering wheel in a car, with the lowest-priority substituent as the steering column.

For the stereocenter adjacent to the aldehyde, the alcohol is the highest-priority substituent, followed by the aldehyde, then the carbon with the other stereocenter, and finally the hydrogen. Because the hydrogen is already oriented away from us, we can go ahead and assign the stereocenter to be *S*, because we "turn the wheel" to the left.

Applying the same methodology to the other stereocenter gives an *S* stereocenter as well.

MCAT Pitfall: Be careful with assigning the second stereocenter because the hydrogen is coming out of the page at you.

Things to Watch Out For

Don't forget that if a substituent is attached to a horizontal bond in a Fischer projection, that means that it is *coming out of the page at you*. If it is attached to a vertical bond, it is *going into the page away from you*.

3) Draw in the substituents in the Fischer projection and make sure that they match the original molecule.

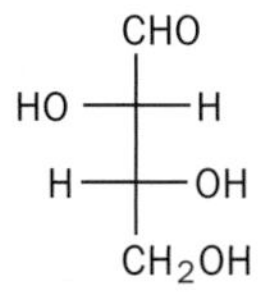

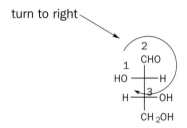

At this point, you can randomly insert the substituents and check to make sure that they match the original molecule. Assign priorities as before.

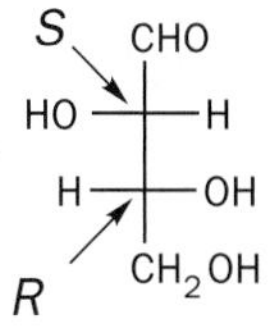

turn to right

For the first stereocenter, we would turn to the right, meaning that you would think it would be *R*. However, note that the lowest-priority substituent, the hydrogen, is coming *out of the page* because it is attached to a horizontal line; we want the hydrogen to be going into the page. So we would flip the assignment from *R* to *S*. The first stereocenter then matches. Applying the same idea to the second stereocenter would give an *R* assignment.

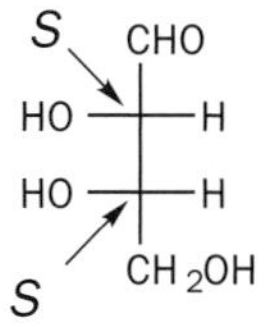

However, we need the *S, S* compound. We can do that by just exchanging the alcohol and the proton in the second stereocenter.

Similar Questions

1) Draw the Fischer projection of the enantiomer compound.

2) Draw the Fischer projection of all the diastereomers for the compound and the compound's enantiomer, diagramming the relationships between each.

3) Fumaric acid (trans-2-butenedioic acid) can undergo *syn* addition with D₂. Draw the Fischer projection of the product(s). If multiple products are produced, what is the relationship between them?

Key Concepts

Chapters 1–3

Acidity and basicity

Resonance

Induction

pK_a

Substituent effects

Acidity Trends

Place the following molecules in order of *decreasing* pK_a of the phenol proton:

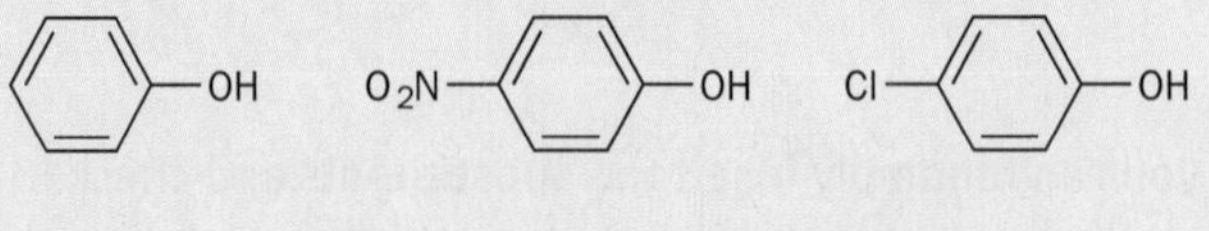

1) Determine the potential stabilizing effects on each molecule.
All of the molecules possess the ability to have their conjugate base stabilized by resonance, but some have more resonance structures than others, as we'll see in a second.

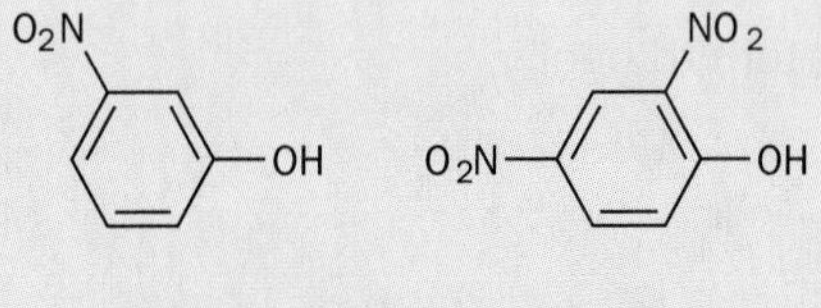

Remember: **Decreasing pK_a** means **increasing acidity** and **increasing stability** *of a negative charge.*

Remember: When it comes to charge stabilization, **resonance stabilization** is **always** more powerful than **inductive stabilization**.

Takeaways

Make sure to *draw* the anions resulting from deprotonation. This will get you thinking about stability and decrease the odds that you will miss some detail.

2) Look for resonance stabilization first.
You should zero in on molecule 5 right away as being the most acidic because it has the most electronegative substituent and the greatest number of electronegative substituents. That means that molecule 1 will have the least stable conjugate base and be the least acidic. When you remove the phenol proton, you can draw a total of six resonance structures:

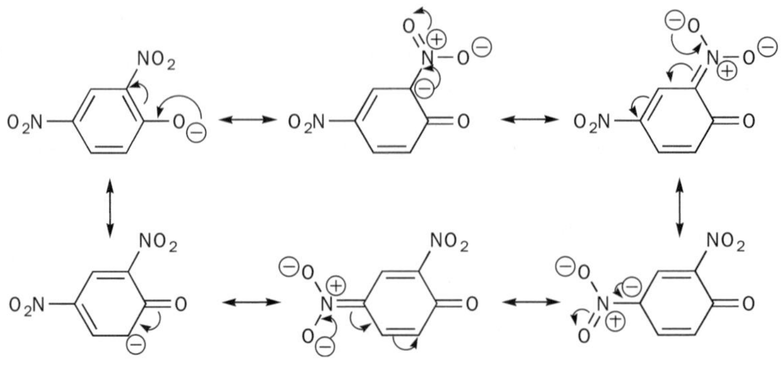

Things to Watch Out For

Don't confuse increasing *basicity* (least stabilized anion) with increasing *acidity* (most stabilized anion).

Notice that the negative charge only appears at the *ortho* and *para* positions on the ring (with respect to the alcohol). Thus, compound 4, with the nitro group in the *meta* position, can't benefit from the resonance stabilization of the negative charge into the nitro group.

Compound 2 has a nitro group at the *para* position, but its conjugate base won't be as stable because it only has one nitro group instead of two.

Remember: *The effects of electron withdrawing (or donating) substituents are additive.*

3) Look for inductive stabilization next.
Molecules 4 and 3 will benefit from inductive stabilization, and 4 will be more acidic than 3 because the nitro group is more electron withdrawing than a chloro group.

4) Place all of the molecules in order of their reactivity.
The unsubstituted phenol is the least acidic, followed by the compounds with only inductive stabilization, and finally the compounds that are resonance stabilized.

1 < 3 < 4 < 2 < 5

Similar Questions

1) How would you compare the acidity of the most acidic proton in each of the following molecules?

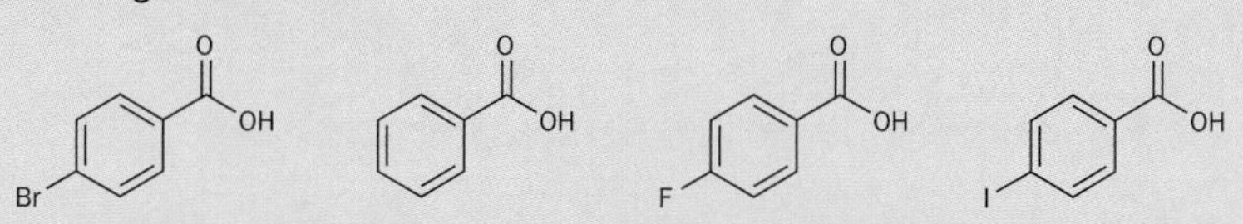

2) How would you compare the acidity of the most acidic proton in each of the following molecules?

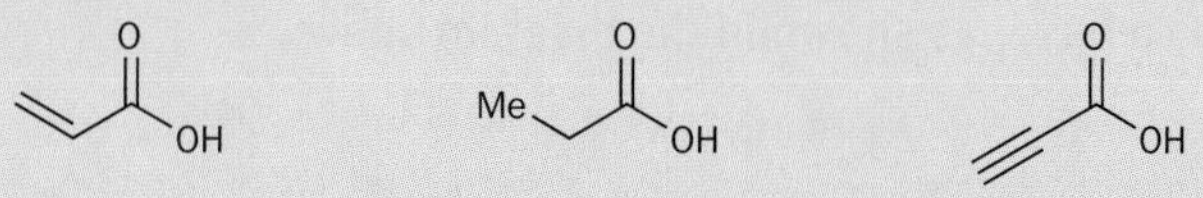

3) How would you compare the acidity of the most acidic proton in each of the following molecules?

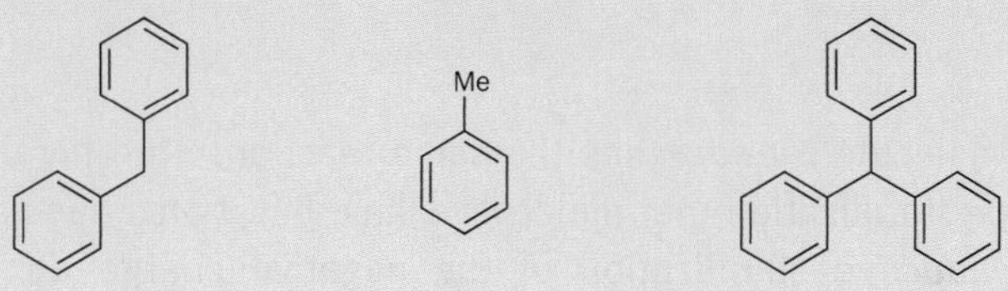

Key Concepts

Chapters 1–3

Acidity and basicity

Hybridization

Resonance

pK_a

Basicity Trends

Place the following molecules in order of *increasing* pK_a of the proton highlighted in bold:

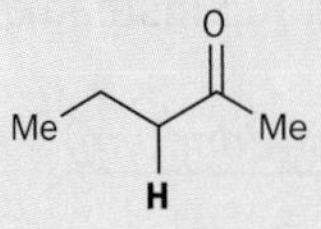

1) Determine the potential stabilizing effects on each molecule.

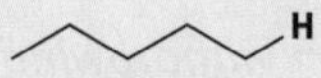

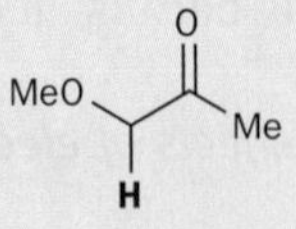

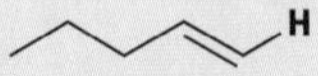

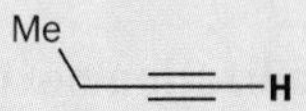

The only molecules that would possess resonance stabilization of the resulting anions if the bold proton were to be removed are 1 and 3, so these will be *less basic* than the others.

*Remember: Increasing pK_a means **increasing basicity** and **decreasing stability** of a negative charge.*

*Remember: When it comes to charge stabilization, **resonance stabilization** is **always** more powerful than **inductive stabilization**.*

---

2) Look for resonance stabilization first.

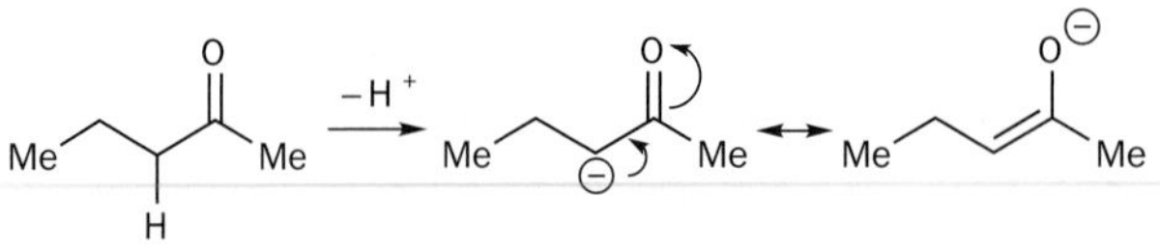

Molecule 1 clearly would have a resonance structure were the α-proton to be abstracted by a base, as shown in the diagram above.

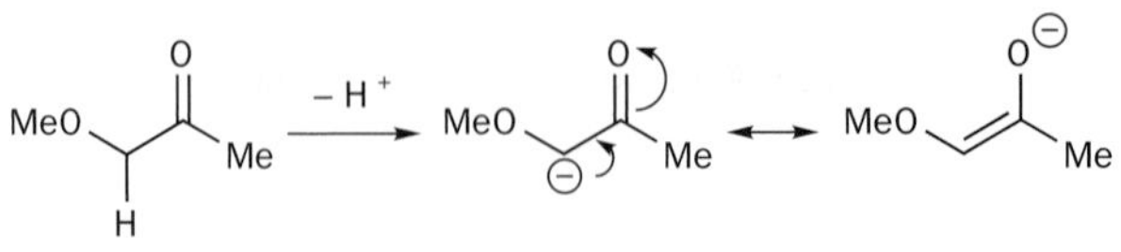

However, if molecule 3 undergoes the same reaction, not only does it have the resonance stabilization that molecule 1 has, but it also has an additional amount of *inductive* stabilization of the negative charge (in the middle

Takeaways

Make sure to *draw* the anions resulting from deprotonation. This will get you thinking about stability and decrease the odds that you will miss some detail.

Things to Watch Out For

Don't confuse increasing *basicity* (least stabilized anion) with increasing *acidity* (most stabilized anion).

resonance structure). The adjacent oxygen will help to stabilize the negative charge due to its electronegativity. Thus, molecule 3 is more stable and therefore *less basic* than 1.

3) Look for inductive stabilization next.

The only significant difference between the remaining molecules is the *hybridization of the carbon* attached to the bold proton. Notice that we have an *sp*-hybridized carbon (5), an sp^2-hybridized carbon (4), and an sp^3-hybridized carbon (2).

In this case, the carbon with the *sp* hybridization has the greatest "*s* character" because it is approximately 50 percent *s* and 50 percent *p*. Increasing *s* character helps stabilize a negative charge more. Remember that the charge distribution of an *s* orbital is spherical, with the electron closer to the nucleus (and therefore more stable) than an electron in a *p* orbital (recall that a *p* orbital has a nodal plane at the nucleus, meaning there is zero probability that an electron can be located there).

Thus, the anion generated from molecule 5 will be more stable than that generated from molecule 4, and finally the anion resulting from deprotonation of molecule 2 will be the least stable and most basic.

4) Place all of the molecules in order of their reactivity.

The final order in increasing basicity is thus the following:

3 < 1 < 5 < 4 < 2

Similar Questions

1) How would you compare the basicity of the protons highlighted in bold of the following molecules?

2) How would you compare the basicity of the protons highlighted in bold of the following molecules?

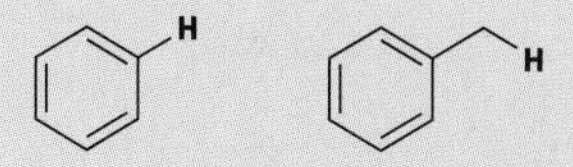

3) How would you compare the basicity of the protons highlighted in bold of the following molecules?

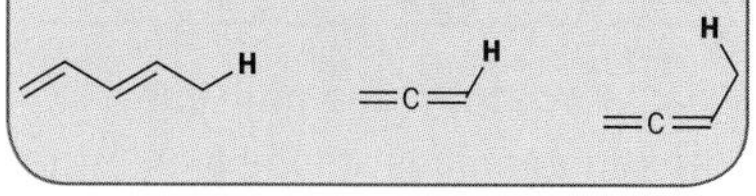

Key Concepts

Chapters 1–3

Polarity

Intermolecular forces

Solubility

Solubility Trends

Place the following molecules in order of *increasing* solubility in *dichloromethane*:

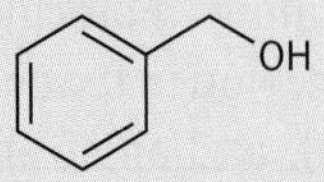

1

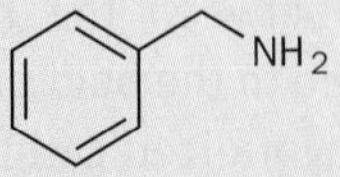

2

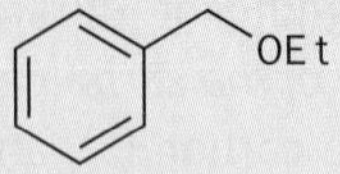

3

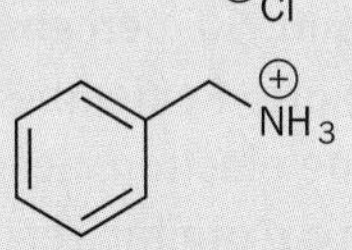

4

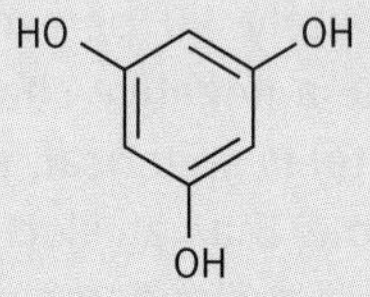

5

1) Determine the nature of the solvent.
In this case, we are concerned about the solubility of these molecules in dichloromethane, which is an organic, *nonpolar* solvent. Thus, the molecules that are most nonpolar will be most soluble in dichloromethane.

Remember: *The key principle with solubility is* ***"like dissolves like."***

Takeaways

Remember that the principle that determines solubility is "*like dissolves like.*" Therefore, polar molecules will be more soluble in polar solvents, and nonpolar molecules will be more soluble in nonpolar solvents.

2) Place the molecules in order of increasing solubility in the solvent of choice.
Here, we want to order the molecules from most polar to least polar.

This means that molecule 4 will be the most polar because it is a salt and bears a formal charge. Next will be molecule 5 because it has three hydroxyl groups (and can make three hydrogen bonds). It should also be clear that molecule 3 will be the least polar (and therefore the most soluble) because as an ether, it has no functional groups that would allow hydrogen bonding.

That leaves molecules 1 and 2. Molecule 1 would be more polar because oxygen is more electronegative than nitrogen.

Things to Watch Out For

Be sure to verify the nature of the solvent before ordering the molecules! Don't ever assume that the solvent is always water.

3) Place all of the molecules in order of their reactivity.
The final order in increasing solubility is thus the following:

4 < 5 < 1 < 2 < 3

Similar Questions

1) How would you compare the water solubility of the following molecules?

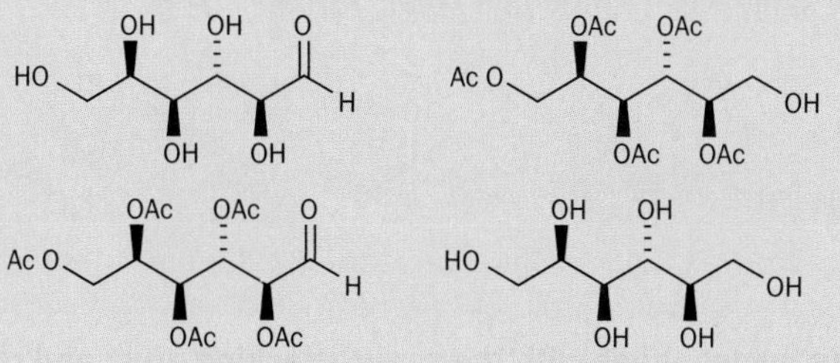

2) How would you compare the solubility of the following molecules in ether?

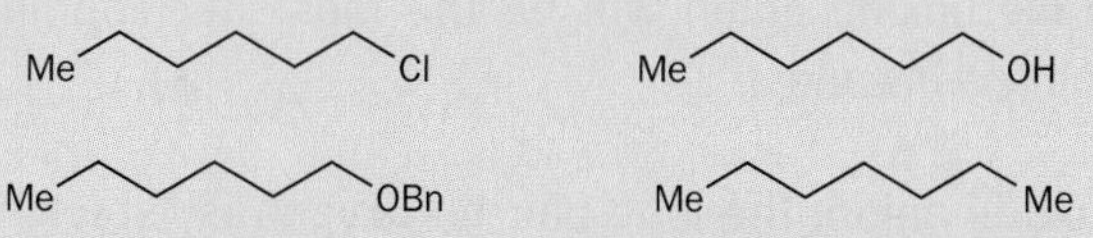

3) How would you compare the solubility of the following molecules in an aqueous solution at pH 1?

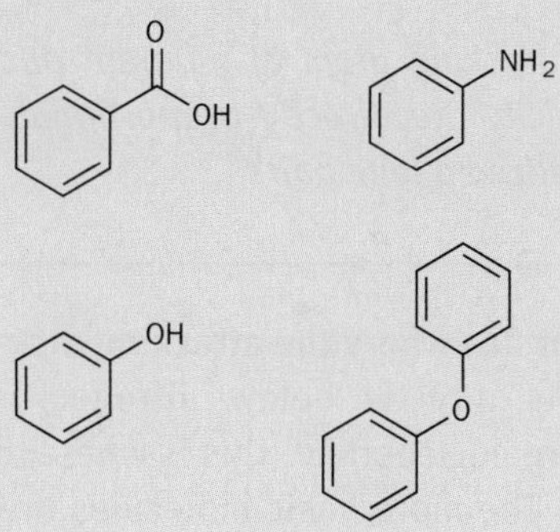

Nucleophilicity Trends

Rank the following compounds in order of *increasing nucleophilicity* toward the same electrophile in a *polar, protic* solvent:

$$CH_3OH \qquad Et_3N \qquad H_3C-CO_2^{\ominus} \qquad Et_3P \qquad CH_3O^{\ominus}$$

1) Separate out nucleophiles with the same attacking atom and rank them first. Look at the oxygen nucleophiles first. Here the methoxide anion is more basic than the acetate anion ($CH_3CO_2^-$), which in turn is more basic than methanol. Therefore, the methoxide anion will be the most nucleophilic of the three oxygen-containing molecules.

With the methoxide anion, the lone pair on oxygen is "stuck" on the oxygen atom, whereas with acetate, the negative charge can be delocalized through resonance; this makes methoxide more basic. Both molecules are more basic than methanol, because methanol lacks a negative charge.

Remember: When the attacking atom of different nucleophiles is the same, nucleophilicity and basicity are **directly proportional**. *Recall that* **basicity** *is proportional to how* **localized a lone pair** *is.*

2) Look next for nucleophiles where the attacking atom is in the same group. Because phosphorus is directly below nitrogen in the periodic table, triethylphosphine is more nucleophilic. This is where the nature of the solvent makes a big difference. The more basic molecules are better hydrogen bond *acceptors,* meaning that they will be surrounded by solvent molecules and therefore less available to attack the substrate. The differences in basicity are *less pronounced* when molecules are in the same period, so this effect is only noticeable when the attacking atoms are in the same group.

If the solvent were *polar aprotic,* then the trend would be *exactly the opposite.* Here, the hydrogen bonding effect is removed, so the molecules with the most localized charge density—the most basic—will also be the most nucleophilic.

Comparing the basicity of triethylphosphine and triethylamine is a bit more complicated. The key to determining basicity is remembering that in triethylphosphine, the lone pair on phosphorus is contained in an sp^3 hybrid orbital that is made up of one *s*- and three $3p$-orbitals. Contrast this with triethylamine, where the nitrogen lone pair is in an sp^3 hybrid composed of one *s*- and three $2p$-orbitals. This means that the electrons in the phosphorus lone pair are in a larger hybrid orbital, as $3p$-orbitals are larger than $2p$-orbitals.

This, in turn, means that the electrons in the phosphorus lone pair are more stable, because they probably have more volume to exist in. If the phosphorus lone pair is *more stable,* then the lone pair is *less reactive* and *less basic* (less likely to want to reach out and grab a proton).

---

3) Look for relationships between nucleophiles in the same period.

Now the question is between the two groups we have ordered separately. Which one is more nucleophilic? In most cases, this question is answered by realizing that for different nucleophiles where the attacking atoms are in the *same period*, *nucleophilicity roughly parallels basicity*. That being the case, triethylamine is more basic than the acetate anion.

$CH_3OH < CH_3CO_2^- < CH_3O^- < Et_3N < Et_3P$ (polar, protic solvent)

This trend is borne out experimentally. The relative reactivities of each nucleophile toward CH_3I in CH_3OH as solvent are as follows:

Nucleophile	Relative Rate
CH_3OH	1
$CH_3CO_2^-$	20,000
CH_3O^-	1,900,000
Et_3N	4,600,000
Et_3P	520,000,000

In a *polar, aprotic* solvent, the order of nucleophilicity would parallel basicity:

$CH_3OH < Et_3P < CH_3CO_2^- < Et_3N < CH_3O^-$ (polar, aprotic solvent)

Similar Questions

1) Place the following molecules in order of increasing nucleophilicity: pyridine (benzene with one of the carbons in the ring replaced by a nitrogen), triethylamine, acetonitrile (CH_3CN), and DMAP (4-dimethylaminopyridine). (Note that the solvent doesn't impact nucleophilicity here, because the same atom is nucleophilic in all four compounds.) Which of the two nitrogens in DMAP is more nucleophilic, and why?

2) How would the nucleophilicity of fluoride, chloride, bromide, and iodide rank in an S_N2 reaction with methyl iodide in methanol? In dimethyl sulfoxide?

3) How would you order the nucleophilicity of the following molecules in methanol: Et_3N, Ph_3P, Et_3P, Ph_3N, and Et_3As? Provide a rationale for your ordering. (*Hint*: What about their structures makes all of the molecules above both basic *and* nucleophilic?)

Key Concepts

Chapter 4

Reaction mechanisms

Carbocation stability

Aromaticity

Solvolytic conditions

Hückel's rule

Substrate Reactivity: S_N1 Reactions

Place the following molecules in order of *increasing* reactivity towards methanol under solvolytic conditions:

1 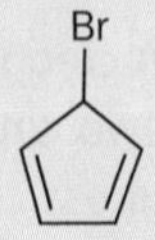   **2** 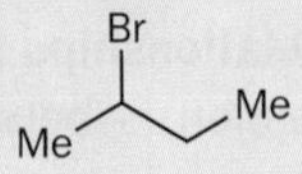   **3**

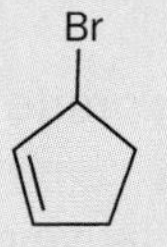

4 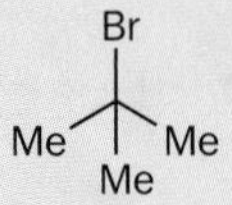   **5**

Takeaways

Reactivity in the S_N1 reaction is determined by carbocation stability because carbocation formation is the rate-limiting step.

1) Determine the potential stabilizing effects on each molecule.

"Solvolytic conditions" is code for an S_N1 reaction. With that in mind, the question is essentially asking you to place the molecules in order of increasing carbocation stability.

Molecules 2 and 4 would benefit from resonance stabilization, so at first glance they will be more stable carbocations than the others.

*Remember: When it comes to charge stabilization, **resonance stabilization** is **always** more powerful than **inductive stabilization**.*

---

2) Look for resonance stabilization first.

Molecule 4 clearly would have a resonance structure were the bromide to leave and form a cation:

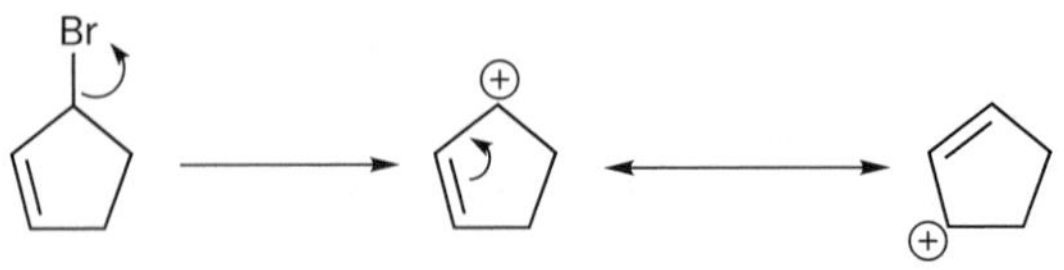

Things to Watch Out For

Don't forget that charged molecules can be aromatic as well!

You might think that if one alkene helps stabilize the carbocation, then *two* alkenes would do it better. Be careful with this, though: Take a look at the carbocation generated from 2:

Even though the carbocation at the right could have five resonance structures, notice that it is *antiaromatic*: It is cyclic, planar, and with conjugated alkenes, but it does not fit Hückel's rule. Therefore, this carbocation will be the *least stable* of all five molecules.

3) Look for inductive stabilization next.

Now we will look at the remaining molecules to determine their carbocation stability. If you draw the carbocations resulting from each bromide, you get the following:

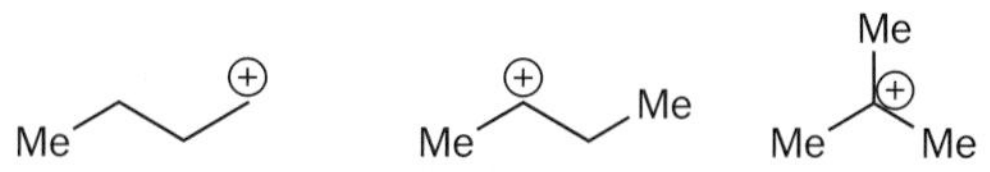

1   **3**   **5**

Because the stability of a carbocation is proportional to its substitution, 5 (tertiary) will be more stable than 3 (secondary) and finally 1 (primary).

4) Place all of the molecules in order of their reactivity.

The final order in increasing reactivity is thus as follows:

2 < 1 < 3 < 5 < 4

Similar Questions

1) 1–Chlorocycloheptatriene is dramatically more reactive in S_N1 reactions than is 1–bromocyclohexadiene. Why is this the case?

2) If 1–bromobutane (molecule **1**) were forced to become a carbocation, what product(s) would be isolated from the solvolytic reaction with methanol?

3) Compare the reactivity of 1–iodocyclopropene to 1–iodocyclopropane in a solvolysis reaction with ethanol, and provide an explanation for your comparison.

Key Concepts

Chapters 4–6

Nucleophilic addition

Oxidation and reduction

Substitution and elimination

Spectroscopy

Takeaways

Again, the key here is to move one step at a time so as not to get overwhelmed. Interpret each clue as you read through the passage and make notes on the reaction scheme, if necessary.

Things to Watch Out For

Be careful with the identities of **A** and **B**. They must be isomeric because they have the same molecular formula and give the same product when exposed to the same reaction conditions.

Identifying Structure of Unknown Hydrocarbon

For every mole of the mixture of **A** and **B** that was reacted, two moles of **C** were obtained. Compound **D** was reacted with a large excess of methyl iodide and potassium *tert*-butoxide in *t*-butanol as solvent. Kinetic studies were performed, and this reaction was found to be second order overall, with the reaction being first order with respect to **D** and potassium *tert*-butoxide. This reaction was heated and the product, 1-butene, was distilled off *in situ*.

Given this information, provide the structures of compounds **A**, **B**, **C**, and **D**.

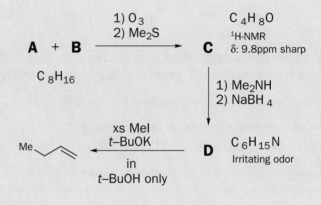

1) Work through the problem one step at a time—backward in this case, because we are given the structure of the final product.

You should immediately suspect that some sort of elimination is going on to furnish 1-pentene. There are a myriad of clues suggesting this: the fact that an alkene is the product; that there is a strong, bulky base present in the reaction; and that the kinetic data specifically tells you that this reaction is an E2 reaction. This probably means that compound **D** is some sort of amine, but which amine is it? Also, amines are poor leaving groups, so how could an elimination occur?

There must be something about adding methyl iodide to the amine that is converting it to a good leaving group. This is exactly analogous to protonating an alcohol to turn it into a good leaving group. Thus, compound **D** must be *N,N*-dimethylbutylamine, given the fact that **C** is reacted with dimethylamine.

2) Determine the relationship between C and D.

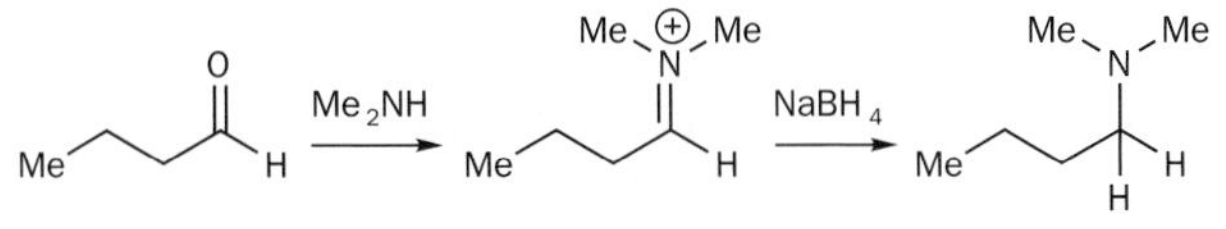

C

C_4H_8O

D

$C_6H_{15}N$

Because you are going from an aldehyde (note the diagnostic aldehyde peak for **C** in the NMR), this must be a reductive amination. Recall that when a carbonyl reacts with a primary amine, an *imine* is formed, but when a secondary amine is used, an *iminium ion* is the key intermediate.

3) Identify compounds A and B.

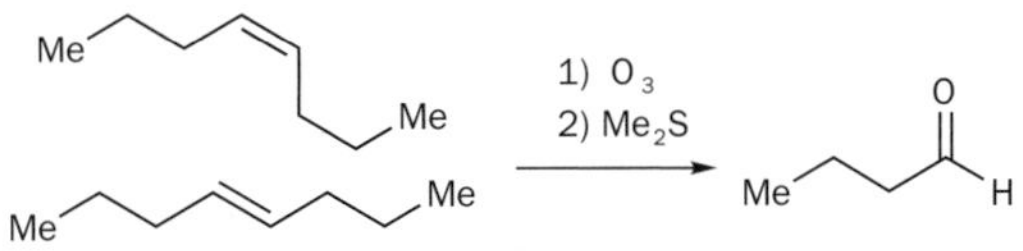

A + B

C_8H_{16}

C

C_4H_8O

The use of ozone should be a tip-off that **A** and **B** are going to be alkenes, and it must be a symmetrical alkene because one mole of the alkene mixture gives two moles of aldehyde. As for the fact that **A** and **B** give the same aldehyde, this should tell you that **A** and **B** must be geometric isomers—the only isomers that could react in the same way to give the same product.

Similar Questions

1) What would happen to compound **C** if it were exposed to sodium borohydride before the amine instead of after?

2) What alkene would you need to start with if 3-methylpentene were the alkene isolated at the end of the process?

3) Compound **C** could be reacted with methyl amine instead of dimethylamine to give the same alkene at the end because there is an excess of methyl iodide in the E2 elimination. However, a stronger reducing agent than $NaBH_4$ would be necessary to give the amine. Why do you think this is the case?

> **Key Concepts**
>
> Chapters 4–6
>
> Substitution vs. elimination
>
> Isomerism
>
> Reaction mechanisms
>
> S_N2
>
> E2

> **Takeaways**
>
> When trying to decide between substitution and elimination, use the following decision pathway:
>
> 1) First, consider the structure of the substrate. If it is primary, you know that either S_N2 or E2 must be occurring. If it is tertiary, S_N2 cannot occur.
> 2) Next, consider the nature of the nucleophile/base. Is it a strong, bulky base? Then elimination is preferred. Is it smaller but still a strong base? Then substitution is preferred.
> 3) Finally, consider the solvent. Remember that S_N1/E1 reactions require polar, protic solvents, whereas S_N2 reactions require polar, aprotic solvents.

Identifying Reaction Mechanisms

When the trimethylammonium salt shown below is treated with a strong bulky base, only demethylation is observed.

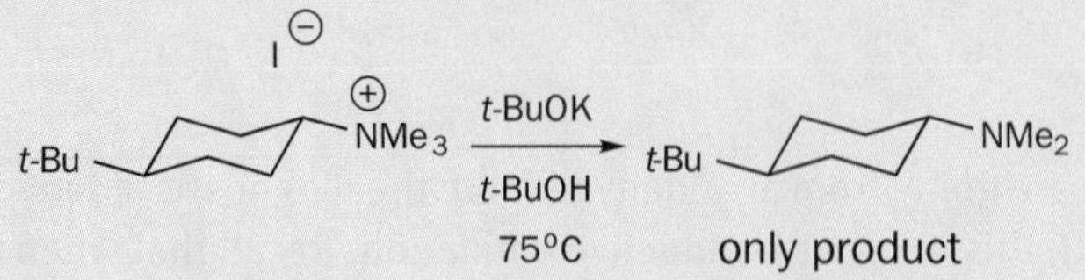

When the isomeric salt shown below is subjected to the same conditions, the product distribution below is obtained.

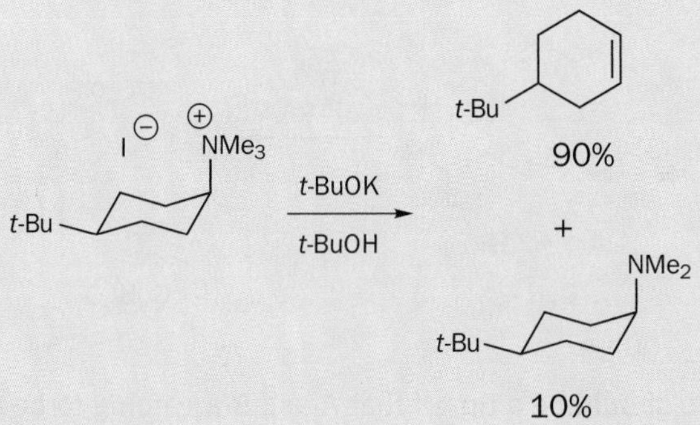

When the *tert*-butyl group is removed, the product distribution shifts back to favor demethylation.

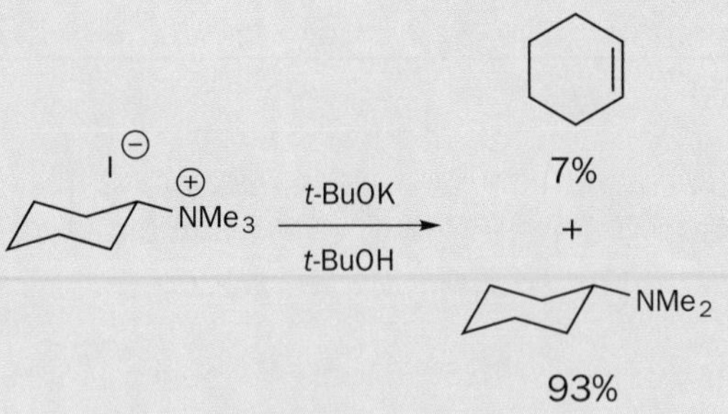

Provide explanations for the results of these reactions.

1) Identify the reactions taking place in each reaction.

Reaction 1: S_N2

For the first reaction, the reaction appears to be an S_N2 reaction with a primary substrate, a good leaving group, and a good nucleophile (*t*–BuOK).

Reaction 2: E2

The second reaction seems to be going mainly through an E2 mechanism because the substrate is secondary and a strong, bulky base is present.

Reaction 3: S_N2

In the third reaction, the major product is again that of an S_N2 reaction (primary substrate, good leaving group, good nucleophile).

---

2) Given the preferences of each reaction and the properties of the substrate, explain the reaction outcome.

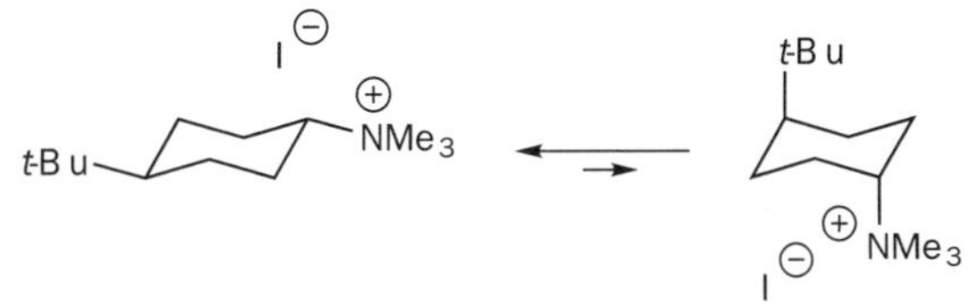

Recall that E2 reactions require antiperiplanar geometry of the substrate. Because the conformation shown above is that of the ring and cannot change without getting the diaxial isomer, substitution is the only path available.

In the first reaction, the ring is essentially locked in the conformation shown because a "ring flip" would generate the diaxial isomer, which is strongly disfavored energetically.

In the second reaction, the molecule starts with the leaving group in an axial position, which is properly aligned for E2 elimination. Elimination is favored over substitution because we have a strong, bulky base.

In the third reaction, the preferred conformer of the molecule is the one shown. This is because the trimethylammonium substituent is essentially the same as a *tert*-butyl group, meaning that the equatorial conformer is preferred. The Newman projection is then similar to that in the first reaction, leading to substitution being preferred.

Remember: *The bulkiest substituent on a cyclohexane ring always goes to the equatorial position.*

Things to Watch Out For

Be sure to take into account all of the factors listed above. Often one small change can completely change the preferred mechanism of a reaction.

Similar Questions

1) Predict the product if the following substituted cyclohexane were subjected to the same conditions as reaction 1 above.

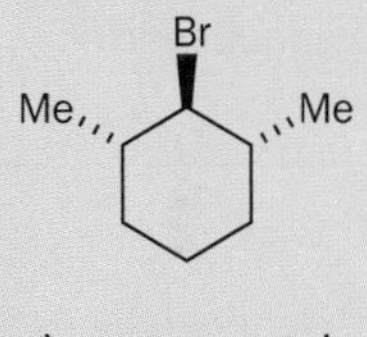

2) Why does neopentyl bromide (2,2-dimethyl-1-bromopropane) not undergo S_N2 substitution, even though it is a primary alkyl halide?

3) Explain why the enantiomerically pure molecule below undergoes racemization when dissolved by itself in a polar, protic solvent.

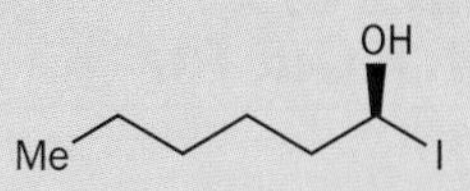

Key Concepts

Chapter 6

Aromaticity

Electrophilic aromatic substitution

Electrophilic Aromatic Substitution

Show how you might prepare *p*-bromobenzoic acid starting from benzene.

1) Identify the substituents on the ring and their regiochemical preferences. Work backward, if necessary.

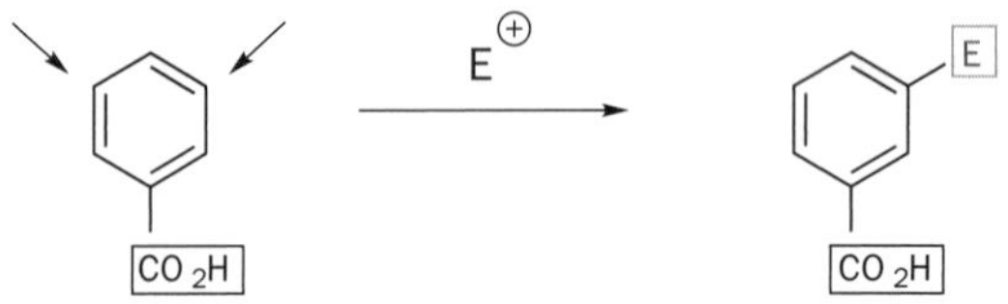

Clearly, we can't put both substituents on the ring at the same time. So we'll have to put one substituent on at a time.

If the intermediate before the last step is the carboxylic acid, when this molecule is substituted, the electrophile will go to the *meta* position, giving the incorrect regiochemistry.

Takeaways

Identify the regiochemical preferences of each substituent on an aromatic ring before thinking about specific reactions.

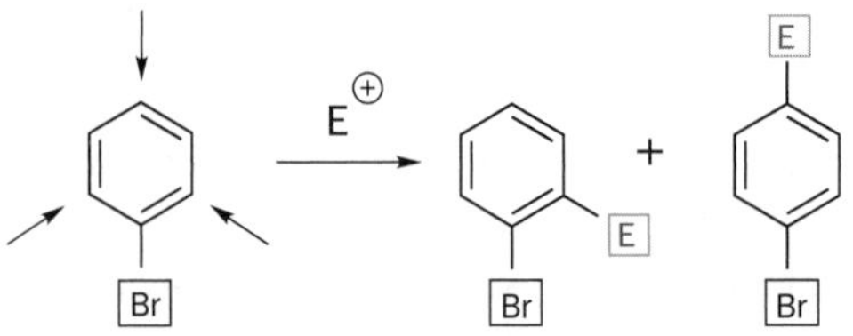

If bromobenzene is substituted, the electrophile will go to the *ortho* and *para* positions. We can then separate the isomers to give the desired *para* isomer.

Remember: *The carboxylic acid is a* meta-*director because it is resonance electron withdrawing. The bromo group is an* ortho, para-*director because it is resonance electron donating.*

---

2) Establish reaction conditions to get to the desired product.

Things to Watch Out For

Be sure to arrange the synthetic steps in the correct order!

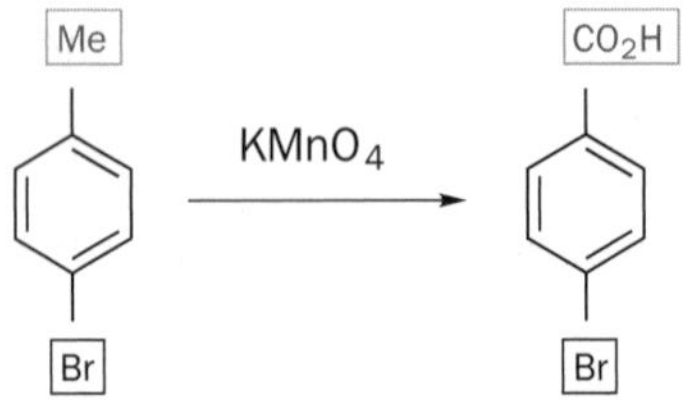

Now that we've decided to brominate first, we have to figure out which electrophile we will place on bromobenzene to get to the carboxylic acid.

The most straightforward way to do this is to place a methyl group on bromobenzene and then oxidize the methyl group to the carboxylic acid.

---

3) Write down the complete synthetic scheme in the forward direction.

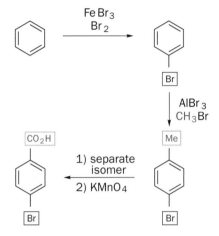

Similar Questions

1) How might *para*-bromobenzoic acid be prepared from *para*-dibromobenzene?

2) If 3-bromomethoxybenzene were nitrated once, where do you expect that the nitro group would appear in the product?

3) Show how triphenylmethane could be prepared from excess benzene and chloroform.

Key Concepts

Chapter 6

Electrophilic aromatic substitution

Nucleophilic acyl substitution

Spectroscopy

^{1}H-NMR

Identifying Structure of Unknown Aromatic

Given the diagram and the ^{1}H-NMR spectra shown below, determine the structures of molecules **A** through **H**.

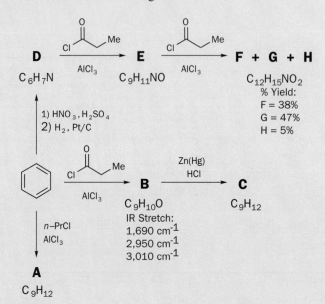

Takeaways

Be sure to move one step at a time with these problems and to use the spectroscopic data together, rather than in separate pieces, if possible.

Things to Watch Out For

Make sure you know the IR stretches that are diagnostic for given functional groups. There aren't that many to learn—perhaps six at the most.

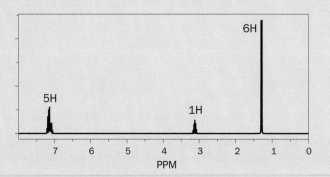

^{1}H-NMR of compound **A**

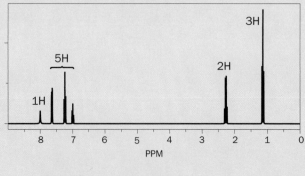

^{1}H-NMR of compound **E**

1) Determine the type of reaction.

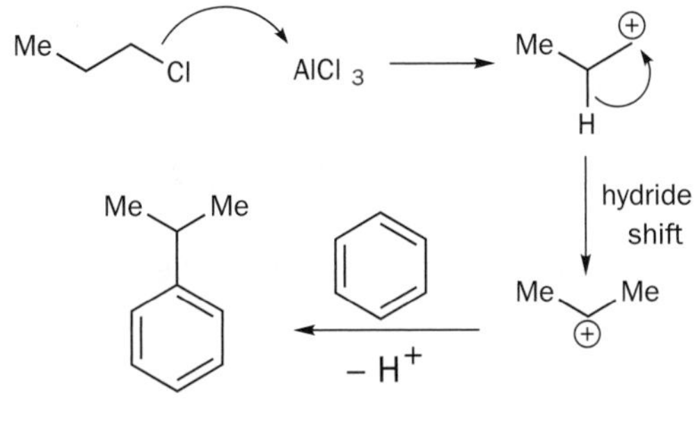

A

For the reaction to form product **A**, you should immediately recognize these conditions as that of a Friedel-Crafts alkylation. However, note from the NMR that the product is not simply propylbenzene because there are only two aliphatic signals in the NMR, not three. Therefore, the product must be isopropylbenzene.

2) Identify product B.

Product **B** is the product of a Friedel-Crafts *acylation*, giving a carbonyl.

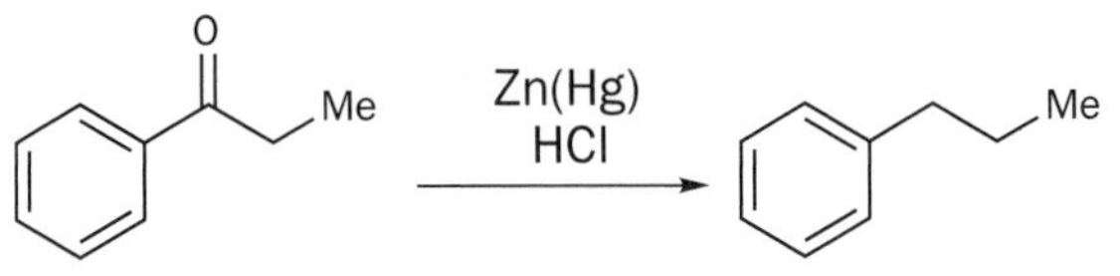

$C_9H_{10}O$

B

C_9H_{12}

C

Even if you didn't remember this, you should know that B contains a ketone from the stretch in the IR [the other stretches are for sp^3 C–H's (just to the *right* of 3,000 cm^{-1}) and the aromatic sp^2 C–H's (just to the *left* of 3,000 cm^{-1})]. In the next step, the carbonyl is removed and replaced with a methylene in the *Clemmensen reduction*.

3) Identify product D.

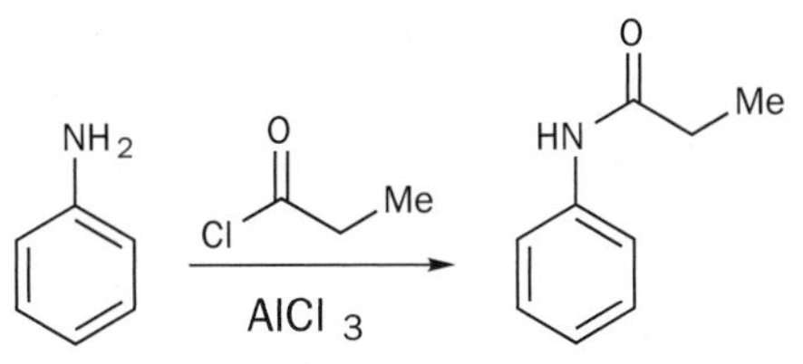

C_6H_7N

D

$C_9H_{11}NO$

E

In the reaction to give molecule **D**, note that benzene is first *nitrate*, then the nitro group is reduced to an *amine*. Remember that if you see a nitrogen-bearing functional group followed by reductive conditions, an amine is almost certainly being generated. You should recognize the conditions to give **E** as another Friedel-Crafts acylation; however, note that in the NMR, there are still five aromatic protons. Therefore, the only other place that the acyl group can go is on the amine.

Remember: *The amino group is much more nucleophilic than the benzene ring, so with a Lewis acid in the reaction, the amine adds to the acid chloride carbonyl and then eliminates chloride to give the amide* ***E****.*

---

4) Rerun the reaction with molecule E.

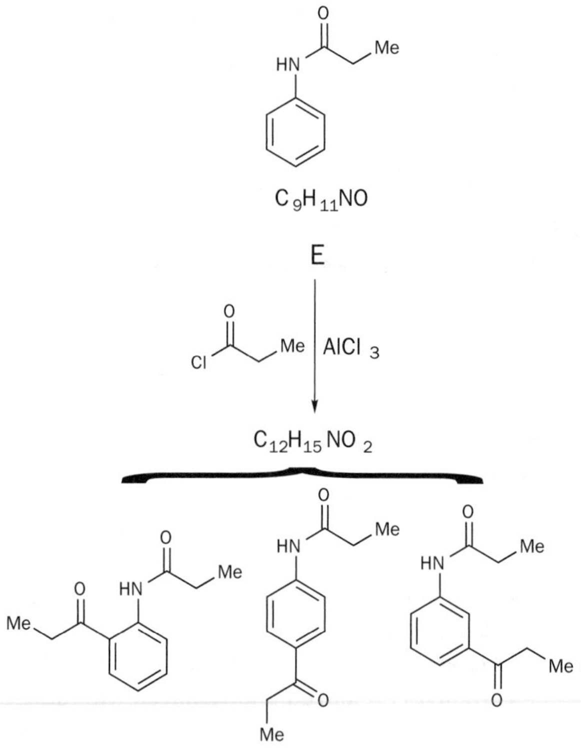
O
HN
Me
$C_9H_{11}NO$
E
O
Cl
Me
$AlCl_3$
$C_{12}H_{15}NO_2$
O
HN
Me
O
Me
O
HN
Me
O
Me
O
HN
Me
Me
O

F G H

The third time seems to be the charm for this grad student. When he repeats the acylation reaction on **E**, this time the reaction works. You should suspect this not only from the molecular formula but from the fact that three products are formed in unequal yield–one of the telltale signs of electrophilic aromatic substitution. Because the nitrogen in **E** is still an *ortho-, para-* director, even with the adjacent carbonyl, the major products **F** and **G** will be the *ortho* and *para* isomers, and **H** will be the *meta* isomer.

Key Concepts

Chapters 7–10

Nucleophilic addition

Resonance

Reaction rate

Substrate Reactivity: Nucleophilic Addition

Place the following molecules in order of *decreasing rate* of nucleophilic addition with lithium aluminum hydride:

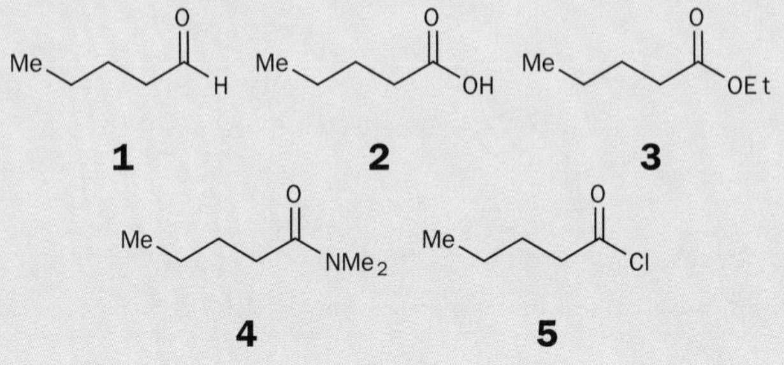

Takeaways

The rate at which a carbonyl compound reacts with a nucleophile is proportional to its electrophilicity—in other words, how much of a partial positive charge exists on the carbonyl carbon.

1) Determine the nature of the nucleophile.
Here, the nucleophile is coming from lithium aluminum hydride, which we can think about as being "H⁻."

---

2) Place the molecules in order of increasing electrophilicity.
Remember that molecules in which the carbonyl carbon is more electrophilic will react faster with nucleophiles. The electrophilicity of the carbonyl carbon is determined by the following resonance structure:

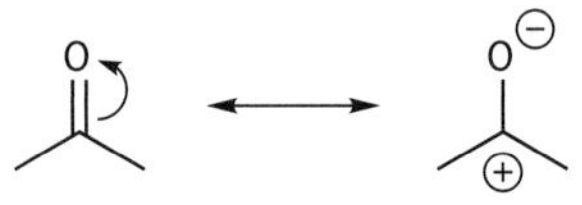

Molecules in which the resonance structure on the right is *more important* will have more electrophilic carbonyl carbons and therefore react the *fastest* with a nucleophile.

With that in mind, it should be clear that molecule 5 will react the fastest. Take a look at its analogous resonance structure:

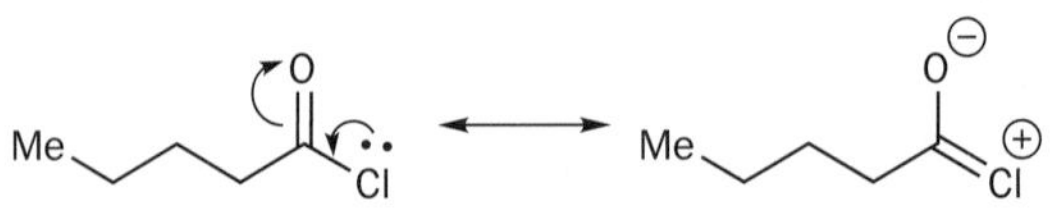

Things to Watch Out For

Don't forget to account for the fact that reactions may be possible other than just the reaction you've been asked about. In general, *acid-base reactions* (proton transfers) are faster than *intramolecular reactions,* which are faster than *intermolecular reactions.*

This resonance structure doesn't seem very reasonable because chlorine ends up having a positive charge on it. This means that the resonance structure with the positive charge on carbon is relatively more important, meaning that this molecule will react relatively quickly.

Hydrogen isn't quite as electronegative as chlorine, meaning that the aldehyde (molecule 1) will be the next most reactive.

Between molecules 3 and 4, 3 will be more reactive. You can figure this out by examining the resonance structures below:

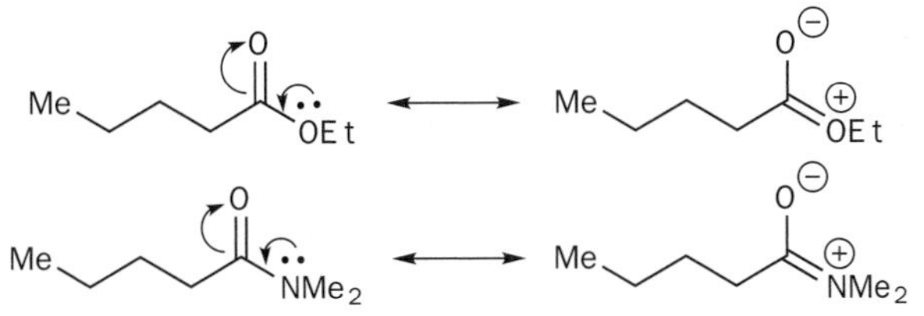

The nitrogen is more stable with a positive charge than oxygen due to its lower electronegativity. So it doesn't mind giving its lone pairs up to the carbonyl as much. When it does give up its lone pairs, though, it helps reduce the partial positive charge on carbon, and therefore the amide is less reactive toward nucleophiles than the ester.

Finally, how do we handle the carboxylic acid? As it turns out, this molecule is the least reactive toward nucleophilic addition, because an *acid–base reaction* occurs before any nucleophilic addition:

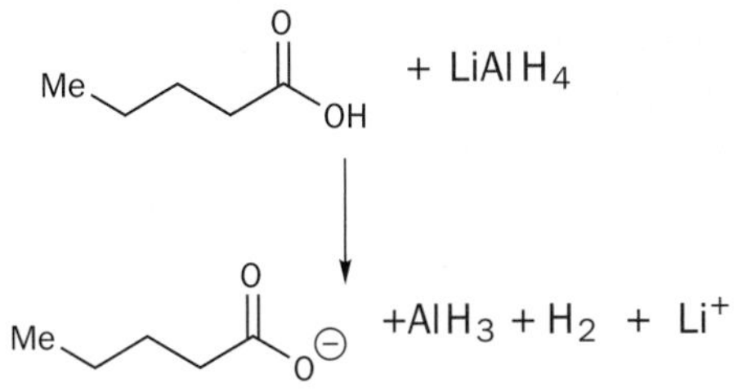

Whereas before, electron donation into the carbonyl occurred through a resonance structure with charge separation, here the carboxylate is already charged. So it can push its electron density into the carbonyl, resulting in a distribution of a negative charge:

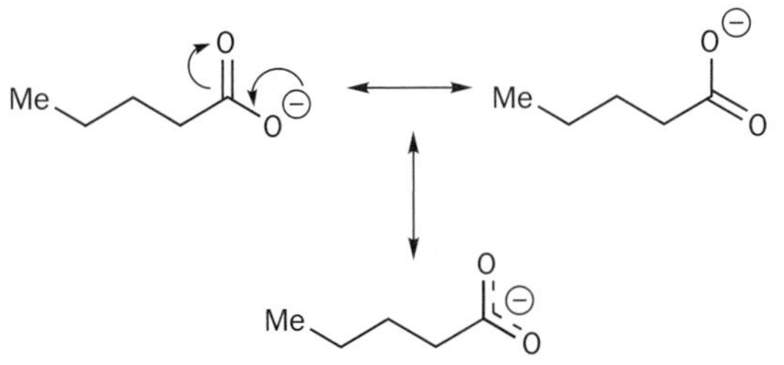

If there's a lot of negative charge floating around in the carbonyl, that's only going to repel the reagent, which is also negatively charged, making the carboxylic acid the least susceptible to attack.

---

3) Place all of the molecules in order of their reactivity.

The final order in decreasing rate of nucleophilic addition is as follows:

5 > 1 > 3 > 4 > 2

Similar Questions

1) Nucleophilic substitutions can also occur with weak nucleophiles under acid catalysis. This requires that the carbonyl oxygen pick up a proton before the nucleophile adds. Rank the compounds above in order of *increasing basicity* of the carbonyl lone pair and explain your rankings.

2) How would you compare the reactivity of the following compounds towards methylmagnesium bromide:

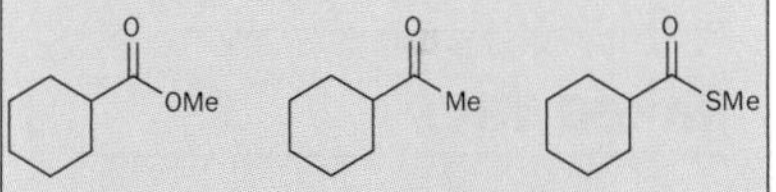

3) In the *haloform reaction*, methyl ketones are converted to their corresponding carboxylates. Provide a detailed, stepwise mechanism for the following haloform reaction:

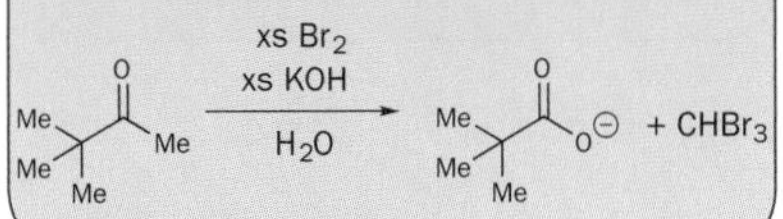

Key Concepts

Chapters 7–10

Oxidation/reduction

Isomerism

Identifying Structure of Unknown Oxy Compound

A student carried out the following series of transformations in the lab.

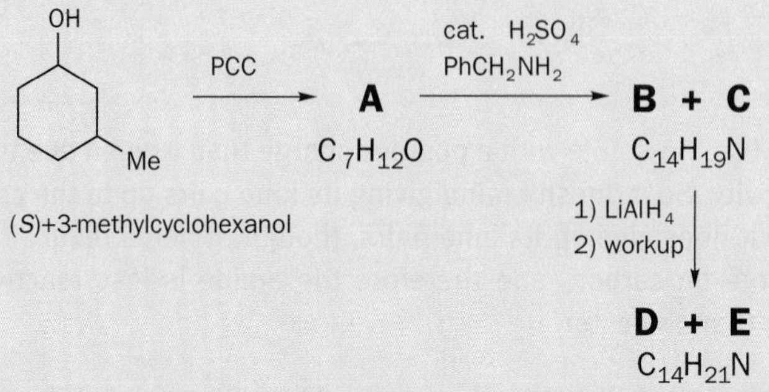

Upon A's reaction with catalytic acid and benzylamine, the student obtained a mixture of two products, B and C. The mixture of B and C is subjected to lithium aluminum hydride. Following a diluted aqueous workup and chromatographic separation, two more products, D and E, are obtained in unequal yield.

Identify the structures of compounds A through E, given their molecular formulas.

Takeaways

The key to these types of problems is identifying the nature of the reagents and then identifying how they would react with the starting materials for each step. Try to look for combinations of *electrophiles* and *nucleophiles*.

1) React alcohol with PCC.

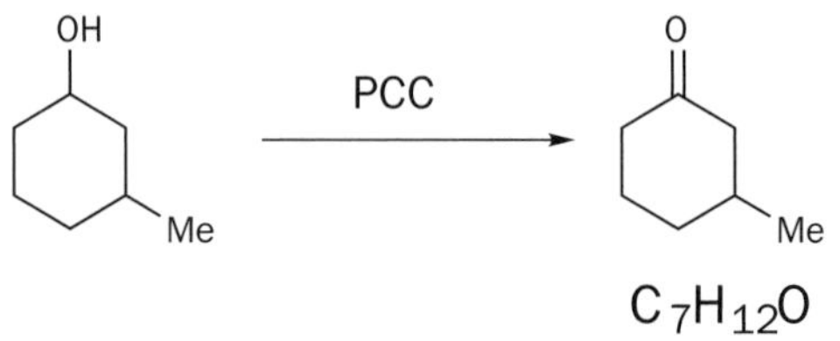

The first step of this process is to take the alcohol and subject it to PCC oxidation, which would give a ketone.

---

2) Subject ketone to an acid catalyst and benzylamine.

Things to Watch Out For

If the molecular formulas are supplied, be sure to check your structure against the given molecular formula.

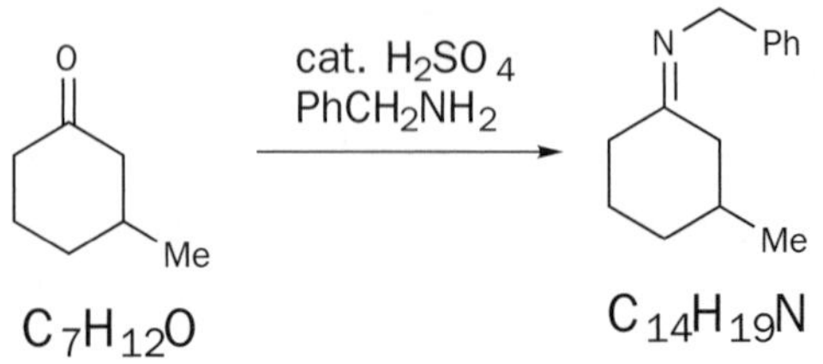

You should suspect that some sort of nucleophilic addition is going to take place. Recall that a ketone that reacts with a primary amine gives an *imine*.

Similar Questions

1) How many total stereoisomers are produced in the last reduction step? (*Hint:* How many stereocenters are there in the molecule?)

2) The final amine products were placed in a polarimeter and found not to rotate plane-polarized light. Why should this be the case?

3) Determine the other product of this reaction.

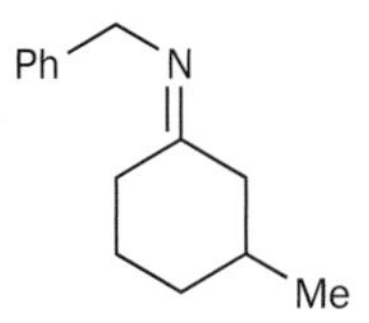

Recall that anytime there is a double bond, there exists the possibility of having *geometric isomers*. The double bond doesn't have to be a carbon–carbon double bond! So the other product must be the other geometric isomer.

4) React imine with LAH.

$C_{14}H_{19}N$ $\qquad$ $C_{14}H_{21}N$

Reacting each of the imines with lithium aluminum hydride (LAH) will afford an amine. Note that you should be able to identify $LiAlH_4$ as a *reducing agent* because there are a lot of H's attached to either B or Al.

The student obtained two products in unequal yield. This suggests that the two products are *diastereomers*. In this case, there are two possible diastereomers:

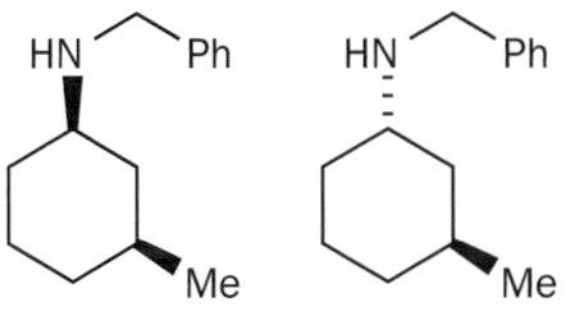

The methyl stereocenter has the same orientation for both molecules because it has been unchanged since the beginning. Therefore, the difference in stereochemistry must be at the nitrogen-bearing stereocenter.

Key Concepts

Chapter 10

Acids and bases

Enolate ion

Claisen condensation

Intramolecular reactions

Intramolecular Ring Closures

Provide a detailed, stepwise mechanism to account for the following transformation:

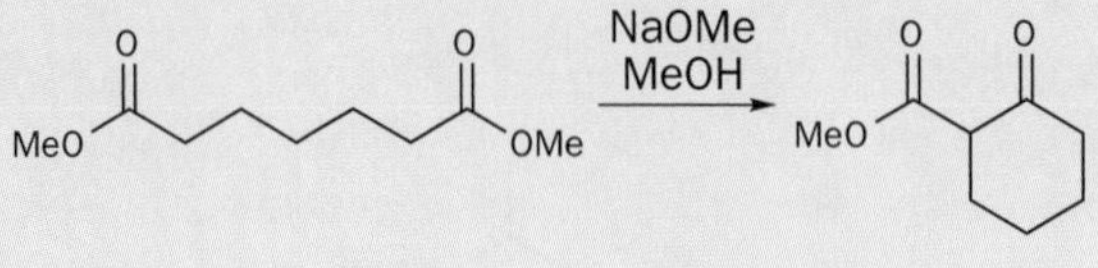

1) Examine the product for clues to the connectivity.

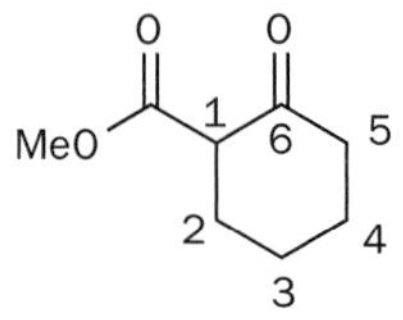

Anytime you see one molecule going to form a ring, you should suspect that there is an intramolecular reaction. Here, note that in the six-membered ring, the α-carbon of one ester is directly connected to a ketone. That, combined with the fact that there is a β-keto ester in the product, should tell you that what is going on is an intramolecular Claisen condensation.

Remember: *Intramolecular reactions are always faster than intermolecular reactions because the reactants are already close together.*

Takeaways

Remember that with mechanism problems, you always want to get toward the specified products. Don't include steps that don't get you any closer to where you want to be.

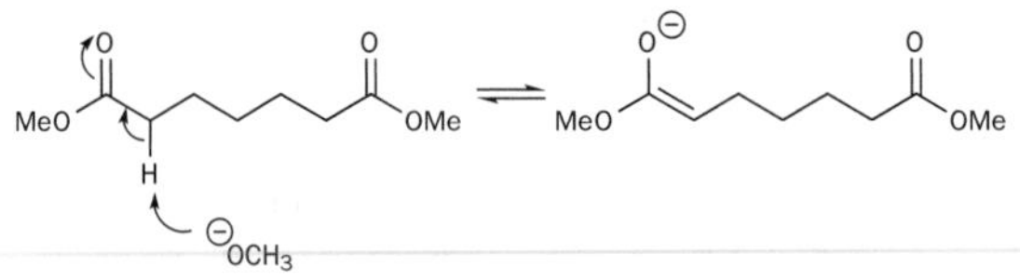

Things to Watch Out For

Make sure that if charged intermediates are involved in your mechanism, they go away before you get to the product, unless the product is charged as well.

Also, be sure that your arrows are pointing in the right direction! The head of the arrow is pointing toward where the electrons are moving, not where they start from.

2) Start pushing electons.

First, generate an enolate for the Claisen condensation, which must take place next to one of the esters.

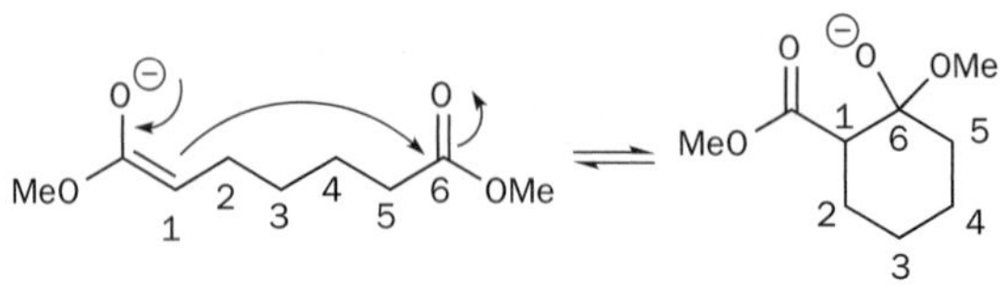

Then, the intramolecular reaction takes place. Numbering along the carbon chain and in the product is always a good idea. This will help you make sure that everything is in the right place.

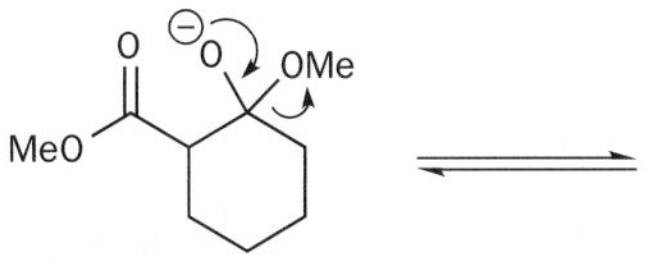

Here, finish the mechanism by generating the keto ester functionality that is in the product.

Similar Questions

1) Provide a detailed, stepwise mechanism for the following transformation:

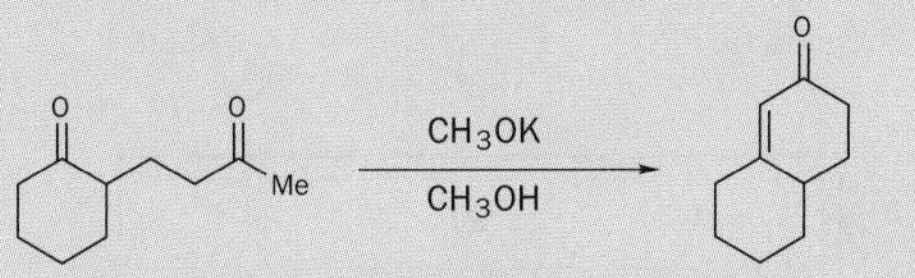

2) Provide a detailed, stepwise mechanism for the same reaction above, except run an *acid* instead of a *base*.

3) Provide a detailed, stepwise mechanism to account for the following reaction:

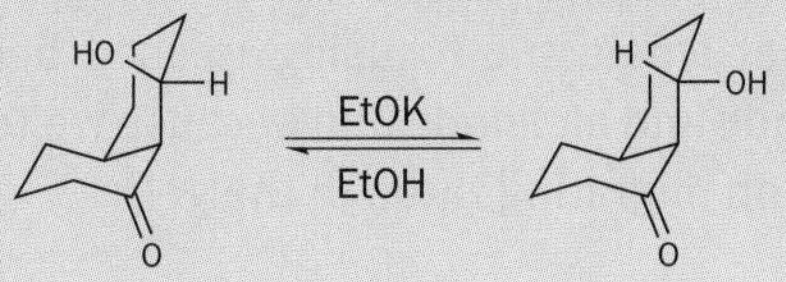

Key Concepts

Chapter 12

Isoelectric focusing

Determining isoelectric point

Electrolytic cell

Isoelectric Focusing

Suppose you are trying to separate glycine, glutamic acid, and lysine given the following information:

	pKa COOH	pKa NH$_3^+$	pKa R group
Glycine:	2.34	9.63	—
Glutamic acid:	2.19	9.67	4.25
Lysine:	2.18	8.95	10.53

Indicate in which region of the gel each amino acid will stop migrating.

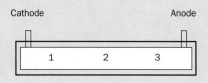

Takeaways

To solve isoelectric focusing questions, determine the pI of the samples being separated. Then, determine the orientation of the pH gradient on the gel. The samples will migrate toward their pI, isoelectric point.

1) Identify if it is an isoelectric focusing problem.

Whenever a question gives you the pK$_a$ of the substance being purified, think ion exchange chromatography or isoelectric focusing. In the above question, we can be certain that isoelectric focusing is used because the separatory apparatus has a cathode and an anode and because we're told that each amino acid will eventually stop migrating through the gel.

2) Determine the isoelectric points of the sample(s).

To find the pI for an amino acid, identify the deprotonation reaction that converts the amino acid with +1 overall charge into the zwitterion with 0 overall charge; also, identify the deprotonation reaction that converts the zwitterion into a form with −1 overall charge. The pI for the amino acid is the average of the pK$_a$'s for these two reactions.

For glycine, the sequence of deprotonation reactions is the following:

$$\underset{\underset{H}{|}}{\overset{\overset{R}{|}}{NH_3^+-C-COOH}} \underset{pK_{a1}=2.34}{\rightleftharpoons} \underset{\underset{H}{|}}{\overset{\overset{R}{|}}{NH_3^+-C-COO^-}} \underset{pK_{a2}=9.63}{\rightleftharpoons} \underset{\underset{H}{|}}{\overset{\overset{R}{|}}{NH_2-C-COO^-}}$$

For glycine, the pKa's for the reactions leading to and from the zwitterion are pK$_{a1}$ and pK$_{a2}$. So the pI for glycine is the average of its pK$_{a1}$ and pK$_{a2}$.

$$\text{pI of glycine} = \frac{(2.34 + 9.63)}{2} = 5.99$$

Things to Watch Out For

Be careful in problems that ask you to separate proteins. Remember that the pI of a protein cannot be determined simply by averaging the pI of the individual amino acids. If the isoelectric point of a protein is not given, then another method must be used to separate the proteins.

For glutamic acid, the sequence of deprotonation reactions is this:

$$\underset{H}{\overset{RH}{NH_3^+-C-COOH}} \underset{pK_{a1}=2.19}{\rightleftharpoons} \underset{H}{\overset{RH}{NH_3^+-C-COO^-}} \underset{pK_{a2}=4.25}{\rightleftharpoons} \underset{H}{\overset{R^-}{NH_3^+-C-COO^-}} \underset{pK_{a3}=9.67}{\rightleftharpoons} \underset{H}{\overset{R^-}{NH_2-C-COO^-}}$$

(The side chain is acidic, so we need to include a reaction for its deprotonation. The conjugate base of an acidic side chain is negatively charged.) For glutamic acid, the pKa's for the reactions leading to and from the zwitterion are pK_{a1} and pK_{a2}. So the pI for glutamic acid is the average of its pK_{a1} and pK_{a2}.

$$pI \text{ of Glutamic acid} = \frac{(2.19 + 4.25)}{2} = 3.22$$

For lysine the sequence of deprotonation reactions is this:

$$\underset{H}{\overset{RH^+}{NH_3^+-C-COOH}} \underset{pK_{a1}=2.18}{\rightleftharpoons} \underset{H}{\overset{RH^+}{NH_3^+-C-COO^-}} \underset{pK_{a2}=8.95}{\rightleftharpoons} \underset{H}{\overset{RH^+}{NH_2-C-COO^-}} \underset{pK_{a3}=10.53}{\rightleftharpoons} \underset{H}{\overset{R}{NH_2-C-COO^-}}$$

For lysine, the pKa's for the reactions leading to and from the zwitterion are pK_{a2} and pK_{a3}. So the pI for glycine is the average of its pK_{a2} and pK_{a3}.

$$pI \text{ of lysine} = \frac{(8.95 + 10.53)}{2} = 9.74$$

3) Determine the relative pH gradient of the gel.
Electrophoresis is always run on electrolytic cells. Recall that electrolytic cells require an outside source of energy. The negative terminal is connected to the cathode, and the positive end is connected to the anode. This means that the anode (acidic end of the gel) will attract negative anions and the cathode (basic end of the gel) will attract positive anions.

Therefore, we know that zone 1 is at a higher pH than zone 2, which is at a higher pH than zone 3.

4) Determine where the samples will migrate.
This means that proteins will migrate toward their pI. At the pI, the protein will not have a net charge (it will be in its zwitterion form) and thus will no longer be induced to migrate in the electric field.

In the above problem, glutamic acid will align itself in region 3, glycine will align itself in region 2, and lysine will align itself in region 1.

Remember: *Amino acids are amphoteric and thus will be positively charged at pH values below their pI and negatively charged above their pI.*

Similar Questions

1) If a segment of polypeptide with a pI of 6.7 is subjected to electrophoresis at pH 5, will the segment move toward the cathode or the anode?

2) What is the isoelectric point of aspartic acid?

3) In what form is an amino acid said to be when it reaches its isoelectric point?

Key Concepts

Chapter 12

Extraction (liquid-liquid separation)

Acid/base properties

Separation

Extraction

A student wishes to separate methyl phenyl ketone, aniline, and phenol from a mixture. To perform the separation, the mixture is dissolved in a solution consisting of 500 ml of H_2O and 500 ml of dichloromethane. The solution is then washed with water three times, and the aqueous layer (A) is extracted. The remaining solution is then washed with 20 percent Na_2CO_3 three times and the aqueous layer (B) is collected. The remaining organic layer is finally washed with 10 percent HCl, and the aqueous layer (C) is once again collected, leaving behind the organic layer (D). What were the contents of samples A, B, C, and D?

1) Determine the difference between the molecules being separated.

Acetophenone, aniline, and phenol are all organic compounds. However, aniline is a weak base whereas phenol is a weak acid. Methyl phenyl ketone is the most hydrophobic of the three compounds because it doesn't possess any functional groups capable of making hydrogen bonds.

2) Determine into what phase each of the compounds will dissolve after the first set of washings.

All three compounds are uncharged organic compounds and as such will dissolve in the organic layer, in dichloromethane. Thus, the first set of washings will not aid in separating any of the three compounds.

3) Determine into what phase each of the compounds will dissolve after the second set of washings.

When the sample is washed with Na_2CO_3, phenol will be deprotonated to yield sodium phenoxide (the conjugate base of phenol). Because this molecule is charged, it will move into the aqueous layer. After the washing, the deprotonated phenol will move to the aqueous phase, whereas methyl phenyl ketone and aniline will remain in the organic layer.

Remember: *Washing a mixture with a base is an effective way to move acidic compounds from the organic layer into the aqueous layer.*

4) Determine into what phase each of the compounds will dissolve after the third set of washings.

At this point, the only remaining compounds in the organic layer are acetophenone and aniline.

When the sample is washed with HCl (a strong acid), aniline will be protonated to an anilinium ion. This positively charged molecule will move into the aqueous layer, whereas acetophenone will remain in the organic layer.

Takeaways

In an extraction problem, each compound will either be dissolved in the aqueous layer or the organic layer. However, if a compound is acidic or basic, it is possible to transpose it to the aqueous layer by using basic or acidic washes, respectively.

Things to Watch Out For

Don't assume that the organic phase will be on top—this depends on the densities of the two phases. For example, dichloromethane (1.3 g mL^{-1}) is denser than water (1.0 g mL^{-1}); dichloromethane will sink to the bottom of the separatory funnel, with the water floating on top.

Remember: *Washing a mixture with an acid is an effective way to move basic compounds from the organic layer to the aqueous layer.*

Similar Questions

1) Design an extraction procedure to separate a mixture of phenol and benzoic acid dissolved in ether.

2) In order to extract *p*-nitrophenol from phenol in an ether solution, a student washes the organic layer with 10 ml of a 5 percent aqueous solution of NaOH. After the washing, what will be left in the organic layer?

Chromatography

In an effort to purify ATCase, a crude cell extract in a potassium phosphate buffer is run on a Q-Sepharose column (mono Q is an anion exchanger: $-CH_2-N(CH_3)_3^+$). What characteristic of ATCase allows it to be separated using an anion exchanger? Are any additives necessary to achieve a successful purification?

1) Determine the difference between the molecules being separated.

In the question stem, we are told that mono Q (the stationary phase in the column) is an anion exchanger. This means that it attracts anions and thus must have a positive charged group. Because we are trying to purify ATCase, it must bind to mono Q; if it doesn't, it will simply pass through the column along with the other positively charged proteins and thus not be purified. So we can conclude that ATCase is a negatively charged protein (an anionic protein), enabling it to be purified using an anion exchanger.

If an antibody or substrate for ATCase were available, affinity chromatography could have been used. Column chromatography could also be used to separate substances based on size.

Takeaways

All forms of chromatography have two phases, a stationary phase and a mobile phase. Separations of compounds take advantage of the different affinities that compounds have for the two different phases.

2) Determine which compound has a higher affinity for the stationary phase.

When the crude cell extract is run through the column, ATCase and other anionic proteins will stick to the stationary phase, whereas the rest of the extract will pass through the column relatively easily.

3) Determine which compound has a higher affinity for the eluent.

Now that the anionic proteins are bound to the Q-sepharose gel, they must be eluted based on their affinities (in this case the strength of their negative charge) for the stationary phase. For this purpose, NaCl is added in an increasing concentration gradient. The least negatively charged proteins will emerge from the column before the proteins with the greatest negative charge.

Things to Watch Out For

Be cautious not to assume that the desired product will attach to the stationary phase. You may be presented with a situation in which purification will be better accomplished if the desired product has a higher affinity for the mobile phase.

Similar Questions

1) Sample A (R_f value of 0.75) and sample B (R_f value of 0.50) were run on silica gel. What is the distance traveled by sample A if sample B traveled 2.0 cm?

2) If the pH of the buffer is increased from 7 to 9, how will the purification be affected?

3) If you want to separate two anionic proteins (protein A and protein B, where protein A is a tetramer of protein B) with the same anionic character, which type of chromatography will be most useful? Assume that the tetramer once formed in the cell does not dissociate and that the monomer cannot form the tetramer *in vitro*.

High-Yield Problems continue on the next page

Key Concepts

Chapter 13

Spectroscopy

Electrophilic aromatic substitution

^{1}H-NMR

NMR Spectroscopy

A grad student performed an electrophilic chlorination of phenol, as shown below.

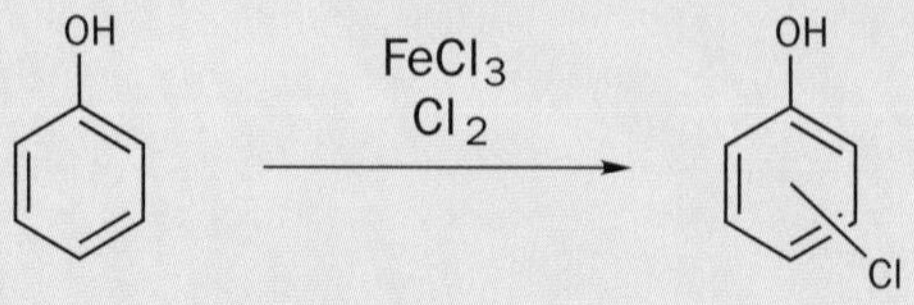

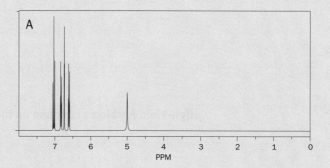

The grad student obtained three products, the *ortho*, *meta*, and *para* isomers, and separated all three. Unfortunately, he forgot to label which compound was which. ^{1}H-NMRs were taken of each product and are shown below. Match each spectrum to its corresponding product.

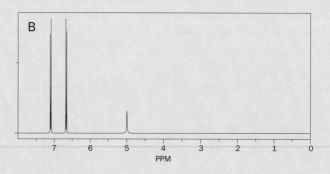

Takeaways

The most effective strategy in these types of problems is to try to eliminate one spectrum at a time by looking at the most general differences between molecules and proceeding to the more specific.

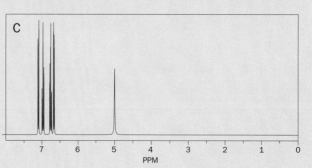

Things to Watch Out For

Be sure to check your assignments by ensuring that each spectrum has the correct number of proton signals.

In the world of molecular genetics, the devil truly is in the details. Seemingly small changes to the genetic code can result in disastrous, life-altering, life-threatening, even life-incompatible alterations to protein structure and function. As protein function necessarily depends on protein structure, protein structure necessarily depends upon the genetic code. One of the clearest examples of this—and a clear example of the dire results of even the smallest errors in the genetic system—is the molecular basis for the pathophysiology of sickle cell disease, also called sickle cell anemia. A disease most prevalent in people of tropical or subtropical origin, sickle cell anemia is a genetic disorder that results in abnormally shaped red blood cells. Rather than having the normal flexible biconcavity, these red blood cells assume a shape that is rigid and sickle shaped (like the curved blade used to cut tall grasses).

Sickle cell disease is caused by a point mutation in the gene for the β-globin chain of hemoglobin. In this particular mutation, a thymine nucleotide is substituted for an adenine nucleotide, resulting in the substitution of valine for glutamic acid at the sixth position from the amino terminus of the β-globin chain. Individuals with sickle cell disease are homozygous for the mutated allele, which is autosomal recessive. The substitution of a nonpolar amino acid for an acidic (charged) amino acid has no effect on the secondary, tertiary, and even quaternary structure of hemoglobin: Under normal physiological conditions, this is a totally benign mutation! However, under low-oxygen conditions, the deoxy form of hemoglobin exposes a hydrophobic patch on the protein with which the nonpolar valine residue can interact by way of hydrophobic interactions. These interactions cause the hemoglobin molecules (called hemoglobin S, for the sickle cell mutation) to aggregate and form precipitates that distort the shape of the red blood cell and decrease its elasticity.

Under conditions of low oxygen tension, the aggregation of hemoglobin and the resulting shape change lead to damage of the erythrocyte membrane. Repeated sickling causes accumulated membrane damage and significantly decreased elasticity. These damaged cells do not return to their normal shape even after oxygen levels have been restored. When these abnormally shaped cells pass into the microvasculature (i.e., the capillaries), they can get stuck, blocking off blood supply to the tissue and causing ischemic tissue damage and high levels of pain.

The last chapter introduced us to genes as the fundamental units of heredity. We briefly noted that they are composed of **deoxyribonucleic acid (DNA)**. We saw that for traits to be inherited, the genes that code for the traits must be passed from one generation of individuals to the next. This ultimately means that the genetic code itself (DNA) must be transmitted. Each cell in the human body contains the complete blueprint for all the proteins that are necessary for life and that make each person unique. In Chapter 4, we noted that DNA replication is critical for cell division and reproduction. The self-replicating nature of DNA, and its ability to direct protein

Combined Spectroscopy: IR and NMR

An unknown compound was discovered in an old, unused laboratory. Its molecular formula was determined to be $C_6H_9NO_2$ by high-resolution mass spectrometry. The following IR stretches were recorded: 3,300 (sharp), 2,890 (m), 2,220, 1,740 (s), 1,220, 984, 700, 650 cm^{-1}.

The ^{1}H-NMR spectrum of the compound is as follows:

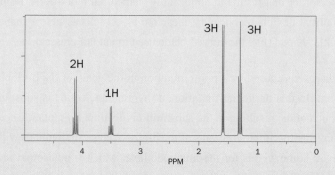

Given this information, determine the structure of the unknown compound.

1) Compute the number of sites of unsaturation.

$$U = \frac{(2n + 2 - m)}{2}$$

n = number of carbons; m = number of protons and/or halogens minus number of nitrogens. Ignore oxygen and sulfur.

Thus, $U = \dfrac{(2 \times 6 + 2 - 8)}{2} = \dfrac{6}{2} = 3$.

This means that the molecule has either three double bonds, one double bond and one triple bond, or some combination of rings and double or triple bonds.

Remember: *If a molecule has four or more sites of unsaturation, you should immediately suspect that an aromatic ring is present.*

2) Look at the IR stretches to determine what functional groups are present.

Here, the stretch at 1,740 cm^{-1} indicates the presence of a carbonyl, and the stretch at 2,220 cm^{-1} indicates the presence of a triple bond (either an alkyne or a nitrile).

The one thing you do *not* want to do with the IR data is to try to interpret every single stretch. The IR is not nearly as informative as the NMR. Just look for the few stretches that are indicative of functional groups.

3) Do a little detective work to narrow down the structural possibilities.

First let's think about the carbonyl. It can't be an aldehyde because there are no aldehyde signals in the NMR, and it can't be a carboxylic acid because there is no alcohol stretch in the IR. Because the stretch is closer to 1,740 than to 1,700, it is probably an ester rather than a ketone (you might also suspect this from the 1,220 stretch in the IR, which indicates a C–O stretch).

As for the triple-bond stretch, it is most likely a nitrile because there are no amine stretches in the IR.

Similar Questions

1) Why is it unlikely that the compound in the original question is cyclic (i.e., contains one or more rings)?

2) If the molecule were a methyl ketone rather than an ester (i.e., replace the ethoxy group with a methyl group), where do you expect that the carbonyl IR stretch would appear, and why?

3) Where would the signal for the methyl ketone protons in the compound described in question 2 show up in the NMR relative to the signal for the protons adjacent to the oxygen in the ester?

4) Look more specifically at the information in the NMR to put the rest of the molecule together.

Look at the signal that's farthest downfield in the NMR. It comes from two protons that are adjacent to a methyl group (because the signal is a quartet). Because we suspect that the carbonyl is an ester, this signal must correspond to two protons that are right next to the ester oxygen. The fact that the signal is farthest downfield indicates that these protons are immediately adjacent to the oxygen, which is the most electronegative atom. We also know that this is an ethyl ester because these two protons are next to a methyl group.

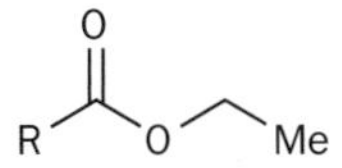

We've accounted for three carbons, two oxygens, and five hydrogens in the structure above, and we also know that the nitrile accounts for an additional carbon and nitrogen.

$$C_6H_9NO_2 - C_4H_5NO_2 = C_2H_4$$

We have two carbons and two hydrogens left to deal with. There can only be two possibilities, structurally:

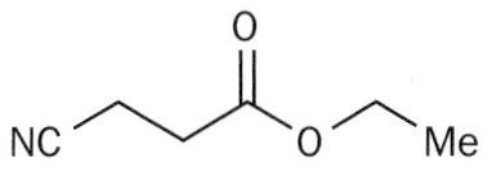

or

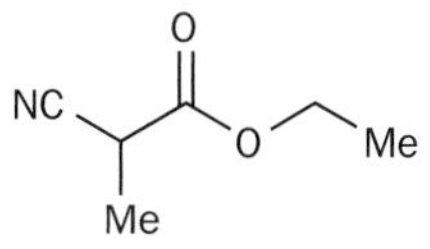

Note that the protons in the structure on the left would have to give rise to two triplets because each is adjacent to a carbon with two protons. However, the only signals we haven't accounted for in the NMR are a doublet integrating for three protons and a quartet integrating for one. These signals exactly match the structure on the right, so that must be the unknown.

Remember: *Once you have made a tentative structural assignment, check it against all of the data available to be sure you have the right molecule.*

Art Credits for Organic Chemistry

Chapter 3 Cover—Image credited to Slim Films. From Proteins Rule by Carol Ezzell. Copyright © 2002 by Scientific American, Inc. All rights reserved.

Chapter 6 Cover—Image credited to Mark A. Reed. From Computing with Molecules by Mark A. Reed and James M. Tour. Copyright © 2000 by Scientific American, Inc. All rights reserved.

Chapter 9 Cover—Image credited to Ken Eward/BioGrafs. From Molecular Lego by Christian E. Schafmeister. Copyright © 2007 by Scientific American, Inc. All rights reserved.

Figure 9.11—Image credited to Bryan Christie. From Working Knowledge: Cleaning Agents by Louis A. Bloomfield. Copyright © 2000 by Scientific American, Inc. All rights reserved.

Figure 12.10—Image credited to Daniels and Daniels. From The Amateur Scientist: Sorting Molecules with Electricity by Shawn Carlson. Copyright © 1998 by Scientific American, Inc. All rights reserved.

Figure 13.3 (Graphs)—Image credited to Lucy Reading-Ikkanda. From The Incredible Shrinking Scanner by Bernhard Blümich. Copyright © 2004 by Scientific American, Inc. All rights reserved.

Figure 13.3 (MRI machine)—Image credited to George Retseck. From The Incredible Shrinking Scanner by Bernhard Blümich. Copyright © 2004 by Scientific American, Inc. All rights reserved.

Figure 13.3 (MRI image)—Image credited to Mehau Kulyk SPL/Photo Researchers, Inc. From The Incredible Shrinking Scanner by Bernhard Blümich. Copyright © 2004 by Scientific American, Inc. All rights reserved.

Part II
Practice Sections

INSTRUCTIONS FOR TAKING THE PRACTICE SECTIONS

Before taking each Practice Section, find a quiet place where you can work uninterrupted. Take a maximum of 70 minutes per section (52 questions) to get accustomed to the length and scope.

Keep in mind that the actual MCAT will not feature a section made up of Organic Chemistry questions alone, but rather a Biological Sciences section made up of both Organic Chemistry and Biology questions. Use the following three sections to hone your Organic Chemistry skills.

Good luck!

Practice Section 1

Time—70 minutes

QUESTIONS 1–52

Directions: Most of the questions in the following Organic Chemistry Practice Section are organized into groups, with a descriptive passage preceding each group of questions. Study the passage, then select the single best answer to the question in each group. Some of the questions are not based on a descriptive passage; you must also select the best answer to these questions. If you are unsure of the best answer, eliminate the choices that you know are incorrect, then select an answer from the choices that remain.

Period	1 IA 1A	2 IIA 2A	3 IIIB 3B	4 IVB 4B	5 VB 5B	6 VIB 6B	7 VIIB 7B	8	9 VIII 8	10	11 IB 1B	12 IIB 2B	13 IIIA 3A	14 IVA 4A	15 VA 5A	16 VIA 6A	17 VIIA 7A	18 vIIIA 8A
1	1 H 1.008																	2 He 4.003
2	3 Li 6.941	4 Be 9.012											5 B 10.81	6 C 12.01	7 N 14.01	8 O 16.00	9 F 19.00	10 Ne 20.18
3	11 Na 22.99	12 Mg 24.31											13 Al 26.98	14 Si 28.09	15 P 30.97	16 S 32.07	17 Cl 35.45	18 Ar 39.95
4	19 K 39.10	20 Ca 40.08	21 Sc 44.96	22 Ti 47.88	23 V 50.94	24 Cr 52.00	25 Mn 54.94	26 Fe 55.85	27 Co 58.47	28 Ni 58.69	29 Cu 63.55	30 Zn 65.39	31 Ga 69.72	32 Ge 72.59	33 As 74.92	34 Se 78.96	35 Br 79.90	36 Kr 83.80
5	37 Rb 85.47	38 Sr 87.62	39 Y 88.91	40 Zr 91.22	41 Nb 92.91	42 Mo 95.94	43 Tc (98)	44 Ru 101.1	45 Rh 102.9	46 Pd 106.4	47 Ag 107.9	48 Cd 112.4	49 In 114.8	50 Sn 118.7	51 Sb 121.8	52 Te 127.6	53 I 126.9	54 Xe 131.3
6	55 Cs 132.9	56 Ba 137.3	57 La* 138.9	72 Hf 178.5	73 Ta 180.9	74 W 183.9	75 Re 186.2	76 Os 190.2	77 Ir 190.2	78 Pt 195.1	79 Au 197.0	80 Hg 200.5	81 Tl 204.4	82 Pb 207.2	83 Bi 209.0	84 Po (210)	85 At (210)	86 Rn (222)
7	87 Fr (223)	88 Ra (226)	89 Ac~ (227)	104 Rf (257)	105 Db (260)	106 Sg (263)	107 Bh (262)	108 Hs (265)	109 Mt (266)	110 --- ()	111 --- ()	112 --- ()		114 --- ()		116 --- ()		118 --- ()

Lanthanide Series*	58 Ce 140.1	59 Pr 140.9	60 Nd 144.2	61 Pm (147)	62 Sm 150.4	63 Eu 152.0	64 Gd 157.3	65 Tb 158.9	66 Dy 162.5	67 Ho 164.9	68 Er 167.3	69 Tm 168.9	70 Yb 173.0	71 Lu 175.0
Actinide Series~	90 Th 232.0	91 Pa (231)	92 U (238)	93 Np (237)	94 Pu (242)	95 Am (243)	96 Cm (247)	97 Bk (247)	98 Cf (249)	99 Es (254)	100 Fm (253)	101 Md (256)	102 No (254)	103 Lr (257)

PASSAGE I (QUESTIONS 1–7)

Alcohols and ethers are functional groups that can also be thought of as substituted water molecules. When one hydrogen of water is replaced with a hydrocarbon, it becomes an alcohol; when both are substituted, the molecule becomes an ether. When substitution of water yields an alcohol, the result is a polar molecule capable of hydrogen bonding in solutions, but its polarity and ability to form hydrogen bonds decrease as the length of hydrocarbon increases. Ethers, in contrast, are relatively nonpolar and the hydrogen bonds that they form are too weak to appreciably affect their boiling points. The reactivity of alcohols is influenced by the electron-releasing property of carbons and electron-withdrawing power of halides attached to the hydrocarbon.

1. Which of the following is the best example of a dehydration reaction through a carbonium ion?

A.

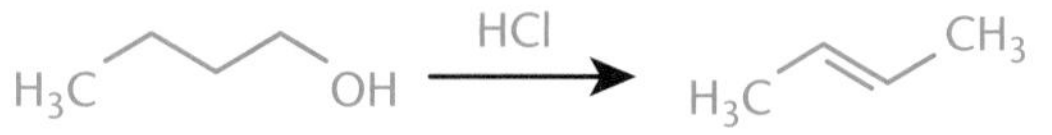

B.

C.

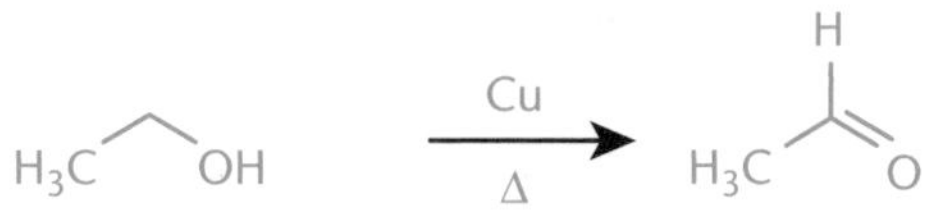

D.

2. Which of the following structures is most amenable to O–H bond cleavage by active metals?

A.
$$CH_3-CH_2-\overset{\overset{\displaystyle CH_3}{|}}{\underset{\underset{\displaystyle H}{|}}{C}}-OH$$

B.
$$CH_3-CH_2-\overset{\overset{\displaystyle CH_3}{|}}{\underset{\underset{\displaystyle CH_3}{|}}{C}}-OH$$

C. CH_3OH

D. $CH_3CH_2CH_2-OH$

3. Which of the following compounds would react to form a tertiary alcohol by the Grignard reaction?

A. $H-\overset{\overset{\displaystyle H}{|}}{C}=O$

B. $CH_3-CH_2-\overset{\overset{\displaystyle H}{|}}{C}=O$

C. $CH_3-\overset{\overset{\displaystyle CH_3}{|}}{C}=O$

D. $CH_3-\overset{\overset{\displaystyle H}{|}}{C}=O$

4. Which of the following compounds would be expected to have the highest boiling point?

A. $CH_3CH_2CH_2CH_2CH_3$
B. $CH_3CH_2-O-CH_2CH_3$
C. $CH_3CH_2CH_2Cl$
D. $CH_3CH_2CH_2OH$

5. In the presence of a nucleophile and an acid, which substrate will undergo an S_N1 substitution reaction most rapidly?

A. CH_3-OH B. CH_3CH_2OH

C. $CH_3-\overset{\overset{\displaystyle H}{|}}{\underset{\underset{\displaystyle OH}{|}}{C}}-CH_3$ D. $CH_3-\overset{\overset{\displaystyle CH_3}{|}}{\underset{\underset{\displaystyle OH}{|}}{C}}-CH_3$

6. A chemist wishes to create a sec-butyl alcohol by using a Grignard reagent. He starts with ethanol and $MgBr_2$. Which of the following compounds would NOT be an intermediate any step of the process?

A. CH_3CH_2Br
B. CH_3CH_2MgBr
C. $CH_3-CH_2C(CH_3)=O$
D. $CH_3CH_2-CH(OMgBr)CH_3$

7. What halide compound is NOT susceptible to attack by an alkoxide during a Williamson synthesis?

A. CH_3Br

B.

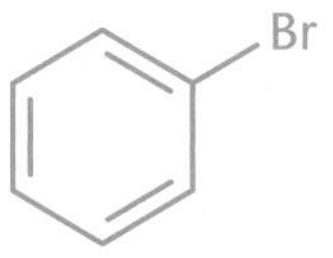

C.

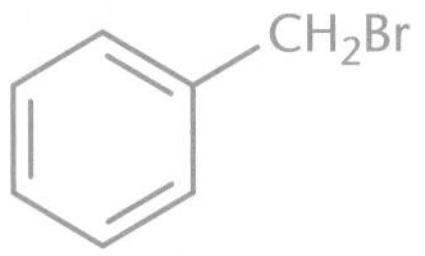

D.

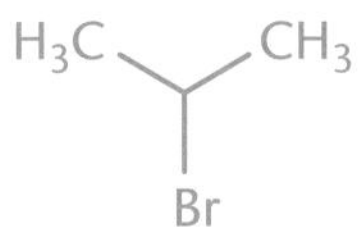

PASSAGE II (QUESTIONS 8–15)

A student investigates the substitution kinetics of two alkyl halides, shown in the figure below (reactions 1 and 2). He uses acetone as a solvent, and finds that the rate equation for both reactions is consistent with S_N2 kinetics. To his surprise, however, the stereochemistry in reaction 1 remains the same throughout the substitution, with no inversion occurring overall.

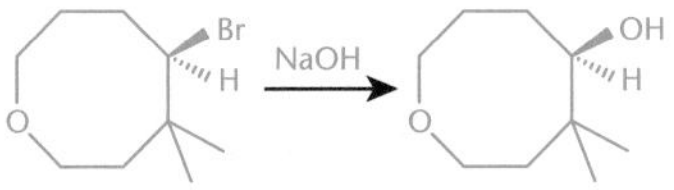

Reaction 1 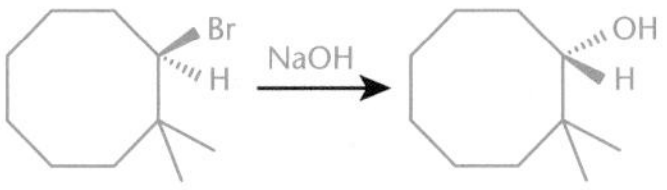   Reaction 2

In a separate experiment, the student switches the solvent to isopropanol, and measures the kinetics of each reaction. He finds that the rate equation for both reactions is consistent with S_N1 kinetics. In addition to the usual S_N1 products, there are several additional products that result from alkyl group shifts. The rates of each substitution reaction are listed in the table below.

Reaction	Rate in Acetone (Ms^{-1})	Rate in Isopropanol (Ms^{-1})
1	2000	175
2	180	175

8. Which of the following is a suitable substitution for acetone?

A. 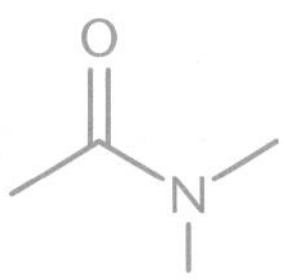
B. 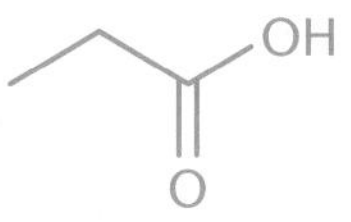
C. 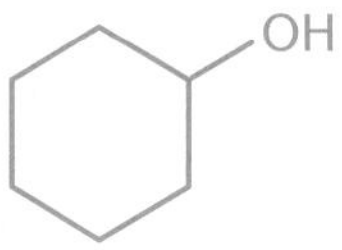
D.

9. The student deduces that in the presence of acetone (reaction 1), the oxygen atom takes part in substitution as a separate nucleophile, before the addition of hydroxide. What is the correct sequence for the change in stereochemistry?

A. S to R to S
B. R to S to R
C. R to R to S
D. S to S to R

10. Which of the following correctly illustrates the intermediate formed from oxygen attack?

A.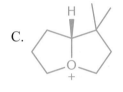

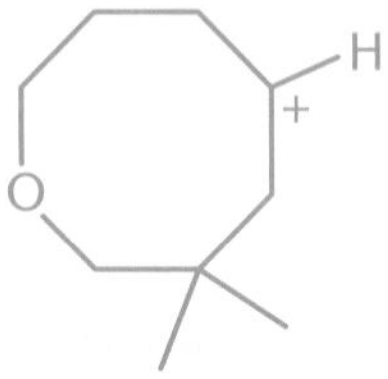

B.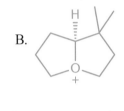

C.

D.

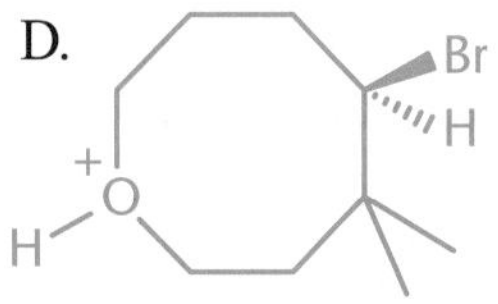

11. For reaction 2, why is the rate in acetone slightly faster than in isopropanol?

    A. S_N2 reactions occur over two steps, while S_N1 reactions occur in one step.

    B. S_N2 reactions occur in one step, while S_N1 reactions occur over two steps.

    C. Acetone is a polar aprotic solvent that forms only weak interactions with nucleophiles.

    D. Isopropanol is a protic solvent that is capable of hydrogen bonding.

12. Why are polar protic solvents preferred in S_N1 reactions?

    A. The solvent stabilizes the negative charge on the leaving group.

    B. The incoming nucleophile is stabilized by solvation.

    C. The carbocation formed is stabilized by protons donated by the solvent.

    D. The leaving group is destabilized by solvation.

13. Why does racemization occur during S_N1 reactions?

    A. The incoming nucleophile racemizes the alkyl halide before any substitution occurs.

    B. The incoming nucleophile can attack from either side of the carbocation, which is sp^2-hybridized.

    C. The incoming nucleophile can attack from either side of the carbocation, which is sp-hybridized.

    D. The alkyl halide racemizes spontaneously before any reaction occurs.

14. What is the driving force for alkyl group shifts during S_N1 reactions?

    A. Formation of secondary carbocations

    B. Formation of primary carbocations

    C. Formation of a stable tertiary radical

    D. Formation of tertiary carbocations

15. Which of the following is possible S_N1 products from the reactants in reactions 1 and 2?

I

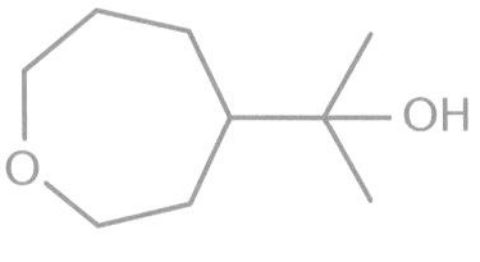

compound I

II

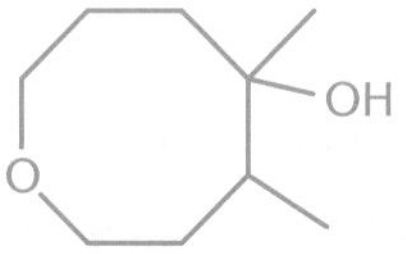

compound II

III

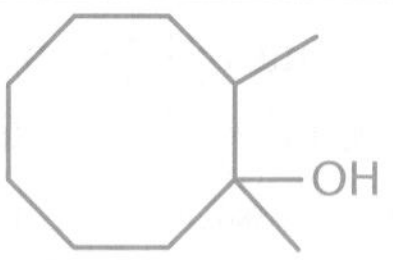

compound III

    A. I only

    B. II only

    C. II and III

    D. I and III

QUESTIONS 16–19 ARE NOT BASED ON A DESCRIPTIVE PASSAGE.

16. The cytosolic aspect of the eukaryotic cell membrane has which of the following chemical properties?

A. Hydrophilic
B. Hydrophobic
C. Nonpolar
D. Insoluble

17. Optically active compounds that rotate plane-polarized light counterclockwise are prefixed with

A. R.
B. S.
C. D.
D. L.

18. Which of the following compounds has one half that's a mirror image of its opposite half?

A. Anomer
B. Epimer
C. Meso compound
D. Geometric isomer

19. What is the degree of unsaturation for a molecule with the molecular formula $C_{20}H_{40}$?

A. 0
B. 1
C. 2
D. 4

PASSAGE III (QUESTIONS 20–29)

Carbohydrates are one of the primary chemical classes that sustain life. Glucose provides energy for cellular respiration and metabolism. *Carbohydrates* is a term that includes both the simple sugars (mono-saccharides) and linked monosaccharides (disaccharides and polysaccharides). Monosaccharides are polyhydroxy aldehydes, or polyhydroxy ketones, and are classified as trioses, tetroses, pentoses, and hexoses, according to the number of carbons in their structure. Monosaccharides can reduce Benedict's or Tollen's reagent and are therefore known as reducing sugars. However, reduction requires that the carbonyl group be in the free form.

20. Which set of descriptors is accurate for the monosaccharide structure shown below in its open and ring forms?

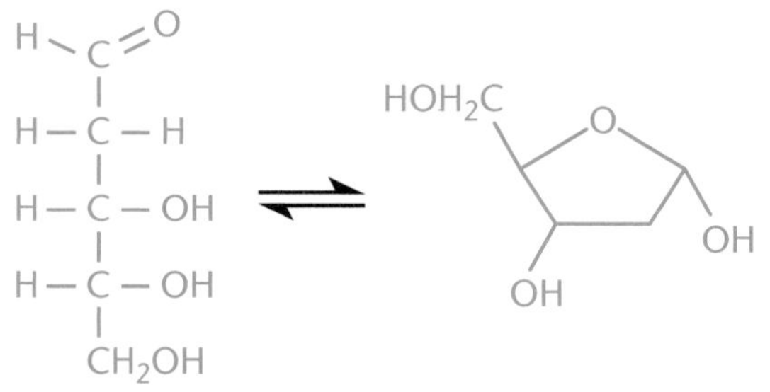

A. D aldose, pentose, pyranose ring, β anomer
B. D aldose, pentose, furanose ring, α anomer
C. L ketose, pentose, furanose ring, α anomer
D. L aldose, hexose, furanose ring, α anomer

21. In the open and ring structures in the previous question, which carbons are chiral centers in the open and ring forms, respectively?

A. C3 and C4; C3 and C4
B. C1, C3, and C4; C1, C3, C4 and C5
C. C3 and C4; C1, C3 and C4
D. C1, C2, and C5; C2 and C5

22. Which of the following structure(s) are nonreducing sugars?

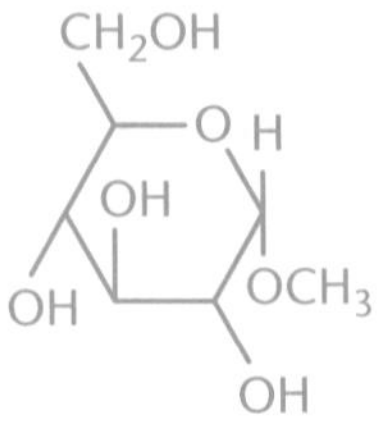

I

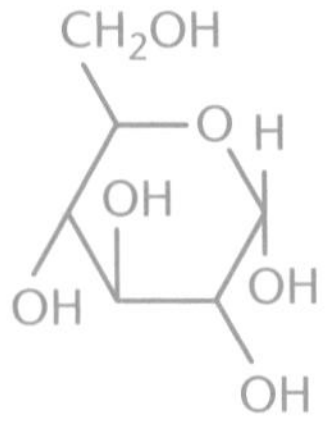

II

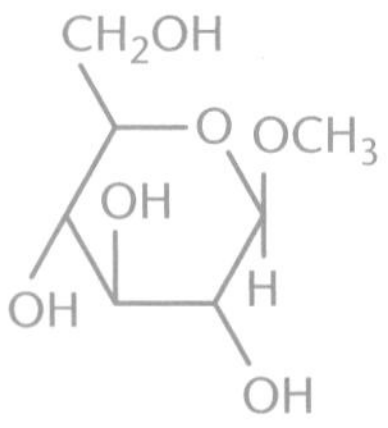

III

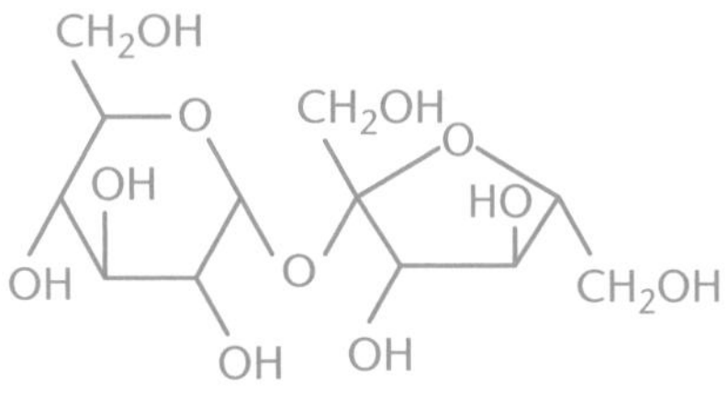

IV

A. I
B. II, III
C. IV
D. I, III, and IV

23. Fehling's solution, Tollen's reagent, and bromine water will all oxidize glucose.

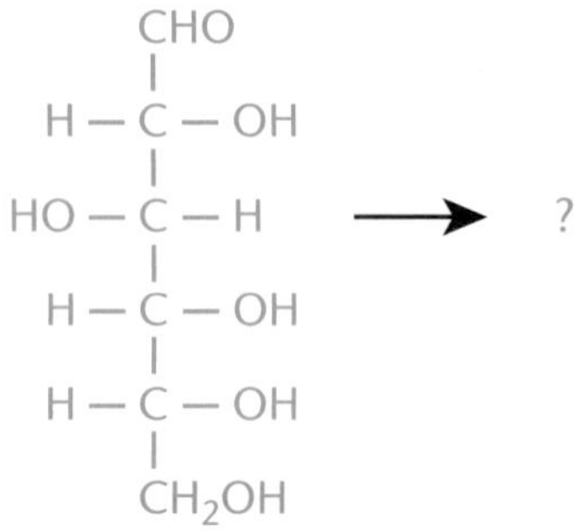

$$\text{CHO}$$
$$\text{H} - \text{C} - \text{OH}$$
$$\text{HO} - \text{C} - \text{H} \quad \longrightarrow \quad ?$$
$$\text{H} - \text{C} - \text{OH}$$
$$\text{H} - \text{C} - \text{OH}$$
$$\text{CH}_2\text{OH}$$

Which of the following structures shown represents the only product produced by oxidizing glucose with bromine water?

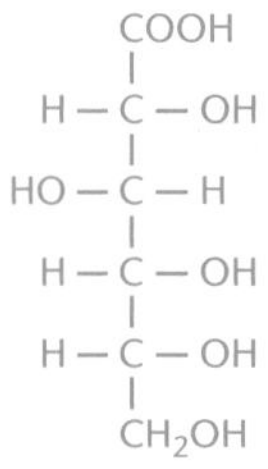

I

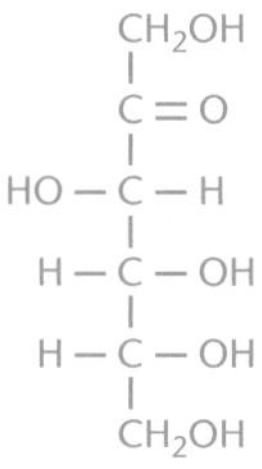

II

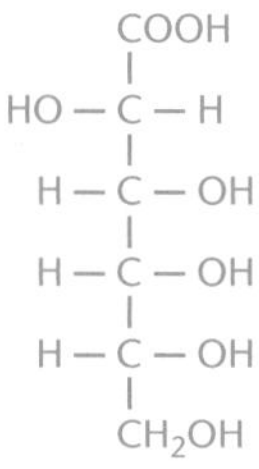

III

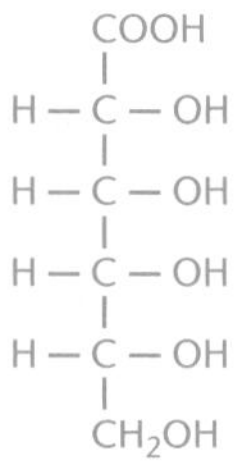

IV

A. I
B. II
C. III
D. IV

24. Which sequence of treatments would yield the structure shown below from fructose?

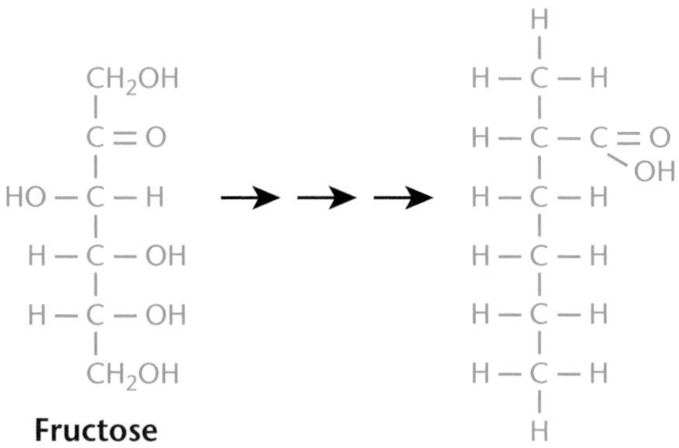

Fructose

A. Acetic anhydride → hydrolysis → HI, heat →

B. HCN → HI, heat → hydrolysis →

C. HCN → hydrolysis → HI, heat →

D. H_2, Ni → HI, heat →

25. What is observed, respectively, by 1) treating glucose with acetic anhydride, and 2) treating glucose with hydrogen and nickel?

A. 4 carbonyl groups; 5 hydroxyl groups

B. 5 carbonyl groups; 4 hydroxyl groups

C. 6 carbonyl groups; 6 hydroxyl groups

D. 1 carbonyl group; 4 hydroxyl groups

26. Which of the compounds shown below will NOT form the same structure as the other three upon treatment with phenylhydrazine followed by warm acid?

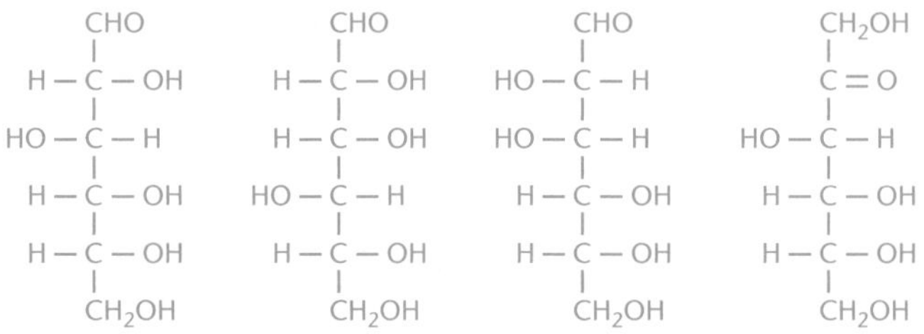

I	II	III	IV
Glucose	Gulose	Mannose	Fructose

A. I

B. II

C. III

D. IV

27. Which of the following statements is true of the ATP molecule shown below?

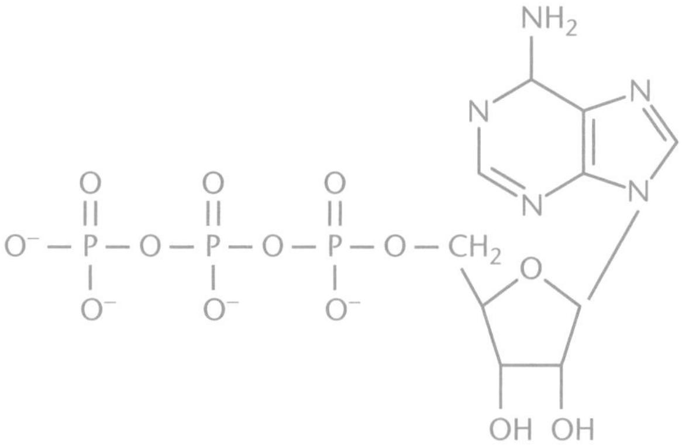

Adenosine Triphosphate (ATP)

A. ATP is a glycoside.

B. ATP is a sugar ester.

C. It has a phosphodiester linkage.

D. A and B only

28. The phosphodiester linkage between sugar and phosphate in DNA is relatively resistant to alkaline hydrolysis compared to the similar linkage in RNA. Which of the factors below contributes to this fact?

A. The triphosphate is a triprotic acid.

B. The –OH group on C2 of ribose can be attacked by an unbound –OH group on the triphosphate.

C. The lack of an –OH group on C2 of deoxyribose removes a target for rearrangement of the triphosphate ester linkage.

D. All of the above

29. What product is expected after treatment of β-D-(+)-glucose with methanol and HCl?

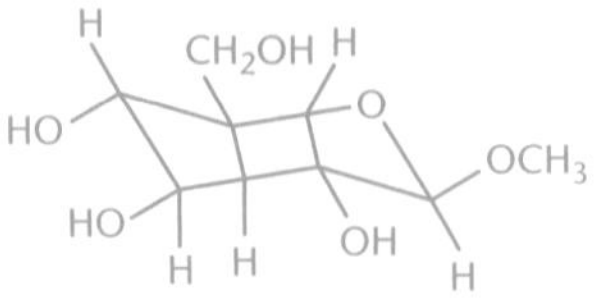

I

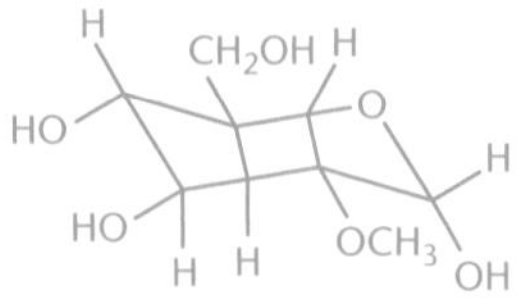

II

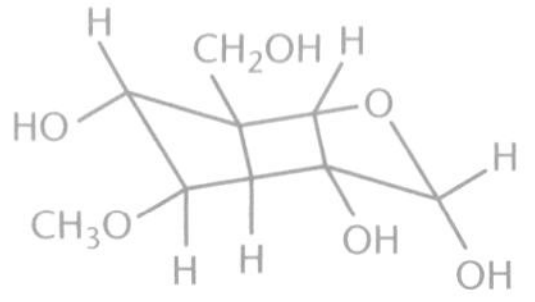

III

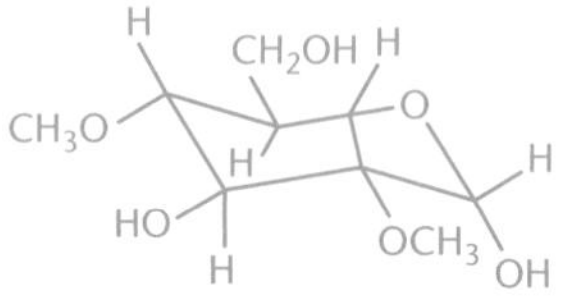

IV

A. I
B. II
C. III
D. IV

QUESTIONS 30–32 ARE NOT BASED ON A DESCRIPTIVE PASSAGE.

30. Which of the following halogens, if reacted with isobutane in the presence of ultraviolet light, will produce a compound with a tertiary carbon?

A. Fluorine
B. Bromine
C. Chlorine
D. Iodine

31. Alcohols most commonly react via bimolecular nucleophilic substitution.

Which of the following does NOT describe this type of reaction?

  I. The rate-limiting step has a molecularity of two.
 II. The reaction produces a racemic mixture of products.
III. An inversion of molecular geometry occurs

A. I and II only
B. II and III only
C. II only
D. I, II, and III

32. Which of the following will most readily react with an amine to form an amide?

A. Acyl chloride
B. Ester
C. Carboxylic acid
D. Acid anhydride

PASSAGE IV (QUESTIONS 33–39)

The citric acid cycle, or Kreb's cycle, is an enzymatic pathway that is important for cellular respiration. The enzymes in this pathway combine acetyl-coA with oxaloacetate to form citrate, which is degraded back to oxaloacetate through a series of reactions. The energy from these reactions is used to generate high-energy molecules such as GTP, NADH, and $FADH_2$. The intermediates of the citric acid cycle include several mono-, di- and tricarboxylic acids, including citric acid, succinic acid, and oxaloacetic acid.

The citric acid cycle is found in various organisms from humans to bacteria, though there are differences in the structure of the intermediates. Herbicides and pesticides have been designed to take advantage of these differences to inhibit the citric acid cycle. Some of these inhibitors are shown below.

Malonic acid

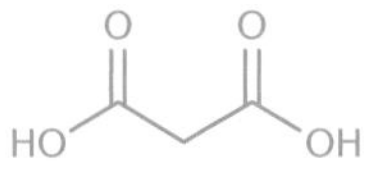

Fluoroacetic acid

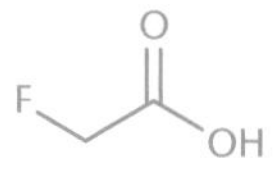

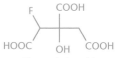
Fluorocitric acid

Various physical and chemical properties have been determined for intermediates of the citric acid cycle as well as for putative inhibitors. Elucidation of these properties is important for chemical and biological applications.

33. Which of the following can most effectively synthe-size malonic acid from acetic acid?

A. Br_2/PBr_3, then NaCN, and finally aqueous acid
B. Excess methanol in aqueous acid
C. Base, followed by formic acid, then acid neutralization
D. $KMnO_4$

34. Although there are known inhibitors of the citric acid cycle, the pH of mitochondrial matrix can alter the charges on various carboxylic acids, based on the pH, which may have an affect on the rate of the reactions taking place within the cycle. Which of the following pairs does NOT describe their relative acidities?

A.

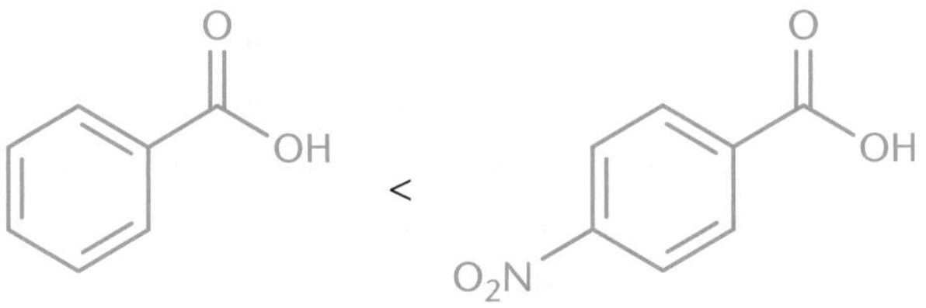

B.

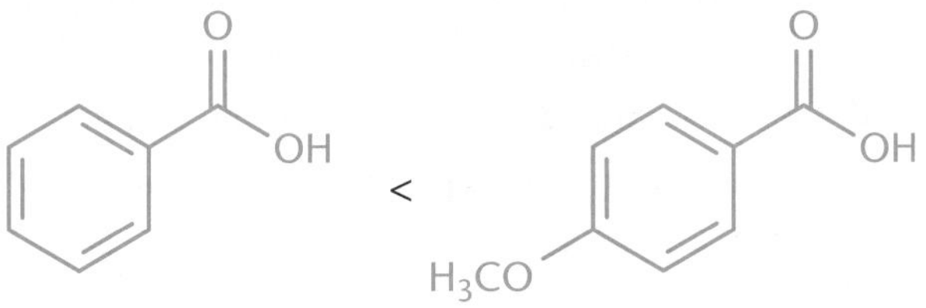

C.

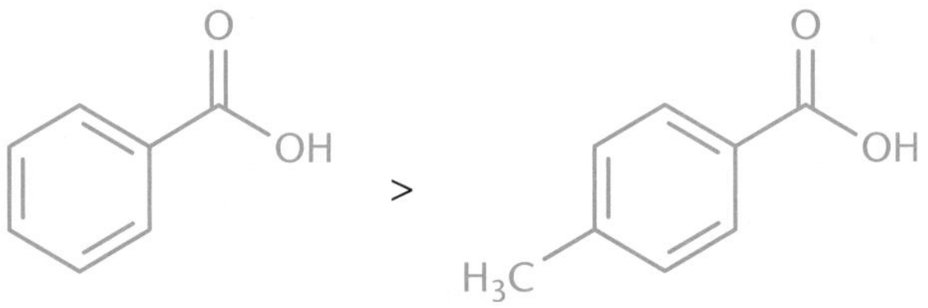

D.

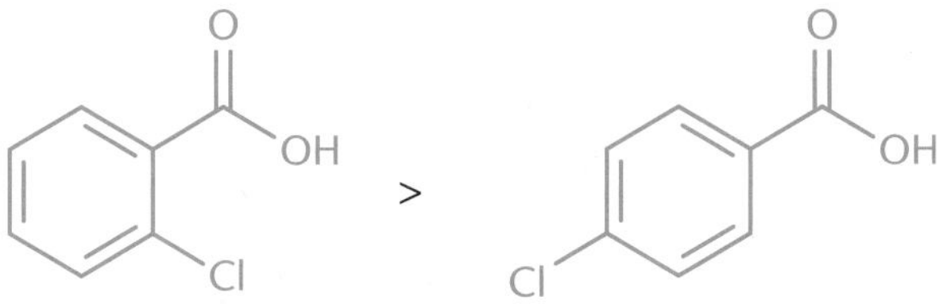

35. Isocitric acid (below) is one of the intermediates of the citric acid cycle. Which of the following names is the correct IUPAC name for isocitric acid?

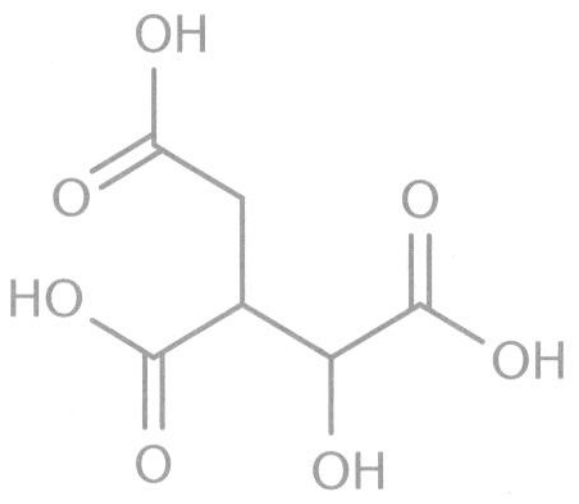

Isocitric Acid

A. Tricarboxyl-2-pentanol
B. 2-hydroxy-3-carboxypentadicarboxylic acid
C. 1-hydroxypropane-1,2,3-tricarboxylic acid
D. 2-hydroxy-3-oxo-pentadicarboxylic acid

36. Which of the following statements is NOT correct?

A. Fluoroacetic acid is more acidic than chloroacetic acid is.
B. Trifluoroacetic acid is more acidic than fluoroacetic acid is.
C. Succinic acid ($HOOCCH_2CH_2COOH$) is more acidic than malonic acid is.
D. 2-fluorobutanoic acid is more acidic than 4-fluorobutanoic acid is.

37. Which of the following reactions described below is NOT likely to occur in the presence of heat?

A. 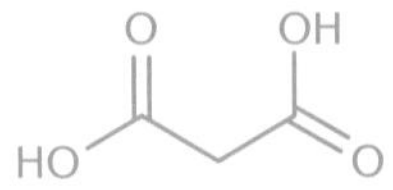 forms a monocarboxylic acid

B. 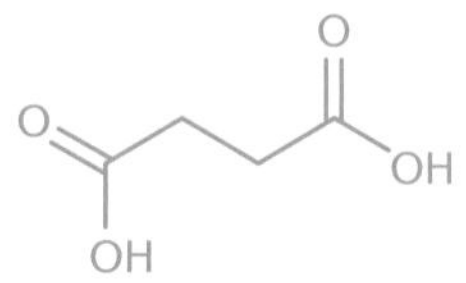 forms a cyclic compound

C. 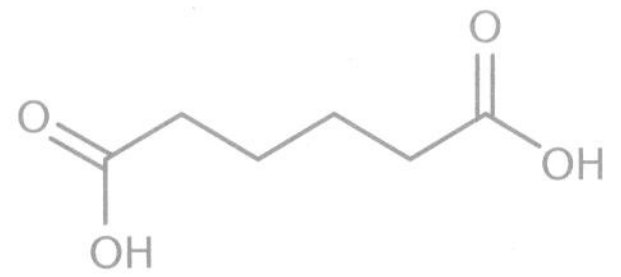 forms a cyclic compound

D. 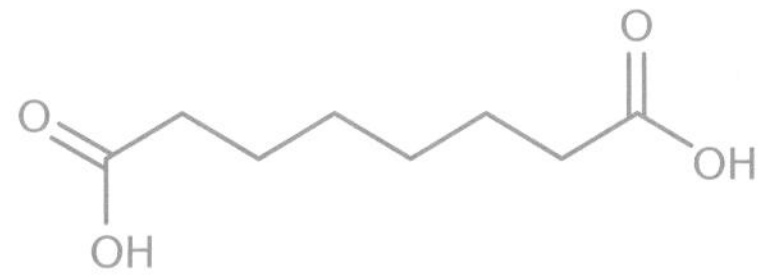 forms a cyclic compound

38. Adipic acid and succinic acid can be synthesized from tetrahydrofuran (below). Which of the following statements is NOT true of these syntheses?

THF 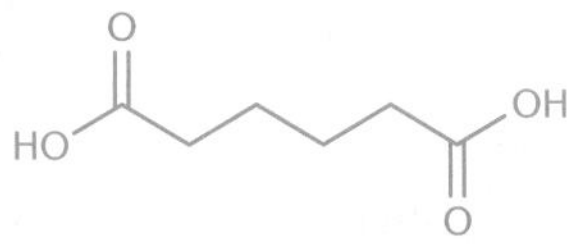   Adipic acid 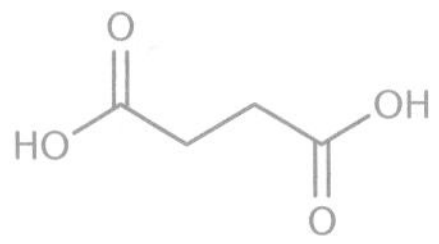   Succinic acid

A. THF is treated with concentrated HI.
B. There is an oxidation step in the synthesis of adipic acid.
C. There is dicarbonation in the synthesis of adipic acid.
D. A diol intermediate forms in the synthesis of succinic acid.

39. A bacterium is found to have an enzyme that cleaves fluorocitric acid into fluoroacetic acid and oxaloacetate. Which of the following is the simplest mechanism leading to cleavage?

A. Removing hydrogen from the alcohol group
B. Nucleophilic attack by threonine side chain on carbonyl carbon
C. Nucleophilic attack by cysteine side chain on carbonyl carbon
D. Fluoride ion acting as nucleophile

PASSAGE V (QUESTIONS 40–46)

Without the aid of spectroscopy or polarimetry, Emil Fischer was able to determine the absolute structure of glucose using several simple reactions. One of these reactions, the *Ruff degradation*, shortens aldoses by removing the aldehyde group as carbon dioxide via oxidation to carboxylic acids (Figure 1). Sugars can also be oxidized to aldaric acids in the presence of nitric acid (Figure 2). Fischer also developed a method of interchanging the end groups of any sugar without affecting the stereochemistry of the other chiral centers (Figure 3). Finally, the *Kiliani-Fischer synthesis* lengthens a sugar molecule by one carbon atom (Figure 4).

CHO
|
(CHOH)$_n$ $\xrightarrow[\text{2. H}_2\text{O}_2,\ \text{Fe}_2(\text{SO}_4)_3]{\text{1. Br}_2,\ \text{H}_2\text{O}}$ CHO
| |
CH$_2$OH   (CHOH)$_{n-1}$ + CO$_2$
                                                         |
                                                         CH$_2$OH

Figure 1

CHO   CO$_2$H
| $\xrightarrow{\text{HNO}_3}$ |
(CHOH)$_n$ (CHOH)$_n$
| |
CH$_2$OH   CO$_2$H

Figure 2

CHO   CH$_2$OH
| $\xrightarrow{\text{Several steps}}$ |
(CHOH)$_n$ (CHOH)$_n$
| |
CH$_2$OH   CHO

Figure 3

CHO   CHO
| $\xrightarrow[\text{2. H}_3\text{O}^+]{\text{1. HCN}}$ |
(CHOH)$_n$ (CHOH)$_{n+1}$
| |
CH$_2$OH   CH$_2$OH

Figure 4

Before determining the structure of glucose, Fischer knew that glucose is an optically active aldohexose that can be degraded to D-(+)-glyceraldehyde. Fischer also devised a two-dimensional representation of three-dimensional molecules, now known as the Fischer projection, which is particularly useful for describing sugars and their derivatives, by readily providing stereochemical information.

40. What is the IUPAC name for D-(+)-glyceraldehyde, shown below?

CHO
H —|— OH
CH$_2$OH

    A. (2R)-2,3-Dihydroxypropanal
    B. (2R)-1,2-Dihydroxypropan-3-al
    C. (2S)-1,2-Dihydroxypropan-3-al
    D. (2S)-2,3-Dihydroxypropanal

41. Ruff degradation of D-(+)-glucose and D-(+)-mannose gives the same aldopentose (D-(-)-arabinose). Which of the following does this suggest?

    A. Glucose and mannose are enantiomers.
    B. Glucose and mannose are C3 epimers.
    C. Glucose and mannose are C2 epimers.
    D. Glucose and mannose are identical.

42. To differentiate between glucose and mannose, Fischer interchanges the end groups of those sugars (Figure 3). When this reaction is performed on D-(+)-mannose, the product is again D-(+)-mannose; which of the following sugars is D-(+)-mannose?

A.
CHO
H —|— OH
H —|— OH
HO —|— H
HO —|— H
CH$_2$OH

B.
CHO
H —|— OH
HO —|— H
H —|— OH
HO —|— H
CH$_2$OH

C.
CHO
H —|— OH
HO —|— H
H —|— OH
H —|— OH
CH$_2$OH

D.
CHO
HO —|— H
HO —|— H
H —|— OH
H —|— OH
CH$_2$OH

43. Suppose that when performing the reaction shown in Figure 1, the reagents in step 1 are replaced by HNO_3. What is the most likely change observed in the product?

   A. The functional groups on either end will be switched.
   B. The products are two smaller carboxylic acids.
   C. The product contains two fewer carbon atoms than the reactant.
   D. The product is optically inactive since all the –OH groups are oxidized.

44. A Kiliani-Fischer synthesis is performed on D-(+)-glyceraldehyde. Which of the molecules below correctly illustrates the intermediate after step 1?

A.
```
      CN
HO ──┼── H
 H ──┼── OH
    CH₂OH
```
B.
```
    CH₂NH₂
HO ──┼── H
 H ──┼── OH
    CH₂OH
```
C.
```
   H    NH
HO ──┼── H
 H ──┼── OH
    CH₂OH
```
D.
```
    CH₂CN
 H ──┼── OH
    CH₂OH
```

45. When a Kiliani-Fischer synthesis is performed on D-(+)-glyceraldehyde, there are two tetroses possible. What is the relationship between them?

   A. They are enantiomers.
   B. They are structural isomers.
   C. They are geometric isomers.
   D. They are diastereomers.

46. Suppose that instead of D-sugars, L-sugars are the most common naturally occurring sugars. How does this affect the optical rotation of the corresponding aldohexoses?

   A. The optical rotation of the L-sugars has the same magnitude as D-sugars, but they have opposite signs.
   B. The optical rotation of the L-sugars is twice the magnitude of D-sugars, but they have the same sign.
   C. The optical rotation of the L-sugars has the same magnitude and sign as the D-sugars.
   D. There is no correlation between optical rotation and L/D designations.

PASSAGE VI (QUESTIONS 47–52)

Carbon is one of the most abundant elements on Earth and is a major component of all organisms. Carbon has four valence electrons available for bonding, making it possible for carbon to join with an array of other elements to potentially form an infinite number of compounds. For these reasons, the analysis and synthesis of carbon-based compounds plays a key role in the pharmaceutical industry.

Some colleagues are attempting to develop a new drug with analgesic and antipyretic properties, which will outcompete those currently on the market. To do this, they have developed several structures in an attempt to increase the absorption rate of the ingested drug. The drug designers hope that the added hydroxyl and carbonyl groups will allow for increased hydrogen bonding with polar water molecules inside the human body. If this is the case, then perhaps it will be easier for the drug to cross biological barriers, such as the lumen of the stomach, and be carried in the blood to its targets.

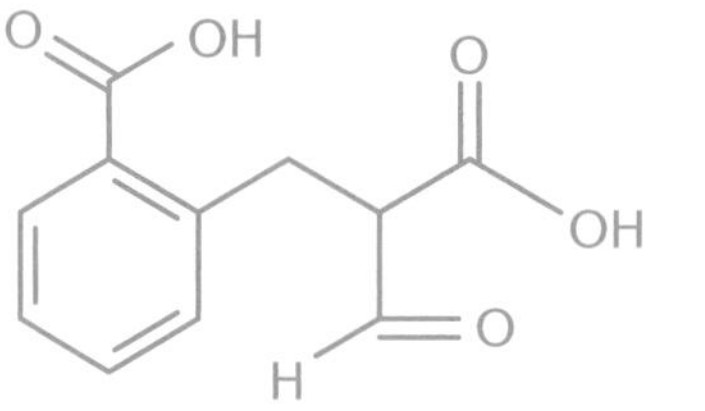

Drug A

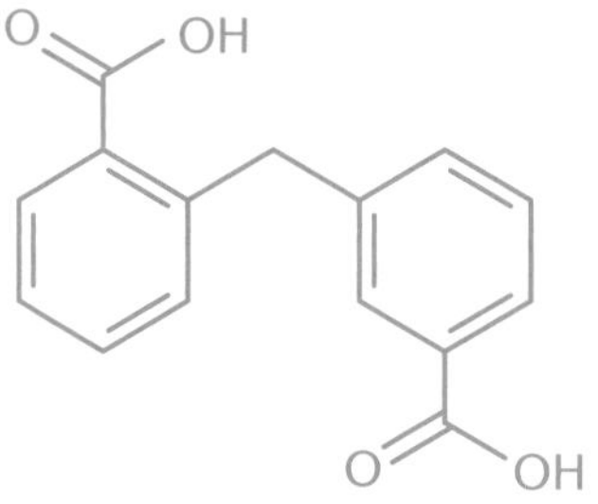

Drug B

47. Despite having different structures, drugs A and B have a common feature on their IR spectra. Which of the following is a correct description of that feature?

A. Both drugs have an absorption band at 2,200 cm^{-1}.

B. Both drugs have a broad absorption centered at 3,500 cm^{-1}.

C. Both drugs have a characteristic double absorption band at 2,850 and 2,750 cm^{-1}.

D. Both drugs have a large overtone that spans 3,500 to 2,500 cm^{-1}.

48. What is the correct electron configuration for carbon?

A. $1s^2\ 2s^2\ 2p^2$

B. $1s^2\ 2s^2$

C. $1s^2\ 2s^2\ 2p^6\ 3s^2\ 3p^2$

D. $1s^2\ 2s^2\ 2p^6$

49. How would one best describe the overlap of orbitals that is required to form pi bonds seen in the structure of drugs A and B?

A. Parallel overlap of two s orbitals

B. Overlap of one s and one p orbital

C. Perpendicular overlap of two p orbitals

D. Parallel overlap of two p orbitals

50. For each hydrogenation reaction below, energy is released per double bond reduced. In which reaction will the energy per double bond be MOST negative?

A.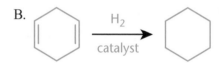

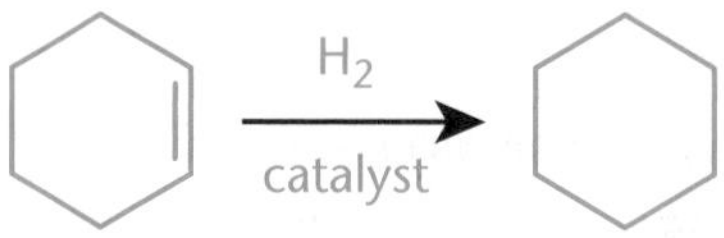

B.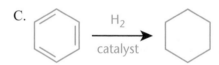

C.

D. The energy is always equal for each individual double bond.

51. While attempting to manufacture drug A, a chemist isolates an impurity. He analyzes the molecule in order to determine the structure of several bonds in question. An image of the molecule can be seen below.

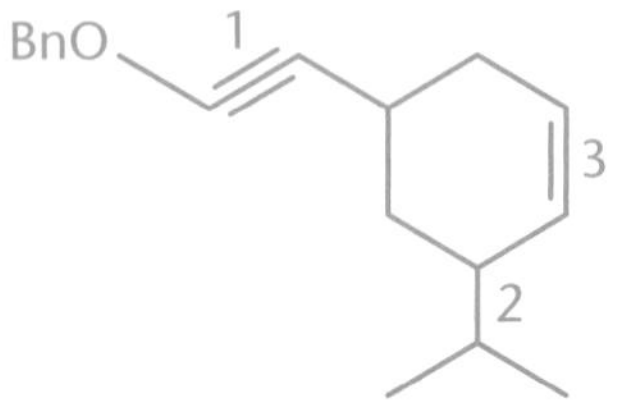

Which of the following is most likely true?

A. The bond lengths increase in the order of 2<3<1, while the bond strengths increase in the order of 1<3<2.

B. The bond lengths decrease in the order of 2>3>1, while the bond strengths decrease in the order of 1>3>2.

C. The bond lengths increase in the order of 1<3<2, while the bond strengths increase in the order of 1<3<2.

D. The bond lengths decrease in the order of 2>3>1, while the bond strengths increase in the order of 1<3<2.

52. A chemist hopes to create a method of deactivating drugs A and B in order to prevent their quick absorption through the lumen of the stomach. Which of the following treatments should he investigate as a basis for this task?

A. Hydrogenation (H_2 over Pd)
B. Forming methyl esters from all the carboxylic acid groups present
C. Reduction with $LiAlH_4$
D. Substitution with $SOCl_2$

Practice Section 2

Time—70 minutes

QUESTIONS 1–52

Directions: Most of the questions in the following Organic Chemistry Practice Section are organized into groups, with a descriptive passage preceding each group of questions. Study the passage, then select the single best answer to the question in each group. Some of the questions are not based on a descriptive passage; you must also select the best answer to these questions. If you are unsure of the best answer, eliminate the choices that you know are incorrect, then select an answer from the choices that remain.

Period	1 IA 1A	2 IIA 2A	3 IIIB 3B	4 IVB 4B	5 VB 5B	6 VIB 6B	7 VIIB 7B	8 ------- VIII ----- -- ------- 8 -------	9	10	11 IB 1B	12 IIB 2B	13 IIIA 3A	14 IVA 4A	15 VA 5A	16 VIA 6A	17 VIIA 7A	18 vIIIA 8A
1	1 H 1.008																	2 He 4.003
2	3 Li 6.941	4 Be 9.012											5 B 10.81	6 C 12.01	7 N 14.01	8 O 16.00	9 F 19.00	10 Ne 20.18
3	11 Na 22.99	12 Mg 24.31											13 Al 26.98	14 Si 28.09	15 P 30.97	16 S 32.07	17 Cl 35.45	18 Ar 39.95
4	19 K 39.10	20 Ca 40.08	21 Sc 44.96	22 Ti 47.88	23 V 50.94	24 Cr 52.00	25 Mn 54.94	26 Fe 55.85	27 Co 58.47	28 Ni 58.69	29 Cu 63.55	30 Zn 65.39	31 Ga 69.72	32 Ge 72.59	33 As 74.92	34 Se 78.96	35 Br 79.90	36 Kr 83.80
5	37 Rb 85.47	38 Sr 87.62	39 Y 88.91	40 Zr 91.22	41 Nb 92.91	42 Mo 95.94	43 Tc (98)	44 Ru 101.1	45 Rh 102.9	46 Pd 106.4	47 Ag 107.9	48 Cd 112.4	49 In 114.8	50 Sn 118.7	51 Sb 121.8	52 Te 127.6	53 I 126.9	54 Xe 131.3
6	55 Cs 132.9	56 Ba 137.3	57 La* 138.9	72 Hf 178.5	73 Ta 180.9	74 W 183.9	75 Re 186.2	76 Os 190.2	77 Ir 190.2	78 Pt 195.1	79 Au 197.0	80 Hg 200.5	81 Tl 204.4	82 Pb 207.2	83 Bi 209.0	84 Po (210)	85 At (210)	86 Rn (222)
7	87 Fr (223)	88 Ra (226)	89 Ac~ (227)	104 Rf (257)	105 Db (260)	106 Sg (263)	107 Bh (262)	108 Hs (265)	109 Mt (266)	110 --- ()	111 --- ()	112 --- ()		114 --- ()		116 --- ()		118 --- ()

Lanthanide Series*	58 Ce 140.1	59 Pr 140.9	60 Nd 144.2	61 Pm (147)	62 Sm 150.4	63 Eu 152.0	64 Gd 157.3	65 Tb 158.9	66 Dy 162.5	67 Ho 164.9	68 Er 167.3	69 Tm 168.9	70 Yb 173.0	71 Lu 175.0
Actinide Series~	90 Th 232.0	91 Pa (231)	92 U (238)	93 Np (237)	94 Pu (242)	95 Am (243)	96 Cm (247)	97 Bk (247)	98 Cf (249)	99 Es (254)	100 Fm (253)	101 Md (256)	102 No (254)	103 Lr (257)

PASSAGE I (QUESTIONS 1–8)

The Wieland-Miescher ketone (Figure 1) is one of the most versatile building blocks in synthetic chemistry, found in the synthesis of many natural products, a majority of which are medically relevant. These products have diverse applications and include compounds ranging from antimicrobial to anticancer agents. The Wieland-Miescher ketone is prepared from two other commonly used building blocks, shown below, via a Robinson annulation.

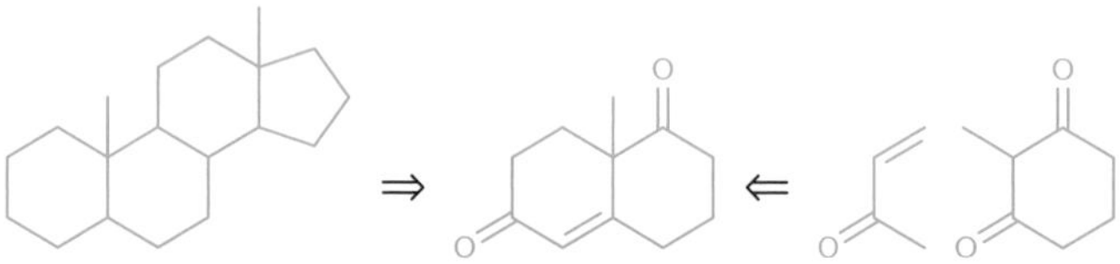

Androstane   Wieland-Miescher ketone   I   II

Figure 1

One of the earliest uses of the Wieland-Miescher ketone was in the synthesis of steroids, because it contains two of the four rings in the steroid skeleton. An example is the synthesis of androstane, the steroid hydrocarbon backbone, accessible from two other precursor molecules (compounds III and V; Figures 2 and 3).

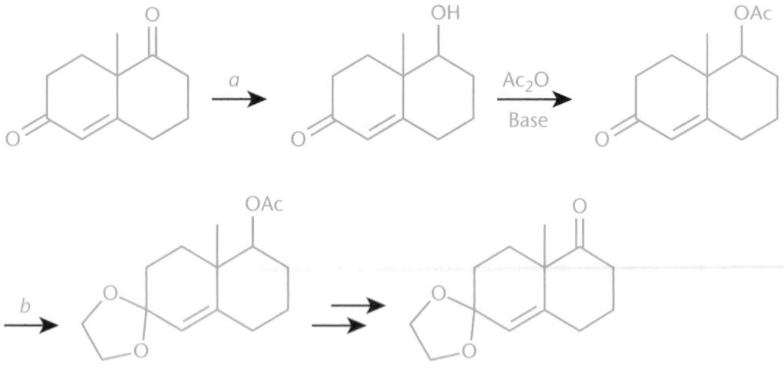

III

Figure 2

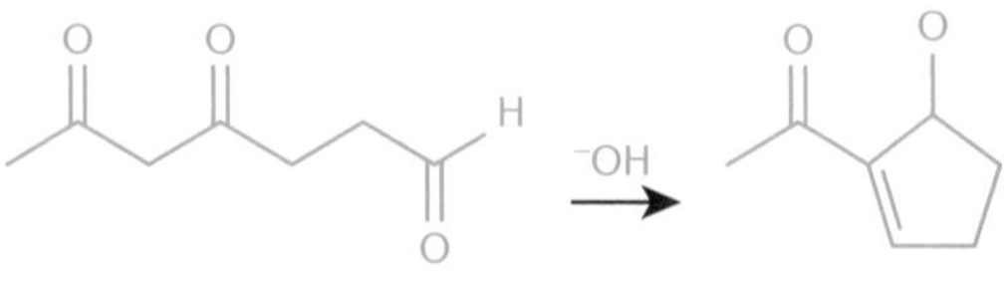

IV   V

Figure 3

1. What is the IUPAC name of compound I?

   A. 3-buten-2-one

   B. 1-buten-3-one

   C. Vinyl methyl ketone

   D. 2-buten-2-one

2. Which of the following can selectively reduce the ketone shown in reaction a in Figure 2?

   A. $LiAlH_4$

   B. Ag_2O

   C. $NaBH_4$

   D. H_2NNH_2

3. After formation of the ester, the remaining ketone needs to be protected (reaction b). Which of the following converts the ketone to the acetal shown in Figure 2?

   A. $2\ CH_3OH,\ H_3O^+$

   B. $HOCH_2CH_2OH,\ H_2O$

   C. $2\ C_2H_5OH,\ H_3O^+$

   D. $HOCH_2CH_2OH,\ H_3O^+$

4. What is the IUPAC name of compound IV?

   A. 3,5-dioxohexanal

   B. 4,7-oxoheptan-2-one

   C. 4,6-dioxoheptanal

   D. 1,4, 6-trioxoheptane

5. Which enol of compound IV contributes to the formation of compound V?

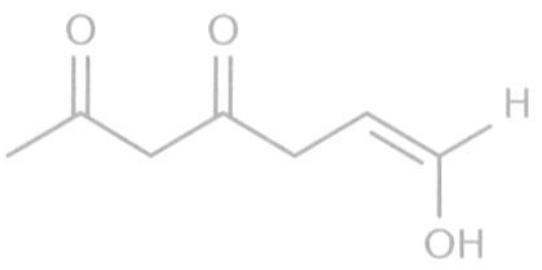

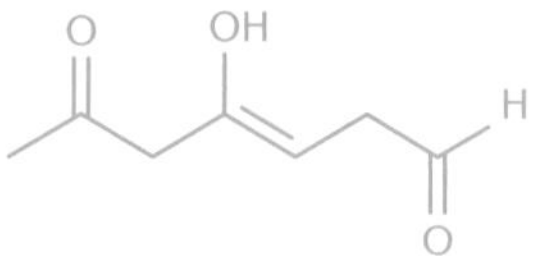

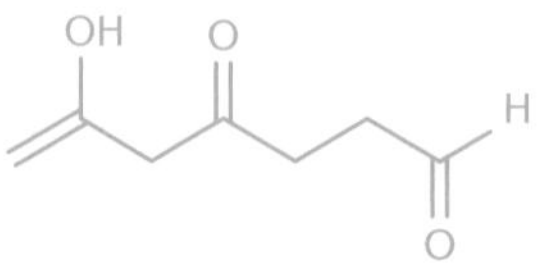

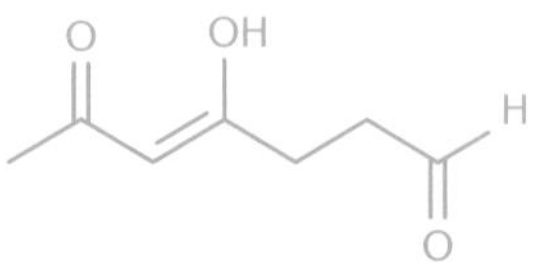

6. In the figure below, what reaction is occurring in the coupling between compounds III and V to form the steroid backbone?

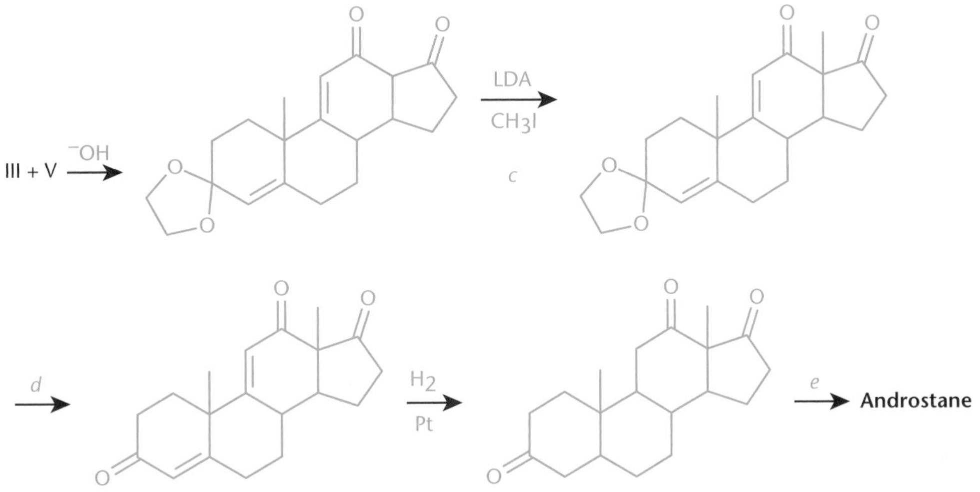

A. Ketal formation

B. Robinson annulation

C. Wolff-Kishner reduction

D. Michael addition

7. What reagent is used to deprotect the ketone (reaction *d*) shown in question 6?

A. H_2O_2

B. NaOH

C. H_3O^+

D. CrO_3

8. The final step to forming androstane involves the complete reduction of all the ketone groups present (reaction *e*). Which of the following reagents can be used?

A. Hg(Zn), HCl

B. $(C_6H_5)_3P=CH_2$

C. Ag_2O

D. HCN

PASSAGE II (QUESTIONS 9–15)

Salicylic acid (Figure 1a) is an important precursor in the synthesis of various pharmaceuticals, artificial flavors, and preservatives. It is formed when sodium phenolate is combined with carbon dioxide under heat and pressure in the presence of a base. Both its carboxyl and hydroxyl groups have proven useful targets for synthetic modification. For example, the hydroxyl group of salicylic acid reacts with acetic acid to form acetylsalicylic acid, better known as aspirin. The versatility of salicylic acid is further demonstrated by the ease with which the carboxyl group forms esters with various alcohols. Some esters of salicylic acid produce molecules that absorb UV light for use in suntan lotions, while other esters are used as antiseptic and antipyretic agents. In addition to esters, amides that are formed from salicylic acid have been shown to have practical applications. A family of compounds related to salicylanilide (Figure 1b) consists of salicylic acid-related amides in which one or more hydrogen atoms are replaced by a benzene ring. Brominated salicylanilides are used as disinfectants with antibacterial and antifungal activities.

Some salicylanilide derivatives are used as pesticides while others, like oxyclozanide and rafoxanide, have antihelminthic properties.

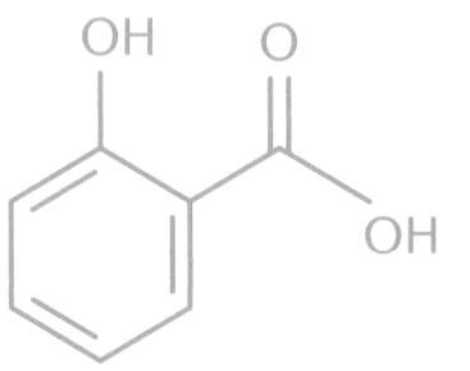

Figure 1a

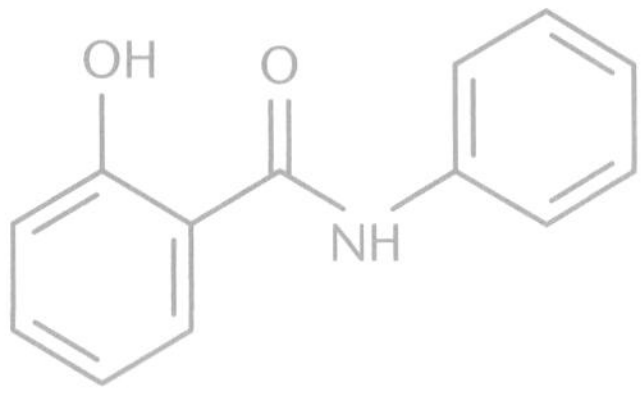

Figure 1b

A compound that is structurally related to salicylanilide and salicylic acid is acetanilide (Figure 2a). Acetanilide has antipyretic and analgesic properties and was previously marketed under the brand name Antifebrin. The well-known analgesic acetaminophen (Figure 2b) differs from acetanilide by only one hydroxyl group.

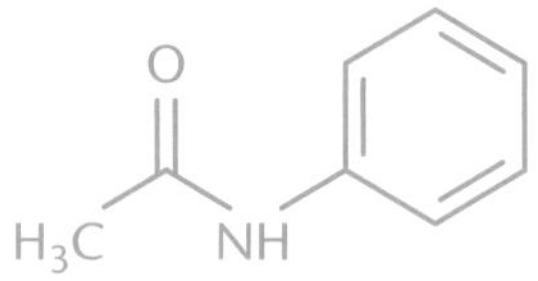

Figure 2a

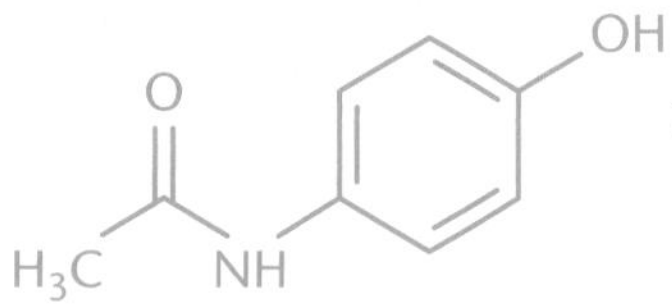

Figure 2b

9. Using a purified enzyme preparation, a scientist discovers that salicylanilide acts as a suitable substrate and is metabolized to aniline. To confirm her observations, she measures the concentration of aniline in the test medium following the assay. Which amino acid residue is LEAST likely to be responsible for the mechanism of enzyme inhibition?

A. Leucine
B. Serine
C. Cysteine
D. Lysine

10. What is the major product of salicylanilide and LiAlH$_4$?

A.

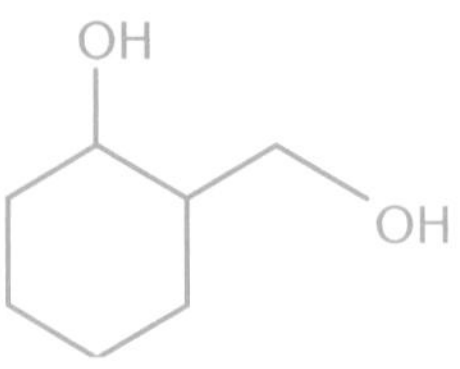

B.

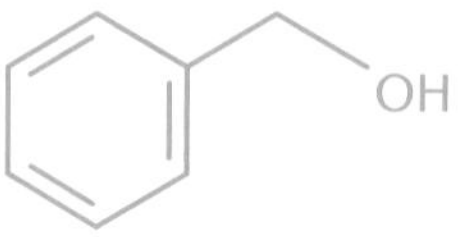

C.

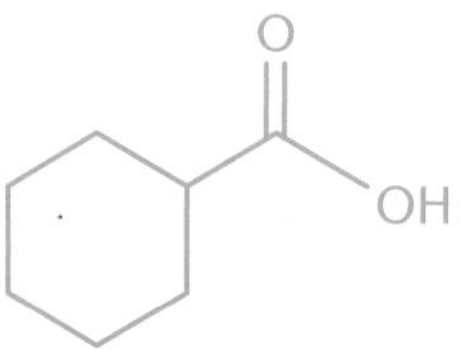

D.

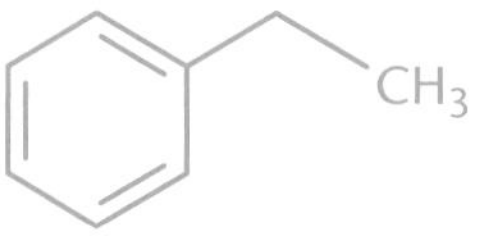

11. A chemist is attempting a novel synthesis of salicylanilide in which benzoic acid is formed from phenol. Which of the following is true?

A. KCr$_2$O$_7$, H$_2$SO$_4$, water → excellent yield
B. Bleach, acetic acid → good yield
C. CrO$_3$-pyridine, CH$_2$Cl$_2$ → good yield
D. None of the above

12. In an analogue of salicylanilide, the amide bond has been replaced with an ester bond (the nitrogen atom is now oxygen). This analogue is heated with NaOH and then acidified. Which of the following are among the major products?

A.

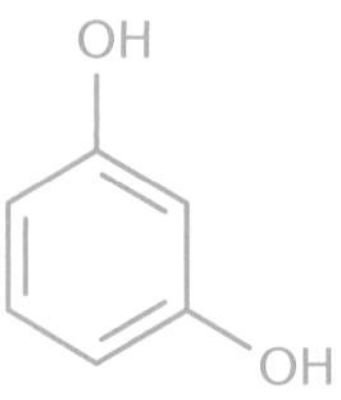

B.

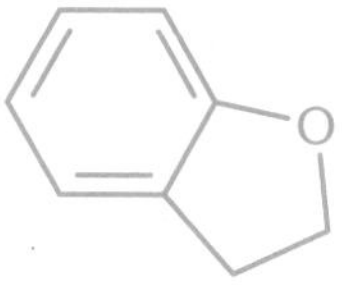

C.

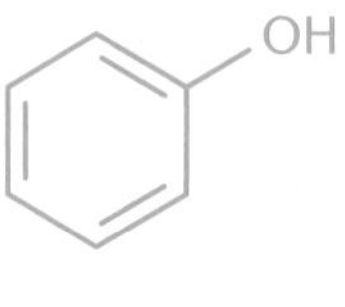

D.

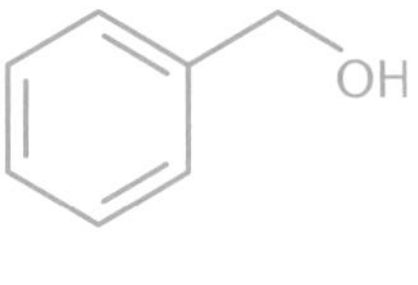

13. If the molecule in Figure 3 below undergoes a Hofmann rearrangement, what is the product?

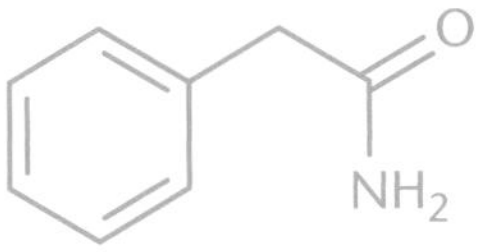

Figure 3

A.

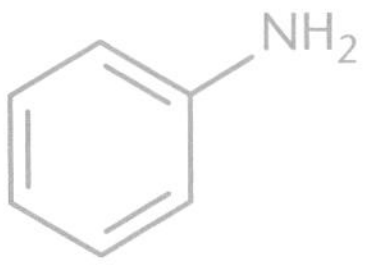

B.

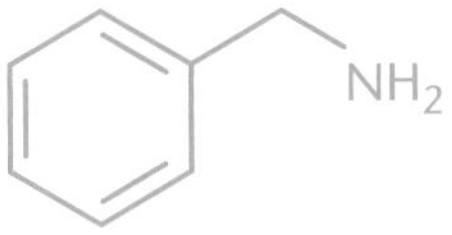

C.

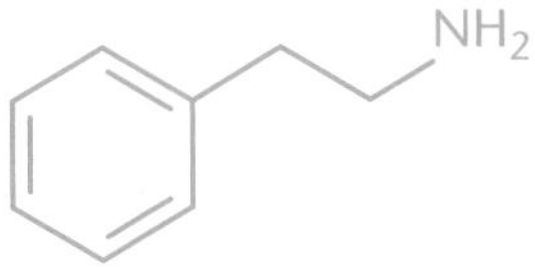

D.

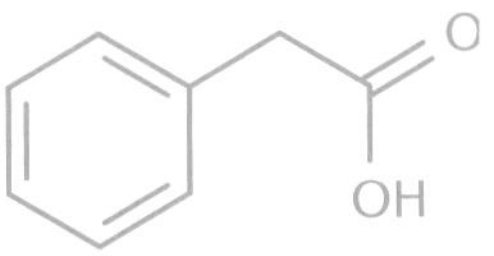

14. What is the IUPAC name for salicylanilide?

A. 2-hydroxy-N-phenyl-benzamide
B. 3-hydroxybenzanilide
C. 3-oxo-3-anilido-phenol
D. 3-hydroxy-1-cyano-N-phenylbenzoic acid

15. Which of the following syntheses gives the highest yield of acetanilide?

A.

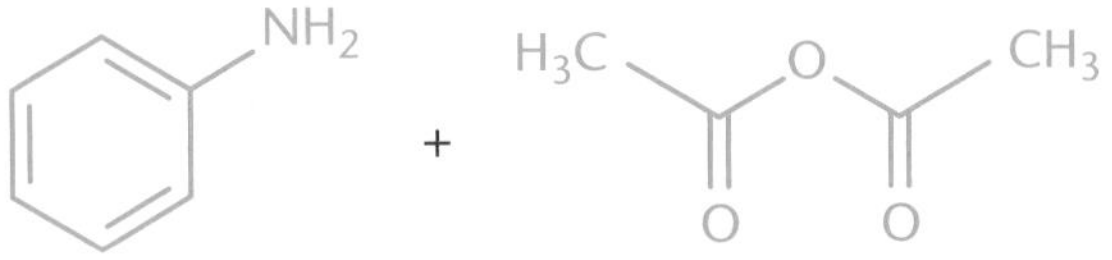

B.

C.

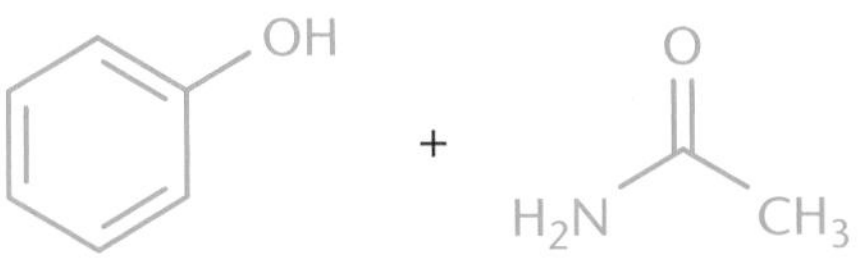

D.

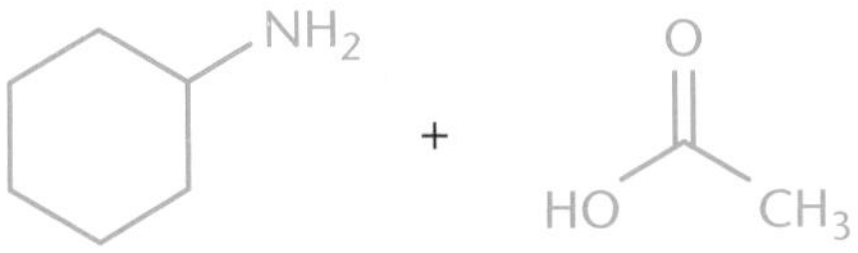

QUESTIONS 16–19 ARE NOT BASED ON A DESCRIPTIVE PASSAGE.

16. Which of the following reactions is NOT characteristic of a carboxylic acid?

A. Nucleophilic substitution
B. Decarboxylation
C. Esterification
D. Nucleophilic addition

17. Nitriles are hydrolyzed to amines under mild polar conditions and mild heat.

What is the product of the same reaction under more extreme polarity (very acidic or basic) and higher temperatures?

A. Aldehyde
B. Ester
C. Carboxylic acid
D. Ketone

18. The partial double-bond character of the peptide bonds formed between amino acids in a polypeptide has its most significant impact on which enzyme structure?

A. Primary
B. Secondary
C. Tertiary
D. Quaternary

19. What is the maximum number of isomeric pairs that can be formed from mononitration of chlorobenzene?

A. 1
B. 2
C. 3
D. 4

PASSAGE III (QUESTIONS 20–28)

Mass spectrometry (MS) involves the bombardment of the original molecule (M) with electrons to form radical cations:

$$M + e^- \rightarrow M^{+\cdot} + 2e^-$$

Radical cations fragment to smaller pieces, and only stable cation fragments are detected for the mass spectrum, at their mass/charge (m/z) ratio (for simplicity, only fragments with charge = +1 will be considered). Several common fragmentation patterns are listed in Table 1.

Table 1

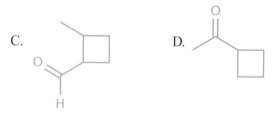

McLafferty Rearrangement	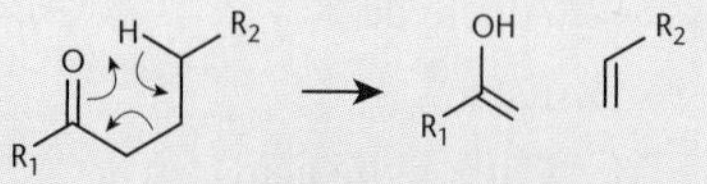
α-cleavage	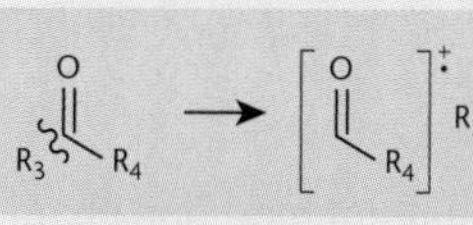
Alkanes	Cleavage to give most stable carbocation
Alkenes	Cleavage to give allylic cations
Alcohols	Cleavage of − OH via loss of H₂O; α-cleavage
Amines	α-cleavage

A student obtains a mass spectrum of compound Y, with molecular formula $C_6H_{10}O$, and key fragments occur at m/z values of 41 and 29, as well as two smaller peaks occurring at m/z 57 and 43. Through more tests on compound Y, the student deduces that compound Y contains a cyclobutane ring, an aldehyde group, and a methyl group. The student also finds from the mass spectrum that:

(1) a McLafferty Rearrangement takes place, *before any fragmentation occurs*;
(2) the parent peak is the base peak.

20. On a mass spectrum, abundances are measured relative to the

A. parent peak.
B. smallest peak.
C. number of possible fragments.
D. base peak.

21. At what m/z value does the base peak for compound Y occur?

A. 94
B. 96
C. 98
D. 100

22. The enol fragment resulting from McLafferty rearrangements typically isomerizes to what type of compound?

A. Carbonyls
B. Alcohols
C. Epoxides
D. Carboxylic acids

23. Given that a McLafferty rearrangement takes place before other fragmentation occurs, what is the most likely structure of compound Y?

A.

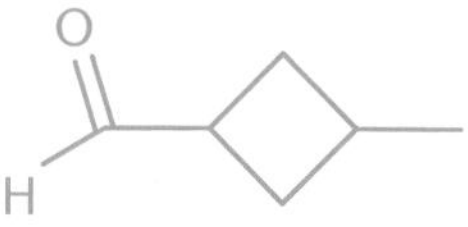

B.

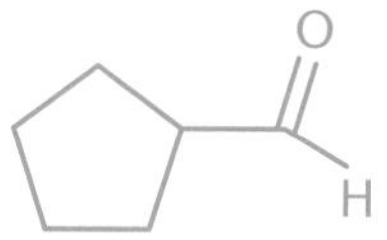

C.

D.

24. The key fragment at m/z 41 corresponds most likely to which structure?

A.    B.

C. 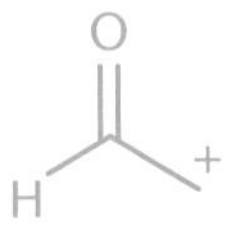   D.

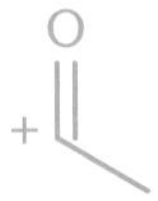

25. The key fragment at m/z 29 corresponds most likely to which structure?

A. $H—\!\!\!\equiv O^+$ B. $H_2C = CH_2$

C. $H_3C —^+$ D. $C \equiv O^+$

26. In a separate experiment, the student obtains the mass spectrum of compound Z, also with the molecular formula $C_6H_{10}O$. To her surprise, there is no parent peak, though there is a base peak at m/z 80 and a peak at m/z 31.

What functional group does compound Z most likely contain?

A. Alcohol

B. Ketone

C. Ether

D. Aldehyde

27. The key fragment at m/z 31 corresponds to which of the following structures?

A. $\left[C_2H_6\right]^{+\bullet}$ B. $\left[H_2C — NH_2\right]^{+\bullet}$

C. $\left[H_2C = O\right]^{+\bullet}$ D. $\left[HN = NH\right]^{+}$

28. The base peak at m/z 80 comes from the most stable carbocation fragment. Which of the following structures corresponds to the base peak?

A. 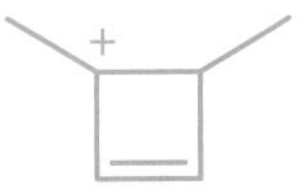   B.

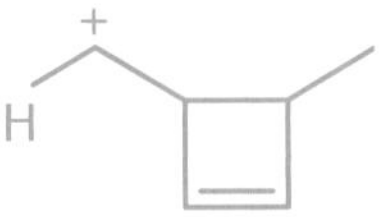

C. 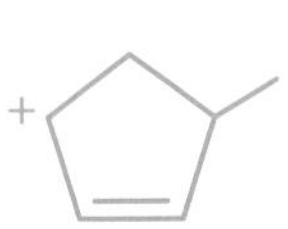   D.

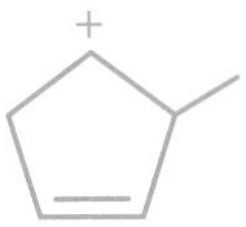

PASSAGE IV (QUESTIONS 29–36)

Compound I, with molecular formula C_7H_{12}, is an optically active molecule with one stereocenter. It is found to react with two molecules of hydrogen to give compound II, also optically active with one stereocenter.

When compound I is reacted with acidic potassium permanganate over heat, carbon dioxide is emitted, and compound III, with formula $C_6H_{12}O_2$, is also formed. Compound III is also optically active and is found to react with acidic methanol to form an optically active compound IV, with formula $C_7H_{14}O_2$.

The IR spectrum for compound III contains a broad absorbance band that spans approximately 1,000 wavenumbers, as well as a sharp absorbance at 1,720 cm^{-1}. The ^{1}H-NMR spectrum for compound III contains a characteristic singlet at 12 ppm. Several IR bond-stretching frequencies and ^{1}H-NMR chemical shifts are listed in the following table.

IR		^{1}H NMR	
Bond	Stretching frequency (cm^{-1})	Type of proton	Chemical shift (ppm)
C — O	1000–1250	—CH$_3$ (aliphatic)	0–1.5
C = O	1650–1740	—CH$_2$— (aliphatic)	1.5–3
O — H (alcohol)	3400	=CH$_2$ (alkene)	5–7
O — H (acid)	2500–3500	CHO (aldehyde)	9–10
C = C	1400–1600	—OH (acid)	10–13

29. What are the degrees of unsaturation of compound I?

A. 0

B. 1

C. 2

D. More information is needed.

30. Which of the following is a possible structure for compound I?

A. 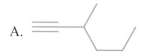 B.

C.  D.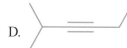

31. Which of the following might be compound II?

A. Heptane

B. 3-methylhexane

C. 2,2-dimethylpentane

D. 2-methylhexane

32. Given compound III's spectral information, what functional group does it most likely contain?

A. Carboxylic acid

B. Aldehyde

C. Ketone

D. Alcohol

33. Which of the following is a suitable catalyst for the conversion of compound I to compound II?

A. Aluminum

B. Magnesium

C. Platinum

D. Lithium

34. Using IR spectroscopy only, what will be an indication that conversion from compound I to compound II was successful?

A. Appearance of a sharp absorbance band at 1,720 cm^{-1}

B. Disappearance of a broad absorbance band at 3,400 cm^{-1}

C. Appearance of a sharp absorbance band at 960 cm^{-1}

D. Disappearance of a sharp absorbance band at 2,200 cm^{-1}

35. Suppose that instead of acidic potassium permanganate with heat, ozone followed by aqueous workup is used on compound I. Which of the following are possible products?

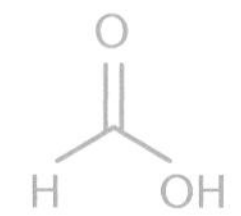

compound V

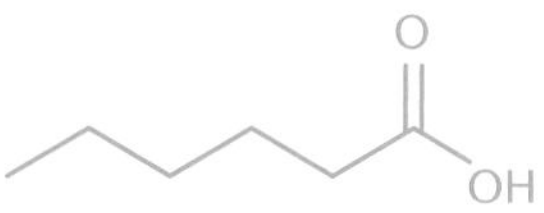

compound VI

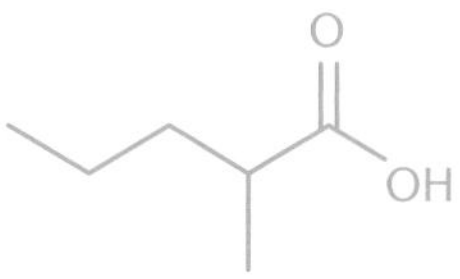

compound VII

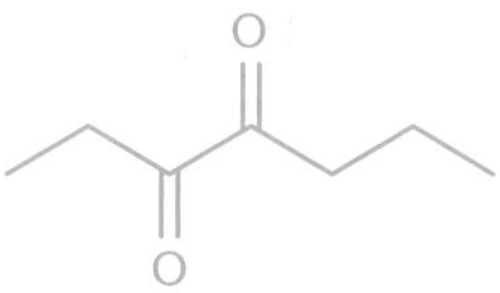

compound VIII

A. V only
B. VIII only
C. V, VI, and VIII
D. V and VII

36. Using ^{1}H-NMR spectroscopy only, what will be an indication that conversion from compound III to compound IV is successful?

A. Appearance of a singlet at 4 ppm, with the singlet at 12 ppm remaining
B. Disappearance of the singlet at 12 ppm only
C. Appearance of a singlet at 4 ppm, with the disappearance of the singlet at 12 ppm
D. Appearance of a doublet at 12 ppm

QUESTIONS 37–39 ARE NOT BASED ON A DESCRIPTIVE PASSAGE.

37. How many peaks are there in an H-NMR spectrum of 2-methyl-2-butene?

A. 2
B. 4
C. 5
D. 10

38. Which of the following is a product of the reaction between propylmagnesium bromide and ethyne?

A. 1-pentyne
B. Propane
C. 1-pentene
D. Propene

39. What is the major product of the following reaction?

$$H_2C = CH - CH_2 - OH \xrightarrow[\text{excess}]{\text{HBr}}$$

A. 1,3-dibromopropane
B. 1-bromoprop-3-ene
C. 2-bromopropan-3-ol
D. 2-hydroxypropan-3-ol

PASSAGE V (QUESTIONS 40–47)

Qualitative organic analysis is a process often employed by chemists in order to identify unknown compounds of interest. Though its origins are in the lab, chemical analysis plays an important and practical role in areas such as medicine, environmental monitoring, and forensic science. Identification of substances revolves around a set of known properties associated with specific functional groups. The difficulty of verifying a substance's identity lies in the fact that there are millions of chemically and structurally unique compounds in the world, which to the naked eye, have very few distinguishable features. In order to simplify the daunting task of sifting through each possibility, it is the chemist's duty to develop a logical and well-planned method for analysis.

As a final assignment for his chemistry lab, a student is given a set of unknown compounds and must identify each one using the techniques he learned throughout the course. The student performs solubility tests to divide the unknowns into broad categories, before testing with several reagents in order to identify functional groups. Brady's reagent (2,4-Dinitrophenylhydrazine) is a commonly used compound, which produces a yellow or red precipitate when in the presence of a carbonyl group of ketones or aldehydes. Once a carbonyl is identified, the Tollen's test can be used to make a distinction between aldehydes and ketones. Silver nitrate (Tollen's reagent) is used to oxidize the carbonyl of an aldehyde forming a carboxylic acid and an easily idenitifiable silver mirror. Once the presence of such functional groups is verified, infrared spectroscopy can then be utilized to further predict the structure. After running a series of tests on each of his unknowns, the student proposes the structures shown in Figures 1a, 1b, and 1c.

| Substance A | Substance B | Substance C |
| Figure 1a | Figure 1b | Figure 1c |

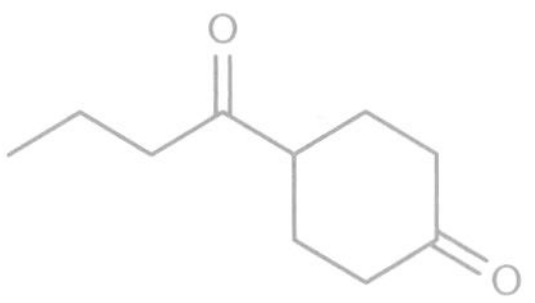

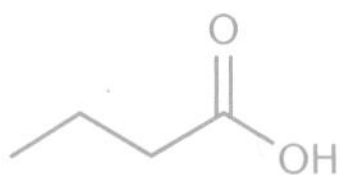

40. What is the appropriate IUPAC name for the predicted structure of substance A?

A. 4,4-dimethyl-5-pentaldehyde
B. 5-(4,4 dimethyl)-pentaldehyde
C. 2, 2-dimethylpentanal
D. 4,4-dimethylpentanal

41. A Grignard reagent is used in the reaction below. What is the IUPAC name for the product that would be produced by this reaction?

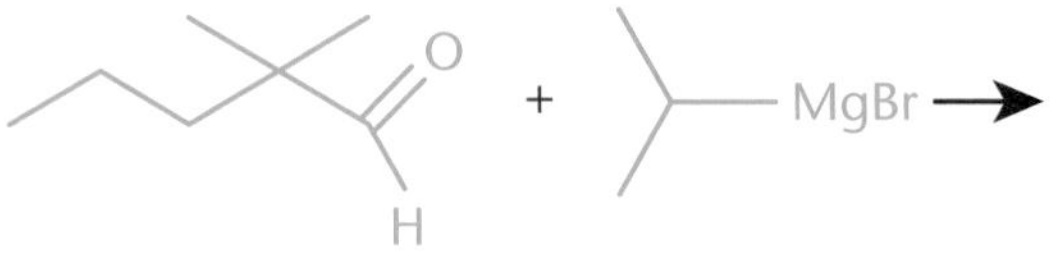

Substance A

A. 2,4,4-trimethylheptan-3-ol
B. 3-(2-ethyl-4-dimethyl)-hexanol
C. 2,4,4 trimethyl-heptane alcohol
D. 5-(4,4,6-trimethyl)-heptanol

42. The student is told that he can synthesize substance C by treating butanenitrile with aqueous acid. Which of the structures below correctly depicts butanenitrile?

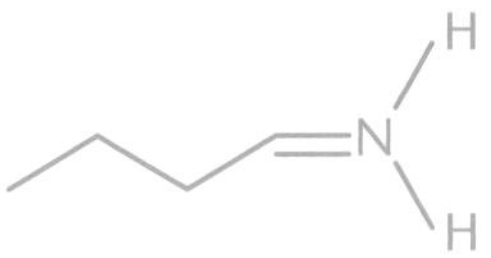

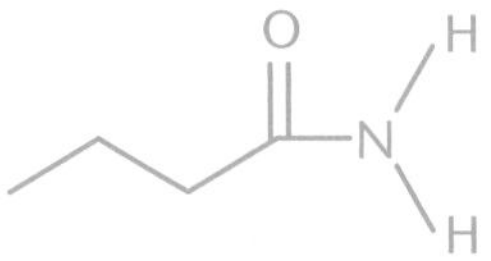

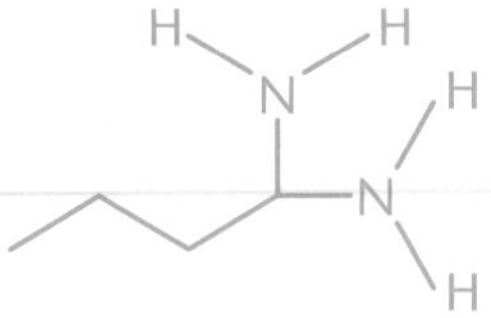

43. Substance B is subjected to a reaction and the product is given below. What is the correct IUPAC name for this product?

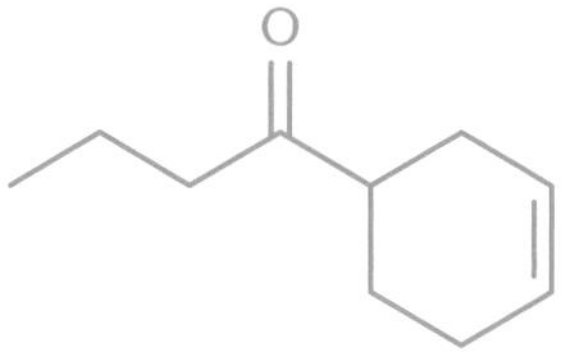

   A. 1-hexane-2-butanone
   B. 5-hexane-4-butanone
   C. 1-(1-butanone)-cyclohex-3-ene
   D. Butanone-cyclohexene

44. The product from the previous question is subjected to a reaction that opens the ring structure by breaking the double bond. This produces a final product that maintains the carbonyl but now has a saturated carbon chain in place of the ring. What is the name of this new product?

   A. 4-decanone
   B. 4-(3-propyl)-heptanone
   C. 5-(4-ethyl)-octanone
   D. 4-(5-ethyl)-octanone

45. During the course of analysis, the student uses Brady's reagent on all three unknowns. Mixing Brady's reagent with which of the following would cause a yellow or red precipitate?

   A. Substance A only
   B. Substances A and C only
   C. Substances B and C only
   D. Substances A and B only

46. A fourth unknown is given to the student and he is told that there is only one functional group on this molecule. When it is mixed with 2,4-DNPH, a yellow crystal falls out of solution. This same unknown is then combined with Tollen's reagent, which fails to produce a silver mirror. If this unknown is mixed with a Wittig reagent, the most likely product to form would be a(n)

   A. aldehyde.
   B. ketone.
   C. alkene.
   D. alkyne.

47. One of the unknowns displayed the following stretches on the IR spectrum:

   $1,200$ cm^{-1} strong
   $1,760$ cm^{-1} strong
   Broad stretch in the region between $3,500$–$2,500$ cm^{-1}

With this information in hand, what can be said about this compound?

   A. Mixing this unknown with Tollen's reagent will produce a silver coat on the test tube glass.
   B. Addition of excess alcohol to this unknown in the presence of acid and heat will result in ester formation.
   C. When reacted with 2,4-DNPH a red precipitate falls out of solution.
   D. Reaction with NaBH$_4$ in a THF solution will result in the formation of an alcohol.

PASSAGE VI (QUESTIONS 48–52)

Some of the most abundant neurotransmitters in the central nervous system (CNS) are amino acids. For example, glutamate and aspartate are responsible for most of the excitatory neurotransmission in the brain and spinal cord, respectively, while glycine, the simplest of the essential amino acids, is a major inhibitory neurotransmitter of spinal cord. In addition, GABA or gamma-aminobutyrate, while not one of the 20 essential amino acids, is the most abundant inhibitory neurotransmitter in the CNS. Disruptions in the regulation of these amino acids can lead to various diseases of the CNS. For instance, excessive stimulation of ionic glutamate receptors can lead to excitotoxic neuron death.

Glutamate is converted to GABA in the brain by the enzyme L-glutamate decarboxylase (GAD). This enzyme removes the carboxylic acid group in the amino acid backbone, as CO_2 (Figure 1). There are two main isoforms of the GAD in the brain: GAD1 and GAD2 or GAD67 and GAD65, where the numbers signify the enzyme's weight in kD. Abnormalities of these enzymes have been discovered in various conditions including epilepsy and schizophrenia.

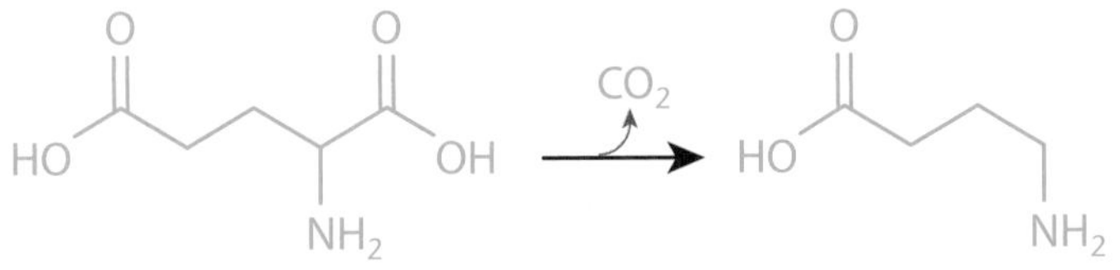

Glutamate   **GABA**

Figure 1

Without an enzyme, simple carboxylic acids rarely undergo decarboxylation. GAD requires pyridoxal 5′-phosphate (PLP) (Figure 2) as a cofactor to effect decarboxylation. A lysine residue in GAD forms a Schiff base with the aldehyde group of PLP. As with many enzymes, after GAD catalyzes decarboxylation, the cofactor remains unchanged.

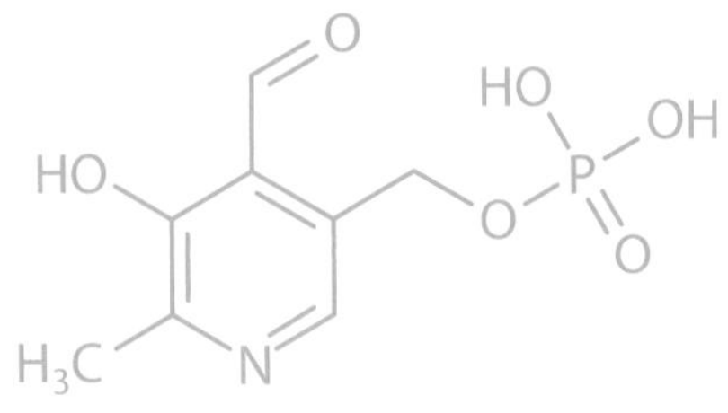

Figure 2

Table 1

Amino acid	pKa_1	pKa_2	pKa_3
Glycine	2.34	9.60	
Aspartic acid	1.88	3.65	9.60
Glutamic acid	2.19	4.25	9.67

48. A mixture of glycine, aspartate, glutamate, and other amino acids is placed in a well in the center of an electrophoresis gel. When current is applied to the bath at pH 4, which of the following accurately describes the action of glycine?

A. Glycine will migrate toward the cathode.

B. Glycine will migrate toward the anode.

C. Glycine will not migrate, because its net charge is zero.

D. Unlike peptides and proteins, single amino acids cannot migrate in an electric field.

49. You plan to separate a solution of glycine and aspartic acid (below) into individual amino acids. What pH would you choose for the electrophoresis buffer?

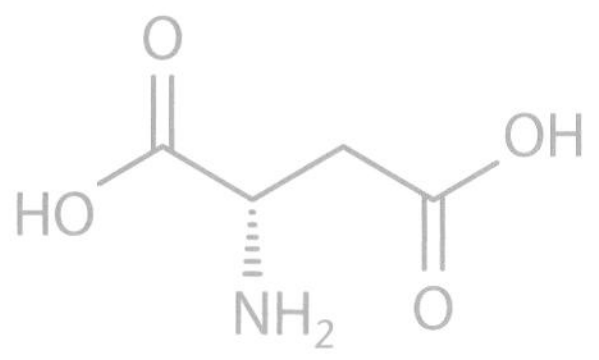

A. 1.88
B. 2.19
C. 2.34
D. 2.77

50. The decarboxylation mechanism requires the formation of a Schiff base. Which of the following most closely resembles a Schiff base?

A. $R_1R_2C{=}N{-}R$
B. $R_1R_2C{=}N{-}NH_2$
C. $R_1R_2C{-}NH{-}R_3$
D. $R_1N{=}NR_2$

51. Mechanistically, how would a lysine residue in GAD most likely begin to form an imine with the aldehyde group in PLP?

A. The amine of the lysine side chain would bond to the carbonyl carbon of PLP by nucleophilic attack.
B. Oxygen in water would nucleophillically attack the aldehyde group of PLP.
C. The carbonyl carbon loses its proton to the amine on the lysine backbone.
D. The carboxylic acid of the lysine residue donates a proton to the carbonyl oxygen to facilitate nucleophilic attack on the carbonyl carbon.

52. In the absence of GAD and PLP, which of the following molecules can undergo decarboxylation with heating only?

A. Glutamic acid
B. 3-oxo-2-aminobutyric acid
C. 2-aminoethanoic acid
D. Aspartic acid

Practice Section 3

Time—70 minutes

QUESTIONS 1–52

Directions: Most of the questions in the following Organic Chemistry Practice Section are organized into groups, with a descriptive passage preceding each group of questions. Study the passage, then select the single best answer to the question in each group. Some of the questions are not based on a descriptive passage; you must also select the best answer to these questions. If you are unsure of the best answer, eliminate the choices that you know are incorrect, then select an answer from the choices that remain.

Period

	1 IA 1A	2 IIA 2A											13 IIIA 3A	14 IVA 4A	15 VA 5A	16 VIA 6A	17 VIIA 7A	18 vIIIA 8A
1	1 H 1.008																	2 He 4.003
2	3 Li 6.941	4 Be 9.012											5 B 10.81	6 C 12.01	7 N 14.01	8 O 16.00	9 F 19.00	10 Ne 20.18
3	11 Na 22.99	12 Mg 24.31	3 IIIB 3B	4 IVB 4B	5 VB 5B	6 VIB 6B	7 VIIB 7B	8	9 ------- VIII ----- --	10	11 IB 1B	12 IIB 2B	13 Al 26.98	14 Si 28.09	15 P 30.97	16 S 32.07	17 Cl 35.45	18 Ar 39.95
4	19 K 39.10	20 Ca 40.08	21 Sc 44.96	22 Ti 47.88	23 V 50.94	24 Cr 52.00	25 Mn 54.94	26 Fe 55.85	27 Co 58.47	28 Ni 58.69	29 Cu 63.55	30 Zn 65.39	31 Ga 69.72	32 Ge 72.59	33 As 74.92	34 Se 78.96	35 Br 79.90	36 Kr 83.80
5	37 Rb 85.47	38 Sr 87.62	39 Y 88.91	40 Zr 91.22	41 Nb 92.91	42 Mo 95.94	43 Tc (98)	44 Ru 101.1	45 Rh 102.9	46 Pd 106.4	47 Ag 107.9	48 Cd 112.4	49 In 114.8	50 Sn 118.7	51 Sb 121.8	52 Te 127.6	53 I 126.9	54 Xe 131.3
6	55 Cs 132.9	56 Ba 137.3	57 La* 138.9	72 Hf 178.5	73 Ta 180.9	74 W 183.9	75 Re 186.2	76 Os 190.2	77 Ir 190.2	78 Pt 195.1	79 Au 197.0	80 Hg 200.5	81 Tl 204.4	82 Pb 207.2	83 Bi 209.0	84 Po (210)	85 At (210)	86 Rn (222)
7	87 Fr (223)	88 Ra (226)	89 Ac~ (227)	104 Rf (257)	105 Db (260)	106 Sg (263)	107 Bh (262)	108 Hs (265)	109 Mt (266)	110 --- ()	111 --- ()	112 --- ()		114 --- ()		116 --- ()		118 --- ()

Lanthanide Series*	58 Ce 140.1	59 Pr 140.9	60 Nd 144.2	61 Pm (147)	62 Sm 150.4	63 Eu 152.0	64 Gd 157.3	65 Tb 158.9	66 Dy 162.5	67 Ho 164.9	68 Er 167.3	69 Tm 168.9	70 Yb 173.0	71 Lu 175.0
Actinide Series~	90 Th 232.0	91 Pa (231)	92 U (238)	93 Np (237)	94 Pu (242)	95 Am (243)	96 Cm (247)	97 Bk (247)	98 Cf (249)	99 Es (254)	100 Fm (253)	101 Md (256)	102 No (254)	103 Lr (257)

PASSAGE I (QUESTIONS 1–8)

The carbonyl group, C=O, is central to the chemistry of aldehydes and ketones. Even though aldehydes are distinguished from ketones by only a hydrogen atom, their reactivities are dissimilar enough that they can be differentiated by chemical means. For example, aldehydes can be more easily oxidized compared to ketones, and aldehydes are more reactive toward nucleophilic addition. The structure of aldehydes and ketones include the central carbonyl carbon being bonded to three other groups: oxygen, by a double (s + p) bond, and two others by s bonds. The three bonds are coplanar, with bond angles of 120°. In addition, the electronegative oxygen atom in aldehydes and ketones unequally shares electrons, creating polar compounds.

Nucleophilic addition is a prominent reaction with aldehydes and ketones. The mechanism includes a transition state where the reactant molecule changes from a trigonal planar to a tetrahedral geometry, after nucleophilic attack at the carbonyl carbon atom, which has a partial positive charge. The Cannizzaro reaction is an example of nucleophilic addition that occurs when an aldehyde containing no α-hydrogen is allowed to react with aqueous or alcoholic hydroxides at room temperature; the aldehyde self-oxidizes, yielding an alcohol and a salt of a carboxylic acid.

1. A mixture of two alcohols, $CH_3CH_2CH_2CH_2OH$ and $CH_3CH_2CH(OH)CH_3$, is treated with pyridinium dichromate (PDC) in the presence of sulfuric acid to give a mixture of compounds. Reaction of this mixture with Tollen's reagent would give which of the following products?

A.

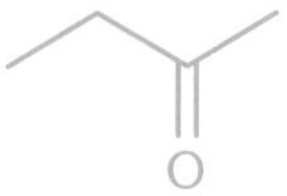

B.

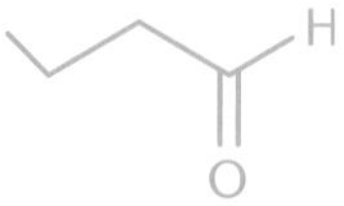

C.

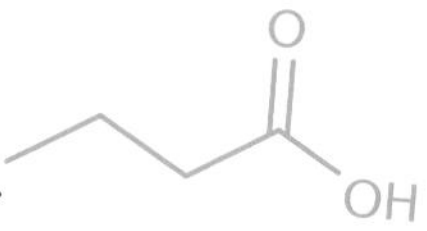

D.

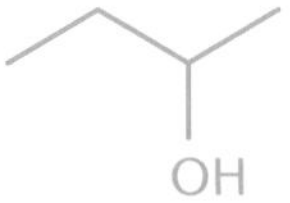

2. Aldehydes and ketones can be reduced to their corresponding alcohols and/or hydrocarbons with suitable reducing agents. What is the final product of the reaction sequence shown below?

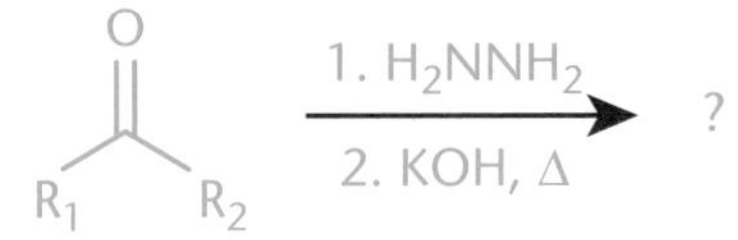

A.

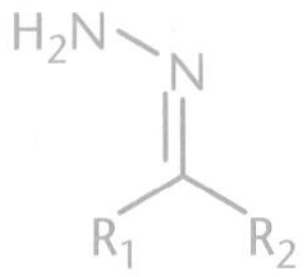

B.

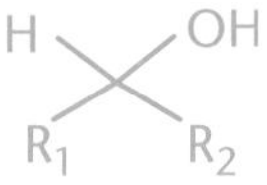

C.

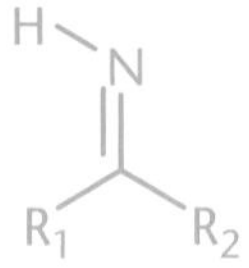

D.

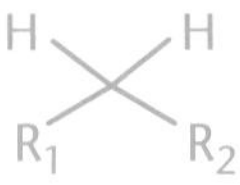

3. What compound results when ethyl methyl ketone reacts with HCN followed by treatment with sulfuric acid and heat?

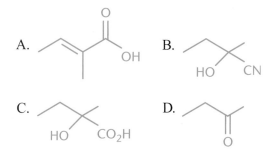

4. Which would be a product of a reaction with aqueous or alcoholic hydroxides and acetaldehyde?

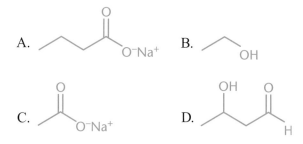

5. In the reaction above, what is the nucleophile involved in the mechanism?

A. ‾OH

B. $[CH_2CHO]^-$

C. 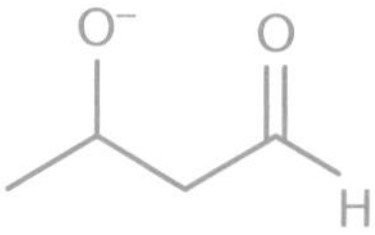 (structure)

D. 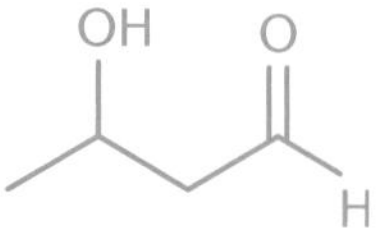 (structure)

6. If β-hydroxybutanal produced from an aldol condensation is reacted with dilute acid, which of the following would be a resulting product?

A. 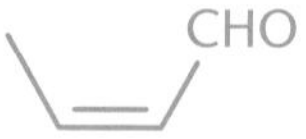 (structure) CHO

B. 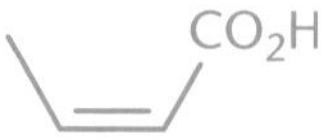 (structure) CO_2H

C. 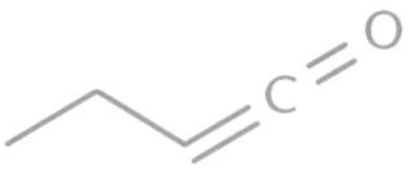 (structure)

D. 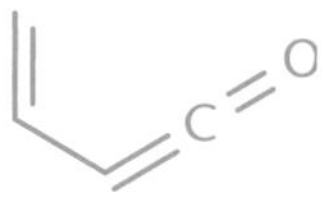 (structure)

7. Aldol condensation is useful in the synthesis of larger molecules from smaller precursors. What sequence of reactions would result in using acetaldehyde to make n-butyraldehyde?

A. Aldol condensation to β-hydroxybutanal, hydrogenation to n-butyl alcohol, oxidation to n-butanal

B. Aldol condensation to β-hydroxybutanal, dehydration to 2-butenal, oxidation to n-butanal

C. Aldol condensation to β-hydroxybutanal, dehydration to 2-butenal, hydrogenation of the alkene to n-butanal

D. Hydrogenation to ethyl alcohol, oxidation to acetone, aldol condensation to n-butanal

8. A Perkin condensation adds anhydrides to aromatic aldehydes in the presence of a base to give α, β-unsaturated acids. The corresponding saturated acid can then be made by hydrogenation of the carbon-carbon double bond. Which compound, in addition to acetic anhydride, represents the starting compound if the end product of a Perkin condensation produces the compound shown below?

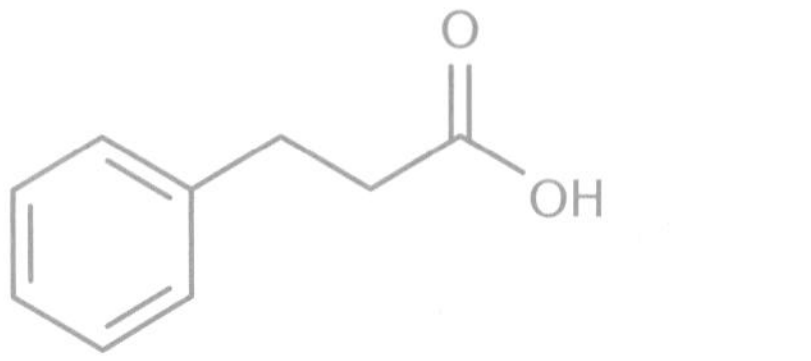

A.

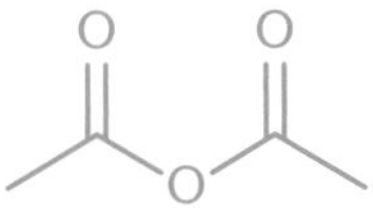

B.

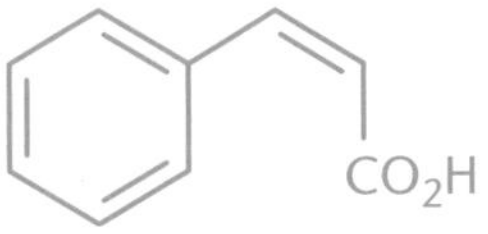

C.

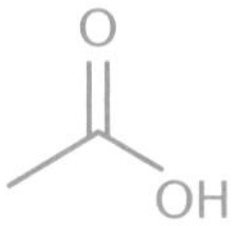

D.

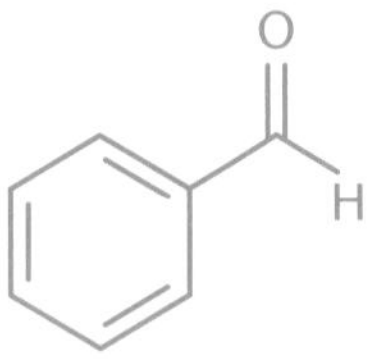

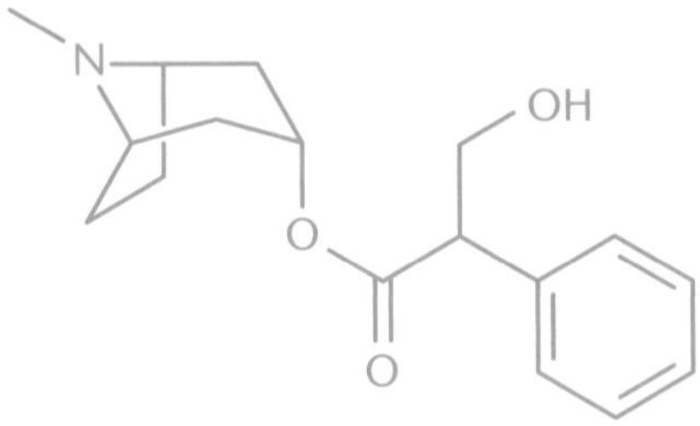

Atropine

Figure 1a

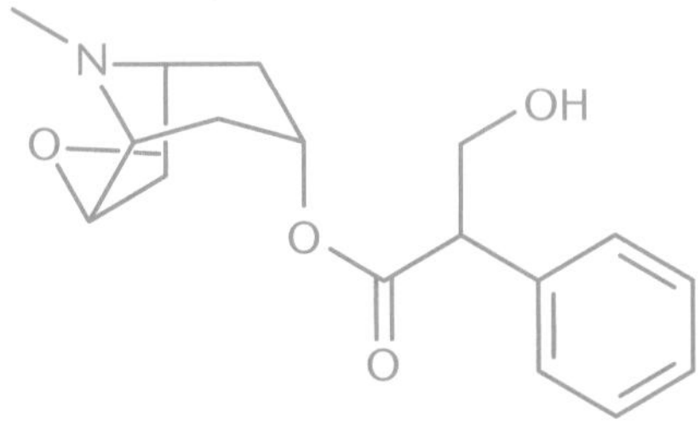

Scopolamine

Figure 1b

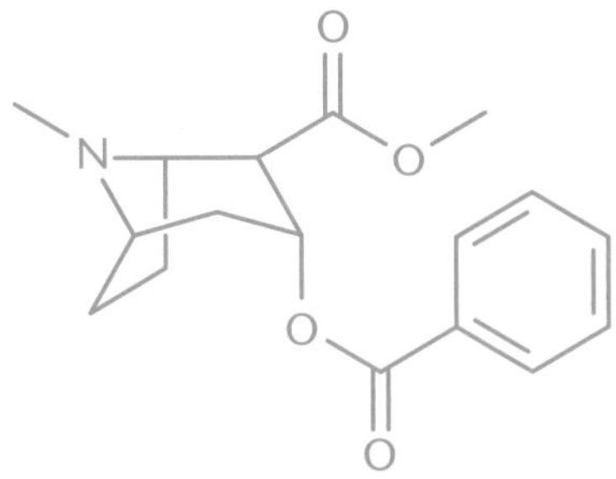

Cocaine

Figure 1c

PASSAGE II (QUESTIONS 9–15)

Atropine (Figure 1a) is a widely administered alkaloid drug used as a depressant of the parasympathetic nervous system, effective in the treatment of cardiac arrest, as well as being a popular drug in ophthalmology for pupil dilation. Atropine is categorized as a tropane alkaloid, in the same group as other drugs such as scopolamine (Figure 1b) and cocaine (Figure 1c).

Atropine and other tropane alkaloids can be conveniently derived from tropinone (figure 2), a symmetric bicyclic nitrogenous ketone. In 1917, Sir Robert Robinson reported a facile synthesis of tropinone from succinaldehyde, methylamine, and acetone dicarboxylic acid.

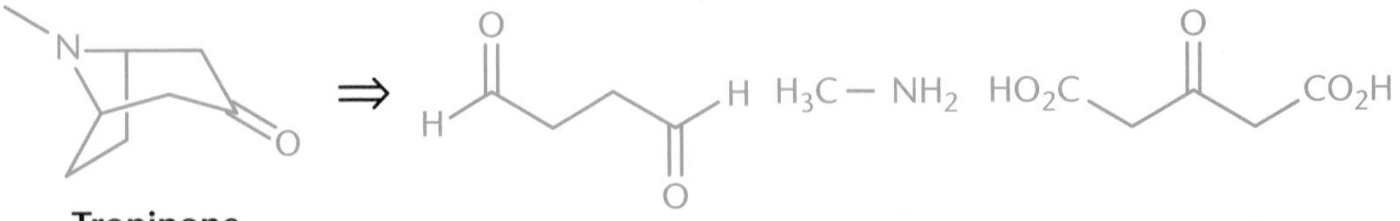

Tropinone

Figure 2

A proposed mechanism begins with the formation of a Schiff base between succinaldehyde and methylamine, followed by nucleophilic addition of the Schiff base to the second aldehyde group to form the five-membered ring (Figure 3). The remaining mechanism is illustrated below.

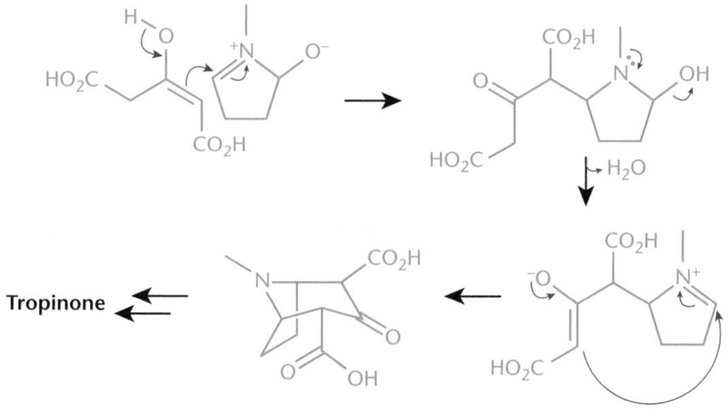

Figure 3

9. Which of the following structures illustrates the Schiff base initially formed between succinaldehyde and methylamine?

A.

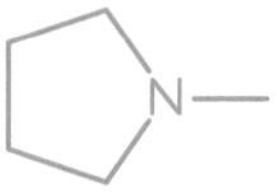

B.

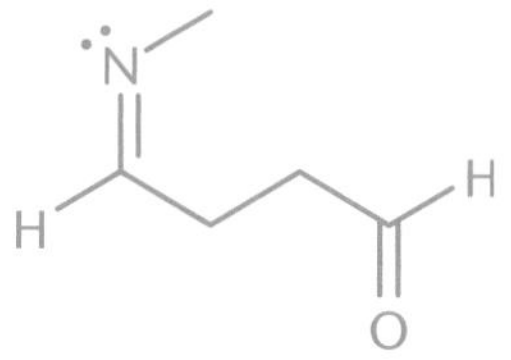

C.

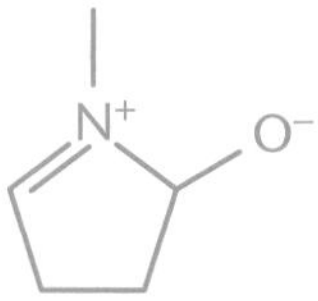

D.

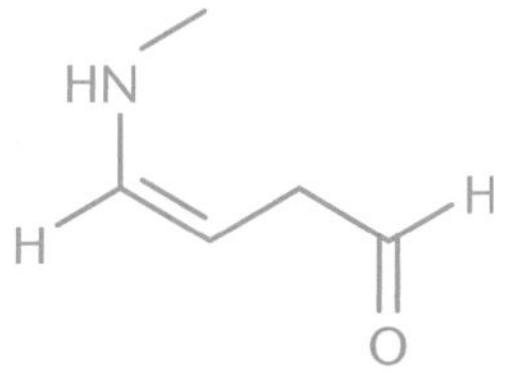

For questions 10 and 11, please refer to the reaction shown below.

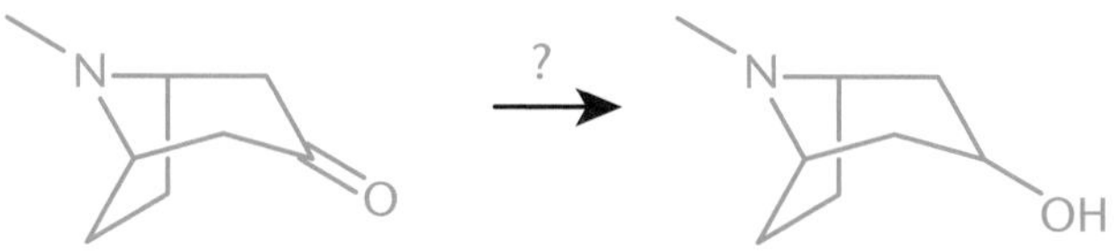

10. Which of the following reagents would be most suitable for the previous transformation?

A. $Na_2Cr_2O_7$
B. $NaBH_4$
C. BH_3/THF, followed by H_2O_2/NaOH
D. HBr

11. What is a suitable name for the product shown?

A. Tropinol
B. Tropane
C. Tropene
D. Tropinamine

12. The active form of atropine is synthesized by the addition of the molecule shown below. What is the IUPAC name?

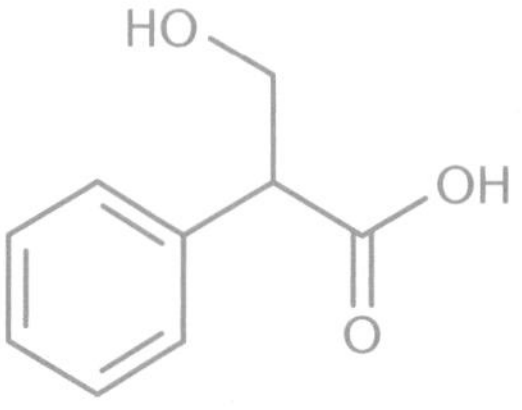

A. (S)-3-Hydroxy-2-phenylethanoic acid
B. (S)-3-Hydroxy-2-phenylpropanoic acid
C. (R)-2-Hydroxy-3-phenylbutanoic acid
D. (R)-3-Hydroxy-2-phenylpropanoic acid

13. How many distinct ^{1}H-NMR signals are observed in the spectrum of tropinone?

A. 7
B. 8
C. 4
D. 5

14. How many distinct ^{13}C NMR signals are observed in the spectrum of tropinone?

A. 5
B. 7
C. 10
D. 8

15. It would seem more logical to use acetone as a starting material, as the final steps to tropinone (not shown) can be avoided. Which of the following explains why acetone dicarboxylic acid is used instead of acetone?

   I. It is a better electrophile than acetone is.

   II. Its enol is more stable than that of acetone.

   III. The α-protons are more acidic than acetone is.

   IV. The β-protons are more acidic than acetone is.

   A. I only

   B. III only

   C. II and III

   D. II and IV

QUESTIONS 16–18 ARE NOT BASED ON A DESCRIPTIVE PASSAGE.

16. How many absorption peaks will the following compound have?

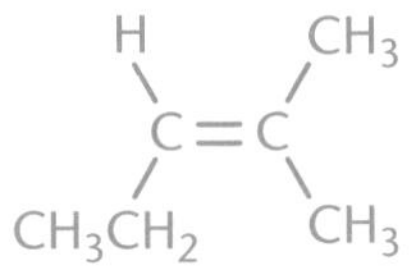

   A. 5

   B. 6

   C. 7

   D. 8

17. Which of the following steps would never form a radical in a radical halogenation reaction?

   A. Initiation

   B. Elongation

   C. Propagation

   D. Termination

18. Triglycerides include which of the following?

   A. Glycerol and fatty esters

   B. Esters, alcohols, and phospholipids

   C. Fatty acids, esters, and alcohols

   D. Glycerol and fatty acids

PASSAGE III (QUESTIONS 19–26)

A student is developing a new "orange azo dye" for a science fair project. He plans to synthesize a part of the dye molecule, which is colorless, and unveil the color at the science fair. He decides to start his synthesis with benzoic acid, but unfortunately, he only has benzene and phenol as aromatic starting materials. The synthesis of the colorless precursor is illustrated below.

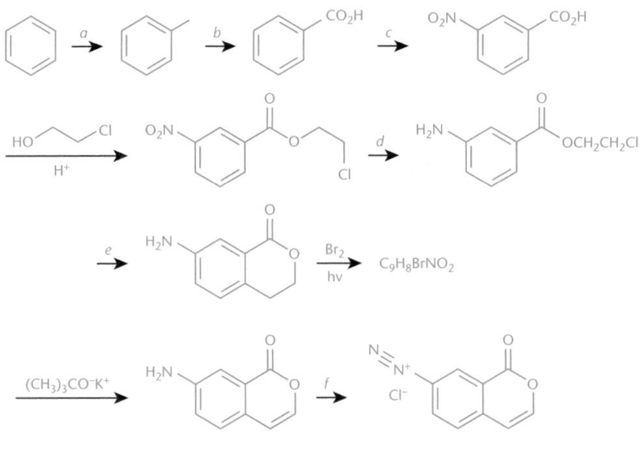

19. As shown in the figure above, benzoic acid can be synthesized from benzene in two steps. What two reactions (*a* and *b*) are needed?

   A. Step 1: CH_3Cl, $AlCl_3$; Step 2: $KMnO_4$, heat

   B. Step 1: CH_3OH, Al_2O_3; Step 2: $KMnO_4$, heat

   C. Step 1: CH_3Cl, $AlCl_3$; Step 2: PCC

   D. Step 1: CH_3COCl, $AlCl_3$; Step 2: CrO_3

20. What reagents are required for reaction *c*?

A. HNO_2

B. Concentrated HNO_3 and H_2SO_4

C. $NaNO_2$

D. Concentrated HNO_3

21. Which of the following reagents can be used in reaction *d*?

   I. H_2, Pt

   II. Sn, H_2SO_4

   III. Zn, HCl

A. I only

B. II only

C. II and III

D. I, II, and III

22. How do amine groups direct subsequent reactions in the benzene ring?

A. Deactivate the ring, *ortho-* or *para*-directing

B. Activate the ring, *meta*-directing

C. Activate the ring, *ortho-* or *para*-directing

D. Deactivate the ring, *meta*-directing

23. Which of the following Lewis acids below can best catalyze reaction *e*?

   I. BCl_3

   II. $AlCl_3$

   III. $PbCl_4$

   IV. $[NiCl_4]^{2-}$

A. II only

B. IV only

C. I and II

D. III and IV

24. Which compound below, with molecular formula $C_9H_8BrNO_2$, is the correct structure of the product of reaction *e* after radical monobromination?

A. 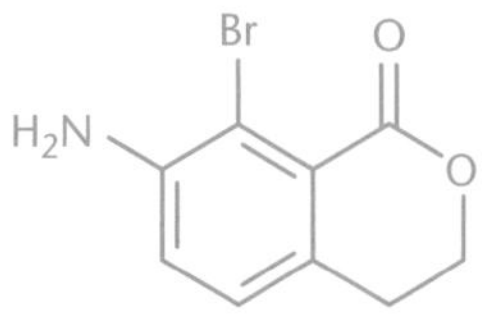 B. 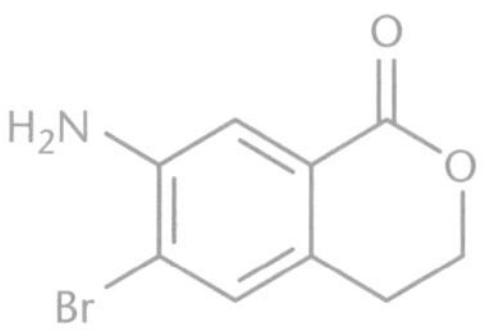 C. 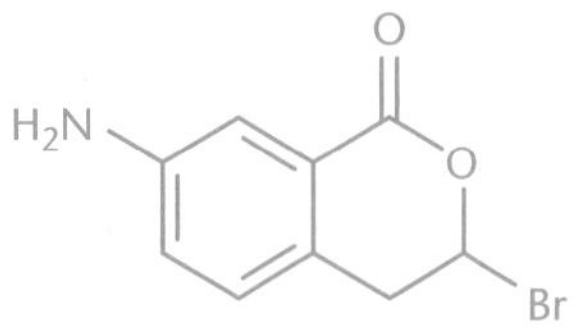 D.

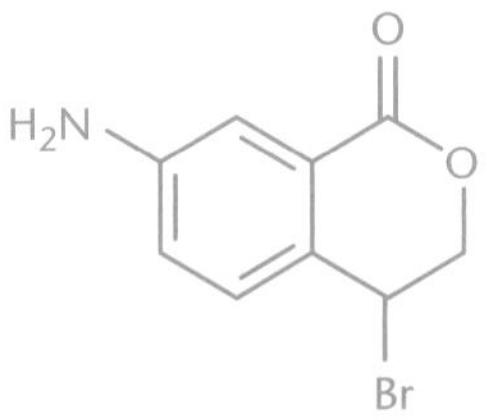

25. At the science fair demonstration, the student treats the diazonium salt with phenol to form the orange azo dye. He knows, however, that he needs to somehow activate the phenol first before nucleophilic aromatic substitution can occur. What reagent can activate phenol?

A. HCl

B. H_2O

C. NaH

D. H_3O^+

26. After working up with mild aqueous acid, what is the structure of the orange azo dye?

A. 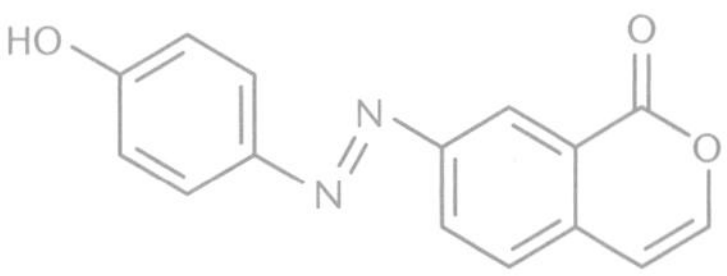 B.

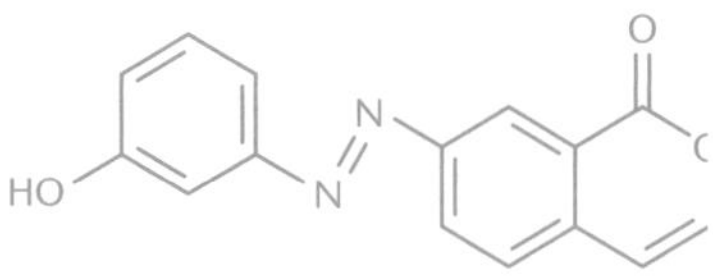

C. 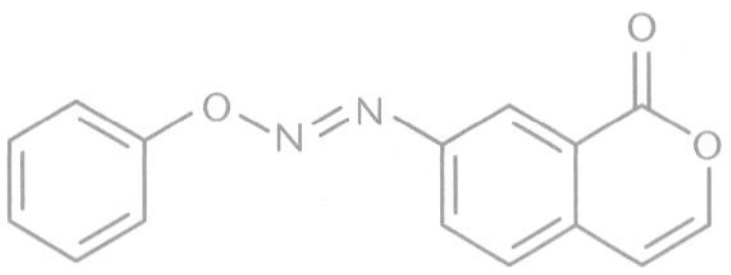 D.

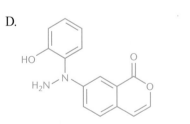

PASSAGE IV (QUESTIONS 27–36)

A student attempts to separate a mixture of acetaminophen, amantadine, aspirin, caffeine, and ethenzamide (Figures 1a, 1b, 1c, 1d, and 1e).

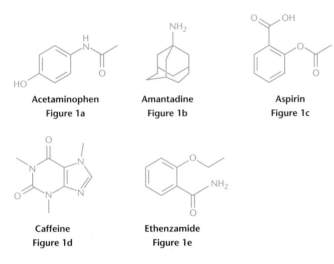

| Acetaminophen | Amantadine | Aspirin |
| Figure 1a | Figure 1b | Figure 1c |

| Caffeine | Ethenzamide |
| Figure 1d | Figure 1e |

At her disposal are several solvents; their densities and boiling points are listed in Table 1.

Table 1

Solvent	Density (g/mL)	Boiling point (°C)
Water	1.0	100
Ethanol	0.8	78.0
Chloroform	1.5	61.0
Diethyl ether	0.7	35.0

As a reference, the student constructs a flow chart illustrating her separation process (Figure 2.)

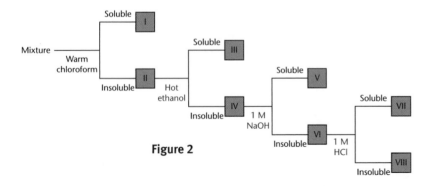

Figure 2

27. What compound belongs in box I of Figure 2?

   A. Amantadine
   B. Aspirin
   C. Ethenzamide
   D. Caffeine

28. What compound belongs in box III of Figure 2?

   A. Acetaminophen
   B. Caffeine
   C. Ethenzamide
   D. Amantadine

29. Which of the following sets of ^{1}H NMR data corresponds to aspirin?

   A. d 2.0 (singlet, 3H), d 6.7 (doublet, 2H), d 7.4 (doublet, 2H), d 9.2 (singlet, 1H), d 9.6 (singlet, 1H)
   B. d 3.2 (singlet, 3H), d 3.4 (singlet, 3H), d 3.9 (singlet, 3H), d 7.9 (singlet, 1H)
   C. d 2.3 (singlet, 3H), d 7.1 (doublet, 1H), d 7.3 (triplet, 1H), d 7.6 (triplet, 1H), d 7.9 (doublet, 1H)
   D. d 1.1 (triplet, 3H), d 4.1 (quartet, 2H), d 7.3–7.5 (multiplet, 4H), d 7.9 (doublet, 2H)

30. Given that aspirin is soluble in 1 M NaOH, which of the structures below corresponds to the dissolved species?

A.

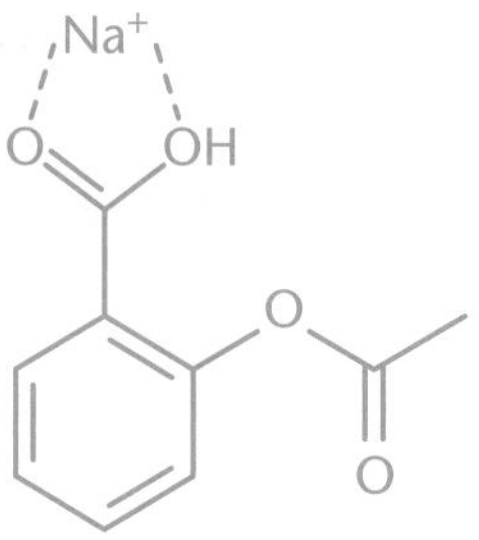

B.

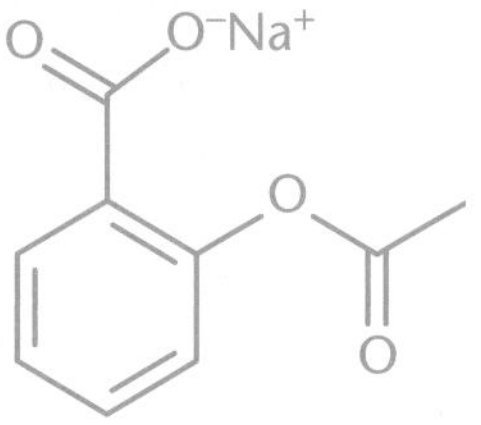

C.

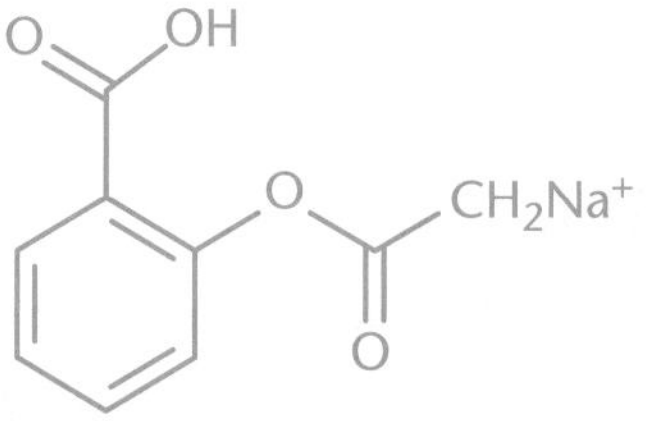

D.

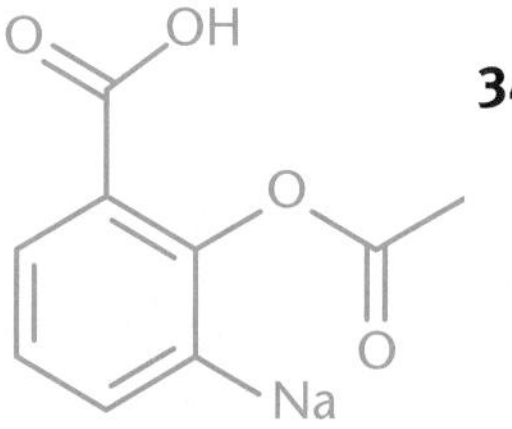

31. What pair of compounds is being separated in the final step (addition of 1 M HCl)?

A. Amantadine and caffeine
B. Amantadine and ethenzamide
C. Acetaminophen and ethenzamide
D. Acetaminophen and aspirin

32. How many different signals are observed in the ^{13}C NMR spectrum for acetaminophen?

A. 8
B. 5
C. 7
D. 6

33. Suppose that the student accidentally adds $LiAlH_4$ to the initial mixture. Which of the following compounds will undergo reduction?

    I. Amantadine
    II. Acetaminophen
    III. Aspirin
    IV. Ethenzamide

A. I only
B. III only
C. II and IV
D. II, III, and IV

34. The structure of ibuprofen is given below. If ibuprofen is added to the initial mixture, at which box in Figure 2 does it appear?

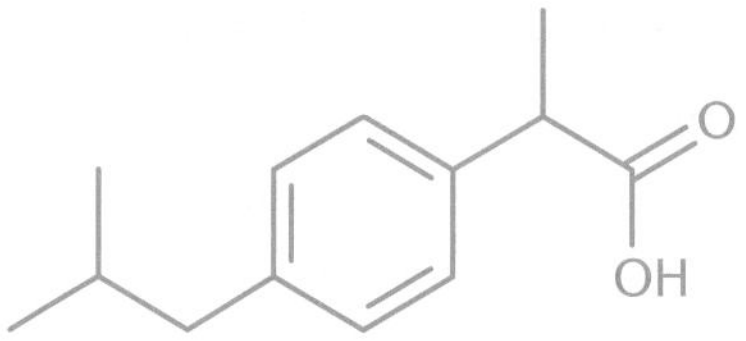

A. I
B. III
C. V
D. VII

35. Suppose the initial mixture is treated with sodium hydride (NaH), followed by methyl iodide. Which of the steps in Figure 2 will not separate any compounds?

    I. 1 M HCl
    II. 1M NaOH
    III. Warm chloroform
    IV. Hot ethanol

A. III only
B. IV only
C. I and II
D. I and IV

36. Another student decides to separate the same mixture of compounds using the same solvents, but in a different order. Which of the variations below can still give complete separation of the mixture into individual compounds?

A. 1 M HCl, followed by hot ethanol, 1 M NaOH, and warm chloroform last

B. 1 M NaOH first, followed by hot ethanol, warm chloroform, and 1 M HCl last

C. 1 M HCl first, followed by warm chloroform, 1 M NaOH, and hot ethanol last

D. 1 M NaOH, followed by 1 M HCl, hot ethanol, and warm chloroform last

QUESTIONS 37–39 ARE NOT BASED ON A DESCRIPTIVE PASSAGE.

37. In a room temperature sample of *cis*-1,2-dibromocyclohexane in a chair conformation, the configuration of the bromines will

A. be axial.

B. be equatorial.

C. alternate between axial and equatorial switching conformations at the same time.

D. alternate between axial and equatorial switching conformations at different times.

38. Which of the following compounds produces the most heat per mole of compound when reacted with oxygen?

A. CH_4

B. C_2H_6

C. Cyclohexane

D. Cycloheptane

39. Using gel electrophoresis, a scientist can separate a mixture of amino acids by subjecting them to an electric field. The strength and direction of the electric field is determined by the net charge of the amino acid. If a solution of four different amino acids at a pH of 8 underwent gel electophoresis, which of the following would move farthest in the direction of the anode?

A. Glutamate

B. Glutamine

C. Lysine

D. Histidine

PASSAGE V (QUESTIONS 40–47)

Methylphenidate is a drug used primarily to treat children with attention deficit hyperactivity disorder. While the precise mechanism of action is unclear, it is known to inhibit monoamine neurotransmitter reuptake in a noncompetitive manner. Paradoxically, when the compound is administered to laboratory animals or healthy human volunteers, it acts as a stimulant and increases locomotor activity. The molecule has two stereocenters and the configuration of these greatly impacts the efficacy and side effects of the molecule. Studies have demonstrated that d-*threo*-methylphenidate is the most potent isomer. In order to study the effects of the various enantiomers and diastereomers, asymmetric syntheses have been employed. Utilizing a starting compound that is chiral can reduce the need to resolve enantiomers and produce an enantiomerically pure product. The various isomers of methylphenidate or methyl-2-phenyl-2-(2′-piperidyl)-acetate are shown on the following page.

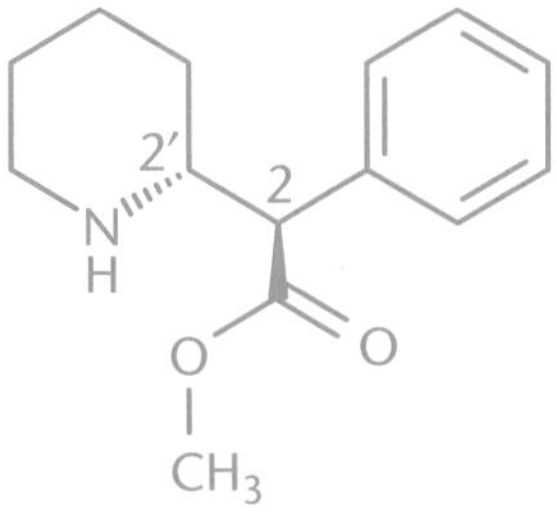

I

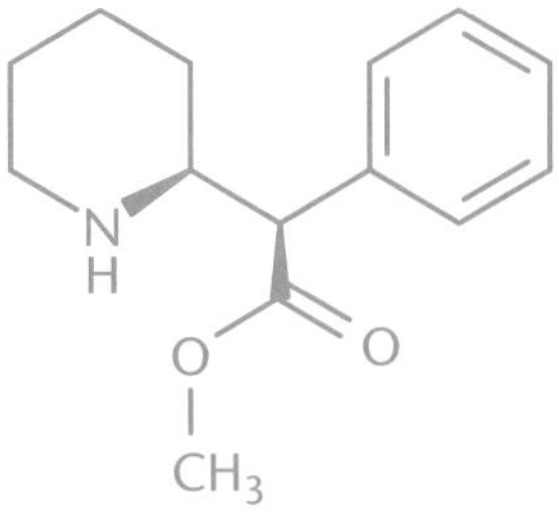

II

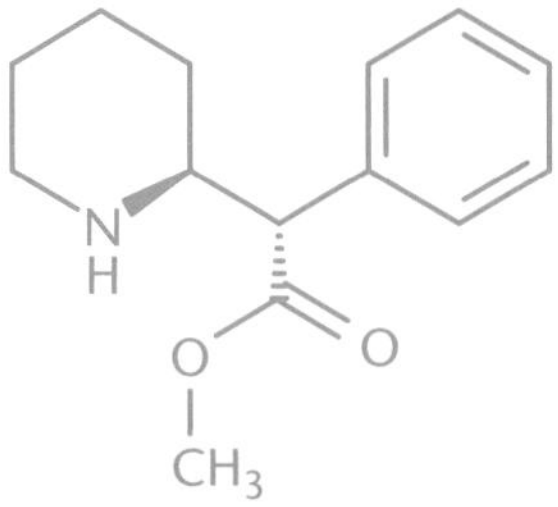

III

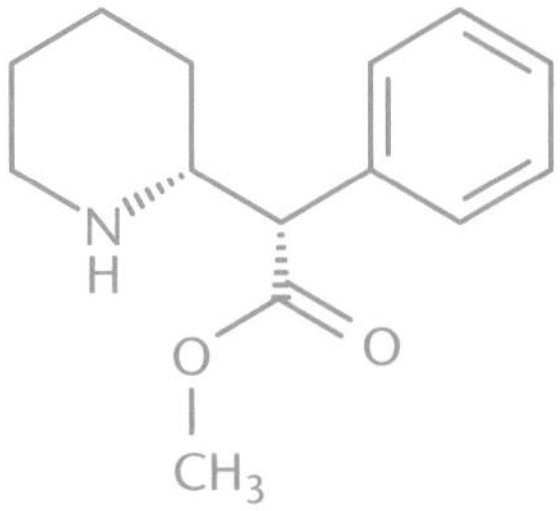

IV

40. For her thesis, a graduate student uses a seven-step chiral synthesis to produce methylphenidate, which will be used in various experiments. After the fourth step, the product has an observed optical rotation. After the fifth step, however, the optical rotation of the product was one-half of the previously observed value. What accounts for this discrepancy?

A. The current solution is half the concentration of previous syntheses.

B. Her starting compound was the opposite chirality.

C. The sample tube of the polarimeter is twice the length.

D. Both B and C

41. Which compound in the figure above is (2R, 2′R)-(+)-*threo*-methyl-α-phenyl-α-(2-piperidyl) acetate, also known as d-threo-methylphenidate?

A. I

B. II

C. III

D. IV

42. Which of the compounds in the figure are structural (constitutional) isomers?

A. I and II

B. II and III

C. I and III

D. None of the above

43. Which of the compounds in the figure are stereoisomers?

A. I and II

B. II and III

C. I and III

D. All of the above

44. Which of the molecules shown are diastereomers?

A. I and II

B. II and IV

C. I and III

D. None of the above

45. While devising an asymmetric, multistep synthesis, a student proposes an S_N2 reaction at a chiral atom. Both the beginning reactant and final product have an R orientation. What will his mentor most likely tell him?

A. Proceed; the dehydration of a tertiary alcohol with strong base is an S_N2 reaction.

B. Halt; the S_N2 will invert the stereocenter.

C. Proceed; the S_N2 will not invert the stereocenter.

D. The stereocenter's configuration will only remain the same if the leaving group has a different priority in the starting molecule than the substituted group does in the final molecule.

46. Which of the following can exist as geometric isomers?

A. 1-bromo-1-pentyne

B. 1, 2-dibromopentane

C. 1-bromo-1-pentene

D. None of the above

47. Which of the following most likely explains why d-*threo*-methylphenidate is the most potent stereoisomer for inhibiting dopamine reuptake *in vitro*?

   A. This isomer most readily crosses the blood-brain barrier.
   B. This isomer binds most effectively to the dopamine reuptake transporter.
   C. This isomer most closely mimics dopamine.
   D. None of the above

PASSAGE VI (QUESTIONS 48–52)

Bonds in organic chemistry are mostly covalent bonds, sharing electrons. Electrons occupy orbitals consisting of electron pairs with opposite spins. Orbitals occupy shells, or energy levels. Electrons in the outer shell of an atom, the valence electrons, largely determine the bonding characteristics of the atom, and usually adhere to the octet rule. The octet rule states that for an atom to be stable, its outer electron shell must be occupied by eight electrons. Covalent bonds also usually obey the octet rule. Thus, eight electrons in the outer shell of each of the bonded atoms form a stable, nonreactive molecule. Lewis structures are commonly used to show the valence electrons with dots representing electrons of the outer shell. For example, the Lewis structure for carbon, as the neutral atom presented in the periodic table, would be represented as shown in Figure 1.

Figure 1

From Lewis structures, the electron domains of a molecule can be counted. According to the valence shell electron-pair repulsion (VSEPR) model, the shape of a molecule can be determined by first drawing its Lewis structure and counting the number of electron domains, then arranging those domains around the central atom such that their repulsions of one another are minimized. Electron domains consist of 1) each single bond; 2) each double bond; 3) each triple bond; and 4) each nonbonding electron pair on the central atom. Finally, the electron domains are positioned such that the atoms form a molecular geometry. Much like balloons (representing electron domains) would position themselves when tied together, electron domains position themselves according to their repulsion to each other. Domain numbers around a central atom determine geometries (see Table 1). (Note: One or two nonbonding domains on the central atom will alter the bond angles due to repulsion of the bonding domains.)

Domain number	Geometry	Depiction
2	Linear	
3	Trigonal planar	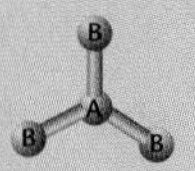
4	Tetrahedral	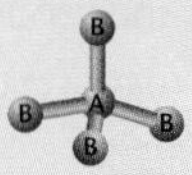
5	Trigonal bypyramidal	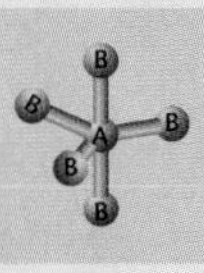
6	Octahedral	

Table 1

Once the geometry of the molecule has been determined, the hybrid orbitals necessary to accommodate their electron's geometric arrangement can be specified.

48. Table 2 shows the categories of electron assignments corresponding to values for the three quantum numbers n (which defines the energy level), l (which defines the shape of the electrons orbitals), and m_l (which defines the orientation of the orbitals is space). Organic molecules are composed mainly of the atoms carbon (atomic number 6), hydrogen (atomic number 1), nitrogen (atomic number 7), and oxygen (atomic number 8). Which of the following atoms has a valence electron possessing a spherical-shaped orbital?

n (shell)	l values	subshell	m_l values	No. orbitals (subshell)	No. orbitals (shell)
1	0	1s	0	1	1
2	0	2s	0	1	
2	1	2p	1, 0, –1	3	4
3	0	3s	0	1	
3	1	3p	1, 0, –1	3	
3	2	3d	2, 1, 0, –1, –2	5	9

Table 2

A. Hydrogen
B. Carbon
C. Nitrogen
D. Oxygen

49. Carbon, with an atomic number of 6, and oxygen, atomic number 8, can form carbon dioxide, a molecule critical for life on earth. When more than one Lewis structure is possible for a molecule, assigning formal charges may help decide which structure is correct. The preferred Lewis structure is the one with atoms bearing the charge closest to zero, and in which any negative charges are assigned to the more electronegative atom(s). What is the preferred Lewis structure for carbon dioxide (CO_2)?

A. O::C::O

B. O:C:O

C. :O::C::O:

D. :O:C:::O:

50. Bonds between any two atoms in a molecule vary little in their energy from molecule to molecule. For example, the bond between carbon and hydrogen in propane varies little in energy from the same bond within methane. Thus, tables of average bond enthalpies between specific atoms can be accurate enough to provide valid comparisons of energies among fuel molecules, expressing the energy as kJ/mole. Remember that the reaction of hydrocarbons in oxygen yields carbon dioxide and water. Given the enthalpy values below, which of the following gases is the most efficient fuel per molecular weight?

Bond	Enthalpy (kJ/mole)
C — H	413
C — C	348
O — O	146
C = O	799
O — H	463

A. Methane
B. Ethane
C. Propane
D. Butane

51. Using the VSEPR model rules, what shape would you predict for the carbon dioxide (CO_2) molecule?

A. Linear
B. Trigonal planar
C. Tetrahedral
D. Trigonal bipyramidal

52. According to the VSEPR model, what shape would you ascribe to the methane (CH_4) molecule?

A. Linear
B. Trigonal planar
C. Tetrahedral
D. Trigonal bipyramidal

Answers and Explanations

Answers and Explanations

PRACTICE SECTION 1

1.	A	19.	B	37.	D
2.	C	20.	B	38.	B
3.	C	21.	C	39.	A
4.	D	22.	D	40.	A
5.	D	23.	A	41.	C
6.	C	24.	C	42.	D
7.	B	25.	C	43.	C
8.	A	26.	B	44.	A
9.	B	27.	D	45.	D
10.	B	28.	D	46.	D
11.	B	29.	A	47.	D
12.	A	30.	B	48.	A
13.	B	31.	C	49.	D
14.	D	32.	A	50.	B
15.	D	33.	A	51.	B
16.	A	34.	B	52.	B
17.	D	35.	C		
18.	C	36.	C		

ANSWER KEY

PASSAGE I

1. A

Dehydration reactions involve the loss of an alcohol –OH group and a hydrogen on an adjacent carbon to form an alkene. This occurs in the presence of a strong acid, and oftentimes heat. In the first step, the acid protonates the alcohol to form ROH^{2+}. An H_2O water molecule then dissociates, leaving a carbocation. Next, an adjacent carbon loses a hydrogen, creating a C=C double bond; in other words, an alkene. Although often, before the alkene forms, the carbocation will rearrange to become more stable. This has occurred in (A)—the primary carbocation stole a hyrdrogen from the adjacent carbon, causing the carbocation now to be located on a secondary carbon. Remember, the more substituted a carbon is, the more it is able to stabilize the positive formal charge of the carbocation. At this point, the molecule loses the hydrogen to form an alkene, resulting in (A). (B) would undergo an S_N2 mechanism. (C) is an oxidation. (D) proceeds by an elimantion mechanism.

2. C

Active metals such as sodium, potassium, and aluminum can react with alcohols. The metals deprotonate alcohols and release the hydrogens as H_2 gas. The remaining alkoxides (RO⁻) bind to the metal. The better an alkoxide is at stabilizing the negative formal charge that forms on the oxygen, the more likely the alkoxide is to form. Since alkyl groups are electron-releasing (the inductive effect), more substituted alkoxides have a greater build-up of negative charge on the oxygen atom, resulting in a less stable alkoxide. Less substituted alkoxides have less inductive effect to destablize the negative formal charge of the alkoxide. Therefore, the primary alcohol in (C) results in the most stable alkoxide. (D), while also a primary alcohol, has a larger alkyl chain and thus has a greater inductive effect than (C). (A) is a secondary alcohol and (B) is a tertiary alcohol.

3. C

Grignard reagents form alcohols by attacking carbonyl carbons as a nucleophile. The oxygen atom of the carbonyl group becomes the –OH group of the alcohol. Only ketones result in tertiary alcohols after reaction with a Grignard reagent. (C) is the only ketone among the choices and will form a tertiary alcohol after nucleophilic attack. (A) would form a primary alcohol, and (B) and (D) would form secondary alcohols upon addition of the Grignard reagent.

4. D

When evaluating boiling points, the two main factors to consider are intermolecular forces and molecular weights. Since all answer choices have similar molecular weights, this property does not account for the difference in boiling points. The answer choice with the strongest intermolecular attractions is (D). Hydrogen bonding between molecules tends to increase the boiling point because greater energy (higher temperature) is required to break the hydrogen bonds. Other intermolecular forces that affect boiling point are much less important when comparing these four molecules.

5. D

The S_N1 mechanism proceeds through a carbocation intermediate, and the stability of that carbocation determines the reactivity. The order of carbonium ion stability is allyl > benzyl > 3° > 2° > 1° > methyl. (D) is correct because, as a tertiary alcohol, it is most likely to react via an S_N1 mechanism. (A) and (B) are primary alcohols and (C) is a secondary alcohol which would more likely undergo an S_N2 reaction.

6. C

Because ethanol is the starting material and the product is sec-butyl alcohol, it would be reasonable to make both the Grignard reagent and an aldehyde from ethanol, since Grignard reagents add to aldehydes to form secondary alcohols. (C) is the correct answer since ketones form tertiary alcohols upon addition of Grignard reagents. Additionally, this ketone already has four carbons and adding a two-carbon Grignard reagent would create a six-carbon molecule. (A) is formed when making the Grignard reagent from ethanol. (B) is the Grignard reagent. (D) is the final intermediate and occurs immediately prior to loss of MgBr to form sec-butyl alcohol.

7. B

The bond between bromine and the aryl ring of bromobenzene is unreactive to nucleophilic substitution, and therefore, an ether cannot be formed by the Williamson synthesis. An alkoxide will react with methyl bromine (A) to form an ether, as will benzyl chloride and 2-bromopropane, (C) and (D) respectively.

PASSAGE II

8. A

(A) is a polar aprotic solvent, like acetone. (B) and (C) are polar protic solvents, so they are not suitable for S_N2 reactions. (D) is nonpolar, so it is unlikely to dissolve the reactants and products.

9. B

For reaction 1 the stereochemistry of both the reactant and the product is R. Only (B) can be correct.

10. B

Information provided in the question immediately discounts (A) (S_N1 intermediate) and (D). The stereochemistry of the intermediate in (C) is R, which is incorrect since an inversion in stereochemistry occurs.

11. B

S_N2 reactions proceed faster in polar aprotic solvents, since they're only able to form weak intermolecular interactions with the nucleophile. (D) is incorrect since protic solvents are able to hydrogen bond. This will result in isopropanol creating a solvation shell around the nucleophile, preventing nucleophile attack. (A) and (B) do not answer the question, and (A) is also an incorrect statement.

12. A

S_N1 reactions are favored by protic solvents because the large positive charge on the solvent's hydrogen can hydrogen bond with the negatively-charged leaving group. This helps the reaction proceed through the transition state to the carbocation intermediate. The incoming nucleophile (B) plays no role in affecting the rate, while protons (C) cannot stabilize another positively charged species. Destabilizing the leaving group (D) will likely slow down S_N1 reactions.

13. B

The carbocation intermediate is flat, with the empty p-orbital perpendicular to the three bond pairs. As such, the incoming nucleophile has access to the carbocation from either side of the plane, leading to racemization. The nucleophile itself has no effect on the initial alkyl halide (A) in S_N1 reactions, while (D) is incorrect since a chiral compound cannot racemize spontaneously. (C) refers to the carbocation as being sp-hybridized, which is incorrect.

14. D

A tertiary carbocation is more stable than primary and secondary carbocations due to inductive effects, so (A) and (B) are incorrect. (C) is incorrect because radicals do not form during S_N1 reactions.

15. D

Possible alkyl shifts leading to more stable carbocations are shown below. Compound III had a methyl group shift so that the carbocation became tertiary. In compound I, the carbon two carbons away from the carbocation attacked the positive formal charge. This creates a tertiary carbocation on an isopropyl group attached to a ring with one less carbon than it initially had. Compound II is incorrect, since the −OH group is in the wrong position, so (B) and (C) are incorrect. (A) is incorrect because it is not the only product possible.

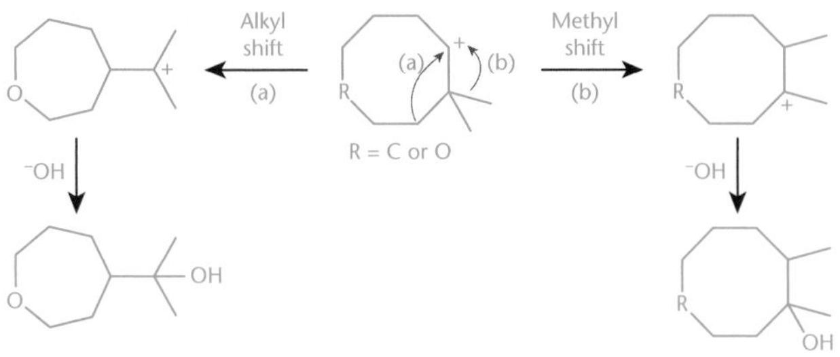

QUESTIONS 16–19

16. A

(B) and (C) are wrong for the same reason and thus the savvy test taker could have eliminated both of them at the same time. The phospholipid bilayer's interior is nonpolar, but the sides that face either the external environment or the internal environment of the cell are polar. (D) is wrong because insoluble is a relative term and no solvent was mentioned the question stem.

17. D

Levorotary compounds are defined as optically active compounds that rotate plane-polarized light in a counterclockwise fashion. Dextrorotatory compounds rotate it in a clockwise direction. Neither the R nor the S designation indicate the direction of rotation of plane-polarized light; rather, they indicate the orientation of groups around a chiral carbon.

18. C

Meso compounds by definition have an internal plane of symetry and thus one side of the molecule is the mirror image of the opposite side. (A) and (B) can be eliminated because an anomer is a special class of epimer. Epimers are diastereomers that differ at only one chiral C, and diastereomers are not mirror images. (D) is wrong because geometric isomers need not be symmetric.

19. B

A completely saturated hydrocarbon has as many hydrogens as possible. This means that carbons in the interior of the molecule are attached to two hydrogens and to two other atoms, and that carbons on the ends are attached to three hydrogens and one other atom. A double bond and a ring both create one degree of unsaturation. A triple bond creates two degrees of unsaturation. The formula for degrees of unsaturation is: Degrees of Unsaturation = $[(2C + 2) + N - X - H]/2$, where C stands for the number of carbons, N stands for the number of nitrogens, X stands for the number of halogens, and H stands for the number of hydrogens. For $C_{20}H_{40}$, the degree of unsaturation = $[(2 \times 20 + 2) - 40]/2 = 1$. This matches (B).

PASSAGE III

20. B

The monosaccharide is a D-aldose because the chiral carbon furthest from the carboxyl group is to the right in the open structure; it is an aldose rather than ketose because the open chain form shows that the carbon atom number one is an aldehyde; it is a pentose because it has five carbons; it is a furanose ring because it is a five-membered ring (including the oxygen). The monosaccharide ring is α. In D-sugars, α carbons have the hydroxyl group on the number one, anomeric carbon pointing downward below the ring. (A) is incorrect because it contains pyranose ring and the β anomer as descriptors. (C) is incorrect because it contains L and ketose as descriptors. (D) is incorrect because it contains L and hexose as descriptors.

21. C

Carbons are numbered with carbon number 1 (C1) as the carbonyl carbon, then carbons are numbered sequentially going away from the carbonyl carbon. Chiral centers are asymmetric carbons, meaning that all four bonds are to different atoms or groups. The open ring has two chiral carbons, C3 and C4, and the ring structure has three (C1, C3, and C4), having gained one when carbons 4 and 1 joined to form the ring structure. (A) is incorrect, as the ring structure has three (C1, C3, and C4) chiral carbons. (B) is incorrect, as C1 is not chiral on the open structure, and C5 is not chiral. (D) is incorrect, as the answers are the reverse of the correct answers, giving the achiral carbons rather than the chiral carbons.

22. D

Monosaccharides are reducing sugars because they are either aldehydes or ketones that form a hydroxyl group on the anomeric (C1) carbon when they take a ring form. This hydroxyl group is able to donate electrons to reduce another molecule and form a new bond. Structures I and III, however, have a methyl group added to the oxygen at the C1 carbon, so the sugar is no longer reducing. The methyl group destroys the reducing power of the hydroxyl group. Therefore, structures I and III are non-reducing. The oxygen

atoms attached to the C1 and C2 carbons in structure IV (which is sucrose) are tied up in the glycosidic linkage and therefore are unable to reduce. Therefore, structures I, III, and IV are all non-reducing sugars. (A) is incorrect because it is incomplete because structures III and IV are not included. (B) is incorrect because it (glucose) is a reducing sugar. (C) is incorrect because it is incomplete because it does not include structures I and III.

23. A

Bromine water is acidic and thus does not allow isomerization to take place as do the alkaline solutions provided by Fehling's (Benedict's) solution and Tollen's reagent. (B) is incorrect because it does not show the C1 carbon to have been oxidized and a double bond to oxygen has formed at C2. (C) is incorrect because it shows isomerization that changes the hydroxyl at C2 to the β orientation, and the orientation of the hydroxyl at C3 has changed to α. (D) is incorrect because isomerization has resulted in the switch to α-hydroxyl from β-hydroxyl at the C3 carbon.

24. C

The first reaction is with HCN to form the cyanohydrin at the C2 carboxyl, which is then hydrolyzed to the hydroxy acid. Upon treatment with hydrogen iodide and heat, the hydroxyls are reduced to hydrogens, yielding the final product, α-methylcaproic acid. (A) is incorrect because acetic anhydride would have added an acyl group to each hydroxyl. (B) is incorrect because after the cyanohydrin is formed by reaction with HCN, reaction with HI next would reduce hydroxyls to hydrogens, but leave the cyanohydrin intact. Hydrolysis treatment would then produce the unsaturated hydroxy acid. (D) is incorrect because if fructose is first reduced with H_2 and nickel, it would change carbonyl to a hydroxyl, then HI and heat treatment would reduce the alcohols to hydrogens, but add iodine to the C2 carbon.

25. C

Acylation of glucose with acetic anhydride results in the formation of an acyl linkage to each hydoxyl group in the glucose molecule, which is 5 hydroxyls in glucose. So there is a total of six carbonyl groups: five from the hydroxyl groups that were acylated and one from the original aldehyde on C1. Reduction of glucose with hydrogen and nickel reduces the carbonyl, changing it to another hydroxyl, to yield 6 hydroxyls per glucose molecule.

26. B

An excess of phenylhydrazine reacts with aldose and ketose sugars to produce an osazone that can then have the phenylhydrazine group removed by warm acid to give an osone. This activity destroys differences based on the C1 and C2 carbon. Because glucose, mannose, and fructose differ only at C1 and C2, they will all yield the same osazone after reacting with phenylhydrazine, and after subsequent treatment with warm acid, the same osone structure will result for the three compounds. Gulose, however, differs at the C3 and C4 carbons, and thus its structure will differ from the other three structures. (A) is incorrect because it will have the same osazone and osone structure as mannose and fructose. (C) is incorrect because it will have the same osazone and osone structure as as glucose and and fructose. (D) is incorrect because it will have the same osazone and ozone structure as glucose and mannose.

27. D

A sugar can be reacted with other compounds to form glycosides through a glycosidic bond, which is basically an ether linkage (R–O–R). The other compound can be an alcohol, a thio, or an amine. The triphosphate is an ester linkage but not a diester linkage, as would be true if one of the O⁻ groups were to form another ester linkage with a second molecule, such as another ribose. The latter occurs in RNA and DNA. (A) and (B) are incomplete. (C) is incorrect as the triphosphate is linked in an ester linkage, not a diester linkage.

28. D

Phosphoric acid is a triprotic acid, because it has three–OH groups. It can form the anhydrides di- or triphosphoric acid, which also have multiple –OH groups that form ester linkages with the –OH groups of sugars. Ribose molecules in RNA and DNA are held together by the phosphodiester bonds from the 5′ carbon of one ribose to the 3′ OH of an adjacent ribose. The –OH groups of the phosphoric acid can form an unstable cyclic bond with the 3′ and 2′ OH groups of ribose under alkaline conditions, resulting in strand breakage in RNA. Because deoxyribose does not have an OH group at the 2′ sugar, it is not susceptible to the cyclic ester formation by phosphoric acid. The other answer choices are correct but incomplete.

2′,3′-cyclic nucleoside monophosphate

29. A

Methylation occurs at the C1 carbon, which is, of course, the aldehyde (strictly speaking, the hemiacetal) group. Methylation of the other carbons occurs under alkaline conditions with methyl sulfate. (B) is wrong because methylation occurs only at the C1 carbon. (C) and (D) are incorrect because methylation occurs only at the C1 carbon under these conditions. (B), (C), and (D) are also wrong because they are all α anomers.

QUESTIONS 30–32

30. B

Bromine is selective for secondary and tertiary carbons whereas fluorine (A) and chlorine (C) prefer primary carbons. Iodine (D) rarely reacts via free radical halogenation because its large atomic radius makes it the most stable halogen in ionic form.

31. C

What are the characteristics of a bimolecular nucleophilic substitution reaction? Because item II appears in all of the choices, it makes sense to evaluate I or III. Both of those are characteristic of S_N2 reactions, so neither can be correct. That leaves (C) as the only valid option.

32. A

Which class of carbonyls is the most reactive? The electronegativity of the halogen group accentuates the nucleophilic character of the already polar carbonyl carbon increasing its susceptibility to electrophilic attack. Furthermore, halogens are among the best leaving groups.

PASSAGE IV

33. A

The methyl group of acetic acid is brominated during the first step, after which the bromide is substituted with a cyanide group. Hydrolysis with aqueous acid converts the −CN to −COOH. Excess methanol in aqueous acid (B) is incorrect, as this reaction forms an ester. While base, followed by formic acid, then acid neutralization (C) is a possible procedure, it is unlikely to synthesize malonic acid in high yields because the carboxylic acids present would affect the reactivities of the base. $KMnO_4$ (potassium permanganate) (D) is a strong oxidizer and can form carboxylic acids; however, it cannot add carbon atoms to acetic acid to form malonic acid.

34. B

The acidity of carboxylic acids increases with increased stability of the conjugate base. Because nitro groups are electron withdrawing, they stabilize the conjugate base by inductive effects, so (A) is a correct inequality, and an incorrect choice. A methyl group in the *para* position is actually destabilizing, as it donates electrons into the benzene ring, resulting in a weaker acid, so (C) is incorrect. A chloride in the *ortho* position stabilizes the base more than when it is in the *meta* or *para* positions, so (D) is incorrect. The oxygen atom in the para-substituted methoxy group in (B) actually donates electron density to the overall

molecule, makes the proton less likely to leave, and makes it less acidic than benzoic acid.

35. C

In molecules that have three or more carboxylic acid groups, the carboxylic acids are no longer counted in the main alkane backbone but are named using a carboxylic acid suffix. In isocitric acid, the alkane chain is propane (three carbons) and the number one carbon has an −OH group. The carboxylic acids are considered substituents at carbons 1, 2, and 3 on the propane chain. Tricarboxyl-2-pentanol (A) incorrectly indicates that an alcohol has higher priority than a carboxylic acid. The *oxo-* in (D) denotes a carbonyl group, not a carboxylic acid. (B) erroneously includes carbons from the carboxylic acids in the main alkane chain.

36. C

Fluorine is more electronegative than chlorine, and its presence near the carboxylic acid is more electron-withdrawing making fluoroacetic acid more acidic. Three electronegative atoms enhance the effect making (B) a true statement. The effect of this electron-withdrawing ability decreases as distance from the acidic proton increases; therefore, 2-fluorobutanoic acid is more acidic than 4-fluorobutanoic acid. The additional alkyl group in succinic acid works to slightly destabilize the conjugate base when compared to malonic acid. Malonic acid is the more acidic compound, thus (C) is the correct choice.

37. D

β-keto acids undergo decarboxylation. When heated, the dicarboxylic acid in (A) forms acetic acid and carbon dioxide. In (B), the structure lends itself to the formation of a cyclic anhydride, namely succinic anhydride. In (C), a seven-membered lactone forms. (D)'s dicarboxylic acid, suberic acid, would not form a nine-membered lactone ring, because a nine-membered ring is not as energetically favorable as it is in the cases with five- or seven-membered rings. Suberic acid is more likely to form straight-chain polymeric anhydrides when heated.

38. B

THF and succinic acid have four carbon molecules while adipic acid contains six carbons. While there is more than one way to perform these syntheses, (B) is incorrect. The oxidation step is not needed in the synthesis of adipic acid. Both reactions start with HI (A), which opens the THF ring and leaves iodide atoms on each end of the chain. The addition of two CO_2 molecules (carbonation) converts the iodinated intermediate into a dicarboxylic acid, namely adipic acid. Because succinic acid does not require additional carbons, base is applied to make a diol (D), which is then oxidized.

39. A

By binding molecules in specific configurations and lowering reaction energies, enzymes are able to catalyze organic reactions. In this case, the simplest organic reaction is to deprotonate the alcohol in fluorocitrate. The oxygen anion that remains forms a carbonyl with the carbon atom it is bonded to, and fluoroacetic acid is the leaving group; oxaloacetic acid is the other product. Because enzymes can sometimes catalyze reactions that are not feasible using other catalysts, complicated mechanisms could exist for (B), (C), and (D). However, if the oxygen in threonine—the sulfur in cysteine—or the fluoride ion were to act as nucleophiles, the products would not be formed in a single step.

PASSAGE V

40. A

At C2, the order of substituent priority in decreasing order is the following: $-OH$, $-CHO$, $-CH_2OH$, and $-H$. The substituents form a counterclockwise turn, which would imply 2S; however, the hydrogen atom is on a horizontal bond in a Fischer projection, which can be represented as a wedge coming out of the page. When the lowest priority group is not pointing away, the designation needs to be reversed. The actual configuration is 2R. In addition, the longest chain contains three carbon atoms, with the aldehyde having higher priority than the alcohol groups, so the compound name is as given in (A).

41. C

Ruff degradation removes aldehyde groups as CO_2, shortening sugars by one carbon atom (see Figure 1); the carbon directly adjacent to the starting aldehyde group now becomes the new aldehyde. If D-(-)-arabinose can be formed from either D-(+)-glucose or D-(+)-mannose, then this implies that only the stereochemistry at C2 is different, which becomes the aldehyde group in arabinose. Therefore, D-(+)-glucose and D-(+)-mannose must be C2 epimers. If glucose and mannose were C3 epimers (B), then one round of Ruff degradation would produce different aldopentoses. If glucose and mannose were enantiomers (A), then all their stereocenters would have opposite configurations to one another, and removing the aldehyde group would still give a distinct pair of enantiomeric aldopentoses.

42. D

Because the passage concentrates on D-sugars only, (A) and (B) can be discounted. (C) is incorrect, as the reactant and products are different (see below).

Interchanging the end groups of (D), followed by 180° rotation, gives the same (see below).

43. C

HNO_3 oxidizes both end groups to carboxylic acids, as seen in Figure 2. Because HNO_3 does not oxidize all $-OH$ groups present, (D) is incorrect. The reagents in the second step of the reaction in Figure 1 oxidize the carboxylic acid into a separate carbon dioxide. A CO_2 is lost from both ends, giving a product with two fewer carbon atoms than the reactant (C). Because the functional groups on both ends of the molecule are fully oxidized to carboxylic acids, switching functional groups (A) would not occur. Ruff degradation does not break up the reactant sugar.

44. A

Addition of HCN to aldehydes forms cyanohydrins, via nucleophilic attack of the cyanide ion on the carbonyl carbon atom. The proton is transferred to oxygen to form an alcohol. (B) results from treatment of a cyanohydrin with lithium aluminum hydride (reduction of the cyanide group), while (C) is the intermediate that leads to (B), so they are both incorrect. Finally, because HCN is not a reducing agent, it cannot readily replace alcohol groups with hydrogen, so (D) is incorrect.

45. D

Because the addition of HCN is not stereoselective, the stereochemistry of the cyanohydrin carbon can be R or S. In addition, the other chiral carbon atom in glyceraldehyde has a fixed stereochemistry (R), so the pair of tetroses are diastereomers, where only one stereocenter has a different configuration. Because the definition of diastereomers excludes enantiomers, (A) is incorrect. Structural isomers (B) have the same molecular formula, but the atoms are connected differently, which is not the case with pairs of sugars. Geometric isomers (C) refer to *cis-*/*trans-*isomerism such as those seen in alkenes, not sugars.

46. D

A common mistake is to assume that once D or L is known for a particular sugar, its optical rotation can be easily predicted. However, the optical rotation for any molecule can only be determined experimentally, and does not depend on D/L, or R/S configurations. For example, it is only by chance that in nature, glucose exists in a D-(+)- configuration.

PASSAGE VI

47. D

Because both drugs contain carboxylic acid groups, which can take part in extensive hydrogen bonding with each other, their IR spectra contains a very broad absorption band that spans 3,500 to 2,500 cm^{-1},which corresponds to the acid O–H bond stretch. (A) describes carbon-carbon bond stretches, while (B) corresponds to alcohol O–H stretches. Finally, (C) describes aldehyde C–H stretches, which is present only in drug A.

48. A

Carbon is a p-block element, so the highest occupied orbital is a p orbital. Elemental carbon contains six electrons (the same number as its atomic number), and filling up the orbitals via the Aufbau principle, there are two electrons in the 1s orbital, two in the 2s orbital, and two in the 2p orbital, i.e., $1s^2 \, 2s^2 \, 2p^6$. (A) is correct.

49. D

A pi bond forms by the parallel (side-to-side) overlap of two p orbitals. No s orbitals are involved in pi bond formation (A) and (B). Perpendicular overlap of p orbitals (C) cannot result in bonds.

50. B

Negative (exothermic) energy is a measure of stability: the more negative a reaction is, the less stable the initial reactant is. Thus, a molecule that is initially very stable will release less energy during an exothermic reaction. (C) is incorrect because benzene rings are more stable than rings with unconjugated pi bonds, so the energy released is less than choices (A) and (B). 1,3-cyclohexadiene (B) is less stable than cyclohexene (A) due to increased ring strain and sterics (double bonds are shorter than single bonds), so (B) releases more energy upon hydrogenation.

51. B

The strength of carbon-carbon bonds is directly correlated to the number of times they are bonded to each other. Triple bonds are strongest, followed by double bonds, and then single bonds. Triple bonds are also the shortest, followed by double bonds, and then single bonds (the longest). (B) correctly describes, in decreasing order, both bond strength and bond length.

52. B

The most convenient way to deactivate the drugs is to reduce their polarity; forming esters can effectively reduce absorption through the lumen. Hydrogenation (A) is unlikely to have any effect on polarity, since the double bonds present are not affected. Reduction to primary alcohols (C) will greatly increase the polarity of the drugs. Substitution with $SOCl_2$ (D) converts the drugs to acid chlorides, which are unreliable as drugs since they are highly reactive.

PRACTICE SECTION 2

ANSWER KEY

1.	A	19.	C	37.	B
2.	C	20.	D	38.	C
3.	D	21.	C	39.	A
4.	C	22.	A	40.	C
5.	D	23.	C	41.	A
6.	B	24.	B	42.	A
7.	C	25.	A	43.	C
8.	A	26.	A	44.	D
9.	A	27.	C	45.	D
10.	A	28.	C	46.	C
11.	D	29.	C	47.	B
12.	C	30.	A	48.	A
13.	B	31.	B	49.	D
14.	A	32.	A	50.	A
15.	A	33.	C	51.	A
16.	D	34.	D	52.	B
17.	C	35.	D		
18.	B	36.	C		

PASSAGE I

1. A

(B) is incorrect because the alkene—part of the longest carbon chain—should not be given priority. (C) is incorrect because the substituents are not in alphabetical order. (D) is incorrect because the numbering is not correct (in fact, the compound would contain a carbon with five bonds.)

2. C

(B) is an oxidizing agent. (D) is incorrect because a hydrazone is formed, with no reduction occurring. $LiAlH_4$ is a much stronger reducing agent than $NaBH_4$, and will reduce both ketones present to alcohols.

3. D

The ketone group is protected as an acetal, and an alcohol in the presence of aqueous acid is used. (B) is incorrect, because acid is a required catalyst.

4. C

The longest chain contains seven carbon atoms, with the aldehyde having a higher priority than the ketone groups. The *oxo* prefix in (B) cannot refer to the aldehyde and only one of the ketones.

5. D

The simplest way to answer this question is to recognize which protons are the most acidic (the ones between the two ketone groups) for enol formation. (B) and (C) are incorrect because those enols will not produce five-membered rings. (A) is incorrect because the aldehyde is not present in compound V.

6. B

The coupling between compounds III and V occurs in the same way as the coupling between compounds I and II. There is no ketone group protection, so (A) is incorrect, and because no reduction of ketone groups is occurring, (C) is incorrect. (D) is incorrect since it is part of (A).

7. C

Aqueous acids are sufficient enough to remove acetals, which are stable in bases (B), as well as oxidizing agents (A) and (D).

8. A

(B) is used for Wittig reactions, which add carbon atoms to carbonyl groups, while (C) is an oxidant. (D) is used for cyanohydrin formation. (A) contains the reagents needed for a Clemmensen reduction.

PASSAGE II

9. A

Given the favorable energies achieved through catalysis by enzymes, salicylanilide is undergoing nucleophilic attack at the carbonyl carbon, because aniline is being formed. Of the residues listed, leucine (A) is least likely to be participating in this reaction because its alkyl side chain does not contain an acceptable nucleophile. In contrast, the other amino acids have potential nucleophiles in their side chains: serine has an oxygen atom, cysteine has a sulfur atom, and lysine has a nitrogen atom, all of which could act as nucleophiles.

10. A

$LiAlH_4$ is an extremely strong reducing agent. It will reduce the carboxyl group all the way down to a primary alcohol and it will reduce all of the aromatic pi bonds. (B) is incorrect because the aromatic pi bonds have not been reduced. (C) is incorrect because the carboxyl has not been reduced. (D) is incorrect because aromatic pi bonds have not been reduced and because there is a methyl group where a hydroxyl group should be.

11. D

The groups of reactants and reagents shown are able to oxidize aliphatic alcohols, not phenol. When combined with the reagents in (A) and (B), primary alcohols are oxidized to carboxylic acids. CrO_3^- pyridine, CH_2Cl_2 (C) would oxidize a primary alcohol to an aldehyde.

12. C

When an ester bond is heated with a strong base such as NaOH, the hydroxide group acts as a nucleophile and attacks the carbonyl carbon. The leaving group is the alcohol formed from the noncarbonyl oxygen (after acidification). In the case of salicylanilide, the major products of this synthesis are phenol (C) and salicylic acid. (A) is close to salicylic acid but incorrect, because it cannot be formed from saponification of phenyl 2-hydroxybenzoate. (D) is too far reduced to be a possible product. It is conceivable that the product salicylic acid goes on to form a ring under these conditions. However, if the OH group were to act as a nucleophile on the carboxylic acid, the ring formed would be four-membered, not five-membered as shown.

13. B

A Hofmann rearrangement converts a primary amide to a primary amine with the loss of one carbon, as in (B). (A) reflects a loss of two carbons. While the amide is converted to an amine, (C) does not account for the loss of a carbon. (D) is incorrect because a Hofmann rearrangement does not convert amides to carboxylic acids.

14. A

The amide group has fairly high priority among functional groups in that it is higher than alcohol, phenyl, and alkyl groups. Because there is an amide group, (A) is correct. An alternate name is 2-hydroxybenzanilide, which is similar to (B) 3-hydroxybenzanilide. (C) does not account for the priority of the amide group over the alcohol group, and (D) erroneously describes a carboxylic acid, which is distinct from an amide.

15. A

Aniline and acetic anhydride (A) combine to form acetanilide. The amino group of aniline attacks one of the carbonyl groups of acetic anhydride with acetate as the leaving group. Amides are relatively unreactive species and (B) and (C) would not result in acetanilide. The reaction in (D) creates an amide group very similar to acetanilide. However, instead of aniline, the reaction uses cyclohexane amine.

QUESTIONS 16–19

16. D

While nucleophilic addition could theoretically occur in a carboxylic acid, many other compounds—even alkanes—undergo this type of reaction, so (D) is not specific to carboxylic acids. (A), (B), and (C) are common reactions for carboxylic acids.

17. C

High temperature and extreme basicity or acidity create highly oxidative conditions. These favor the formation of the most oxidized compound: a carboxylic acid.

18. B

A peptide bond is said to have partial double bond character. To answer this question, you must understand that pi bonds prevent rotation about the axis of the bond. The α-helices and β-pleats that compose a protein's secondary structure are explained by this rigidity of peptide bonds.

19. C

The addition of one nitrate group breaks the symmetry of chlorobenzene. Because the nitrate group can add on to the 1,2,3,4 carbons (5,6 are indistinguishable from 2,3). One might initially think (D) to be correct. However, the chlorine at position one forces the incoming nitrate, were it to add there, into one conformation. If the nitrate added at position one, then it would be on the opposite side of the carbon skeleton (remember that benzene is planar) and so both 'isomers' would appear exactly the same. However, for addition at positions 2, 3, 4 the nitrate group could add on either *cis* or *trans* to the chlorine thus creating an isomeric pair.

PASSAGE III

20. D

The base peak is by definition designated 100 percent abundant and all other peaks are measured relative to it. (C) is incorrect, because the number of possible fragments are different for different compounds, while (A) is incorrect, because the parent peak is not always evident on a mass spectrum. Finally, (B) is incorrect, because the smallest peak will give relative abundances of larger peak at more than 100 percent, which is impossible.

21. C

According to the passage, the base peak is the parent peak of compound Y, so this is a simple calculation based on the molecular formula $C_6H_{10}O$:

$$m/z = (6 \times 12) + (10 \times 1) + (16 \times 1) = 72 + 10 + 16 = 98$$

22. A

An enol isomerizes to carbonyl compounds due to keto-enol tautomerization. (D) is incorrect, because a carboxylic acid cannot be formed with a single oxygen atom, while (B) is incorrect, because the alkene will have to be reduced to form an alcohol, and reduction does not happen spontaneously. (C) is incorrect, because an epoxide is strained, and isomerization to it represents an uphill (unfavorable) climb in energy.

23. C

A very particular arrangement of atoms (see Question 6) is needed for a McLafferty arrangement. (A), (B), and (D) are incorrect, since the arrangement of atoms does not allow a McLafferty rearrangement to take place. We also know that (D) is incorrect since the passage says that compound Y contains a cyclobutane ring.

24. B

An allylic cation from an α-cleavage (see below) is stable due to resonance, and corresponds to m/z 41. (A) is incorrect, because its m/z is 43, not 41. (C) and (D) are incorrect for the same reason.

25. A

The fragment at m/z 29 comes from an α-cleavage of the aldehyde group, forming a carbocation which can be resonance stabilized by the lone pairs on oxygen. (B) and (D) are incorrect, because their m/z values are 28, not 29, while a primary ethyl carbocation (C) cannot stabilize by resonance, and thus is unlikely to appear on a mass spectrum.

26. A

According to the passage, alcohols readily lose the –OH group (as water) in the mass spectrum, and so the parent peak will either be small or not present. Another hint comes from m/z 80, which happens to correspond to m/z 98 – 18, or the molecular ion losing water. No ether group (C) would have a mass of 18. A methoxy group, the smallest possible ether, would result in 31 being subtracted from the molecular ion peak. Similarly, ketone (B) and aldehyde (D) do not readily lose their oxygen atom as water.

27. C

The m/z 29 fragment comes from the α-cleavage of the carbonyl. (B) is incorrect because compound Y does not contain a nitrogen atom.

28. C

(B) and (D) are incorrect because primary and secondary carbocations are less stable than allylic cations (A) and (C.) However, (A) is incorrect; a cyclobutene ring will have a much higher ring strain than a cyclopentene ring, and so it is less stable than (C).

PASSAGE IV

29. C

Because compound I reacts with *two* molecules of hydrogen, compound I has two degrees of unsaturation. A more definitive way to deduce the answer is to follow the equation below:

$$\text{Degrees of unsaturation} = \frac{2C + 2 - H - X + N}{2}$$

Where C is the number of carbon atoms, H is the number of hydrogen atoms, X is the number of halides, and N the number of nitrogen atoms.

30. A

Compound I is optically active because it has a chiral carbon (i.e., a carbon with four different substituents). (B), (C), and (D) are incorrect because they don't contain a chiral carbon.

31. B

There are two ways of solving this problem. One way is to recognize that two molecules of hydrogen (H_2) is 4 hydrogen atoms. Adding these to the molecule we determined to be the structure of Compound I in the previous problem will reduce the alkyne to an alkane, leaving (B). Another way of solving this problem is to recognize that (B) is the only molecule with a chiral carbon atom. The other answer choices are not optically active.

32. A

The structure can be verified by information provided in the table: a sharp absorbance at 1,720 cm^{-1}, combined with the broad overtone between 2,500–3,500 cm^{-1} is indicative of a carboxylic acid. The single piece of ^{1}H-NMR information also points to (A). (D) is incorrect: alcohols indeed have an IR absorbance at 3,400 cm^{-1}, but there is no large overtone. (B) and (C) are incorrect because the IR spectra for those also lack the broad absorbance.

33. C

Hydrogenation is occurring, so a suitable metal is needed for an adsorbent surface. Platinum is a relatively inactive metal, making it an excellent catalyst. All the other metals are too reactive themselves to be catalysts.

34. D

The IR spectrum for compound II should not have an absorbance band corresponding to the carbon-carbon triple bond stretch, which occurs at approximately 2,200 cm^{-1}. (A) implies that a carbonyl group has formed. (B) refers to an alcohol group. (C) is incorrect because carbon-carbon triple bonds stretches do not occur at such a low wave number.

35. D

Ozone cleaves triple bonds, and with aqueous workup yields two carboxylic acids. Because compound III is chiral, at least one of the products from ozonolysis should also be chiral, which in this case is compound VII. (B) and (C) are incorrect because VIII comes from an internal alkyne, while VI comes from an achiral terminal alkyne. Compound V (A) is not the sole product formed from the cleavage of a terminal alkyne.

36. C

An esterification is occurring, so disappearance of the hydrogen singlet of the carboxylic acid proton (at 12 ppm) indicates that the reaction is successful. (A) is incorrect, while (B) is only partially correct, because the ^{1}H-NMR spectrum for compound IV (see below) will also include a singlet for the methyl group protons; (C) sufficiently includes both the disappearance and appearance of the corresponding singlets. (D) is also incorrect: the carboxylic acid proton singlet does not couple to other protons, and the presence of that signal implies that no reaction takes place.

Compound IV
(C$_7$H$_{14}$O$_2$)

QUESTIONS 37–39

37. B

The unique hydrogen environments are as follows: one hydrogen bonded immediately to the alkene and each of the three methyl groups occupies a unique environment because there is no free rotation around a double bond thus preventing symmetry in the local electronic environment. (A) assumes that all methyls are electronically equivalent.

38. C

This is an example of a Grignard reaction. Because the products of such reactions have a carbon chain equal to the sum of the carbon chains of the reactants, (B) and (D) can be eliminated. Because the Grignard reaction is a reduction

reaction, ethyne should be converted into ethene, making (C) more likely than (A).

39. A

Both the alcohol and alkene moieties react with HBr. The alkene reacts to form the more stable carbocation and the alcohol reacts by the S$_N$2 mecha-nism to substitute the halogen for the hydroxyl group.

PASSAGE V

40. C

The longest chain contains five carbon atoms, and because the aldehyde group has the highest priority, the parent compound is a pentanal. In addition, because the aldehyde has the highest priority, it is assigned as carbon 1, which implies that the adjacent carbon with two methyl groups bonded to it is carbon 2. IUPAC naming requires that numbering redundancies be included for all substituents, giving 2,2-dimethyl-pentanal, or (C). The other choices don't give the aldehydes group the highest priority.

41. A

This question gives you the mechanism with which Grignard reagents work. The nucleophile in this case is the isopropyl group, which attacks the carbonyl carbon atom, which ultimately forms a secondary alcohol upon acidic workup.

To name this alcohol, the longest chain contains seven carbon atoms, and labeling the rightmost carbon atom as number 1 gives three methyl groups (on carbons 2, 4, and 4), while the hydroxyl group is on carbon 3, to give 2, 4, 4-trimethylheptan-3-ol (remember that substituents are named alphabetically, and that the numbers give the lowest possible sum). (D) is incorrect because the numbers are counted from the leftmost carbon atom, while (B) fails to account for the longest chain present. (C) fails to provide the position of the alcohol group.

42. A

The question provides a reaction that nitriles can undergo, namely, hydrolysis of the C−N triple bond by aqueous acid to form carboxylic acids. A nitrile contains cyanide ($-C\equiv N$) as the main functional group. (C) is an amide, while (B) is an imine. (D) is a diamine.

43. C

We have a six-member ring that has one double bond. This is classified as a cyclohexene (*cyclo-* for the ring structure; *hex-* meaning six carbons; *-ene* indicating the double bond). The ring is our main structure and thus the carbon chain will be treated as a substituent. (A) and (B) are incorrect; butanone is identified as the main structure and the cyclohexene is misidentified. We see that it is composed of four carbons and has a carbonyl attached with and adjacent alkyl group. Thus, the name of the substituent will be 1-butanone (*but-* meaning four; *-one* indicating a ketone; and 1 indicating that the ketone is positioned on the first carbon). Now that we know the substituent's name, we can complete it by referencing location. Because the butonone is the only substituent, the carbon it attaches to will be carbon 1 by default. If the 1-butanone is on the first carbon, then that means our double bond is on the third carbon. This should be indicated before the *-en* ending when identifying the cyclohexene molecule. Thus, the complete name of the structure is 1-(1-butanone)-cyclohex-3-ene. (D) is incorrect as there is no reference to substituent location.

44. D

This question requires you to draw out a new structure for the proposed product. The question tells you that the double bond has been broken, opening the hexe-3-en ring. This leaves the previous butanone structure with a saturated carbon chain (no double bonds) in place of the ring. So you need to draw out the new structure and name the molecule. Because the double bond was between the third and fourth carbon of the hexane ring, there will be two new carbon chains of differing lengths.

Remember to choose the carbon chain that is longest when naming your structure. Here you see that the longest chain consists of eight carbons. (A) is incorrect because all 10 carbons are not part of one continuous chain; in (B), the seven-member chain is not the longest continuous chain. If we number the carbons so that the high priority substituent has the lowest number, we are left with 4-(5-ethyl)-octanone. (C) is incorrect as the carbonyl is given the higher number.

45. D

Brady's reagent will produce a yellow or red precipitate when in the presence of aldehydes and ketones. (D) is the only choice that includes both of these functional groups.

46. C

According to the question, the fourth unknown forms a precipitate with Brady's reagent, but no silver mirror is observed with Tollen's reagent, so the unknown most likely contains a ketone group. One of many reactions that ketones can undergo is the Wittig reaction, which forms alkenes (C). (A) and (B) are meant to confuse you; several of the tests would first lead you to the conclusion that the molecule may be an aldehyde or ketone and you may forget to consider the Wittig reaction. (D) tests your knowledge of the difference between an alkene (double bond) and an alkyne (triple bond).

47. B

A strong absorbance at $1,200$ cm^{-1} indicates the presence of a C−O single bond. The strong absorbance at $1,760$ cm^{-1} indicates a carbonyl group (C=O stretching.) The broad stretch that spans $3,500$–$2,500$ cm^{-1} indicates the O−H bond of a carboxylic acid (do not confuse this with a strong absorbance at 3,400 cm^{-1}, which indicates an alcohol or phenol O–H stretch.) Information from the IR spectrum points to substance C, the carboxylic acid. Were this mixed with Tollen's reagent, no silver mirror (A) would be produced (because it's not an aldehyde). Adding alcohol to a carboxylic acid and applying heat does indeed form an ester (B). Carboxylic acids do not react with Tollen's reagent (2,4-DNPH) and thus there should be no precipitate (C). NaBH$_4$ would cause an alcohol formation when mixed with a ketone or an aldehyde, not a carboxylic acid (D).

PASSAGE VI

48. A

Charged molecules such as amino acids will migrate to either electrode when placed in an electric field, so (D) is not correct. The motility of molecules in an electric field also depends on their net charge: glycine exists in one of three states that change with increasing pH (low pH: NH$_3^+$CH$_2$COOH, pI: NH$_3^+$CH$_2$COO$^-$, high pH: NH$_2$CH$_2$COO$^-$). For glycine, the isoelectric point is the mean of pKa$_1$ and pKa$_2$ or (9.60 + 2.34)/2 = 5.97. Because the electrophoresis is taking place at pH 4, glycine is in its fully protonated form (NH$_3^+$CH$_2$COOH), and will migrate toward the cathode (A), or the negative terminal. (B) would be correct at a pH above 5.97, while (C) would be correct at a pH of 5.97.

49. D

The pH of the electrophoresis buffer should be configured so as to draw one amino acid toward the cathode, one to the anode (or one to remain stationary). The isoelectric point for glycine is (9.60 + 2.34)/2 = 5.97, and the pI of aspartic acid, using pKa$_1$ and pKa$_2$, is (1.88 + 3.65)/2 = 2.77. Performing the electrophoresis at pH 2.77 would draw glycine toward the cathode, and glutmate would remain stationary. Any pH less than 2.77 would draw both amino acids toward the cathode.

50. A

A Schiff base, also known as an imine, has a general formula like that of (A). (C) is a secondary amine, and (D) is a diazene group. (B) is incorrect, because the structure corresponds to a hydroazone.

51. A

The aldehyde group in PLP must be converted into a Schiff base in order to decarboxylate glutamic acid. Without knowing the reaction mechanism, it can be surmised that the active site lysine in GAD participates in the decarboxylation of glutamate via Schiff base formation, using its side chain amine group. The mechanism begins with the N atom of lysine's ε-amino group (side chain amino) making the nucleophilic attack on the aldehyde as described in (A). (C) and (D) can be ruled out since the α-amino group and the carboxylic acid are in the peptide backbone, and are unlikely to participate in catalysis. (B) does not make sense mechanistically as a geminal diol is being formed, which does not contribute to the progress of the reaction.

52. B

In the absence of the appropriate enzyme and cofactor, aspartic and glutamic acid does not decarboxylate spontaneously, even with heating, so (A) and (D) are incorrect. For this question, a beta-keto acid (B) can effectively be decarboxylated upon heating. 2-aminoethanoic acid (C) is the IUPAC name for glycine, which like aspartic and glutamic acid, does not lose CO$_2$ readily.

PRACTICE SECTION 3

ANSWER KEY

1.	C	19.	A	37.	C
2.	D	20.	B	38.	D
3.	A	21.	D	39.	A
4.	D	22.	C	40.	A
5.	B	23.	C	41.	A
6.	A	24.	D	42.	D
7.	C	25.	C	43.	D
8.	D	26.	A	44.	A
9.	B	27.	D	45.	D
10.	B	28.	A	46.	C
11.	A	29.	C	47.	B
12.	B	30.	B	48.	A
13.	C	31.	B	49.	C
14.	A	32.	D	50.	A
15.	C	33.	D	51.	A
16.	B	34.	C	52.	C
17.	D	35.	B		
18.	D	36.	A		

PASSAGE I

1. C

Tollen's reagent oxidizes aldehydes but not ketones to give the corresponding carboxylic acid. Because $CH_3CH_2CH_2CH_2OH$ is a primary alcohol, it is oxidized to a mixture of an aldehyde and a carboxylic acid, in contrast to $CH_3CH_2CH(OH)CH_3$ which, as a secondary alcohol, is oxidized to a ketone. (A) is the unreacted ketone formed from oxidation of the secondary alcohol. (B) is the reactant upon which Tollen's reagent reacts, not the product of the reaction. (D) is unreacted secondary alcohol.

2. D

In the presence of base and heat, the addition product, a hydrazone, is unstable and progresses to the alkane. (A) is incorrect, though it would be correct if the reaction environment were acidic. In basic environment, however, it is

an unstable intermediate. (B) is the alcohol and would not be made under the conditions shown. (C) is incorrect, as the complete molecule of hydrazine adds to the reactant in the intermediate step, as in (A).

3. A

(D) is the starting methyl ethyl ketone. Nucleophilic addition of –CN to the carbonyl carbon results in 2-butanone cyanohydrin. Next, acid hydrolisis yields 2-methyl-2-butenoic acid (A). (C) is the unstable intermediate formed from hydrolysis of the cyanohydrin leading to the final product.

4. D

When a α-hydrogen exists on the aldehyde or ketone, the presence of a dilute base or dilute acid results in an aldol condensation, and two molecules of acetaldehyde combine to form β-hydroxybutaldehyde. (A) is a salt of the carboxylic acid of butaldehyde.

5. B

The reaction is done in a basic environment, and the hydroxide ion removes a hydrogen ion from the α-hydrogen of acetaldehyde to create a carbanion, the nucleophilic reagent which attacks a second acetaldehyde's carbonyl carbon. (A) is the hydroxide ion that abstracts the hydrogen ion from the α-hydrogen of acetaldehyde to form the nucleophilic reagent. (C) is the resulting ion formed by the nucleophilic attack but before protonation to the final product. (D) is the final product.

6. A

The aldol is dehydrated to form 2-butenal. The reaction places the double bond between the α and β carbons, (i.e., C2 and C3). The double bond forms between these two carbons because it creates a conjugated system with the carbonyl C=O double bond. If the double bond formed between the beta and gamma carbons, no conjugation would result. (B) is a carboxylic acid, which is not the type of product expected from dehydration from an aldol. (C) and (D) place the double bond incorrectly.

7. C

Aldol condensation of two molecules of acetaldehyde is the first step to yield the 4-carbon compound under basic conditions, and hydrolysis yields 2-butenal followed by hydrogenation of the alkene to give butyraldehyde. (A) skips the dehydration to 2-butenal step. (B) skips the hydrogenation to n-butyl alcohol step. (D) is incorrect because, for one thing, acetone cannot be accessed from ethyl alcohol via aldol condensation.

8. D

Benzaldehyde reacts with acetic anhydride to give cinnamic acid (B), which can then be hydrogenated with molecular hydrogen and nickel catalyst to give hydrocinnamic acid. (A) is incorrect because, although a starting material (acetic anhydride), the question asks for the other starting compound. (B) is the result of the condensation reaction but not of the hydrogenation reaction. (C) accepts the hydrogen released in the condensation, but is not the product of the condensation or the hydrogenation.

PASSAGE II

9. B

A Schiff base (aka imine) is formed between a primary amine and carbonyl group, with the loss of a water molecule. (A) is not an imine (it is just a regular amine). (C) is incorrect because the five-membered ring is formed after initial Schiff base formation. (D) is incorrect. The molecule is an enamine, formed between a secondary amine and carbonyl group.

10. B

A reduction is occurring and (B) is the only reducing group among the choices. (A) is an oxidizing agent, (C) is used for hydroboration and hydroxylation of alkenes, and (D) is typically used for, among other reactions, bromination of alkenes.

11. A

The product contains an alcohol functional group, so the name should contain the suffix –ol, in keeping with naming

tropinone with the suffix –one implying the ketone group. Tropane (B) is correct only if the ketone group is removed, while tropene (C) is incorrect because no alkenes are present. Tropinamine (D) implies that an additional amine group is present.

12. B

The longest chain contains three carbon atoms, with the carboxylic acid having the highest priority, so the parent compound is propanoic acid; (A) is incorrect. The stereochemistry of C2 (see below) is S, so (C) and (D) are incorrect.

13. C

Because tropinone is a symmetric molecule with a plane of symmetry that bisects the carbonyl group and nitrogen, there are several signals that occur at identical chemical shifts. Starting at the carbons alpha to the carbonyl group (see below), there is one signal for the alpha protons, one for the beta protons, one for the gamma protons, and one for the methyl group on the nitrogen atom, for a total of 4 ^{1}H-NMR signals.

14. A

Using the same plane of symmetry that bisects the carbonyl group and the nitrogen as above, and starting from the carbonyl carbon, there is one signal for the carbonyl, one for carbons in the alpha position, one for the beta-carbons, one for the gamma carbons, and one for the methyl group on nitrogen, for a total of five distinct ^{13}C NMR signals.

15. C

Because the enol is attacking, it cannot be an electrophile, so item I is incorrect. The formation of an enol depends on the acidity of the protons alpha to the carbonyl group, and more carbonyl groups that flank such protons increases their acidity. Therefore, item III is correct. Finally, if the α-protons are more acidic, then the enol will be formed more easily, implying an increase in stability, making item II correct. β-protons (item IV) are too distant from the carbonyl group to affect acidity. With items II and III correct, that means (C) is the answer.

QUESTIONS 16–18

16. B

The unique environments are as follows: the hydrogen common immediately off the alkene, each methyl group immediately attached to the alkene has its own peak as there is no free rotation around a double bond and because the other groups attached to the alkene group obviate symmetry, there are two distinct chemical environments, the ethyl group gives three peaks, one for the methyl hydrogens and one for each hydrogen of the intermediate carbon.

17. D

The question requires you to know that in a radical halogenation reaction, the initiation and propagation steps (A) and (C) give rise to molecules with unpaired electrons. Only termination (D) will end the process, yielding molecules with no free radicals. Elongation (B) is not a step in radical halogenation.

18. D

The question requires you to know the chemical structure of a triglyceride. Triglycerides are composed of fatty acids and the three-carbon backbone of glycerol.

PASSAGE III

19. A

The two reactions used to convert benzene to benzoic acid in this case is a Friedel-Crafts alkylation, followed by side-chain oxidation. Only (A) contains the required reagents for those reactions. PCC (C) is not strong enough an oxidant, (D) lists a Friedel-Crafts *acylation* as the first step, and the first step of (B) does not lead to alkylation.

20. B

Two concentrated acids (nitric and sulfuric) are needed for nitration to occur; the actual active species is a nitroso ($^+NO_2$) cation. (A) and (C) are incorrect because, in those cases, NO_2 exists as an anion. (D) is incorrect because a nitroso ion cannot form spontaneously from nitric acid (sulfuric acid is required for activation of nitric acid).

21. D

The reduction of aromatic nitro compounds to amines can be performed by either hydrogenation (item I) or treatment with an active metal in an acidic media (items II and III). Because all items are correct, (D) is correct.

22. C

Meta-directing groups deactivate benzene rings by withdrawing electron density, so (B) is incorrect. Conversely, *ortho*- and *para*-directing groups activate benzene rings by donating electron density by resonance and/or inductive effects, so (A) is incorrect. Because an amine group contains a lone pair on nitrogen, it can donate electrons into the benzene ring by resonance, so (D) is incorrect.

23. C

A good Lewis acid, for example, is one where the molecule is electron deficient, such as salts formed by Group III elements, including boron (item I) and aluminum (item II). Items III and IV are weaker Lewis acids than items I and II, because the metals are less electron deficient. Because items I and II are correct, the answer is (C).

24. D

Benzene rings rarely undergo radical reactions, since aromaticity is destroyed to give a very high energy radical, so (A) and (B) are incorrect. Radicals that can delocalize into the benzene ring, such as a benzyl radical, however, are highly stable, and (D) comes from the radical bromination of its corresponding benzyl radical. (C) is incorrect because bromine is in the wrong position.

25. C

Among the choices, only NaH (sodium hydride) can activate phenol via deprotonation of the alcohol group, to form sodium phenoxide and gaseous hydrogen. A negatively charged phenoxide is more likely to undergo electrophilic aromatic substitution (*para*-directed) than phenol itself, which has no charge. HCl and H_3O^+ [(A) and (D)] protonate phenol, giving it a positive charge, which will deactivate the benzene ring. Phenol is not activated in water (B), and is only sparingly soluble.

26. A

Phenol (or phenoxide) is an *ortho*-/*para*-directing group by resonance, so (B), a *meta*-substituted product, is incorrect. The oxygen atom is unlikely to attack the nitrogen atom, both electronegative elements, directly, so (C) is incorrect. In (D), phenol has been added to the wrong nitrogen atom (besides, the product is not an azo compound).

PASSAGE IV

27. D

Of the compounds in the starting mixture, caffeine is the most nonpolar, so it will dissolve in warm chloroform. The other choices contain some sort of polar functional group or arrange the slightly polar groups such that the molecule overall has a degree of polarity (amine group in amantadine, carboxylic acid in aspirin, and amide and ether groups in ethenzamide).

28. A

With caffeine already separated, (B) is incorrect. For this question, it is sufficient to realize that hot ethanol will most likely dissolve acetaminophen over the other two choices, due to the presence of the phenol group.

29. C

Because none of the choices lists a signal which corresponds to a carboxylic acid proton—which occurs between $\delta 10$–13—it may be easier to discern which choices are incorrect as a result of specific signals. (D) is incorrect, as the first two signals (triplet and quartet) are indicative of an ethyl group, which is present only in ethenzamide. (B) is also incorrect, since the singlets that integrate to three protons correspond to the N-bonded methyl groups in caffeine. (A) is incorrect because the two doublets that occur in the phenyl proton region strongly suggest a *para*-substituted benzene, which is observed in the structure for acetaminophen.

30. B

The solubility of aspirin in NaOH is a result of deprotonation leading to formation of a charged species in an aqueous solution. The most acidic proton is in the carboxylic acid group, rather than the α-protons (C) or the phenyl protons (D). While the association of sodium ions to oxygen atoms does occur (A), no actual deprotonation is occurring, so it is incorrect.

31. B

The answer should be apparent from your work in answering the previous four questions. Aspirin (D) cannot appear in the final separation. Caffeine (A) is separated after the addition of warm chloroform. Acetaminophen (C) dissolves in hot ethanol.

32. D

Because acetaminophen is a *para*-substituted benzene, some of the phenyl carbon atoms will have identical ^{13}C NMR signals. There are a total of six distinct signals (see below). The other answers fail to account for symmetry.

33. D

$LiAlH_4$ is a strong reducing agent, able to reduce amides, esters, and carboxylic acids into their corresponding amines and alcohols. Because acetaminophen and ethenzamide contain amides, and aspirin contains a carboxylic acid and an ester, they can be reduced by $LiAlH_4$. Amines groups are unaffected by $LiAlH_4$, so item I is incorrect. (D) is correct.

34. C

Ibuprofen contains a carboxylic acid group, so it is expected that, like aspirin, it will dissolve in NaOH. In addition, it is insoluble in chloroform, ethanol, and HCl.

35. B

The reaction sequence of sodium hydride, followed by methyl iodide is able to form ethers (with the hydroxyl group in acetaminophen) or esters (with the carboxylic acid group in aspirin.) As such, hot ethanol will unlikely be able to dissolve the methyl ether of acetaminophen. The methyl ester of aspirin, however, can be converted back to the carboxylate via saponification, so (C) is incorrect. As for (A) and (D), the reaction conditions in the question will not affect caffeine, amantadine, and ethenzamide.

36. A

NaOH will dissolve in both aspirin and acetaminophen (NaOH will deprotonate the hydroxyl group in acetaminophen), so any answer choice which uses NaOH before hot ethanol is incorrect [(B), (C), and (D)].

QUESTIONS 37–39

37. C

Because the substituents are bulky, both will want to be equatorial; however because the compound is *cis* on two adjacent carbons, only one substituent can exist in either configuration. They will switch at the same time because the change in one's configuration provides the energy to simultaneously change the other's configuration.

38. D

In the combustion reaction, the hydrocarbon is usually the limiting reagent. Because carbon is present in at least an equimolar amount with hydrogen in all hydrocarbons, the compound that has the greatest moles of carbon will produce the greatest heat (the combustion of a hydrocarbon is an exothermic reaction). The fact that both (C) and (D) have ring structures is not relevant, as cycloheptane clearly has more carbons than any of the other choices.

39. A

What type of amino acid moves toward the anode? Any acidic amino acid. The only acidic amino acid listed is glutamate, the ionized form of glutamic acid. Lysine (C) and histidine (D) are basic (i.e., cations) at or near physiologic pH. Glutamine (B) is uncharged.

PASSAGE V (QUESTIONS 40–47)

40. A

The observed optical rotation is dependent on the concentration of the solution and the length of the polarimeter tube. As the concentration of the solution increases, the number of molecules that can alter the path of light increases. By the same principle, the longer the polarimeter tube, the more molecules there will be in the light's path. Therefore, observed rotation is proportional to solution concentration and tube length. If the solution is half the concentration as before, the student's reading is reduced by a factor of two. Doubling the length of the polarimeter tube (C) doubles the optical rotation. If she starts with a molecule of the opposite chirality, her polarimeter reading will have the same magnitude but in the opposite direction.

41. A

It would be convenient to draw the hydrogen atoms of C2 (with a dash) and C2′ (with a wedge) before designating their stereochemistry. Ignoring the (+) and the *threo*-prefixes, the stereochemistry of C2 in compound I is R (priority of groups at C2 in decreasing order being the carbon bound to the ester oxygen, the carbon bound to the piperidine nitrogen, the carbon bound to the benzene ring, and the hydrogen atom), while the stereochemistry of C2′ is also R (priority being the nitrogen atom, the carbon bounded to the ester and the benzene, $-CH_2^-$, and the hydrogen atom).

42. D

A structural or constitutional isomer is one in which the chemical formula is the same, though the atoms/molecules are connected differently (for example, C_4H_{10} could describe n-butane or 2-methylpropane). The listed compounds are stereoisomers of each other, not constitutional isomers.

43. D

Stereoisomers have the same structure overall, but different stereochemistry at chiral carbon atoms. The theoretical number of stereoisomers for any molecule is 2^n, where n is the number of stereocenters. Because methylphenidate has two stereocenters, there are 2^2, or four stereoisomers, or compounds I–IV in Figure 1.

44. A

To identify diastereomers, the most straightforward way is to decide which pairs of compounds only have *one* of their chiral configurations switched, as opposed to both; i.e., diastereomers, not enantiomers. Of the molecules listed, I and II are diastereomers, as are I and IV, III and IV, and II and III.

45. D

When the leaving group in the original molecule and the newly substituted group in the new molecule have the same priority, the stereocenter configuration does switch (R to S or S to R). But if the leaving group and new substituent have different priorities in the molecule, the stereochemistry is not changed (R remains R or S remains S). (B) and (C) cannot be chosen because we do not know the starting molecule or the attacking nucleophile. (A) is describing the first step of an E1 reaction, not an S_N2 reaction.

46. C

By definition, geometric isomers refer to *cis-/trans-* or E-/Z-isomers of substituted alkenes, which applies only to (C). Furthermore, alkenes prevent the rotation of the atoms bonded to the carbons in the double bond. In this case, H and Br are the atoms bonded to the one carbon of the double bond, and H and C_3H_7 are bound to the other carbon.

47. B

According to the passage, methylphenidate acts at monoamine transporters in a noncompetitive manner. This means that its mechanism of action does not involve competition with dopamine. Because the molecular similarities of methylphenidate to dopamine are irrelevant (and nonexistent, really), (C) is incorrect. Because the activity is being assessed *in vitro*, the ability of methylphenidate to cross the blood-brain barrier is not relevant to the question, so (A) is incorrect.

PASSAGE VI

48. A

Hydrogen is the correct answer. The valence electrons are those in the outer electron shell of the atom. The atomic number provides the value for the number of electrons in the atom. Pauli's exclusion principle restricts the number of electrons in an orbital to two. Therefore, hydrogen's one electron is in the 1s orbital which also composes the outer shell. The s orbitals are spherically shaped by definition.

49. C

Each dot in a Lewis structure represents one electron, and each atom can be shown to have eight valence electrons, satisfying the octet rule that an outer electron shell of eight electrons is needed for chemical stability. (A) does not account for eight valence electrons for both carbon and oxygen. (B) and (D) are incorrect because carbon and oxygen should each have eight electrons.

50. A

Methane has the maximum ratio of hydrogens to carbons of any molecule since all four valence electrons of carbon are bonded to a hydrogen. C–H bonds are higher in energy than C–C bonds. Thus, any substitution of hydrogens for carbons reduces the bond energies contained in the molecule; the longer the molecule, the lower its potential energy compared to methane. Ethane has two carbons per molecule, propane has three, and butane has four.

51. A

The Lewis structure for the CO_2 molecule is:

$$:O::C::O:$$

The number of electron domains around the central atom is two, and they are bonding domains. There are no nonbonding domains on the central atom. The electrons on the two oxygen atoms are not on the central atom and thus do not define the geometry of this molecule. (A) is correct.

52. C

The CH_4 molecule has four electron domains, one each for the four carbon-hydrogen bonds around the central atom carbon. There are no nonbonding electron pairs. Thus, the four electron domains dictate a tetrahedral shape. A linear shape is dictated by two electron domains, a trigonal planar by three, and a trigonal bipyramidal shape by five. The Lewis structure for the CH_4 molecule is:

$$\begin{array}{c} H \\ H:\overset{..}{\underset{..}{C}}:H \\ H \end{array}$$

Glossary

Absolute configuration Three-dimensional orientation in space of the four substituents on a chiral center (i.e., the R or S configuration of a chiral carbon).

Acetals Stable compounds of the general formula $R_2C(OR')_2$, resulting from the nucleophilic addition of two moles of an alcohol to an aldehyde. Acetals are often used as a protecting group for aldehydes, because they are stable to basic and nucleophilic reagents but easily removed by acid hydrolysis.

Achiral A molecule that does not possess optical activity.

Activating group Activating groups make an aromatic ring more susceptible to electrophilic substitution. Activating groups, except for alkyl groups, have at least one pair of nonbonding electrons on the atom directly attached to the ring; these electrons stabilize the carbocation intermediate. Activating groups direct substituents to the *ortho* and *para* positions. Typical examples are $-NH_2$, $-OH$, $-CH_3$, and $-OCH_3$.

Activation energy Energy barrier that must be overcome in order for a reaction to occur. The activation energy required determines the rate of the reaction at a particular temperature.

Addition reaction Reaction in which an electrophile and then a nucleophile add to a pi bond, resulting in a more saturated compound.

Alcohols Compounds of the general formula ROH.

Aldehydes Compounds of the general formula RCHO.

Aldol condensation The nucleophilic addition of an enolate ion to a carbonyl compound to yield an aldol (a β-hydroxy aldehyde). The reaction is called a condensation because two molecules join to form one large molecule. This reaction can also be used for ketones but is less efficient.

Aliphatic compounds Nonaromatic hydrocarbons.

Alkanes The simplest organic molecules, consisting only of carbon and hydrogen and containing only single bonds. The general formula for alkanes is C_nH_{2n+2}. Also called paraffins.

Alkenes Hydrocarbons with at least one carbon–carbon double bond (C=C). Their general formula is C_nH_{2n}. Also called *olefins*.

Alkynes Hydrocarbons with at least one carbon–carbon triple bond (C≡C). Their general formula is C_nH_{2n-2}.

Allenes Dienes whose two C–C double bonds are adjacent (not separated by any single bonds). See *dienes*.

Allylic cation $RCH=CH-CH_2^+$: A carbocation with a positive charge adjacent to a double bond. This cation is more stable than a tertiary carbocation because of resonance stabilization from the p-orbital on the central carbon, which can overlap with the p-orbital on either carbon adjacent to it.

Alpha carbon A carbon adjacent to a carbon containing the functional group under consideration.

Alpha hydrogen The hydrogen bonded to an α carbon, which is usually affected by the nearby group. For instance, a hydrogen α to a carbonyl group is more acidic than other carbon-bonded hydrogens because of the resonance stabilization effect of the carbonyl on the resulting carbanion.

Amides Compounds of the general formula $RCONH_2$, $RCONHR$, or $RCONR_2$.

Amines Compounds of the general formula RNH_2 (primary), R_2NH (secondary), or R_3N (tertiary).

Amino acids Compounds of the general formula $NH_2CRHCOOH$. The 20 amino acids found in nature are the building blocks of proteins.

Angle strain Occurs in molecules when bond angles are forced from their ideal values.

Anhydrides Compounds of the general formula RCO_2COR. They are the dimeric products of two carboxylic acids, or acid derivatives, that have lost water or hydrogen halides.

Anion Negatively charged ion. Compare *cation*.

Anomeric carbon Hemiacetal or hemiketal carbon (the carbon attached to two oxygens) in a furanose or pyranose ring.

Anomers Diastereomers that differ in the configuration about the anomeric carbon (usually C-1 in hexoses). Anomers can be either α or β, depending on the orientation of the hydroxyl or alkoxy substitutent on the C-1 carbon.

anti **addition** Addition in which two atoms or molecules add on opposite sides of a double bond. For instance, when Br_2 is added to an alkene, a bromonium ion intermediate is initially formed, and then Br^- attacks from the other side. See *syn addition*.

Anti **conformation** The most stable conformation of straight-chain alkanes, in which the two largest R-groups are staggered by 180°.

Aromatic compounds (arenes) Cyclic compounds that fulfill the following criteria:

1) $4n + 2$ pi electrons (Hückel's rule)
2) Every atom of the ring is associated with at least one pi orbital.
3) Planar configuration
4) Pi electrons above and below the plane of the ring
5) Delocalized pi electrons

Aromatic compounds are unusually stable due to increased resonance. Examples are benzene, pyridine, and the cyclopentadiene carbanion.

Axial bonds Bonds perpendicular to the plane of a ring.

Base peak The most intense peak in a mass spectrum.

Beta carbon A carbon two carbons away from the functional group under consideration.

Boat conformation Transition-state conformation of cyclohexane, in which all hydrogens are eclipsed and the "flagpole" hydrogens repel each other because of their proximity. The boat conformation is less stable than the chair conformation because of steric hindrance.

Boiling point Temperature at which the vapor pressure of a liquid is equal to atmospheric pressure and the liquid and gas phases are in equilibrium.

Buffer solution Solution whose pH changes only slightly upon addition of either acid or base. The solution contains a conjugate acid-base pair that consumes any added base or acid.

Carbanion Carbon atom that possesses a formal negative charge (has an extra electron).

Carbocation Carbon atom that possesses a formal positive charge (lacks an electron).

Carbohydrates Compounds of the general formula $C_n(H_2O)_n$.

Carbonyl group C=O group found in aldehydes, ketones, and carboxylic acids, among others.

Carboxylic acids Compounds of the general formula RCOOH. The hydrogen is acidic due to resonance stabilization of the conjugate base.

Catalyst Any material that reduces the activation energy of a reaction and thus increases its forward and reverse reaction rates. Catalysts are neither altered nor consumed during a reaction.

Cation Positively charged ion. Compare *anion*.

Chain reaction A reaction involving several steps, each leading to a reactive substance that is necessary for the next step to occur. For example, in a free-radical reaction, each step after initiation of the radical produces a new radical that makes the reaction continue.

Chair conformation The most stable conformation of cyclohexane, in which all C–C bonds are 109.5° and all the substituents on alternating carbons are staggered.

Chiral center Atom, usually carbon, with four different substituents attached to it.

Chiral molecule A molecule not superimposable on its mirror image and that exhibits optical activity. A chiral center is usually but not necessarily present.

Chromatography Technique used to separate a complex mixture, based on the fact that different compounds will adhere to a particular adsorbent to a lesser or greater degree. A solvent elutes compounds in a mixture through the adsorbent at different rates, separating (resolving) them.

cis **isomers** Configuration about a double bond in which the two largest groups are on the same side of the molecule. See *geometric isomers*.

Condensation reaction Combination of two or more molecules, often with the loss of a small molecule such as water or alcohol (e.g., aldol condensation).

Conformation Orientation of atoms in a molecule that can be altered by rotation about a C–C single bond.

Conjugated dienes *Dienes* whose two C–C double bonds are separated by one single bond and are therefore subject to electron delocalization.

Covalent bonding Bonding in which the half-filled orbitals of two atoms

overlap such that both constituents share the resulting electron pair.

Cycloalkanes Saturated cyclic hydrocarbons of the formula C_nH_{2n}.

Deactivating groups Substituents that, when attached to benzene rings, make the ring less susceptible to electrophilic attack. These are compounds that withdraw electrons from the aromatic ring, destabilizing the carbocation intermediate. Examples include $-NO_2$, $-COOH$, $-CHO$, and halogens. Most are *meta* directors, except for the halogens, which are *ortho/para* directors.

Decarboxylation A reaction resulting in the loss of a molecule of CO_2. β-dicarboxylic and β-keto acids undergo decarboxylation easily.

Dehydration A reaction resulting in a net loss of H_2O, often observed in the elimination reactions of alcohols.

Dehydrohalogenation Reaction of alkyl halides resulting in the loss of HX and producing alkenes.

Delocalization of electrons Distribution of electron density over several atoms because of conjugation of pi bonds.

Denaturation Loss of secondary and tertiary structure of a protein, caused by an increase in temperature or a pH change. Denaturing agents disrupt hydrogen bonding, inactivating proteins.

Dextrorotatory Term used to describe the rotation of plane-polarized light by

an optically active molecule in a clockwise or positive (+) direction.

Diastereomers Stereoisomers that are not mirror images of each other (e.g., the *S, R* and *R, R* forms of tartaric acid).

Dicarboxylic acids Compounds of the general formula $HOOC(CH_2)_nCOOH$.

Dienes Compounds containing two double bonds. See *allenes*; *conjugated dienes*.

Diols Compounds with two alcohol groups. Geminal (gem) diols have the two –OH groups on the same carbon atom; vicinal (vic) diols, also known as glycols, have the two –OH groups on adjacent carbons.

Dipole moment Measure of the net polarity of a bond or molecule.

Eclipsed conformation The least stable conformation of a straight-chain alkane, in which the bulkiest R-groups are at an angle of 0° relative to an adjacent hydrogen atom.

Electron affinity Measurable energy change accompanying the addition of an electron to an atom.

Electronegativity Ability of an atom to attract electrons, resulting in polarized bonds.

Electrophiles Species that "love" electrons and therefore seek them out. They often are positively charged and seek electrons in order to fill their outer shells. Many typical electrophiles are Lewis acids.

Electrophilic addition Addition of an electrophile to an electron-rich species. A typical example is the addition of Br_2 to an alkene.

Electrophilic aromatic Substitution of an electrophile into the electron-rich pi system of an aromatic compound. Typically, a Lewis acid is used as a catalyst.

E1 (unimolecular elimination) Elimination reaction whose kinetics are first-order. The rate-limiting step is the departure of a leaving group, which produces a carbocation; a base then abstracts a proton to form a double bond.

E2 (bimolecular elimination) Elimination reaction whose kinetics are second-order. A base removes a proton, and the leaving group simultaneously departs, forming a double bond.

Enantiomers Stereoisomers that are nonsuperimposable mirror images of one another. For example, if there is one chiral center, then the *R* and *S* isomers are enantiomers.

Enols Compounds in which a hydroxyl group is located on the carbon atom of a double bond. They are tautomers of ketones, and an equilibrium exists between the two forms. The enol form is generally less stable than the keto form. (One exception is phenol, which is more stable in its enol form because of resonance stabilization.)

Epimers Stereoisomers of sugars that differ only in the configuration about the C-2 carbon atom.

Epoxides Compounds containing a three-membered cyclic ether.

Equatorial bonds Bonds lying in the plane of a ring.

Esterification The formation of an ester by reaction of an alcohol with an acid.

Esters Compounds of the general formula RCOOR.

Ethers Compounds of the general formula ROR.

Fatty acid Long-chain aliphatic carboxylic acids derived from the hydrolysis of fats.

First-order reaction Reaction whose rate depends on the concentration of only one reactant (rate = k [reactant]).

Fischer projection The representation of a three-dimensional chiral structure in two dimensions. The vertical lines indicate bonds that project into the plane of the paper, whereas the horizontal lines represent bonds that project out of the plane of the paper.

Formal charge The difference in the number of electrons possessed by an atom in a molecule and in its elemental state.

Free radical Highly reactive species possessing an unpaired electron.

Free radical substitution Chain reaction in which a radical abstracts a substituent from a molecule (usually hydrogen) and replaces it with another substituent, often a halogen, forming the product and a free radical. Free-radical substitutions are characterized by three steps: initiation, propagation, and termination.

***Gauche* conformation** Conformation of straight-chain alkanes in which the largest R-groups are staggered by 60°.

Geminal (gem) Term describing compounds with two of the same functional groups attached to one carbon. See *vicinal*.

Geminal diol A compound that has two alcohol groups on the same carbon and is a hydrate of an aldehyde or ketone.

Geometric isomers Compounds that differ only in the geometry of the groups around a double bond (i.e., *cis* and *trans*).

Halogenation Reaction in which a halogen atom is incorporated into a substrate through an addition, free-radical, or substitution reaction.

Haworth projection Flat depiction of cyclic molecules. For sugars, the oxygen atom is always at the back, right corner of a Haworth projection, and the hemiacetal carbon is at the far right.

Heat of combustion Amount of heat released when a compound is burned.

For the combustion of a hydrocarbon:

$$C_nH_m + O_2 \rightarrow nCO_2 + \frac{m}{2}H_2O$$

Hemiacetal Unstable intermediate between aldehyde and acetal, containing one –OR group and one –OH group attached to the same carbon atom.

Hemiketal Unstable intermediate between ketone and ketal, containing one –OR group and one –OH group on the same carbon atom.

Hückel's rule Rule defining aromaticity, stating that cyclic conjugated molecules will exhibit unusual stability if they contain $4n + 2$ pi electrons.

Hydrocarbons Organic compounds containing only carbon and hydrogen.

Hydrogen bonding Weak electrostatic interaction between a hydrogen atom bonded to an electronegative atom, such as N, O, or F, and the lone pairs of other electronegative atoms.

Hydrogenation Reaction in which hydrogen is added to an unsaturated compound, usually performed with a catalyst.

Imines Compounds of the general formula $RCH = NC$ or $R_2C = NH$; the condensation products of aldehydes and amines.

Inductive effect An electron-withdrawing or electron-attracting effect transmitted through sigma bonds in response to a dipole.

Initiation reaction A reaction generating a free radical; for example,

$$Br_2 \rightarrow 2Br\bullet$$

Ion An atom or molecule with a net negative or positive charge. See *anion*; *cation*.

Ionic bond Bond between compounds with very different electron affinities, involving the transfer of an electron to the more electronegative atom (e.g., LiF).

Isoelectric point pH at which the number of positive charges and the number of negative charges on a compound (e.g., an amino acid) are equal.

Isomers Compounds with the same molecular formulas but different structures. See *geometric isomers*; *stereoisomers*; *structural isomers*.

IUPAC nomenclature Standardized system of nomenclature promoted by the International Union of Pure and Applied Chemistry.

Ketals Compounds of the general formula $R_2C(OR)_2$, formed from the reaction of a ketone and two alcohols and often used as protecting groups.

Ketones Compounds of the general formula RCOR.

Kinetic order of reaction Sum of the exponents of all the reactants present in a rate equation.

Leaving group Group that is replaced in a substitution reaction, which must be a weaker nucleophile than the species that will replace it. The best leaving groups form the most stable anions in solution.

Levorotatory Term used to describe the rotation of plane-polarized light by an optically active molecule in a counterclockwise or negative (−) direction.

Lewis acid Electron-pair acceptor (e.g., BF_3 or $AlCl_3$).

Lewis base Electron-pair donor (e.g., NH_3).

Lipids Triacylglycerols (1,2,3-triesters of glycerol) found in tissue and cells; classified as fats, terpenes, prostaglandins, or steroids.

Markovnikov's rule The rule stating that the addition of a protic acid (HX) to an alkene occurs such that the proton attaches to the carbon atom with the smallest number of alkyl groups, producing the most stable carbocation.

Mechanism Pathway by which a reaction occurs, describing all reactants, intermediates, and products and the conditions that must be present for the reaction to take place.

Melting point Temperature at which the solid and liquid phases of a compound are in equilibrium.

***meso* compounds** Compounds with at least two chiral centers but with a plane of symmetry resulting in a mirror image that is superimposable on the original molecule.

Meta configuration In disubstituted benzene rings, the configuration in which the two functional groups are oriented in the 1,3 or 1,5 positions on the ring.

Micelles Clusters of molecules possessing hydrophilic ionic heads facing the surface of a sphere, where they can interact with water, and possessing hydrophobic hydrocarbon tails in the interior. Soap forms micelles, facilitating the dissolution of oils and fats.

Mobile phase Gaseous or liquid solvent used to move components through the adsorbent (stationary) phase in chromatography.

Monosaccharides Simple sugars that cannot be hydrolyzed to simpler compounds.

Mutarotation Exchange of position between the axial and equatorial substituents of the anomeric carbon of a cyclic sugar. Mutarotation is acid-catalyzed and results in a change in the direction of optical rotation.

Newman projection Representation of a molecule along a carbon-carbon axis, showing the different rotational conformers possible for the compound.

Nucleophile Species that is a "nucleus lover" and thus tends to donate an electron pair to an electrophile.

Olefins Another name for *alkenes*.

Optically active Term describing a compound that can rotate the plane of polarized light.

ortho **configuration** In disubstituted benzene rings, the configuration in which the two functional groups are oriented in the 1,2 or 1,6 positions on the ring.

Oxidation Loss of electrons. Compare *reduction*.

para **configuration** In disubstituted benzene rings, the configuration in which the two functional groups are oriented in the 1,4 positions on the ring.

Peptide bond Amide bond between the nitrogen of the amino group of one amino acid and the carbon of the carbonyl group of another amino acid. Characterized by partial double-bond character and thus imparts rigidity to peptide chains.

Peptides Molecules that consist of two or more amino acids linked to each other by peptide bonds.

Pi (π) bond Covalent bond formed by parallel overlap of two unhybridized atomic *p*-orbitals, as in a carbon–carbon double bond.

Polar covalent bond Bond formed by the sharing of electrons between two atoms of different electronegativities, resulting in the attraction of electrons toward the more electronegative atom.

Polarity Charge separation due to asymmetric distribution of electrons.

Polarized light Light in which all electric fields vibrate in one plane.

p-orbital: A dumbbell-shaped electron orbital centered on the nucleus. They exist for atomic numbers two and higher.

Primary amine An amine with two hydrogen and one hydrocarbon substituents (i.e., RNH_2).

Primary (1°) atom A carbon atom attached to only one other carbon atom, or a hydrogen atom or other group attached to such a carbon.

Primary structure The amino acid sequence of a protein.

Propagation Series of events immediately following initiation in a chain reaction. A reactive intermediate reacts with a stable molecule to form another reactive intermediate, thereby continuously regenerating the reacting species. This enables the reaction to continue until completion.

Proteins Long-chain polypeptides with high molecular weights.

Protonation Acceptance of a proton by an electron-pair donor.

Quaternary structure Interaction of protein subunits to form a large complex; the highest form of protein structure.

Racemic mixture A 50:50 mixture of the (+) and (−) enantiomers of an optically active substance.

Rate-determining step Slowest step in a multistep reaction. The rate of the reaction is dependent only on this step.

Reactive intermediates Reactive molecules or molecule pieces that are formed during a reaction and quickly proceed to subsequent steps of the reaction sequence.

Rearrangement Shifting of substituents with their electrons to a new location on the same molecule, leaving behind a more stable molecule (e.g., methyl and hydride shifts).

Reduction Gain of electrons. Compare *oxidation*.

Resonance Delocalization of electrons within a compound. Such compounds may be represented by various electron configurations and have a true electron configuration somewhere between the various possibilities. Because the electrons are spread out over the molecule, the structure gains added stability. See *tautomerism*.

Ring strain Tension experienced by cyclic compounds due to the bending and stretching of bonds in order to fulfill geometric (angular) and steric requirements.

Salts Positive and negative ions linked by electrostatic attraction. A salt is the neutralization product of an acid and a base.

Saponification Hydrolysis of an ester with a base, forming a carboxylic acid salt.

Saturated hydrocarbon A hydrocarbon with only single bonds.

Secondary amine An amine with one hydrogen and two hydrocarbon substituents (i.e., R_2NH).

Secondary atom A carbon atom attached to two other carbon atoms, or a hydrogen atom or other group attached to such a carbon.

Secondary structure Level of protein structure characterized by inter- and intramolecular hydrogen bonding. Examples of 2° structure are the α-helix and the β-pleated sheet.

Sigma (σ) bond Head-to-head overlap of hybridized or *s*-orbitals from separate atoms to form a bonding orbital.

S_N1 Unimolecular nucleophilic substitution. It is characterized by two steps: (1) dissociation of a molecule into a carbocation and a leaving group; (2) combination of a nucleophile with the carbocation. No inversion of configuration occurs, but a loss of stereochemistry does occur because of the formation of a planar intermediate.

S_N2 Bimolecular nucleophilic substitution. It occurs in one step, involving two principal reactants. A strong nucleophile pushes into a molecule, dislodging a leaving group. These reactions are characterized by an inversion of absolute configuration.

s-orbital A spherically symmetrical electron orbital centered on the nucleus.

Staggered conformation Arrangement of atoms about a carbon–carbon single bond such that the greatest spacing of adjacent groups is obtained. *Anti* and *gauche* conformations are special cases of staggered conformations.

Stationary phase Solid support used in chromatography to which compounds adsorb.

Stereoisomers Isomeric compounds that possess the same atomic connectivity but differ in their spatial orientation.

Steric hindrance Strain in a molecule produced by repulsion of groups adjacent or close to one another. Hindrance increases as size and bulk increase.

Structural isomers Compounds with the same molecular formula but different connections between atoms.

Sugars Carbohydrates; compounds containing the elements C, H, and O, with H and O in a 2:1 ratio. Simple sugars are called monosaccharides and can dimerize or polymerize into disaccharides and polysaccharides. Examples of mono-, di-, and polysaccharides, respectively, are glucose, maltose, and cellulose.

syn addition Addition in which two atoms or molecules add to the same side of a double bond. See anti *addition*.

Tautomerism Equilibrium rearrangement in which a compound exists as two distinct structures differing in the position of both a proton and a double bond. See *resonance*, in which atoms retain their positions and electrons change location.

Termination The step in a chain reaction in which two reactive species join together to form a nonreactive species.

Tertiary atom A carbon atom attached to three other carbons, or a hydrogen atom or other group attached to such a carbon.

Tertiary amine An amine with three hydrocarbon substituents (i.e., R_3N).

Tertiary structure Level of protein structure dictated by hydrophobic and hydrophilic interactions, causing the molecule to fold into a complex shape.

Totally eclipsed conformation Eclipsed conformation in which the substituent pairs that eclipse each other are the same group or groups of equal priority.

Twist-boat conformation Intermediate between the two chair conformations in cyclohexane; similar to the *boat conformation* except it is more stable, because the twist relieves eclipsing.

Unsaturated compound Compound with double or triple bonds.

van der Waals forces Weak intermolecular interactions such as dipole–dipole interactions, hydrogen bonding, and London forces.

Vicinal (vic) Term describing compounds that have the same substituent on adjacent carbons. See *geminal*.

Vinylic Substituent on a double-bonded carbon atom (e.g., an enol is a vinylic alcohol).

Zwitterion Neutral dipolar molecule in which the charges are separated. Some amino acids are zwitterions.

Index